M000211800

DICTIONARY OF CORRESPONDENCES

DICTIONARY OF CORRESPONDENCES

The Key to Biblical Interpretation

George Nicholson

Fifteenth Edition

Swedenborg Foundation Press
West Chester, Pennsylvania

Originally published in folio in 1800 by George Nicholson
First bound edition, revised by Charles Bolles, published
    by Otis Clapp in 1841 as the *Dictionary of Correspondences,*
    Representatives, and Significatives derived from the Word of
    the Lord; extracted from the Writings of Emanuel Swedenborg
Revised second edition published in 1847
Revised tenth edition published in 1910 by the
    Massachusetts New Church Union
Thirteenth edition published in 1931
Tri-centennial (fourteenth) edition published in 1988 by the
    Swedenborg Foundation
Fifteenth edition published in 2010

ISBN 978-0-87785-116-5

Library of Congress Catalog Number 88-43279

Cover by Karen Connor
Interior text design by Brad Allan Walrod, High Text Graphics

Manufactured in the United States of America

Swedenborg Foundation
320 North Church Street
West Chester, PA 19380
www.swedenborg.com

PREFACE

The *Dictionary of Correspondences* was compiled as a key to the writings of Emanuel Swedenborg (1688–1772), a Swedish scientist, inventor, and mystic whose volumes of theological material provided a unique insight into the nature of the world, the afterlife, and Scripture. This book provides a comprehensive reference to one of the basic principles of Swedenborg's teachings: that there is an inner spiritual meaning underlying the literal text of the Bible, and that this meaning can be understood through a complex system known as correspondences.

The original text of this volume was published in folio form in 1800 under the title *A new and comprehensive dictionary of correspondences, representatives, and significatives: contained in the Word of the Lord; arranged under distinct heads, with proper references; including a full explanation of each article, or subject, with the reason, cause, and ground of its signification; the whole being an infallible key to the internal sense of the Holy Word, and an universal system of evangelical theology; faithfully extracted from all the theological works of the hon. Emanuel Swedenborg; with an introductory preface.* The author was the Reverend George Nicholson, an early minister of the Church of the New Jerusalem or New Church, which was founded based on the writings of Emanuel Swedenborg.

Nicholson was first introduced to Swedenborg's writings in 1790 and quickly became an enthusiastic convert. He attended the New Church society in Great Eastcheap, London, and participated in a number of lectures and events there, as well as contributing regular articles to the *New Jerusalem Journal*, an early New Church *publication*. In 1794 he also published his first book on New Church topics, *Essays on the Most Essential Theological Subjects*.

On December 25, 1800—less than a month after completing his *Dictionary of Correspondences*—Nicholson was ordained into the New Church by the Reverend Robert Hindmarsh and the Reverend Manoah Sibly. Upon his ordination in 1800, he became minister of the New Church society in Kingston-upon-Hull in Yorkshire, England. The history of his involvement with this group is unclear; a biographical article about Nicholson in the October 1919 issue of *The New-Church Review* refers to "misunderstandings with, and among, his Society at Hull," and notes his need to find "secure anchorage" to support his wife and six children. For whatever reason, in 1809 Nicholson left his New Church society at Hull and was ordained into the Church of England, spending the rest of his working life in various Anglican churches. He maintained his association with the New Church, however, until his death in March 1819.

Nicholson's legacy lived on in the form of his master work, the *Dictionary of Correspondences*. The original folio edition seems to have been based on a much shorter *New Dictionary of Correspondences, Representations, etc.* published in London 1794 by the Reverend James Hindmarsh, but it was Nicholson's work that became the standard reference in the New Church community. It was reprinted many times both before and after his death and distributed internationally among New Church followers.

In 1841, a revised version of the dictionary was printed by Otis Clapp, a publishing company in Boston. The reviser, Charles Bolles, had edited Nicholson's original work and abridged it by approximately two hundred pages. In the introduction to the new edition, Bolles wrote:

> In preparing the work in its present form it is believed that very little, if anything, has been omitted which could not well be spared in a work of this character; for the writings of Swedenborg are now distributed to a considerable extent throughout this and other countries, and there is not at this day the same necessity of embodying in the work many long passages of Scripture which existed at the time the work was originally compiled. Much additional matter has been added from the different Works of Swedenborg, and considerable care has been bestowed in revising and correcting the whole.

A second edition of this work was published in 1847, correcting errors from the previous edition, adding some new information from Swedenborg's writings, and including some new entries from indexes of Swedenborg's works.

The *Dictionary of Correspondences* underwent another major revision in 1910 for the tenth edition, this time by the Massachusetts New Church Union. This tenth edition added approximately 1,200 new entries for a total of 5,400, and at the same time included some editorial changes. In an effort to save space, words which occurred frequently were abbreviated (see the Key to Abbreviations on page ix).

In 1988, the Swedenborg Foundation re-released the text of the 1910 edition, without revision, to celebrate the tri-centennial of Swedenborg's birth. The current edition is identical to the text of the 1988 edition, reprinted by popular demand.

KEY TO ABBREVIATIONS

Works by Emanuel Swedenborg

The writings of Emanuel Swedenborg are abbreviated through-out the text as follows. Where various translations have different titles, alternative titles are noted in parentheses. Throughout the text, where a number is given with no title, it refers to *Arcana Coelestia (Secrets of Heaven)*.

Adv	Adversaria (The Word Explained)
A.C.	Arcana Coelestia (Secrets of Heaven)
A.Cr.	Athanasian Creed
A.E. or Ap. Ex.	Apocalypse Explained (Revelation Explained)
A.R.	Apocalypse Revealed (Revelation Unveiled)
A.V.C.R.	Appendix to the True Christian Religion (Coronis)
B.E.	Brief Exposition of the New Church Doctrines (Survey)
C. or C.D.	Doctrine of Charity
C.L.J.	Continuation Concerning the Last Judgment (Supplements)
C.L. or C.S.L.	Conjugial Love (Marriage Love)
D.L.	Doctrine of Life
D.L.W.	Divine Love and Wisdom
D.P.	Divine Providence
E.U.	Earths in the Universe (Other Planets)
Exp.	Spiritual Experiences
F.	Doctrine of Faith

G.E.D.	General Explication of the Decalogue from Apocalypse Explained
H. & H.	Heaven and Hell
I.	Influx (Soul-Body Interaction)
L.	Doctrine of the Lord
L.J.	Last Judgment
N.J. or N.J.D.	New Jerusalem
N.Q.	Nine Questions
S.E.L.P.	Summaries of the Internal Sense of the Prophets and Psalms
S.D. or Sp. Dia.	Spiritual Diary
S.S.	Doctrine of Sacred Scripture
T.C.R.	True Christian Religion (True Christianity)
U.T.	Universal Theology (True Christianity)
W.H.	White Horse

Commonly Used Words

Words that are used frequently throughout the text are abbreviated as follows:

c.	correspondence
ch.	church
con.	concerning
cor.	corresponds
den.	denotes
der.	derived
des.	describes
exp.	explained
ill.	illustrates
int.	internal
opp.	opposite
pred.	predicated
rep.	representative
s.	signifies
sp.	spiritual

A

A, in the angelic language, is one of the vowels used in the third heaven, to express a sound cor. with affection. S.S. 90.

Aaron, a mountain of strength. The first high-priest of the Jews. A., as a priest, rep. the Lord in respect to the good of love. Sometimes he rep., in the opposite sense, idolatrous worship; as when he made the golden calf for the children of Israel. In Exod. iv. 14, A. den. the doctrine of good and truth. A.C. 6998. The garments of A. rep. the spiritual kingdom of the Lord, adjoined to his celestial kingdom, and since that exists by this, therefore it is said, in Exod. xxviii. 3, "That the wise in heart should make the garments of A. and his sons." A.C. 9817. A. rep. the external of the church, of the Word, and of worship. A.C. 10468. A. and his sons rep. the Lord as to divine good, and as to divine truth. A.C. 9375. A. and his garments rep. the superior heavens, thus the celestial kingdom; and his sons and their garments rep. the inferior heavens, thus the spiritual kingdom. A.C. 10068.

Abaddon (Rev. ix. 11), the destruction of spiritual truth and good. A.R. 440.

Abdeal s. things pertaining to the spiritual church. A.C. 3268.

Abdication of bodily gratifications is not the self-denial the Lord requires. A.C. 9325.

Abdomen. Spirits who affect too nice a scrupulousness of conscience in trivial matters have communication with the a., and occasion pain there. A.C. 5724.

Abel s. charity or love. (Gen. iv. 2.) D.P. 242. A.C. 325, 341. Good conjoined with truth. Ap. Ex. 817. Celestial love. Ap. Ex. 817. His offering s., that the worship preceeding from charity was acceptable; while that proceeding from faith alone, which Cain s. was not so. A.C. 326. See *Cain*.

Abib, the month, s. the beginning of a new state. A.C. 9291.

Abide, to, in the Lord, s. to a. in faith and love. A.E. 84.

Abide here, to (Gen. xxii. 5), s. to be separated for a time. A.C. 2792.

Abihu and **Nadab**, the sons of Aaron, rep. the doctrine of truth; N., doctrine drawn from the internal sense of the Word, and A., doctrine from the literal sense of the Word. A.C. 9375.

Abimael (Gen. x. 28), a ritual of the church called Eber. A.C. 1245.

Abimelech, and Ahusath his companion, and Phicol, the chief captain of his army (Gen. xxvi. 26), rep. the doctrinals of faith as grounded in the literal sense of the Word. A.C. 3447. A. rep. the Lord as to doctrine. A.C. 3393. A., king of Gerar (Gen. xx. 2), is the doctrine of faith, which has respect to things rational. A.C. 2510. They who place salvation in truths without the good of life. Ap. Ex. 537.

1

Abiram

Abiram s. damnation and immission in hell. A.C. 8306.

Abodes of the Lord des. D.L.W. 170. Of Angels. D.L.W. 92.

Abomination of **Desolation**, spoken of in Daniel, is the grand fundamental error of the old church, which is the doctrine of three divine persons in the Godhead, separately existing from eternity. U.T. 135.

Abominations and **Detestable Things.** (Ezek. vii. 20.) A. s. goods profaned, and d. t. are truths profaned. Ap. Ex. 827.

Abortion, when goods and truths do not succeed in their order. A.C. 9325.

Above and **High** s. what is internal or inmost. A.C. 1735, 2148. See *Altitude*.

Abraham rep. the divine celestial, or divine good. Also the celestial church, and the celestial man. A.C. 1965. When Jehovah, or the angel of Jehovah, speaks with A., then Jehovah, or the angel of Jehovah, is the essential divine, and A. the divine human. A.C. 2833. The angels by A. perceive a saving faith rep. thereby. A.C. 64. A. rep. both the essential divine, which is called father, and the divine human, which is called son; thus the Lord as to both, but the divine human which is from eternity, from which existed, and to which he reduced the human born in time, when he glorified this. A.C. 3251. A., by whom the Lord was rep., when he is named man (vir.), s. celestial truth, which is the same thing as doctrine from a celestial origin. A.C. 2533. A., divine good, and Sarah, divine truth. A.C. 2063. A. rep. the Lord as to rational good, and Sarah the Lord as to rational truth. (Gen. xviii.) A.C. 2198. A. (Gen. xxxi.) rep. the genuine church. A.C. 4207. A., Isaac, and Jacob mean all those who are principled in love. A.C. 1032. Wherever A., Isaac, and Jacob are treated of in the Word, the subject relates to the Lord's human how it was made divine. A.C. 3245. A., Isaac, and Jacob rep. the divine trinity in the person of the Lord. A.C. 2630. A. and Keturah (Gen. xxv.) rep. the Lord as to the divine spiritual. A.C. 3235. A. bosom (Luke xvi. 19, etc.) s. divine truth, which is in heaven. Ap. Ex. 118.

Abram rep. the Lord as to his human essence; and by being called Abraham, he rep. him as his divine essence. A.C. 1416. The letter H being inserted from the name Jehovah, that he might rep. the divine of the Lord. A.C. 1416. The Lord's divine celestial and spiritual. A.C. 1950. The celestial church, the celestial man, and also the essential celestial principle. A.C. 1965. In Gen. xiv. 15, the Lord's interior, or rational man. A.C. 1732, 1791. The knowledge of good. A.C. In Gen. xiv. 23, the Lord now a conqueror, consequently the things appertaining to celestial love, which he procured to himself by victories. A.C. 1749. A. and Nahor taking to themselves wives, Sarah and Milcah (Gen. xi. 29), s. marriages of evil with the false in idolatrous worship. A.C. 1369. A., Nahor, and Haran, the three sons of Terah (Gen. xi. 26), s. the three universal kinds of idolatry; viz., that which is grounded in self-love, the love of the world, and the third in the love of pleasures. A.C. 1357.

Abrech (Gen. xli. 42) den. adoration, for A. in the original tongue is, bend the knees, and the bending of the knees is adoration; for internal efforts which are of the will, thus which are of the love or affection, consequently which are of the life, have external acts or gestures cor. to them, which acts or gestures flow from the very cor. of things exterior with things interior. A.C. 5323.

Abroad s. in externals. A.C. 1806. See *Afar off.*

Absalom s. truths from the divine destroyed. A.C. 4763.

Absence, of the Lord, is in proportion to the a. of good. 10, 146.

Abstract. How ideas can be seen in the a., exp. D.P. 46.

Abstract, sense of the Word, is its true or genuine Spiritual Sense. A.E. 236.

Abstraction. The natural mind cannot by mere a. of thought, perceive the celestial. 5110.

Absorbd, to be, or swallowed up of the earth, as Korah, Dathan, and Abiram were, s. damnation and immission in hell. A.C. 8306.

Abundance is pred. of truth from good. A.E. 357.

Abyss, in old time, s. hell. A.C. 756. In Gen. vii. 11, den. lusts and the falses therein originating. A.C. 756. In Psalm cvi. 9, 11, temptation in the will. A.C. 756. Great a. (Ps. xxxvi. 7) s. divine truth. Ap. Ex. 946. The divine wisdom of the Lord is an a. which neither angels nor men can ever fathom. In the opposite sense, a. s. the hell of those who have confirmed themselves in justification by faith alone. U.T. 32, 290. A. and many waters (Ezek. xx. 19) s. the extreme of temptation. Also Ps. xlii. 7. A.C. 756.

Accad s. variety of worship. 1182–3. See *Babel.*

Acceptable Year s. when nourished by love. A.S. 295.

Access to the Father by the Son, means a. to the divinity, by approaching the humanity; just as one man finds a. to the soul of another by approaching his body. A.R. 484.

Accident. Strictly speaking there is no such thing. Every occurrence in life, however accidental it may appear, is brought to pass by some cause originating in the spiritual world. See D.P.

Accommodation. There must be a. before there can be communication. T.C.R. 125. Truths have to be accommodated to angels and men. 8644.

Accumulation of hereditary evil, exp. D.P. 328.

Accuser s. to call forth the evils and falses which are in man, and so condemn him. This is a common practice with wicked spirits in the spiritual world, who take particular delight therein. A.R. 554.

Accuser of the brethren means the dragon, or those in faith alone. A.R. 554.

Achan, the deed of (Josh. vii.), s. the profanation and consequent taking away of good and truth. A.C. 5135.

Achor, valley of (Isa. lxv. 10), s. the external good of the celestial church. A.C. 10610.

Acknowledgment and true worship of the Lord, is to obey and do his commandments. A.C. 10143. Nothing can be acknowledged without the consent of the will. D.P. 231 Truths and goods cannot be acknowledged, unless with those whose interior mind is opened. A.C. 3524. They who acknowledge God, and his divine providence, constitute heaven; but they who acknowledge nature, and human prudence alone, constitute hell. D.P. 205. So far as man acknowledges all the truth and good which he thinks, and does, to be from the Lord, and not from himself, so far he is regenerated. D.P. 87. A. of a God causes a conjunction of God with man, and of man with God; and the denial of a God causes a disjunction. D.P. 326. It is one thing to know, another to acknowledge, and another to have faith. A.C. 896, 4319, 5664. Unless the Lord is acknowledged by man, and that all good proceeds from him, no man can be saved. Ap. Ex. 893. The first and principal thing is the a. of the Lord. A.C. 10083. A. of a God, arising from a true knowledge of him, constitutes the life and essence of every part of theology. U.T. 5. A. and adoration of the divine human of the Lord, is the life of religion. A.C. 4733. All a. and confession are from the perception of influx. A.C. 3120. See *Adoration.*

Aconite, cor. to evil uses. D.L.W. 339.

Acquisition (Gen. xii. 5), all things which are sensual truths or things of science which are the ground of thought in man. A.C. 1453. In Gen. xv. 14, celestial and spiritual good. A.C. 1851. In Gen. xxxi. 18, it den. truth, and substance, good. A.C. 4105. A. and purchase (Gen. xxxiv. 22) s. truths. Also good and truth. A.C. 4487.

Act, to. Reaction derives its force from the active cause which it reciprocates. 6262. An a. derives its essence from love. D.W.L. 406.

Action. The angels who are with man, and who are in the cor. of all things

Activity

belonging to him, know from a. alone, which is effected by the hands, the state of the man as to his understanding and will, likewise as to charity and faith, and consequently as to the internal life of his mind. D.L. and W. 220. See *Hand.*

Activity is one of the moral virtues which regard life, and enter it. C.L. 164. The a. of love makes the sense of delight. 461. The influx of love and wisdom from the Lord, is a. itself. 461. Essential worship is nothing but a certain principle of a. which derives existence from the celestial principle within; the essential celestial principle cannot be without a principle of a. Worship is the first principle of a.; for thus it brings itself into manifestation, because it has a perception of joy in so doing. All the good of love and charity is the very essential principle of a. A.C. 1561.

Activities, all, are changes of state, and variations of form. A.Cr. 45.

Actually, degrees, opened in man according to his life in the world. D.P. 32.

Actual Evil is distinguished from that which is hereditary, just as the inclination to a thing is from the thing itself. A.C. 719. A. e. is not only that which a man has acquired to himself by acts, but also by thoughts without acts, for if external bonds had not prevented, he would, from cupidity confirmed by reasonings and in reasonings from cupidity, have voluntarily and without conscience rushed into evil. *Spirit. Diary.*

Adah (Gen. iv. 20), the mother of the celestial things of faith. A.C. 413.

Adah and **Zillah,** the two wives of Lamech, s. a new church; A. the internal of the church, and Z. its external. A.C. 333.

Adam. The reason why he is called A. is, because the Hebrew word a. s. man. A.C. 478. A. and his wife do not mean the first of all the men that were created in this world, but the men of the most ancient church. D.P. 241. A.C. 478, 482. See *Red.* See *Most Ancient Church.*

Add. To add (Rev. xxii.) s. to destroy. A.R. 957.

Adder den. evil in general. A.C. 197. See *Serpent.*

Adhere has relation to the good of love and mercy. 3875. A.E. 696.

Adjoined. Charity may be a. to a tripersonal faith, but never conjoined. U.T. 451. The external adjoins itself to the internal, and the internal conjoins itself to the external. C.L. 176.

Adjunction is relatively external, conjunction is relatively internal. "Spiritual good cannot be conjoined to those who from infancy are in externals, but only adjoined to them while in conflict, and after the conflict it recedes." A.C. 8981. A. is the presence of the Lord with man. A.R. 55.

Admah and **Zeboim,** in general, s. the lusts of evil, and the persuasions of what is false. A.C. 1212.

Administrations. There are many employments and a. in every heavenly society. H. and H. 388.

Admiration s. the reception and acknowledgment of a thing both in thought and affection. A.R. 578.

Admission to heaven not from immediate mercy. D.P. 338.

Admonition is an invariable law of divine order. A.C. 2387.

Adolescence, that state when man begins to think and act from himself, and not from the instruction or direction of others.

Adoption s. reception into the spiritual kingdom of the Lord. A.C. 2834, 3494.

Adoration, true, or humiliation of heart, is always attended with a prostration of the body on the face to the earth before the Lord. A.C. 1999.

Adorations offered to men is demoniacal worship. Ath. Cr. 79.

Adore, to (Rev. xiii.), s. to acknowledge and believe. Ap. Ex. 805.

Adorn has respect to divine truths, because all ornaments are external, and truth is the external form of good. A.C. 10536.

Adulla s. truth which is from good, and the opposite. 4816.

4

Adullam, a city mentioned in Josh. xv. 35, and Micah i. 15, s. truth from good, and in the opposite sense, false from evil. A.C. 4816, 4886.

Adult, the, who does not come into rationality in the world, cannot do so after death. D.P. 99.

Adults. Those who die a. acquire from the material a plane which they carry with them. H. and H., 345.

Adulteration is pred. of good being perverted into evil, as falsification is applied to the perversion of truth into false. A.C. 4552.

Adulterous and **Treacherous Men**. (Jer. ix. 2.) The former appellation means they who falsify the knowledges of truth, and the latter, they who falsify the knowledges of good. Ap. Ex. 357.

Adulteries are of three kinds. D.L. 74–79. To commit a., in the natural sense, is to commit whoredom, to be guilty of obscene practices, to indulge in wanton discourse, and to entertain filthy thoughts. In a spiritual sense, it means to adulterate the goods of the Word, and to falsify its truths; and, in a celestial sense, it s. to deny the divinity of the Lord, and to profane the Word. U.T. 236. He who is in natural a., is also in spiritual a. Dec. 74. When any person commits a. on earth, heaven is instantly closed against him. A.C. 2750. The conjunction of truth with the affection of evil cor. to the a. of a son with a mother; but the Lord provides against the existence of this as much as possible. Ap. Ex. 736. All the various kinds or degrees of a. are spiritually understood by the prohibited conjunctions. Lev. xviii. 24, 28. Ap. Ex. 235.

Adultery and **Whoredom**, to commit, s. to adulterate and falsify the goods and truths of the Word; because in the Word and in every part thereof there is a marriage of the Lord and the church. Also, a marriage of good and truth, which constitutes the church. A.R. 134, 958.

Adustion, or **Burning**, s. concupiscence, or the loss and extinction of the good of love. A.C. 9055.

Advent, the Lord's, in the clouds of heaven, s. that he will appear in the Word. L.J. 28.

Advent, second, of the Lord is effected by a man, before whom he has manifested himself in person, and whom he has filled with his spirit to teach the doctrines of the New Church through the Word from him. U.T. 779. See *Second Coming, Redemption.*

Adversary s. evils and falses which oppose man in his regeneration. It was likewise used in another sense in Matt. v. 25: "Agree with thine a. quickly," etc.

Advocate. Jesus Christ is said to be an a. with the Father for the whole human race; because divine truth, signified by the Son, which proceeds from divine good, signified by the Father, is the only medium of salvation, and, as it were, pleads, intercedes, and mediates for man. See *Intercede.*

Adytum (1 Kings vi. 24, 29, 32–35) s. the inmost of heaven and the church. Ap. Ex. 277.

Afar off s. remoteness of state, that is, removed from such things as constitute states of goodness and truth, and thence appertain to the church. And to stand a. o., and to lament over damnation, s. to be in a state remote from damnation and in fear. A.R. 769, 787. A. o. den. in externals. Ap. Ex. 1133. A. o., in an opposite sense, den. to be in evil, for this is in the external man. A.Ex. 1133. See Isa. v. 26; xiii. 5; Jer. iv. 16; v. 15; xxxix. 3.

Affect. Cor. clean things a. the good; and the opposite, the evil. D.P. 40.

Affectation obscures the thing treated of. 6924.

Affection. All conjunction of truth with good takes place by a.; for no truth ever enters into man's rational, and is thence conjoined, except by a. A.C. 3024. Charity is the a. of good, and faith the a. of truth. Ap. Ex. 736. A. is the good of love which conjoins. A.C. 3024. The a. of spiritual truth, which

Affinity

is to love truth, because it is truth, is not given to any others than to those who are conjoined to the Lord by the acknowledgment and faith of his divinity in his humanity; because all the truth of heaven and the church solely proceeds from him. Ap. Ex. 115. A., or love, is what constitutes the life of every person; for whatever the a. is, such is the whole man. A.C. 288. D.L.W. 1. Every a. of good and truth is an extension into heaven, and every a. of evil and false is also an extension into hell. L.J. 9. The a. of good and the a. of truth in the natural man are as brother and sister; and the a. of truth, called forth out of the natural man into the rational and there conjoined with good, is as a married woman. A.C. 3160. There can be no thought or idea without a., for their very soul and life is thence derived. H. and H. 236. When the ardor of a. fails, then liberty ceases. A.C. 4031. The a. of good constitutes the celestial church; and the a. of truth, the spiritual church. A.C. 2362. They who are in no a. of truth for its own sake, utterly reject the things appertaining to the internal sense of the Word, and nauseate them. A.C. 5702. The first a. of truth is not genuine, but is purified as man is further perfected in the spiritual life. A.C. 3040. The celestial angels perceive the Word such as it is in an internal sense, as to a.; whereas the spiritual angels perceive it, such as it is in an eternal sense as to thing. A.C. 2157. A. are rep. by lambs, goats, sheep, etc. A.C. 3218.

Affinity and **Consanguinity.** All and singular the things appertaining to a man truly rational, that is, a regenerated man, whether they be the things of his affections, of his perceptions, or his thoughts, are connected with each other, as it were, by c. and a.; for they are so arranged, that they mutually respect each other as families of one house, and this in a most distinct manner; in consequence whereof, they are reproduced according to the a. in which they are constituted, which is an effect of the influx of heaven. A.C. 2556. A. differs from c. in that the former has respect to faith, or to what is external: and the latter to charity, or to what is internal. A.C. 3815.

Affirmation of truth and good is the first common principle of the church.

Affirmative. There is a doubtful a., and a doubtful negative; the former taking place with some good men, and the latter with evil men. A.C. 2568.

Afflict, to. For a person to a., or to humble himself in an internal sense, means to compel himself. A.C. 1937.

Affliction, "Such as was not from the beginning of the world, no nor ever shall be" (Matt. xxiv. 21), means the infestation from falses, and thence the consummation of every truth, or the desolation which at this day prevails in the christian churches. B.E. 74. The a. of souls on festival days (Lev. xvi. 19) rep. the humiliation of the rational man, or his a. from a principle of freedom. A.C. 1947. By a. is meant the state of the church, when there are no longer any goods of charity, or truths of faith, but instead of them, evils and falses. A.R. 33, 95, 100. A. den. temptations both external and internal: external are persecutions from the world, internal from the devil. A.C. 1846.

Afflux differs from influx, in that it is an exterior reception of the truth and good proceeding from the Lord; whereas influx is the interior reception of the same. A.C. 7955. It also s. the sphere proceeding from evil spirits. A.C. 7990.

Afore, or **Before,** has respect to what is internal, or prior. A.C. 10550.

Africa. The new church is planted in the centre thereof, amongst those who live a good life, according to the best of their knowledge, and worship one God under a human form. C.S.L. 114. A., in a spiritual or angelic idea, den. the east. Ap. Ex. 70. See *Asia.*

Africans, the, are principled in obedience, and receive goods and truths more easily than other Gentiles. 2604.

6

After. To walk a. another s. to obey. A.R. 578. A. den. near, because a. den. succession of time, and in the spiritual world, consequently in the spiritual sense, there is no notion of time, but instead thereof such a quality of state as cor. thereto. A.C. 5216.

Agag s. the false arising from interior evil, which infests and opposes good affections. A.C. 8593.

Agate (one of the precious stones in Aaron's breastplate) s. the spiritual love of good. (Exod. xxviii. 19.) A.C. 9870. A., ligure, amethyst, den. the spiritual love of good, or the spiritual kingdom. A.C. 9870.

Age, an, when spoken of the Lord and of his kingdom of heaven, and of the life therein, of which there is no end, s. eternity; but ages of ages (Matt. vi.) is also expressed respectively as to the churches on earth, which have succeeded each other. A.R. 22. An a. in the Word, is ten years. A.C. 433. A complete state, when spoken of the church. A.C. 9788, 10248, 10371. Old a. s. a state of wisdom, also what is new. A.C. 3254, 3843. See *Consummation of the Age, Old Age, Silver Age.*

Ages of Ages and **Eternity**. (Rev. vii.) The reason why it is not said to e., but to a. of a., is because it is natural to say a. of a., but it is spiritual to say e., and the literal sense is natural, but the internal sense is spiritual, and the former sense includes and contains the latter. Ap. Ex. 468.

Ages, the, which have their names from gold, silver, and copper passed away before the time when writing came into use. C.L. 73. See *Golden Age.*

Ague, or **Cold Fever**, is a disorder occasioned by evil spirits of the most malignant class, whenever it is permitted them to infuse their sphere into the impure substances of the human body. A.C. 5716.

Ahab (1 Kings xxii. 39) s. man as to the rational principle. Ap. Ex. 1146.

Ahio den. instruction from the Word, and Uzzah one who instructs from self-derived intelligence, and not from the Word. A.C. 879.

Ahola (Isa. xxiii. 5), the spiritual church, which is also called Samaria. A.C. 1368.

Aholiab (Exod. xxxi. 6) s. those who are in the good and truth of faith, like the first or lowest heavens. A.C. 10335.

Aholibamah, or **Oholobamah**, one of Esau's women (Gen. xxxvi. 2), s. the affection of apparent truth, which is first conjoined to natural good rep. by Esau. A.C. 4643.

Ahusath. Those who are in doctrine from the literal sense of the Word. 3447.

Ai s. the knowledges of good, and in an opposite sense, the confirmations of evil. Ap. Ex. 655. Ai, or Hai, s. the knowledges of worldly things. A.C. 1453.

Aid, or **Help**, when pred. of the Lord, den. his mercy and h. 8652.

Air or **Spirit** of the **Day** (Gen. iii. 8) s. the time when the church had as yet somewhat of perception remaining. A.C. 221.

Air s. perception and thought, consequently faith. A.R. 708.

Air Vessels in the lungs cor. to perceptions. D.L.W. 412.

Ajalon, the valley of, has respect to faith: by the sun standing still upon Gibeon, and the moon in the valley of A. (Josh. x. 12), is s. the total vastation of the church as to good and truth. Ap. Ex. 401.

Alabaster (*onyx*). Spiritual love of truth. 9841. See *Precious Stones.*

Alas, Alas, s. grievous lamentation. A.R. 415, 769, 788.

Alien s. falses destructive of truths. A.C. 10287.

Aliens s. falses destructive of truths. 10287.

Alive is that which possesses love and wisdom, which are the constituents of spiritual life. A.C. 687. In another life, it is very manifestly perceived what is a., and what is not: truth which is not a. is instantly perceived as somewhat material, shaggy, and shut up. Good which is not a. is perceived as somewhat woody, bony, and stony; but truth and good, vivified by the

All-Provident

Lord, are open, vital, full of what is spiritual and celestial, reaching even from the Lord, and this in every particular idea and action, even the least of each. This is the reason why it is said, in Gen. vi. 19, that pairs should enter into the ark to be made a. A.C. 671.

All-Provident. God is a.-p. Ill. D.W.L. 21.

Allelujah s. celebration of the Lord from joy of heart. A.R. 803.

Allon-Bachuth (Gen. xxxv. 8) literally means the oak of weeping; by which, in the spiritual sense, is s. the total expulsion of all hereditary evil from the lowest natural principle of the Lord's humanity. A.C. 4565.

Allowable. What man thinks a. he does continually in the spirit. D.P. 81, 278.

Almodad. (Gen. x. 26.) A ritual of the ancient church amongst the posterity of Eber. A.C. 1245.

Almonds (Num. xvii. 17, 25) s. the good of charity. Ap. Ex. 727. A. s. goods of life cor. to truths of good of the interior natural principle; the tree itself s. in the spiritual sense, the perception of interior truth which is from good, its flower interior truth which is from good, and its fruit the good of life thence derived; in this sense mention is made of the almond-tree in Jeremiah. A.C. 5622.

Alms, the exercise of charity, which consists in the performance of every duty of life, from the love of justice with judgment. U.T. 425.

Almsgiving and **Prayer.** (Matt. vi. 2, 6.) By a. in a universal sense is s. all the good which man wills and does; and by p. in the same sense is s. all the truth which man thinks and speaks. Ap. Ex. 695.

Aloes s. divine truth in the external. A.C. 10252.

Alone. (Gen. ii. 18.) In old time they were said to dwell a., who were under the Lord's guidance as celestial men; because such were no longer infested by evils or evil spirits; this was also rep. in the Jewish church by the children of Israel dwelling a. when they had driven out the nations; wherefore it is in some parts of the Word said of the church of the Lord, that she is a. See Jer. xlix. 31; Deut. xxxiii. 28; Num. xxiii. 9. This posterity of the most ancient church (Gen. i. 18) was not disposed to dwell a., or to be under the Lord's guidance as a celestial man, but to be amongst the nations like the Jewish church; therefore it is said, that it was not good for man to be a.; for whosoever has a disposition towards evil, is already in evil, and it is granted him. A.C. 139.

Alpha and **Omega**, the beginning and the ending, s. that the Lord is the self-subsisting and only subsisting from principles to ultimates from whom all things proceed, and consequently the all in all of heaven and the church. A.R. 29. A. and O. s. the Lord's divinity and infinity; and also, the Lord's divine love, and Beginning and End, relate to his divine wisdom. A.R. 29, 38.

Alphabet. In the a. of spiritual language, used by angels, every letter s. a complete thing; and this is the reason why the 119th Psalm is written according to the letters of the Hebrew a., beginning with aleph, and ending with tau. Something similar appears in Psalm 111, but not so evidently. A.R. 29, 38. D.L.W. 295. The vowels refer to good, and the consonants to truth. Ibid. Whereas each letter of the spiritual a. is thus significative, it is evident from what ground the Lord is called Alpha and Omega. C.S.L. 326.

Altar s. worship of the Lord out of love. A.R. 392, 295, 648. External worship, or idolatrous worship, and sometimes it means the divine human of the Lord. A.R. 393. A. rep. divine good, horns of the a. divine truths. That horns should be cut out of the a., shows that there is no other truth but what is grounded in good. A.C. 2832. Under the a. s. the inferior earth, where good spirits were guarded by the Lord. A.R. 325. Golden a. before God (Rev. ix.) s. the divine spiritual. Ap. Ex. 567. A. of burnt offerings, s. worship from celestial love, and the golden a. of incense, worship from spiritual love. A.R. 395. A. to burn incense upon (Exod. xxx. 1), in an internal sense, s. the hearing

8

and reception of all worship by the Lord, which is from love and charity. A.C. 10175. To build an a. (Gen. xxii. 9) s. to prepare the Lord's human divine. A.C. 2811. A. s. all worship in general, and particularly the Lord's divine human; for that is all worship and all doctrine. A.C. 921, 2813.

Alternate Reciprocation, by which conjunction is effected, differs from mutual r., in this; that the former is like the conjunction of the heart with the lungs, and the lungs with the heart; whereas the latter, or mutual r., is like the conjunction of the soul with the body, or the will with action, and of thought with speech. The conjunction of the Lord with man, is of this latter kind. U.T. 371.

Altitude s. the degrees of good and truths, from their supreme or inmost, to their ultimate or lowest. Ap. Ex. 627. The uses of all things which are created, ascend by degrees of a. to man, and by man to God the creator, from whom they are. D.L.W. 316. D.P. 32.

Am den. the esse and existere of all things in the universe. The reason why "I a." is twice mentioned in Exod. iii. 14: "I a. that I a.," is because the first "I a." s. the esse, or divinity, which is called father, and the second the existere, or divine humanity, which is called the son. The distinction, however, is to be understood of the Lord before his humanity was made divine; but when the Lord became, or was made the divine esse or Jehovah, even as to his humanity, then the divine truth proceeding from his humanity was and is the divine existere from the divine esse. A.C. 6880.

Amalek (Gen. xiv.), or Amalekites, s. those who are in false principles. A.C. 1679, 3762.

Amalekites and the **Amorites,** dwelling in Hazezon-Tamar (Gen. xiv. 7) s. falses from which evils are derived. A.C. 1679.

Amazed, to be (Gen. xxiv. 21), s. acknowledgment. A.C. 3100.

Amazement, den. a state of perception. 3100. Sudden change of state. 5705.

Amaziah rep. the perverted church. A.C. 624.

Ambassador, or messenger, s. to communicate. 4339.

Amber, the color of (Ezek. i. 4), has respect to the external divine sphere of the Word. S.E.L.P. p. 30.

Amen s. divine confirmation from truth, consequently from the Lord himself. A. s. truth, because the Lord was truth itself, therefore he so often said A. I say unto you (Matt. v. 18, 26), and alibi. And (Rev. iii. 14) he is called the A., the faithful and true witness. That the Lord is the truth itself. See John xiv. 16; xvii. 19. A.R. 592. A. s. the consent of all. A.R. 375.

Amethyst s. the spiritual love of good. (Exod. xxxiii. 19.) A.C. 9870.

Ammon, children of (Jer. xlix. 1), s. those who falsify the truths of the Word, and of the church. S.E.L.P. p. 27.

Ammonite and **Moabite,** an (Deut. xxiii. 3), s. the profanation of the celestial and spiritual things of faith. A.C. 576.

Amorite, in the Word, s. evil in general. A.C. 1857, or evils originating in falses.

Amphitheatre, where the dragons held their diversions. A.E. 655.

Amraphel, king of Shinar and Arioch, king of Ellasar (Gen. xiv.), s. truths and goods in the Lord's external man. A.C. 1685.

Anakims. *See Giants.* Den. persuasions of the false. 1673.

Analytically. To think a., and form conclusions, exp. D.P. 317.

Anamim den. rituals merely scientific. A.C. 1193.

Anatomy. All the viscera and organs are disposed in series and in series of series, analogically as goods and truths, and the arrangement of heaven in societies. 10, 303.

Ancients, the, worshipped one God until monarchical power; when worldly and corporeal affections began to close up the superior understanding. T.C.R. 9.

Ancients

Ancients, the, being principled in celestial good, dwelt in houses made of wood. A.C. 3720. They celebrated their religious worship on mountains. A.C. 796. A. of the people, and the princes thereof (Isa. iii. 14), have a similar signification with the twelve disciples. Ap. Ex. 851.

Ancient Church was a spiritual c., and had a revealed Word, which has been long since lost. A.C. 597, 2897. In the a. c. there were doctrinals, and there were scientifics; the doctrinals treated of love to God, and of charity towards the neighbor; but the scientifics treated of the cor. of the natural world with the spiritual world, and of rep. of spiritual and celestial things, in things natural and terrestrial. These scientifics were principally cultivated and taught in Egypt. A.C. 4064. The a. c. was not constituted by Noah, but by his three sons, Shem, Ham, and Japheth. A.C. 915.

Ancient of Days. (Dan. vii. 9, 10.) The Lord as to divine good or divine love, who is called the A. of D. from the most ancient times, when the church was celestial, being in love to the Lord; that church and the heaven of those who were from thence is understood by a throne, which was as a flame of fire, but the wheels, which were as a fire burning, s. the doctrine of celestial love; and the divine love itself, proceeding from the Lord, is s. by a fire emanating, and going forth from before him. A. Ex. 504. A. of D., is the Lord from Eternity. Ap. Ex. 195. Dan. vii. 9.

Ancient Time, the people of the, never, on any account, ate the flesh of any beast or bird, but fed solely on grain, and on fruits, milk, etc. (Gen. i. 29, 30.) A.C. 1002.

Ancient Word. The ancient church had an inspired W., consisting of historical and prophetical books cited by Moses. 2686. The W. has been in every period of time, but not such as we have it at this day. 2895. In the period of the most a. church, it was not written, but revealed to each individual, and inscribed on their hearts. 2896.

Ancle. A. s. what is sensual and natural. A.C. 629.

Andrew (Simon Peter's brother) s. the obedience of faith. Ap. Ex. 821.

Aner s. the angels attendant upon the Lord. A.C. 1705.

Angel, in a supreme sense means the Lord, and in a relative sense the heaven of a.; as also an angelic society. But when mentioned by name, as in Rev. xii. s. a ministry in heaven. A.R. 548. A. s. divine truths. Ap. Ex. 687. In Gen. xxiv. 7, the divine providence. A.C. 3039. A. from heaven (Luke xxii. 43) s. the divine principle which was in the Lord. A.C. 2821. A strong a. descending from heaven (Rev. x. 1) s. the Word as to its quality in the internal sense. A.C. 2162. A. of the covenant (Mal. iii. 1) s. the Lord as to divine truth. A.C. 1925. A. (Rev. xiv. 6) s. the gospel which is of the Lord alone. A.C. 1925. A. of the waters (Rev. xvi. 5) s. the divine truth of the Word. A.R. 685. A. of Jehovah (Gen. xvi. 7) s. the thought of the Lord's interior man. A.C. 1925. The a. of Jehovah is sometimes mentioned in the Word, and everywhere when in a good sense rep. and s. somewhat essential with the Lord and from the Lord. This is the reason why a. were sometimes called Jehovah. See Exod. iii. 2, 4, 14, 15, and alibi. A.C. 1925. By the a. which stood at the altar (Rev. viii.) is s. the inmost or third heaven. Ap. Ex. 490. By the a. who rolled away the stone from the door of the Lord's sepulchre, and sat upon it (Matt. xxvii. 66), is s. that the Lord removed every false which closed up the passage to himself, and opened divine truth, which stone cor. to, and which was falsified by, the traditions of the Jews, for it is said that the chief priests and Pharisees sealed the stone, and set a watch, but that the a. from heaven removed it, and sat upon it. (Matt. xxviii. 2.) Ap. Ex. 400. A., a strong, descending from heaven (Rev. x. 1), s. the Lord as to the natural or ultimate sense of the Word. Ap. Ex. 593. A., the four, bound at the river Euphrates (Rev. ix.), s. ratiocinations from fallacies of the sensual man, and their being loosened s. that they were at liberty to exercise those reasonings. Ap. Ex. 570. The celestial a. dwell in expanses above others, and in gardens where there are arbors and flower-gardens, thus in perpetual representatives of celestial things; and what is wonderful, there is not a stone to be found there, because stone s. natural truth, but wood s. good, tree, perception, and flower, implantation. Ap. Ex. 828. A., in an opposite sense, den. falses. See Matt. xxv. 41. Rev. xii. 7. Ap. Ex. 739. A. of the third heaven are perfected in wisdom by hearing and not by sight. H. and H. 271. The affection of a. is communicated to young people, in knowing and thinking of the historicals of the Word, and causes their pleasure and delight thence arising. A.C. 3665. The two a. coming to Sodom s. the Lord's divine human principle and holy principle. (Gen. xix. 15.) A.C. 2319. There are a. who do not live consociated, but separate, house and house. Such dwell in the midst of heaven, as being the best of a. H. and H. 189. The a. of the third heaven dwell upon mountains; the a. of the second heaven upon hills; and the a. of the ultimate heaven in valleys, between the hills and mountains. Apoc. Rev. 896. The seven a. mentioned in the Revelation sounding their trumpets, describe the successive changes of the state of the church. Ap. Ex. 566. A. in the Word are called Gods, from their reception of divine truth and good from the Lord. A.C. 4295. The a. are not present with the Lord, but the Lord is present with the a. A.C. 9415, 9680, 9682, 9683. The celestial a. do not reason of truths like the spiritual a. See Matt. 5, 37. A.C. 202, 597, etc. Every man has a. associated to him from the Lord; and such is his conjunction with them, that, if they were taken away, he would instantly fall to pieces. C.S.L. 404. A. have a pulse like that of the heart, and respiration like that of the lungs in men, but more interior. A.C. 3884, 3887. The spiritual a. understand the Word in its internal sense, and the celestial in its inmost sense. A.C. 2157, 2275. The a. of the Lord's Celestial kingdom imbibe the internal sense of the Word from the affection alone of man, when he reads the Word resulting also from the sound of the words in the original language. But the a. who are in the spiritual kingdom of the Lord imbibe the internal sense from the truths which the words contain; therefore from the celestial kingdom proceeds joy of heart to the man who is in spiritual affection, and from the spiritual kingdom proceeds the confession of man from that joy. Ap. Ex. 326. The celestial a. do not write by letters, but by curved lines and inflections which contain arcana, which transcend the understanding of the a. in the inferior heavens. S.S. 90. A. of the celestial kingdom are clothed in purple garments, and a. of the spiritual kingdom in white linen garments. D.L.W. 380. The a. of the inmost heaven are naked. H. and H. 178. A. cannot utter one word of any human language. H. and H. 246. A. and spirits know nothing of man, no more indeed, than man knows of them; because they are consociated by correspondences, which cause them to be together in affections, but not in thoughts. A.R. 943. A. are consociated with men, but the Lord only is conjoined with them. A.R. 946. A. have in heaven the very same Word, or Scriptures, that men have in the world. L. 2. The a. can express more in their language in a moment, than we can in half an hour. A.C. 1641. A. are called powers because of their reception of divine truth from the Lord. A.C. 9639.

Angels, Elders, and the **Four Animals.** (Rev. vii.) The a. s. they who are in the first heaven; the e., they who are in the second heaven; and the f. a., they who are in the third heaven. Ap. Ex. 462.

Angelic Spirits. He who is preparing for heaven, in the world of spirits, is called an angelic spirit. D.L. and W. 140.

Angels from the Lord by whom man is led and protected. For a particular description of their office and efforts, see A.C. n. 5992.

Anger. In all evil there is a. against the Lord and against the holy things of

11

Anguish

the church; hence a. in the Word s. evil, in the whole complex. Ap. Ex. 693. A. is violence of passion pred. of the will, as wrath is violence of passion pred. of the understanding. S.S. 84. The overflowing of a. (Isa. liv. 8.) den. temptation. A.C. 5585. A. of heat. (Exod. xi. 8.) Heat is pred. of falses, and a. of evil. A. is pred. of the punishment of evil, and wrath of the punishment of what is false, and fervor of the punishment of both. (Jer. xxi. 5, 6.) A.C. 3614. See *Indignation*.

Anguish of conscience, is temptation. A.C. 4299. There is no a. of c. with those who are in hell, on account of their evils done in this world. A.C. 695-6.

Animal s. affections of the will and understanding, in a good and evil sense. 9331.

Animalcules cor. to evil uses. D.W.L. 341.

Animal Kingdom, relation of man to the. D.L.W. 61. See *Man*.

Animal Spirit. There are spirits who cor. to the corrupted principles of the purer blood with man, which blood is called the a. s., and wheresoever they diffuse themselves, they are as poisons, which induce cold and torpor in the nerves and fibres, from which break forth the most grievous and fatal diseases; these spirits, are they who in the life of the body, had taught by art and deceit, to subdue to themselves the minds of others, with a view to rule over them, especially with the powerful and the rich. A.C. 4227.

Animals taken from the herd den. celestial natural things; and those from the flock celestial rational things. A.C. 2180. The lives of a. are dissipated after death. A.C. 1633. The four a. (Rev. v.) specifically s. the third or inmost heaven, and the twenty-four elders the second or middle heaven. Ap. Ex. 322. All the greater and lesser a. derive their origin from the spiritual principle in its ultimate degree, which is called its natural degree; man alone from all the degrees, which are three, and are called celestial, spiritual, and natural. D.L.W. 346. Noxious a., vegetables, etc., derive their origin from man, and so from hell; but the mild and useful a., etc., are from the Lord. D.L.W. 339, 345. A. s. the Word in its ultimates. A.R. 972. In Rev. vii. 11; xix. 4, a. s. those who are nearest to the Lord in heaven. A.C. 46. With brute a. there is influx from the spiritual world, and afflux from the natural world. A.C. 3646. The life of a. is a life merely natural, and cor. to the life of such in the spiritual world. D.P. 161. See *Beasts, Nature, Sacrifices*.

Animus, that which affects the mind as eminence and opulence. Ath. Cr. 76.

Anointed of Jehovah, the, is the Lord alone, as to his divine humanity, for in himself from conception was the divine good itself of divine love, and from that he made his humanity divine truth itself, when in the world, and moreover by union with his essential divinity he made that also the divine good of his divine love. Ap. Ex. 375. See *Christ*.

Anointing of Aaron and his sons, rep. the divine good of divine love in the Lord, and impletion of their hands, divine truth and thence divine power. A.C. 10019. See *Unction*.

Answer, to (Ps. xlix. 8), s. to bring assistance and to do good. Ap. Ex. 295. When pred. of the Lord, s. influx, inspiration, perception, and information, moreover also, mercy and help. Ap. Ex. 471. To a. (Apoc. vii. 13) s. influx; and, to say, perception. Ap. Ex. 471. To a., when assent is given to what is asked, s. what is reciprocal, and consequently reception. (Gen. xxiii. 5.) A.C. 2919.

Antediluvian Church. In that church all the understanding of truth and will of good perished. This was the case to such a degree with the antediluvians, who were infected with direful persuasions and filthy lusts, that there did not appear the smallest vestige or trace of understanding and will; but with those who were called Noah, there was a reserve of remains, which nevertheless could not form any thing of understanding and will, but only rational truth, and natural good. A.C. 635, 560.

Antelope s. natural affection of truth. 6413.

Antipas, my faithful Martyr (Rev. ii. 13), in the spiritual or angelic language, s. those who are hated on account of acknowledging the divine human of the Lord. Ap. Ex. 137. A.R. 112.

Antipathy, those who have hated others in this world, conceive an a. for their spheres, and seek to do them injury in the other life. 5061. The delight of heaven is insupportable in hell, and vice versa. D.P. 303.

Antipodes, cited in ill. 1378, 2196. Heaven and hell are like two a. D.P. 300.

Antiquities (Ezek. xxxvi. 10, 11) s. the most ancient church. Beginnings, the ancient church. The house of Israel, and people Israel, the primitive church, or church of the Gentiles. A.C. 477.

Anxieties before the rest of the viscera, affect the stomach. A.C. 5179. If any a. is felt when man thinks evil, it is from conscience. A.C. 5470. See *Temptation.*

Aorta. The great artery. Its cor. exp. D.L.W. 412.

Apes s. those who pervert the understanding of the Word. A.R. 839.

Apocalypse. Forasmuch as all things of heaven and the church among men are from the divine human of the Lord, therefore in the first chapter of the A., he is described by various rep., and from that description are taken exordiums to the seven particular churches mentioned in the subsequent chapters. Ap. Ex. 113, 151. The first sixteen chapters of the A. treat of the reformed, the seventeenth and eighteenth of the Roman Catholics, and the succeeding chapters of the last judgment and the new church. A.R. 567. The A., from beginning to end, treats solely of the state of the former heaven and church, and of their abolition, and afterwards of the new heaven and new church, in which one God will be acknowledged, in whom there is a trinity, and that the Lord Jesus is that God. A.R. 523. All things in the A. relate to the acknowledgment, that the Lord is the God of heaven and earth, and to a life according to his commandments. A.R. 903, 957. The A., in series, treats of the falses in the church, inasmuch as the truths of the new church cannot be received before those falses are discovered and removed. A.R. 700. The A. was manifested to John by the Lord, and it is now opened by the Lord. A.R. 953. That nothing shall be added to or taken away from what is written in the A., s. that nothing shall be added or taken away from the truths of the new church, which contain prophecies, and are now revealed. A.R. 958. The last words in the A. are the words of desponsation between the Lord and the church to marriage. A.R. 960. Seven chapters of the A. treat more particularly and expressly of the perverted state of the church among the reformed. B.E. 88. All things, which are contained in the A. have respect to that which is s. by the seven golden candlesticks; viz., the new heaven and new church, as to its end and conclusion: those things therefore in the last chapters are treated of; the rest which come in between, are such things as oppose, and which are to be removed, as those things which are recorded of the dragon and the beasts of Babylon; which things not opposing or being removed, the new heaven and new church rise out and appear. Ap. Ex. 91. The A. does not treat of those who deny truth, but of those who falsify it; for they who deny truths are not among those who were in the former heaven, and from thence in the day of the last judgment were cast into hell, for these immediately after death were cast in thither. But they who falsify truths from various causes, are treated of in this book, because they made to themselves a heaven which was afterwards destroyed. Ap. Ex. 535.

Apollyon, den. reasoning from falses appearing as from truths, and from things philosophical perversely applied. 7643.

Apostles

Apostles, the twelve, s. all divine truths in the christian church. A.R. 70. The a. sitting upon twelve thrones to judge the twelve tribes of Israel, s. that the Lord will proceed in judgment according to the truths and goods of faith and love. A.C. 2129, 6397. The Lord's twelve a. who were with him in the world, were again commissioned by him to preach the gospel of his new church and kingdom throughout the universal spiritual world. This was done on the 19th day of June, 1770. See Matt. xxiv. 31. U.T. 791. A. are they who teach the goods and truths of the church, and in an abstract sense the goods and truths themselves. A.R. 79. The a. thought the kingdom of heaven was like the kingdoms of this world. A.C. 3857. The a. are called holy, because they rep. holy things. A.R. 790. See *Disciples, Peter, Prophets*.

Apparel s. truths in common. A.R. 328. See *Garment, Robes, etc.*

Apparent Truth. Divine t. is latent under the a. t. of the Word. 6997.

Appearances. In the Word many things are expressed according to a. 589, 626.

Appear, to. The Lord appears to every one according to his state. A.C. 934. That man does not live of, or from himself, is an eternal truth; but yet, unless it appeared as if he lived of himself, it would be impossible for him to live at all. A.C. 1712.

Appearance in the Word. Evil and wrath are attributed, in the Word, to the Lord; when notwithstanding nothing but good proceeds from him. A.C. 2447. When apparent truths are taken for real truths, then they are confirmed, and become fallacies. D.L.W.

Appearances of Truth are genuine goods and truths invested or clothed. Ap. Ex. 778. It is not sin and blasphemy to interpret the Word according to appearances, provided such interpretations are not formed into the principles of a system, and these confirmed to the destruction of divine truth in its genuine sense. Ap. Ex. 778. When man perceives the Word according to appearances of truth therein, the angels who are round about him understand it spiritually; thus the spiritual of heaven is conjoined with the natural of the world, as to such things as conduce to the life of man after death. If the Word had been written otherwise, no conjunction of heaven could have been given with man. Ap. Ex. 816.

Appearances. Essential divine truths are such that they cannot in any sort be comprehended by any angel, still less by any man; inasmuch as they exceed every faculty of the understanding both of men and angels; in order therefore that they may have conjunction with the Lord, truths divine flow in with them in a., and then they can be received and acknowledged: this is effected in a manner adequate to the comprehension of every one. Wherefore a. of truth, that is, truths angelic and human, are of a threefold degree. A.C. 3362. There are a. in the hells which are not real existences, but only the effects of fantasy and insanity, like the wild imaginations of a person in a delirious fever. Ap. Ex. 553.

Apperception in the writings of E.S. den. the exterior views or apprehensions of truth existing in the natural mind of man; whereas perception is a term applied to the more interior views thereof. See A.C. 3549. The a. of truth is from good, inasmuch as the Lord is in good and gives a.; when it hence receives truth, it then increases indefinitely; the case herein is like that of a little seed, which grows into a tree, and produces little seeds, and these next produce a garden, etc. A.C. 5355.

Appetite and **Taste** cor. with the desire of sciences (in the world of spirits). A.C. 1480.

Apple of the **Eye**. "He kept him as the a. of his e." (Deut. xxxii. 10), s. that the Lord fights (together with man) against evils and falses from hell. Ap. Ex. 730.

14

Apple Tree s. joy of heart originating in natural good derived from spiritual good. Ap. Ex. 458. Sensual good and truth, which is the ultimate of the natural principle. (Joel i. 12.) Ap. Ex. 458.

Approach s. influx and communication. 8159.

Application. Interior truths in the natural are the a. of celestial and spiritual truths to use. 4973.

Appropriate, to. Divine providence does not a. good or evil to any one, but self-derived prudence a. both. D.P. 308. The love of good and truth cannot be a. to man apparently as his own, unless he is in a state of freedom. H. and H. 293. A.C. 4031. Appropriation of good is its implantation in the will. A.C. 10109. Whatsoever man from his will thinks, speaks, and acts as well good as evil is a. to him and remains. D.P. 226, 227.

Approximations in the spiritual world are similitudes. H. and H. 193.

Ar (Deut. ii. 17) s. good not as yet defiled with falses. A.C. 2466.

Ar of **Moab** (Isa. xv. 1) s. the doctrine of those who are in truths from the natural man. Ap. Ex. 652.

Arabia (Jer. xlix. 29) s. the church which is in truths from good. Ap. Ex. 799. A. s. the same as Kedar. Also the natural man. Ap. Ex. 405. In Jer. xliv. 28, s. those who pervert the knowledges of good. S.E.L.P. p. 28. A. s. spiritual good, and the Princes of Kedar, spiritual truths. (Ezek. xxvii. 21.) A.C. 3268. A. s. wisdom, and the Princes of Kedar, intelligence. (Ezek. xxvii. 21.) A.C. 2830.

Arabia and the **Kingdoms** of **Hazor** (Jer. xlix. 28), in an opposite sense, s. those who are principled in the knowledges of things celestial and spiritual, for no other end or use than that they may be reputed wise and intelligent by themselves and the world. A.C. 3048.

Arabia and the **Sons** of the **East** (Jer. xlix. 28, 30) s. the possession of celestial riches or of the things that relate to love, which things, if wasted, are said to flee and to wander, etc., when they yield no good fruit. A.C. 382.

Arad (threshing-floor) s. first state. 6537.

Aram or **Syria**. The knowledges of good and of truth. A.C. 3676. Aram, in the opposite sense, s. the knowledges of good perverted. See Isa. vii. 4–6, ix. 12. Deut. xxvi. 5. A.C. 1232.

Aram-Naharaim (Gen. xxiv. 10) s. the knowledge of truth. A.C. 3051.

Ararat, Mount (Gen. viii. 4), den. the light of a regenerate person. This light is the first light after temptation, and is consequently obscure. A.C. 854.

Arcana, the, of the christian church were contained in the rituals and rep. of the Jewish church. A.C. 3478. The a. of justification by faith alone, can scarcely be comprehended by any, except the rulers of the church who teach it. A.R. 426. He who knows the formation of good from truths, knows the greatest a. of heaven. A.C. 8772. All the a. of the world of nature are contained in man. A.C. 3702, 6057. The a. of the internal sense of the Word are such that they can scarcely be explored as to a ten thousandth part to the apprehension of man, except only in a most general way. A.C. 3085.

Archangels exercise no arbitrary authority. A.E. 735.

Archer. A member of the church spiritual was of old so called, because he defends himself by truths and disputes about them. A.C. 2709.

Architectural Art, among the angels, is art herself realizing her own skill. A.Cr. 82.

Architecture of the other life des. 1627–29. H. and H. 185.

Arianism took its rise from thinking of God as three persons. D.P. 262.

Arians. Condition in the other life des. D.P. 262.

Ariel (Isa. xxix. 1–2) s. the true church destroyed. S.E.L.P.

Arioc, king of Ellasar, so many kinds of goods and truths with the Lord's external man. A.C. 1660.

Arise

Arise. To arise is to be elevated from a state of evil to a state of good. A.C. 2388, 2401.

Aristotle, concerning his thoughts on the Lord, man, etc. 4658.

Arm den. power. 878. 9937.

Ark, the, rep. heaven, in the supreme sense the Lord, consequently the divine good. A.C. 4926. A. s. the inmost heaven. A.C. 9485. The translation of the a. (2 Sam. vi. 1–17) s. the progression of the church among men, from its ultimates to its inmost principles. Ap. Ex. 700. By the a. going forward, were rep. combats and temptations. A.C. 85. By the a. resting, is s. regeneration. A.C. 850, 851. By reason of the decalogue therein contained, the a. was the most holy thing of the church. D.L.W. 53, 61. Its going forth s. liberty. A.C. 903. In Gen. viii., it s. the man of the ancient church who was to be regenerated. A.C. 896. A. of Jehovah (Num. x. 31–36) s. the Lord as to divine truth. Ap. Ex. 700. The a. (in 2 Sam. vi. 6, 7) rep. the Lord, consequently all that is holy and celestial. A.C. 878. Noah's a. (Gen. viii. 18) s. the state of the man of the most ancient church, before regeneration. A.C. 876.

Ark of the **Strength of Jehovah** s. heaven and the church. A.E. 684.

Arkite s. different kinds of idolatry. A.C. 1205.

Arm of **Jehovah** s. the humanity which he assumed. U.T. 84.

Armageddon. A state and desire of mind to wage war under the influence of falsified truths, arising from the love of eminence and universal dominion. A.R. 770. There was a combat in A., at the time of the last judgment on the church in 1757, with respect to the understanding of the Lord's prayer in its beginning. A.R. 839.

Armies, in the Word, mean the truths and goods of the church, also the falses and evils thereof. A.R. 862. A. of the heavens and the sands of the sea (Jer. xxxiii. 15–22) s. the knowledges of truth and good in the spiritual and natural man. Ap. Ex. 444.

Arms s. such things as belong to spiritual war. A.R. 436. A. and Feet (Dan. x. 6) s. the exterior things of the Word, which are its literal sense. A.C. 2162. A. and hands, in the Word, s. power; and the right hand superior power. D.L.W. 220. A.C. 878, 3091. Those who are in the province of the a. and hands are in eminent power of truth from good. H. and H. 96. The same may be said with respect to the shoulders. A.C. 4932.

Army, an, s. doctrinals. A.C. 3448. A.R. 447.

Aroer s. the knowledges of truth and good. A.E. 911.

Aromatic Wax (Gen. xliii. 11) s. the truth of good, for all aromatics, inasmuch as they have a sweet scent, in the internal sense s. truths which are grounded in good; this may be manifest from the consideration that truths grounded in good in heaven are perceived as pleasantly as sweet-scented objects are in the world; on which account also, when the perceptions of the angels are turned into odors, which frequently is the case by virtue of the Lord's good pleasure, on such occasions the senses are gratified as it were with fragrances arising from aromatics and from flowers; hence it is, that frankincense and perfumes were made of such substances as had a grateful odor, and that they were applied to holy uses, and hence also it is, that aromatics were mixed with anointing oil. A.C. 5621.

Around s. what is distant in degree of intelligence and wisdom, thus what is below. A.E. 335.

Arphaxad (Gen. x. 24) s. science. A.C. 1235.

Arrange, to, truths and goods which constitute the church in man, can only be effected by the Lord. A.R. 364.

Arrangement. The heavens and hells were arranged and underwent changes from one judgment to another. A.E. 702. D.P. 302. A. of societies according to genera and species of affections in heaven and hell. A.Cr. 34.

16

Arrayed s. to be instructed in truths. A.E. 1222.

Arrogate, to, to one's self divine power, is to say that we can open and shut heaven, remit and retain sins, etc. D.P. 257.

Arrow and **Bow**. (Isa. vii. 24.) A. is the false destroying truth, and b. is the doctrine of the false. Ap. Ex. 357. Polished a. den. the truth of doctrine. A.C. 2680, 2709, 2799. A. den. truths. A.R. 299. Also spiritual truths. A.C. 2686. See *Quiver.*

Arsenals den. truth combating against falses, and in the opposite sense, the false combating against truth. A.C. 6661.

Art. A. of magicians described. A.C. 831.

Arteries and **Veins** of the heart cor. to affections, and a. and v. of the lungs, to the affections of truth. D.L.W. 412.

Artificer den. one who is wise, intelligent, and knowing. A.C. 424. S. wisdom, intelligence, and science. A.E. 1186.

Arvadites falsities and evil lusts. A.C. 1205.

As it were from himself, exp. D.P. 76, 88, 92.

Ascend, to, involves elevation to truth and good, and to descend involves dejection to what is false and evil. A.C. 4815.

Ascending and **Descending** on the ladder (Gen. xxviii. 12) s. infinite and eternal communication and thence conjunction. A.C. 3701.

Ascension. There are six degrees of a.; three in the natural and three in the spiritual world. D.L.W. 66–7.

Asenath. "And gave him A. the daughter of Potipher the priest of On for a woman." (Gen. xli. 45.) That hereby is s. the quality of the marriage of truth with good and of good with truth, appears from the signification of giving for a woman, as den. marriage; the reason why it is the marriage of good with truth and of truth with good is, because no other is meant by marriages in the spiritual sense, and hence no other by marriages in the Word. By the daughter of the priest of On is s. the truth of good, for daughter is the affection of truth, and priest is good. A.C. 5332.

Aser, in a supreme sense, s. eternity; in a spiritual sense, eternal beatitude; and in a natural sense, the affection of goodness and truth. Also the love of being useful, which is called mutual love. A.R. 353.

Ashamed (Gen. ii. 25) s. to be in evil. A.C. 163. To be a. and confounded (Jer. xxii. 22) s. to be destitute of every good and truth. Ap. Ex. 811. See *Naked.*

Asher, reasonings. D.L.W. 325. A.C. 1186. A. s. the internal, and Manasseh the cor. external. Ap. Ex. 441. See *Aser.*

Ashes (Ezek. xxvii. 30) s. what is condemned; because fire from which they are derived s. infernal love. Ap. Ex. 1175. A. of the Furnace (Exod. ix. 8) s. the falses of lusts. A.C. 7519. Ap. Ex. 962. See *Dust and Ashes.*

Ashteroth, Karnaim, and **Shaveh Kiriathaim** (Gen. xiv. 5) s. the hells of such as were in persuasions of the false, and whom the Lord conquered in his childhood. A.C. 1673.

Ashur or **Assyrian** s. the rational principle. A.C. 119, 1186. The spiritual church. A.C. 776.

Asia (Rev. i. 4) s. those who from the Word are in the light of truth. A.R. 11. The angels when A. is named perceive the south; when Europe is named, they perceive the north; and when Africa is named, they perceive the east. Ap. Ex. 21. The science of correspondences was known a long time in A. A.C. 202–3.

Aside, to be, is pred. of the Gentiles, because they are in collateral good. A.C. 4189.

Ask, to (Gen. xxv. 23), s. communication. A.C. 3291. In Gen. xliii. 7, it den. to perceive another's thought, because in heaven there is a communication of all thoughts, insomuch that no one has any need to a. another what he thinks; hence it is that to a. s. to perceive another's thought; for the quali-

Askenas

ty of any thing on earth, in the internal sense, is its quality in heaven. A.C. 5597.

Askenas (Jer. li. 27) den. idolatrous worship, or external worship separate from internal. A.C. 1154.

Asking s. searching into or examination. 3385.

Asleep. (Matt. viii. 23–26.) When the man of the church is in a natural state, and not yet in a spiritual state, natural affections, which are various cupidities arising from the loves of self and of the world, rise up and cause various emotions of the mind (which is s. by the tempest on the sea); in this state the Lord appears as absent, and this apparent absence is s. by that the Lord was a. in the ship. Ap. Ex. 514.

Aspect, when pred. of the Lord, den. the divine presence, and thence providence. A.E. 25.

Aspersion, s. truths destroyed by falses. A.E. 519.

Asps. (Deut. xxxii. 33.) Dragons and a. s. the sensual principles, which are the ultimate of the natural man, full of abominable evils and their confirming falses. Ap. Ex. 714.

Ass. Natural truth. A.C. 2781. The scientific principle in particular. A.C. 1486. A she-a., the affection of natural truth. A.C. 2781, 1486. Son of a she-a. den. rational truth. A.C. 1895, 1896, 1902, 1910. By wild a. is meant truth separated from good. A.C. 1949. A. and the foal of an a. (Luke xix. 28, 41) s. the natural man as to good and truth. A.C. 2781. He-a., natural exterior truth. A.C. 4244. See *Wild A.*

Assemble s. to be arranged into order. 6338, 10397.

Assembly s. that the tent of a. den. where the presence of the Lord is. 9784.

Asses. Truths of good of the inferior or external order. A.C. 403. A. s. the things relating to the self-intelligence of the sensual man; and camels, the things of self-intelligence in the natural man. (Isa. xxx. 6, 7.) Ap. Ex. 654. Wild a. s. rational truths. A.C. 1947.

Association of Ideas, ill. 3336.

Assume, to. The Lord could not a. the human, without nativity. A.C. 3030. The Lord a. the human essence when he was seen by the prophets. A.C. 1573. The one God, who is invisible, a. the human by coming into the world, not only that he might redeem men, but also that he might become visible, and so conjoined to man. U.T. 786.

Assyria, the king of (Isa. vii. 11, 14), rep. the external or natural principle of the church. Ap. Ex. 706. The kings of A. (Isa. viii. 7, 8) s. fantasies, principles of what is false, originating therein, which desolate man. A.C. 705.

Astonishment and **Blindness.** (Zech. xii. 4.) A. is pred. of the understanding when there is no perception of good, and b., when there is no perception of truth therein. Ap. Ex. 355.

Asylum, an, was provided for those who had been hurt by falses of religion. 9011.

Atad, s. initiation, and the first state of the church. A.C. 6537.

At Hand s. nearness of state. A.R. 947.

Athanasian Creed was permitted to be written by divine providence, because although it is inconsistent with itself and with the true idea of the divine unity; yet it agrees with the truth with respect to the union of the divinity and humanity in the person of Christ. Ap. Ex. 1006. A. doctrine of the trinity has perverted the whole christian church. D.L.W. 146. U.T. 177.

Atheists are the subjects of infernal spirits. 1308. Their position in the spiritual world. D.L.W. 357.

Atmosphere cor. to use, because it is the receptacle and continent of heat and light, as use is the continent of love and wisdom. D.L.W. 183, 299. A.C. 1621.

18

Atmospheres, which are three in both worlds, the spiritual and the natural, in their ultimates close in substances and matters, such as there are in the earths. D.L.W. 302. A., water, and earth, are the three general principles by which and from which all things exist. D.L.W. 178. All the societies in the spiritual world appear surrounded with a., cor. to their affections and thoughts. Those which are in the third heaven appear in a pure ethereal a.; those in the second heaven, in an aerial, or less pure a.; but those in the ultimate heaven appear encompassed with a watery a. Ap. Ex. 342. A. exist in another life, with innumerable varieties, and of inexpressible beauty. A.C. 2297.

Atoms. It is a fallacy of the natural senses to suppose there are simple substances, such as a. 5084.

Atonements (Exod. xxviii. 36) are the receptions of the good of love and faith from the Lord, after the removal of evils and thence of falses. A.C. 10122.

Attention. He who is wise, attends to the end. 9407. A derivation from wisdom or understanding. D.L.W. 363.

Attraction. All love is a. 8604, 6476. With the good after death, there is a. to the Lord, as to a common centre. A.E. 646. All conjunctions and associations are regulated by a. T.C.R. 365, 350.

Attribute, the proper, of the human of the Lord, is redemption and salvation; which is called righteousness and merit. L. 34.

Attributes, the divine, were changed by idolatries into so many gods. S.S. 117.

Aura's, adamantine a. of precious stones in the other life. 1621. The atmosphere of the inmost heaven is a pure a. A.E. 538.

Auricles. The heart and lungs are conjoined by the a. and cor. to the conjunction of will and understanding. D.L.W. 403.

Aurora (day dawn). Dawn or redness den. when conjunction begins. 4300.

Authority. The sphere of a. is tempered with goodness with those who have lived in faith and charity. 1508. When pred. of the Lord, s. the salvation of the human race. A.E. 293. Those who think from a., think as a crab walks, the sight following the tail. C.L. 295.

Autumn in the Word, s. the decline of the church. D.L.W. 73.

Avel Mitzraim. Mourning of the Egyptians. 6543.

Avarice, in, there is not only the love of the world, but also self-love, and, indeed, the most filthy self-love. The Jewish nation has been in such a. from the beginning. A.C. 4751.

Aven, the high places of, s. principal falses, and thence ratiocinations, which are from those who are in that worship which, considered in itself, is interior idolatry; for they who are in evil of life and in falses of doctrine, worship themselves and the world. Ap. Ex. 391. Also, self-love. A.C. 273.

Avenged seventy and seven-fold (Gen. iv. 24) s. the complete extinction of both faith and charity, whence cometh damnation, s. by slaying a man and a little child. A.C. 433.

Aversion. Those who live in evils are averse to truths. 7951. Concerning the a. from the Lord of the spirits of hell. A.E. 1143.

Avims, the, who were expelled by the Caphtorites (Deut. ii. 23), s. falses and evils which infest the regenerate man. A.C. 1868.

Authority, arbitrary, does not exist in the heavens, for there no one acknowledges, in heart, any above himself, but the Lord alone. A.E. 735.

Autumn and **Evening** s. the decline of the church. D.L.W. 73.

Awake, to (Gen. xli. 4), den. a state of illustration. A.C. 5208.

Awl den. affixtion or adjunction, and the like is s. by a peg or nail. A.C. 8990.

Axe, an. (Jer. x. 3.) The work of the hands of the workman with the a., s. that which is from man's proprium and from his proper intelligence. Ap. Ex. 458. The false principle originating in self-derived intelligence. A.R. 847.

Axis. The sphere of divine good is in the midst like an a. A.C. 10190.

Azal (Zech. xiv. 5) s. separation and liberation, here separation from the falses of evil. Ap. Ex. 405.

Azarel s. the natural man not purified. A.E. 730.

Azure Stone den. the spiritual love of good. 9870.

Azzah (Gen. x. 19), s. those things which are revealed concerning charity. A.C. 1207.

B

Baal s. worship from the evils of self-love and the love of the world. Ap. Ex. 160.

Baale of Judah (2 Sam. vi. 2) s. the ultimate of the church, which is called its natural principle. Ap. Ex. 700.

Baalim and her **Lovers** (Hosea ii. 13) s. those things which belong to the natural man, and are loved; viz., lusts and falsities thence derived. Ap. Ex. 730.

Baal-peor (Num. xxv. 5) s. the adulteration of good. Ap. Ex. 655. To commit whoredom after B.-p., and to worship their gods, s. to profane worship. A.C. 5044.

Babel, or **Babylon**, s. those whose externals appear holy, whilst their internals are profane. A.C. 1182, 1325. In Jer. xx. 4, 5, s. those who deprive others of all knowledge and acknowledgment of truth. A.C. 1327. In Jer. li., s. those, who, by traditions or reasonings of the natural man, pervert the truths and goods of the church. S.E.L.P. p. 48. In Rev. xviii., s. the profanation of good and truth. In the prophets of the Old Testament, B. s. the profanation of good, and Chaldea, the profanation of truth. A.C. 4922. Those who, by application to their own loves, falsify truths and adulterate goods, are much treated of in the Word, where B. is mentioned, but most especially in the Apocalypse. A.C. 10307.

Babel, Erech, Accad, and **Calneh** (Gen. x. 10), s. different kinds of worship, whose externals appear holy, whilst their internals are profane. A.C. 1082.

Babylon s. the Roman Catholic religion, as to its tenets and doctrinals. A.R. 631. B., or Babel, s. corrupt worship, in which self-love and the love of the world have dominion. Such is the worship of the church of Rome. D.L.W. 65.

Babylonians, the, have transcribed the merit and righteousness of the Lord unto themselves. A.R. 758.

Babylonish Captivity, the, rep. the change of the state of the church, which change consisted in its worship becoming external, uninfluenced by any internal principle. A.C. 1327.

Back. The wicked appear in the light of heaven, as having their b. turned towards the celestial sun which is the Lord. See Jer. ii. 27. A.C. 10307.

Back parts of Jehovah (Exod. xxxiii. 23) s. the externals of the Word, of the church, and of worship. A.C. 10584.

Backwards, to go (Gen. ix. 23), s. not to attend to error and perverseness. A.C. 1086.

Badgers' Skins s. knowledges of good. A.E. 1143.

Baggage s. knowledge and scientifics in the natural man. Ap. Ex. 434.

Bake s. preparation for the conjunction of good. 8496.

Baker s. the good of love, and butler, the truth of doctrine. Ap. Ex. 55. B. (Gen. xl.) den. the external sensual principle, or that of the body, which is subordinate or subject to the will part of the internal man; because every thing which serves for food, or which is eaten, as bread, meat in general, and all the work of the b., is pred. of good, and thereby hath relation to the will part. A.C. 5078, 5157. Those who blend truths or falses together, so

Balaam

that they cohere, appear in the spiritual world as b. kneading dough, and beside them also there appears an oven. Ap. Ex. 540.

Balaam s. those who, as to their understanding, are illustrated and teach truths, but nevertheless love to destroy those who are of the church. Ap. Ex. 140. By the angel of Jehovah standing in the way against Balaam, with a drawn sword (Num. xxii. 22, 31) was s. the principle of truth, which opposed the false principle in which B. was. A.C. 2799. The doctrine of B. s. those who do works by which worship was defiled. A.R. 114.

Balances (Rev. vi. 5) s. the estimation of goodness and truth. A.R. 313.

Baldness s. the Word without its ultimates. A.R. 47. The natural principle, in which there is nothing of truth. A.C. 3301. The deprivation of exterior truth, or truth of the external man. A.C. 10199.

Balm. (Gen. xliii. 11.) The truth of exterior natural good, and its pleasantness. A.C. 5615.

Balsam s. truths which are grateful by virtue of good. A.E. 654.

Band, a, conjoining the goods and truths of the church. A.R. 46.

Bands of their **Yoke** (Ezek. xxxiv. 27) are the pleasantnesses of evil derived from self-love and the love of the world. Ap. Ex. 365.

Banquets and **Feasts** s. conjunction, specifically, initiation to conjunction. A.C. 5698.

Baptism neither gives faith nor salvation; but is a sign and testimony that the person baptized belongs to the church, and that he may become regenerate. N.J.D. 203, 207. B. is a sacrament of repentance. A.R. 224. Adults, as well as infants, may be baptized. N.J.D. 206. The waters of b. s. temptations. A.C. 10239. By washing, which is called b., is meant spiritual washing, consisting in purification from evils and falses, and regeneration is thereby effected. B. was instituted in the place of circumcision, because by the circumcision of the foreskin was rep. the circumcision of the heart, to the end that the internal church might succeed the external, which in all and every thing figured the internal church. The first use of b. is introduction into the christian church, and insertion at the same time amongst christians in the spiritual world. The second use of b. is, that the person baptized may know and acknowledge the Lord Jesus Christ the Redeemer and Saviour, and may follow him. The third use of b., which is the final use, is, that man may be regenerated. U.T. 670, 691. See *Gates*. See *Cross*.

Baptism of John. By it a way was prepared, in order that the Lord Jehovah might come down into the world, and accomplish the work of redemption. U.T. 688, 691.

Baptism of the Lord s. the glorification of his human. A.C. 10239.

Barak and Deborah s. the truth of good. Ap. Ex. 447. See *Deborah*.

Barbarians and **Enemies** (Ps. lxxii. 9) s. those who look towards earthly and worldly things. A.C. 249.

Bared (Gen. xvi. 14) s. what is beneath, consequently, scientific truth, from which also the rational principle is derived. A.C. 1958.

Bark s. the ultimate of the stem, exp. D.L.W. 314.

Barley cor. to truth and also to the good of the natural exterior principle. A.R. 315. A.C. 7600. B. den. natural good, and meal (farina) from b., truth from a natural origin. Ap. Ex. 1153. B. (Isa. xxviii. 26) s. truth, and rye the knowledge thereof. Ap. Ex. 374.

Barn, or **Granary** (Matt. xiii.), s. heaven. Ap. Ex. 911.

Barren, the, s. those who are not in good, because not in truths, and yet who desire that truths may be in good, like as the well-disposed Gentiles do who are without the church. The b. also s. the Gentiles who are called to the church, and to whom the church is transferred, when the old church perishes; that is, when they, who have been before of the church, are no more in faith, because in no charity. See 1 Sam. ii. 5; Ps. lxiii. 7, 8, 9;

Isa. liv. 1, and A.C. 9325. "Sarai was b., she had no child" (Gen. xi. 30), s. that evil and the false were not productive. A.C. 1371. The b., is the church of the Gentiles, and she that had many children is the church of the Jews who had the Word. (1 Sam. ii. 5.) A.R. 10. Barrenness and abortions s. perversions and denials of the goods and truths of heaven. A.C. 9226.

Bars (Lam. ii. 9) s. doctrinals. A.C. 402.

Basemath, the daughter of Elon, the Hittite (Gen. xxvi. 34), den. truth from another source than what was real and genuine. A.C. 3470.

Bases, the ten, round Solomon's temple (1 Kings, vii. 30), s. the receptacles of truth by which man is purified and regenerated. A.C. 8215.

Basin, truths of faith in the natural. 10, 243, 10.235.

Basons den. things of the memory. A.C. 9394.

Bashan s. the external of the church, that is, the natural. Ap. Ex. 163. Mount of B. (Ps. lxviii. 15) s. the good of the will-principle, which is amongst those who are in the externals of the church. Ap. Ex. 405. B. and Gilead (Micah vii. 14) have respect to the goods and truths of the Word from the natural sense thereof. Ap. Ex. 727.

Basilisk (Isa. xiv. 29) s. the destruction of all the truth in the church. F. 53. They who confirm themselves in the principle of faith alone in doctrine and life, in the spiritual world, are seen as b., and their ratiocinations as fiery flying serpents. (Isa. xiv. 29, 30.) Ap. Ex. 386.

Basis s. truths in ultimates. 4618, 9433.

Basis. The natural world is the b. of the spiritual world; the body is the b. of the soul; the church on earth is the b. of the angelic heaven; the ultimate delights of married partners are the b. of conjugial love; the actions of man's life are the b. of his will and understanding; and the literal sense of the Word is the b. of its spiritual and celestial senses. U.T. 210; A.C. 10235; L.J. 65; C.L.S. 44. Just before the Lord came into the world and thereby took upon himself the ultimates of humanity, there was no b. to the heavens, for there was no divine truth in ultimates with the men of the church among them in the world, and altogether none in the church among the Jewish nation, unless falsified and perverted; wherefore, unless the Lord had come, all the human race in this earth would have perished in eternal death. Ap. Ex. The b. and foundation of the heavens is the human race. A.C. 4618.

Baskets den. the things of the will, because they are vessels to contain meats, and because meats s. celestial and spiritual goods, and these are of the will, for all good appertains to the will, and all truth to the understanding; as soon as any thing proceeds from the will, it is perceived as a good. In Gen. xl. 16, and Exod. xxix. 3, b. s. the sensual principle, or the ultimate of the life of man, which contains all his interior principles in order. A.C. 9996. B. (canistrum) (Num. vi. 15, etc.) den. the will-principle as that which contains; the cakes, wafers, oil, meat-offering, boiled shoulder of the ram, are the celestial goods which were rep.; for the Nazarite rep. the celestial man. At that time similar things, which were for worship, were carried in b. (canistris), or in b. (calathis), as also the kid of the goats by Gideon, which he brought forth to the angel under the oak (Judges vi. 19), and this by reason that b. rep. the things containing, and the things contained, which were therein. A.C. 5144.

Bath, a (Isa. v. 10), s. the same as vine; namely, truth from good. Ap. Ex. 675.

Bats rep. those who are in the light of infatuation. A.R. 566.

Battle, dissension concerning truths and goods. A.E. 1003.

Battle Axe (Jer. li. 20) s. the Lord with respect to divine truth. A.C. 2547.

Be, to, in God, s. the Lord's presence. A.C. 10, 154.

Beam (Gen. xix. 18; 2 Kings vi. 2, 5, 6; Hab. ii. 11; Matt. vii. 3, 5) s. the false of evil. Ap. Ex. 746. B. in the eye s. a great false from evil; and mote, or straw in the eye, s. a lesser false from evil. Ap. Ex. 746. B. of a ship from the Isles of Kitthin (Ezek. xxviii. 6) s. the externals of worship: consequently, rituals which respect the class of things celestial. A.C. 1156. See *Shadow of a Beam.*

Beans and **Pulse** s. the less noble species of good. A.C. 3332.

Bear or **Carry**, to, is to contain in its own state. A.C. 9836.

Bear or **Bring Forth**, to, s. acknowledgment. A.C. 3919.

Bear False Witness, to, s. lies and hypocritical artifices. U.T. 321.

Bear Sins, to, is not to take them away. L. 15–17.

Bear Bereaved of her **Whelps**, a (Hosea xiii. 8), s. the power of evil from the false. Ap. Ex. 388.

Bear, a, s. power from the natural sense of the Word, as well amongst the evil as the good. Ap. Ex. 781.

Bears s. the natural sense of the Word separated from its spiritual sense. They who separate them appear at a distance like b. in the spiritual world. A.R. 48, 573. White b., in the spiritual world, rep. the power of the spiritual natural man by the Word. Ap. Ex. 781.

Bears and **Doves**. (Isa. lix. 11.) B. have relation to the natural man, and d. to the spiritual man. Ap. Ex. 781.

Bears out of the Wood (2 Kings ii. 24) s. power from the natural or literal sense of the Word. Ap. Ex. 781.

Beard s. the most external part or principle. A.C. 9806. In Lev. xx. 5, s. the ultimate of the rational man. Ap. Ex. 557.

Bearing our Diseases and Carrying our Sorrows (Isa. liii. 3, 4) does not mean that the faithful are to undergo no temptations, or that the Lord took sin upon himself, and thereby removed it, but that, by temptation, combats, and victories, he conquered the hells, and thus alone, even as to his human essence, endured the temptations incident to the faithful. A.C. 1846.

Bearing Iniquities, by the Lord's, is meant dire temptations. He suffered the Jews to do unto him as they had done unto the Word. L. 15.

Beast. This expression, in the original tongue, s. properly life, or what is alive, but in the Word it not only s. what is alive, but what is, as it were, not alive; wherefore, unless a person is acquainted with the internal sense of the Word, he sometimes cannot know what is s. A.C. 908. B. in the Word is often des. by these two words, fera, and bestia, sometimes only fera, and often fera terræ, or fera agri, and when it is said fera and bestia, then is s. the affection or love of false and evil; by fera, the affection of the false, and by bestia, the love of evil; or in an opp. sense, by fera, the love of truth, and by bestia, the affection of good; but when fera is mentioned alone, or when bestia is mentioned alone, then by fera is understood the affection, as well of falses as of evil, and in an opp. sense, the affection of truth and good, but by bestia, the affection of evil, and thence of the false, and in an opp. sense, the affection of good, and thence of truths; when b. of the earth (fera terræ) are mentioned, the wild b. are understood which devour animals and men; but when b. of the field (fera agri) are mentioned, then are understood the b. (fera) which consume seeds; consequently, b. of the earth s. those who destroy the goods of the church; and b. of the field those who destroy the truths of the church. Ap. Ex. 388. In many places of the Word, b. and wild b. are used; and by wild b., fera is not understood. Wild b. in that sense which is received concerning wild b. for fera, in the Hebrew language, is derived from a word which s. life; thence for fera, in such places, it is rather to be called animal (see Rev. chap. i., chap. x.); but, nevertheless, there is a distinction to be made between bestiæ and feræ, and by bestia are s. the affections of the natural man, which are of his understanding, but forasmuch as fera, in the Hebrew language is derived from a word which s. life, therefore Eve, the wife of Adam, was named from that word. Ap. Ex. 650. By man and b., both named together, is s. man with respect to spiritual affection and natural affection. A.R. 567. In Gen. ix. 10, b. (bestia) s. the affection of good, and b. (fera) the affection of truth. Ap. Ex. 701. B. ascending out of the sea (Rev. xiii. 1) s. reasonings from the natural man, confirming the separation of faith from life. Ap. Ex. 773. The b. which rose out of the earth (Rev. xiii. 11) s. the faith among the clergy of the churches of the reformed. A.R. 594. B. ascending out of the earth (Rev. xiii. 11) s. confirmations by the natural man of faith, separate from charity, from the literal sense of the Word. Ap. Ex. 774. The scarlet-colored b. s. the Word. (Rev. xvii. 3.) A.R. 740. B. and creeping thing (Gen. viii. 19) s. the goodnesses of the internal and external man. A.C. 916. The b. (Rev. xix. 19) s. the good things of love profaned. A.C. 2015. Forasmuch as b. s. affections in both senses, and the posterity of Jacob were in externals, without the internal, therefore they were prohibited from making any figure or image of b., etc., for if they had, they would have made idols of them, and worshipped them. See Deut. iv. 17, 18. Ap. Ex. 650. There are b. of various kinds, by which the things of the will which relate to good are s., as lambs, sheep, kids, she-goats, cows, and oxen. A.C. 1823, 2179. There are also b., by which are s. things of the understanding, which relate to truth; viz., horses, mules, wild asses, camels, asses, and all birds. A.C. 2781, etc., etc. B. of the south (Isa. xxx. 6) s. those who are principled in the knowledges of good and of truth, but who do not apply them to life, but to science. A.C. 2781. The clean b. s. the affections of goodness, but b. not clean, lusts. A.C. 45, 46.

Beasts which were sacrificed s. various kinds of good and truth. Ap. Ex. 741. B. from a herd s. exterior affections, and b. of a flock, interior affections. Ap. Ex. 710. B. of the fields (Ps. civ. 11) s. the Gentiles who are in the good life. Ap. Ex. 483. B. (feræ) in Ezek. xxxi. 2, 9, s. affections of truth. Ap. Ex. 588. Daniel's four b. (Dan. vii. 3, 7) rep. the successive states of the church, from the beginning to the end of it, until it is entirely wasted as to all good and truth of the Word, and then the Lord comes. A.R. 471. B., in Mark i. 13, s. devils, with whom the Lord fought, and whom he subdued. A.V.C.R. 3. B. have no thoughts from understanding, but merely science from affections; they can only utter sounds, expressive of their affection, and vary them according to their appetite. W. II. B. are born into the sciences cor. to the love of their life; for as soon as they drop from the womb, or are excluded from the egg, they see, hear, walk, know their food, etc.; but man alone, at his birth, knows nothing of this sort, for nothing of science is connate with him, only he has the faculty of receiving those things. C.L.S. 350. The lives of b. are nothing else than affections, for they follow their affection from instinct without reason, and are thereby carried each to its use. A.C. 5198. B. have no reception and appropriation of the divine being. A.C. 5114. B. have no ideas or thoughts. U.T. 335.

Beat, to, or pound any thing as in a mortar (Exod. xxx. 36), s. the disposition of truths in their order. A.C. 10303.

Beatitude. Those in the life of heaven are in eternal b. A.E. 484.

Beatitudes, the, of heaven cannot be des. in words, though in heaven they can be perceived by the sense. D.P. 39.

Beautiful in form (Gen. xxxix. 6) s. the good of life hence; and b. in aspect s. the truth of faith hence; for form is the essence of a thing, but aspect is the existence thence derived. And whereas good is the very essence, and truth is the existence, thence, by b. in f. is s. the good of life, and by b. in aspect the truth of faith. A.C. 4985.

Beautiful in aspect. (Gen. xlii. 2.) Spiritual beauty is the affection of interior truth, and spiritual aspect is faith; hence by b. in a. is s. the affection of the truth of faith. A.C. 5199.

Beauty

Beauty. All b. is from good, in which is innocence. Good, when it flows in from the internal man into the external, constitutes what is beautiful, and hence is all human beautifulness. A.C. 3080. The affection of wisdom is b. itself. C.S.L. 56. B. of his ornament (Ezek. vii. 20) s. the church and its doctrine. Ap. Ex. 827.

Bdellium and the **Onyx Stone** s. truth. A.C. 110.

Bed s. doctrine, because as the body rests in its b., so does the mind in its doctrine. "There shall be two in one b., the one shall be taken (or accepted), the other left." Luke xvii. 35, meaning two in one doctrine, but not in similar life. A.R. 137. Every one's b. in the spiritual world is conformable to the quality of his science and intelligence; the wise have them magnificent, the foolish have mean ones, and false speakers have filthy ones. A.R. 137. B., in Rev. ii. 22, s. the natural man, and also the doctrine of falses. Ap. Ex. 163. Inasmuch as Jacob rep. the doctrine of the church, therefore, sometimes, when he was thought of by Swedenborg, there appeared to him, in the spiritual world, a man above, towards the right, lying in a b. A.R. 137. B., couch, and bedchamber, have a similar signification. A.R. 137. B. of ivory (Amos vi. 4) are doctrines apparently from rational truths. Ap. Ex. 1146.

Bedchamber s. interiors of man. 5694.

Bee (Isa. vii. 19) s. ratiocinations of the false. Ap. Ex. 410. Forasmuch as the rational principle derives its all from the scientifics of the natural man, from thence his reasonings are s. by b., because as b. suck and draw their nourishment from flowers, so does the rational principle from the scientifics of the natural man. Ap. Ex. 410.

Beech Trees s. natural good. C.S.L. 270.

Beelzebub s. the god of all falses. A.E. 740.

Beeri, the **Hittite**, truth from another source than what is real and genuine. A.C. 3470.

Beer-la-hai-roi (Gen. xxiv. 62) den. divine good rational born from essential divine truth. A.C. 3194, 3261.

Beer, or **Beersheba** (Gen. xxi. 33), s. the doctrine of faith, also divine doctrine. (Gen. xxviii. 10.) A.C. 2722, 3690. B. (Gen. xxi. 31) s. the state and quality of doctrine. A.C. 3466. In Gen. xxvi. 23, the doctrine of faith, which is the very literal sense of the Word. A.C. 3436. In Gen. xxvi. 33, human rational things, again adjoined to the doctrine of faith. A.C. 2723.

Beetle, or **Locust**, s. the false which vastates the extremes of the natural. 7643.

Befall, to. (Gen. xlii. 29.) The things which b. are the things which were of providence, or which were provided, because every thing which b., or happens, in other words what is called fortuitous, and is ascribed to chance, or to fortune, is of providence. A.C. 5508.

Before has respect to what is internal or prior. A.C. 10, 550.

Beginning of the **Work** of God (Rev. iii. 14) s. the faith of the church. Ap. Ex. 229.

Beginning (Gen. i. 1) s. the most ancient time. By the prophets it is usually called the day of antiquity, and also the day of eternity. B. also implies the first time when man is regenerated, for then he is born anew and receives life. It is from this ground that regeneration is called a new creation of man. A.C. 16. B. (initium), (Gen. xiii. 3) and b. (principium), (Gen. xiii. 4); every state previous to man's instruction is an initium, and when he begins to be instructed it is a principium. A.C. 1560.

Begotten, truth in act and operation. A.R. 17.

Begotten of the Father. See *Only Begotten*. A.E. 1069.

Behemoth (Job xl. 15), or the **Elephant**, as some think, s. the natural man as to good. Ap. Ex. 455.

Behind, to be (Gen. xviii. 10), s. not to be joined together, but at his back. What is separated from any one, this is rep. in another life, by a kind of rejection, as it were, to the back. A.C. 2196. B., or after (Gen. xvi. 13), s. within or above, or an interior or superior principle. A.C. 1955.

Behold, to, s. perception. A.E. 354.

Being, (esse.) Every person and thing has its b. or esse from conception; but its existing from birth. As conception is prior to birth, so is b. prior to existing. A.C. 2621.

Bela, or **Zoar**, den. the affection of good. 1589.

Bel (Isa. xlvi. 1) s. the profanation of truth. S.E.L.P. p. 12.

Belief. Matters of b. called faith, which are not joined with love and charity, vanish into nothing in another world. A.C. 553, 2364, 10153. H. and H. 474.

Believe, to, in **Jesus**, is to go to him, and to have faith that he can save, because he is the Saviour of the world. A.R. 839. To b. in Jesus, and not to approach him, but to pray to the Father for his sake, is not to b. in him, for all faith approaches him in whom man b. Ap. Ex. 805. To b. in the Lord, is to approach him immediately, and to have confidence that it is he who saves, and since no one can have this confidence, who does not lead a good life, therefore this also is implied by b. in him. A.R. 553. To b. in the Son, is to b. in the Father. U.T. 107. To b. the Word, is the first thing with the man of the church. A.C. 9222. To b. in the Lord, is derived from him and not from man. A.C. 10731. No one can b. in God, and love him, unless he can comprehend him under some particular form. A.C. 9356. To b. in God is the faith which saves, but to b. those things which are from God, is historical faith, which without the former will not save. Ap. Ex. 349. A.C. 9239.

Believe in God, to, is to know, to will, and to do. A.E. 349.

Bells, the sound of, s. divine spiritual truths. A.C. 9926. B., s. all things of doctrine and worship, passing over to those who are from the church, because by them the presence of Aaron in his ministration, was heard and perceived by the people; for by the people are s. they who are of the church, and by Aaron the minister, is s. all things of doctrine and worship. A.C. 9921. B. of gold (Exod. xxviii. 33) s. all things of doctrine and worship from good, passing over to those who are of the church. A.C. 9921. B. of the horses (Zech. xiv. 20), s. the understanding of the spiritual things of the Word, which are holy. A.C. 2761. Also, scientifics and knowledges, and from thence predications, which are from the understanding of truth. Ap. Ex. 355.

Belly, the (Ps. xvi. 4), s. the interior understanding. Ap. Ex. 622. In Gen. iii. 14, those things which are nearest to the earth. A.C. 247. Natural good. A.C. 10030. B., in Matt. xv. 17, from cor., s. the world of spirits, from whence thoughts flow into man, and the draught there mentioned, s. hell. Ap. Ex. 580. The b. (John vii. 37), cor. to the interiors of the understanding and of thought. Ap. Ex. 518, 622. The reason why walking upon the b. to the earth, s. the infernal falses, is, because under the earths in the spiritual world, are the hells, which send up an exhalation of the falses of evil, and the interiors of the understanding and thought (to which the b. cor.) would thereby be infected, and imbue those falses; wherefore nothing in the spiritual world goes with his b. upon the earth; but to walk upon the earth with the feet, has no such cor. connection, except only with those who are merely natural and principled in evil, and the false. Ap. Ex. 622. The b. of the great fish, into which Jonah was cast, s. the lower parts of the earth. A.C. 247. See *Womb*.

Belly and **Thigh**. (Num. v. 29.) B. s. conjugial love; also spiritual love; and t. s. natural love. Ap. Ex. 618.

Beloved of **Jehovah**, the (Deut. xxxiii. 12), s. spiritual truth derived from celestial good. A.C. 4586.

Beloved

Beloved, or **well-beloved** (Isa. v. 1), s. the Lord. Ap. Ex. 375.

Below, that which is above is within, and that which is b. is without. A.E. 283.

Belt den. a common bond, that all things may look to one end, and may be kept in connection. A.C. 9828.

Beltshazzar. His kingdom being divided, s. the dissipation of goods and truths; and he himself being slain that night, s. the privation of the life of truth and good, consequently, damnation. A.C. 9093.

Belzebub, who was the god of Ekron, s. the god of every false. Ap. Ex. 740.

Bemoan, to (Gen. xxxvii. 35), s. the ultimate of grief and sorrow. A.C. 4786.

Bend, to, the knee, s. adoration. 5323.

Beneath. The things which are b. are nothing but derivations and consequent compositions, inasmuch as the inmost principle is all in all in whatever is b. it, for whatever is b. unless it exists from things interior, or what is the same, from things superior, as an effect from its efficient cause, has no existence at all. A.C. 3562.

Benediction, acknowledgment, glorification, and thanksgiving. A.E. 340–3.

Benevolence, exp. 2949–54.

Benjamin s. the spiritual of the celestial principle, which is the medium proceeding from the internal rep. by Joseph. A.C. 5469. The spiritual celestial man. A.C. 3969. In Num. ii. 18–24, the conjunction of good and truth. Ap. Ex. 449. In Ps. lxviii. 28, the innocence of the natural man. Ap. Ex. 449. Also, the Word in its ultimate sense (Deut. xxxiii. 43.) Ap. Ex. 449. The conjunction of the spiritual natural and the celestial natural angels, in the ultimate heaven. Ap. Ex. 449. In Rev. vii. 8, a life of truth originating in good. A.R. 361.

Benjamin and **Joseph**. B. s. the conjunction of good and truth in the natural man, and consequently the conjunction of the spiritual man with the natural; and J. s. the conjunction of the celestial man with the natural. Ap. Ex. 449. The medium which B. rep., is the medium between the internal and the external, or between the spiritual and the natural man, and is the truth of good which proceeds from the truth derived from the divine which is rep. by J.; that truth of good is called the spiritual of the celestial principle; B. is the spiritual of the celestial principle. A.C. 5566. Sons of B. (Jer. vi. 1, 2) s. those who, in the ultimate heaven, have conjunction with the Lord. S.E.L.P. p. 19. J. could not be conjoined with his brethren, nor with his father, but by B., for without an intermediate, conjunction cannot have place, and this was the reason why J. did not sooner reveal himself. A.C. 4592.

Benoni, in the original tongue, s. a son of my grief. 4591.

Bera den. the Lord's Temptations. 1651.

Bereave of **Children**, to, den. to deprive the church of its truths and goods, because the church is compared to a marriage, its good to the husband, and its truth to the wife, and the truths born from that marriage to sons, and the goods to daughters, and so forth; when therefore mention is made of being made childless or being b. of c., it s. that the church is deprived of its truths, and thence becomes no church. A.C. 5536.

Bereavings, sons of (Isa. xlix. 18), den. truths restored to the vastated church. A.C. 536.

Beryl, the, s. the good of charity and faith or the spiritual love of truth. A.C. 6135, 9873.

Bethaven, those things which relate to spiritual truth, derived from celestial. 4592.

Bethel (Gen. xii. 8), s. the knowledge of things celestial. A.C. 1451. In Gen. xxviii., the natural principle, or the good of that principle; also the knowledges of good, and truth, in a proximate sense: also, the divine in the natu-

28

ral principle, or in the ultimate of order. A.C. 3720, 3729. In Amos iii. 14, divine good. A.C. 2832.

Bethlehem, the spiritual of the celestial principle. This is the reason why the Lord was born there, for he alone was born spiritual celestial, the divine principle being in him. A.C. 4592. Truth conjoined with good in the natural man. Ap. Ex. 449. The ultimate of good, and Dan the ultimate of truth. Ap. Ex. 391.

Bethograma, those who are in internal worship. A.E. 355.

Bethsaida (Mark viii. 22) s. condemnation from non-reception of the Lord. Ap. Ex. 239.

Bethuel (Gen. xxiv.), the origin of the affection of good. A.C. 3160. In Gen. xxii. rep. the good of the Gentiles of the first class. A.C. 268, 311.

Betrothed, agreement of minds preceding conjunction of marriage. A.C. 8996.

Bezaleel rep. those who are in the good of love. A.C. 10329.

Bilhah (Rachel's handmaid) s. the affection subservient to the affection of interior truth as a medium. A.C. 3849. B. (the concubine of Israel) (Gen. xxxv.) s. good. A.C. 4802. See *Reuben.*

Bind, to (Gen. xxii. 9), s. to put on a state of undergoing the last degrees of temptation. A.C. 2813.

Binding Together s. truths arranged series within series; also aggregations of falses. 7408.

Bird of Abominations (Dan. ix. 27) s. faith alone, or separate from charity. Ap. Ex. 684.

Birds in general s. things spiritual, rational, and also intellectual. A.C. 40, 1832. Those who have an immediate perception of truths are rep. by eagles; those who arrive at truths by a series of proofs, by singing b.; those who accept it on authority, by the pie kind; those who have no inclination to perceive truths, by b. of night. T.C.R. 42. He who draws wisdom from God is like a b. flying aloft enjoying a wide and extensive view, and directing its flight to whatever is required for its use. T.C.R. 69. B. know each other by their notes and cries, and by the sphere of life which exhales from their bodies. T.C. 459. See *Fowl.*

Birds of Paradise, a pair of, rep. conjugial love of the middle or spiritual region of the human mind. C.S.L. 270.

Birsha den. the Lord's temptations. 1651.

Birth, in the Word, relates to the work of regeneration. A.C. 613, 1255.

Birthright. See *Primogeniture.*

Bite, to, s. to cleave unto, and to bring an injury upon any one. A.C. 6400.

Bitter, cor. to truth falsified. A.R. 411, 481. B., in the Word, s. unpleasantness; but the bitterness of wormwood s. one kind of it, the bitterness of gall, another kind, and the bitterness of hemlock, a third kind. There is one kind of unpleasantness s. by the bitterness of unripe fruit, and another kind by that bitterness which is neither from herbs nor fruit; this bitterness s. grief of mind and anxiety from many causes. Ap. Ex. 522. When man applies the literal sense of the Word to the evils of earthly loves, then it becomes to the angels who are in the internal or spiritual sense like the unpleasant (taste) of bitterness. Ap. Ex. 618. See *Grapes of Gall.*

Bitter Herbs, things undelighted, injucundities of temptations. 7854.

Bittern s. affections of the false, interior and exterior. A.E. 650.

Bitumen den. good mixed with evils. 6724.

Black (Gen. xxx. 32) s. proprium. A.C. 3994. In Rev. vi. 5, s. what is false. A.R. 312.

Black Garment rep. the Word in the letter. A.C. 1872.

Blackness. There are in the spiritual world two kinds, which proceed from a twofold origin; one from the absence of flaming light, which is the light of

Bladder

those who are in the Lord's celestial kingdom, and the other from the absence of white light, which is the light of those who are in the spiritual kingdom. A.R. 312. B. (Gen. iv. 23) s. the devastation of charity. A.C. 43.

Bladder. They who are in the hells cor. to such things as are excreted by the intestines and by the b., inasmuch as the falses and evils in which they are principled, are nothing but urine and excrement in the spiritual sense. A.C. 5380. There are companies of spirits who wander about, and by turns return to the same places; evil spirits are much afraid of them, for they torment them with a certain kind of torture; it was told me that they cor. to the bottom or lower part of the b. in general, and to the muscular ligaments, thence concentrating towards the sphincter, where the urine is extruded by a mode of contortion. A.C. 5389. See *Gall-Bladder*, and *Kidneys*.

Blasphemies s. truths of the Word falsified, or scandals. A.C. 584.

Blasphemy (Rev. xiii. 1) s. the falsification of the Word. Ap. Ex. 778. The denial of the Lord's divine human, and church doctrine of the Word. A.R. 571. The commonly received doctrine concerning three persons in the Godhead and the atonement is b. Ap. Ex. 778. In Rev. ii. 9, s. false assertion. A.R. 96.

Blasphemy against the Holy Spirit. They are guilty of it who exclude the works of charity from the means of salvation, and assume the doctrine of faith exclusively from them, as the one only medium, and confirm this not only in doctrine, but also in life, saying in their heart that good works cannot save them, nor evils condemn them, because they have faith. Ap. Ex. 778. To speak a word against the son of man, s. to interpret the natural sense of the Word according to appearances, but blasphemy against the Holy Spirit s. falsification of the Word, even to the destruction of divine truth in its genuine sense. Ap. Ex. 778.

Blast of the Breath of his Nostrils (Ps. xviii. 16) s. the same as by his anger and wrath, elsewhere mentioned in the Word, which to the evil appear as from the Lord. Ap. Ex. 741.

Blasting and Mildew (Amos iv. 9) s. evil and the false in the extremes, or from the sensual corporeal principle. Ap. Ex. 638.

Bleatings of the Flocks s. perceptions and thoughts. A.E. 434.

Bless, to (Gen. xxiv. 60), s. devout wishes. A.C. 3185. In Gen. xxv. 11, a beginning of rep. A.C. 3260. Gen. xxxi. 55, to testify joy when one departs. A.C. 4216. To b. (Deut. x. 8, and xxi. 5), worship from spiritual truths, and to minister, worship from good. Ap. Ex. 340. To b. (Jer. iv. 2) in an opp. sense, s. to love and imbue evil and the false. Ap. Ex. 340.

Blessed, the, s. those who have the felicity of eternal life. A.R. 639, 951. B. (Rev. i.) is pred. of one who with respect to his spirit is in heaven, consequently, who while he lives in the world, is in communion with the angels of heaven. A.R. 8.

Blessed of Jehovah, to be enriched with every good of love. A.C. 3406.

Blessedness s. eternity. A.C. 3938. B. is internal delight, and delight is external b. C.L.S. 51.

Blessing, when pred. of the Lord's human (Gen. xxiv. 1), s. to dispose all things into divine order. A.C. 3017. The Lord's b. in the Word, s. fructification and multiplication, because it gives birth thereto. A.C. 43. B. s. celestial, spiritual, natural, worldly, and corporeal good, which things are good when they thus succeed each other in orderly arrangement, and in these good things is happiness. A.C. 1422.

Blessing of God (Gen. ix. 1), s. the presence and grace of the Lord. A.C. 981.

Blessing, and Glory, and Wisdom, and Thanksgiving (Rev. vii.), s. divine spiritual things of the Lord. A.R. 372. The reception of divine truth in the first heaven, is called b.; the reception of divine truth in the second heaven is called g., and the reception of divine truth in the third heaven is called w. Ap. Ex. 465.

Blessing and **Righteousness**. (Isa. xxiv. v.) B. s. the reception of divine truth, and r., the reception of divine good. Ap. Ex. 340.

Blessing of Jehovah. The b. of J. in the general sense s. love to the Lord and charity towards the neighbor. A.C. 4981.

Blessings of the **Breasts** and of the **Womb** (Gen. xlix. 25) s. spiritual and celestial goods. Ap. Ex. 340. B. of the b. (Gen. xlix. 25) s. the affections of good and truth, and b. of the w., the conjunction of good and truth, thus regeneration. Ap. Ex. 7.

Blind and **Naked**. (Rev. iii.) By b. is understood they who are in no understanding of truth, and by n. they who are in no understanding and will of good. Ap. Ex. 238. B. s. falsity. A.C. 2383, 1008. Also, ignorance of truth. A.C. 1328, 1059.

Blood, s. divine truth, and in an opp. sense, divine truth falsified. A.R. 332. The holy principle of charity. (Gen. ix. 6.) A.C. 1010. B., s. things celestial, and in a supreme sense the human essence of the Lord, consequently essential love or his mercy towards mankind. B. was therefore called the b. of the covenant, and was sprinkled upon the people in the Jewish rep. church. A.C. 1011. The redness of the b. is occasioned by cor. of the heart with love and its affection. D.L.W. 380. B. sometimes means violence, according to the subject. A.R. 237, 379. B. of the Lamb means divine truth proceeding from the Lord, which is the divine truth of the Word. A.R. 379. The Lord's b. s. the divine truth proceeding from the divine good of his divine love. A.C. 4795, 4978. The unmercifulness and hatred of the last times. (Rev. xvi. 3, 4.) A.C. 374. B., as of one dead (Rev. xvi. 3), s. the internal false principle. A.R. 681. By drinking b. is s. not only to falsify the truths of the Word, but also to imbibe such falsifications in life. A.R. 688.

Blood of Grapes (Gen. xlix. 11) s. what is celestial in respect to spiritual churches. A.C. 1071.

Blood and **Water**, which issued from the breast of the Lord (John xix. 34–5), s. the conjunction of the Lord with the human race by divine truth spiritual and natural proceeding from the divine good of his love. Ap. Ex. 329.

Bloods s. violence offered to the truths and goods of the Word and of the church. Ap. Ex. 329. The abominations of Jerusalem (Ezek. xvi. 6, 22.) A.C. 374. Evil. (Ezek. xvi. 9.) A.C. 3147. See *Cry.*

Blood-Shedding s. violence offered to good. A.C. 3400.

Blossom rep. second state of the re-birth of man. A.C. 5116.

Blue s. truth from a celestial origin. A.C. 9933. U.T. 220. B., in an opp. sense, s. the diabolical love of the false, and also the love of the world. Ap. Ex. 576.

Blue and **Purple** s. celestial goods and truths, and scarlet double-dyed and fine-twined linen, spiritual goods and truths. (Exod. xxviii. 33.) A.C. 4922. B. and P. from the Isles of Elishah (Ezek. xxvii. 7) den. rituals cor. with internal worship, consequently, those rep. of things celestial. A.C. 1156.

Boanerges, or sons of Thunder (Mark. iii. 17), s. truths from celestial good. A. Ex. 821.

Boar in the **Wood** (Ps. lxxx. 11) s. the false, and the wild beast of the fields, is the evil which destroys the church as to faith in the Lord. A.C. 5113.

Body, the (Matt. vi. 22), s. the man (homo). Ap. Ex. 1081. The good of love, which is the good of the will. (Matt. vi. 25.) Ap. Ex. 750. The form of the b. cor. to the form of the understanding and the will. D.L.W. 136. All who are in good, although as to b. dispersed throughout the universe, form as to life, but one b.; so also the church, and all members in it. A.C. 2853, 2854. The b. which clothes the inmost of the life of man is from the mother. A.C. 1815, 6716. "His b. shall not remain all night upon the tree" (Deut. xxi. 23),

Body of the Lord

s. lest it should be rep. of eternal damnation. Ap. Ex. 655. The b. (Luke xvii. 37) s. the world of spirits where all men are together for a time, both the evil and the good: and the eagles in this passage s. those who are in truths, and in an opp. sense, those who are in falses. Ap. Ex. 281. The spiritual b. appears before those who are spiritual like as the natural b. does to those who are natural. C.L.J. 3. Into the interiors of their b. flow the heat and light of heaven whose interior mind is opened and elevated by actual conversion to the Lord. D.L.W. 138. The b. is an organ composed of all the most mysterious things which are in the world of nature. A.C. 4523.

Body of the Lord. The human b. of the L. cannot be thought of as great, or small, or of any particular stature. D.L.W. 285. The Lord's glorified b. was not a material but a divine substantial b. L. 35. The Lord arose with his whole b., for he left nothing in the sepulchre, and although he was a man as to flesh and bone, still he entered through the doors when shut. A.C. 10825. B. and flesh of the L., s. the divine good of his divine love, which is that of his divine human. A.C. 3813.

Bogs cor. with filthy loves. C.S.L. 431.

Boil, to (Gen. xxv. 29), s. to heap up. A.C. 3316. To b. in water, is to reduce truths into doctrine, and so to prepare them to the use of life. A.C. 10105.

Boils and **Sores** s. interior evils and falses destructive of goodness and truth. A.R. 678.

Bolsters s. communication of divine things with outermost. A.C. 3695.

Bondage s. infestations from falses. A.C. 7120, 7129.

Bondmen s. those who know and understand from others. A.R. 337, 832.

Bonds. All affections are b., because they rule the man and keep him bound to themselves. A.C. 3835.

Bones, a fire of (Ezek. xxiv. 5), s. the affection of truth. A.C. 3812. B. s. falses, and sepulchres evils. (Num. xix. 16, 18.) A.C. 3812. The spreading out of b. (Jer. viii. 1) s. the infernal things attendant on lusts. A.C. 2441. Intellectual propriety in the external man, as to truth. A.C. 156. The societies of spirits, to whom the cartilages and b. cor., are very many in number; but they are such as have in them little of spiritual life; as there is very little of life in the b. compared with what is in the soft substances which encompass them; for example, as there is in the skull and the b. of the head compared with what is in each brain, and the medulla oblongata, and the sensitive substances therein; and also as there is in the vertebræ and ribs, compared with what is in the heart and lungs, etc. A.C. 5560.

Bonnets (Exod. xxviii. 40), being a covering for the head, s. intelligence and wisdom, the same as mitre, which see. A.C. 9949.

Book. (Rev. x. 9.) "And I went unto the angel, saying, give me the little b.," s. the faculty of perceiving the quality of the Word from the Lord. Ap. Ex. 616. Little b. (Rev. x.) s. the doctrine of the New Jerusalem concerning the Lord. A.R. 472. By taking and eating the little b., which shall make thy belly bitter, but in thy mouth it shall be sweet as honey, is s. that the reception of the doctrines of the New Jerusalem, so far as that his humanity is divine, would be unpleasing and difficult by reason of falsifications. A.R. 481, 482. The b. which the angel had in his hand (Rev. x.) s. the Word, and the eating thereof, the exploration of its quality. Ap. Ex. 614. By book (Rev. vi.) is understood a roll, for in ancient times there were no types and thence b., as at this day, but only rolls of parchment. Ap. Ex. 404.

Books s. the interiors of the mind of man, because in them are written all things appertaining to his life. A.R. 867.

Book of the Covenant (Exod. xxv. 7) s. the divine truth which they had at that time. A.C. 4735.

Book of Generations (Gen. v. 1), an account of those who were of the most ancient church. A.C. 470.

Book of Life s. the Word of the Lord, and all doctrine respecting him. A.R. 588. B. of l. (Rev. v.) s. the states of the life of all in heaven and earth which is inscribed or implanted in the spirit of man. Ap. Ex. 299.

Book of the Word. In order to constitute a genuine b. of the W., it is necessary that it treat, in an internal sense, of the Lord Jesus Christ alone, and his kingdom. See Luke xxiv. 27, 44; John v. 39, etc., etc. A.C. 3540.

Border (Isa. liv. 12) s. the scientific and sensual principle. A.C. 655. "And thou shalt make unto it a b. of an hand-breath round about." (Exod. xxv. 25), s. conjunction there with truth from the divine; for b. is the ultimate of termination; consequently, conjunction with truth from the divine. A.C. 9534. See *Hem.*

Bore, to, the ear through with an awl (Exod. xxviii. 6) was a rep. of obedience. A.C. 8990.

Born of God, the (John i. 11, 13), are those who are principled in love, and thence in faith. A.C. 2531.

Born of the House (Gen. xvii. 12) s. the celestial, and bought with silver s. the spiritual; consequently, those who are within the church. A.C. 2048.

Born from Eternity. See *Divine Human.* See A.C. 2803.

Born in Time. See *Divine Human.* See A.C. 2803.

Borne from the Belly and carried from the Womb. (Isa. xlvi. 3, 4.) Man who is regenerated by the Lord, is first of all conceived, and afterwards born, and at length educated and perfected, and since regeneration in this respect is like the natural generation of man, therefore, by being b. from the b., is s. the state of man whilst he is regenerating, from conception to nativity, and that nativity itself and afterwards education and perfection is s. by being brought forth from the womb. Ap. Ex. 710.

Borrow and **Lend** den. to communicate the goods of heaven from the affection of charity, and also the goods of the Word according to the laws of charity. A.C. 9174. To l. den. instruction. A.C. 9209.

Bosom, the, or **Breast**, s. spiritual love, which is love in act. Ap. Ex. 821.

Bottle (Jer. xiii. 12) s. the mind of man, because that is the recipient of truth or false, as a b. contains wine. Ap. Ex. 376.

Bottles s. the knowledges which contain truths. Ap. Ex. 195. Also the exterior worship of the church. A.R. 316. Old b. (Matt. ix. 17) s. the statutes and judgments of the Jewish church, and new b., the precepts and commands of the Lord to the Christian church. Ap. Ex. 376. See *Vials.*

Bottomless Pit s. hells where the Word is falsified. A.E. 536.

Boughs of thick Trees (Lev. xxiii. 40) s. scientific truth with its good. Ap. Ex. 458.

Bought from the Earth (Rev. xiv. 3) are they which could be regenerated. A.R. 619, 622.

Bought with Silver s. the spiritual in the church. A.C. 2048.

Bound, the, or those who are in prison (Matt. xxv. 35), s. those who acknowledge that in themselves there is nothing but what is false, or who are in the false. A.C. 4956, 4958. B. (Gen. xlii. 16) den. to be separated, for he who is kept b. is separated, viz., from the spiritual good, which is s. by the father Israel. A.C. 5452. To be b., or be a surety for another (Gen. xliii. 10), s. to adjoin to himself. A.C. 5839.

Boundary, the ultimate ground or principle into which interior things fall and terminate. A.E. 403.

Boundaries, ground into which things interior fall and terminate. A.E. 403.

Bow, to (Gen. xviii. 2), s. to humble. A.C. 2153. To b. one's self (Gen. xxiii. 7) s. to rejoice. A.C. 2927. To b. the head (Gen. xliii. 28) s. adoration, or the effect of humiliation. A.C. 4689.

Bow s. doctrinals. A.C. 3899. Also the doctrine of truth. A.C. 2685, 2686. To handle or bend the b. s. to reason. A.C. 1195. B. s. the false of doctrine

Bow of Jonathan

destroying truth, and spear, the false of evil destroying good. (Jer. vi. 23.) Ap. Ex. 357. See *Quiver, Shooter.*

Bow of Jonathan s. doctrine, and the sword of Saul, is truth from good. (2 Sam. i. 22.) Ap. Ex. 357.

Bow in a Cloud, the (Gen. ix.), rep. regeneration. A.C. 1042, 1048. See *Rainbow.*

Bow Himself, to, when pred. of a lion, s. to put himself into ability. 6369.

Bowels, in the Word, s. love or mercy, by reason that the b. (viscera) of generation, especially the mother's womb, rep. and thereby s. chaste conjugial love, and, consequently, love towards infants. B. s. essential love or essential mercy and the Lord's compassion towards mankind. A.C. 1803. To come forth out of the b. (Gen. xv. 4) s. the state of those who are principled in love to the Lord and towards their neighbor. A.C. 1803.

Bowels (Exod. xxv. 33) s. scientific truths derived from the good of charity. A.C. 9557.

Box Tree (Isa. xli. 19) s. the understanding of good and truth. Ap. Ex. 830.

Boy and **Boys** in the Word have various significations, because they are pred. as well of home-born sons as of the sons of a stranger, and also of servants. A.C. 2782. What is interior is in the Word, respectively called b., because there is more of innocence in what is interior, than in what is exterior, and innocence is signified by an infant, and also by a b. A.C. 5604. B. (Gen. xviii. 7) s. the natural man, and consequently, him who ministers and administers. A.C. 2181. In Gen. xxi. 14, the spiritual principle. A.C. 2677. In Gen. xxii. 5, the Lord's divine rational principle in a state of truth prepared for the most grievous and inmost temptation combats. A.C. 2793. In Isa. xi. 6, innocence and love to the Lord. Ap. Ex. 780. In Gen. xxii. 17, spiritual truth. A.C. 2691. It is said (Isa. ix. 5), "unto us a b. is born and unto us a son is given." By b. is here s. divine good; and by son, divine truth. Ap. Ex. 365. B. (Gen. xxii. 3) s. the Lord's former rational principle merely human which he adjoined and which was to serve the divine rational. A.C. 2782. In Gen. xxii. 19, things human rational. A.C. 2858. In Gen. xxv. 26, good and truth. A.C. 3308. The b. who were torn in pieces by the two she-bears (2 Kings ii. 23, 24) rep. those who blaspheme the Word by denying that truth is contained therein. A.C. 2762, 3301. B. and girls (Zech. viii. 5) s. the truths and goods of innocence, such as the truths and goods of the Word which essentially constitute the church. Ap. Ex. 863. B. playing in the streets, den. truths in the first stage of their growth; and girls den. goodnesses in the first stage of their growth, and the affections thereof, together with the joys thence derived. A.C. 2348. B. and old men, in a bad sense, den. falses and evils, both such as are in an early stage of growth, and such as are confirmed. A.C. 1259, 1260, 2349.

Boyhood, or **Childhood,** s. the affections of good and truth. 3254.

Bozrah (Isa. lxiii. 1) s. a vintage, which is pred. concerning truth. Ap. Ex. 9, 22. B. has respect to the divine truth, and Edom, to the divine good of the Word. (Isa. lxiii. 1.) Ap. Ex. 922.

Bracelets (Gen. xxv. 22) s. truth, and in this passage divine truth, because the Lord is treated of. A.C. 310. B. upon the arms, s. the power of truth from good. A.C. 358.

Brain, the, is the primitive formation in man. D.L.W. 432. An organical recipient of the interior senses. A.C. 444. In the heavens there are heavens and societies, which have reference to the cerebrum and cerebellum, in common and in parts. A.C. 4045. All things in the b. are according to a heavenly form. A.C. 4040. The indurated humors of the b. answer to those societies which regard no use, and induce stupidity. A.C. 4054. The b., like heaven, is in the sphere of ends which are uses. A.C. 4054. The human b. is a recipient form of divine truth and divine good, spiritually and naturally organized. U.T. 224, 351. Those who have reference to the glands, or cortical substances of the b., are in the principles of good, but those who are in the principles of truth, have reference to those things in the b. which flow forth from those principles, and are called fibres. A.C. 4052. The cortical substances are full of glands, answering to the heavenly societies, and the medullary, full of fibres, answering to the rays of goods and truths, issuing from thence; as those of the light of the stars on the earth. D.L.W. 366. The b. consist of two hemispheres, the cerebellum for the will, and the cerebrum for the understanding. D.L.W. 42, 384. It is the b. and the interiors thereof, by which descent from the heavens into the world, and ascent from the world into the heavens is made, for therein are the very principles, or first and last ends, from which all and singular the things that are in the body flow forth and are derived; thence also come the thoughts of the understanding, and the affection of the will. A.C. 4042, 4053.

Bramble (Exod. iii. 2) s. scientific truth, because all small shrubs of every kind s. scientifics, but the greater shrubs themselves s. perceptions and knowledges. A.C. 6832. B. (Judges ix. 13) s. spurious good. A.C. 9277.

Branch (Matt. xxiv. 32) s. affection, for affection springs and flourishes from good as a b. from its trunk. A.C. 4231. B. (Mal. iv. 1) den. truth. A.C. 1861. B. s. spiritual truth, and bulrush, that which is sensual and scientific. (Isa. xix. 15.) Ap. Ex. 559. B. of a tree s. sensual and natural truths in man. A.R. 936.

Brand s. but little of truth remaining. A.E. 740.

Brass s. natural good. A.C. 421, 425. Also rational good. A.C. 2576. Fine b. (Rev. i.) the good of truth natural. A.R. 49.

Brass and **Iron** (Isa. xlviii. 4, and Dan. vii. 19) s. what is hard. Ap. Ex. 70.

Brazen Sea, the, was ten cubits from laver to laver, and five cubits in height, and thirty cubits in circumference, to the intent that holy things might be s. as well by the numbers ten and five, as by thirty, which number of the circumference does not indeed geometrically answer to the diameter, but still it spiritually involves that which is s. by the compass of that vessel. For all numbers s. things in the spiritual world. A.C. 5291. See *Laver*.

Brazen Serpent, the, s. the Lord, as to his divine humanity. A.R. 469. The b. s. which was set up in the wilderness, s. the sensual of the Lord, who alone is a celestial man, and alone is circumspect and provident over all, so that all who look upon him are preserved. A.C. 197.

Breach (Gen. xxxviii. 29) s. the infraction and perversion of truth, by separation from good. A.C. 4926. In Ps. lx. 3, 4, the undermining of the church, and thence the perversion of truth, and irruption of the false. Ap. Ex. 400. B. s. the false of doctrine, and the stroke of their wound, evil of life. (Isa. xxx. 26.) Ap. Ex. 962. B. (Amos iv. 3, etc.) s. the false which exists by the separation of truth from good. A.C. 4926.

Bread s. the Lord himself, and of course his love towards the whole human race, and whatever appertains thereto. As also man's reciprocality to the Lord, and towards his neighbor, thus it s. all things celestial. A.C. 2165. B. s. every good that is for spiritual food to man. All the burnt offerings and sacrifices in the Jewish church, were called by the single name b., although they had each respectively a particular rep., therefore when sacrifices were abolished, and other things succeeded instead thereof, for external worship, it was commanded that b. and wine should be used for this purpose. A.C. 2165, 2177. B., in Gen. xxxvii. 25 s. evil derived from the false principle. A.C. 4745. In Ezek. iv. 16, both good and truth. Ap. Ex. 727. To break b. s. to communicate one's own good with another. Ap. Ex. 617. By eating b. in the sweat of the face, is s. to have an aversion to what is celestial. A.C. 275, 279. To eat the b. of the Lord (Ps. xli. 10) s. appropriation of divine truth, here, its communication, because it could not be

Bread

appropriated to the Jews. B. s. the Word from which spiritual nutrition is derived. Ap. Ex. 617.

Bread and **Wine.** Goods and truths in the spiritual man. A.E. 340.

Breadth s. the truth of the church, because in the spiritual world or in heaven, the Lord is the centre of all things, for he is the sun therein; they who are in a state of good, are more inward according to the quality and quantity of the good in which they are; hence altitude is pred. of good; they who are in a like degree of good, are also in a like degree of truth, and thereby, as it were, in a like distance, or in the same periphery. This is the reason why by b. in the Word, the angels understand truth. A.C. 4482. See *Length.*

Break, to, bread is rep. of mutual love. 5405. A breach den. the infraction and perversion of truth. 4926.

Break Forth, to (Gen. xxviii. 14), s. extension. A.C. 3708. To b. f. to a multitude (Gen. xxx. 30) s. fruitfulness. A.C. 3985.

Break the **Neck,** to (Exod. xiii. 13), s. separation and ejection. A.C. 8079.

Breast, the, s. goodness and truth, by reason of the heart and lungs being therein. A.C. 1788. The b. cor. to the second or middle heaven. Ap. Ex. 65. The b. s. things rational. A.C. 2162. By the Lord's b., and especially by the paps, his divine love is s. A.R. 46. The b. cor. to the affections of good and truth of that order, viz., the spiritual: the right, to the affection of good, and the lefts to the affection of truth. A.C. 6745. B. fashioned (Ezek. xvi. 7), s. natural good. A.C. 3301.

Breast of Consolations (Isa. lxvi. 11) s. divine good; and the splendor (or abundance) of her glory, divine truth from which doctrine is derived. (Isa. lxvi. 11.) Ap. Ex. 365.

Breastplate of Judgment (Exod. xxviii. 15) s. divine truth shining forth from the divine good of the Lord in the ultimates. A.C. 9823. The twelve precious stones therein rep. all the goods and truths of heaven in their order. A.C. 9873.

Breastplates (Rev. ix. 9) s. argumentations. A.R. 450.

Breath of the **Lips** (Isa. xi. 4) s. doctrines which with the wicked is false. A.C. 1286.

Breath of the **Nostrils** (Lam. iv. 20) is the essential celestial life which is from the Lord. Ap. Ex. 375.

Breathe, to, in **Man's Nostrils** the **Breath** of **Lives** (Gen. ii. 7) s. to give the life of faith and love. A.C. 94.

Breathing and a **Cry.** (Lam. iii. 56.) B. is pred. of truths, and c. concerning goods. Ap. Ex. 419.

Breeches of Linen s. the external of conjugial love. 9959.

Brethren (Gen. xxvii. 29) s. the affections of good. A.C. 3582. My b. and thy b. (Gen. xxxi. 37) s. what is just and equitable. A.C. 4167. See *Accuser Joseph's Brethren.*

Briars and **Thorns** den. falsities and lusts. 2831.

Brick s. what is false, being an artificial imitation made by man of stone, which cor. to truth. A.C. 1296.

Brick Kiln, to repair the (Nahum iii. 14), s. worship grounded in falses. A.C. 1276. See *Clay.*

Bride. The church is a b. when she is desirous to receive the Lord; and a wife, when she actually does receive him. A.R. 895. See *Spirit and Bride.*

Bridegroom and **Bride.** By virtue of the marriage of the Lord with the church, the Lord is called b., and the church, b. Hence the new church, which is the New Jerusalem, is called the b., the Lamb's wife, and at the end of the Apocalypse, the b. and b. speak, i.e., the Lord and the church, as if it were during the desponsation. A.R. 797, 895, 960.

Bridles of the **Horses** (Rev. xiv. 20) s. truths of the Word, by which the understanding is guided. A.R. 298, 653.

Briers s. falses of evils. A.R. 439. B. and thorns (Isa. ix. 17) s. falsity and lust. A.C. 2831. B. s. evil, and thorns what is false. (Isa. xxxii. 13.) Ap. Ex. 304.

Brightness. They are exterior truths which are rep. by the b. of garments in the heavens, and interior truths by the b. and splendor of the countenance. A.C. 5319.

Brimstone (Isa. xxxiv. 9, etc.) s. filthy lusts. A.C. 643.

Bring away, to (Gen. xxi. 18), s. to separate. A.C. 4105.

Bring back, to (Gen. xxviii. 15), s. to join together again. A.C. 3712.

Bring back upon a station, to (Gen. xl. 21), den. to reduce into order, that they may be in the last place. A.C. 5165.

Bringing Forth (Gen. xviii. 13) s. that the rational should be made divine. A.C. 2208. To b. f. (Gen. xix. 16) s. to withhold. A.C. 2413. To acknowledge in faith and in act. (Gen. xxx. 1.) A.C. 3905. The existence of the spiritual things which are of truth, and of the celestial things which are of good. A.C. 4586. To b. f. has respect to the existence of good and truth. A.C. 3298. To b. f. (Micah i. 8, 9) is pred. of the restoration and reformation of the church. Ap. Ex. 721. To b. f. is pred. of the truth, and to burn of the good, which were to be extirpated. A.C. 4906. To b. f. and travail in birth, s. to conceive and b. f. those things which appertain to spiritual life. A.R. 535.

Bring Forth Abroad, to (Gen. xv. 5), s. the vision of the interior man, which from things external sees things internal. A.C. 1806.

Bring, to (Gen. xxxvii. 28), s. consultation. A.C. 4760.

Bring to his House, to (Gen. xxix. 3), s. conjunction. A.C. 3809.

Bring himself near, to (Gen. xxxiii. 3), s. to conjoin himself. A.C. 4348.

Bring up upon the Knees, to (Gen. l. 23), s. conjunction of good and truth. A.C. 6585.

Broad Place, or **Way,** s. truth of doctrine and truths of life. A.E. 652.

Broidered Work (Ezek. xvi. 10, 13) s. genuine scientifics. A.C. 5954.

Broken Cisterns, doctrines in which are no truths. A.C. 2702.

Bronchia, and their ramifications, cor. to will and understanding. D.L.W. 405.

Brooks of Honey and Butter (Job xx. 17) are things spiritual and celestial, which reasoners were not to see. Reasonings are called the poison of asps and the viper's tongue. A.C. 195.

Brother s. the affection of good, and sister the affection of truth. A.C. 3129. B. s. goods, and sons s. truths. (Deut. xxxiii. 9.) Ap. Ex. 444. B. s. good in the natural man. A.C. 3166. The truths of faith. (Gen. xii. 5.) A.C. 1434. B., in the Word, s. the same thing as neighbor. A.C. 2360. External worship is called b. to internal worship, in the Word. A.C. 1244. B. s. such as are in the good of charity. A.R. 32. It is not allowable for any man to call the Lord b., because he is God as to his humanity, and God is not b., but father. The only reason why he calls his disciples his brethren (Matt. xxv. 40, John xx. 17, etc.), is because he is father, from divine love, but b. from the divine proceeding from himself. Ap. Ex. 746. B. delivering up b. to death, s. that the false shall destroy good; specifically, that faith shall alone destroy charity. Ap. Ex. 315.

Brother and **Companion.** (Jer. xxiii. 35.) B. means he who is principled in the good of love, and c. he who is principled in the truth of doctrine. S.S. 84.

Brother-in-Law, to perform the duty of a, was a law enjoined in the Jewish church, not merely for the sake of preserving a name and thence of inheritance, but in order to rep. the conservation and continuation of the church. A.C. 4835.

Bruised s. what is broken and not in coherence with interior truth. A.E. 627.

Bruised Reed, divine truth sensual with the simple. A.E. 627.

Buckets (Num. xxiv. 7) s. knowledges. A.C. 3079.

Buckler, defence against falses. A.E. 734.

Bud forth

Bud forth, to, is pred. of goodnesses and truths, and, consequently, of every thing relating to the church. A.C. 2452.

Budding, or producing leaves and afterwards blossoms, s. the first of re-birth: the reason why influx is also den. is, because when man is in the act of being re-born, spiritual life flows in into him, as life by heat from the sun into a tree, when it is in the act of b. He who is born a man, in the Word throughout is compared to the subjects of the vegetable kingdom, especial-ly to trees, and this because the whole vegetable kingdom, as also the ani-mal kingdom, rep. such things as appertain to man, consequently, such as are in the Lord's kingdom, for man is a heaven in the least form. A.C. 5115.

Build, to, s. to raise up that which is fallen, and is pred. of evils and some-times of goods. A.C. 153. To b. s. to collect scientifics. A.C. 1488. To b. an house (Gen. xxxiii. 17) s. to instruct the internal man in intelligence and wisdom. A.C. 4390. To b. is applied to the old waste places, and to erect, to the former desolations. (Isa. lxi. 4.) A.C. 153.

Bullock s. the good of innocence in the natural man. A.C. 5391.

Bulrushes (Exod. ii. 3) s. what is vile, but nevertheless derived from truth. A.C. 6723. See *Branch.*

Bulwarks (Isa. xxvi. 2) s. truths. A.C. 402.

Bundle (Gen. xlii. 3) s. orderly arrangement, because the truths appertaining to man are disposed and arranged into serieses: those which are in the greatest agreement with the loves, are in the midst; those which are not in so much agreement, are at the sides, and lastly, those which are in no agreement, are rejected to the remotest circumferences; the things out of the series are those which are contrary to the loves. A.C. 5530.

Burden (Jer. xvii. 4) s. that which is from the proprium of man. Ap. Ex. 208. B. s. infestations from falses, and from thence combats. A.C. 7109. B. (Judges v. 15) (in the common version, sheepfolds) s. knowledges and sci-entifics in the natural man; and the bleatings of the flocks s. the percep-tions and thoughts arising from them. Ap. Ex. 434.

Burial, by, wheresoever mentioned in the Word, the angels understand res-urrection. A.C. 4016. See *Death.*

Buried, to be (Gen. xxxiv. 8), s. to be rejected. A.C. 4564. To be b. s. to rise again, and to continue life, because all earthly and impure things are rejected. And not to be b. s. to continue in things earthly and unclean, and for that reason to be rejected, as damned. A.R. 506.

Burning (Rev. xviii. 18) s. damnation and punishment of evils arising from earthly and corporeal loves. Ap. Ex. 1173.

Burning, Fire, Sulphur, and **Pitch,** are pred. of evil lusts, especially of those which are derived from self-love. A.C. 1297.

Burnt Offerings and **Sacrifices,** the, in the Jewish church, rep. nothing else by celestial things appertaining to the Lord's kingdom in the heavens and in the earth, general and particular, consequently, all the things of love and charity. A.C. 2165. B. o. and s. s. all worship: b. o. worship from love, s. worship from faith proceeding from love. A.C. 916, 924. The Lord's divine human. A.C. 10057.

Bus, or **Buz.** Various religious persuasions. 2860–4.

Bush (Exod. iii. 2) s. scientific truth. A.C. 6832.

Butler den. the sensual principle which is subject or subordinate to the intellectual part of the internal man, because every thing which serves for drinking, or which is drunk, as wine, milk, water, has relation to truth, which is of the intellectual part, and whereas the external sensual princi-ple, or that of the body, is what subministers, therefore, by b. is s. that subministering sensual principle, or that which subministers of things sen-sual. A.C. 5977. The chief B. (Gen. xl. 1) is the sensual part of the under-standing in a state of subjection. A.C. 5227.

Butter (Isa. vii. 14, 16) s. the Lord's celestial principle, and honey that which is derived from thence. A.C. 2184. Celestial good. (Isa. vii. 22.) A.C. 5620. B. of the herd (Deut. xxxii. 13) s. the celestial natural principle, and milk of the flock, the celestial spiritual principle of the rational. A.C. 2184. B. and Honey (Isa. vii. 15) s. the good of celestial and spiritual love, and the good of natural love, which the Lord should appropriate to himself. Ap. Ex. 304, 617. B. and oil (Isa. lv. 21): b. s. the good of external affection, and o. the good of internal affection. Ap. Ex. 537.

Butterflies. He that confirms himself in favor of the divine from the visible things of nature, sees a certain image of the earthly state of man in these creatures as worms, and an image of his celestial state in them as b. D.L.W. 354.

Buy, to, s. to procure for one's self, and thereby to appropriate; procuration and appropriation is effected spiritually by good and truth; to this cor. the procuration and appropriation which in the world is effected by silver and gold, for silver is truth, and gold is good in the spiritual sense, hence buying s. appropriation. A.C. 5374. To b. s. redemption. A.C. 6549. To b. (Rev. iii. 18) s. to procure or acquire to one's self. A.R. 211.

C

Cadesh (Gen. xiv. 7) s. truths, and also contentions about truths. A.C. 1677. The affection of interior truth, proceeding from things rational. (Gen. xx. 1.) A.C. 2503.

Cage. The c. of unclean spirits s. the hell of those who are in evils from the adulterated goods of the Word, and obstructed by the evils themselves, which are adulterated goods. Ap. Ex. 1099.

Cain s. faith separate from love. D.P. 242. The knowledges of truth and good, separate from a life according to them. Ap. Ex. 817. C. saying, "Am I my brother's keeper?" means faith making light of charity. A.C. 370, 372. The mark set upon C. was faith, by which charity might be implanted; and therefore C., that is, faith, was to be preserved for the sake of charity. A.C. 330, 392. C. speaking to Jehovah s. a kind of confession from internal pain. "His iniquities greater than he could bear," s. desperation, and that "every one who found him would slay him," s. that every evil and false would destroy him. (Gen. iv. 13, 14.) A.C. 383, 385. See *Tubal-Cain.*

Cainan (Gen. v. 12) s. a fourth church from Adam. A.C. 506.

Cake s. the good of celestial love. Ap. Ex. 147. C. den. the conjunction of the spiritual and celestial principles, which appertained to the Lord. (Gen. xviii. 16.) A.C. 2177. See *Baskets.*

Calah (Gen. x. 12) s. the false derived from evil lusts. A.C. 1184. See *Ninevah* and *Resin.*

Calamus, sweet (Exod. xxx. 23), the perception and affection of interior truth, but when mentioned alone by itself it s. good. A.C. 10256.

Caleb (Num. xiv. 24) rep. those who are introduced into the church, and, accordingly, his seed s. the truth of the doctrine of the church. Ap. Ex. 768.

Calf s. the affection of knowing divine truth. A.R. 242, 244. The good of exterior innocence. (Isa. xi. 6.) A.C. 10132. Male c. the natural principle which the Lord put on, conformable to his spiritual and celestial principles. (Gen. xviii. 7.) A.C. 2137. See *Calves.*

Call, to, without the addition of name, in the internal sense of the Word, s. to be of such or such a quality. A.C. 3421. To c. on the name of Jehovah is a customary and general form of speaking, expressive of all worship of the Lord. A.C. 440. Also s. internal worship. (Gen. xii. 8.) A.C. 1455. To c. to any one, s. perception of quality. A.C. 3650.

Call Forth, to. Angels c. f. truths and goods in man. A.C. 5992. The internal sight of man c. f. from scientifics those things which are derived from his love. A.C. 9394. Truths are c. f. from the natural memory, or the external of man, into the internal, by the Lord. A. C. 10252.

Called. By the c. in a general sense, are meant all throughout the world, because all are c. By the c. in a particular sense, are meant those who are with the Lord. The c. to the marriage supper of the Lamb, s. those who receive the things of the new church, and the c., the chosen, and the faithful, s. those who are in the externals, the internals and inmost principles of the church. A.R. 744, 816. To be c. by Jehovah, in the historical parts of the Word, s. influx from the Lord. A.C. 6840.

Callosity, profanation of the Word, induces c. A.C. 571.

Candlestick

Calneh, a variety of worship, s. by Babel. A.C. 1183.

Calves of **Egypt** and of **Samaria** (Jer. xlvi. 20, 1 Kings xii. 28, 32) s. the affection of knowing falses. A.R. 242. C. of the lips (Hos. xiv. 2) are confessions from the affection of truth. A.R. 242. C. of the stall (Mal. iv. 2), or fatted c., s. those who are filled with knowledges of things true and good from the affection of knowing them. A.R. 242.

Calves or **Sherp**. A he-c. den. the external good of innocence, a s. the internal, a lamb the inmost. 10, 132.

Camel (Matt. xxii. 24) s. scientific knowledge. A.C. 3048, 10227. C. s. the scientific principle in general, and ass, the scientific principle in particular. A.C. 2781. C. in the word, s. common scientifics in the natural man. A.C. 3048. Common principles in the natural scientific principle. A.C. 4104. C. are confirming scientifics, and cattle are the knowledges of good and truth. (Jer. xlix. 32.) Ap. Ex. 417.

Camel's Hair, the ultimate principle of the natural man. A.E. 619.

Camp s. all the truths and goods of the church. A.R. 862. To sacrifice in the c. was holy, but out of the c. profanation. A.C. 1010. C. of God (Gen. xxxii. 2) s. heaven. A.C. 423. C. of the saints (Rev. xx. 8) s. the good things of love and charity. A.C. 2418. C. of the sons of Israel (Deut. xxiii. 14, 15) rep. the church. C.S.L. 431. In the opp. sense, c. s. evils and falses and consequently hell. A.C. 4236. C. in a good sense, den. genuine order, and in an opp. sense, order not genuine. A.C. 4236.

Cana of **Galilee** (John ii. 1) s. the church among the Gentiles. Ap. Ex. 376.

Canaan (Gen. ix. 18), a worship in things external without internal, which arose out of the internal church corrupted, called Ham. Thus it is that Ham is named the father of C. A.C. 1060, 1167. Daughters of C. (Gen. xxviii. 8) s. affections of truth from a ground not genuine, whereas in Gen. xxviii. 1, they s. the affections of what is false and evil, the reason of which distinction is, that the Hittites were in the land of C. of the church of the Gentiles and not so much principled in what is false and evil, as the other nations therein; viz., the Canaanites, the Amorites, and the Perizites. A.C. 3662, 3686. The land of C. in the Word s. the church, because the church had been in that land from the most ancient time, first the most ancient church which was before the flood, next the ancient church which was after the flood, afterwards the other ancient church which was called the Hebrew church, and at length the Jewish church; and that the Jewish church might be there instituted, Abram was commanded to betake himself thither out of Syria, and it was there promised that that land should be given to his posterity for an inheritance. A.C. 5136.

Canaanite and **Perizite**, the, being in the land (Gen. xiii. 7), s. hereditary evils and falses in the Lord's external man. A.C. 1414, 1570.

Cancer, a, cor. to the consummation of the church in the manner of its progress and fatal termination. A.T.C.R. 13. U.T. 120.

Candle. (Luke xv. 8.) By the woman lighting a c. to find the piece of silver she had lost, is s. inquisition in herself from affection. Ap. Ex. 675. See *Lamps*.

Candlestick s. intelligence and faith in particular. A.R. 493. The spiritual heaven, or the divine spiritual in heaven and in the church from the Lord. (Exod. xxv. 31.) A.C. 9558. The shaft, branches, bowls, knobs, and flowers belonging to the c. (Exod. xxv. 31), s. spiritual things in natural, for the natural is produced and derived from the spiritual, as the spiritual is from the celestial, and as the external appendages of the c. proceed from the c. itself. A.C. 9551, 9552. C. rep. the church as to illumination from the Lord through the Word. A.R. 43. C., in an extended sense, s. the spiritual kingdom of the Lord, and thence the spiritual church; also the truth of doctrine and of faith. Ap. Ex. 638. Seven golden c. (Rev. i. 12), s. the New Church which will have her light from the Lord. A.R. 43.

41

Cane

Cane (sweet) **from a far Country** (Jer. vi. 20) s. adorations of the Lord, destitute of charity. A.C. 1171.

Canker-Worm, Caterpillar, and **Palmer-Worm** (Joel ii. 25), s. falses and evils vastating or consuming the truths and goods of the church. Ap. Ex. 573.

Canons for the use of the New Church. I. That no one can shun evils as sins, and do goods, which are good in the sight of God, from himself; but that as far as any one shuns evils as sins, so far he does good, not from himself, but from the Lord. II. That man ought to shun evils as sins, and to fight against them as from himself; and that if any one shuns evil from any other cause whatever, than because they are sins, he does not shun them, but only causes them not to appear before the world. T.C.R. 330.

Canticles. See *Solomon's Song* and A.C. 3942.

Captains over a Thousand (Rev. xix. 18) s. those who are in knowledges of things good and true, and abstractedly, those knowledges. A.R. 337. C. and Rulers (Jer. li. 23) s. principal evils and falses. Ap. Ex. 863. C. and Rulers (Ezek. xxxiii. 6) s. principal truths. Ap. Ex. 576. See *Chief Captains*.

Carthorium, scientific, or external rituals of worship. 1193.

Captives, in the Word, s. the Gentiles. Ap. Ex. 811. The same as those who are bound. Ap. Ex. 811.

Captivity, in the Word, s. spiritual c., and generally has respect to the seclusion and deprivation of truth. Ap. Ex. 811. The c. of the tribe of Judah in Babel, seventy years, rep. the plenary destruction of truth, and devastation of the church. Ap. Ex. 811. C. s. being seduced, and so led away from truths and goods. A.R. 591. C. and spoil (Dan. xi. 33) s. the deprivation of every truth and good. Ap. Ex. 811.

Carbuncle (Exod. xxviii. 17) s. the good of celestial love. A.C. 9865.

Carcase (Matt. xxiv. 28) s. the church void of the life of charity and faith. A.C. 3900.

Cardiac Kingdom s. that in which love reigns. D.W.L. 381.

Care, impedes and obstructs the perception of spiritual things. 6408.

Carmel (Isa. xvi. 10) s. the good of the church. Ap. Ex. 376. Mount C. (Isa. xvi. 10) s. the spiritual church. A.C. 1071. Also the celestial church. (Isa. xxxv. 2.) A.C. 5922.

Carried from the Womb s. education and perfection. A.E. 710.

Carriages s. doctrinals. 5945, 8215.

Carry, to, s. to hold together in a state of good and truth. 9500.

Carry Iniquities, to, s. to sustain dire temptations. L. 15.

Cart, the new (Sam. i. 5, 6), upon which the Philistines sent back the ark, s. new but natural doctrine. D.P. 326.

Cartilages cor. to truths and goods of the lowest natural kind. A.C. 6380.

Cask (Gen. xxiv. 20) s. truth which was initiated into good divine. A.C. 3095. C., or water pot (Gen. xxiv. 14), s. scientifics. A.C. 3068.

Casluhim, name of a nation, and s. doctrinals. 1196.

Cassia (Exod. xxx. 24) s. interior truth from good, or interior truth of the internal man. A.C. 10258. C. and Calamus (Ezek. xxvii. 19) s. natural truth from which good comes. A.C. 3923.

Cast out, to (Gen. xxi. 10), s. to exterminate. A.C. 2657. To be c. o. of the garden of Eden (Gen. iii. 24) s. to be deprived of all intelligence and wisdom. A.C. 306.

Cast Lots, to, to disperse truths by falses. A.E. 863.

Cast Dust on the Head, to, interior grief and mourning. A.R. 778.

Castles (Gen. xxv. 17) s. the intellectual things of faith and of the church. A.C. 2371. Rational and natural truths are called c., when the truths of faith are called cities. A.C. 3271.

Cataracts of Heaven, falses of the understanding. A.C. 843.

Caterpillar (Joel i. 4) s. the evil of the sensual man. A.E. 543.

Celestial Good

Catholic Church of the Lord, the, consists of all throughout the world who lead good lives, and believe in a Supreme Being. A.C. 2589–2604.

Catholics. The Roman Catholic religion is external without internal. 10.040.

Cats. They who confirm themselves in the negation of the things of the church are like c. who can see in the dark, for they acquire to themselves a deceitful light, which is excited by the activities of their concupiscences. A.R. 566.

Cattle (Gen. xxii. 7, 8) s. those of the human race who may be sanctified. A.C. 2807. The goods and truths of churches. (Gen. xxix. 7.) A.C. 3807. C. of the earth (Gen. ix. 2) den. lusts. A.C. 987. C. and beasts of the field in the Word, have a distinct signification. A.C. 46. C. s. the celestial affections, and fowls of the air, spiritual affections. A.C. 142. See *Oxen*.

Caught up, to be, to God and his throne. See *Child*.

Caul above the liver; interior good of the external man. 10,031.

Cause, the, of natural things is an inmost spiritual principle, of which natural things are its effect, and both together act as one, like soul and body in man. A.R. 1. The c. principal is the all in all of the c. instrumental. U.T. 442. The Lord is not the c. of evil, but only the wicked themselves. D.R. 292, 330. God would be the c. of evil, if men were without free will in spiritual things. U.T. 489. C. explain effects, and to know effects from c. is to be wise; but to inquire into c. from effects is not to be wise. D.L.W. 119. C. produce effects, not by continuous but by discrete order. D.L.W. 185.

Cause and Effect. The end is the all, in the c. and e. A.C. 3562.

Cave s. an obscure principle, because it is a dark place; when it is said the c. of a mountain, it then s. an obscure principle of good, but when it is said the c. of a field, it then s. an obscure principle of truth. A.C. 2935. In Gen. xix. 30, it s. the good of a false principle, and in 1 Kings xix. 9, it s. such an obscure state of good as exists in temptations. A.C. 2463. See *Den of Thieves*.

Caverns, confirmations from scientifics. A.E. 388.

Cedar s. the spiritual man. A.C. 776. The church spiritual rational. Ap. Ex. 1100.

Cedars of Lebanon s. the knowledges of truth. A.R. 242.

Celebration and Glorification of the Lord, is a living acknowledgment that the humanity of the Lord is divine, and that he has all omnipotence and omniscience. Ap. Ex. 321.

Celestial as well as **Spiritual** is pred. both of the rational and of the natural principle, that is, of the internal man, which is the rational man, and of the external, which is the natural man; for the s. principle in its essence is the divine truth which proceeds from the Lord, and the c. is the divine good which is in that divine truth. A.C. 4980. It is c. to think and act from the affection of good. A.C. 2718. The c. in the grand man constitute the head. A.C. 4938. The c. are distinguished from the s. by regarding the goods of faith, while the latter regard its truths. 1155.

Celestial Angels reason not concerning the truths of faith, but the spiritual a. do. H. and H. 25. A.C. 202. C. a. far excel the spiritual a. in wisdom. A.C. 2718. H. and H. 25.

Celestial Church, the, is the truth of good implanted in the voluntary part which was before the proper seat of good. A.C. 5733.

Celestial Divine Good. See *Rational Principle*. A.C. 2557.

Celestial Doctrine, love towards the Lord. A.C. 7257.

Celestial Form. See *Lord*.

Celestial Good consists in looking to the Lord; and in believing that from him alone is all good and truth; and that from man, or his proprium, there is nothing but evil. Ap. Ex. 324. C. g. is the same with the good of love in the will, and in act. Ap. Ex. 821.

43

Celestial Love

Celestial Love is love to the Lord, received in the celestial kingdom; and spiritual love is love to the Lord received in the spiritual kingdom. Ap. Ex. 433. The good of c. l. immediately proceeds from the divine human of the Lord. Ap. Ex. 364.

Celestial Man, a, believes and perceives spiritual and celestial truth and goodness, nor does he acknowledge any other faith, but what has its ground in love, which love is also the principle of his actions. A.C. 81. The ends which influence him regard the Lord and thereby his kingdom and eternal life. He is engaged in no combats, and in case he is assaulted by evils and falses he despises them, and is therefore called a conqueror. A.C. 81. A c. m. does nothing of his own pleasure but of the good pleasure of the Lord which is his pleasure: thus he enjoys peace and internal felicity, which is expressed by "riding on the high places of the earth," and he enjoys at the same time tranquillity and external delight, which is signified by feeding on the "heritage of Jacob." (Isa. lviii. 13, 14.) A.C. 85. The c. m. is the interior rational man. A.C. 4402. The Lord came into the world not to save the c., but the spiritual; the most ancient church, which was called m., was c., and if this had remained in its integrity, the Lord would have had no need that he should be born m. A.C. 2661.

Celestial Mysteries. There is not a single expression in the Word which does not involve them. A.C. 4136.

Celestial Natural Principle, the, is the good in the n. p. which cor. to the good of the rational, that is, which cor. to the c. of the spiritual p. from the rational. A.C. 4980. The c. n. p. is natural good. A.C. 2184. The inmost c. cor. to gold, the inferior to brass, and the corporeal, or lowest, to wood. A.C. 643. The c. p. consists in love towards the Lord. The c. p. consists in perceiving solely the affection of the things contained in the internal sense. A.C. 2275. All laws relating to what is true and right flow from c. p., or from the order of life in the c. man; for the whole heaven is a c. man from this, that the Lord alone is a c. man; and this is the true ground of their being called c. A.C. 162.

Celestial and **Angelical Proprium** from the Lord. It is by virtue thereof that the church is called a woman, and also a bride, a wife, a virgin, and a daughter. A.C. 253. In order that man may receive a c. p., he ought to do good from himself, and to think truth from himself, but still to know that all good and truth is from the Lord. A.C. 2883. The c. p. exists from the new will which is given by the Lord, and differs from man's p. in this, that they no longer respect themselves in all and singular the things which they do, and in all and singular the things which they learn and teach, but they respect the neighbor, the public, the church, the kingdom of the Lord, and thereby the Lord himself. A.C. 5660.

Celestial Sense, the, of the Word, is the highest or most interior; but this sense cannot easily be unfolded, not being so much the object of intellectual thought, as of will affection. S.S. 19.

Celestial Spirits are intermediate angelical societies, called c. spiritual. A.C. 4047. H. and H. 26.

Celestial spiritual is that which is s. from a c. origin. A.C. 1001.

Celestial, the, of the spiritual principle is truth from the divine, because the Lord's internal human before it was fully glorified, inasmuch as it was the receptacle of the divine itself, was the c. of the spiritual principle, so to be called, because it cannot be expressed in other terms. A.C. 5471. All men whatsoever are born natural, with the ability to become *either c. or spiritual.* A.C. 4592. The Lord alone was born a spiritual c. man, but all others natural, with the faculty or ability that by regeneration from the Lord they may be made either c. or spiritual. A.C. 4594.

Celestial and **Spiritual**. The divine love of the Lord in the heavens is called c. and s. with respect only to its reception by the angels and not from any divisibility in itself. Moreover, s. love exists from c. love, as an effect from its efficient cause, and as truth from good. Ap. Ex. 496.

Celestial Things. In them alone the Lord is present, and from them all perception is derived. A.C. 1442. When c. t. have the dominion, they ill. worldly things, place them in a clear light, and take away doubts. A.C. 4099. C. t. exterior, appertain to the external man; c. t. interior, appertain to the internal man; and c. t. spiritual are what are thence derived. The essential c. principle is love to the Lord and neighborly love; and in the interior man is called the c. interior principle. In the exterior man it is called the c. exterior principle which is every affection of good, and also every pleasure thence derived, and the c. spiritual principle is every affection of truth which is generated from the affection of good. A.C. 1824. C. t. are not clothed, but spiritual and natural things are. A.C. 5248.

Celibacy. Chastity cannot be pred. of those who have renounced marriage by vows of perpetual c., unless there be and remain in them the love of a life truly conjugial. C.L. 155. C. has place only among those who are in external worship, and who do not address themselves to the Lord, or read the Word. Ib. 155. The reason why they who live in c. are on the side of heaven, is because the sphere of perpetual c. infests the sphere of conjugial love, which is the very essential sphere of heaven. C.S.L. 54.

Cellular. Substance of the lungs, exp. D.L.W. 413.

Censer, a, s. worship from spiritual good. Ap. Ex. 491. To cast the c. upon the earth (Rev. viii. 5) s. influx into the parts beneath. A.R. 395. A golden c., s. conjunction of celestial good with spiritual good, and a brazen c., conjunction of spiritual good with natural good. Ap. Ex. 491.

Centre. The c. from the expanse of nature ought to be viewed from the c. and expanse of life. U.T. 35. The Lord is the common c. whereunto all the angels in heaven turn themselves. A.C. 3633. The nearer the c., the more beautiful are the angels. A.C. 3475. Every one in his society, has an influx from the universal heaven. Every one is a c. of all influences, and a base in which terminates the influx of all. A.C. 4226. In the universal heaven, every individual is a c. of the blessednesses and happinesses of all, and all together are the c. of the blessednesses and happinesses of each individual. A.C. 2872.

Centre of Gravity. The c. of g. in the spiritual world is determined with man from the love in which he is principled; downwards if his love is infernal, and upwards if his love is celestial. Ap. Ex. 150.

Cerebellum. In the c., which is in the hinder part of the head, dwells the will. I. 13. The angelic spirits who diligently watch over man during sleep, belong to that province. A.C. 1977. The c. is awake when the cerebrum is asleep, for the will or love of man never sleeps. A.C. 1977. See *Brain*.

Cerebreus den. a guard to prevent any one passing from the delight of conjugial love to the delight of adultery. 2743.

Cerebrum. The left part thereof cor. to rational or intellectual things, and the right part to affections or the things of the will. A.C. 3884. In the c., which is under the forehead, dwells the understanding. I. 13.

Ceremonies, are of no moment by themselves. 2342.

Chafer and **Locust** s. the false which vastates the extremes. 7643.

Chaff (Matt. iii. 12) s. the false of every kind, derived from an infernal origin. Ap. Ex. 374. The faith of the false, is as c. before the wind. Ap. Ex. 740. See *Stubble*.

Chains. Things conjoined, or coherences of good, of truth, of falses, etc. 9852, 9879.

Chain in the **Hand**, to have a (Rev. xx. 1), s. the endeavor proceeding from the power of binding and loosing. A.R. 840.

Chain

Chain of **Gold**, a (Gen. xli. 42), s. conjunction by good. A.C. 5320. C. for the neck s. the conjunction of the interiors and exteriors. Ap. Ex. 195.

Chalcedony. A stone consisting of several varieties. See *Precious Stones.*

Chaldea s. worship in which inwardly are falses. See *Babel.*

Chaldeans s. those who are principled in knowledges profaned. A.C. 3079.

Chalice s. spiritual truths. A.R. 672.

Chamberlain, the interior things of scientifics. 4789. Such as accede closely to spiritual. 4965.

Chambers, or inner apartments of a house, s. such things as are more interior. A.C. 3900.

Chambers of **Jehovah** (Ps. civ. 3) s. the heavens and the church. Ap. Ex. 594.

Chance. Things ascribed to c. are of the divine providence. 5508.

Change, to (Gen. xli. 14), s. to remove and reject. A.C. 5248. To c. the garments, was a rep. that holy truths were to be put on. A.C. 4545. The state of the life of man from infancy to the end of life, and afterwards to eternity, is continually changing, and in like manner the internal form of man, which is that of his spirit. C.S.L. 185, 186.

Changes of **State** have respect both to the thoughts and the affections. A.C. 1463. There are c. relative to things spiritual and celestial, both in general and in particular. Life without such c. and varieties would be one or uniform, consequently none, nor would goodness and truth be known or distinguished, much less perceived. These c. are in the prophets called ordinances. A.C. 37.

Channels. The c. of the waters s. the truths of the church. Ap. Ex. 741.

Charcoal Fire rep. the life of lusts, and the obscure light thence proceeding cor. to the falsities thereof. A.C. 1666.

Chariot s. doctrine; also the being grounded in spiritual truth. D.P. 326.

Chariots (Rev. xviii. 13) s. goods from a rational origin. Ap. Ex. 1155. See *Coaches, Horses.*

Chariot of an **Ass**, a heap of particular scientifics. A.C. 3048.

Chariot of a **Camel**, a heap of common scientifics. A.C. 3048.

Charity, or **Good**, is actually the first principle or constituent of the church, and truth or faith the secondary principle, although it appears otherwise. A.C. 3424. C. is the very ground of the seeds of faith; truth and g. agree together, but truth and evil do not agree. A.C. 2343. C. is an internal affection of the soul, proceeding from the Lord Jesus Christ, as its proper fountain, and prompting a man to do g., and to act uprightly from a pure love of goodness and uprightness, without any regard to reward or recompense; for it brings its own reward along with it, and in its exercise is attended with the highest and purest satisfactions of life. N.J.D. 104. C. the genuine goods of, are all from a spiritual origin. A.C. 5119. C. alone is a natural, not a spiritual, affection. Ap. Ex. 232. C. with the spiritual appears like the affection of g., but it is the affection of truth, and is the g. of their faith. A.C. 2088. C. is the alone medium of loving the Lord. A.C. 4776. C. is the uniting medium of the rational, natural, and sensual. A.C. 5133. The state of c. with man is according to the quality and quantity of truth. A.C. 2189. The offices exercised towards the hungry, thirsty, strangers, naked, sick, and bound in prison, which are spoken of by our Lord (Matt. xxv. 34, 36), comprehend the whole doctrine of c. A.L. 4954, 4959. C. is of the internal man, and is the internal man himself. A.C. 1012. C., which is the life of the Lord, is not in man, but with him. A.C. 1010. C. gives the faculty of receiving influx from the Lord, and salvation thereby. A.C. 8321. The doctrine of c., in the ancient church, was chiefly insisted on, which constituted a great part of their wisdom. A.C. 2417. The life of c. consists in man's thinking well of others, and desiring g. to others, and perceiving joy in himself at the salvation of others. A.C. 2284. The first part of c. consists in putting away what is evil, and the second in doing what is g. and profitable to our neighbor. By c., there is conjunction of the Lord with man, and by faith there is conjunction of man with the Lord. A.R. 571. All things which are of the doctrine of faith lead to c., are in it, and are derived from it. A.C. 2228. C. is the essence of faith, and faith separated therefrom is merely natural, but conjoined thereto becomes spiritual. A.R. 417. C. may be adjoined to any heretical faith. U.T. 450. C. and g. works are two distinct things, like willing what is g., and doing what is g. C. consists in acting justly and faithfully in whatsoever office, business, or employment a person is engaged, and with whomsoever he has any commerce or connection. U.T. 420.

Chaste Love of the **Female Sex**, the, s. to love them for their beauty, virtue, and intelligence, free from all allurements of libidinous desire. Conjugial love is another thing, but with those who are principled in it, there is also the c. l. of the sex in general. C.L. 55, 138.

Chaste Principle, the, and the **non-chaste**, are pred. only of marriages, and of such things as relate to marriages. C.S.L. 139, 140. The c. p. is pred. only of monogamical marriages, or the marriage of one man with one wife. C.S.L. 141. The Christian conjugial p. alone is c. 142. Love truly conjugial, is essential chastity. C.S.L. 143. All the delights of love truly conjugial, even the ultimate are c. C.S.L. 144.

Chasten, to admit into temptations. A.E. 246.

Chastity, cannot be pred. of those who abstain from adulteries, only for various external reasons. C.S.L. 153. C. cannot be pred. of those who believe marriages to be unchaste. C.S.L. 154. C. cannot be pred. of those who have renounced marriage by vows of perpetual celibacy, unless there be and remain in them the love of a life truly conjugial. C.S.L. 155.

Chaunting (of the Land) (Gen. xliii. 11) den. things excellent, land den. the church, and vessels den. the truths of faith. The expression c. is used, because in the original tongue it is derived from singing; hence the c. of the land s. productions chaunted and commended, consequently, in the internal sense, things more excellent. A.C. 5618.

Chedorlaomer (Gen. xiv. 4, 5) den. apparent good and truth in the Lord's external man. A.C. 1669. C. (Gen. xiv.) rep. the divine good and truth of the Lord in childhood, consequently, the human essence of the Lord as to goodness and truth, by which he destroyed the persuasions of the false, which tended to lay waste the world of spirits and mankind. A.C. 1675. C., king of Elam (Gen. xiv. 9), s. truths; and Tidal, king of Goiim, goods. A.C. 1682.

Cheek (Matt. v. 39) s. the perception and understanding of interior truth. The right c., the affection, and thence perception, and the left c., its understanding. Ap. Ex. 556.

Cheek-bone. (Ps. iii. 8.) To smite the c.-b., and to break the teeth, s. to destroy interior and exterior falses. Ap. Ex. 556.

Chemosh, false principles of those in natural good. A.C. 2468.

Chemoth, the people of (Jer. xlviii. 46), s. those who are in natural truth. Ap. Ex. 811.

Cherethims. See *Egypt*. S. external rituals. 1193–5.

Cherez, the city of (Isa. xix. 18), commonly rendered "the city of destruction," s. the doctrine of the good of charity. See Ap. Ex. 654.

Cherub (Ps. xviii. 11) s. the inmost heaven. Ap. Ex. 529.

Cherubim s. the providence of the Lord, to prevent man, who is in a bad state, entering into the things of faith; also the guards which are set by the Lord to preserve the spiritual sense of the holy Word from being violated and profaned. A.C. 306, 308.

Chesed den. various religious principles and worship. 2864.

Chide, to (Gen. xxxi. 36), s. zeal. A.C. 4164.

Chief Captains

Chief Captains or **Commanders** of one thousand men (Rev. vi. 15) s. external goods. Ap. Ex. 408.

Chiefs of the People (Num. xxi. 18) s. inferior truths, such as are contained in the literal sense of the Word. A.C. 3424.

Chiefs, primary things of truth. A.C. 2089.

Child, to be with (Gen. xxxviii. 24), s. to produce something. A.C. 4904. Being with c., travailing in birth, and pained to be delivered (Rev. xii.), s. the doctrine of the new church, in its birth, and the difficult reception thereof. A.R. 535. The c. was caught up unto God and his throne (Rev. xii. 5), s. the protection of the doctrine of the New Church by the Lord. A.R. 545. The woman with c. (Jer. xxxi. 8) s. those who receive truths, and "her that travaileth with c." those who do them. Ap. Ex. 721. The c. is perfected in the womb by the ministry of angels. A.C. 5052.

Child of Light (John xii. 35, 36) s. the spiritual man. A.C. 51.

Childbirth, birth of the faith of heaven. H. and H. 382.

Childhood, the good of, is not spiritual good, but becomes so by the sowing of truth in the mind. H. and H. 277.

Children s. innocence. A.C. 429. Good spirits, and angelic spirits. (Gen. xiv. 23.) A.C. 1752. The regenerate who have the understanding of goodness and truth. (Isa. xxix. 22–24.) A.C. 489. C. or infants (Lam. ii. 19) s. those who love truths and desire them. Ap. Ex. 187. C. of the desolate, the truths of the primitive church, or Gentiles. A.C. 489. C. of the married wife, the truths of the Jewish church. A.C. 489. C. that are corrupters (Isa. i. 4) s. the falses which are of the understanding or persuasions. A.C. 622. C. rising up against their parents, and causing them to be put to death (Mark xiii. 12), s. that the falses of evil would oppose and destroy the goods and truths of the church. Ap. Ex. 315. C. of delight (Micah i. 17) are the genuine truths of the church from the Word. A.R. 47. All the little c. of christians are in the new heaven. A.R. 876. All c. go to heaven, whose number amounts to the fourth or fifth part of the human species on earth. H. and H. 416. C. as soon as they die are taken up into heaven, and delivered to such of the female angels as, when in this world, were more particularly fond of c., and who also loved God. H. and H. 332. C. are instructed in heaven by the most exquisitely delicate rep. adequate to their tender capacities. H. and H. 335, 336. C. are born with inclinations to such things as their parents were inclined to. C.S.L. 202, 205. C. born from parents who are principled in love truly conjugial, derive from their parents the conjugial principle of good and truth, by virtue whereof, they have an inclination and faculty, if sons, to perceive the things appertaining to wisdom; and if daughters, to love those things which wisdom teaches. C.S.L. 202, 205.

Chiliads, or thousands, s. goods, and myriads, or ten thousands, s. truths. Ap. Ex. 336.

Chinese, the, in the spiritual world present at a distance an appearance of a wholly he-goat, a cake made of millet, an ebony spoon, and likewise the idea of a native city. A.C. 2596.

Chittim, land of (Isa. xxiii. 6), s. falses. Ap. Ex. 406.

Choice, Choosing, and **Chosen,** s. what is wished for, or well pleasing. A.C. 2922.

Choirs, by, inauguration into unanimity is effected. 5182.

Chosen, those who are in the life of good and truth. 3755.

Christ, or the Messiah, is the Son of God, the divine human of the Lord, or the divine truth. And by false C. are meant divine truths falsified. A.R. 520, 595. See *Jesus Christ.*

Christian, a, is one who is principled in truth grounded in good. A.C. 3010. A c. is one who acknowledges the Lord Jesus Christ as the only God of heaven and earth, and follows his commandments. U.T. 682. No c. can be admitted into heaven, unless he believes in the Lord God and Saviour, and approaches him alone. U.T. 107, 108.

Christian Church, the, is one with the church instituted with the Jews, only the latter was external, but the former was internal. A.C. 4868. The c. c. in its essence is the same as to its internal form, with the rep. church. A.C. 4489. The true quality of the c. c. is almost the same as was that of the sons of Shem. A.C. 1141. The c. c. founded by the Lord when he was in the world, is now, for the first time, built up by himself. U.T. 674. The christian or new church is instituted, which not like the former, was led by rep. to internal things, but knows them without rep. A.C. 4904. The former c. c. is at an end. U.T. 757. The c. c. which is in possession of the Word, is as the heart and lungs in the grand man, with respect to those who are without the pale of the church. A.C. 4217. The universal c. c. is founded upon the worship of Jehovah in human form. U.T. 94. The c. c. at this day, is in the extremes, or at the lowest degree. A.C. 3489, 4649. The rituals and rep. of the Jewish church contained the arcana of the c. c. A.C. 3478. There is no c. c. amongst the Papists. N.J.D. 8.

Christian World, the, is in works alone, and in no truths of doctrine, wherefore they cannot be called any thing else but Gentiles; they know the Lord indeed, but yet do not apply to him, and are possessed of the Word, but yet do not search for truths in it. A.R. 110. In the c. w. at this day, there is neither church nor religion. A.R. 675. They are the worst of all in the spiritual world, who come from the c. w. A.C. 1032.

Christians. The greater part at this day are either Arians or Socinians, and such, if they worship Christ as God, are hypocrites. A.R. 294. C. are in the midst of the other nations in the spiritual world. U.T. 268. C. have so extinguished the good of love and charity, that they cannot be informed by influx, and ill. from the Word. A.C. 10.355. The reason why they have acknowledged three divine persons, is because there is a threefold principle in the Lord, which is apparently distinguished by appropriate names in the Word. L. 55. C. were examined in the spiritual world, and they were not able to pronounce this expression, Divine human. U.T. 111.

Chrysolite. See *Precious Stones.*

Chrysoprasus (Exod. xxviii. 18) s. the celestial love of truth. A.C. 9868.

Church, the, is called a c. from doctrine, and religion is so called from a life according to doctrine. A.R. 923. All things of the c. in length of time are changed into the opposites. A.C. 1151. The c. in the Lord's kingdom is like the heart and lungs in man, the interiors of man being joined with his externals by means of the heart and lungs, whence life is derived to all the neighboring viscera; so also it is with the human race. A.C. 2054. When the c. is near to its end, evil and the false reign, and then good spirits retire. A.C. 8054. The genuine things of the c. could be rep. by the Jews. A.C. 4208. The c. does not really exist with man before its truths are implanted in his life, and thus formed into the good of charity. A.C. 3310. Every c. is at first spiritual, and commences from charity. L.J. 38. The state of the c. after the advent of the Lord was entirely changed. S.S. 99. The c. goes through its several successive ages like man. A.C. 4672. The essential of the c. is to acknowledge the divine of the Lord, and his union with the father. H. and H. 34. The most ancient c. was altogether unacquainted with sacrifices. The ancient c. which was after the flood was likewise unacquainted with sacrifices; it was indeed principled in rep., but sacrifices were first instituted in the succeeding c., which was called the Hebrew c. A.C. 2180. There are two things which conjoin the men of the church; viz., life and doctrine; if life conjoins, doctrine does not separate, but if doctrine only conjoins, then they mutually separate. A.C. 4468. All the states of the c. were rep. with the Lord in the world, and in what manner by him men should be saved. A.C. 2661, 2672. The successive states of the c. des. in the Word, do not appear to any one in the world, for they are successive states, as to the understanding of truth from the Word, and these no one can see but the Lord alone. Ap. Ex. 361. The internal of the c. is charity, and thence faith, but the external of the c. is the good of life. Ap. Ex. 403. Wheresoever there is a c. there must of necessity be both an internal and an external. A.C. 1083. In the end of the c., when there is no faith, because no charity, the interior things of the Word are then manifested, which shall serve the new c. for doctrine and for life; this was done by the Lord himself, at his first advent in a considerable manner and degree at the end or consummation of the Jewish c., as the new christian c. was able to bear it. Ap. Ex. 670. When the c. is vastated, i.e., when it is no longer in any good of faith, it principally perishes as to the states of its interior, thus as to states in another life, in such case heaven removes itself from them, and, consequently, the Lord transfers himself to others who are adopted in their place. A.C. 4432. The c. of the Lord is compared with the time of the day, its first age with the dawn or sunrise and the morning, its last age with the sunset or evening, and the shades which then take place; for the cases are exactly similar; in like manner it is compared with the seasons of the year, nay, it is also compared to metals. See Dan. ii. 31–33. A.C. 1837. The c. is in a perfect human form, as well as heaven, from the divine humanity of the Lord 4837. At this day there is no c. in the christian world, neither among the Roman Catholics, nor among the reformed. A.R. 263. The c. appears before the Lord as a man, beautiful or deformed, according to its doctrine, and at the same time conformity of life to it. A.R. 601. The c. in process of time decreases, by receding from the good of love, and truth of faith, even until evil is supposed to be good, and falsehood truth. A.R. 658. Every c. has a threefold principle, called celestial, spiritual, and natural, hence it is that Noah had three sons. A.V.C.R. 39. The c. in heaven could not subsist without the c. in the earths. A.R. 533. Upon every c. there has been a last judgment executed, after which there has been a new heaven, and a new hell. A.V.C.R. 36. The c. is the marriage of the good of love, and of the truth of doctrine. A.R. 349. The c. is not a c. from externals, or ritual observances, but from internals. A.C. 4831. Every c. in its beginning, is only acquainted with the general [principles] of doctrine. A.C. 468. The c. is formed by the Lord, in man (vir), and through the man (vir) in the wife, and afterwards it is formed with both, and is complete. C.S.L. 63, 125. The c. with its truths and goods can never be given among any others than those who live with one wife in love truly conjugial. C.S.L. 76. Wherever the c. is treated of in the Word, there the Lord also is treated of. S.S. 89. The c. of the Lord is internal and external; in the internal c. are they who are in intelligence and wisdom, and thence are in the superior heavens; but in the external c. are they who are in sciences and the knowledges of truth and good from the Word, and not in any interior intelligence and wisdom, and are thence in the inferior heavens, these are called spiritual natural, but the former spiritual. Ap. Ex. 629. The Lord's c. everywhere is internal and external; the internal is of the heart, and the external is of the mouth; or the internal is of the will, and the external is of action; when the internal makes one with the external in man, then that which is of the heart is also of the mouth, or that which is of the will is also of action. A.C. 9375. The c. which falsifies the truths of the Word, is therein des. by Cain, by Reuben, the Philistines, the goat in Daniel and by the dragon and his two beasts in the Apocalypse; and the c. which has adulterated all the goods of the c., is des. by Babylon and by Chaldea, in the Word. Ap. Ex. 817. It is always provided by the Lord, that some c. shall remain, and when the old c. perishes, a new c. is raised up. A.C. 4069. Without a c. somewhere upon earth, which is in possession of the Word, no communication could be given with heaven, and the human race would perish. A.C. 4423, 9276. The c. of the Lord as to doctrine, is rep. as a city and sometimes as an espoused virgin. (Rev. xxi. 2.) A.R. 881. The angels of heaven lament when the c. on the earths is destroyed, and pray to the Lord, that it may be brought to an end, which is effected by the last judgment. Because the c. on the earths is the foundation of heaven. A.R. 645. In every c. there have been four following changes of state, in the first of which there was the appearance of the Lord Jehovah, and redemption, and then was its morning or first rise; the second was its instruction, and then was its day or progression; the third was its decline, and then was its evening or vastation: the fourth was its end, and then was its night or consummation. A.V.C.R. 6. The c. of the Lord in the earths cannot be otherwise than various and diverse. A.C. 3451. All things of the c., from the first degree to the last are s. by the cities of Judah, the circuit of Jerusalem, the land of Benjamin, the plain, the mountain. A.C. 4592. There is nothing of the c. without the conjugial union between good and truth, and unless the internal be in the external. A.C. 4899. The c. exists by virtue of the Word and acquires a nature and quality amongst men, according to their understanding of the Word. U.T. 243. In the most ancient c. there was immediate revelation, in the ancient c. revelation by cor., in the Jewish c. by a living voice, and in the christian c. by the Word. A.C. 10.355. See *Ancient* and *Most Ancient Church.*

Church-Militant, Lord's church so called before regeneration. A.C. 59.

Churches. In the ancient c. charity was the essential and principal of the church. A.C. 4680. The most ancient and ancient c. were in the land of Canaan. N.J.D. 5. All the four former and general c. were not in the truth of knowledge and acknowledgment of the one God. U.T. 786. All things of the c. before the Lord's advent were rep., because the Lord was rep. by angels. U.T. 109. The ancient and christian c. were entirely the same as to their internal state, they only differed as to externals. A.C. 4772. There were three c. successively after the deluge. A.C. 1285. The seven c. s. all who are of the church in the christian world and every one according to reception. A.R. 10, 41, 69. There were three c. which are particularly mentioned in the Word, viz., the first ancient church called Noah; the second ancient church called Eber; and the third ancient church which had its name from Jacob, and afterwards from Judah and Israel. A.C. 1327. Four c. have existed on this earth since the day of its creation; viz., the first, called Adam; the second, called Noah; the third, called the Israelitish; and the fourth, called the christian: after these four c., a new church arises, which will be the true christian church, foretold in Daniel vii. 14, and in the Apocalypse, chap. xxi. and by the Lord himself in the Evangelists, which church was expected by the Apostles. U.T. 760, and A.V.C.R. 2.

Chyle, purification of the blood; c., etc., cor. to the various modes of spiritual vexation and inauguration. 5173.

Cicero, discourse with. 2592. H. and H. 322.

Cinders of a Furnace s. the falses of lusts. 7519.

Cinnamon s. natural truth. A.C. 10.254. Truth derived from good or the spiritual principle of worship. (Rev. xviii. 13.) A.C. 4748. C. also s. the good of celestial love. Ap. Ex. 1150.

Circle, the, of communication between good and truth compared with the circulation of the blood. 9300.

Circle of the Earth (Isa. xl. 22) s. heaven. Ap. Ex. 799.

Circle of Life. The circle of the life of man is to know, to understand, to will, and to do. Ap. Ex. 242.

Circuit s. what is outermost. A.C. 2973.

Circuit

Circuit of **Israel** den. exterior knowledges. A.C. 264.

Circumcision (Gen. xvii. 10) s. purity. A.C. 2039. C. was a rep. of regeneration by love. A.C. 1025. Purification from filthy loves, or the removal of self-love and the love of the world. A.C. 2040, 2045. C. was the principal thing which distinguished the Israelitish from the other Asiatic, and christian churches. U.T. 674.

Circumferences s. such things as are round about or beneath, which are the truths of good in the natural man. Ap. Ex. 449. C. of Jerusalem s. the truths of doctrine in the natural man. Ib.

Circumgyration, exp. D.L.W. 270.

Cisterns, dug or hewn, s. the interiors of the natural mind full of the knowledges of good and truth. Ap. Ex. 617. Broken c. (Jer. ii. 13) s. false doctrines. A.C. 2702.

Citadel, or **Castle**, den. internals of the church. 3270, 1.

Cities den. the interiors of the natural mind; c., in the universal sense, s. the doctrinals of the church, but in the singular sense, they s. the interiors of man where doctrinals are, or rather where truths are conjoined to good; for the truths and goods appertaining to man form as it were a city, hence the man himself, in whom the church is, is called the city of God; the s. of a city is as the s. of a house; in the universal sense, a house s. good, but in a singular sense, it s. a man, and specifically his mind as to good and truth there conjoined, and a house, with its apartments, circumjacent buildings, and courts, is a city in the least form. A.C. 3538, 5297. C. of the mountain and c. of the plain (Jer. xxxiii. 13) s. doctrines of charity and faith. A.C. 2418. C. of the nations (Rev. xvi. 19) s. heretical doctrines. A.R. 712. See *Villages*.

City s. the doctrine of the church and of religion. A.R. 402. C. without inhabitants s. truths without good. A.C. 2451. C. of God (Ps. xlvi. 5) s. the church as to doctrine. Ap. Ex. 518. C. of habitation (Ps. x. 7) s. the doctrine of life which constitutes the church among men. Ap. Ex. 730. C. of holiness (Dan. ix. 25) s. divine truth which is the Word. Ap. Ex. 684. C. of praise and of joy (Isa. xlix. 25, 26) s. the things appertaining to the church. A.C. 1664. See *Gate*.

City of **Destruction**. See Cherez.

City of **Judah**, love towards the Lord and neighbor. A.E. 850.

City of the **Samaritans**, false doctrine of those who reject the Lord. A.E. 223.

Civil Good is that which a man does under civil law. D.L. 12.

Civil Life cor. with spiritual life. 4366.

Civil Man, a, is one who knows the laws of his kingdom whereof he is a citizen, and lives according to them; and he is called a moral man, who makes those laws his morals and his virtues, and lives conformably to them from reason. D.P. 322.

Clause, concluding. A general concluding c. frequently occurs in the Word, which includes all that went before. A.C. 804.

Clay s. the lowest natural good. A.C. 1300, 1301. The good whereof the mind or man of the church is formed, consequently, the good of charity. (Gen. xi. 3.) A.C. 1300. To tread the c. (Nahum iii. 14) s. falses, and to repair or make strong the brick-kiln den. worship grounded therein. A.C. 1290. See *Spittle*.

Clean is spoken of goods, and shining of truths. (Rev. xix. 14.) A.R. 814.

Clean Beast s. the affections of goodness. A.C. 45, 46.

Cleansed, to be, s. to be sanctified. A.C. 4545.

Cleave, to, **unto a Wife** (Gen. ii. 24), s. that the internal is in the external. A.C. 160.

Cleft of a **Rock**, obscurity and false of faith. 10.582.

Clemency of **Jehovah** (Gen. xix. 16) s. grace and mercy. A.C. 2412.

Clergy. The c. rep. the internal of the church, and the laity is external. A.R. 567.

Climate. Changes of state, like variations of c. H. and H. 157.

Cloak s. exterior truth. A.E. 566.

Cloaks s. truths in common. A.R. 328.

Clothe, to, s. to instruct in truths. A.E. 240.

Closed. The internal of perception is c. when there is no intermediate [principle] through which influx may pass. A.C. 4692. So long as man keeps his external c. the Lord cannot purify him from any concupiscence of evil in his spirit or internal man. D.P. 120. The Word is said to be c. when it is understood only as to the sense of the letter, and when all that is assumed for doctrine, which is contained in the letter, and it is still more c. when doctrinals are formed therefrom which favor self-love and the love of the world. A.C. 3769.

Closets (Luke xii. 3) s. the interiors of man; viz., that which he thinks, intends, etc. A.C. 5194. The ancients compared the mind of man to a house, and those things which are within in man to c. The things contained in the mind are distinct, nearly resembling the distinction of a house into its c. (or chambers). Those things which are in the midst are the inmost there, those which are at the sides are more external; these latter were compared to courts, and the things without which cohered with the things within were compared to porticos. A.C. 7353.

Closure s. conjunction with truth from the divine. 9534.

Clothed. Celestial good is that which is not c., because it is inmost, and is innocent; but celestial spiritual good is that which is first c., and also natural good, they being of an exterior nature, on which account they are compared to garments in the Word. A.C. 297.

Clothing den. the support of exterior life by interior scientifics. 9003. S. every thing external which clothes the soul. A.Cr. 83.

Cloud s. an obscure light in which the spiritual man is, with respect to the celestial. A.C. 1043. In some parts of the Word it s. divine truth in the superior heavens, because they appear before the eyes of them who are in the inferior heavens as covered round with a thin white c. Ap. Ex. 594. The divine presence. (1 Kings viii. 11.) A.C. 10.574. A light c. (Isa. xix. 1, 17) s. divine truth natural spiritual from which the quality of man as to his natural principle is derived. Ap. Ex. 654. C. in an opp. sense, s. the Word, with respect to its literal sense falsified. A.R. 24. C. s. the written Word in its literal sense. A.C. 4060, 10.574. It is said of Jehovah, that "the c. are the dust of his feet" (Nahum i. 3), because those things which are in the literal sense of the Word, which is natural, appear scattered. Ap. Ex. 69. White c. s. the Word in the literal sense translucent by virtue of its spiritual sense. A.R. 642. "To cover the heavens with c.," s. to preserve and defend the spiritual things of the Word which are in the heavens by the natural truths which are in the literal sense of the Word. Ap. Ex. 594. The discourses of angels are sometimes rep. by c., and by their forms, motions, and translations; affirmatives of truth, by bright and ascending c., negatives, by dark and descending c.; affirmatives of what is false, by dusky and black c.; consent and dissent, by various consociations and dissociations of c., and these in a sky color, like that of the heavens in the night. A.C. 3221. See *Bow in a Cloud, Pillar of a Cloud, Literal Sense.*

Cluster, to eat the (Micah vii. 1, 2), den. the good of charity in its beginning, or what is holy and the primitive [c.] or first ripe den. the truth of faith. A.C. 1071, 517. C., or bunches of grapes, properly, s. the variations of the state of spiritual good, or the good of charity, because many grapes cohere together in them. Ap. Ex. 918. C. den. the truth of spiritual good, and grapes, the good of celestial truth. (Gen. xl. 10.) A.C. 5117.

Clusters of Bitterness

Clusters of Bitterness, evils from dire falsities. A.E. 433.

Coaches, arched (Isa. lxvi. 20), s. the knowledges of truth. Ap. Ex. 355. See *Horses.*

Coal, a burning (Ezek. i. 26) s. the celestial principle of the Lord, and the brightness of fire round about, is the celestial spiritual principle. A.C. 1042. A live c. from the altar (Isa. vi. 6), s. divine love, from which all purification is derived. Ap. Ex. 580.

Coals, burning (Ps. cxl. 10), s. the pride of proper intelligence. Ap. Ex. 455. C. of fire being scattered over the cities (Ezek. x. 1, 7), s. that men were to be left to their wild lusts, rather than they should incur the dangers of profanation. A.C. 308.

Coat (Matt. x. 10) s. interior natural truth, or truth of the natural principle. A.C. 4677. Aaron's c. s. truth from a celestial origin. A.C. 9942. The Lord's c. without seam, woven from above throughout (John xix. 23), s. the Lord's divine truth, which is one only, and derived from good, and as it was not divided, but for it they cast lots who should have it entire; this rep. that the Lord did not suffer divine truth to be violated or pulled asunder into parts, as was done to the inferior truths of the church by the Jews. The like was s. by Aaron's c. (Exod. xxxix. 27.) A.C. 4677. A c. of skin (Gen. iii. 21) s. spiritual and natural good. A.C. 294. A c. of various colors (Gen. xxxvii. 3), s appearances of truth, whereby the spiritual of the natural principle is known and distinguished. A.C. 4677. C. s. interior truth, and cloak, exterior truth. (Matt. v.) Ap. Ex. 566. See *Robe, Garment.*

Coat of **Mail** s. defence against evil and falses in combats, and in the opp. sense defences of evil and falses against goods and truths. Ap. Ex. 657.

Cockatrice (Isa. xiv. 29) s. evil originating in the false, derived from the sensual scientific principle. A.C. 251.

Cock-crowing, as well as the twilight, s. the last time of the church. A.C. 10.134. See *Evening.*

Coffer, something vile, but still derived from truth, and capable of being an enclosure and protection. 6723.

Coffin (Gen. l. 26) s. that wherein something is shut up or concealed. A.C. 6596.

Cohabitation (Gen. xxx. 20) s. the Lord's essential divine and his divine human. A.C. 3960. See *Zebulon.*

Coition, to be next in (Gen. xxx. 42), s. things compelled or not free. A.C. 4031.

Cold s. no love, or no charity in faith; and heat, or fire, s. love, or charity and faith. A.C. 934, 936. Infernal love. Ap. Ex. 231.

Collateral Good, or that which does not flow in directly, is that good which is also called middle good, for this good derives much from worldly things, which appear as good but are not; whereas good directly flowing in, is what comes immediately from the Lord, or immediately through heaven from the Lord, and is good divine, separate from such worldly good. A.C. 4145.

Collect, to store the memory with truths, and to c. them into unity. 679, 6112.

Collections (Gen. xli. 47) den. serieses; in regard to serieses, the case is this; with the man who is reformed, at first are insinuated common [or general] truths, next the particulars of common [or general] truths, and lastly the singulars of particulars; particulars are arranged under common [or general] truths, and singulars beneath particulars; those arrangements or ordinations are in the Word s. by fascicles [bundles]. A.C. 5339.

Collyrium, an ointment made of flour and oil, because flour s. the truth of faith, and oil the good of love. A.E. 245.

Colon and **Rectum,** the, answer to the hells in which are those who are savage and wild, composed of the soldiery, etc. A.C. 5394.

Color could not exist unless there were something obscure and something whitish. A.C. 1042. Obscurity itself is turned into c. by the shining of the rays of the sun. A.C. 1043. There are two c. fundamental of the rest, in the spiritual world, red and white. And so far as they partake of red, they s. good; and so far as they partake of white, they s. truth, because the heat of the spiritual sun is of a fiery red, and the light thereof, of a shining white. But black c. derive their origin from the hells, which are also two in number, one in opp. to white, which is with those who have falsified the truths of the Word, and the other in opp. to red, which blackness is with those who have adulterated the goods of the Word. A.R. 231. A.C. 9476. C. in the other life, are in their essence the variations, or the modifications of intelligence and wisdom. They derive their splendor from truth appertaining to intelligence, and their brilliancy from good appertaining to wisdom. A.C. 4530. C. in the spiritual world are modifications of celestial light, thus of the intelligence and wisdom which is with the angels in heaven. Ap. Ex. 576. There are c. in another life, and in heaven most beautiful, which were never seen here on earth. A.C. 1055, 1624.

Comb, to, the hair, s. to accommodate natural things that they may appear decent. Spirits can know from the hair, its color, length, and the manner in which it is spread, what had been the qualtiy of the natural life in the world. A.C. 5570. In the spiritual world there were seen some children, who were combed by their mothers so cruelly, that the blood flowed out, by which was rep. that such is the education of infants [in the Christian church] at this day. A.C. 2125.

Combat. Temptation is a c. between good and evil. N.J.D. 199.

Combustion, is pred. of the love of self, because that love is s. by fire. A.E. 405.

Come, to, when pred. of the Lord, s. to reveal himself. Ap. Ex. 36. To c. in the spiritual sense, s. to approach in sight, that is to attend with the understanding. Ap. Ex. 354. To c. when pred. of God, as in Gen. xx. 3, s. to perceive, for perception is nothing else but the divine coming, or influx into the intellectual faculty. A.C. 2513.

Come Down, to (Gen. xi. 5), is pred. of Jehovah, by reason of his being called the Highest. This is spoken according to appearance. A.C. 1311. To c. d. to see (Gen. xi. 5), s. judgment. A.C. 1311.

Come Forth, to, transition from one state to another. 1853.

Come, to, **in strength** (Isa. xl. 10), s. to execute judgment, thus to subjugate the hells. Ap. Ex. 850. To c. to any one (Gen. xxxv. 27), s. conjunction. A.C. 4612. To c. to the Lord, causes his presence and to live according to his commandments, causes conjunction with him. C.S.L. 341.

Come up, to (Gen. lxi. 3), s. progression from what is exterior towards interior things. A.C. 5202.

Comeliness s. divine truth in its external form and splendor. 9815.

Comfort or **Consolation**, is an influx from the Lord, into the affection of truth. 2692.

Comforter or **Paraclete** s. the divine truth proceeding from the Lord. Ap. Ex. 16, 27.

Coming (Gen. xli. 14) den. communication by influx. A.C. 5249.

Coming of the Lord, etc., the, is the revelation of the Lord in the Word, or the spiritual s. of the Word. H. and H. 1. The c. of the L. is not to destroy the visible heaven and the visible earth, and to create a new heaven and a new earth, according to the notions which many have heretofore entertained in consequence of not understanding the spiritual sense of the Word. U.T. 768. See *Celestial.*

Coming to Drink s. the affection of truth. A.C. 4017.

Command

Command, to, with the Lord, is to prepare and do. A.C. 783. To c. (Gen. xxviii. 1) s. to reflect. A.C. 3661. To give c. over his house (Gen. xl. 3) den. to apply itself thereto; viz., to scientific or natural truth. A.C. 4977.

Commanders s. principal truths. A.E. 576.

Commandments, the ten, are the precepts of doctrine and of life, comprising the sum and substance of all religion, and are therefore to be understood in a threefold sense, celestial, spiritual, and natural. U.T. 282. In the first three of the ten c. are the laws of the spiritual life, in the four following the laws of the civil life, in the three last the laws of the moral life. H. and H. 531. See *Decalogue*.

Commencement s. a state when man begins to be instructed. 1560.

Commerce is a general good, when the love of it is the end, and that of money the means subservient. D.P. 220.

Commixion. Good and evil, and truth and the false are commixed, when evil and the false are in the spirit of man, but good and truth in his bodily actions and speech; but this c. of good and evil, and of truth and the false is not the profanation of good and truth; for profanation is only with those who first have received truth and good in faith and heart, and afterwards in faith and heart deny them. Ap. Ex. 519.

Common, every thing contains thousands of particulars, and every particular thousands of singulars. A.C. 865.

Common Principle. In all and singular things which exist, not only in the spiritual world, but also in the natural, a c. [or general] p. precedes, into which things less common, and finally particular things are afterwards successively inserted; without such insertion or infitting, nothing can possibly have inherence, for whatsoever is not in some c. [or general] p. and depends upon such principle, is dissipated. A.C. 5208.

Communication of the divine, is by the divine human, and the c. of this is by divine truth; otherwise c. would be impossible. A.C. 4724, 6880. C. of man with heaven and the Lord is by the internal; when this is shut, man has only c. with hell. A.C. 10.698. C. with heaven in the Christian church, is effected by the internals and not by external rep. A.C. 8792.

Communion, the, of the church, ill. by c. of parts in the human body. 2853. Heaven is a c. of all goods. H. and H. 73.

Companion den. goods and its truth. 10.490.

Company, a, congregation, and a multitude, in the Word, are pred. of truths. A.C. 4574.

Comparisons in the Word, are from cor. A.R. 334. All c. in the Word, are made by significatives. A.C. 3901.

Compass, to (Gen. ii. 12), s. to enter by influx. And hence it is said (Exod. xxviii. 11), that the onyx stones on the shoulders of Aaron's Ephod should be set [encompassed] in ouches of gold, which s. that the good of love should enter by influx into the truth of faith, and so in other instances. A.C. 115.

Compassed About. All and singular the things of nature are c. a. with spiritual things from the sun of the spiritual world. D.L.W. 157, 158. The nation which descended from Jacob was c. a. (while engaged in worship) with evil spirits. A.C. 4311.

Compassion. To be moved with c. is to have mercy from love. 5691.

Compel. Man ought to c. himself to resist evil and do good. 1937. For a man to c. himself, is freedom. 1937.

Complaint, is more or less evil according to the end. 5388.

Complex of Truths. Faith is the c. of t. shining in the mind of man. U.T. 347–349.

Compulsion. If it were possible for man to be reformed by c., all mankind would be reformed. A.C. 2881. C., in holy things is dangerous. A.C. 4031. Nothing is conjoined to man which is done by c. A.C. 2875.

56

Confirmation

Compute, to (Rev. xiii. 18), s. to know. A.R. 608.

Conate, the loves and knowledges of animals are c. with them. T.C.R. 48.

Conceal, to, is to reject, and bury as dead. 4552.

Conceit. The proprium of man's understanding is the c. of self-derived intelligence. D.P. 321.

Conceive, to, s. reception, and to bear or bring forth, acknowledgment. (Gen. xxx. 5.) A.C. 3919.

Conception is the first period of the reception of the faith of heaven. A.C. 4904. The c. of man from his father is not a c. of life, but only a c. of the first and purest form receptible of life, to which as a stamen, or beginning successively accede in the womb, substances and matters in forms adapted to the reception of life, in their order and degree. D.L.W. 6. See *Birth.*

Conclusion, the divine, and determined execution of a thing, is providence. A.C. 5124. C. formed from objects under the first view of the external senses, are natural truths. A.C. 8861.

Concubinage was permitted formerly to external men of the church, for the sake of rep. the celestial church by a wife, and of the spiritual church by a concubine, and because such men were not principled in conjugial love. A.C. 3246. C., apart from a wife, when it is engaged in from causes legitimate, just, and truly conscientious, is not illicit. C.S.L. 467. A concubine den. the Gentiles who are in idolatrous worship. A.C. 2867. Concubines (Gen. xxv. 6) s. the members of the Lord's spiritual kingdom, for they are not sons born from the essential marriage of good and truth, but from a kind of covenant not so conjugial in its nature; they are indeed from the same father, but not from the same mother; i.e., they are from the same divine good, but not from the same divine truth, which is the characteristic of celestial men. A.C. 3246.

Concubine of **Israel** s. good. 4802. See *Billah.*

Concupiscences are of the love of evil, and desires and affections are of the love of good. G.E.D. p. 124. C. with man are spiritual fires, which consume him in the life of the body. U.T. 328. Every evil c. presents the similitude of itself seen at a distance [in the spiritual world]. C.S.L. 521.

Condemnation. Spirits come into c. before they are in hell. A.C. 8333.

Condemned. No one in another world is c. before he knows himself, and is interiorly proved to be in evil, etc. A.C. 7705. Man is c. by himself to hell. A.C. 10.367. They are c. who have not lived according to the precepts of the Word, and thence could not receive faith in the Lord. A.R. 874.

Confess, to, s. the Lord, the Word, doctrine thence der. the divine principle of love, and the Lord's celestial kingdom. A.C. 3880.

Confession, interior, is that of the heart, which exists in humiliation, and at the same time in the affection of good; but exterior c. is that of the lips, which it is possible may exist in a feigned humiliation and in a feigned affection of good, which in reality is no humiliation and affection at all. A.C. 2329. The oral c. of one God does not abolish the idea of three Gods. U.T. 173. C. of sins implies a perception of evils, a discovery thereof in ourselves, an acknowledgment of them, and a conviction of guilt proceeding from them, and self-condemnation in consequence of guilt. But this alone is not repentance. N.J.D. 160.

Confidence. There can be no c. of salvation except in the good of life. 2982. Genuine c. is der. from charity. 3868.

Confirmed. Every thing c. by the will, and at the same time by the understanding, is permanent to eternity; but not that which is only c. by the understanding. D.P. 318, 319. They who have c. themselves in faith separated from charity, falsify the whole Word. A.R. 136, 467.

Confirmation, the light of, is a natural light, and not spiritual, and in the power of bad men to attain unto. A.C. 8780. There is a false light arising

Confirmations

therefrom, and it appears to those who are in falses, as light, but it is the light of infatuation, which is of such a nature that it is converted into darkness on the flowing in of the light from heaven; and the light of their eyes is like that of owls and bats. A.R. 566, 695. They who confirm faith separate from charity, and yet live a life of charity, are those who are in intellectual c., and not at the same time in voluntary c.; but they who confirm the false of doctrine and live according to it, are those who are in voluntary, and at the same time in intellectual, c. The reason is, because the understanding does not flow into the will, but the will into the understanding. D.P. 318.

Confirmations in first principles concerning God, cannot be taken away after death. U.T. 110. C. of evil by the thoughts, are called falses from the life of lusts. A.C. 4729. C. of evil, and what is false, are nothing else but removals of good and truth, and if they increase, they are rejections; for evil removes and rejects good, and what is false rejects truths. D.L.W. 268.

Confirmators are those who can make truths appear falses, and falses truths. C.S.L. 233.

Confound, to (Gen. xi. 7), s. in an internal sense, not only to darken, but also to obliterate and dissipate, so that there remains no longer any truth. A.C. 1321.

Confounded or Ashamed. (Zech. x. 5.) The riders on horses shall be confounded, s. the annihilation of ratiocinating argumentations and confirmations which are from the intellectual proprium of man. Ap. Ex. 355.

Confused. All imperfection of form results from what is confused or indistinct. D.P. 4.

Congeries. Man is a mere c. and composition of evils and falses. A.C. 761.

Conglutination, how the deceitful are punished by. A.C. 960.

Congregations, are pred. of truths. 4574. Opp. sense of falses. 6355.

Congregation of God (Ps. lxxxii. 1) s. heaven, and in the midst of the gods, s. among all the angels there, that is in the whole heaven. Ap. Ex. 313. Congregation of Jehovah (Deut. xxii. 30), s. heaven. A.C. 2468. Congregations, in the Word, are pred. of spiritual truths. Ap. Ex. 340.

Coniah (King of Judah) and his seed s. the same as Satan and his seed; viz., the internal false principle. Ap. Ex. 768.

Conjoined. No one can be c. to the essential Divine, by love and faith, without the divine human. A.C. 10.067. All are c. in another life, according to the love of good and truth from the Lord. A.C. 9378. Truth is c. with good when man perceives pleasure in doing well to his neighbor on account of truth and good, but not on account of himself and the world. A.C. 5340.

Conjugal is applied by Swedenborg to express the opposite to conjugial love; viz., the conjunctive principle of evil and the false. See C.S.L. 203.

Conjugial Love is the conjunction of love and wisdom. C.S.L. 65. It is implanted in every woman from creation, and together with it, the love of procreating, which is determined to, and has its conflux into the procreated offspring, and from the woman is communicated to the men. C.S.L. 400. With those who are principled in love truly conjugial, conjunction of minds increases, and therewith friendship; but both friendship and conjunction of minds decrease with those who are not so principled. C.S.L. 214. They who are principled in love truly conjugial, are continually desirous to be one man; but they who are not so principled, are desirous to be two. 215. They who are principled in love truly conjugial, in marriage have respect to what is eternal, but the case is reversed with those who are not principled in c. l. 216. C. l. resides with chaste wives, but still their love depends upon their husbands. 216. Its delights are the delights of wisdom; but those of scortatory love are the pleasures of insanity. 442. C. l. makes a man more and more a man (homo). 432, 433. It is the inmost heaven, through which the Lord insinuates c. l., the inhabitants thereof being

58

Conjunction

at peace above all others; peace in the heavens is comparatively as the spring season in the world, which gives delight to all things; it is the celestial principle itself in its origin; the angels who inhabit there are the wisest of all, and from innocence appear to others as infants; for they love infants much more than their parents and mothers do; they are present with infants in the womb, and by them the Lord takes care that infants be nourished and perfected; thus they preside over those who are with child. A.C. 5052. C. l. is not the love of the sex, but the love of one of the sex. C. l. was the love of loves with the ancients who lived in the golden, silver, and copperages. C.S.L. 73. C. l. derives its origin from the divine marriage of good and truth; consequently, from the Lord himself. A.C. 2728. C. l. dwells in the supreme region, in the midst of mutual love, in the marriage chamber of the will; and also in the midst of the perceptions of wisdom in the marriage chamber of the understanding, etc. The husband is in the marriage chamber of the understanding, and the wife in the marriage chamber of the will. C.S.L. 270. C. l. with its virtue, power, and delights, is to every one according to the study of genuine use in which he is. 207. True c. l. is heaven itself with man. A.C. 9961. C. l. opens the interiors of the minds of the married partners more and more. C.S.L. C. l. does not appertain to the male sex, but solely to the female sex, and from this sex is transferred into the male. 161, 223. C. l., which is genuine, cannot exist but between two, that is, in the marriage of one man and of one wife, and in no wise between more together. The men of the most ancient church, who were celestial, had only one wife. A.C. 2740. Matt. xix. 3–12. In c. l., the wife is the love of the husband's wisdom, and the husband is the wisdom of her love. C.S.L. 75. During the implantation of c. l., the love of the sex inverts itself, and becomes the chaste love of the sex. 99. Conjunction is effected from the first days of marriage successively; and with those who are principled in love truly conjugial it is wrought more and more thoroughly to eternity. 162. Love truly conjugial may have place with one of the conjugial partners and not at the same time with the other. 226. C. l. has conjunction with the love of infants. 385. C. l. appertains to the internal or spiritual man, and hence this love is proper to man. 95. With man c. l. is in the love of the sex as a diamond in its matrix. 97. If the conjugial partners have lived in true c. l., when one of them dies, the spirit of the deceased cohabits continually with the spirit of the partner not deceased, and this even to the death of the latter, when they again meet and reunite, and love each other more tenderly than before. C.S.L. 321.

Conjugial Principle, the, is capable of being ingrafted into christians, and of being transplanted hereditarily into the offspring from parents who are principled in love truly conjugial, and hence both the faculty and inclination to grow wise in the things of the church and of heaven may become connate. C.S.L. 142.

Conjugial Semblances. In the natural world where spiritual affections do not conjoin, there are given external affections, which assume a semblance of internal, and tend to consociate; hence comes apparent love, friendship, and favor, between conjugial partners. C.S.L. 272.

Conjugial Sphere, the, is what flows from the Lord through heaven, into all and singular the things of the universe, even to its ultimates. C.S.L. 222. This sphere is received by the female sex, and through that sex is transferred into the male sex. Where love truly conjugial is, this sphere is received by the wife, and only through the wife by the husband. Where love not conjugial is, that sphere is received indeed by the wife, but not by the husband through her. C.S.L. 223–225.

Conjunction, all, requires an object, and according to the quality of the object, c. is effected. A.C. 8705. C. with God and man is only given by the

Conjunctive Principle

union of the divine and human natures in the Lord. U.T. 98. A.C. 2112. C. with God the Father is not allowable, but with the Lord, and by him with God the Father. U.T. 370–372. C. of the Lord with man is effected by truths of the Word, and by a life conformable to them. A.R. 883. No one can be conjoined to the Lord, except he immediately approaches Him, because the aspect which is of the understanding derived from the affection which is of the will, conjoins. A.R. 933. C. of the Lord with man, and reciprocal c. of man with the Lord, is effected by man's loving his neighbor as himself, and loving the Lord above all things. D.P. 94. C. between the Lord and man is effected by all and every part of the Word, and herein the Word is marvellous beyond all other writings. R.C. 10.632–4. The c. and presence of the Lord and heaven is given in all the earths by the Word. U.T. 267, 268. C. with the Lord by the literal sense of the Word is in the affection of truth and its perception. S.S. 62. C. of the Lord with man, is the spiritual in the natural, and of man with God, is the natural from the spiritual. U.T. 369. The c. of the Lord with man is according to the state of his thought, and thence of his affection. A.C. 4211. C. of man with the Lord is not with his supreme divinity but with his divine human. A.C. 4211. The c. of man with heaven and hell, is not immediate, but mediate through spirits in the world of spirits. H. and H. 600.

Conjunctive Principle. Divine celestial good is the essential c. p. of all things. A.C. 10.262.

Connection. All things are continued in a chain of c. from first to last. A.C. 9822. When the ultimates of the heavens have a c. with those who are conjoined to hell, then the light and intelligence of the angels of heaven is diminished. Ap. Ex. 744. There is a c. of all spiritual truths, which is like the c. of the viscera, organs, and members in man's body. A.R. 916.

Connubial connections only are beneath heaven, which are entered into and put off. C.S.L. 192.

Conquer, to, s. the removal of evils and falses. Ap. Ex. 359. To c. or overcome (Rev. iii. 5) s. to abide constantly in the spiritual affection of truth, even unto the end of life. Ap. Ex. 197. To c. when pred. of the Lord, s. to unite divine good with divine truth, because this was done by temptations and victories. Ap. Ex. 254. Conquering s. the removal of evils, and thence falses to the end of life; and to c. s. afterwards to eternity. (Rev. vi.) Ap. Ex. 359.

Conqueror, the celestial man is called a. A.C. 81.

Consanguinities. All relationship takes its origin from good. In the spiritual world, or in heaven, no other c. and affinities exist, than those of love to the Lord and love to the neighbor, or what is the same thing, of good. A father does not know a son or a daughter, nor a brother a brother or sister, nor indeed a husband a wife, unless they have been in similar good. They meet indeed when they first come into another life, but they are soon dissociated, for good itself, or love and charity, determines and assigns every one to his own society. A.C. n. 3815.

Conscience is formed in every man from the principles of his particular religion, according to his internal reception thereof. N.J.D. 130. C. is to do no evil in any manner to any person, and to do well to every one in every possible way. A.C. 1076. Real c. is the plane on which temptations operate. A.C. 762. They who have no c. do not know what it means. H. and H. 300. They, and they only, have c. who love God and their neighbor. A.C. 831. C. is that frame or fitness of subject which is accommodated to the reception of heavenly influx. N.J.D. 130. The Lord rules those who have no c. by external restraints. A.C. 1077. C. may be rendered more perfect in those who are in a particular illumination and clear perception of divine truths, than in those who are less illuminated, and whose perception is more obscure. N.J.D. 132. They who have no c. in this world cannot be endowed with c. in the other life; hence they who are in hell are in no anguish of c. for the evils they did in the world. A.C. 965. Man is endowed with a c. of what is good, and a c. of what is right; the former pertains to his internal man, and the latter to his external man. N.J.D. 134. C. was the new will and understanding given to the church called Noah. A.C. 431. Some are not aware that they are endowed with a principle of c. at the time they have it. A.C. 2380. They who do good from a natural principle and not from religion, have no c. A.C. 6208. C. is the acknowledgment of truth from an interior principle. A.C. 4015. C. is formed in the intellectual part of the spiritual, otherwise than in that of the celestial. N.J.D. 139. Cannot be first received in another life. N.J.D. 138. The Lord alone operates all good by means of c. A.C. 4459.

Consent to (Gen. xxxiv. 23), s. to condescend. A.C. 4490. C. is essential acknowledgment, whereby reception is effected. A.C. 3157. C. from the understanding and the will is required to form the conjunction of truth with good. N.J.D. 23.

Consociation. All things are consociated most exquisitely, in the heavens, according to all the difference of love to the Lord, and of mutual love and faith, originating therein; and in the hells, according to all the differences of lusts, and of fantasies, thence derived. A.C. 2449. In the hells, the evil spirits, although they appear by the light of heaven, to the angels, in the most hideous forms, yet amongst themselves they appear as men, and this is permitted for the sake of c. U.T. 281. C. are made in another life according to spheres. A.C. 6830.

Consolation, all, is by good and from good. 2822.

Console s. to protect. A.E. 727.

Consonants. The speech of celestial angels is without hard c. Exp. H. and H. 241.

Consort, or conjugial companion, the, of natural love, is science, of spiritual love, is intelligence; and of celestial love, is wisdom. A.R. 351.

Constant. Variety cannot exist except in things c., stated, and certain. D.P. 190.

Constellations cor. to heavenly abodes. 5377. See *Stars.*

Consternation, terror and despair experienced in regeneration. 8310.

Consume, to perish by reason of evil. 10.431.

Consume away, to (Ezek. iv. 17), is pred. concerning the destruction of spiritual life. Ap. Ex. 617.

Consuming Fire, testification that they were in evils and falses. A.R. 599.

Consummation s. the last time when there is no longer any good. A.C. 1857. A state when evil is come to its summit. A.C. 2243. C. is treated of in the Word throughout, and the state which precedes is des. by vastation and desolation, which is succeeded by visitation. A.C. 2243. C., in the Word, is also called devastation and decision, which is effected by the deprivation of goods and truths, in consequence whereof man enters into evils and falses. A.R. 676.

Consummation of the **Age** (which is commonly translated the end of the world) is the last time or end of a church, and the first of a new church. A.C. 4535. See *Word.*

Consummation and **Decision** (Dan. ix. 27) s. the last state of the church, when there is no more truth; because no more good. Ap. Ex. 684.

Contagion, of evil, resulting from the lust of seducing. D.P. 328.

Contain, to, one's self (Gen. xiv. 21) s. to wait in expectation concerning the reality of a thing. A.C. 3100.

Contained and **Containing**. The thing containing s. the same with the thing contained. A.R. 672. See *Vessel.*

Contempt, those who despise others. 4949.

Contend

Contend, to, with God and man (Gen. xxxii. 28) s. to be tempted as to truths and goods. A.C. 4287. To c. with God (Gen. xxxii. 28), in the internal historical sense, s. to be urgent that a rep. of the church might be amongst them. A.C. 4317.

Content, a mind contented in God. 4981.

Contiguity. What is living in man or angel is from the proceeding divine, which is joined to him by c. D.P. 57.

Contiguity, by, there is conjunction with the Lord. D.W.L. 56.

Continent. The literal sense of the word is the basis, and the c. of its spiritual and celestial sense. U.T. 210–13.

Continent and **Complex**. See *Ultimate Degree*.

Contingencies, or in other words, the things ascribed to chance and fortune, are of the divine providence. A.C. 5508.

Continually den. all and in all. 10.133, 3994.

Continuous, or **Continual**, is a term applied by the schoolmen to den. quantity or co-extension, whose parts are not divided, but joined and connected together, so as to leave no room to determine where one begins and the other ends; in which sense it is used by Swedenborg in C.S.L. 125. It is also used by him in some of his theological works, in contradistinction to the term discrete, as applied to degrees; the term c. being applied to degrees of purer and denser, higher and lower, greater and less, etc., whilst the term discrete is applied to what he calls degrees of altitude, where one is within another, as in the case of three degrees of the atmosphere. Glossary to C.S.L. See *Discrete*.

Continuous and **Discrete Degrees**. All and singular the things of both worlds co-exist from c., and at the same time d., d. D.L.W. 185.

Contraction of the spiritual degree exp. D.L.W. 254.

Contrition, which is said now-a-days to precede faith, and to be followed by evangelic consolation, is not repentance. U.T. 512. Is not temptation. U.T. 597.

Contrive den. to will from a depraved mind. 4724. Den. intellectual part. 9598.

Controversy of Zion (Isa. xxxiv. 8) s. the rejections of the truths and goods of the church. Ap. Ex. 413.

Conversations of spirits and angels with man. See *Language*.

Conversion. By c. all conjunction in the spiritual world is effected. H. and H. 255. Man is continually held in state of the possibility of c. U.T. 720. Angels and good men, as to their spirit, continually turn themselves toward the Lord as a sun, and thus they have the Lord continually before their faces, and thus, which way soever they turn, which is wonderful; but the devils continually turn themselves from the Lord. A.R. 380.

Conversion of the **Jews**. See *Jews*. Exp. A.C. 4847.

Converted and **Healed**, to be (John xii. 40), s. to profane. Ap. Ex. 706.

Conviction. The existence of the faith of the N. C. is, 1st, spiritual light; 2d, harmonious agreement of truths; 3d, conviction. U.T. 344.

Convocation, the holy (Exod. xii. 16), was made in order to rep. heaven. A.C. 7891.

Cook s. to congest doctrine. 3316.

Co-operation. Regeneration is effected by the Lord alone through charity and faith, during man's c. U.T. 576.

Copper s. natural good, which is the good of the last heaven. U.T. 609.

Copper Age, the, is inferior to the golden and silver ages. 5658.

Coral s. knowledges of good. A.C. 1232.

Cords and **Nails**. (Isa. liv. 2.) C. s. the conjunction of good and truth, and n. the confirmation thereof. Ap. Ex. 799. See *Curtains*.

Coriander Seed (Exod. xvi. 31), because it is white, is pred. concerning truth. A.C. 8521.

Cormorant and **Bittern** (Zeph. ii. 14) s. the affections of the false and the false itself, interior and exterior. Ap. Ex. 650.

Corn den. good of the natural principle, also the good of truth which is in the natural principle; which is truth in the will and act. The reason why c. den. good, is because a field in the spiritual sense den. the church, and hence the things appertaining to a field, as seed, seedtime, harvest, standing c., grain, and also a spike or ear of c., besides wheat, barley, and several other specific kinds of grain, den. such things as appertain to the church; and the things appertaining to the church have all of them reference to good and truth. A.C. 5295. Ripe c., in the Word, s. the state of reception and increase of truth derived from good. A.C. 9291. Standing c. s. truth in its conception. A.C. 9146. See *Ears of Corn.*

Corn-Floor s. the doctrine of the church. A.E. 543.

Cornelian. See *Precious Stones.*

Corner-Stone s. all divine truth upon which the church is founded; therefore also the Lord as to his divine humanity, because all divine truth proceeds from him. The builders who rejected that stone (as it is read in the evangelists), are they who are of the church, there, of the Jewish church, for with them there were nothing but vain traditions from the literal sense of the Word, in which the truths of the Word were falsified, and its goods adulterated. Ap. Ex. 417.

Corner and **Extremity** (Amos iii. 12) s. what is more remote. A.R. 137.

Corners, in an historical sense, s. the quarters in the spiritual world, but in a spiritual sense, all the truths and goods of the church. Ap. Ex. 417. By the four c. of the earth mentioned (Rev. vii.), is s. the universal world of spirits, which is in the midst, between heaven and hell. The four c. s. the four quarters or points of the compass, because c. s. quarters, therefore they s. all things; as all things relating to heaven or hell, or to goodness and truth. C. s. the ultimate which sustains things superior, as its foundation does a house, and thus also every thing. A.R. 342. C. of the earth (Rev. vii. 1) s. the universal spiritual world. Ap. Ex. 417. See *Quarters.*

Cornet s. manifest perception of good. A.E. 357.

Cornucopia s. truths from good. A.E. 316.

Corporeal. Every man is by birth merely c., and yet from c. he may become natural more and more interiorly, and thus rational, and at length spiritual. The reason why this is effected progressively, is because the c. principle is like the ground, wherein things natural, rational, and spiritual, are implanted in their order. C.S.L. 59, 447.

Correspondence is the appearance of the internal in the external, and its rep. therein. A.C. 5423. The c. of forms or of rep. in the heavens in every manner is with divine celestial and spiritual things themselves. A.C. 9739. All and singular things in man cor. to the Lord. A.C. 4524. No distinct idea can be had of c., without a previous knowledge concerning heaven as the grand man. H. and H. 67. The spiritual things with which natural things cor., assume another appearance in nature, so that they are not distinguished, but seem incongruous and irrelative. A.C. 1887, 2396, 8920. The case with c., is almost like any one speaking a foreign language, and another instantly understanding the sense of the words, etc. A.C. 4337. C. is between those things which appertain to the light of heaven, and those things which appertain to the light of the world: that is, between those things which appertain to the internal or spiritual man, and those which appertain to the external or natural man, and rep. is whatever exists in the things appertaining to the light of the world, that is, whatever exists in the external or natural man, considered in respect to the things appertaining to the light of heaven, or to the internal or spiritual man. A.C. 3225. The c. of the universe in its three kingdoms, with all and singular things of man,

Correspondence

is not with those things as substances, but as uses. D.L.W. 324. All things which cor., are likewise rep., and thereby significative, so that c. and rep. are united in one subject. A.C. 2890. No one can understand the internal sense of the Word, unless he is acquainted with the nature of c. A.C. 2895, 4322. All things which appear in heaven are according to c., and called rep. A.C. 3213–3226, 9576, 9577. There is a c. between all things in heaven, and all things in man. H. and H. 87–102. The things in man, which have the greatest life, cor. to those societies in the heavens which have the greatest life, and in consequence thereof the greatest happiness, as are those to which man's external and internal sensories cor., and the things which are of the understanding and the will; but the things in man, which have lesser life, cor. to such societies in heaven as are in lesser life, as are those to which the cuticles cor., which encompass the whole body; also the cartilages and the bones, which support and sustain all things that are in the body; and also the hairs which spring forth from the cuticles. A.C. 5552. All c. is natural and spontaneous. H. and H. 262. The conjunction of the spirit of man with his body, is by the c. of his will and understanding with his heart and lungs, and their disjunction by the want of c. D.L.W. 390. From the c. of the heart with the will, and of the understanding with the lungs, may be known all things which can be known of the will and the understanding, or of love and wisdom, consequently, all that can be known of the soul of man. D.L.W. 394. Without c. with the grand man, that is, with heaven, or, which is the same, with the spiritual world, nothing whatever could exist and subsist. A.C. 5377. And unless there was a c. of man with heaven and through heaven with the Lord, he could not subsist a moment, but would flow out into nothing. A.C. 3628. There is a c. of sensual things with natural things, of these with spiritual things, of these with celestial things, and of celestial things with the divine of the Lord. A.C. 5131. Man is continually preserved in c. with heaven by the Lord, that he may, if he chooses it, be led from hell to heaven, and by heaven to the Lord. A.C. 4323. There is not given the least thing with man, with which there is no c. A.C. 4791. The first divine c. of love and wisdom is the fiery sun of heaven. D.L.W. 93. The following c. were derived from the ancient church to the gentiles, viz.: The sun, love. Apollo, the god of wisdom and intelligence, des. in a chariot and four fiery horses. Neptune, the sea, sciences in general. Pegasus, the birth of the intellectual principle, des. by a flying horse, who with his hoof burst open a fountain, where were virgins, who were the sciences. Horse, the understanding. Fountains, truths, also erudition. A.C. 2762, 3251. W.H. 4. The science of c. has been concealed since the time of Job, but is now made known. C.S.L. 532. By derivation from the ancients it is still a custom that kings, at their coronation, should sit on a silver throne, should be clad in a purple robe, be anointed with oil, should wear on their heads a crown, and carry in their hands a sceptre, a sword, and keys, should ride in royal pomp on a white horse, and under whose feet shoud be hoofs of silver, and should be waited on at table by the most respectable personages of the kingdom, etc. These ceremonies are called emblematical, from an entire ignorance of every thing relating to correspondency and rep. A.C. 4966. Whatsoever cor., this also s. N.J.D. 216. According to the quality of man's c. with heaven, such he appears in another life in the light of heaven. A.C. 5377. C. are natural truths and the mirrors of spiritual truths. A.C. 9300. C. are rep. of spiritual and celestial things in natural. U.T. 204. By the knowledge of some c., a man may falsify the Word, by conjoining and applying them to the confirmation of particular opinions rooted in his mind. U.T. 230. The science of c., after the times of the Jewish church, was not disclosed to Christians, because in the primitive church they were persons of great simplicity, so that, had it been discovered, it would have been useless and unintelligible. S.S. 24. C., rep. and significatives conjoin the natural world to the spiritual. A.C. 7290.

Correspondent, every thing is a c. which exists and subsists in nature from divine order. H. and H. 107.

Corrupt and **Violence** (Gen. vi. 11.) C. is pred. of the understanding when it is desolate; v., of what relates to the will, when it is vastated. Thus c. is pred. of persuasions, and v. of lusts. A.C. 621.

Cortical Substances of the **Brain** s. they who are in the will of good, and thence are good. 4052.

Costliness s. the holy things of the church. A.R. 789.

Cottages den. what is holy pred. of truth. 4391.

Cotton s. truths from a celestial origin, the same as fine linen. Ap. Ex. 1143.

Couches, the natural mind is s. by a bed. 6188.

Council of **Nice**. See *Imputation*. U.T. 632.

Councils, the deliberations of, are vain, unless supplication is made to the Lord for ill. U.T. 188.

Counsellors den. primary scientifics. 1482.

Counsel has respect to the thought. A.E. 687.

Countenance fallen (Gen. iv. 5) s. that the interiors were changed. A.C. 358. The c. of animals which appear in the spiritual world, most especially indicate with extensive variety the peculiar affections there which are terminated and presented in the forms of such animals as appear in our world. Ap. Ex. 582.

Country (Gen. xii. 1) s. things corporeal and worldly, because such things appertain to the external man. A.C. 1411. A far c. (Luke xix. 12) s. the spiritual world. Ap. Ex. 675. See *Nobleman*.

Courses s. truths. A.E. 97, 405. See *Ways*.

Court s. the external of the Word, and thence of the church, and of worship. Ap. Ex. 630. C. of the tabernacle (Exod. xxvii. 9), etc., s. the external of heaven, or the first, which is also called the ultimate heaven. A.C. 9741. The two c. of the temple at Jerusalem rep. the church as to its internal and external. A.R. 487. C. of the temple s. the external heaven and heaven in ultimates. Also the church on earth. A.R. 487. C. s. the external things of the church, and palaces the internal things thereof. A.C. 3271. The memory and understanding are like the outer c. of a house. A.C. 9230. See *Heavens, Temple*.

Covenant. Things internal are what appertain to a c., because they are effective of conjunction, but not things external, unless by things internal; things external were only signs of a c. or tokens of conjunction, whereby a remembrance of internal things might be excited, and thus conjunction might be effected by such internal things. A.C. 2037. C. (Ps. lxxxix. 34, 35) s. the divine good, and the declaration of the lips, the divine truth. A.C. 2842. To make a c. has respect to irrevocable confirmation from divine good; and to swear, the same confirmation from divine truth. A.C. 2842. C. of brethren (Amos i. 9) s. the union of faith and charity. A.C. 367. C. of the calf (Jer. xxxiv. 18, 20), the c. s. conjunction, the calf, good; the calf, being divided into two parts, s. the good proceeding from the Lord, on one part, and the good received by men on the other, from whence there is conjunction. Ap. Ex. 279. C. of the day, is conjunction by love; and c. of the night, conjunction by faith. Ap. Ex. 444. C. of the day and night (Jer. xxxiii. 20–26) s. all the statutes of the Israelitish church, prescribed in the Word, by which there was conjunction with heaven and the Lord. They are called the c. of the day, in relation to the church in heaven; and the c. of the night in relation to the church on earth, and spiritual things are rep. and s. for heaven, but natural things are rep. and s. for the church. Hence, also, the c. of the day and night are in this chapter called the statutes of heaven

Cover

and earth; and the c. of the night, is called the statutes [or ordinances] of the moon and stars. Ap. Ex. 532. See *Token.*

Cover. The reason why it is said (Deut. xxiii. 14, 15) that they were to c. their excrements, lest Jehovah God should see the nakedness of the thing and should return, was, because things c. and closed up den. all those places in hell where troops of [lascivious and unclean] spirits have their abodes; on which account also it is said, lest he see the nakedness of the thing. C.S.L. 431. To be c. (Gen. xxxviii. 14) s. not be acknowledged. A.C. 4860. To be c. (Isa. xxix. 10) s. to know nothing and to see nothing of truth. A.C. 2534. "High mountains being covered" (Gen. vii. 19) s. that all the good things of charity were extinguished. A.C. 795. See *Clouds.*

Covering, to remove a (Gen. viii. 13), s. to take away those things which obstruct the light. A.C. 896. Rational truths are like a c. or clothing to spiritual truths. (See Gen. xx. 16.) A.C. 2576. A c. of precious stones (Ezek. xxviii. 4, 13) s. the truths of intelligence. A.R. 90.

Covet, to, den. to will from an evil love. The precept not to c. or lust after those things which belong to the neighbor, den. that they should not pass into the will. A.C. 8910.

Cow, a red (Num. xix. 1–10), s. the good of the natural man, and the water of separation made from its burning, the truth of the natural man. Ap. Ex. 364. C. s. natural truths, A.C. 5198. See *Oxen.*

Craft takes away the perception of good and truth. 5058.

Creatable. Love and wisdom, life, light, heat, and activity, considered in themselves, are not c. U.T. 40, 364, 471.

Create, Form, and **Make,** to, s. to regenerate. A.C. 16. To c., f., and m. are three distinct terms of application. (See Isa. xliii. 7.) A.C. 88. To c., properly relates to man when he is created anew or regenerated; and to m., is used when he is perfected. To c. also relates to the spiritual man, and to m. to the celestial man. A.C. 472. In every thing created, there is a certain united image of the divine love and wisdom proceeding from the Lord. D.L.W. 47–51. Man is so created that the divine things of the Lord may descend through him even to the ultimates of nature, and from these may also ascend up to him again. A.C. 3702. Man created in the f. of God, has been changed into the f. of a devil. C.S.L. 153. All created things which are in the world are according to cor. A.C. 9272. All things are created by the living sun from the Lord, and nothing by the sun of this world, which is dead. D.L.W. 116. All things which are seen in the spiritual world are created instantaneously by the Lord, but in the natural world, they exist and grow from seed. U.T. 794. Man, as to his internal, is created after the image of heaven, and as to his external, according to the image of the world. A.C. 9776. H. and H. 202. No angel or spirit is created such immediately. D.P. 220. The divine truth proceeding from the Lord created all things. A.C. 8200. The Lord created the universe and all things therein by means of his own sun, which is his first proceeding emanation. D.L.W. 151. All things were created by the divine wisdom from the divine love. D.L.W. 52. All created things in a certain image rep. man. D.L.W. 61. The uses of all created things ascend by degrees from ultimates to man, and through man to God the creator, from whom they proceeded. D.L.W. 65.

Creation, all, proceeds from first principles to ultimates, and from ultimates to the first [cause] from whom it was derived. D.P. 56. There is no c. given, without order. U.T. 500. In order that an idea of c. may be formed, space and time must be removed from the thought. D.L.W. 155. C. commenced from the supreme or inmost, because from the Divine, and proceeded to ultimates or extremes, and then first subsisted. L.J. 9. Jehovah could not have created the universe, unless he had been a Man. D.L.W. 285. For no one could be immediately created from the uncreate infinite, the esse, and the life itself. D.L.W. 4, 5. The Lord from eternity, who is Jehovah, created the universe and all things therein from himself, and not out of nothing. D.L.W. 282. The c. of the universe and of all things therein, is upheld by continual mediums. D.L.W. 303. No c. could have been effected unless there had been something of freewill in all created things. U.T. 499. C. of the universe is produced, as it were, from the influx of the divine of the Lord through an angel. D.L.W. 326. The end of c. exists in its ultimates, which is, that all things may return to the creator, and that there may be conjunction. D.L.W. 167. C. of heaven and earth, in the first chapter of Genesis, in a spiritual sense, des. the new c. or regeneration of the man of the most ancient church. Ap. Ex. 650. In the order of c. the Lord governs what is last from what is first, and what is first from what is last; and this is the reason why he is called the First and the Last. A.C. 3702, 6040. At the c., when all things were pronounced by God to be good, the meaning was, that they all mutually cor. to each other; that is to say, nature and the world cor. with man and his mind, and the human mind cor. with the deity; so that there was no occasion for instruction, inasmuch as every thing subsisted in perfect harmony. H.K. Ex. 9.

Creator of the Universe. See *Image*. C.S.L. 479.

Creatures s. those who are capable of being reformed. A.R. 290, 405. The difference between human and brute c. consists in this: the soul of every man, by virtue of its origin, being celestial, receives the influx of light and heat, or love and wisdom, immediately from the Lord; but a brute receives light and heat immediately through heaven or hell. C.S.L. 482. U.T. 473.

Creeping Things which the Waters Produce (Gen. i. 20) s. scientifics belonging to the external man. A.C. 40. The c. t. of the ground (Gen. vi. 20) s. both things intellectual and voluntary in their lowest state. A.C. 674. C. t. (Gen. vi. 7) s. pleasures as well corporeal as sensual. A.C. 594. C. t., in a proper sense, are what were the vilest of all which are named (Lev. xi. 22, 29, 30) and were unclean; but in an enlarged sense, as in Gen. ix. 3, they are animals which are given for meats. Here, however, they are called c. t., because they s. pleasures. A.C. 994. C. t. (Ezek. viii. 10) s. filthy pleasures, whose interiors are lusts. A.C. 994. See *Beasts, Fowls.*

Crew. Conversation with the infernal c. A.C. 968.

Crimson s. spiritual good. 4922, 9833.

Critics, how they appear in the other life. 6621.

Crocodile, a, s. the guileful or deceitful. A.R. 624.

Crooked made straight (Isa. xl.) s. the evil of ignorance turned into good. A.C. 3527.

Cross s. temptations. Ap. Ex. 893. The Lord, by the passion of the c., did not take away sins, but he bore them. L. 15–17. To take up the c. is to fight against concupiscences; and to follow the Lord is to acknowledge him to be God. D.L. 66. The quality of the human of the Lord, as it hung upon the cross, is not to be thought of, when he is approached in the holy supper. U.T. 728. At baptism an infant receives the sign of the c. upon the forehead and breast, which is a sign of inauguration into the acknowledgment and worship of the Lord. U.T. 682; also 685. See *Passion of the Cross.*

Crowd s. all who are in the good of life, according to their religion. A.E. 452.

Crowing, cock, s. the last state of the church. 10, 134.

Crown s. an ensign of warfare and victory; hence it was an ensign of victory to martyrs, because they had conquered in temptations. A.R. 103, 300. C. on the head s. wisdom, and a golden c., wisdom proceeding from love. A.R. 189, 235, 252, 643. C. of glory in the hand of Jehovah (Isa. lxii. 3) s. wisdom which is of good, and a royal diadem in the hand of God, the intelligence which is of truth. Ap. Ex. 272. C. (Rev. iv.) s. the good of love and charity. Ap. Ex. 292.

Crows

Crows (young), or **Ravens** (Ps. xiv. 7, 9), s. natural men, who are in the thickest darkness from fallacies concerning divine truths, of which quality are many of the Gentiles. Ap. Ex. 650.

Crucified. It is said in Rev. xi. that the Lord was c. in Sodom and Egypt, which was not literally true, but only spiritually so; for by Sodom is s. the love of dominion, originating in self-love; and by Egypt, the pride of self-derived intelligence, by which loves the Lord is c. A.R. 502. See *Mocked*.

Crucify, to. Crucifixion or suspension upon wood s. condemnation and the curse on account of the destruction of good in the church. Ap. Ex. 655. To c. the Lord, is to blaspheme him, and to deny that he is the son of God, and that his humanity is divine. A.R. 504. See *Cross*.

Cruel. It is surprising that they who have been c. during their life in the body, have also been adulterers above all others. A.C. 824.

Cruelties originate in the love of self. D.P. 276.

Cry, in the Word, is said of every affection that breaks out from the heart, wherefore it is the voice of lamentation, of imploring, of supplication, grounded in indolence, of contestation, of indignation, of confessions, yea, of exultation. A.R. 885. As a c. [or shout] also is an act, which cor. to a living confession or acknowledgment from faith, therefore also amongst the ancients, the ritual of crying [or shouting] was received when such a thing was s.; and on this account mention is made of crying [or shouting] in the Word throughout, when confession and acknowledgment from faith are treated of. A.C. 5323. C., in a good sense, has respect to truths; but in a bad sense, to falses. A.C. 2240, 2243. C. of Sodom and Gomorrah becoming great, and their sin being grievous (Gen. xviii. 20) s. that the false and evil principle and self-love, were grown to every consummation. A.C. 2237. To c. out of heaven (Gen. xxii. 11, etc.) den. consolation. A.C. 2820. C. den. what is false, and sin what is evil. (Gen. xviii. 20.) A.C. 2239. To c. with a great voice, s. interior affection according to the subject pred. Ap. Ex. 459. Crying, or a c. is spoken of grief and fear of falses from hell, and thence of damnation. A.R. 885. The Crying of Bloods (Gen. iv. 10) s. guilt. A.C. 373.

Crystal s. divine truth. (Rev. xxii. 1.) Ap. Ex. 253.

Cubit (a measure of eighteen inches) s. quality. A.R. 909.

Cucumbers, Melons, Leeks, Onions, and **Garlick** (Num. xi. 5), all s. such things as are of the lowest natural, or the sensual or corporeal part of man. Ap. Ex. 513.

Cultivate, to, or till, is to become corporeal. A.C. 345, 381.

Cummin den. scientifics. 10.669.

Cunning. The perceptions of concupiscences are all sorts of craft and c. D.P. 206.

Cunning Sleights in the hand (Num. xxii. 4, 7) s. falsifications of truth. A.C. 3242.

Cup. In the Word frequent mention is made of c., and thereby is s. in the genuine sense spiritual truth, that is, the truth of faith which is from the good of charity, the like as by wine; and in the opp. sense, the false which gives birth to evil, and also the false derived from evil; the reason why c. s. the like as wine is, because a c. is what contains, and wine is what is contained, and hence they constitute one thing, and thus the one is meant by the other. The c. of the wine of anger (Jer. xxv. 15–17, 28), den. the false which gives birth to evil; the reason why the false which gives birth to evil is s., is because as wine intoxicates and makes insane, so does the false, spiritual intoxication being nothing else but insanity induced by reasonings concerning what is to be believed, when nothing is believed which is not comprehended, hence come falses and from falses evils, wherefore it is said, that they may drink and stagger, and be insane by reason of the sword which I shall send. A.C. 5120. C. (Matt. xxiii. 26, Luke xi. 39), in the internal sense, s. the truth of faith, to cultivate which without the good thereof is to purge the exterior of the c., and especially when the interiors are full of hypocrisy, deceit, hatred, revenge, and cruelty, for in such case the truth of faith is only in the external man, and nothing at all thereof in the internal; and to cultivate and imbue the good of faith causes truths to be conjoined to good in the interior man, in which case even fallacies are accepted for truths, which is s. by purging first the interior of the c., and the exterior becoming also clean. A.C. 5120. C. s. temptations. See Matt. xxvi. 39, xx. 22, and John xviii. 11. Ap. Ex. 960. To receive c. of salvations (Ps. cxvi. 12, 13), s. the appropriation of the goods of faith. A.C. 5120. To give the c. of the wine of the fierceness of the wrath of God (Rev. xvi. 19), s. to devastate the church until there is nothing but evil and falsehood. A.R. 713.

Cup and **Platter** (Matt. xxiii. 27) s. the interiors and exteriors of man which receive truth and good. Ap. Ex. 474.

Cup of Trembling s. mere falses, from which evils are derived. A.E. 724.

Curdle. See *Milk.*

Cure den. the restoration of spiritual life. 9031.

Curse and **Blessing,** a. (Zech. viii. 13.) The church devastated is called a c.; because therein is evil and the false; but the church restored is called a b.; because goodness and truth are therein. Ap. Ex. 340.

Cursed Thing s. evil and the false. A.E. 1340.

Curtains (Exod. xxvi.) s. the interior truths of faith, which are of the new intellectual principle. A.C. 9595. C. of the tent (Exod. xxvi.) rep. natural or external things. A.C. 3540. C. and cords (Jer. iv. 20, and x. 20), s. spiritual things from a celestial origin. A.C. 414. C. (Jer. x. 20) s. truths proceeding from good, and serving as a covering thereto. Ap. Ex. 799. See *Loops.*

Cush (Ezek. xxix. 10) s. the interior knowledges of the Word, applied to confirm false principles originating in scientifics. A.C. 1164. The fallacies of the senses. Ap. Ex. 240. C. s. the same as Ethiopia. Ap. Ex. 304. C. and Egypt, also stand simply for knowledges and sciences, which are truths useful to those who are principled in faith grounded in charity. See Isa. xlv. 14. Dan. xi. 43. Zeph. iii. 10. Ps. lxviii. 31, and Ps. lxxxvii. 4. A.C. 1164. C. and Phut (Ezek. xxx. 4–6) s. knowledges collected from the Word. A.C. 1164. C. and the Sabæans (Isa. xlv. 14) s. knowledges. A.C. 2508. See *Egypt, Land of Cush.*

Custody, to shut up in, s. rejection and separation. A.C. 5456. See *Brother.*

Custom, the, in the ancient church, was, to give a name significative of a state. 2643.

Custom of the Ancients. See *History.*

Cut, to, stones is to fashion truths from the proprium. 8941.

Cut Off, to be (Gen. xli.), s. to perish. A.C. 5302. To cut asunder with swords s. the destruction of truths by falses. Ap. Ex. 315.

Cut Wood, to, s. to place merit in the good of works. A.C. 2784.

Cuttings off of the Mountains (Jonah ii. 7) s. where there are the most damned, for the dark, thick mists, which appear around them are the mountains. A.C. 4728.

Cuticles. The societies, to which the c. cor., are in the entrance to heaven; and to them is given a perception of the quality of the spirits who crowd to the first threshold, whom they either reject or admit; so that they may be called the entrances or thresholds of heaven. A.C. 5553.

Cuticulars, such as acquire truth without delight. 8977.

Cymbal, used to den. joy of heart. 8337, 9.

Cyrus (Isa. xliv. 28), s. the Lord, as to his divine human principle. Ap. Ex. 298.

D

Dagger den. doctrinals destroying truth and good. 6353.

Dagon (1 Sam. v. 6), being the idol of the Philistines, s. their religion, which also was faith separate from charity. D.P. 326.

Daily den. what is perpetual. 2838.

Daily Bread. It is given to the angels by the Lord every moment, what to think and this with blessedness and happiness, which is implied also in the internal sense, by the d. b., mentioned in the Lord's prayer; and likewise by the Lord's precept to his disciples, not to be solicitous about what they eat or drink, or with what they are clothed. A.C. 2493. See *Day.*

Damascus. A principal city of Syria, where there were the remains of worship, as practised in the ancient church, and from whence came Eber or the Hebrew nation. A.C. 1796. D. s. nearly the same as Syria, which see. A.C. 1715. D. and Aroer (Isa. xvii. 1, 2) s. the knowledges of truth and good. A.E. 911. See *Eliezer of Damascus.*

Damnation is to perish by reason of evil. 2395. To suppose any one predestined to d. is a cruel heresy. D.P. 330. Whoever denies God, is already among the condemned. T.C.R. 14.

Damsel den. affection in which is innocence. 3067. D. of Rebecca (Gen. xxiv. 61) s. subservient affections. 3189. See *Daughter.*

Dan. (Jer. viii. 16) s. truth in its own ultimate degree of order, here truth in the church, which is contained in the literal sense of the Word. He who remains in this alone and does not read it from the doctrine of genuine truth, which leads and enlightens, is liable to fall into all kinds of errors and such are understood by D. The confirmation of the false thence, by the snorting of his horses, and the falsifications of truth, by the sound of the neighing of his strong ones. That from thence the church is vastated, is understood by the whole land trembled, etc. A.E. 355. The reason why this tribe is not mentioned among the rest, in Rev. vii., is because by this tribe they are rep. and s., who are treated of in the subsequent parts of that chapter, verse 9, etc.: viz., they who have not been in the real truths of heaven and the church, but in the good of life, according to their doctrinals of religion, which, for the most part, were not genuine truths, but falses, which were, however, accepted by the Lord as truths, because they were in the good of life, from which the falses of their religion were not tinctured with evil, but inclining to good. The reason why these were received instead of the tribe of D., is because this tribe was the ultimate of all, and therefore, in the kingdom of the Lord, s. the ultimate [heaven] in which they are, who are of the above description. A.E. 450. 10.335. D. s. those who are in truth, and not at the same time in good. 6395. D. is the first state of one about to be regenerated, but the ultimate or last of him, who is regenerated. 3923.

Dances (Exod. xv. 20) are pred. of the affection of spiritual good, or the good of truth, and s. its pleasantness and joy. 8339.

Dancing is pred. of truths, and joy of goods. (Ps. xxx. 11.) 5779.

Danger. There is no d. in departing from evil to good; the d. is in departing from good to evil. A.Cr. 55.

Daniel rep. every thing prophetical concerning the Lord's coming, and concerning the state of the church. 3652. See Matt. xxiv.
Daniel's Four Beasts rep. the successive states of the church. A.R. 574.
Darius the Mede, requiring to be worshipped as a God (Dan. vi.), rep. profanation. 1326.
Darkened, the perversion of the church by falsity. A.E. 368.
Darkness (tenebræ) s. natural light (lumen), for, in respect to spiritual light (lux), it is as d. This light (lumen) is s. by d. (tenebræ) Gen. i. 2, 5. D. also s. mere ignorance from the deprivation of truth, as in Ps. xviii. 29, Ps. cxxxix. 11, 12. A.E. 526. D. (Matt. iv. 16) den. the falses of ignorance. 1839. D. (thick) (Gen. xv. 17) s. hatred, instead of charity. 1860. The light of heaven effectively appears as d. to those who are in the love of self and of the world. 2441. Thick d. or blackness s. the falses of evil. 1839, 7711. D. and thick d. (Zeph. i. 15) s. falses and evils. 1839.
Dark Sayings of Old. See *Representatives*. A.C. 66.
Dart s. doctrinals of truth. 2686.
Dates. The branch on which they hang, s. the good of faith. 7093.
Dathan, swallowed up, s. damnation. 8306.
David rep. the Lord, as to divine truth proceeding from his divine human. A.E. 316. D. in the Word, den. the Lord. 2159, 1888. Also the divine sovereignty or royalty. H. and H. 526. 1888, 9954. And he rep. the Lord who was to come into the world. D.P. 245. Doct. Lord. 43, 44. D. in a supreme sense, s. divine truth proceeding from the Lord's divine good, and in an internal sense all truth which is from good derived from the Lord. A.E. 206. Root of D. s. the Lord as to divine good united to divine truth in his humanity. A.E. 310.
David and **Israel**. D. s. those who are in divine spiritual truth, and I. those who are in divine truth spiritual natural, which is the medium between divine truth natural and spiritual. A.E. 768.
Daughter, a (Gen. xxx. 21), s. a church of faith in which is good. 3693.
Daughter of Jacob (Gen. xxxiv. 19) s. the superstitious principle of the ancient church. 4475.
Daughter of Zion s. the celestial church; and daughter of Jerusalem, the spiritual church. (Isa. xxxviii. 22.) 2362.
Daughter, Young Woman, and **Damsel**. D. s. affection in common; y. w., affection in which is charity; and d., affection in which is innocence. 3067. See *King's Daughter*.
Daughters of Canaan s. the affections of what is false and evil. 3683. Two d. of one mother (Ezek. xxii.) are the Israelitish and Jewish churches. A.R. 134. D. and virgins s. the affections of goodness and truth. A.R. 620. D.-in-law s. good associated to its proper truth. 4843. "Behold I have two d.," etc. (Gen. xix. 8), s. the affections of good and truth, and the blessedness perceivable from the enjoyment thereof, by those who do not violate the divine and holy principle of the Lord. 2362.
Daughters of the **Night-Monster**. Devastation of truth. A.E. 141.
Daughters of **one Mother**. The Israelitish and Jewish churches. A.E. 141.
Daughters of the **Owl** s. self love, or proprium. 1326.
Daughters of **Rabbah** s. those who are in natural good, and falsify the truths of the church. A.E. 637.
Dawn s. when conjunction is at hand. 4300.
Day s. what is perpetual and eternal. 2838. Also good and charity. 38, 862. D. (Gen. i. 18) s. good, and night, evil. 38. D. and year, in the Word, s. the states of life in general. H. and H. 155. A.C. 23, 487. D. s. time and state in general, and years, times and states in particular. 486, 487. Mid-d. s. a state of light or of the knowledges of truth, or of wisdom and intelligence. 1548, 5672, 9684. "Give us this d. our daily bread." By this d. and to-d. is s. the

Day Before Yesterday

perpetuity and eternity of a state. That daily and to-d. s. what is perpetual, appears from the sacrifice which was offered every d., and which, by reason of the s. of d., of daily and to-d., was called the continual or perpetual sacrifices. (Num. xxviii. 3, 23, etc.) This appears still more evident from the manna which rained from heaven. (Exod. xvi. 4, 19, 20, 23.) 2838.

Day Before Yesterday den. from eternity. 6983. Also a prior state. 7114.

Day Dawn Ascending (Gen. xxxii.) s. when conjunction is at hand. 4300.

Day of the **Anger** and **Wrath** of **Jehovah**, in the Old Testament relates to the judgment which he executed by his incarnation; but the day of his wrath, mentioned in the Revelation, relates to the last judgment executed at his second advent, Anno 1757. A.E. 413.

Day of **Jehovah**, or Great day of **Jehovah** s. the coming of the Lord, and the establishment of a new church, by him; and as there is a consummation of the age, that is, an end of the old church, at the coming of the Lord, and commencement of a new church, therefore, by the d. of Jehovah, in many passages, is also s. the end of the former church; and it is said, that there will then be rumors, tumults, and wars, etc. L. 45. A.R. 704. D. of Jehovah (Joel i. 15) s. vastation. 488. D. of Jehovah (Zeph. i. 14) s. the last time and state of the church. 1839.

Day of **Ruin** (Ezek. xxvii. 27) s. the last judgment. A.E. 538.

Day and **Night** s. the state of the regenerate person, as to things intellectual; and summer and winter, are pred. of things belonging to the will. 936.

Day of **Vengeance** s. a state of damnation. 488.

Day-spring from on High s. the Lord; and they who are without the church, are understood by those "who sit in darkness and in the shadow of death;" their illustration in divine truth by their reception of the Lord and conjunction with him, from whence heaven and eternal felicity are derived, is understood by the way of peace; and by guiding our feet therein, is s. instruction. (Luke i. 79.) A.E. 365.

Days, to come to (Gen. xxiv. 1), s. when the state was at hand. 3016.

Days of **Eternity** and the **Years** of **Generation** and **Generation** (Deut. xxxii. 7, 8) den. the most ancient and the ancient churches. 1259. See *Ancient of Days.*

Days of **Old** (Ps. lxxvii. 5) s. states of the most ancient church, and years of ancient times, states of the ancient church. 488. The most ancient church which was before the flood, and in love to the Lord, is understood by the d. of o., of an age, or of eternity (Mal. iii. 4); and the ancient church which was after the flood, which was the spiritual church, is understood by former years. A.E. 433. A.C. 486. See *Seventh day.*

Dead. They are so called, in the Word, who have only natural life, but not spiritual life also. A.E. 694. D. (Gen. xxiii. 8) s. night, in respect to the goodnesses and truths of faith. 2931. D. (Rev. vi. 8, and xi. 18) has respect to what is infernal. A.R. 321, 525. When it is said of the Lord, that he was made d. (Rev. i. 18), it does not mean that he was crucified, and so died, but that he was neglected in the church, and his divine humanity not acknowledged; for so he became d. among men. A.R. 93. A d. man s. one who is unregenerate. 81. A d. man acknowledges nothing to be true and good, but what regards the body and the world, and this he adores. 81.

Dead Worship. The external worship of the church without the internal is infernal. 10.546. To imitate affections in worship is infernal. 10.309.

Deaf, the, in the spiritual sense, s. those who are not in the truth of faith, because not in the knowledge and thence the apperception of it. 9397. The d. (Dan. iv. 10–16) s. those who are not in the understanding of truth, and thence not in obedience. A.E. 455.

Death s. extinction of concupiscences, which is the crucifixion of the flesh, and thus a renewal of life. Also, a rejection by the world. Also, the devil

Decalogue

and hell, and thence evil of the will. A.R. 866. D. in the Word, s. resurrection. H. and H. 445. 3498, 6035, 6222. The second d. s. spiritual d., which is damnation. A.R. 853. By men seeking d. (Rev. ix. 6) is s. that in matters of faith, the understanding should be shut up; and shall not find it, s. that it is provided of the Lord, that this should not be done; and shall desire to die, s. that they shall wish to have the will closed in them; and d. shall flee from them, s. that it is provided that neither should this be done. A.R. 429. "They loved not their soul unto d." (Rev. xii. 11) s. that they loved not themselves more than the Lord. A.R. 556. A separation or d. ensues, when the body comes into such a state, from whatsoever disease or accident it be, that it cannot act as one with its spirit. The pulse and respiration of the body ceases, when the correspondence with the pulse and respiration of the spirit ceases, and then his spirit departs and continues its life in the spiritual world. D.L.W. 390. As d. is from no other source than from sin, and sin is all that which is contrary to divine order, it is from this ground that evil closes the smallest and altogether invisible vessels [of the human body], of which the next greater vessels, which are also invisible, are composed; for the smallest and altogether invisible vessels are continued to man's interiors; hence comes the first and inmost obstruction, and hence the first and inmost vitiation in the blood; this vitiation, when it increases, causes disease, and at length d. But if man had lived the life of good, in this case his interiors would be open to heaven, and through heaven to the Lord; thus also the smallest and invisible vascula (it is allowable to call the delineaments of the first stamina, vascula, by reason of correspondence) would be open also, and hence man would be without disease, and would only decrease to ultimate old age, until he became altogether an infant but a wise infant; and when in such case the body could no longer minister to its internal man, or spirit, he would pass without disease out of his terrestrial body, into a body such as the angels have, thus out of the world immediately into heaven. 5726.

Death and **Burial**. When the d. of man is mentioned in the Word, the angels only perceive his transmigration from one world to another; and when b. is named, they perceive man's resurrection unto life. A.E. 659.

Death and **Hell**. (Rev. vi. 8.) D. s. the extinction of spiritual life, and h., damnation thence. A.R. 321. By d. and h. gave up the dead which were in them (Rev. xx. 13), is s. the men of the church who were impious at heart, and who in themselves were devils and satans called to judgment. A.R. 870, 872.

Death of the **Waters**. See *Jericho.* 10, 300.

Debility s. diminution of potency. 8616.

Deborah, the nurse of Rebecca (Gen. xxxiv. 8), s. hereditary evil in the Lord's maternal humanity. 4564.

Deborah and **Barak** s. the truth of good. A.E. 447. The prophecy of D. and B., in the spiritual sense, treats concerning the victory of truth from good over the false from evil, and concerning the purification and reformation of the church. A.E. 447.

Debt, internal, or charity between man and man. 4190. Conjugial d. s. conjunction. 9003.

Decalogue, the precepts of the, were promulgated by Jehovah, and were not only precepts of society, but also of religion. A.R. 529. The precepts of the d. are in every religion, and man should live according to them from religion. A.R. 272. The first step to reformation, is to live according to the commandments of the d. A.R. 628. Through a life conformable to the precepts of the d., conjunction is effected with the Lord. A.R. 490. The second table of the d. is the universal doctrine of repentance. A.R. 531. The d. is, at this day, like a little book shut up. D.P. 329. The d., in the literal sense,

Deceit

contains general precepts of doctrine and life, but in the spiritual and celestial senses, all things universally. U.T. 287. There are two tables of the d., one for God, the other for man. D.P. 326. See *Commandments.*

Deceit and **Profanation**. There are two things, which not only close up the way of communication, but also deprive man of the faculty of ever becoming rational, which are d. and p.: d. is like a subtle poison which infects the interiors; and p. is what mixes falses with truths, and evils with goods; by these two things the rational principle is destroyed; there are with every man goods and truths from the Lord stored up from infancy, which goods and truths in the Word are called remains, these remains are infected by d., and are mixed together by p. 5128.

Decision den. the end of the church. 1857.

Declare, to (Ps. iv. 13), s. to flow in. A.E. 405.

Decline, to, is to fall into what is false and evil. 4815.

Decoration s. the divine truth of the church. A.E. 272.

Decorum. Honesty is the complex of all moral virtues; d. the form. 2915.

Decrease of spiritual heat and light exp. D.L.W. 94.

Decrepit Old Men and **Women**. Such of them as lived in this world in conjugial love, or in goodness and truth, in the other world are in the fullest beauty and flower of age. C.S.L. 137.

Dedan (Gen. x.) s. the knowledges of celestial things of an inferior order, such as consist in ritual observances. 1172. D. (Gen. xxv.) den. those who are principled in the good of faith, properly, those who are principled in the truth of faith grounded in good. 3240. D. (Jer. xlix. 8) s. rituals wherein there is no internal worship. 1172.

Deep, the, that lieth under (Gen. xlix. 25), s. scientifics in the natural principle. 6431. See *Face of the Deep.*

Deeps (Ps. cxlviii. 7) s. the ultimate heavens, in which the spiritual natural angels are; also divine truths in abundance, and arcana of divine wisdom. See Ps. lxxvi. 15, xxxvi. 7, etc. A.E. 538.

Deer, male, natural affection of truth; female, of good. 6413.

Defence. Ultimate truth is a d. to spiritual truth. 5008.

Defend, to. The spiritual man is unable to d. himself against the natural man, when ultimate truth is withdrawn. 5008.

Defiled with **Women**, to adulterate and falsify the divine good and truth of the Word. A.R. 620.

Deflux, or **Flowing Down**, produces a different effect with the good, from what it does with the evil. A.E. 502.

Deformity. He with whom the internal and external man are opposed is black and deformed as to his spirit. 3425.

Degrees. There are three d. in man, answering to the three heavens. 4154. There are three d. both in the spiritual and in the natural world, hitherto unknown, according to which the laws of influx have their operations. I. 17, 18.

Degrees of **Altitude** are discrete or disjunct, and d. of latitude are continuous. I. 16. There are three d. of a. or discrete d. in every man from his birth; each of which has also d. of latitude or continuous d. D.L.W. 236. D. of a. are ascending and descending, and d. of latitude are of increase and decrease. D.L.W. 184. D. of a. or discrete d. are as things prior, posterior, and postreme, or as end, cause, and effect. D.L.W. 184, 189. The d. of a. in their ultimate, are in their fulness and power. D.L.W. 217. There are three infinite and uncreate d. of a. in the Lord, and there are three finite and created d. in man. D.L.W. 230. Three d. of a. are in every man from his birth, and they can be opened successively, and as they are opened, man is in the Lord and the Lord in him. D.L.W. 236. These three d., with the angels are named *celestial, spiritual,* and *natural;* and their celestial d. is their d. of love, their spiritual d. is their d. of wisdom, and their natural d. is their d. of uses. D.L.W. 232.

Degrees of **Ascent**. See **Man**. D.L.W. 67.

Deists. See *Deity*. Those who profess to acknowledge the supreme ens, acknowledge no God but nature. 4733.

Deity. No conception can be had of the D. but in a human form; and whatsoever is incomprehensible can be no object of thought or idea. 9359. See *Human Form*.

Delicacies (Lam. iv. 5) s. genuine truths from the Word. A.E. 652. D. (Jer. li. 34) s. the knowledges of faith. 42. Sons of d. (Micah i. 16) are so called from the love of them, and pleasures thence derived, and have relations to truths. A.E. 724.

Delight which a man has, is from his love. D.P. 73. D. is the universal of heaven, and the universal of hell. C.S.L. 401. The d. wherein there is good from the Lord, is alone a living d., for in such case it has life from the essential life of good. 995. Every d. is of such a nature, that it becomes viler, the more it proceeds to external things, and happier, the more it proceeds to things internal. 996. D. carries light along with it, and to those who love divine and celestial things, light shines from heaven and gives ill. H. and H. 265. The whole of an angel may be called d. D.P. 93. They who have taken d. in the Word, in another life receive the heat of heaven, wherein is celestial love. 1773. Every one is allowed the d. of his evil, provided he does not infest those who are good; but forasmuch as the evil cannot do otherwise than this, they are remanded to hell. D.P. 324. D. of every one's life are changed after death to things cor. thereto. H. and H. 485, 490.

Deliver, to, up a brother to death s. that the false shall destroy good. A.E. 315.

Delivered, to be, **in Childbirth** s. the doctrines of the N.C., in its birth, and the difficult reception thereof. A.R. 535.

Delivery of the **Woman** in **Childbirth**, the, shows the difficulties attending the birth of the faith of heaven and its life, consequently, regeneration. H. and H. 382. 613, 10.197.

Deluge den. desolation or devastation. 705.

Demons which were cast out by the Lord, when on earth, s. all kinds of falsities, with which the church was infested. A.E. 586. D. s. concupiscences of evil originating in the love of the world. A.R. 458. When man in his worship does not regard the Lord nor his neighbor, but himself and the world, that is, when he worships God, to the end that he may be raised to honors and riches, or that he may bring loss to others, then he worships d. (Rev. ix.), for then the Lord is not present, but only infernal spirits, who are consociated, among whom there is also such madness, that they believe themselves to be Gods, which indeed is the case interiorly with every man who is principled in self-love. A.E. 586. They become d. of the worst kind, who were in the concupiscence of exercising dominion from the love of self, over the holy things of the church. A.R. 756.

Den of **Thieves**, a (Matt. xxi. 13), s. the profanation of the church and of worship. A.E. 325. Old dens, or dungeons s. hells. A.R. 757. Dens or caves s. evils, for they who have been in evil loves, are in hell, in dens, and hence dens s. those loves. A.R. 338.

Denarius, the smallest Roman coin, s. the last price. A.E. 374.

Denial of the **Lord's Divinity**, heaven is shut by. G.E.D. p. 36.

Denial of the **Sanctity** of the **Word**, heaven is shut by. G.E.D. p. 36.

Deny Himself, to (Mark viii. 34), s. to reject evils which are from proprium. A.E. 122. To d. h. s. not to be led by self, but by the Lord, and he d. h., who turns himself away from evils, because they are sins. A.E. 864.

Depart

Depart, to, in the internal sense, s. the institutes and order of life. 1293. To d. (Gen. xi. 2) s. to recede. 1290.

Depend, to. Every thing, unless it depended upon one, would divide and fall to pieces. U.T. 10.

Deposite, to store up for use. 5299.

Deprivation, the, of spiritual truth and good produces anxiety. 2682.

Depth s. what is exterior. D.L.W. 206.

Depths of **Satan** s. interior falses. A.R. 143.

Derivations, in the inferior degrees, are only compositions, or more properly confirmations of the singulars and particulars of the superior degrees successively, with such things added from purer nature, and afterwards from grosser, as may serve for containing vessels, etc. 5114.

Descend, to. That which d. into the body from the spiritual man presents itself therein under another shape, but nevertheless is similar and unanimous thereto. H. and H. 373.

Desert s. the state of the church among the gentiles, and also the state of those who are in temptation. A.E. 730. Man is like a d. when charity and faith are not conjoined in him. 7626.

Desert of the Sea s. the vanity of the sciences, which are not for use; the chariot of an ass s. an heap of particular scientifics; the chariot of a camel s. an heap of common scientifics, which are in the natural man. The van reasonings which appertain to those who are s. by Babel are thus des. (Isa. xxi. 1, 6, 7, 9.) 3048.

Desirable Things, in the Word, are pred. concerning truths. A.E. 799. D. good t. (Joel iii. 4–6) den. knowledges. 1197.

Desire, to (Rev. ix. 6), is pred. of the will, and to seek, of the understanding. A.R. 429.

Desolation, in the Word, is pred. of truths, and falses. A.R. 747. D. is for the end, that man may be regenerated, that is, that evils and falses being separated, truths may be conjoined to goods and goods to truths; the regenerate man as to good is what is compared to Eden, and as to truths, to the garden of Jehovah. The vastation or d. of the man of the church, or of the church with man, was rep. by the captivity of the Jewish people in Babylon, and the raising up of the church by a return from that captivity; see Jeremiah throughout, especially xxxii. 37, to the end; for d. is captivity, man in such case being kept, as it were, bound, wherefore also by the bound in prison, and in the pit, are s. those who are in d. 5376.

Desperation. Temptations are generally carried on to a state of d., which is their period and conclusion. 1787. Man is held in a state of d. in the combat against the false. 8567.

Desponsation. The last words in the Apocalypse. A.R. 960.

Destroy, to, "every substance which I have made from off the faces of the ground" (Gen. vii. 4), s. man's proprium which is, as it were, destroyed, when it is vivified, or made alive by the Lord; but whereas the subject here treated of, is also concerning the final vastation of those who were of the most ancient church, therefore by destroying every substance which I have made from off the faces of the ground, are s. those who perished. 731. To d. (Gen. xix. 13), when pred. of the Lord, s. for man to perish by evil, that is, to be damned. 2395.

Destroyers and **Devastators** (Isa. xliii. 17) s. the falses of evil. A.E. 724.

Destruction, great (Jer. vi. 1), s. the dissipation of good and truth. A.E. 449.

Detained. Unless the Lord d. every man in general from evils and falses he would cast himself headlong into hell, and in the moment he is not so d., he violently rushes there headlong. 789. All men whatsoever are d. from evils by the Lord, and this by a stronger force than can be believed. 2406. Angels as well as men, are d. from evil, and preserved in good by the Lord. 4564.

Determinations, there are two d. of the intellectual and voluntary parts of man; the one outward towards the world, the other inward towards heaven. 9730. D. of angels is from the reigning love. H. and H. 25.

Devastation and **Desolation**. (Ezek. xxiii. 33.) The former is pred. of good, and the latter, of truth. The common version reads it "astonishment and desolation." A.E. 960.

Devil s. self-love. D.P. 302. D. and his crew s. the love of ruling in hell. Concupiscences are called the d.; and thoughts of what is false are called his crew, in the Word. D.L.W. 273. D. and Satan do not s. any one particular evil spirit, but all in hell are called d. and satans, on which account, hell in the complex has such appellations. A.R. 550. Every d. can understand truth when he hears it, but cannot retain it; because the affection of evil when it returns, casts out the thought of truth. A.R. 655. D. and satans sometimes understand arcana as well as angels, yet only when they hear them from others; but when they return into their own thoughts, they do not understand them; the reason is, because they will not. D.P. 99. D. may be thurst down to their infernal abodes by a little child. 1271. It is a false notion to suppose that d. have existed from the beginning of creation, except what were once men. 968.

Devotion, external, and piety have no communication with heaven, when evils are cherished in the heart. 10.500.

Devour, to, or **Eat** the **Book** (Rev. x.), s. to read and perceive the Word, for to d. and to c., is to conjoin and appropriate to one's self; and the Word is conjoined to man by reading and perception. A.E. 617. To d. (Rev. xii. 4), s. to destroy. A.E. 722.

Devouring or **Consuming Fire**, the Lord appears to the evil as a. 9434.

Dew, in a genuine sense, is the truth of good, which is derived from a state of innocence and peace. 3579. D. (Deut. xxxii. 2) s. the multiplication of truth from good, and the fructification of good by truth. 3579. D. of Hermon (Ps. cxxxiii. 3) s. divine truth. A.E. 375.

Diadems, seven, upon the head of the dragon, s. all the truths of the Word falsified and profaned. A.R. 540. See *Crown.*

Diamond. The Word is like a d., by virtue of its spiritual light. U.T. 216. D., or precious stones, s. the truths of the literal sense of the Word. A.R. 540. S.S. 43–35.

Diaphanous forms transmit spiritual light, as crystal transmits natural. Exp. D.L.W. 245.

Diastole and **Systole** change and vary according to the affections. Exp. D.L.W. 378.

Dibon, Daughter who inhabits, s. the external of the church, and thence the external of the Word, which is its literal sense. A.E. 727.

Dictate, the interior, of truth flows in from the Lord by the medium of the angels. 1308.

Die, to, when the subject treated of, is concerning the rep. of any one, s. an end of his representation. 3259. To d. (Gen. v. 5) s. that perception no longer existed. 494. To d. (Gen. xxiii. 2) pred. of the church, s. its last time, when all faith and charity has expired. 2908. To d. (Gen. xxv. 33) s. to rise again afterwards into superiority and dominion. 3326.

Diet, or meat and drink, den. the knowledges of good and truth. 1480, 9003.

Dig, to (Gen. xxvi. 18), s. to open. 3419. To d. s. to investigate or search thoroughly into any thing. 7343.

Digestions of Food rep. temptations. 5174.

Dignities and riches are stumbling-blocks to the wicked, but not to the good. D.P. 250.

Dignity is adjoined to every employment, according to use. H. and H. 389.

Diklah (Gen. x. 27), a ritual of the church called Eber. 1245.

Dilated

Dilated (Gen. xxvi. 22) s. to receive increments of truth. 3434.

Dimensions, viz., length, breadth, and height, cannot be pred. of celestial and spiritual things; when they are pred. abstracted from d., they den. greater and lesser perfection, and also the quality and quantity of a thing. 650.

Dinah s. the affection of all things of faith and of the church thence derived. 4427. Also, the external church such as was instituted amongst the posterity of Jacob. 4429.

Dinner, Supper, and **Feast,** a, are the good of charity, in which the Lord cohabits with man. A.E. 2371. D. and s. s. all conjunction. A.E. 391. D. and s. were significative of consociation by love. 3596, 3832.

Dip, to, or **Dye** (Gen. xxxvii. 31), s. to defile. 4770.

Disagreement, between the understanding and will des. A.Cr. 65.

Disciple (Matt. x. 41) s. charity and at the same time, faith from the Lord. A.R. 8. To be the Lord's d. is to be led by the Lord, and not by self. 10.490. D. s. truth of life, and prophet truth of doctrine. (Matt. x. 40–42.) 10.683. D. mean all who worship the Lord and live according to the truths of his Word. A.R. 325. By the d. of the Lord, are meant those who are instructed by the Lord in goods and truths of doctrine, but by apostles, they who, after they are instructed, teach them. See Luke ix. 1, 2, 10. Mark vi. 7, 30. A.R. 70.

Discourse. When the d. in a superior heaven is concerning good, there is an appearance of what is golden beneath amongst those who are in the first or ultimate heaven below them, and when the d. is concerning truth, there appears there what is silvery, sometimes to such a degree, that not only the walls of the rooms which they inhabit glitter with gold and silver, but even the atmosphere itself; likewise amongst the angels of the first or ultimate heaven, who are principled in good from good, there appear tables of gold, candlesticks of gold, and several other things; but with those who are principled in truth from truth, there appear such things of silver. 5658.

Discrete Degrees exist, when one is formed from another, and by means of the other a third, which is called composite, and each degree is distinct from another. D.L.W. 190. See *Degrees.*

Discerption, all, consists in separating good from evils and falses. 5828.

Discord, the natural man is so discordant with the spiritual, that they are the opp. of each other. 3913.

Diseases cor. to the lusts and passions of the mind (animus); these therefore are the origins of d.; for the origins of d. in common are intemperances, luxuries of various kinds, pleasures merely corporeal also envyings, hatreds, revenges, lasciviousnesses, and the like, which destroy the interiors of man, and when these are destroyed, the exteriors suffer, and draw man into d., and thereby into death; that man is subject to death by reason of evils, or on account of sin, is a thing known in the church, thus also he is subject to d., for these are of death. From these considerations it may be manifest, that d. also have cor. with the spiritual world, but with unclean things here, for d. in themselves are unclean, inasmuch as they originate in things unclean. 5712. All the infernals induce d., but with a difference, by reason that all the hells are in the lusts and concupiscences of evil, consequently, contrary to those things which are of heaven, wherefore they act upon (or into) man from an opp. principle; heaven, which is the grand man, contains all things in connection and safety; hell, as being in the opp. principle, destroys and rends all things asunder; consequently, if the infernals are applied, they induce d., and at length death; but it is not permitted them to flow in even into the solid parts of the body, or into the parts which constitute the viscera, the organs, and members of man, but only into the lusts and falsities; only when man falls into d., they then flow

78

in into such unclean things as appertain to the d.; for as was said, nothing in any wise exists with man, unless the cause also be in the spiritual world; the natural principle appertaining to man, if it was separated from a spiritual principle, would be separated from all cause of existence, thus also from every principle of life. Nevertheless, this is no hindrance to man's being healed naturally, for the divine providence concurs with such means of healing. 5713.

Disgraced. To be ashamed and d., s. to be destitute of all good and truth. A.E. 811.

Disjunction from the Lord is s. by evils and sins. 4997.

Dish s. the things contained in them. A.R. 672.

Disperse, to, den. to be dissipated. 1328.

Disposition. Truths are disposed into order when spiritual good begins to act in the natural mind. 4543.

Disputation concerning Faith and Charity in the Spiritual World. The d. c. f. alone, was heard at a distance, like the gnashing of teeth. And the d. c. c., like a beating noise. A.R. 386.

Dispute, to (Gen. xxvi. 20), s. to deny. 3425.

Dissensions and **Heresies,** the permission of, is according to the laws of divine providence. D.P. 259.

Dissimulation. See *Simulation.* Sphere like the smell of a vomit. 1514.

Dissipate s. to cast into hell. A.E. 639.

Dissociations in another life, are made according to spheres. E.U. 64.

Dissolute den. aversion from what is internal. 10.479.

Distance, in another life, is only an appearance. A.E. 731. See *Space, Place, Time.*

Distil, to, s. influx and instruction. A.E. 594.

Distinctly One, in God-man indicates cause and effect are. D.L.W. 169.

Distinguish, to. Men can with difficulty d. between good and truth; because of the difficulty there is in distinguishing between thinking and willing. N.J.D. 35. 9999.

Distress in the **Land** and **Wrath** upon the **People.** (Luke xxi. 23.) D. s. here the dominion of evil, and w. the dominion of the false from evil. A.E. 693.

Disturb. In the beginning of ill. the mind is disturbed, and only becomes tranquil when truths are disposed into order by good. 5221.

Ditch or **Moat,** a (Dan. ix. 25), s. doctrine. A.E. 652.

Diversity arises from infinite things in God-man. D.L.W. 155.

Dives s. the Jewish nation, which had the Word. A.R. 725. U.T. 215, 246, 595. S.S. 40. See *Rich Man and Lazarus.*

Divide, to (Gen. xv. 10), s. parallelism and cor. 1831, 1832. To d. over to (Gen. xxxiii. 2) s. arrangement. 4342. To d. (Matt. xxiv.) s. separation and removal from goods and truths. 4424. To d. and disperse, s. to separate and extirpate. 4052.

Divided. What is d. does not become more and more simple, but more and more multiple. C.S.L. 329. It is not suffered by the Lord that any thing should be d.; wherefore, it must be either in good and at the same time in truth, or in evil and at the same time in the false. D.P. 16.

Divided Mind, a, is contrary to the laws of the other world. 250.

Dividing the Lord's Garments s. the Word in the letter. A.E. 375.

Divine is that which is infinite and eternal. D.P. 51. In every thing d., there is a first, a middle, and a last. U.T. 210. The d. only flows into those things which are of affection. 5044. The d. fills all spaces of the universe without space. D.L.W. 69. The d. is in all time without time. D.L.W. 73. The d. in the greatest and least things is the same. D.L.W. 77. The d. cannot be appropriated to man as his own, but may be adjoined to him, and thereby appear as his own. D.P. 285. The d. of the Church is Jehovah God, etc. 7311. The d.

Divine

of the father constitutes the soul. The d. of the son constitutes the body; and the d. of the holy spirit constitutes the operation of the Lord. U.T. 168. The d. itself, in its descent, was made adequate to the perception of angels, and at length of men, from thence there is a spiritual sense within the natural. U.T. 193. A.R. 959. The essential d., the d. rational, and the d. natural, are one in the Lord. 4615. The d. itself which appeared in human form, was the d. human. 5110. The d. itself, before the Lord came into the world, flowed into the universal heaven, and by that influx from his d. omnipotence, light was produced; but afterwards that light could no longer be produced, so as to penetrate to the human race; till the Lord made the human in himself d. 4180. That which is from the Lord is d., but the proprium of man can in no wise be so made. A.R. 758. The d. of the Lord is distinguished into d. good and d. truth; that is called the father, this the son; but the d. of the Lord is nothing but good, yea, good itself. D. truth is the d. good of the Lord, so appearing in heaven, or before the angels. 3704. The whole of the d., from first principles in heaven to ultimates in the world, tends to the human form. L. 32. H. and H. 73, 453. The d. is not perceptible nor receptible, unless when it has passed heaven. N.J.D. 305. The d. passes into the world by the ultimates of order. 4618. The d. which comes from the Lord, in the supreme sense, is the d. in himself; and in the rep. sense, it is the d. from himself. D. good is celestial, and d. truth is spiritual. 4696. The d. is the same in one subject as in another, but the subject changes, etc. D.L.W. 54. The d. above the heavens is d. good itself, but the d. in the heavens, is the good which is in the truth which proceeds from the d. 8328. The d. passing through the heavens, is a d. man. 8705. Those things which are in the d. can never appear to any one, but those things which are from the d., and these appear most common and obscure. 4644. The d. of the father is the soul of the son. U.T. 112.

Divine, to, den. to know what is hidden. 5748. Divination, when it relates to the prophets, den. revelation which respects life; seeng has respect to doctrine. 9248.

Divine Celestial. Whatsoever proceeds from the Lord's divine love, is called the d. c., and all that is goodness. U.T. 195.

Divine Doctrine is divine truth, and all the Word of the Lord is divine truth. 3712.

Divine Esse, the, is one, the same, itself, and individual. A.R. 961.

Divine Essence united to the Human Essence. Unless the Lord had come into the world, and united the d. e. to the h. e., salvation could no more have reached to man. 1999, 2016, 2034. The d. e. is divine love, and the divine existence is divine wisdom. D.L.W. 14–16.

Divine Good cannot be applied to any other vessels than genuine truths, for they mutually cor. to each other. 4247. D. g. cannot be received by man nor angel, but only by the Lord's divine human. But divine truth may be received, yet of a quality such as the man who receives is capable of admitting; in which truth may dwell d. g., with a difference according to reception. 4180. D. g. is the supreme divine, but the divine word is what is from the d. g., and is also named son. 4207. D. g. united with divine truth, proceeding from the Lord, in the third or inmost heaven, is received as divine providence; in the second or middle heaven, as divine wisdom; and in the first heaven, as divine intelligence. A.E. 458. D. g. and truths are wholly separate from those goods and truths which derive any thing from humanity, for the former transcend and become infinite. 4026.

Divine Human, the, was what the ancient churches adored; Jehovah also manifested himself amongst them in the d. h.; and the d. h. was the divine itself in heaven, for heaven constitutes one man, which is called the grand man: this divine in heaven is no other than the divine itself, but in heaven as a divine man; this man is he whom the Lord took upon him, and made divine in himself, and united to the divine itself, as he had been united from eternity, for from eternity there was oneness; and this, because the human race could not otherwise be saved; for it could no longer suffice that the divine itself through heaven, thus through the d. h. there, could flow into human minds, wherefore the divine itself willed to unite to itself the d. h. actually by the human principle, assumed in the world; the latter and the former is the Lord. A.C. 5663. The d. h. existing from eternity, was the divine truth in heaven; of consequence the divine existence, which was afterwards made in the Lord the divine essence, from which the divine existence in heaven was derived. 3061, 6280, 6880, 10579. The d. h. which was born from eternity was also born in time, and what was born in time, and glorified, is the same. 2803. It is absolutely impossible for any thing of doctrine to proceed from the divine itself, except by the d. h., that is, by the Word, which in the supreme sense is the divine truth from the Lord's d. h. What proceeds immediately from the divine itself cannot be comprehended even by the angels in the inmost heaven; the reason is, because it is infinite, and thus transcends all comprehension, even the angelical; but what proceeds from the Lord's d. h., this the angels can comprehend, for it treats of God as of a divine man, concerning whom, some idea may be formed from the human, and the idea which is formed concerning the human is accepted, of whatsoever kind it is, if so be it flows from the good of innocence, and be in the good of charity; this is what is meant by the Lord's words in John i. 18, and Matt. xi. 27. 5321. The most ancient inhabitants of the earth could not worship the infinite essence, but the infinite existence which is the d. h., and they acknowledged the divine because of its appearing in a human form. 4687, 6847, 10.737. The d. h. before the advent of the Lord, was not so one with the father, as after it. 6000, 5663.

Divine Love. Such is the nature of the Lord's love, that if it were possible, his love would desire all to be in the third heaven, yea with himself, and in himself. 1798. The fire of d. l., in its full ardor, does not enter into heaven, but appears in the form of radiant circles round the sun of the spiritual world. 7270. The d. l. towards the human race is infinite. 8672. The d. l. towards the whole human race is, that it may save them, make them blessed and happy to eternity, and appropriate to them its own divine [quality], so far as it can be received. 4735. D. l. disposes all in the heavens into a celestial form, and conjoins them, so that they may be as one. H. and H. 405. The d. l. and the d. wisdom are substance and form in themselves, consequently, the self-subsisting and only subsisting [being or principle]. D.L.W. 44. All things in the universe were created from the d. l. and the divine wisdom of God-man. D.L.W. 52. All things in the created universe are recipients of the d. l. and the divine wisdom of God-man. D.L.W. 55.

Divine Natural. The Lord from eternity, or Jehovah, was divine love and divine wisdom; and he then had a divine celestial and a divine spiritual, but not a d. n., before he assumed the humanity. N.Q. No. 2.

Divine Operation, s. by the holy spirit, consists in general, in reformation and regeneration. U.T. 142.

Divine Order. What is against d. o. is impossible; as that a man who lives in evil can be saved by mere mercy. 8700. D. o. is a perpetual commandment of God; wherefore to live according to the commandments, is to live according to d. o. 2634. D. o. requires, that man should prepare himself for the reception of God, and prepare himself to be a receptacle and habitation, whereinto God may enter, and dwell as in his own temple; man ought to do this of himself, but yet to acknowledge, that it is an effect of divine

Divine Presence

influence; this he should acknowledge, because he does not perceive the presence and operation of God, although God by his most immediate presence and operation produces in man all the good of love, and all the truth of faith. According to this order every man proceeds, and ought to proceed, who from natural, wishes to become spiritual. U.T. 105.

Divine Presence, the, of the Lord is pred. according to the state of neighborly love, and of faith, in which man is. 904.

Divine Principle, the, which is called the father, is the divine esse. A.Cr. 17.

Divine Providence hath for its end an angelic heaven out of the human race. D.P. 27.

Divine Spiritual. Whatsoever proceeds from the Lord's divine wisdom is called the d. s. and all that is truth. U.T. 195.

Divine Truth. All power proceeding from the Lord is by d. t. 6948. D. t. was that principle whereby the Lord united the human to the divine; and divine good was that principle whereby he united the divine to the human. 2004, 2665. D. t. is the order itself of the universal kingdom of the Lord. 1728. D. t. itself with the angels, is the human of the Lord. 10.265. D. t. proceeding from the Lord in heaven, is man (homo). 9144. D. t. which proceeds from the Lord, does nothing of itself but from the divine good. 8724. D. t., in the literal sense of the Word, is in its fulness, in its sanctity, and in its power. U.T. 214–223. D. t. is not in the Lord, but proceeds from the Lord; as light is not in the sun, but proceeds from the sun. 3969. D. t. is not in divine good, but from divine good. 2704. D. t. which flows into the third heaven, also without successive formation, flows into the ultimate of order. 7270. D. t. in heaven, in a genuine sense, is the good of love towards our neighbor or charity. 5922. D. t. from the Word can alone oppose, conquer, subdue, and reduce into order, etc. U.T. 86. D. t. proceeding from the Lord has innocence in its inmost self. 9127. D. t. which appears before the eyes of the angels as light, and illuminates their understanding, is a thousand times more white than the meridian light of this world. 5400. All d. t. in the universal heaven, proceeds not immediately from the divine essence, but from the divine human of the Lord. 4724. D. t. in its most common or general [form] is according to appearances. 6997. D. t. not divine good, terrifies those who are not good. 4180. D. t. may be received by the evil; but only by their external man. 4180.

Divine Worship. In all d. w., it is a general rule or law, that man should first will, desire, and pray, and then that the Lord should answer, inform, and do; otherwise, man does not receive any thing divine. A.R. 376. D. w., in heaven, is not unlike that on earth, as to externals. H. and H. 221, 222.

Divinity, the, called the Father, and the divine humanity called the son, are one, like soul and body. A.R. 613. The d. of the father belongs to the humanity of the son, and the humanity of the son to the d. of the father; consequently, in Christ, God is man, and man is God, and thus they are one person as soul and body are one. U.T. 112.

Divisions and **Searchings of Heart** (Judges v. 15) are all things, which from good in the spiritual man, are determined and ordained in the natural. A.E. 434.

Divorced, that a woman, s. good rejected by truth. A.E. 768.

Do, to, when pred. of God, den. providence. 5284. To d., when pred. of the Lord's divine, s. the all of effect, consequently, of state. 2618.

Do Well, to (Gen. iv. 7), so to be well disposed, or to have charity. 363. To d. w. (Gen. xxiii. 12) s. to gain life. 4258.

Doctor, or **Rabbi** (Matt. xxiii. 8), s. truth. A.E. 8746.

Doctrinal. Every general d. of faith is from divine good and divine truth, and has in itself, a celestial marriage. 2516. There is a twofold d., one of charity, another of faith, although in reality they are one. 2417. D. are the truths

Dodanium

of the spiritual man, in his natural man. 3726. They who are in the affection of truth for truth's sake, when they arrive at mature age, and ripeness of judgment, do not blindly rest in the d. of their own particular church, but examine the truth thereof by the Word. 5402, 6047. D. from the Word are scientific, so long as they are in the external or natural memory; but they become of faith and of charity, when they are in the internal memory, which comes to pass, when they are lived according to; and are called spiritual. 9918. D. or knowledges of good and truth cannot be communicated to the natural man, thus neither be conjoined and appropriated, unless by the delights and pleasures accommodated to him. 3502. The supreme amongst all d. is this, that the human of the Lord is divine. 4687. D. are general things to which truths are referred. 6146. All d., when they are true, look to charity, as to their fundamental [end and use.] 1799. D. are nothing else than the means of arriving at good, as an end. 5997. He who is arrived at spiritual good, has no more need for d. 6997. All d. from the literal sense of the Word possess interior truths. 3464. D. of faith are not purely divine truths, but appearances of truth. 3364. D. of faith from the Word are spiritual laws and precepts of life. 5826.

Doctrine. All the truth of the d. of the church from the Word, is the good of love in form. A.R. 917. The Word is unintelligible without d. 9025, 9409, 9424, 10.582. The Lord is d. itself, for the all of d. proceeds from him, and the all of d. treats of him; for the all of d. treats of the good of love and the truth of faith, which things are from the Lord, wherefore the Lord is not only in them, but also is each; hence it is manifest, that the d. which treats of good and truth, treats of the Lord alone. 5321. D. of the New Jerusalem Church is derived solely from the literal sense of the Word. A.R. 898. The d. of genuine truth may be fully drawn from the literal sense of the word. SS. 55. The genuine truth of d. does not appear in the literal sense of the Word, except to those who are in ill. from the Lord. S.S. 57. D. is not to be acquired by the spiritual sense of the Word, etc. U.T. 230. The holy things of d. are in the extreme or lowest [principles], and also therein, and from thence, there is a hearing and a perception. 9921. D. concerning what is good, is called the d. of charity, and d. concerning what is true, the d. of faith. 2227. The spiritual d. of the church is not the d. of divine truth itself. 7233. D. is not in itself truth, but truth is in d. as the soul is in its body. 4642. The d. of celestial love, which is love towards the Lord, is contained in the inmost sense of the Word; but the d. of spiritual love, which is love towards our neighbor, is in the internal sense. 7257. It is to be noted that the internal sense of the Word contains the genuine d. of the church. 9424.

Doctrine of Faith, the, is the same as the understanding of the Word as to its interiors or its internal sense. 2762. The d. of f. without the d. of love and charity, is like the shade of night. 9409. To respect the d. of f. from things rational, is very different from respecting rational things from the d. of f. 2568. The d. of f. derives its origin either from the rational, or from the celestial principle. 2510.

Doctrines of Charity are called cities of the mountain, and d. of faith, cities of the plain. (Jer. xxxiii. 13.) 2418.

Doctrines, the, of churches, in many things recede from the literal sense of the Word, etc. 9025. D. of the New Church are diametrically opp. to those of the old church, so that they do not agree together in one single point or particular, however minute. B.E. 10, 96. All the d. of the New Jerusalem refer to these two things—the Lord and a life according to his commandments. A.R. 903.

Doctrine of Balaam, those who do work, by which worship is defiled. A.R. 114.

Dodanium s. a species of ritual or external worship. 1156.

Dog

Dog (Exod. xi. 7) s. the lowest or meanest of all in the church, also those who are without the church, also those who babble or prate much about the things of the church, and understand but little; and in an opp. sense, those who are altogether without the faith of the church, and treat the things appertaining to faith with reproaches. (See Matt. xv. 26, 28; Mark vii. 27, 28; Luke xvi. 21; Isa. lvi. 10; Ps. lix. 7, 15, etc.) 7784. A great d., with his jaws horribly extended, like him who is called Cerberus by the most ancient writers, appears in the spiritual world, and s. a guard to prevent man passing over from celestial conjugial love to the love of adultery, which is internal, or vice versa. 2743, 5051. D., in general, s. those who are in all kinds of concupiscences, and indulge them; especially in the pleasure of eating and drinking. A.R. 952. D. s. those who render the good of faith impure by falsifications. 9231. (Exod. xxii.) D. (2 Kings ix.), which eat the flesh of Jezebel, s. cupidities or lusts. A.R. 132. Greedy d. (Isa. lvi. 11), or d. obstinate in soul, who do not know satiety, s. those who have no perception of good, and no understanding of truth. A.E. 376. The d. who licked the sores of Lazarus den. those who out of the church are in good, although not in the genuine good of faith; to lick sores den. to heal them as far as possible. 9231.

Dogmatic principle in religion never induced by any good spirit, still less by any angel. D.P. 134–5.

Domestic Good. See *Natural Domestic Good.*

Dominion, to have, is pred. of the Lord, as to divine good, and to reign, is pred. of him, as to divine truth. See Micah iv. 8, etc. A.E. 685. A.C. 4973. The d. of self-love is infernal, but the love of d. grounded in the love of uses, is heavenly. C.S.L. 261, 267.

Done s. to be consummated. A.E. 1013.

Door s. that which introduces, or lets in, either to truth or to good, or to the Lord; hence it is, that d. also s. truth itself, and likewise good itself, and also the Lord himself; for truth leads to good, and good to the Lord, such things were rep. by the d. and veils of the tent, and also of the temple. 2356. D. in the side of the ark (Gen. vi. 16) s. hearing; for the ear, with respect to the internal organs of sense, is as a d. on the side in respect to a window above; or what is the same thing, hearing, which is of the ear, in respect to the intellectual which is of the internal sensory. 656.

Doors. There are actually d. in the spiritual world which are opened and shut to those who ascend to heaven, and therefore they s. entrance, admission, or introduction. But the Lord alone opens and shuts the d. there, on which account he is called the d., by which man is to enter in, that he may be saved. (John x.) A.R. 916.

Dothan (2 Kings vi. 13) s. the doctrinals of good and truth from the Word. 4720. Dothan (Gen. xxxvii. 17), s. special or particular principles of doctrine. 4720.

Doubt. In all temptation there is a d. concerning the presence and mercy of the Lord. 2334.

Dove (Gen. viii.) s. goodness and truth. 876. The holy principle of faith, or the truth of faith. 869, 871, 875. One that is about to be regenerated. 869–871. D. (Hosea xi. 11) s. rational good. A.E. 601. Or the rational principle. A.E. 275.

Double is pred., in the Word, concerning retribution and remuneration, and s. much. A.E. 1115. D. and to d. s. to be done according to quantity and quality. A.R. 762.

Double-Dyed (Gen. xxxviii.) s. spiritual good. 4922.

Dough (Exod. xii. 34) s. truth from good. 7966. See *Bakers.*

Down. To come d. s. judgment. 1311.

Downward. Those who are in falses look d., and outwards, that is, into the world and to the earth. 6952.

84

Dowry den. a ticket of consent and confirmation of initiation. 4456.

Drachms, or pieces of silver (Luke v. 8), s. truths. A.E. 675.

Dragon s. an acknowledgment of three Gods, or three divine persons, and of justification by faith alone. A.R. 537, 542. The great red d. mentioned in the Revelation, does not s. those who are in hell, or they who deny God and blaspheme the Lord and the Word, who love themselves and the world, etc., but it rep. those, who while they live in the world have external communication with heaven, from the reading of the Word, preaching and external worship, while at the same time they are not in a life according to the Lord's commandments. A.E. 713. The d. (Rev. xii.) properly s. the learned who are confirmed in the doctrine of faith alone. A.E. 714. They constitute the head of the d., who believe in three divine persons, and the atonement, and are in faith separate from charity; they who frame to themselves dogmas from the Word, from their own proper intelligence, form the body of the d.; they who study the Word without doctrine and are in self-love, make the external of the d.; all those who constitute the d. adore God the Father above or separate from the Lord's humanity; and by the tail of the d. is s. the false fiction and adulteration of the Word. A.E. 714. D., in a good sense, s. the same as serpent; viz., the sensual principle, which is the ultimate of the natural man, not evil, or malicious. See Exod. vii. 9–12. Isa. xliii. 20, and Jer. xiv. 6. A.E. 714.

Dragon, Beast, and **False Prophet**. (Rev. xvi. 13.) The d. s. those who are in faith alone, both as to doctrine and life. The b., those who, by reasonings from the natural man, confirm faith alone. And the f. p. s. the doctrine of the false, from the truths of the Word being falsified. A.E. 998, 999.

Dragon and **Daughters** of the **Night-Monster**. (Micah i. 8.) D. have respect to the devastation of good, and d. of the n.-m. to the devastation of truth. A.E. 714.

Dragonists rep. those who are in faith alone. F. 57, 61.

Draught s. hell. A.E. 580.

Draw Back, to (Gen. xxxviii. 28), s. to conceal. 4924.

Draw Near s. to be enjoined by love. A.E. 331.

Draw Water, to (Gen. xxiv. 11), s. to be instructed. 3057.

Drawers of Water, in the Jewish church, rep. those who are continually desirous of knowing truths, but for no other end than to know, without any regard to the use thence to be derived. Such were rep. among the most vile. They were rep. by the Gibeonites. Josh. ix. 21–27. 3058. See *Hewers of Wood*.

Drawn Sword s. the principle of truth, which opposed the false. 2799.

Dread is pred. of those who are in falses. 9327.

Dream (Gen. xx. 3) s. somewhat obscure. 2514. D., in the supreme sense, den. foresight, because the d., which flow in immediately through heaven from the Lord, foretell things to come; such were the d. of Joseph, the d. of the butler and the baker, the d. of Pharaoh, the d. of Nebuchadnezzar, and, in general, the prophetic d.: the things to come, which are foretold thereby, are from no other source than from the Lord's divine foresight: hence also it may be known that all and singular things are foreseen. 5091. To d. a d. (Gen. xxxvii.) s. to preach. 4682. To d. (Isa. xxix. 8) s. erroneous opinion and faith. A.E. 750. To d. dreams s. to receive revelation, and to see visions s. to perceive revelation. (Joel iii. 1.) A.E. 624.

Dreams. The men of the most ancient church had the most delightful d. and visions, and it was insinuated to them what they s. 1122. There are three sorts of d., the first sort come immediately through heaven from the Lord, such were the prophetical d. recorded in the Word; the second sort come by angelic spirits, particularly by those who are in front above to the right, where there are things paradisiacal, hence the men of the most ancient

Dream of Nebuchadnezzar

church had their d., which were instructive; the third sort come by spirits who are near when man is asleep, which also are significative. But fantastic d. have another origin. 1976.

Dream of Nebuchadnezzar des. the restoration of the celestial church and its advancement, even to its summit, and afterwards its destruction, on account of its dominion also over the holy things of the church, and on account of its claiming to itself a right over heaven. A.E. 650.

Dregs (Jer. xlviii. 11) s. the false principles wherewith the good which is called Moab is defiled. 2468.

Dregs of the **Cup of Trembling** (Isa. li. 17) s. mere falses from which evils are derived. A.E. 724.

Drink, to, s. to perceive and appropriate truths or falses. A.R. 635. A.C. 5113, 9960. To d. s. to be communicated and conjoined, and is pred. of what is spiritual. 3089.

Drink Offerings s. the divine good of truth. 4581.

Drinking Troughs s. goods of truth. 4017.

Drink Blood, to, s. to falsify the truths of the Word, and imbibe them in life. A.R. 688.

Driven from the Faces of the Ground, to be (Gen. iv. 14), s. to be separated from every truth of the church. 386.

Dromedaries of **Midian** and **Ephah** (Isa. lx. 6) s. doctrinals. 3242. The knowledges of truth and good. A.E. 324.

Drones cor. to evil uses. D.L.W. 338.

Drop, to, or **Distil** (Judges v. 4), s. influx and instruction. A.E. 594.

Drops upon the grass and herb s. intelligence and wisdom. A.E. 644.

Dross (Isa. i. 22) s. the false. A.E. 887.

Drought s. deprivation of truths. A.E. 481.

Drove, Troop, or **Company**, den. scientifics, also knowledges. 3767, 4266. D. (Gen. xxix. 3) s. churches and their doctrines. 3770. D. (Gen. xxx. 40) s. goods and truths, and by setting them for himself alone, s. separation by virtue of self-derived ability: in a supreme sense, those goods and truths which the Lord made divine in himself, are here the d. which he set for himself alone. 4025.

Drum (Gen. xxxi.) s. spiritual good. 4138.

Drunk s. infatuated or insane with regard to spiritual things. A.R. 721. They are called drunkards in the Word who believe nothing but what they comprehend, and in this spirit inquire into the mysteries of faith, in consequence of which they must needs fall into many errors. 1072. Drunken without wine (Isa. xxix. 9), are they who are unconcerned about the Word, and the truths of faith, and thus have no inclination to know any thing about faith, denying first principles. 1072.

Dry Ground (Gen. vii. 22) s. those in whom all the life of love and faith was extinguished. 806.

Drying up of the Waters from off the Earth (Gen. viii. 7) s. the apparent dissipation of falsities in regeneration. 868. To dry up the waters (Jer. l. 38) s. the vastation of truth. A.E. 131.

Dryness (Jer. xiv. 6) s. where there is no good and truth. 1949.

Ducts s. intelligence from truths. A.E. 401.

Dudaim, or **Mandrakes**, a plant said to render barren women fruitful. 3942.

Dukes (Exod. xv. 15) s. chief things or principles, thus also all and singular things.

Dumah s. all things appertaining to the spiritual church. 3268.

Dumb, the (Isa. xxxv. 6), s. those who on account of ignorance of the truth, cannot confess the Lord, nor the genuine truths of the church. A.E. 455.

Dung on the **Faces** of the **Earth** (Jer. xvi. 4) s. the filthy infernal principle, which is evil defiling the good and truth of the church. A.E. 650.

Dungeon or **House** of a **Pit**. (Exod. xii. 22.) By being captive therein, is understood he who is in the corporeal sensual principle, thus in mere darkness concerning truths and goods, because not so much as in the faculty of perceiving, like they who are interiorly sensual: thence it is, that they are s. who are in the last place. 7950.

Dunghills (Lam. iv. 5) s. the falses of evil. A.E. 652. D. and bogs cor. with filthy loves. C.S.L. 431.

Dura Mater. They who belong to that province, are such as during their lives, when men thought nothing concerning spiritual and celestial things, neither spake about them, because they were such as believed nothing else to be, but what was natural, and this because they could not penetrate further; still, however, like others, they had stated times of divine worship, and were good citizens. 4046.

Duration of the first state after death. H. and H. 498. D. in the world of spirits. H. and H. 426.

Dust s. things terrestrial. 249. Also, what is damned or infernal. A.R. 788. D. (Ezek. xxvi. 12) s. the lowest things which are of the sensual principle of man. A.E. 1145. D. of the earth (Gen. xxviii.) den. good. 1610, 3707. Exterior or natural truths and goods, both of heaven and the church. (Isa. xl. 12.) A.E. 373.

Dust of the **Feet**. (Matt. x. 12–14.) In the spiritual world, when any of the good come among the evil, evil flows into them and disorders or disturbs them a little while, but only with respect to the ultimates, which cor. to the soles of the feet; hence when they turn themselves away and depart, it appears as if they shook off the d. of their feet behind them, which is a sign that they are liberated, and that evil adheres only to them who are in evil. A.E. 365. See *Cloud*.

Dust and **Ashes** (Gen. xviii. 27) s. the Lord's merely human principle from the mother, in respect to his essential divine principle. 2265. To cast d. on the head, s. interior grief and mourning on account of damnation. A.R. 778.

Dutch, the, in the spiritual world, are more firmly fixed in their religion than others. T.C.R. 802. They are under the influence of the spiritual love of trade. T.C.R. 801.

Dwell, to, s. to live a good life, and consequently, conjunction of the Lord with man. A.R. 883. To d. and possess (Ps. lxix. 35, 36) is pred. of celestial good, but to d., when used alone, is pred. of spiritual good. 2712.

Dwelling-Places and **Assemblies** of **Mount Zion**. (Isa. iv. 5.) The former means the good of the celestial church, and the latter the truths of that good. A.E. 594.

E

E and I. In the third heaven, they are not able to express these two vowels, but instead of them Y and Eu, because the vowels E and I properly belong to the spiritual class of affections. S.S. 90. H. and H. 241.

Eagle, an, s. the affection of divine truth as to knowledge and understanding. A.R. 244. Also, intellectual sight, and consequent thought. A.R. 245, 561. The face of an e. s. circumspection and providence. 3901. E., in a good sense, s. man's rational principle, and in a bad sense, his rational principle perverted. Matt. xxiv. 31. D.P. 20. The two e. (Ezek. xvii. 1, 8) rep. the Jewish and Israelitish churches, both as to knowledges of truth and consequent intelligence. A.R. 244. Or the first e. des. the process of the regeneration of the natural or external man, by scientifics and knowledge from the Word, and the other e. des. the process of the regeneration of the spiritual or internal man, by truth from good. A.E. 281. Flying e. s. knowledges from whence understanding is derived; because when they fly they know and see things; and by flying is s. to perceive and instruct. See Rev. iv. 7. A.R. 244. E. wings (Dan. vii. 3) s. rational principles grounded in man's proprium. 3901.

Ear. They who are dutiful and obedient in another life, belong to the province of the e., yea, cor. to hearing itself. 2542. Those answering to the cartilaginous parts of the e., attend but little to the sense of a thing; but those answering to the more interior parts, attend more perfectly. The nature of the interior parts may be known from their uses. 4656. The region where the e. is, cor. to obedience alone, without affection. 4326.

Ear of Corn den. exterior natural principle. 5212.

Ears and **Eyes**, when pred. of Jehovah, s. infinite will and infinite intelligence. Infinite will is providence, and infinite intelligence is foresight. 3869.

Early Rising s. to perceive clearly, also the light of confirmation from celestial good. 2540.

Earrings were of two sorts, viz., such as were applied above the nose to the forehead, and such as were applied to the ears; those which were applied above the nose to the forehead, were badges rep. of good; and those which were applied to the ears, were badges rep. of obedience, and are e. but in the original tongue, both sorts are expressed by the same term. 4551. E. (Gen. xxxv.) are insignia rep. of obedience; consequently, they s. things actual, for to obey, involves to do a thing in act. 4551. E. of gold s. those things which appertain to simple good. 3103.

Ears of Spikes of Corn (Gen. xli.) s. scientifics of the natural principle. 5212.

Earth s. all inferior things cor. to internal and superior things, as inferior, rational, and natural things, whereof also things celestial and spiritual are pred.; by reason of cor., these inferior things are such as are in the inferior heavens, and also in the church, and in external worship, and likewise such as are in the literal sense of the Word; in short, all things which proceed from things internal, and are fixed and exhibited in things external, as being things natural, are called e. and the Lord's footstool. 2162. E. is sometimes used to den. the people or men who are out of the church; it is rarely used in the Word to den. the whole globe of the e., unless at the same time it s. the whole human race, with respect to their state as a church, or as not a church. 1066. E., in an opp. sense, s. damnation, because when there is no church in man, there is damnation; in the last sense, e. is mentioned in Isa. xiv. 12, xxi. 9, xxvi. 19, 21, xxix. 4, xlvii. 1, lxiii. 6; Lam. ii. 10; Ezek. xxvi. 20, xxxii. 24; Num. xvi. 29, 33, xxvi. 10, and in other places. A.R. 285. E. s. the church, and sometimes the church in a desolate state, or where there is no church. 620. The e. s. the church as to good, or the good of the church. A.E. 365. E. empty and void (Gen. i. 2) s. man before regeneration. 17. E. (Gen. ii. 5) s. the external of the spiritual man. 90. E. (Gen. viii. 13) s. the will of man which is nothing else but lust: his ground is in his intellectual part, wherein truths are sown, and not at all in his will part, which in the spiritual man is separated from the intellectual. 895. E. (Isa. lx. 80) s. the internal spiritual man, because therein the church is, which, in general, by e. is s. A.E. 365. The e. which helped the woman, and swallowed the flood which the dragon cast out of his mouth (Rev. xii. 16), s. those in the old church who are not dragons (although amongst the dragons who separate faith from charity), because they are in ignorant simplicity, and live the life of faith, which is charity. A.E. 764. E. s. the church as consisting of the nations and people there; and field, the church as to the dissemination of divine truth and its reception. A.E. 388. E. is distinguished from ground, as the man of the church and the church itself are distinguished from each other, or as love and faith are distinguished. 662. E., land, ground, and field are frequently mentioned in the Word, and by e., when applied in a good sense, is s. the Lord's kingdom in the heavens and in the e. The same is s. by ground, but in a more confined sense; the same is also s. by field, but in a sense still more confined. 3310. The e. and sea (Rev. xi. 6) s. the inferior heavens. A.E. 609. The spirits of this e., in the grand man, have relation to the external sense. E.U. 89. The principal reason why the Lord was willing to be born on our e., and not on another, was because of the Word, in that it might be written on our e., and when written, be afterwards published throughout the whole e., and when once published, be preserved to all posterity, and thus that it might be made manifest, even to all in another life, that God was made man. E.U. 113. In every other e. (besides this) divine truth is manifested by word of mouth, by spirits and angels, but this manifestation is confined to families; for mankind in most e. live distinct according to families, wherefore, divine truth, thus revealed by spirits and angels, is not conveyed far beyond the limits of families, and unless a new revelation constantly succeeds, truth is either perverted or perishes; it is otherwise on our e., where divine truth, which is the Word, remains forever in its integrity. E.U. 120.

Earth, lower, is proximately beneath the feet, and the region about to a small distance; there most persons are after death, before they are elevated into heaven; mention is made also of this e. in the Word throughout; beneath it are the places of vastation, which are called pits; below those places and round about, to much extent, are hells. 4728.

Earthquakes s. concussions, paroxysms, inversions, and distractions, i.e., separations or tearings away from heaven, of all things appertaining to the church. The end of the church is likewise des. in the prophets by concussions, overturnings, and sinkings of the earth, and other circumstances, which attend e. Consequently, e. s. changes of the state of the church. A.R. 331, 711. E. happen in the spiritual world. A.R. 315, 331.

Ease. The joy and blessedness of heaven does not consist in e., but in active exercises of use. 6410.

East, the, s. the Lord. 101. Jehovah himself, as to love. 1451. Love in a clear perception. H. and H. 150. Land of the e. (Gen. xxv. 6) s. the good of faith. 3249. E., in an opp. sense, s. self-love. A.E. 422.

East Wind

East Wind, the, and the **East**, in the genuine sense, den. love to the Lord, and love towards the neighbor; hence, in the opp. sense, they den. self-love, and the love of the world. 5215. The e. w. s. the dispersion of falses and evils. 842. The e. w. s. those things which are of lusts and of fantasies thence derived, which is manifest from the passages in the Word where it is named. 5244.

Eat, to, den. communication, conjunction, and appropriation. 2187. The act of eating with man, cor. with scientifics in the world of spirits. 1480. To e. of the tree of life, in a spiritual sense, is to be intelligent and wise from the Lord; and to e. of the tree of the knowledge of good and evil, is to be intelligent and wise from self. C.S.L. 353. To e. and drink s. appropriation and conjunction by love and charity. 2187, 2343. To e. and to drink (Luke xvii. 28) s. to live to self and the world, and to appropriate to self evils and falses; to buy and to sell, s. to acquire to themselves those things, and to communicate them to others; and to plant and to build, s. to confirm themselves in them, and to live in them. A.E. 840.

Eber s. a new church, which may be called another ancient church. 1217. The external things of worship. A.E. 514.

Ebony (1 Kings x. 18) s. divine truths in ultimates. A.E. 253.

Ecclesiastic, its necessity and limits defined. 10.793.

Eden, the garden of, s. love from the Lord, heaven, and the church, and the Lord himself in a supreme sense. 99, 4447. E., in a bad sense, s. the love of self and of the world. 130. E. s. love to the Lord, and the garden of Jehovah, wisdom thence derived. (Isa. li. 3.) A.E. 721. A.C. 5376.

Eder, the tower of (Gen. xxxv. and Joshua xv. 21), s. the progression of what is holy to interior things. 4599.

Edge of the **Sword** (Gen. xxxiv. 26) s. what is false and evil in a state of combat. 4501.

Edge. To have the teeth set on e. (Ezek. xviii. 24) s. the appropriation of the false from evil. A.E. 556.

Edom, in a good sense, s. the Lord's human essence; also the strength, power, or good of the natural principle. In an opp. sense, the natural man originating in self-love, which despises and rejects all truth, whence comes the devastation thereof. 3322. E. (Obad. ver. 11) s. the truth of the natural man, and in an opp. sense, the false. A.E. 811. The field of E. (Gen. xxxii. 3) s. truths derived from good in the Lord's divine natural principle. 4241. E. and Moab, in many passages are named together, because they s. those who are principled in good; but the difference is, that E. den. the good of the natural principle, to which are adjoined the doctrinals of truth; whereas Moab den. natural good, such as has place with those, with whom such doctrinals are not conjoined. The former and the latter appear alike in their external form, but not in their internal. 3322.

Education. The order of progression by e., is apparent from scientific to celestial truths, but in reality it is the celestial which flows in through the successive degrees, and adapts rational and scientific truth to itself. E. of infants in heaven. H. and H. 334–44. 1495.

Effect, the, is the continent and basis of causes and ends, and these actually are in the e. D.L.W. 212. All e. in the universe are produced by two things; viz., life and nature. I. 10.

Effigy, the, of man such as he is in general, is such also in the least things of his will. 6571. A spirit is known by his ideas; and, what is wonderful, there is in each of his ideas his image, or e. 1008.

Effluvium. There is an e. around every vegetable, animal, and man. With man after death, it is his sphere or love. 10.130.

Efflux. Influx adapts itself to e. T.C.R. 814.

Effort, is in first principles and lost, in the spiritual world, and thence in the natural. A.Cr. 96.

Egg, an. Spiritual life successively comes forth from whatsoever age, as from an e.; the age of infancy is, as it were, an e. for the age of childhood, and the age of childhood is, as it were, an e. for the age of adolescence and youth, and this latter is an e. for adult age. 4378.

Egypt s. the natural man in conjunction with the spiritual, and in such case the affection of truth. But in the opp. sense, it s. the natural man separated from the spiritual, and in that case, insanity in spiritual things. For the Egyptians cultivated the science of correspondences, whence came their hieroglyphics, which science they afterwards turned into magic, and made it idolatrous. A.R. 503. E. in a good sense, s. faith conjoined to charity, but in a bad sense, faith separate from charity. A.E. 654. E., in a bad sense, s. the scientifics of the natural man, which of itself endeavors to enter into heavenly arcana, and hence perverts, denies, and profanes truths divine. 1164, 4735. E. s. scientifics, and Ethiopians knowledges. (Dan. xi. 43.) 117. The rivers E. and Euphrates (Gen. xv. 18) s. the extension of things spiritual and celestial. 1866. The labor of E. s. sciences, and the merchandise of Cush, and the Sabeans, s. the knowledges of things spiritual, which are serviceable to those who acknowledge the Lord. (Isa. xlv. 14.) 1164.

Egypt and **Memphis** (Hosea ix. 6) s. those who wish to be wise in things divine, by a power in themselves and their scientifics. 273.

Egypt, Sin, and **No** (Ezek. xxx. 15, 16) s. the scientifics and fallacies, which are of the natural man, and oppose the reformation of man by truths from the Word. A.E. 721.

Egyptians, the, rep. those who are in natural science, thus the natural, but the Hebrews, those who are of the church, thus respectively the spiritual; the E. also held the Hebrews so vile, as servants, that it was an abomination to them to eat with the Hebrews (Gen. xliii. 32), and also the sacrifices offered by the Hebrews were an abomination to them. (Exod. viii. 26.) 5013.

Eight s. good. A.R. 739.

Eighteen (3 × 6) s. things of combat. 1709.

Eighteen Thousand s. all the truths from doctrine encompassing and defending the church. A.E. 438.

Eighth Day, the, den. every beginning, consequently, continuation. This is one reason why the sabbath was changed from the seventh day to the first, that is, by way of continuation, the e. d., which den. the beginning of a new christian church, at the end of the Jewish church. 2633.

Eighth Mountain. (Rev. xvii. 11.) By the beast being the e. m. is s. divine good. A.R. 739.

Eighty s. temptations. 1963.

Eject s. to exterminate. 2657.

Ekron. Belzebub the god of E., s. the god of every false. A.E. 740.

El and **Elohim** s. the divine spiritual principle, but with this difference, that El s. truth in the will and act, or the good of truth; whereas Elohim, in the plural, is used to s. all truths which are from the Lord. 4402.

Elam (Isa. xxi. 1) s. faith originating in charity, consequently, the internal church. 1228. E. (Jer. xlix. 34) s. the falsification of doctrine. S.E.L.P. p. 28. E. (Jer. xlix. 35) s. the science of the natural man, and thence faith. A.E. 357. E. (Jer. xlix. 36) s. those who are in the knowledges of faith, and not at the same time in any charity. A.E. 411.

El-Bethel (Gen. xxiv. 7, and xxxv.) s. an holy natural principle; for when the Lord made his human divine, he first made it holy; the difference between making divine, and holy, is this, that the divine is Jehovah himself; whereas the holy is, what is from Jehovah, the former is the divine esse, but the latter, is what thence exists. When the Lord glorified himself, he also made his human the divine esse, or Jehovah. 4559.

Elder Brother

Elder Brother (Gen. x. 21) s. the internal church. 1222.

Elder Servant of the **House** (Gen. xxiv. 2) s. the Lord's natural principle. 3019.

Elders of **Israel**, the (Deut. i. 13, 15). rep. celestial men. 121.

Elders, the twenty-four (Rev. iv.), s. all the truths and goods of the church in heaven and in earth, or all who are of the Lord's church. A.R. 233, 251. The twenty-four e. (Rev. xi.) s. all in heaven, specifically in the spiritual heaven. A.R. 521. The twenty-four e. and the four animals (Rev. vii. and xix.) s. the superior heavens. A.R. 369, 808. E. and disciples (Matt. xix. 28) s. the same as tribes. A.E. 253. The e. (Joel ii. 16) s. the wise, and those that suck the teats, the innocent. 5608.

Elealeth s. men of the external church who explain the Word, to favor the loves of the world. A.E. 911.

Eldaah den. truths according to which they live. 3240-2. See *Midian*.

Eleazer, the son of Aaron, s. doctrinals derived from the essential doctrine of charity. 7230.

Eleazer and **Ithamar**, the two sons of Aaron, s. the Lord as to his divine natural. 9812.

Elect. The Lord is so called, as to his divine good, and servant, as to his divine truth. A.E. 409. By the chosen, or e., is not meant that any are elected by predestination, but they who are with the Lord are so called. A.R. 744. By the e., spoken of in the Word, are understood those who are in the life of good, and in that of truths from thence. 3755. "To gather his e. from the four winds, from one extreme of heaven to the other," s. the institution of the new church; the e. are they who are in the good of love and faith; the four winds are all the states of good and truth, and from the one extreme of heaven to the other, are the internals and externals of the church. A.E. 418. A.C. 4060.

Elect and **Men-Servants** (Isa. lxv. 9) s. the good things and truths of the church. 2567.

Election. All are elected and predestined to heaven. T.C.R. 664. After death the Lord elects those who have lived well. T.C.R. 664.

Elephant s. the natural man as to good. A.E. 455.

Elevation, all, is derived from things spiritual and celestial, inasmuch as by these things, man is e. towards heaven. 3171. All e. in a state of temptation, is made by divine truth. 8710.

Eleven s. a state not yet full, but still a receptible state, such as exists with well-disposed boys and infants. A.E. 194.

Eliakim (Isa. xxii. 21, 22) s. those who have the faith of charity. A.E. 206.

Elias den. the prophetical books of the Old Testament. 2606.

Eliezer (Exod. xviii. 4) s. the quality of the good of truths among those who are within the church. 8651.

Eliezer of **Damascus** (Gen. xv. 2) is the external church. 1790.

Elijah rep. the Lord as to the Word. 2762.

Elim (Exod. xv. 27) s. a state of illustration and of affection, thus of consolation after temptation. 8367.

Elisha, as well as Elijah, rep. the Lord as to the Word. A.R. 47.

Elishah, Tarshish, Kitthim, and **Dodanim** (Gen. x. 4), s. so many several doctrinals respecting ritual observances, and derived from external worship prevailing with Javan. 1156.

Elm s. same as oak, perceptions grounded in scientifics. 1442, 2466.

Elohim s. all truths which are from the Lord. 4402. See *El*.

Elon the **Hittite** den. truth from another source than what was real and genuine. 3470.

Eloquence. Eloquent words s. joy of mind. 6414.

Elparan s. extension of persuasions of the false. 1674.

Emaciate, or to make lean, s. to remove evils from falses not of evil. A.E. 406.

Embalm, to, s. a preservation from the contagion of evil. 6595.

Emblems cor. to sacred things. 4581, 4967.

Embrace, to, s. affection. 3807.

Embitter den. resistance by falses. 6420.

Embroidered. What is e. s. the scientific principle of the natural man. 9688. A.E. 242.

Embroiderer, Inventor, and **Weaver**, s. the three principles, called natural, spiritual, and celestial. 9915.

Embryo, an, in the womb, cor. to the truth of the doctrine derived from the good of celestial love. A.E. 810. Embryos and new-born infants, have not sensation or voluntary action, until their lungs are opened and thereby an influx be given of the one into the other. 3887.

Emerald (Rev. iv. 3) s. the appearance of the divine sphere of the Lord in the lowest heavens. A.R. 232. E., purple, broidered-work, fine linen, coral, and agate (Ezek. xxvii. 16), s. the knowledges of good. 1232.

Emerods, the, whereby the Philistines were smitten (1 Sam. v. 6), s. natural loves, which, when separated from spiritual love, are unclean. And since gold cor. to good, therefore the golden e., mentioned in the same passage, s. natural loves purified and made good. D.P. 326. A.C. 3322. E. and mice (1 Sam. v. 6) s. falses and evils. A.E. 700.

Emims, Rephaims, Enakims, and **Samsummims** (Deut. ii. 9, 10, 11, 18, 19, 21), s. those who were tainted with persuasions of evil and the false. 2468.

Eminence, if, and opulence are ends, they are curses, if means, they are blessings. A.Cr. 76.

Emissary Spirits. The communications of societies with other societies are effected by the spirits whom they send forth, and by whom they speak; these spirits are called *subjects*. 5856.

Empires. Societies have been transformed into e., by the loves of self, the world ruling. 7364.

Empty s. where there is nothing true, because nothing good. 4744. To e. (Gen. xxiv. 20) s. to separate. 3095. E. s. where there is nothing true, and void, where there is nothing good. (Gen. i. 2.) 17.

Emptying Out (Gen. xlii. 35) den. to do use from truths. 5529.

Emulation, envy, s. to emulate and to chide. 4702.

Enakims s. those tainted with persuasions of evil and false. 2468.

Encamp, to, s. to arrange according to heavenly order. 4236. To e. s. the ordination of truth and good. 8130.

Enchantment. To persuade in falses. A.R. 462. S. the perversion of good. E. are also mentioned in a good sense in the Word. Such the prophets were skilled in, by which they excited good affections, hearing, obedience, etc. But inasmuch as evil affections were excited by the evil, they were severely prohibited. A.E. 590.

Encompass, to (Gen. xix. 4), s. to be contrary, or to attack and assault with an hostile intention. 2347. To. e. (Gen. xxxvii. 7) s. access to adore. 4688.

End. The e. regarded makes the man, and such as the e. is, such is the man, consequently, such is the human principle appertaining to him after death. 4054.

End or **Extremity** of the **Field** (Gen. xxiii. 9), s. a little of the church, which may appear from the description of land, of ground, and of fields, in the Word. Their middle s. much, but their extreme s. little. This extreme is also called circuit; the reason is, because about the extreme the rep. expires. 2936.

End of **Creation**, the, exists in its ultimates, that all things may return to the creator. D.L.W. 167.

End of **Days** s. process of time. 347.

End, Cause, and Effect

End, Cause, and **Effect** cor. to the three discrete degrees of simultaneous order. I. 18. See *Degrees*.

Ends of the **Earth**. (Isa. iv. 15.) The isles and the e. of the earth, in the Word, s. those who are more remote from the truths and goods of the church, because they have not the Word, and are thence in ignorance. A.E. 304. See *Isles*.

Endeavors are internal acts of the will in which good works must be, in order that they may exist, and these internal acts ought to close in external acts, in order that they may abide. A.R. 868, 875.

Endurance (Rev. ii. 19) s. study and labor in acquiring and teaching truth. A.R. 129. Word of e. (Rev. iii. 10) s. spiritual combat, which is temptation. A.R. 185. To endure to the end (Matt. xxiv. 8) s. not to yield in temptations. 3488.

Eneglaim s. those who shall instruct the natural man. 40.

Enemies are evil and false principles. 2851. E. (Ps. cx. 1) s. things natural and rational, perverted and defiled. 2162. Those who are inwardly against the good of love, and the truth of doctrine, but not outwardly so. (Rev. xi. 12.) A.E. 671. E. s. the falses of evil, and foes the evils themselves. A.E. 642.

Enemies and **Haters** (Num. x. 31, 36) s. falses and evils from hell. A.E. 700.

Engedi, fishers from, s. those who shall instruct in the truths of faith. 40.

English. The best of the E. in the spiritual world, are arranged in the centre, because they have interior intellectual light, which they derive from the liberty of speaking and writing, and thereby of thinking. T.C.R. 806. Conversation with E. bishops, and George II. A.R. 716.

Engraver in **Stone** (Exod. xviii. 11) s. the good of love, thus the things pertaining to the will of the regenerate man, for this is from the good of love; because the voluntary principle of the regenerate man receives the good of love, and his intellectual principle receives the truths of faith. 9846.

Engravings of a **Signet**, or **Seal** (Exod. xxviii. 11), is the celestial form of all truths, as it exists in the understanding of the regenerate man; for therein the truths of faith are disposed into a celestial form, and from thence it is, that the regenerate man is an heaven in a little form. 9846.

Enlarge and **Extend**, to (Isa. liv. 2), s. the fructification of good, and the multiplication of truth. A.E. 799.

Enlighten. To ill. in truths. A.E. 391.

Enlightened, to be. Those who love and will truths from the Lord are e., when they read the Word, for the Lord is present in it, and speaks to every one according to his capacity. A.Cr. 75.

En-Mishpat, or the Fountain of Judgment, or the Fountain of Mishpat-Cadesh (Gen. xiv. 7), s. contention about truths, and thus continuation. 1678.

Enmity s. the e. between man's proprium, and the Lord. C.D. 211.

Enoch (Gen. v. 18) s. the seventh church from Adam, and which consisted of those who had framed doctrines out of the things which had been objects of perception in the most ancient and the following churches, with design that such doctrine should serve as a rule whereby to know what was good and true; which is s. by these words: ver. 22, "E. walked with God." And by the translation of E., ver. 24, is s. that as such doctrine at that time was not allowable, it was preserved for the use of posterity. 513, 516–521. The state and quality of perception with those who were called E., was a kind of general obscure perception, without any distinctness; for the mind in such case determines its intuition to doctrinals, out of or without itself. 522.

Enos the **Son of Seth** (Gen. iv. 26) s. a church which accounted charity to be the principal of faith. 438, 439.

Ensign, a sign of combat. A.E. 411.

Ensnared den. destruction of spiritual life. 9348.

Entangled. Confusion as to things of the church. 8133.

Equilibrium

Enter, to (Gen. vii. 1), s. to be prepared. 711. To e. into the ark (Gen. vii. 9) s. protection. 748. To e. in (Rev. iii. 20) when pred. concerning the Lord, s. to conjoin himself with man. A.E. 251. A.R. 219.

Enthusiasm. Visions caused by false persuasions. 1968.

Enthusiasts. None but enthusiastic spirits speak with e. A.Cr. 74.

Entire, to be, den. without blemish, unspotted. 7837.

Entity. Exp. D.L.W. 43.

Entrails. "And they came to their e." (Gen. xli. 21), s. interior extermination. 5258.

Entrance. To enter in, s. communication. 6901.

Entwisted Tree, an (Ezek. xx. 28), s. those things which are not dictated by the Word, but by the scientific proprium of man. 2831. Entwisting (Ezek. xxxi. 1) s. scientifics. 2588.

Enunciations. The historical and prophetical parts of the ancient Word. A.R. 11.

Envelope, or covering. Exp. D.L.W. 194.

Environs. The things which constitute the e., in the internal sense, s. things suitable and proper, because all truths joined to good, are arranged into serieses, and the serieses are such that, in the midst, or in the inmost of every one, there is a truth joined to good, and round about this midst, or inmost, are the truths proper and suitable thereto. 5343.

Envy, to (Gen. xxvi. 14), s. not to comprehend. 3410.

Ephah, an, has respect to good. 8540. See *Omer.*

Ephesus, the church of (Rev. ii. 1), s. those in the church who primarily respect truths of doctrine, and not good of life. A.R. 73.

Ephod, Aaron's, s. all the external of the spiritual kingdom, or divine truth in an external form. 9824. The conservation of good and truth in the spiritual kingdom, or, which is the same, the conservation of the spiritual kingdom in the whole work and power is s. by the two onyx stones placed upon the shoulders of Aaron's e., in which were engraved the names of the sons of Israel. 9855.

Ephraim, in the prophetic Word, s. the intellectual principle of truth and good, pertaining to the spiritual church. 3969. E. s. the understanding of the Word in the church, both true and false. U.T. 247. E. and Manasseh rep. faith and charity. 367. E., Benjamin, and Manasseh (Ps. lxxx. 1, 2) are the three principles proper to the spiritual church. 3969. E. s. the intellectual principle of the church, Israel its spiritual principle, and Judah its celestial principle; and because the intellectual principle of the church is s. by E., therefore, it is often said of E., that he goes away into Egypt and into Assyria, for by Egypt are s. scientifics, and by Assyria the reasonings therein grounded; both the former and the latter are pred. of the intellectual principle. 5354.

Ephrata s. the Word as to its natural sense, and Bethlehem, the Word as to its spiritual sense, and there the Lord was willing to be born, because he is the Word. A.E. 700. E. (Gen. xxxv. and Ps. cxxxii. 6) s. the spiritual of the celestial principle, in a former state, the new state succeeding that, is called Bethlehem. 4594. E. and the fields of the wood (Ps. cxxxii. 6) s. the spiritual and natural senses of the Word. A.E. 684.

Ephron (Gen. xxiii. 8, 17) s. those with whom the good and truth of faith, which are the constituents of the church, might be received. 2933, 2969.

Epistles of the Apostles. See *Evangelists.*

Equilibrium. Man is kept (as to his mind) in a state between heaven and hell, and thus in a state of e., to the intent that he may be in a free state for reformation. 5982. E. itself is in the world of spirits. H. and H. 600. Everywhere in the spiritual world there is an e. between heaven and between hell, and where there is an e., then two contrary forces continually act against one another; the one acts, and the other reacts; and where there is continual action and reaction, there is a continual combat. Hence all things of heaven are called an army, and also all things of hell. A.E. 573.

Er (Gen. xxxviii. 3) s. the quality of the false derived from the evil of self-love, which prevailed in the Jewish church, or the false principle of faith. 4822, 4830.

Erech s. different kinds of worship. 1082.

Erect, to be, s. to look to things celestial. 248.

Ernesti, communication by an intermediate spirit. 3749.

Error, if there be sin in it, s. what is adverse. 5625.

Esau, in a good sense, s. the good of the natural man, and in an opp. sense, the evil of self-love. 3322. E. first rep. the natural good of the Lord's infancy, which was divine from the father, but human from the mother. 3599. E. (Gen. xxv.) s. the Lord's divine natural principle, as to his divine good. 3302. E. (Gen. xxviii. 5, etc.) s. the truth of good in the natural principle. 3677. E. (Gen. xxxii. 3) s. celestial good in the natural principle. 4239.

Esau and Edom, in an opp. sense, rep. those who turn away from good, and altogether despise truth in consequence of self-love. 3322.

Esau and Jacob. (Gen. xxvii.) E. rep. natural good in the Lord, which should be made divine. 3599. E. and J. (Gen. xxvii.) rep. the divine good and divine truth of the Lord's divine natural principle, as conjoined with each other like brethren, which principles, considered in themselves, are nothing else but one power (or potency) together to form and receive actual good and truth. But this rep. was after that the Lord had reduced to order the natural principle as to good and truth in himself, so that it might receive the divine principle, and after that he had successively expelled all the human principle which was from the mother. 3599.

Escape, to, den. liberation from damnation by remains. 5899.

Esek [Contention] (Gen. xxvi. 20) s. a denial of the internal sense of the Word. 3427.

Eshchol rep. the angels who were attendant on the Lord. 1705.

Espousals, love of thine (Jer. ii. 2), s. the state of the reformation and regeneration of man, while from natural he is made spiritual. A.E. 730.

Esse, the, of man, is from his father. 5041. The e. of the life of every one is that from which he is conceived, and the existere of life from that e., is the human in form. This was the case with the Lord. 10.738. The e. of truth is good, and the e. of thought is will. 9995. The essential e. of all things is the divine good of divine love. 10.125, 10.262.

Essence. There is one only e., one only substance, and one only form, from which all the e., substances, and forms which were created, are. D.P. 157. The divine essence is divine love and divine wisdom. U.T. 36–48. The divine e. is one and individual. D.L.W. 35. That which is supreme, being also the inmost, constitutes the very e. of all that is derived from it; and the e., like a soul, forms them into a body after its own image. B.E. 40. E. without form, and form without e., is not any thing. U.T. 367.

Essentials. There are three e. in the church; viz., an acknowledgment of the Lord's divinity, an acknowledgment of the holiness of the Word, and the life which is called charity. D.P. 259. There are three e. in the Lord, which are called father, son, and holy spirit. U.T. 139.

Essentials of **Faith**, the, which are necessary to salvation, are expressed in the letter of the Word, such as they are in the internal sense. (See Deut. 4–6 and several other passages.) 2225. S.S. 55.

Eternal, is a term specifically applicable to the Lord's divine existere, or to his divine wisdom. 3701. E. is also pred. of the divine celestial or good, when generation is pred. of the divine spiritual, or truth. (See Exod. iii. 15; xxvii. 21, etc.) 9789.

Eternity. In the other life, they can think of the essence and omnipresence of God from e., that is, of God, before the creation of the world, inasmuch as they think of the essence of God from e. abstracted from time, and of his omnipresence abstracted from space, and thus comprehend such things as transcend the ideas of the natural man. C.S.L. 326, 329.

Etham. The children of Israel journeying to E., den. the second state of the spiritual after their liberation. 8103.

Ethers are natural forces. Exp. A.Cr. 96. Varieties of sight would not be given unless the e. in its laws were constant. D.P. 190.

Ethiopia s. the knowledges of love and faith. 117. E. (Zeph. iii. 10) s. those who are in possession of celestial things, such as love, charity, and works of charity. 349. E., in a bad sense, s. the interior knowledges of the Word applied to confirm false principles. 1164.

Ethiopian and **Leopard**. (Jer. xiii. 23.) E. s. evil in its form, and l. the false of evil. A.E. 708.

Eucharist den. the celestial things of faith and love. 3880.

Eunuch den. the natural man as to good, and as to truth; but specifically, the natural man as to good. 5081. E. (Isa. lvi. 3, 5) den. the natural man as to good, and the son of the stranger, the natural man as to truth; for the church of the Lord is external and internal; they who are of the external church are natural, and they who are of the internal church are spiritual; they who are natural, and yet are in good, are e., and they who are in truth, are the sons of the stranger; and whereas the truly spiritual or internal [men] cannot be given, except within the church; therefore, also by the sons of the stranger, are s. they who are out of the church, or the Gentiles, and who yet are in truth, according to their religious principle, and by e. they who are in good. 5081. E. (Matt. xix. 12) s. those who are subjects of the celestial marriage; born from the womb, those who are like the celestial angels; made of men, those who are like the spiritual angels; and made of themselves, those who are like angelic spirits, not so much influenced by charity, as by obedience. 394. Those who are in the natural marriage of good and truth (or in the natural degree of regeneration), are understood by those who make themselves e. for the kingdom of heaven's sake; for the natural, by knowledges and sciences, acquire to themselves natural light (lumen), and thereby the good of life, according to that, the affection, and thence conscience. A.E. 710. C.S.L. 156.

Euphrates, the river, s. interior reasonings, whereby those who are in the doctrine of justification by faith alone confirm themselves. A.R. 444. The all of the church as to good, and also as to evil. A.E. 410. The interiors of man's mind, which are called rationals. A.R. 444. A.C. 118. Rational things bordering upon, or bounding the spiritual things of the church. A.R. 444. E. in a bad sense, s. reasonings full of falses, and thence insanities. A.R. 444. E. (Ps. lxxx. 9, 10) s. the sensual and scientific principle. 120.

Europe s. those to whom the Word is about to come. A.R. 34. In a spiritual or angelical idea, Europe den. the north. A.E. 21.

Evangelists. The Lord spake the Word, written by the E., in many cases, from his own mouth, and the rest from the spirit of his mouth. S.S. 2. In their writings are contained the Lord's words, which include a spiritual sense, by which there is given immediate communication with heaven, but the writings of the apostles, do not contain such a sense, nevertheless, they are useful books to the church. A.E. 813.

Evangelize, to. Where mention is made of evangelizing and of the gospel, in the Word, thereby is s. the advent of the Lord. A.E. 612.

Eve is a name which s. life, which has relation to love. 201, 476.

Evening, in a general sense, s. whatever constitutes man's proprium, or self-hood, but morning, whatever is of the Lord. 22. E. s. an obscure principle.

Evening and Autumn

3693. E. (Gen. xix. 1) s. the time of visitation. 2318. E. (Gen. xxiv. 63) s. what is beneath. 3197. The Lord instituted the holy supper in the e., because the e. rep. the last state and time of the church. A.R. 816.

Evening and **Autumn** s. decline of the church. D.L. 73. A.C. 10.135.

Evening and **Morning**. E. s. every preceding state, having relation to shade, or falsity; m. is every subsequent state, having relation to truth. (Gen. i. 5.) 22, 3693.

Evening, Night, and **Cock-Crowing**. The e. s. a state of the ending of faith and charity, which takes place; when man causes his own day of judgment, and extinguishes those things which he has imbibed in his childhood; n. is a state of no faith and charity; c.-c., or the dawn, is a state of the beginning of faith and charity, which takes place when man loves truths and reformation by them, in which state, if man dies, he remains therein, and is judged according thereto. A.E. 187.

Even So s. confirmation of what precedes that it would be so. A.E. 40, 979.

Every One (Gen. xx. 7) s. every thing or all things. 2538.

Evil, all, has its rise from the sensual principle, and also from the scientific. 251. The origin of e. is from the abuse of the faculties which are proper to man, and which are called rationality and liberty. D.L.W. 264. E. derived from an hereditary principle, and acquired by actual habit, adheres close to man, in all his particular thoughts, yea in the smallest constituents of thought, and draws him downwards. 2410. All e. is conceived from the devil, as a father, and is born from atheistical faith, as a mother; and on the contrary, all good is conceived from the Lord, as a father, and is born from a saving faith, as a mother. A.V.C.R. 35. Every e. into which man is born of his parents, is implanted in his natural man; but not any in his spiritual man, because into the spiritual man, he is born of the Lord. C.S.L. 345. Every e. has its limit, which it is not allowed to pass; when a wicked person passes this limit, he plunges himself into punishment. 1857. There is an e. derived from the false, and a false from e.; the former exists, when any one from the assumed false principle, that some one particular e. is not a sin, commits that sin accordingly. But the false from e. exists, when a man is naturally inclined to the love of some e., and confirms the propriety thereof, in his understanding, by arguments drawn from appearances. 1212, 1679.

Evil Spirits, in another life, are scarce any thing else but lusts and fantasies, having acquired to themselves no other life; their fantasies are such, that they perceive them as realities. 1969.

Evils, the, attendant on man, have several origins, the first from ancestors to the father, and from the father into man's self; another from what is actual, which has several origins, in general two; first, that he receives e. from others, without his own fault; and secondly, that he receives from himself, thus with his own fault; what man receives from others, without his own fault, is s. by what is torn, in the Word; but what he receives from himself, thus with his own fault, is s. by carcass. See Lev. xvii. 15, 16; xxii. 8. 4171. E. which a man thinks allowable, although he does them not, are appropriated to him. D.P. 81. D.L.W. 118. The interior e. of man, are derived from the father's side, and the exterior, from the mother's. 3701. The decalogue teaches what e. are sins. All kinds of murder, adultery, theft, false witness, with the concupiscences prompting thereto, are e. which are to be shunned as sins. No one can shun e. as sins, so as to have them inwardly in aversion unless he fights against them. If any one shuns e. from any other motive, than because they are sins, he does not shun them, but only conceals them from the world. Dec. 18–114. It is a law of divine providence, that man as of himself, should remove e. as sins in the external man, for thus and no otherwise the Lord has power to remove e. in the

Exploration

internal man, and at the same time, in such a case, in the external man. U.T. 510–566. D.P. 100–129. N.J.D. 159–173.

Evils and **Falses**. Angels excuse e. and f. in man, which e. spirits excite and condemn. 1088. E. and f. are in all opp. to goods and truths, because e. and f. are diabolical and infernal, and goods and truths are divine and celestial. D.L.W. 271. E. with f. are with the wicked, as it were, in the centre, and goods with truths, in the circumference; but goods with truths, with the good, are in the centre, and e. with f. in the circumference. D.P. 86.

Ewe Lambs s. the holiness of innocence. 2720.

Exactors s. those who violate truths. A.E. 555.

Exalt, to, s. worship from good by truths. A.E. 411.

Exaltation s. power from an interior principle. 2832.

Examination, self, man is reformed by. D.P. 152, 278.

Excellency of **Jacob** s. the love and faith of the falses. A.E. 675.

Excision, the land of, s. hell. A.E. 740.

Excommunicate, to be cast from the good of the church. A.E. 741.

Excretions, the, and secretions of the human body, are in cor. with certain spirits. 5380–6.

Excrement of **Filth** s. evils. (Isa. iv. 4.) 3147.

Exhalation. By the e. of sphere every deed becomes manifest. 7454.

Exile and **Captivity.** To go into e. s. the dissipation of truth, and to go into c., s. occupation by falses. (Ezek. xii. 11.) A.E. 811.

Exinanition is a term applicable to the Lord's voluntary state of humiliation in the world. U.T. 104–110. E. also s. a state of desolation and vastation [in man]. 5360.

Exist, to, nothing can e., unless its esse be in it. 4523, 34.524, 6040, 6056. All and singular the things of nature not only e. from the divine, or first being, but also continually subsists from him, through the spiritual world. 775.

Existere or **Existence,** the, is the external manifestation of the essence, or esse in a subject and form. U.T. 18, note. E. is pred. of the Lord, only when he was in the world, and there put on the divine esse, but when he was made the divine esse, e. could no longer be pred. of him, otherwise than as somewhat proceeding from him, which appears as an e. in him, whereas it is not in him, but from him. 3938.

Exodus, book of. The quality of the natural man, when subordinate to the spiritual, and its quality when separated from the spiritual, is fully des. in the internal sense of that book. A.E. 654.

Expanse, the, over the heads of the cherubim (Ezek. i. 26, and x. 1) s. heaven. A.R. 14. See *Earth, Heavens.*

Expanses. There are six e., viz., the third, middle, and first heaven; the first, middle, and third hell. The spirits of the third hell are held in bonds by those in the third heaven; those in the middle hell by those in the middle heaven; those in the first hell by those in the first heaven. A.Cr. 34.

Expectation of Jesus Christ (Rev. i. 9) s. the new church established by the Lord, where the divinity of his humanity will be known and acknowledged. A.E. 49. A.R. 33.

Expel, to be removed. 7980. Cast down and destroyed. 8295.

Expiation or **Propitiation** is protection from the overflowing of evil. 645. So long as man is in e., he cannot receive the good of love and the truth of faith. 10.177.

Explications of the **Word** must be made, as to its internal sense; because the inmost or supreme sense transcends the human understanding. 6827.

Explore. To inquire into and search out. A.E. 100.

Exploration, consists in an exquisite weighing or liberation, to prevent the least minimum of the false being conjoined to good, or of truth to evil. 3116.

Expressions

Expressions. How the affections treated of in the internal sense fall into natural e. 3605.

Expulsion from the garden, s. the deprivation of wisdom. D.P. 313.

Expurgation, the spiritual affection of truth. A.E. 475.

Extended. Every thing e. belongs to matter. Exp. A.Cr. 33.

Extension, the, of the sphere of perception, or its limits, is proportionate to opposites. 2694. Thought diffuses itself into the societies of spirits and angels round about, and the faculty of understanding and perceiving is according to that e. 6599.

Exterior Man. If the e. m. wholly perverts, or extinguishes that which flows in by the interiors, then the interior man is deprived of his light from heaven, and that part which is towards heaven is shut, and a communication opened with hell. 5427. Whatsoever was from the e. m. of the Lord, had with it something hereditary, and thus also evil. 1921.

External, the, exists from, and has its essence from the internal, but it may appear otherwise than according to its essence from the internal. D.P. 224. The e. is regenerated much later, and with greater difficulty, than the internal. 3469.

External Man. Three things constitute the e. m.; viz., the rational, the scientific, and the sensual e. 1580. The e. m., properly so called, consists of, and is constituted by, scientifics appertaining to the memory, and by affections appertaining to the love, wherein man is principled, and also by the sensual things which are proper to spirits, together with the pleasures which appertain unto spirits. 1718. The e. m. is formed of things sensual; not such as belong to the body, but such as are derived from bodily things; and this is the case not only with men, but also with spirits. 976.

External Worship, without internal, is only a foolish babbling, and often conceals the most abominable wickedness. 1094.

Extreme, the, of the heavens to the e. thereof (Matt. xxiv. 31), s. the internal and external things of the church. 4060.

Exultation s. delight from good, and gladness s. delight from truth. A.E. 294.

Eye, the, s. the understanding, because they cor.; for as the e. sees from natural light, so does the understanding from spiritual light, wherefore to see, is pred. of both. A.R. 48. The right e. den. the affection of good, and the left the affection of truth. The sight of the left e. cor. to the truths of faith, and the sight of the right e. to their goods. 4410, 6923. The left e. is the intellectual principle, but the right e. is the affection of that principle. 2701. The e., or rather its sight, cor. especially to those societies in the other life, which are in paradisiacal scenery; these appear above in front, a little to the right, where there are presented gardens in living view, with trees and flowers of so many genera and species, that those which grow throughout the whole earth, bear but a small proportion to them in number. This heaven is distinguished into several heavens, to which cor. singular the things which are in the cameras of the e. 4528. The heaven of those who appertain to the province of the interior e., and who are to the right in front, in a small degree of elevation, are encompassed with an atmosphere of very small continued rainbows. 1623. E., when spoken of the Lord, s. divine wisdom, omniscience, and providence. A.R. 48.

Eyes, in the Word, s. the understanding, and thence by the eyesight intelligence, and when spoken of the Lord, his divine wisdom is understood. A.R. 48. To have the e. opened, s. an impression from the interiors. (Gen. iii. 7, Num. xxiv. 34, and 1 Sam. xiv. 27, 29, etc.) 212. E. (Gen. xix. 14) s. the rational principle. 2403. It is said the cherubims were full of e. before and behind (Rev. iv.), which s. the divine wisdom and divine love contained in the Word. A.R. 240, 246. The spiritual heavens cor. to the e. A.E. 831. All infants in the grand man are in the province of the e.; those in the right are of a celestial genius; and those in the left of a spiritual genius. H. and H. 333. Those in that province are in great powers of intellection and lucid perception, and are more keenly intellectual than others. H. and H. 96.

Eye-Salve (Rev. iii. 18) s. a medicine whereby the understanding is healed. For e.-s. is an ointment composed of meal and oil; and by the cor. of these in a spiritual sense, the spiritual eyes of man are opened. A.R. 214. A.E. 245.

Eyes and **Teeth.** (Gen. xlix. 12.) "His e. being redder than wine," s. divine wisdom, and "his t. being whiter than milk," s. justice. 4007.

Ezekiel (the prophet) and **John** rep. the doctrine of truth and the Word, and thence exploration, made amongst the men of the church, as to their internal state of reception: hence they were both commanded to eat a book. A.E. 619.

Ezion-Geber (1 Kings xix. 26) s. the ultimates of the church, which are sciences comprehending the knowledges of truth and good. A.E. 514.

F

Face, the, cor. to the mind. 4791, 4805. The f. (Rev. iv.) cor. to affection. A.E. 280. F., when pred. of the Lord, s. mercy, peace, and good. 222, 223, 2434. In an opp. sense, anger and aversion, because a bad man is angry and turns himself away. A.R. 939. They in the other life appear without a f., who have nothing of rational life; for when no f. appears, it is a sign that there is no cor. of the interiors with the grand man, inasmuch as every one appears in the light of heaven, in the other life, according to cor.; hence the infernals appear in horrible deformity. 5387. The f. rep. spiritual and celestial things existing interiorly with man. 5571. To cover the f. (Ezek. xii. 12) s. that truth should not at all be seen. 5044. To fall upon the f. of any one s. influx. 6499.

Face of the **Deep** (Gen. i. 1) s. the lust of the unregenerate man, and the falsities thence originating. 18.

Face of the **Earth**, the, in the spiritual world is altogether like the face of the church, among the spirits and angels there; the most beautiful face is where the angels of the superior heavens dwell; and it is also beautiful where the angels of the inferior heavens dwell; but unbeautiful where evil spirits are. A.E. 417.

Face of the **Father**, to see the (Matt. xviii. 10), s. to receive divine good from the Lord. A.E. 254.

Face of **Jehovah**, or of the **Lord**, the, s. the divine principle itself in its essence, which is divine love and divine wisdom, consequently, himself. The same is s. by the sun shining in his strength. (Rev. i. 6.) A.R. 53. The f. of J. (Num. vi. 25) s. divine love; by making his face to shine is s. the influx of divine truth; and by lifting up his face upon us is s. the influx of divine good. A.E. 340. The f. of the L., in a proper sense, is the sun of the angelic heaven. A.E. 412.

Face of a **Man**, the, s. divine truth of the Word as to its wisdom. A.R. 243.

Face of the **Waters** (Gen. i. 2) s. the knowledges of good and truth. 19.

Faces s. all the interior things of man, as well evil as good, by reason that they shine forth from the face. 2219. "I have seen God f. to f." (Gen. xxxii. 30), s. to sustain the most grievous temptations. 4299. All societies [in the spiritual world] have f. proper to them; when they go out the face changes; it is so with both the evil and the good. 4797.

Faces of the **Ground** being **Dried** (Gen. viii. 13) s. regeneration, when falsities no longer appeared. 898.

Faculties, the two, from the Lord with man are reason and freedom, or rationality and liberty. The Lord guards these as inviolate and sacred. D.P. 73, 96. When these two f. are one, they are called one mind. 65. They are what distinguish man from beast. D.L.W. 240.

Faint, to (Isa. li. 21), s. to be dissipated. A.E. 724. The f. of the earth s. those of the church who are not in truths, but yet desire them. A.E. 219. See *Swoonings*.

Fair, to be (Ps. xlv. 3), s. to be wise. A.E. 684. The fairness of the angels originates from a love of inward truth, and exists according to the state of it. 5199.

Faith

Fairs and **Markets** (Ezek. xxvii. 19) s. acquisitions of truth and good. 3923.
Faith s. the implantation of truth. A.E. 813. F., in the internal sense, is nothing
else than charity. 3121. F. (Rev. iii. 15) is called the beginning of the work of
God. A.E. 226. There are three causes why they were healed who had f. in
the Lord; first, that they acknowledged his divine omnipotence, and that
he was God; secondly, that f. is acknowledgment, and an intuitive acknowledgment in the spiritual world, brings one present to another; thirdly, that
all diseases which the Lord healed cor. to spiritual diseases, which could
be only cured by the Lord, through the medium of the above acknowledgment, and by repentance of life, wherefore he often said, "Thy sins are
remitted; go and sin no more." This f. also was rep. and s. by this miraculous f., but the f. whereby the Lord healed the spiritually diseased, is not
given, except by truths from the Word, and by a life according to them.
A.E. 815. The reason why the Lord called his disciples men of little f., when
they could not do miracles in his name, and why he himself could not
work miracles in his own country, on account of their unbelief, was
because the disciples indeed believed the Lord to be the Messiah, or
Christ the son of God, and a prophet as it was written in the Word, but had
not as yet believed him to be the omnipotent God, and that Jehovah the
father was in him, and so long as they believed him to be a man, and not
also God, his divine, which is omnipotent, could not be present by f., for f.
brings the Lord present, but not a f. in him as a man only; which also is the
cause why he could not perform miracles in his own country, because
there they saw him from infancy as another man, wherefore they could not
associate the idea of his divinity, and when this is not approached, the
Lord indeed is present, but not with his divine omnipotence in man. A.E.
815. No one can have f., till he comes to exercise his thinking faculty. A.R.
776. Saving f. is a f. in the Lord God the Saviour Jesus Christ, because
directed towards a visible God, in whom is the invisible. U.T. 337. Man
receives f., in consequence of approaching to the Lord, of learning truths
from the Word, and of living a life in conformity thereto. U.T. 343. The
internal acknowledgment of truth which is f., does not take place in any
but those who are in charity. F. 13. Historical f. always precedes, before it
becomes saving f., for then historical f. becomes saving f., when man
learns truths from the Word and lives according to them. A.E. 815. Miraculous f. was the first f. with those among whom the new [or first Christian]
church was instituted; it is also the first f. with all in the Christian world at
this day, wherefore the miracles of the Lord were wrought, are described,
and also preached. A.E. 815. Natural f. without spiritual is to think those
things which are in the Word from self, and f. natural from spiritual, is to
think those things which are in the Word from God, although this also
appears as of ourselves. A.E. 790. F. induced by miracles is not f., but persuasion. D.P. 131, 133. F. is compared to the night, and love to the day, as
in Gen. i., where, speaking of the great luminaries, it is said that the greater
luminary, or the sun, which s. love, rules by day, and the lesser luminary,
or the moon, which s. f., rules by night. (Vs. 14, 16.) 709. F. brings the Lord
present, but love conjoins. A.E. 815. F. is the eye of love. 3863.
Faith of the **New Heaven** and **New Church**, in its universal form, is this: that
the Lord from eternity, who is Jehovah, came into the world to subdue the
hells, and glorify his humanity, and that without him no flesh could be
saved, and that all will be saved who believe in him. U.T. 2. The esse of the
f. of the new church is confidence in the Lord God the Saviour Jesus
Christ; secondly, a trust that he who lives a good life, and believes aright,
is saved by him. The essence of the f. of the new church, is truth from the
Word. The existence of the f. of the new church, is, first, spiritual light; secondly, an harmonious agreement of truths; thirdly, conviction; fourthly,

Faith of Persuasion

acknowledgment inscribed on the mind. States of the f. of the new church, are, first, infant f., adolescent, or youthful f., adult f.; secondly, f. of genuine truth, and f. of appearances of truth; thirdly, f. of memory, f. of reason, f. of light; fourthly, natural f., spiritual f., celestial f.; fifthly, living f., and miraculous f.; sixthly, free f., and forced f. U.T. 344.

Faith of Persuasion. Those who are under its influence, are alluded to, in Matt. vii. 22, 23, xxv. 11, 12, and Luke xiii. 26, 27. N.J.D. 119. The f. of p. has no residence in the interiors of the soul, but stands, as it were, in an outer gate in the court of the memory, where it is ready for service, whensoever it is called upon. N.J.D. 118.

Faith Alone. They who are therein, and pray from the form of their faith, cannot do otherwise than make God three, and the Lord two, because they pray to God the father that he would have mercy for the sake of the son, and send the holy ghost. A.R. 537, 611. It is of the divine providence of the Lord, that they who have confirmed themselves in f. a. falsify truths, lest, if they knew holy truths, they should profane them. A.R. 688. The second table of the decalogue is a blank table to those who are in f. a. A.R. 461. F. separated from charity, is destructive of the church, and of all things appertaining thereto. F. 69. They who are principled in f. separated from charity, were rep. in the Word by the Philistines, and by the dragon in the Revelations and by the goats in Daniel and Matthew. F. 57, 61.

Faithful unto Death, to be (Rev. ii. 10), in the natural sense, s. that they [who are here alluded to] must not depart from their fidelity, until the end of their lives; but in the spiritual sense, that they must receive and acknowledge truths, until falses are removed, and, as it were, abolished by them; for this sense is properly for those who are in the spiritual world, who are not liable to death; wherefore, by death is here meant the end of their temptations. A.R. 102.

Faithful Witness (Rev. i. 5) s. the Lord with respect to divine truth. A.R. 18.

Fall, to (Rev. xiv. 3), s. to be dispersed. A.R. 631. To f. down on the knees (Gen. xxiv. 11), s. to dispose to what is holy. 3054. To f. on the faces of his brethren (Gen. xxv. 18), s. contentions about truth, in which superiority is gained. 3277. To f. upon the faces and to adore God (Rev. vii.), s. testification of humiliation of heart, from the good of love, and by truths from that good. A.E. 463. To f. prostrate, s. humiliation, reception, and acknowledgment. A.E. 290.

Fallacies are those things which man reasons and concludes from the natural man without spiritual light, which is the light of the understanding ill. from the Lord; for the natural man takes the ideas of his thought from earthly, corporeal, and worldly things, which in themselves are material, and when the thought of man is not elevated above them, he thinks materially of spiritual things, which thought without spiritual light is wholly derived from natural loves and their delights. A.E. 781. F. overshadow and lusts suffocate [the things of faith]. There are f. of the senses merely natural, and also of a spiritual kind. 5084.

Fallow Deer s. affection of good and truth. 6413.

False, the. The evil of the will of man when it forms itself in his thoughts, so that its quality may be manifested to others, or to himself, is called the f.; wherefore the f. is the form of evil, as truth is the form of good. A.E. 543. There is a f. derived from evil, or a f. of evil; and there is an evil derived from the f., or an evil of the false, and again a f. thence derived, and thus in succession. 1679, 2243. The f. which is not of evil can be conjoined with good, but not the f. of evil; because the f. which is not of evil, is the f. in the understanding, and not in the will; but the f. of evil is the f. of the understanding from evil in the will. D.P. 318. A.C. 2863. There are three origins of what is f.; viz., one from the doctrine of the church, another from

104

the fallacies of the senses, and a third from the life of lusts. 4729. The extirpation of f., must first take place among the clergy, and by their means among the laity. U.T. 785.

False Christs (Matt. xxiv.) are falses, or truths not divine. 3010.

False Prophet s. the doctrine of the false, from the truths of the Word being falsified. A.E. 998.

False Witness. Lies of every kind. A.E. 10.

Falsify, to, the Word is pred. of those who acknowledge the Word, but apply it to favor their own loves and the principles of their own proper intelligence. A.E. 535. To f. the Word, is to take truths out of it, and apply them to confirm what is false, which is to extract truths from the Word, and to destroy them. A.R. 566. To f. the Word, and to profane the Word, are two distinct things. A.R. 541.

Falsification of the Word, to the destruction of its genuine sense, shuts heaven. A.E. 888.

Families, in an internal sense, s. probity, and also charity and love, for all things relating to mutual love are regarded in the heavens as consanguinities and relationships. 1159. F. (Gen. viii. 19) s. goodnesses and truths arranged in man by the Lord, according to order. 917. F. (Nahum iii. 4) have respect to truths. A.E. 354. F. s. goodnesses when pred. of nations, but truths when pred. of people. (Ps. xxii. 27, 28. Ps. xcvi. 7.) 1291.

Families, Tongues, Countries, and **Nations.** (Gen. x. 20.) F. have respect to manners [or morals]; t., to opinions; c., in general, with respect to opinions; and n., in general, with respect to manners [or morals]. 1216. F. have respect to charity; t. have respect to faith; c. have respect, in general, to the things appertaining to faith; and n. have respect, in general, to the things appertaining to charity. 1251.

Famine s. a deprivation and rejection of knowledges of good and truth proceeding from evils of life; it also s. ignorance of the knowledges of truth and good, proceeding from a want or scarcity thereof in the church and likewise s. a desire to know and understand them. A.R. 323. A.C. 2799. Men of f. s. a scarcity of celestial knowledges, and a multitude dried up with thirst s. a scarcity of spiritual knowledges. (Isa. v. 12.) 1460. F. s. the privation of the knowledges of truth and good, and pestilence s. infections from falses. A.E. 734.

Fan (Matt. ii. 12) s. the separation of falses from goods. A.E. 374.

Fantasy exists from sensual thought, while the ideas are closed to interior thought. T.C.R. 80.

Farina of **Fine Flour** (Gen. xviii. 6) s. the spiritual and celestial which at that time appertained to the Lord. 2177.

Fare, to, **sumptuously** every **Day** (Luke xvi. 19, 20) s. the satisfaction and delight which the Jewish people had in reading and possessing the Word. S.S. 40.

Farthing. To pay the uttermost f. (Matt. v. 21, 26) s. the punishment which is called eternal fire. A.E. 1015.

Fashion, in general, is what a man fashions from the heart or will, and also what he fashions from the thought or persuasion, as in Ps. ciii. 14, and Deut. xxxi. 21. 585.

Fascicle. Multiplied truths disposed and arranged in the mind. 5339.

Fast, to (Mark ii. 19), s. to mourn on account of the defect of truth and good. A.E. 1189. Fasting cor. to temptation. A.E. 730.

Fat s. the celestial principle. 350, 354. F. things, full of marrow, s. goodnesses. 353, 2341. F. and blood s. interior goods and truths, and hence the Israelites, prior to the Lord's incarnation, were prohibited from eating thereof, because they were only in externals. A.E. 617. F. s. celestial life, and blood celestial spiritual life. (Lev. iii. 16.) 1001. To be f. and flourishing

Fate

(Ps. xcii. 15) s. to be in the goods and in the truths of doctrine. A.E. 1159. F. is pred. of good, and plenteous, of truths. (Isa. xxx. 23.) A.E. 644. F. and splendid things (Rev. xviii. 15) s. affections of celestial and spiritual goods and truths. A.R. 782. See *Feast of Fat Things*.

Fate. There is no such thing as a predestined or fated course of action, but man is free. 6487.

Fatlings s. celestial goods and the affections thereof, and the delights of those affections. A.R. 782. F. of Bashan (Ezek. xxxix. 11) s. goods of the natural man from a spiritual origin. A.E. 650.

Fatness and the **Fountain** of **Lives** (Ps. xxxvi. 8, 9) s. the celestial which has relation to love. 353.

Father s. the Lord as to divine good. A.E. 32, 200, 254. The Lord as to his all-creating divinity, and also as to his divine human, is called the f. A.R. 31, 613, 839. In heaven they know no other f. than the Lord; because the f. is in him, and he is one with the f., and when they see him, they see the f. 15, 2004. "No man cometh unto the f. but by me" (John xiv. 6), s. that the f. is approached when the Lord is approached. A.E. 200. F. (Gen. xxxvii. 11) s. the Jewish religion derived from the ancient. 4703. F. (Gen. xxxvii 12) s. the ancient and primitive christian churches. 4706.

Father-in-Law den. good, from which exists good conjoined to truth. 6827, 6844.

Father and **Lord**. (Mal. i. 6.) Jehovah is here called f., from divine good, and L., from divine truth. A.E. 695. A.C. 3703.

Father and **Mother**, which a man is to leave (Gen. ii. 24, and Matt. xix. 4, 5), in a spiritual sense, are his proprium of will, and proprium of understanding. C.S.L. 194. In the spiritual sense by f. and m. is meant God and the church. U.T. 306.

Father and **Son**. The f. is in the s., and the s. in the f., and they are one, like soul and body in man, and thus they are one person. U.T. 112.

Father, Son, and **Holy Spirit** s. the three essentials of the one and only God, Jesus Christ our Lord, in whose divine human person alone the whole divine trinity is concentrated, like soul, body, and operation in man. U.T. 164, 184.

Father, Son, Mother, and **Daughter.** (Luke xii. 51, 53.) By f. against s., and by s. against the f., is understood evil against truth, and truth against evil; and by m. against d., and by the d. against the m., is understood the lust of the false against the affection of truth, and vice versa. A.E. 504.

Fatherless, the, s. those who are in good without truth, and are desirous by truth to be led to good. 4844.

Fathers (Gen. xv. 5) s. the same thing as daughters and sons conjointly; viz., goodnesses and truths. 1853. F. (Deut. x. 15) s. the ancient and most ancient churches. 3703.

Fault. Man himself is in f., if he is not saved. D.P. 327.

Fear has various significations according to the thing which causes it. A.R. 511. F. s. love. 5459. F. (Gen. xxviii. 17) s. an holy alteration. 3718. Holy f., which sometimes is joined with a sacred tremor of the interiors of the mind, and sometimes with horripilation, supervenes, when life enters from the Lord, instead of man's proper life; in this holy f. was the prophet Daniel, John in the Apocalypse, Peter, James, and John, when the Lord was transfigured, the woman who saw him at the sepulchre, and others. A.R. 56.

Fear Not (Rev. i. 17; Dan. x. 5, 12; Matt. xvii. 5, 7; xxviii. 10, etc.) s. resuscitation to life, and at the same time adoration from the most profound humiliation. A.R. 56. What is introduced from f. does not remain. A.R. 164. To f. (Gen. xx. 8) s. aversion. 2543. To f. s. to disbelieve, or not to have faith and love. (See Isa. xliii. 1, 5; xliv. 8; Mark v. 36; Luke i. 73, 75; iv. 40; viii. 49; xii. 7, 32.) 2826.

Fear of God, the, as used in the Word, s. worship, either grounded in f., or in the good of faith, or in the good of love; worship grounded, in f., when the subject treated of is concerning the unregenerate; worship grounded in the good of faith, when the subject treated of is concerning the spiritual regenerate; and worship grounded in the good of love, when the subject treated of is concerning the celestial regenerate. 2826. The f. of God (Gen. xx. 10) s. a regard for divine or spiritual truth. 2553. To f. God, s. not to do evil. A.R. 527, 628. To f. God and give glory to him, s. to worship the Lord from holy truths, and to worship, or adore him, s. to worship the Lord from the good of love. A.E. 606. To f. the Lord is to worship and revere him, for in worship and all things appertaining to worship, there is a holy and reverential f., which is grounded in the consideration that the object of worship is to be honored, and not by any means to be injured. A.E. 696.

Fear and **Dread**. F. has relation to evils, and d., to falses. 986. F. here is mentioned for the spiritual man, and d. has respect to the natural man. (Isa. viii. 13.) A.E. 696.

Fear and **Straitness** are the first beginning of temptations. 4249.

Fearful, the, s. those who have no faith. A.R. 891.

Feast (Gen. xix. 3) s. cohabitation. 2341. To make a f. (Exod. v. 1) s. worship of the Lord from a joyful mind. 7093. F. s. the good of charity. 2371. F. (Jer. li. 39) s. the adulterations of good and truth. A.E. 481.

Feasts of Charity. Meeting together in cordial joy, and friendly union. T.C.R. 433.

Feast of Fat Things full of Marrow, and of **Wine on the Lees well refined**. (Isa. xxv. 6.) Feast of fat things full of marrow, s. good both natural and spiritual, with joy of heart, and lees well refined, s. truths from that good, with felicity derived from them. A.E. 1159.

Feast of the Passover s. celebration of the Lord on account of liberation from damnation. 3994.

Feast of Tabernacles s. the implantation of good by truths. A.E. 458. The f. of t. was instituted in memory of the most holy worship of the Lord, in t., by the most ancient people, and of their conjunction with him by love. A.R. 585.

Feast of Weeks, instituted amongst the children of Israel, s. the implantation of truth in good. A.E. 911.

Feathers, spiritual good, from which truth is derived. A.E. 283.

Feed, to, s. to teach. A.R. 383. To f. (Rev. xii. 6) s. to make provision for the increase of the New Church. A.R. 547.

Feel, the sense of touch, cor. to the affection of good. 4404.

Feeling is the inmost and the all of perception; for the taste, smell, hearing, and sight, are no other than the genera thereof. 3528.

Feet, the, s. the natural principle, and when pred. of the Lord, his divine natural. 3761. A.R. 49. The f. cor. to the first, or ultimate heaven. A.E. 65. The place of his f. (Isa. lx. 13) being spoken of the Lord, in a general sense, s. all things of heaven and the church, because the Lord as a sun is above the heavens; but in a particular sense, it s. the church in the natural world. A.E. 606. The reason why the moon was seen under the woman's f. (Rev. xii. 1), is because the church on earth is understood, which is not yet in conjunction with the church in the heavens; moon s. intelligence in the natural man, and faith, and its appearing under the f. s. that it is about to be upon earth; otherwise, by f. is s. the church itself when in conjunction. A.R. 533. To stand upon the f., s. to be reformed, as to the external or natural man. A.R. 510.

Feet of the Angel, the (Rev. x. 1), s. the natural or literal sense of the Word. A.E. 600.

107

Feet and Hoofs

Feet and **Hoofs** (Ezek. xxxii. 2, 13) s. scientifics grounded in things sensual and natural, from which men reason concerning the mysteries of faith. 2163.

Felicities, the, of heaven, enter as man removes the love of evil and falsity. Exp. D.P. 39.

Female s. good. 4005.

Female Angels, those who are fond of children and love God. H. and H. 332.

Female Principle, the, is good grounded in truths. C.S.L. 61. A feminine p. produced from a male soul is from intellectual good, because this in its essence is truth; for the intellectual can think that this is good, thus that it is true, that it is good; it is otherwise with the will; this does not think what is good and true, but loves and does what is good and true, therefore by sons, in the Word, are s. truths, and by daughters, goods. C.L.S. 220.

Ferment (Hosea vii. 4, and Luke xii. 1, etc.) s. the false of evil. D.P. 284. See *Leaven.*

Fermentations, by spiritual, heterogeneous things are separated, and homogeneous conjoined. D.P. 25.

Fervor of Jehovah, the (Isa. xxxiv. 2), s. repugnance. 3614.

Fever. A f. burns from unclean heats collected together. When man falls into such disease, which he had contracted from his life, instantly an unclean sphere cor. to the disease, adjoins itself, and is present as the fomenting cause. 5715. See *Ague, Swoonings.*

Fibres and **Nerves.** F. s. the inmost forms proceeding from good, and n. s. truths. 5435. Ends are also rep. by the principles from which f. proceed, such as they are in the brain; the thoughts thence derived, are rep. by the f. from those principles; and the actions thence flowing, by the n., which are from the f. 5189. All the f. and all the vessels of those who are in hell, are inverted. D.P. 296.

Field s. doctrine and whatever respects doctrine. 368. F. s. the good of life, wherein are to be implanted the things appertaining to faith; i.e., the spiritual truths of the church. 3310. F. s. the church, because the church as a f. receives the seeds of good and of truth; for the church is in possession of the Word, from whence those seeds are received; hence also it is, that whatever is in a f. s. also somewhat appertaining to the church, as sowing, reaping, ripe corn, wheat, barley, etc., but this with a difference. 3766. F. (Ps. xcvi. 12) s. the good of the church. A.E. 326. F. (Joel i. 12) s. the church as to reception and procreation of truth and good. A.E. 374. By the part of the f. on which it rained (Amos iv. 7), is s. the doctrine of f. originating in charity; and by the part, or globe, on which it did not rain, is s. the doctrine of faith without charity. 382. To come from the f. (Gen. xxv.) s. the studious application of good. 3317.

Fiery Chariot (2 Kings ii. 11) s. the doctrine of love and charity. 2762. See *Chariot.*

Fiery Flying Serpent. Those who confirm themselves in faith alone, are seen as the f. f. s. A.E. 386.

Fiery Horses (2 Kings ii. 14) s. the doctrine of faith derived from love and charity. 2762.

Fifteen (Gen. vii. 20) s. so few as to be scarce any thing. 792.

Fifth Part, to take a, s. to make remains. 5291.

Fifty s. what is full, and in Gen. xix., truths full of goodnesses. 2252.

Fig, from cor., s. the natural good of man, in conjunction with his spiritual good; but in an opp. sense, the natural good of man, separated from his spiritual good, which is not good. A.R. 334. The external good of the spiritual church. A.E. 638.

Fig Leaves, with which Adam and Eve covered themselves, s. moral truths, under which they concealed the things appertaining to their love and pride. D.P. 313. See *To Sew.*

Fig Tree s. natural good, also the Jewish church. A.R. 334, 875. A.E. 386. F. t. (Judges ix. 13) s. the external good of the celestial church. 9277.

Fight and War (Ps. cxliv. 1, 2), relate to temptations, and, in an internal sense, to the temptations of the Lord. 1788.

Fill, to (Gen. xlii. 25), den. to be gifted. 5487. To f. the mouth with good (Ps. ciii. 5), is to give understanding by means of knowledges. A.R. 244.

Filth of the **Daughter of Zion** (Isa. iv. 4) s. the evil of self-love. A.E. 475.

Find, not to be found any more, s. not to rise again. A.E. 1183.

Fine, a, s. amendment, because inflicted for that end. 9045.

Finger of God (Exod. viii. 19) s. power from the divine principle. 7430.

Fingers, ten, s. all things terminated in ultimates. A.E. 675.

Finite. Every created thing is f. U.T. 33, 34.

Fir Tree, the, s. the natural principle, as to good. 4014. Also, natural truth superior. A.E. 730. F. t. (Ezek. xxxi. 8) s. the perception of the natural man. A.E. 654. F. t., pine tree, and the box tree (Isa. lx. 13), s. the celestial natural things of the Lord's kingdom and church, consequently, such things as relate to external worship. 2162.

Fire, in the scriptures, s. love, both in a good and bad sense. 934, 4909, 5215. The f. which was to be continually burning upon the altar, rep. the love, that is, the mercy of the Lord perpetual and eternal. 2177. F. in Luke iii. 16, s. divine good. A.R. 378. In the spiritual world, love appears at a distance as f. A.R. 422. It was on account of its cor. with divine love, that the Greeks and Romans amongst their religious ceremonies had a perpetual f., to which the vestal virgins were assembled. A.E. 504. F. from heaven s. testification, yea, an attestation that truth is truth; moreover f. s. celestial love, and hence zeal for the truth; and in an opp. sense, infernal love, and consequently, zeal for falsehood. A.R. 468, 494, 599. A consuming f. from heaven was a testification that they were in evils and falses. A.R. 599. Infernal f. is no other than the mutation of divine love into evil love, and into the lusts of doing evil and hatred. A.E. 504. Strange f. (Lev. x. 1, 2) s. all self-love and love of the world, and every lust arising from those loves. 934. F. s. self-love, and flame the pride of self-derived intelligence. (Joel i. 19.) A.E. 730. F. s. the good of celestial love, and flame the good of spiritual love. A.E. 504. Celestial love is respectively as a f., and the truth of doctrine as an oven, or furnace, in which bread is prepared. (Isa. iii. 9.) A.E. 504. F. and hail, snow and vapors (Ps. cxlviii. 8), s. the pleasantnesses of the loves of the natural man, and their scientifics and knowledges. A.E. 419. F. and sulphur (Ezek. xxxviii. 23) s. evil of the false, and the false of evil. A.E. 644. F. and sulphur s. infernal love, and concupiscences thence derived. A.R. 452. To be burnt with f., s. the punishment of the profanation of what is sacred and holy. A.R. 748.

Fire Hearth of **Jehovah** s. celestial love. A.E. 504.

Fire Brand, a smoking (Isa. vii. 4), s. the concupiscence of the false, and thence great wrath and anger against the truths and goods of the church. A.E. 559.

Firmament (Gen. i.) s. the internal man. 24. The f. of heaven is mutual love. 2027.

Firmament and **Waters** above and beneath it. (Gen. i. 6.) The knowledges in the internal man are called the w. above, and scientifics pertaining to the external, beneath the f. 24.

First and Last s. all and every particular, consequently, the whole. 10.355. The f. and the l. s. that the Lord is the only God. A.R. 92.

First Begotten. The church then first exists with man, when the truth of doctrine conceived in the internal man, is born in the external. A.R. 17. F. b. from the dead (Rev. i. 5) s. the Lord, because with respect to his humanity, he is divine truth itself united to divine good, from whom all men, who in

First-Born

themselves are dead, are made alive. A.R. 17. F. b. from the dead (Rev. i. 5) s. truth in act and operation, which is the good of life, and which is the primary of the church. A.R. 17.

First-Born, in a supreme sense, rep. the Lord as to divine celestial love, and also those respectively who were of the celestial church. 3325. Inasmuch as the Lord alone is f.-b., being essential good, and from his good is all truth, therefore, that Jacob, who was not the f.-b., might rep. him, it was permitted him to buy the primogeniture from Esau his brother, etc. 4925. The f.-b., in the spiritual sense of the Word, is good, for with infants the good of innocence is first infused by the Lord, by virtue of which man first becomes a man: now, since good is of love, and man does not reflect upon his own love, but only upon the thoughts of his memory, and since good has not at first a quality, but acquires one when it is formed in truths, and without a quality nothing is perceived, hence it was unknown that good was the primary principle or f.-b., for good is first conceived from the Lord in man, and is produced by truths, in which good is manifested, in its own form and effigy. A.E. 434. The sanctification of the f.-b. (Exod. xiii.) s. faith in the Lord. 8038. F.-b. (Ps. lxxxix. 28) s. the Lord's humanity. A.R. 17.

First-Born of Egypt, the, which were all cut off, because condemned, s. in a spiritual sense, truth in doctrine and in faith, separate from the good of life, which truth in itself is dead. A.R. 17. (See also Ps. lxxviii. 51, and 1063.)

First-Born of Worship, the, s. the Lord, but the f.-b. of the church s. faith. 352.

First Fruits, the, s. that which first springs up, and afterwards grows as a child grows up to a man, or as a young plant grows up to a tree, and hence they s. all which follows, till a thing is complete; for every thing that follows is in the first, as the man is in the infant, and the tree in the young plant; and whereas this first exists before its successions, in like manner in heaven and in the church, therefore, the f. f. were holy unto the Lord, and the feast thereof was celebrated. A.R. 623. The f. f. of the land (Exod. xxiii. 19) s. the state of innocence which is in infancy. 3519.

Firstlings of the Flock (Gen. iv. 4) s. the holy principle which is of the Lord alone, for the f., or first-born, in the rep. church were all holy, because they had respect to the Lord, who is alone the first-born. 352. A.R. 290.

Fish s. sensual affections which are the ultimate affections of the natural man. Also, those who are in common truths, which are also ultimates of the natural man. Also, those who are in external falses. A.R. 405. F. laid upon the fire (John xxi. 9) rep. the reformation of the natural man by the good of love, of which description were all the men of that time, in consequence of the complete vastation of the church. A.E. 513. Broiled f. (Luke xxiv. 42) s. the truth of good appertaining to the natural and sensual man, and honeycomb, the good of the same truth. A.E. 619. Fishes s. scientifics. 42, 991. Fishes (Hab. i. 14–16) s. those who are in faith separate from charity. A.R. 405. To make as the fishes of the sea, s. to make altogether sensual. A.R. 991.

Fish-hook. To draw out with f.-h. (Amos iv. 2) s. to lead away from truths by the fallacies of the senses. A.E. 560.

Fish Pool. The higher and lower f. p. (Isa. xxii. 9, 10) s. such truths as are in the interior and exterior senses of the Word. A.E. 453.

Fisher, in its spiritual meaning, s. one that searches out and teaches first natural truths, and afterwards such as are spiritual, in a rational way. I. 19. Fishers from Engedi unto Eneglaim (Ezek. xlvii. 10) s. those who shall instruct the natural man in the truths of faith. 40.

Fitches and **Cummin** (Isa. xxviii. 25) s. scientifics. 10.669.

Five s. much. 10.253. And also every thing, when two and three follow; but it s. some and few, when ten or twenty precedes or follows. A.E. 532. F. s. a

Flesh and Bones

sufficient quantity. 9689. Also, all things of one part. 9604. Also, some certain part. U.T. 199. F. (Gen. xiv. 9) s. disjunction. 1686. F., specifically, has a double s.; it s. a little, and hence somewhat, and it s. remains; the reason why it s. a little, is from its relation to those numbers which s. much; viz., to a thousand and to a hundred, and hence also to ten: from this ground it is that f. s. a little and also somewhat; the number f. s. remains when it has relation to ten, for ten s. remains. 5291.

Five Hundred and Four Thousand, and **Eighteen Thousand**. (Num. xlviii. 34, 35.) The former of these numbers s. all truths from good, and the latter all the truths of doctrine encompassing and defending the church. A.E. 438.

Five Thousand Men besides **Women** and **Children** (Matt. xiv. 15, 21) s. all who are of the church in truths from good; m., those who are in truths; w. and c., those who are in goods. A.E. 430.

Fix, to, a **Tent** s. a state of holy love. 4128.

Fix Firm, the heart, is pred. of evil. 7616.

Flagon of **Water**, a (Gen. xxi. 14), s. a small portion of truth with which the spiritual are first gifted, or so much as they are then capable of receiving. 2674.

Flags (Exod. ii. 3) s. scientific falses. 6732.

Flame s. spiritual good, and the light of it truth from that good. 3222, 6832. F. is the appearance of the love of evil. A.R. 384. A f. of fire (Rev. i. 14) s. spiritual love, which is charity, and when spoken of the Lord, his divine love. A.R. 48. A flaming fire (Ps. xiv. 4), s. the celestial spiritual principle. 934. F. in the hells, is an appearance of the love of what is false, and fire there, is an appearance of the love of evil. A.R. 282. F., in the Word, s. the good things appertaining to love, and lights, the truths appertaining to faith. 3222.

Flame of a **Sword Turning Itself** (Gen. iii. 24) s. self-love, with its wild lusts, and consequent persuasions, which carry man to things corporeal and worldly, and thus prevents the profanation of holy things, which is the tree of lives. 306.

Flatterers and **Hypocrites** have double thought. Exp. D.P. 104.

Flax (Exod. ix. 31) s. truth of the natural exterior principle. 7600. Smoking f. (Isa. xlii. 3), s. a little of truth from good. A.E. 951. F., or linen (Hosea ii. 5, 9), properly s. truth from the literal sense of the Word. A.E. 951. Fine f. (Isa. xix. 9) s. spiritual truth; and networks or tapestries are natural truths from a spiritual origin; and to make and to weave here s. to teach. A.E. 654.

Flee s. to escape, and be rescued. A.E. 405. To be overcome. 1689.

Flesh, in a good sense, s. the good of the will-principle, and in an opp. sense, the evil proprium of man. A.E. 1082. Every man in general, and the corporeal man in particular. 574. F. (John i. 14) s. the Lord's divine humanity. A.E. 1069. F. s. the good of the Word and of the church. A.R. 832. F., in the place of the rib (Gen. ii. 21), s. man's proprium, in which there is a vital principle. 147. One f. (Matt. xix. 5) s. one man (homo). C.S.L. 156. The will of the f. (John i. 13), s. the evil will-principle in man, also the corporeal man. 574. The f. of the sacrifice and burnt offering specifically s. spiritual good, but the bread of proposition, celestial good, and therefore not only f., but also bread was offered. 10.079. The f. of asses s. the proprium of the will, and the issue of horses, the proprium of the understanding thence, which perverts all things. (Ezek. xxiii. 20.) A.E. 654.

Flesh and **Spirit**. (Isa. xxxi. 3.) F. s. the proprium of man, and s. is the life from the Lord. A.E. 654. F. s. man, and s. the influx of truth and goodness from the Lord. (Joel ii. 28.) 574. To eat the f. of another s. to destroy his proprium. A.R. 748.

Flesh and **Blood** of the **Lord**. Divine good and divine truth. 3813.

Flesh and **Bones**. See *Body of the Lord.*

111

Flesh Pots

Flesh Pots. To sit by them (Exod. xvi. 3) s. a life according to pleasure, and what is lusted after; for this life is the life of man's proprium. 8408.

Flies, swarms of (Exod. viii. 21), s. the falses of malevolence. 7441. The f. that were sent upon Egypt, s. the falses in the extremes of the natural man, which are called sensual. A.E. 410.

Flight (Matt. xiv. 20) s. removal from a state of the good of love and innocence. 3755. F. (Mark xiii. 18) s. the last time, which, when applied to each particular person, is the time of his death. 34.

Flint s. truths. 2039.

Flock (Gen. xxvi.) den. interior or rational good. 343, 2566. Those who are in spiritual good. 3008. Natural interior good. (Gen. xxxii. 5.) 4244. The church where they are who are in simple good. 6828. F. of thine heritage s. those of the church who are in the spiritual things of the Word, which are the truths of its internal sense. A.E. 727. F. of Kedar s. divine celestial things, and the rams of Nebaioth, divine spiritual things. (Isa. lx. 7.) 2830. They within the church are called f., who are truly rational or internal men; hence it is, that by f. are s. also, in the abstract, essential, rational, or internal goodnesses; but they within the church are called herd, who are natural, or external men; hence also by herd are s. in the abstract, essential, natural, or external goodnesses. 2566. F. s. the spiritual things and herds, the natural things of man. (Ps. viii. 8.) A.E. 513. F., herds, and tents (Gen. xiii. 5), s. those things with which the external man abounds, and here, those which could agree with the internal man. 1564.

Flood, a, s. truths in abundance. A.R. 564. The f. (Gen. vii.) not only s. the temptations which the man of the church called Noah must needs sustain, before he could be regenerated, but likewise the desolation of those who were not in capacity to be regenerated; both temptations and desolations are in the Word compared to f., or inundations of waters, and are so called. 705. The f. s. damnation. 842. F. no more to destroy the earth, s. that such a deadly and suffocating persuasion should not any more exist. 1031. The f. was the end of the most ancient, and the beginning of the ancient church. 1263. The f. which the serpent cast out of his mouth (Rev. xii. 15) s. reasonings in abundance grounded in fallacies and appearances, which, if they are confirmed, appear externally like truths, but conceal within them falses in great abundance. A.R. 563.

Floor (Matt. iii. 12) s. the world of spirits which is between heaven and hell, and where the separation of evils and falses from goods and truths takes place. A.E. 374. F. (Hosea ix. 2) s. the Word as to the good of charity; and wine-press, as to the good of love; and by the wine-press here is understood oil, because there were wine-presses for oil as well as for wine. A.E. 695.

Flour, fine, **made into Cakes,** in general, rep. the same thing as bread; viz., the celestial principle of love, and its farina, the spiritual principle. 2177. Fine f. (Ezek. xvi. 19) s. the spiritual principle of charity. 2177, 5619. F., or meal, s. celestial truth; and wheat, celestial good. A.R. 778. F. and oil s. truth and good from a spiritual origin, and honey, good from a natural origin. (Ezek. xvi. 13.) A.E. 1153.

Flowers. The budding and fructification of a tree rep. the rebirth of man, the growing green from the leaves rep. the first state, the blossoming the second, or the next before regeneration, and the fructification the third, which is the state itself of the regenerate; hence it is that leaves s. those things which are of intelligence, or the truths of faith; for these are the first things of the rebirth or regeneration, but the f. [or blossoms] are those things which are of wisdom, or the goods of faith, because these proximately precede the rebirth or regeneration, and the fruits those things which are of life, or the works of charity, inasmuch as these are sub-

112

Food

sequent, and constitute the state itself of the regenerate. 5116. F. (1 Kings vi. 29–32) s. spiritual natural good, which is the good of the ultimate heaven. A.E. 458. The f. of a tree s. spiritual primitive truths in the rational man. A.R. 936. F. and flower-gardens s. scientific truths. 9558.

Flower of Glory, and **Head** of the **Fat Valleys**. (Isa. xxviii. 1.) F. of g. is truth in its first formation falling or perishing, and the head of the fat valleys is the intelligence of the natural man. A.E. 376.

Flowing Down. The deflux of divine good produces a different effect with the good than with the evil. A.E. 502.

Flow into. All which flows in through the spiritual mind comes from heaven, all through the natural mind from the world. D.L.W. 261.

Flows in, all thought or affection, from heaven or hell. D.P. 251, 288.

Fluctuations of the **Ark** (Gen. vii.) s. the changes of state in regeneration. 785–790.

Flux pred. of those who are in natural love. A.E. 163.

Fluxion, the, of the form of heaven is derived from the love of the Lord flowing in. 3889.

Fly, to, when spoken of the Lord, s. to foresee and to provide. A.R. 244. To f. when pred. of the Lord, also s. omnipresence. A.E. 529. To f. from the face of any one (Gen. xvi. 6) s. indignation. 1923. To f. and to fall (Gen. xiv. 10) s. to be conquered. 1689. To f. and go forth abroad (Gen. xxxix. 12) s. that separation was made, or that there was no longer any thing common. 5009. To f. (Ps. xviii. 11) s. to ill. the middle heaven. A.E. 529. To f. as a cloud, and as doves to their windows (Isa. lx. 7, 8), s. inquiry and investigation into truth, from the literal sense of the Word. A.E. 282. To f. in the midst of heaven (Rev. viii. 13) s. to instruct and foretell. A.R. 415. To f. into the wilderness, into her place (Rev. xii. 14), is pred. of the new church here s. by the woman clothed with the sun, and s. the divine circumspection and care and protection thereof while it is yet confined to a few. A.R. 561.

Foal and the **Son** of an **Ass**. (Gen. xlix. 11.) F. s. the external of the church, and the s. of an a. the internal of the church, both as to truths from the Lord. A.E. 433.

Foam upon the Face of the Waters (Hosea x. 7) s. that which is made void and separate from truth. A.E. 391.

Foes, or **Adversaries**, den. the falses of evil. 9314. When pred. of the Lord, s. to avert falses derived from evil. 9313.

Fœtus. Its formation, as to all and every part thereof, is a work of heaven. 5052. Its formation shows the formation of spiritual good by truth. 9042. While in the womb, it is in the province of the heart, but when separated from the womb, it enters by conjunction into the kingdom of the lungs. 4931. It has no voluntary motion before the lungs are opened. 3887.

Folds and **Pastures** (Ezek. xxxiv. 14) s. the good things of love. 415.

Follow, to, the **Lord** s. to acknowledge him, and to live according to his precepts. A.E. 864. See *Cross*.

Folly, Iniquity, Hypocrisy, and **Error**. (Isa. ix. 17.) F. has respect to the false, i. s. evil, h., the evils spoken against goods, and e., the falses which are spoken against truths. A.E. 386.

Food s. those things which are of use; f., in the internal sense, properly s. those things which nourish the soul of man, that is, which nourish him after the life of the body, for he then lives a soul or spirit, and has no longer need of material f. as in the world, but of spiritual f., which f. is all that which is of use, and all that which conduces to use; what conduces to use is to know what is good and true, what is of use, is to will and to do what is good and true; these are the things whereby the angels are nourished, and which are therefore called spiritual and celestial f. 5293. That goodnesses and truths are man's genuine f. or meat, may appear to every

113

Food and Raiment

one, inasmuch as whosoever is deprived of them has not life, but is dead. The f., or meat, which the wicked want in another life, are the delights arising from evils, and the pleasantnesses arising from falses, which are the meats of death; but the good in another life have celestial and spiritual f., which are the meats of life. 680, 681. F. is given from heaven by the Lord to every one in the spiritual world, according to the uses which he performs, and are like the f. in our world, but from a spiritual origin. A.R. 153. U.T. 281. F. is celestial, spiritual, and scientific. 1480. Every man has his peculiar and, as it were, his proper f., which is provided for him by the Lord before he is regenerated. 677. When man is eating f., the angels with him are in the idea concerning good and truth, according to the species of such f. 5915.

Food and Raiment. F. s. all the internal which nourishes the soul, and r., all the external which as the body clothes it. All the internal refers to love and wisdom, and all the external to opulence and eminence. A.E. 1193.

Fool. By a f. is s. he who is in falses and evils from the love of self; consequently, from self-derived intelligence. A.E. 386. To say "thou f." s. entire aversion to the good of charity. A.E. 746.

Foot (Deut. xxxiii. 3) s. an inferior principle. 2714. To set the right f. on the sea, and the left on the earth (Rev. x. 2), s. that the Lord has the universal church under his intuition and dominion as well those therein who are in its externals, as those who are in its internals. A.R. 470.

Footstool (Ps. cxxxii. 7) s. the Lord's church in the earths. A.E. 607. F. (Ps. cx. 1) s. the lowest region under the heavens, under which are the hells. A.E. 687. "To make thine enemies thy f." (Ps. cx. 1), s. to subjugate and keep under the hells. A.E. 850.

Force, to. Man ought to f. himself to do good, as of himself, but believing that all good is from the Lord. H. and H. 271. Man ought to f. himself to resist evil. D.P. 129.

Forces. There are three f. inherent in every thing spiritual; the active, which is the divine love, or living f.; the creative f. which produces causes and effects from beginning to end through intermediates; and the formative f., which produces animals and vegetables from the ultimate substances of nature, collected in the earth. A.Cr. 97. F. den. the power of truth. 6343–4.

Forehead, the, cor. to heavenly love. 9936. A.R. 729. The f. s. love both good and evil; because the face is the inmost of man's affections, and the f. is the supreme part of the face; the brain, from which is the origin of all things of man's life, is next under the f. A.R. 347. The Lord looks at the angels in the f., and the angels look at the Lord through the eyes, because they look from the understanding of truth, hence proceeds conjunction. A.R. 380.

Foreigner, a (Exod. xii. 45), s. one who does good from his own natural disposition alone. 8002.

Foreknowledge. See *Providence.*

Foresight, where providence is, there is f. 5195. He provides the good and the evil their places by f. D.P. 333.

Foreskin, the, cor. to corporeal love, because that member which the f. touches cor. to spiritual and celestial love. A.E. 817. The f., inasmuch as it covers the genital, cor. in the most ancient church, to the obscuration of good and truth, but in the ancient church to their defilement. 4462. Also self-love. 205.

Forest, a (Isa. xxxii. 15), is pred. of the natural man, but a garden, of the spiritual man. A.E. 730. In hell there appear f. in some places, consisting of trees which bear evil fruits, according to cor. A.R. 400. F. of the South (Ezek. xx. 46, 47), s. those who are in the light of truths, and extinguish it; consequently, it s. those in the church who are such. 1458.

114

Forget, to. That to f., in the internal sense, s. nothing else but removal and apparent privation. 5170, 5278.

Forgive, to. Whensoever sins are removed, they are remitted or forgiven. D.P. 280.

form den. the essence or substance of a thing. 3821.

Form, to, man, is pred. of the external man when made alive, or when he becomes celestial. 472.

Form of Heaven is like the f. of the human mind, the perfection of which increases according to the increase of truth and good, from whence are its intelligence and wisdom. L.J. 12.

Former from the womb (Isa. xliv. 2, 24; xlix. 1, 5) s. the reformer. A.R. 535.

Former Things, the, **have passed away** (Rev. xxi. 4) s. all grief of mind, fear of damnation, of evils and falses from hell, and of temptations arising from them, occasioned by the dragon who is cast out. A.R. 884.

Former Years (Mal. ii. 4) s. the ancient church. 349.

Forms, all natural, both animate and inanimate, are rep. of spiritual and celestial things in the Lord's kingdom. 3002.

Fornication is lust, but not the lust of adultery. C.S.L. 448, 449. The lust of f. is grievous so far as it looks to adultery. C.S.L. 543. F. of Babylon with the kings of the earth (Rev. xviii. 3) s. the falsification of the truth of the church. A.R. 21.

Fortifications den. truths so far as they defend good. 7297. Defence against falses and evils. A.E. 727.

Fortress, or **Bulwark,** is pred. of divine good. A.E. 316.

Forts and **Caves.** (Ezek. xxxiii. 27.) F. are confirmations from the Word, and c. are confirmations from scientifics. A.E. 388.

Fortune is the divine providence in the ultimates of order, agreeing with the particular state of man. D.P. 212. See *Contingencies.*

Forty s. a plenary state of temptation. 730.

Forty Days and **Nights.** Whereas whilst man is in temptation, he is in the vastation of all things appertaining to proprium, and which are corporeal (for the things of proprium and such as are corporeal must die by combats and temptations, before man is born again anew, or becomes spiritual and celestial), therefore also f. d. and n. s. further, the duration of vastation. 730.

Forty-five s. conjunction, the same as nine. 2269.

Forty-two (2 Kings ii. 24) s. blasphemy. A.E. 781. A.R. 573. F.-t. months (Rev. xi. 2) s. until there is an end, and when there is no truth left. A.R. 489. F.-t. months (Rev. xiii. 5) s. plenary vastation and consummation. A.E. 796. F.-t. months (Rev. xiii. 5), or three days and a half, or a time and times, and half a time, or one thousand two hundred and sixty days (which make up the same time), s. until there is an end of the former church, and a beginning of the new. A.R. 583.

Foul and **Filthy Water** cor. to that state in which a person is when he acts on account of his own glory and renown. S.D.

Foundation s. truth on which heaven and the church, and its doctrines are founded. 9643. A.R. 902.

Foundation of the **Heavens.** The basis and f. of the h. is the human race. 4618.

Foundation of the **World.** s. the institution of the church. A.E. 391.

Foundations of a **Wall** s. the knowledges of truth, whereupon doctrinals are founded. 9642. A.R. 902.

Foundations of the **Mountains** (Deut. xxxii. 22) s. the hells, because self-love and the love of the world (here s. by mountains) reign there. 1691.

Founder (Jer. x. 9) s. the same as workman, which see. A.E. 585.

Fountain s. the Lord and the Word. A.R. 360, 384. F. s. superior truth, and well, inferior truth. 3096. F. (Ps. civ. 10) den. knowledges. 1949. F. of waters

Four

(Rev. xvi. 7) s. all truths of the Word serving the church for doctrine and life. A.R. 630. F. of the abyss den. evils of the will, and cataracts of heaven den. falses of the understanding. 843–845.

Four s. the conjunction of good and truth, and it derives this signification from the f. quarters in heaven. A.E. 384. A.R. 322. All respecting good. A.R. 348. See *Sixteen*.

Four Animals, the, s. the superior heavens. A.R. 369.

Four Beasts seen by **Daniel** s. successive states of the church, until it is entirely wasted as to goods and truths. A.R. 574.

Four-Five (Isa. xvii. 6) s. few who are in good. A.E. 532.

Four Hundred s. vastation, temptations, and the duration thereof. 2959.

Four Hundred and Thirty (Gen. xv. 18) den. temptations. 1847.

Four Quarters in **Heaven**. The Lord appears to the celestial angels as a sun, and to the spiritual as the moon. A.E. 422. See *Quarters*.

Four Square s. what is just, because it has f. sides, and its f. sides look towards, or respect equally, the f. quarters, which is to respect all things from justice; and it is owing to this signification of f. s., that in common discourse a man is said to be s. when he is a man who does not from injustice incline either to this or that party. Moreover, the altar of burnt offering, the alter of incense and the breastplate of judgment were f. s., etc. A.R. 905.

Four Thousand s. all truths from good. A.E. 438.

Four Winds of **Heaven** (Dan. viii. 8) s. every good and truth of heaven and the church, and the conjunction of them; but, in an opp. sense, every evil and false, and their conjunction. A.E. 441. See *Elect*.

Four and Six. F. s. celestial good, and s., spiritual good; for f. s. conjunction, and intimate conjunction with the Lord is by love towards him; but s. s. communication, and communication with the Lord is by charity towards our neighbor. A.E. 283.

Fourscore Men, the, who came from **Shechem, Shiloh**, and **Samaria** (Jer. xli. 5), rep. the profanations of good and truth. A.E. 374.

Fourteen (Gen. xxxi. 40) s. a first period. 4177. The fourteenth year (Gen. xiv. 5) s. the first temptation of the Lord in childhood. 1669.

Fourth Part, a, s. the same as four. A.R. 322.

Fowl s. spiritual truth; bird, natural truth; and winged thing, sensual truth. 777. F. s. intellectual things. 40. F. s. thoughts, and all that creeps on the ground, the sensual principle. 776, 998. F. of heaven (Hosea ii. 18) s. the affections of truth; and reptiles of the earth, the affection of the knowledges of truth and good. A.E. 357.

Fox. If man closes up the middle natural degree, which cor. to the middle spiritual, he becomes, with respect to love, like a f., and with respect to intellectual sight, like a bird of the evening. U.T. 34. They who are in self-derived prudence, are like f. and wolves. D.P. 311.

Fracture, a, in the feet and **Hands** (Lev. xxi. 19, 21) s. perverted external worship. 2162.

Fragments, twelve baskets of (Matt. xiv. 20), s. knowledges of truth and good in all abundance and fulness. A.E. 430.

Fragrance. The affection of truth derived from good. 10.295.

Fragrant s. the truth of good. 5621.

France, the kingdom of. The state of the church there is more particularly alluded to in the internal sense of Rev. xvii. 12–14. A.R. 740–745.

Frankincense, by reason of its odor, rep. what is agreeable and acceptable. 2177. F. s. spiritual good. A.R. 277. F. (Matt. ii. 11) s. internal truth from good. 10.252.

Fraud is evil opinion and intention. 4459. The love of self regards itself alone, and out of it grow thefts and frauds. D.P. 276.

Freedom is to think and will from affection. 2874. There is a heavenly f. and an infernal one. 2870, 2873. Man cannot be saved, but in the perfect exercise of f. 1937, 1947. Man's f. is more vigorous in the combats of temptations, in which he conquers; inasmuch as he then inwardly compels himself to resist evils, although it has a different appearance. 1937, 1947. Man is left free even to think and will evil, and also to do it, so far as the laws of his country do not forbid him. 10.777. Natural f. is with beasts, but natural and spiritual f. together are possessed by man. U.T. 205.

Freely. For man to will f., as of himself, is from liberty given him by the Lord. D.P. 96.

Freemen and **Bondmen** (Rev. vi. 15) s. those who know and understand from themselves, and those who know and understand from others. A.R. 337, 832.

Free-Will. The Lord is continually present, and gives the faculty of doing good, but man should open the door, that is, should receive the Lord, and he then receives him, when he does good from his Word; this, although it appears to man to be done, as it were, of himself, nevertheless it is not of man, but of the Lord with him; the reason why it should so appear to man is, because he perceives no other, than that he thinks and acts from himself. A.E. 741. Man, during his abode in this world, is held in the midst between heaven and hell, and this in a spiritual equilibrium, wherein f.-w. consists. U.T. 475–478. Without f.-w., in spiritual things, the Word of God would be of no manner of use, and consequently, no church could exist. U.T. 483, 484. Without f.-w., in spiritual things, there would be nothing about man, whereby he might join himself by reciprocation with the Lord, and consequently, there would be no imputation, but mere absolute pre-destination, which is shocking and detestable. U.T. 485. On a supposition of man's wanting f.-w., in spiritual things, it would be possible for all men throughout the world in the compass of one day to be induced to believe on the Lord; but the impossibility of such an effect taking place is grounded in this circumstance, that nothing remains or continues with man, but what is received freely, or from a free principle. U.T. 500–503.

French Nation, noble, so called because it holds the Word holy, and has not gone under the yoke of priestly domination. D.P. 257.

Friend (John xv. 14, 15) s. the spiritual man. 51.

Friendship of Love, the, contracted with a person without regard to the nature and quality of his spirit is detrimental after death. U.T. 446, 449, 454, 455.

Frogs s. ratiocinations proceeding from cupidities, because they croak and have pruriences. A.R. 702. F. were produced from the waters of Egypt, because the waters of Egypt s. falses of doctrine upon which their reasonings were founded. A.R. 702.

Frontlets between the **Eyes** (Deut. vi. 8) s. understanding. 1038.

Frost (Exod. xvi. 14) is pred. of truth being made good, which is the good of truth. 8459. See *Hoar Frost.*

Froth den. what is evil and false. 4744.

Fructifications and **Multiplications** have not failed from the beginning of creation, neither will fail to eternity. D.P. 56.

Fruit s. the state of will in good. 3668. F. (John xv. 4, 5) s. good works which the Lord works by man, and which man works of himself from the Lord. A.R. 463. First ripe f. s. faith. 1071. F. is what the Lord gives to the celestial man, but seed producing f., is what he gives to the spiritual man. (Gen. i. 29.) 57. F. s. wisdom, and leaf intelligence, which shall be for their use, and this use is medicine. (Ezek. xlvii. 12.) 57. F. of works (Jer. xxxii. 19) s. a life derived from charity. 627. F. rep. and s. charity. 2039. F. of the desire of the soul (Rev. xviii. 14) s. beatitudes and felicities of heaven. A.R. 782.

Fruit Trees

The fruits of a tree s. the goods of love and charity. A.R. 936. See *First Fruits.*

Fruit Trees s. man, as to the affection of good and the perception of truth. 401.

Fruitful, to be, is pred. of goodnesses, and to be multiplied, of truths. 1014, 1018.

Fruitful One s. spiritual good, which is the good of charity. A.E. 357.

Fugitive and **Vagabond in the Earth**, a (Gen. iv. 14), s. one who does not know what is true and good. 382.

Fulfilled. When the Lord said that all things which were written concerning him were f., he meant that all things were f. in their inmost sense. 7933.

Full, or **Perfect before God** (Rev. iii. 2), is pred. of works when the interiors and exteriors of man are in conjunction with the Lord. A.R. 160.

Fulness is pred. of the natural ultimate and external principle. A.E. 448. F. (Ps. lxxxix. 12) s. goods and truths in the whole complex. A.E. 741.

Fulness of Times s. the devastation of all the goods and truths of the church when the Lord came into the world. A.E. 922.

Fulness, Sanctity, and **Power of the Word**. See *Divine Truth.*

Functions. There are spiritual ones cor. to every natural one in the body, for the latter cannot exist but from the mind. D.P. 296. It is principally to the f. of the organs and viscera in the body, that the spiritual societies cor. 4223.

Furlongs s. progressions in a series according to thoughts proceeding from affection. A.E. 924. F., being measured ways, s. leading truths. A.R. 176.

Furnace and **Iron**. (Ps. lxxxi. 7; 1 Kings viii. 51.) F. is the natural man, and i., the scientific false. (See also Deut. iv. 20.) A.E. 540. See *Iron.*

Furnace of Smoke s. the falses of concupiscences. A.R. 422.

Fury is a receding from good, and anger is a receding from truth. 3517, 3614, 4052.

Fuse, or **Melt**. See *Engraving.*

Future. Solicitude about the f. makes dull, and retards the influx of spiritual life. 5177, 8.

Future Events. See *Providence.*

G

Gabriel s. an angelic society consisting of those who teach from the Word, that Jehovah came into the world, and that the human which he there assumed, is the Son of God, and is divine. A.R. 538.

Gad, in a supreme sense, s. omnipotence; in a spiritual sense, good of life, or use; and in a natural sense, works. A.R. 352. G., in an opp. sense, s. the quality of those who are not in the good of faith, and thus not in good works. 3935.

Gahom den. various religious principles grounded in idolatrous worship. 2868.

Gain den. every false principle derived from evil, which perverts the judgment of the mind. 8711. See *To Trade.*

Galbanum (Exod. xxx. 34) s. the affection of interior truth in the internal man. 10.294.

Galeed, a heap and a witness (Gen. xxxi. 47), s. quality on the part of good of the divine natural principle. 4196.

Galilee, Cana of, s. the church among the Gentiles. A.E. 376.

Gall s. the same as wormwood, infernal falsity. A.R. 410.

Gall of Asps s. the enormous false which exists from falsified truths of the Word. A.E. 433.

Gall and **Wormwood** s. evil and the false commixed with good and truth. A.E. 519. To turn judgment into g. s. to turn truth into the false; and the fruit of righteousness into w. s. to turn good into evil. (Amos vi. 12.) A.E. 355.

Gall-Bladder. They who constitute that province are to the back, they are they who in the life of the body have despised what is virtuous, and in some measure what is pious, and also who have brought virtue and piety into discredit. 5186.

Galley, with oars, s. intelligence from man's proprium. A.E. 514.

Gammadims, the, **in the Towers** (Ezek. xxvii. 11) s. the knowledges of interior truth. 4599.

Ganglia. Spirits des. having reference to the g. 5189.

Garden (Isa. i. 30) s. the rational man destitute of rational truth. A.E. 504. G., in a bad sense, s. things sensual and scientific. 130. In the midst of the g. (Gen. ii. 9) s. in the will of the internal man. 105. See *Forest, Eden, Cast out.*

Garden and **Paradise** s. intellect and wisdom. 100, 108. G., grove, and plantation, s. intellectual knowledge. 100, 108, 3222. To plant g. (Jer. xxix. 5, 28) has respect to the understanding. 710. The man of the church is like a g., as to intelligence, when he is in the good of love from the Lord, because the spiritual heat which vivifies him is love, and spiritual light is intelligence thence derived; that by means of these two principles, heat and light, g. flourish in this world, is well known, and it is the same in heaven, where there appear g. paradisiacal with fruit trees, according to the wisdom of the inhabitants derived from the good of love from the Lord. But around those who are intelligent and not in the good of love, there do not appear g., but grass; and around those who are in faith separate from charity, not even grass, but sand. A.R. 90. See *Flowers.*

119

Garden in Eden Eastward

Garden in Eden Eastward (Gen. ii. 8), in a supreme sense, is the Lord; in its inmost sense, it is the kingdom of the Lord, or heaven, wherein man is placed when he is made celestial. 99. To dress and keep the G. of E. (Gen. ii. 15) s. to enjoy all things belonging to the celestial man, but not to possess them as his own, because they are the Lord's. 122.

Garden of God (Ezek. xxviii. 13) s. the rational principle of the spiritual church. 1588.

Garden of Jehovah (Gen. xiii. 10) s. the things appertaining to the rational principle from a celestial origin, as was the case with the most ancient church. 1588.

Garlic s. the corporeal part of man. A.E. 513.

Garment. It is said (Deut. xxii. 11), "Thou shalt not wear a g. of divers sorts; as of woollen and linen together," which words involve that the states of good and truth ought not to be confounded; for those who are in the spiritual kingdom of the Lord, cannot be also in his celestial kingdom at the same time, and vice versa. 10.669. G. of the intwinings of gold and of needlework (Ps. xlv. 13) s. the Lord's divine truth. 5044. A g. down to the foot (Rev. i. 13) s. the proceeding divine, which is divine truth. A.R. 43. It is a peculiar circumstance in the spiritual world, that a spirit thinks himself to be such as the g. is which he wears; the reason is, because in that world the understanding clothes every one. C.S.L. 354. See *Black Garment.*

Garments and **Vesture.** That no injury should be done to the internal or spiritual sense of the Word was s. by the g. of the Lord being divided by the soldiers, and not the v., which was without seam, woven from the top throughout (John xix. 23), for by the g. of the Lord is s. the Word; by the g. which were divided, the Word in the letter; by the v., the Word in the internal sense; and by the soldiers are s. those who fought in favor of the goods and truths of the church. A.E. 375.

Garments. Frequent mention is made of g. in the Word, and by them are meant those things which are beneath or without, and which cover those things that are above or within; wherefore by g. is s. the external of man, consequently, the natural principle, for this covers his internal and spiritual principle; by g. are specifically s. the truths which are of faith, because these cover the goods which are of charity; this significative has its origin from the g. with which spirits and angels appear clothed; spirits appear in g. without splendor, but angels in g. with splendor, and, as it were, from splendor, for splendor itself appears around them as a g., like the Lord's., when he was transfigured, which were as the light (Matt. xvii. 2), and as white lightning (Luke ix. 29), from their g. also, spirits and angels may be known, as to their quality. 5248. The g. of the angels not only appear such, but really are what they appear to be; and also they have change of raiment, which they put on and off, and lay by for future use. H. and H. 177, 181, 182. The infernal spirits have g., but such only as are ragged and filthy. H. and H. 182. G. of holiness which Aaron wore (Lev. xvi. 2, 4; Exod. xxviii. etc.), rep. the Lord's divine human principle. 2576. G. of honorableness (Isa. lii. 1) s. the holy things of faith. 2576. G. of the Lord (Isa. lxiii. 1) s. the Word in the literal sense. A.E. 922. G. of the Lord, at his transfiguration s. divine truth proceeding from his divine love. 9212, 9216. G. of needlework, fine linen, and silk (Ezek. xvi. 10, 18) s. the spiritual inferior things and doctrinals of the spiritual church perverted. 2576. G. of salvation s. the truths of faith, and the robe of righteousness, the good of charity. (Isa. lxi. 10.) 2576. G. of wrought gold (Ps. xlv. 13) s. the quality of truth derived from good. 5954. G. and clothing (Isa. lxiii. 1, 3) s. the Lord's human. 2576.

Garner, Granary, or **Barn** (Matt. iii. 12, and xii. 30) s. where there is a collection of the good. A.E. 426.

120

Gas. The inhabitants of Mars know how to make fluid fires, from which they have light. 7486.

Gate (Amos v. 15) s. the passage to the rational mind. 2943. G. of a city s. doctrine by which there is an entrance into the church. 2943, 4447, 4478. G. of heaven (Gen. xxviii. 17) s. the ultimate principle in which order closes. 3721. G. s. introductory knowledges of what is good and true, out of the literal sense of the Word. A.R. 899, 901, 904. With every man there are two g., one leads to hell, which is open to evils and false principles therein originating, in this g. are infernal genii and spirits; the other g. leads towards heaven, and is open to goodnesses and truths therein originating, and in this g., are angels. The rational mind is the middle point to which these two ways tend. 2851. See *Ways.*

Gates. Baptism and the holy supper are, as it were, two g. to eternal life. Every christian man, by baptism, which is the first g., is admitted and introduced into the things which the church teaches from the Word concerning another life; which all are means by which man may be prepared for and led to heaven. The other g. is the holy supper, through which every man, who has suffered himself to be prepared and led by the Lord, is admitted and introduced into heaven. There are no more universal g. T.C.R. 721.

Gath s. the spiritual principle of the church. A.E. 700.

Gather, to (Gen. vi. 21), is pred. of those things which are in the memory of man, where they are gathered; it also implies, that goodnesses and truths should be gathered together in man before he is regenerated. 679. To g. together in a place to battle (Rev. xvi. 16) s. to excite combat against truths in defence of falses. A.R. 707, 858. To be gathered to his people (Gen. xxv. 10), in the internal sense of the Word, where the subject is concerning the life of any one, as being rep., s. that he is no longer treated of; the ancients were accustomed to say when any one died, that he was gathered to his fathers, or to his people, and they understood thereby, that he actually came to his parents, his relations and kinsfolk in another life; for they knew that all who are in the same good meet and are together in another life; and likewise all who are in the same truth; of the former they said that they were gathered to their fathers, but of the latter that they were gathered to their people. 3255. A.E. 659.

Gatherers, grape, s. falses. A.E. 919.

Gaza, or **Azza,** s. things revealed concerning charity. 1207.

Gebal (Ps. lxxxiii. 7) s. those who are principled in the externals of worship and doctrine. 2468.

Gedahlia, King of **Babel** (Jer. xli. 1, 8) s. the profanation of good and truth. A.E. 374.

Gehenna, is the hell of those in the concupiscences of adultery. 9010.

Gems are pred. of truths grounded in good. 3812.

Genealogy. It was customary with the most ancient people to give names, and by names to s. things, and thus to institute a g.; for whatever has relation to the church may be considered in such a genealogical view, wherefore such names are common in the Word. 339.

Genera and **Species.** Goods and truths, celestial and spiritual, are distinguished into their g. and s. with indefinite variety. 775.

General, or common things, precede, into which particulars are insinuated. A.E. 904.

Generate, to (Isa. lxv. 23), is pred. of things that are of faith; and to labor, of the things that are of love; the latter are called the seed of the blessed of Jehovah, and the former are called offspring. 613. Generation in the Word, relates to the work of regeneration. 613, 1145. Generation of generations (Ps. lxxii. 5) s. the churches after the flood. 337. Members or organs of gen-

Generated

eration cor. to celestial love, which is the love of the third or inmost heaven. 5062. A.R. 213. Generations of the heavens and of the earth (Gen. ii. 4) s. the formations of the celestial man. 89. Perpetual generations or generations of an age (Gen. ix. 12) s. all who are perpetually created anew. 1041.

Generated s. to be regenerated according to a life of divine truth. A.E. 419.

Generation. The soul is the seed of the father, and is clothed with a body in the womb of the mother. T.C.R. 92.

Genesareth, lake of (Luke v. 1), s. the knowledges of truth and good in the whole complex. A.E. 514.

Genesis. The whole of the historical parts of the Word summarily involve the things which are treated of in the spiritual sense of the first sixteen chapters of G. S.E.L.P. p. 70.

Genii s. such as are principled in evil; and spirits are such as are principled more especially in what is false. C.S.L. 71. A.C. 5035. G. (the infernal) greedily draw in concupiscences, and inhale their sphere. A.R. 837.

Genitals cor. to the marriage of good and truth. 4462. In an opp. sense to the loves of hell. A.E. 1009.

Genius. From the hereditary g., in a long succession, children inherit a particular g. 2300–1.

Gentiles, the, who have thought well of their neighbor, and lived in good-will to him, receive the truths of faith in another life better than they who are called christians; and more of the g. are saved than of the christians. 2284. Some of the g. spirits who lived a good life in this world, in one night are initiated into choirs, or into the company of spirits who speak together all as one, and each as all; whereas with many christians it requires the space of thirty years to effect the same purpose. 2595. The g. cannot profane holy things like christians. 1327. Amongst the g., in another life, the Africans are most beloved, inasmuch as they receive the good things and truths of heaven more easily than others. 2604.

Gerar (Gen. x. 19) s. those things which are revealed concerning faith. 1207.

Germans. Concerning the spiritual characteristics of the G. T.C.R. 8145. The G. in the spiritual world are arranged towards the north. L.J. 48.

Germinations are the productions of wisdom, originating in love. A.Cr. 66–9.

Gershom (Exod. xviii. 3) den. the quality of the good of truth, among those who are without the church. 8650.

Gestures cor. to affections. 4215.

Gether den. various knowledges concerning good. 1233.

Ghost. See *Spirit.*

Giants (Gen. vi. 4) s. those who, through a persuasion of their own height and pre-eminence set at naught whatever is holy and true. 580–583.

Gibeah (2 Sam. vi.) s. the natural or ultimate principle of the church. A.E. 700. G. s. the same as Baale Judah, which see. G., Ramah, and Bethaven (Hosea v. 8), den. those things which appertain to spiritual truth, derived from celestial. 4592.

Gibeon. Sun standing still upon G. s. total vastation of the church. A.E. 401.

Gibeonites (Josh. ix. 21–27) s. those who are continually desirous of knowing truths; but for no other end than to know, without any regard to the use thence to be derived; such were reckoned amongst the most vile. 3058.

Gift, an hidden (Gen. xliii. 23), den. the truth and good which are given by the Lord, whilst man is ignorant of it. 5664. The g. which Abraham gave to the sons of the concubines which he had (Gen. xxv. 6) s. lots in the Lord's spiritual kingdom. 3246. To send g. (Rev. xi. 10) s. to be associated by love and friendship, because a g. consociates, for it begets love, and causes friendship. A.R. 508.

122

Gihon, the river (Gen. ii. 13), s. the knowledge of all things relating to goodness and truth. 116.

Gilead, mount (Gen. xxxi. 21, 23), as being a boundary, in a spiritual sense, s. the first good, which is that of things appertaining to the bodily senses, for it is the good, or pleasurable enjoyment of these, into which man is first of all initiated who is regenerated. In this sense, G. is taken in the prophets, as Jer. viii. 52; xxii. 6; xlvi. 11; l. 19; Ezek. xlvii. 18; Obad. ver. 19; Micah. vii. 14; Zech. x. 10; Ps. lx. 7; and, in an opp. sense, Hosea vi. 8; xii. 11. 4117. G. and Lebanon (Zech. x. 10) s. the good of charity, and the good and truth of faith. A.E. 328.

Gilgal s. the doctrine of natural truth, serving for introduction into the church. A.R. 700.

Gins s. enticement and deception of evils. 9348.

Gird One's self, to (John xxi. 18), s. to know and apperceive truths in the light from good. 10.087.

Girdle, or **Zone**, a, in the Word, s. a common band, whereby all things are kept in their order and connection, or a band conjoining the goods and truths of the church. A.R. 46. Golden g. (Rev. i. 13) s. the proceeding and conjoining divine which is divine good. A.R. 46, 671. A linen g. (Jer. xiii. 1–7) s. all the truth of doctrine from the Word. A.E. 951. The leathern g. about the loins, worn by Elijah, rep. the literal sense of the Word, as to the goods thereof. 5247. To make themselves g., or things to gird about (Gen. iii. 7), s. to be effected with shame. 216.

Girgashite and **Jebusite** (Gen. xv. 21) s. falses derived from evils. 1867.

Girls and **Boys** s. the goods and truths of innocence. A.E. 863.

Give, to, **Food** (Gen. xli. 48) s. to store up. 5342.

Give us this Day our Daily Bread s. the perpetuity and eternity of a state. 2838.

Glad. To make g. influx and reception from joy of heart. A.E. 518.

Gladness and **Songs** (Gen. xxxi. 47), are pred. of truths. 4137.

Gland. Those who have reference to the g., are in the principle of good. 4052.

Glass, sea of, like unto crystal (Rev. iv. 6), is so called from the lucidity of the divine truth proceeding from the Lord. A.R. 238.

Glass, pure. (Rev. xxi. 18.) The City of New Jerusalem is here said to be pure gold, like pure g., because gold s. the good of love from the Lord, and like pure g. s. pellucid from divine wisdom, and whereas the latter appears in heaven as light, and flows from the Lord as a sun; by being like clear g. is s. flowing in together with light out of heaven from the Lord. A.R. 912. See *Sea of Glass.*

Globe does not s. the g. of the earth, but the church in it; but when g. and earth are mentioned together, g. s. the church with respect to good, and earth s. the church with respect to truth. A.R. 551.

Glorification, the Lord's, is spoken of in the Word, and in the internal sense it is everywhere spoken of. 2249, 2523, 3245, 10.828. G. of the Lord's humanity s. the union of his humanity with his divinity; for to glorify is to make divine. 1603, 10.053, 10.828. The g. of the Lord (Rev. v.) takes place first in the superior heavens, then in the inferior heavens, then in the lowest heavens; and lastly confirmation and adoration by the superior heavens. A.R. 275. The g. of the Lord by man, when proceeding from the Lord, is the perpetual influx of divine good united to divine truth, with angels and men; with these the g. of the Lord is the reception and acknowledgment in heart, that all good and truth is from the Lord, and thence all intelligence, wisdom, and felicity; this, in a spiritual sense, is s. by thanksgiving. All g. of the Lord which is made by angels of heaven and men of the church, is not from themselves, but flows in from the Lord. The g. which is

Glorifications and Celebrations

from man only, is not from the heart, but only from the memory and mouth, and what proceeds from these is not heard in heaven. A.E. 288. G. of the Lord in the heavens sometimes resembles an irradiation, flowing downwards, and affecting the interiors of the mind. This g. is celebrated, when the angels are in a state of tranquility and peace, for it then flows forth from their inmost joys and very essential felicities. 2133.

Glorifications and **Celebrations** of the **Lord**, in heaven, are made from the Word, because in such case, they are made from the Lord, for the Lord is the Word, that is, essential divine truth therein. C.S.L. 81.

Glory s. divine truth as it is in heaven, because divine truth is the light of heaven, and from that light all the splendor and magnificence and g. is derived there. 4809, 9429. A.E. 42. In proportion as a society in heaven is in divine truth, in the same proportion all things there are resplendent, and in the same proportion the angels are in the splendor of g. A.R. 629. G. (Isa. iv. 5) s. spiritual good and truth. A.E. 594. G. (Matt. xxiv. 30) s. the Word in its spiritual sense. A.R. 24. G., originating in pride, is in them who are in the love of self, and g., not originating in pride, is in them who are in the love of uses. This latter g. is from spiritual light, but the former from mere natural light. A.R. 940. To give g. (Rev. xix. 7) s. to acknowledge and confess that all truth is from the Lord; also to acknowledge that the Lord is God of heaven and earth, here, therefore, it s. to glorify, because this includes both. A.R. 812. To give g. to God s. to live according to divine truth. A.E. 874. G. of the Gentiles (Isa. lxvi. 22) s. the conjunction of good and truth. A.E. 365. The g. of God (Rev. xxi. 11) s. the Word in its divine light, which shines from the Lord by means of the spiritual sense, because the Lord is the Word, and the spiritual sense is in the light of heaven which proceeds from the Lord as a sun, and the light which proceeds from the Lord as a sun is, in its essence, the divine truth of his divine wisdom. A.R. 897.

Glory and **Praise**. (Isa. xlii. 12.) To give g. to Jehovah is to worship him from internals; and to declare his p. is to worship him from externals. A.E. 406.

Glory and **Strength**. By g., in the Word, when spoken of the Lord, is meant divine majesty, and it is pred. of his divine wisdom, and by s. is meant divine omnipotence, and it is pred. of his divine love. A.R. 22.

Glory and **Virtue**. (Rev. xv. 8.) G. s. divine spiritual truth; and v., divine celestial truth. A.R. 674.

Glory and **Wisdom**. (Rev. vii.) The reception of divine truth in the middle or second heaven is called g., and the reception of divine truth in the third heaven is called w. A.E. 465.

Glory, **Wisdom**, and **Thanksgiving** s. the Lord's divine spiritual principle; and **Honor**, **Virtue**, and **Might**, his divine celestial principle. (Rev. vii. 12.) A.R. 372.

Gnashing of Teeth. Disputation heard at a distance like. A.R. 386.

Gnaw, to, the **Tongue** s. to detain the thought from hearing truths. A.R. 696.

Go, to. Inasmuch as to g. and to be moved s. to live, therefore it was said by the ancients, that "in God we are moved, we live, and are," and by being moved is meant the external of life, by living, its internal, and by being, its inmost. 5605. A.E. 768.

Go after, to or **to Follow** (Gen. xxiv. 8), s. to be separated from the natural, and conjoined to the rational principle. 3042.

Go down, to, **to see** (Gen. xviii. 21) s. judgment, and consequently, visitation. 2242.

Go forth, to (Gen. xix. 14), s. to recede from, or not to remain in [evil]. 2401. To g. f. (Gen. xli. 45) den. influx, or to flow in. 5333.

Go near, to (Gen. xxxiii. 12), s. adjunction and conjunction. 4376.

Go out, to, **from the Face of Jehovah** (Gen. iv. 16) s. to be separated from the good of faith grounded in love. 398. To g. o. to meet (Gen. xiv. 17) s. to submit themselves. 1721. To *g*. *o*. (Gen. xxviii. 10) s. to live more remotely. 3690. To *g*. *o*. and to come in (Zech. viii. 10) s. the states of life from beginning to end. A.E. 695.

Go to the Father, to (John xvi. 28), s. to unite the human to the divine essence. 3736.

Go up over, to (Rev. xx. 9), s. to climb over and pass by, consequently, to despise, or hold in contempt. A.R. 861.

Go up, to, and **to go down.** In the Word throughout, mention is made of going up, and going down, in speaking of going from one place to another, not by reason of one place being more elevated than another, but because going up is pred. of going towards interior or superior things, and going down, of going towards exterior or inferior things, that is, because going up is pred. of going towards spiritual and celestial things, for these are interior things, and are also believed to be superior; and going down is pred. of going towards natural and terrestrial things, for these are exterior things, and are also to appearance inferior. 5406. The divine love flows into the affection of good, and thence into the affection of truth, and vivifies and ill. the things which are in the natural man, and in this case, disposes them to order; this is s. by going down. Hereby truths are elevated out of the natural man into the rational, and are conjoined with good therein, and this is s. by going up. 3084.

Goat, from cor., s. the natural man. The g. which was sacrificed (Lev. xvi. 5–10) s. the natural man as to a part purified, and the g. which was sent into the wilderness, the natural man not purified. A.E. 730. G. (Lev. xvi. 21, 22) s. faith; and because by the truth of faith man is regenerated by the Lord, and consequently, his sins are removed and cast into hell, therefore it is said, that "Aaron made the g. bear upon him all the iniquities of the children of Israel unto the land of separation, or into the wilderness." 9937. G. and ram (Dan. viii.); g. s. those who are in falses of doctrine because in evils of life, and ram, those who are in truths of doctrine because in goods of life. A.E. 734. He-g. of the she-g., in the Word, s. natural truths, i.e., truths of the external man, from which the delights of life are derived; also external truths grounded in delights. The truths of the external man, from which the delights of life are derived, are truths divine, such as are those of the literal sense of the Word, in which the doctrinals of a genuine church are grounded. These are properly s. by he-g., and the delights which are thence derived are s. by she-g.; thus by he-g., of the she-g., in a genuine sense, are s. they who are in such truths and consequent delights; but in the opp. sense, they who are in external truths, i.e., in appearances of truth derived from the sense of the letter, which are agreeable to the delights of the mind [animus], which, in general, are honors and gains favoring self-love and the love of the world. 4769. She-g. (Gen. xxx. 32) s. the good of truth, or the charity of faith. 3995. G. s. the good of innocence in the external and natural man. 9470. G. s. faith separate from charity. A.R. 586.

Goblets. Scientifics of the memory, as receptacles of truth. 9394.

God, in the supreme sense, is the divine which is above the heavens, but G., in the internal sense, is the divine which is in the heavens; the divine which is above the heavens is divine good, but the divine in the heavens is divine truth, for from the divine good proceeds the divine truth, which constitutes heaven and disposes it in order. 7268. G. is the term applied (Gen. vi. 11), and in the subsequent parts of that chapter, because there was now no church. 619. The word G. is used, and not Jehovah (Gen. viii. 1), because as yet man was in a state before regeneration; but when he is regenerate, and faith is joined with charity in him, then mention is made of Jehovah, as at vs. 20, 21. 840. G. (Gen. xxii. 8) s. the divine human. 2807. G.

God Tempted Abraham

(Dan. xi. 38) s. the truth of the Word falsified. A.E. 714. The Lord's internal man, which is Jehovah himself, is called G. most high, and before a plenary conjunction or union was effected, is called possessor of the heavens and the earth. (Gen. xiv. 19.) 1733. The Lord is called G. of Israel, because Israel is the spiritual church, and he is called rock, because rock s. divine truth, which is in the spiritual church from him. (2 Sam. xxiii. 3, 4.) A.E. 179. G. is love itself, and wisdom itself, and these two constitute his essence. U.T. 37. G., by reason of his being love itself, and wisdom itself, is also life itself, which is life in himself. U.T. 39. G. is in all space, without space, and in all time without time. U.T. 30. D.L.W. 69, 73. The humanity whereby G. sent himself into the world, is the son of G. U.T. 92. G. was made man, and man G., in one person. U.T. 101. That which man loves above all things is his G. U.T. 293. Upon a just idea of G. the whole heaven and the whole church, and all things of religion are founded, because thereby conjunction is effected with G., and by conjunction heaven and eternal life. Preface to A.R. and n. 469. G. is to be thought of from essence to person, and not from person to essence, for they who think concerning G. from person make G. three, but they who think of him from essence make G. one. A.R. 611. The thought only of G. as a man, in whom is the divine trinity of father, son, and holy spirit, opens heaven; but, on the contrary, the thought concerning G. as being not a man (which appears in the spiritual world as a little cloud, or as nature in its least principles), shuts heaven, for G. is a man (homo) even as the universal angelic heaven in its complex is man (homo) and every angel and spirit is thence a man (homo). A.E. 1097.

God Tempted Abraham (Gen. xxii. 1) s. the Lord's grievous and inmost temptations. 2766, 2768.

God of **Jacob**. Goods in act. A.E. 405.

God and **Christ**. (Rev. xii. 10.) G. s. the essential all-creating divinity, which is called Jehovah the father, and C. s. his divine humanity, which is called the son of G. A.R. 553.

God and the **Father**. In the spiritual sense two persons are not s. thereby, but by G. is understood the divine or divinity, with respect to wisdom, and by f., the divine or divinity with respect to love. A.R. 21.

God and **Jehovah**. The term G., as applied in the Word, is grounded in ability, or potency, but the term J., in esse, or essence; hence it is that the term G. is used in speaking of truth, and the term J. in speaking of good, for ability is pred. of truth, when esse is pred. of good, inasmuch as good has power by truth, for by truth, good produces whatsoever exists. 3910.

God and the **Lamb**, in the Revelation, do not mean two persons, but divine good and divine truth in heaven, both proceeding from the Lord. A.E. 287. A.R. 584.

Gods. In the Word it is occasionally said that there is none as Jehovah God, also that there is no God as he. It was so said in the Word because at that time they worshipped several G. in the land where the church was, as also in the lands where the church was not; and every one preferred his own God to the God of another; they distinguished them by names, and the God of the Israelites and Jews by the name Jehovah; the Jews and Israelites themselves believed also that several G. were given, but that Jehovah was greater than the rest by reason of miracles; wherefore when miracles ceased they instantly lapsed into the worship of other G., as is evident from the historicals of the Word. 7401. (See *Shaddai*.) "Thou shalt have no other G. before me," s., in the spiritual sense, that no other God is to be worshipped but the Lord Jesus Christ, inasmuch as he is Jehovah, who came into the world and accomplished the work of redemption, without which, neither man nor angel could have been saved. The celestial sense of this commandment is, that the Lord Jehovah is infinite, immense, and eternal; that he is omnipotent, omniscient, and omnipresent; that he is the first and the last, the beginning and the end, who was, who is, and will be; that he is essential love, and essential wisdom, or essential good and essential truth, consequently, essential life; and thus the individual one from whom are all things. U.T. 294, 295. To be as G. (Gen. iii. 5) s. to be under the guidance of self-love. 204. G. (Gen. xxxv. 2) s. falses. 4581. G. of the kings of Ashur (Isa. xxxviii. 19) s. reasonings from falses and evils, which agree with the proprium of man. A.E. 585. G. of silver s. falsities, and G. of gold, evil lusts. (Exod. xx. 23.) 1551. The angels cannot speak the word G., but God. A.R. 961. The angels are called G. from the divine truth which they receive from the Lord. A.E. 313, 688.

God and **Magog** s. those who are principled in external natural worship, and not in internal spiritual worship. A.R. 858.

Goiim s. goods. 1685.

Gold (Rev. xxi. 18) s. the good of love from the Lord. A.R. 912. G., when twice mentioned, s. the good of love, and the good of faith originating in love. (See Gen. ii. 11.) 110. G. of Sheba (Ps. lxxii. 14) s. wisdom derived from divine truth. A.R. 379. G. tried in the fire (Rev. iii. 18) s. the good of celestial love. A.R. 311. G. s. spiritual good, and fine g. celestial good. (Ps. xix. 11.) A.E. 619. G. and precious stones (Rev. xvii. 4) s. divine spiritual good, and divine spiritual truth, both derived from the Word. A.R. 726. G. s. the knowledges of things celestial, and silver, the knowledges of things spiritual. (Ezek. xvi. 17.) 1551. G., brass, and wood, rep. the three celestial principles; the inmost principle is rep. by g., the inferior by brass, and the lowest by wood. (Isa. lx. 17.) 113, 1551, 9881.

Golden Age. The ancients distinguished the times, from the first age of the world to the last, into golden, silver, copper, and iron ages, to which also they added an age of clay. The g. a. they called those times when there was innocence and integrity. (See *Most Ancient Church*.) But they called silver those times when there was no longer innocence, but still a species of integrity; the copper and iron ages they called those which were still inferior. They gave these names from cor., not from comparison. 5658. See *Silver Age*.

Golden Altar s. the very essential divine good and truth in the Lord's divine human. 3210.

Golden Calf, the, in a spiritual sense, s. carnal pleasure. U.T. 849.

Goliah the **Philistine** rep. those who are in truths without good; or those who are in the pride of self-derived intelligence. A.E. 781.

Gomer den. those who are in external worship. 1131.

Gomorrah s. the lust of bearing rule from a principle of the false. 2141.

Good, with man, is from a twofold origin; namely, from what is hereditary, and thence adscititious; and also, from the doctrine of faith and charity; in the case of the gentiles from their religious principles. 4988. G. from the Lord is continually flowing in; and, as it were, presses and solicits to be received. 5471, 5497. G. is essentially the holy divine proceeding from the Lord, and flows by a superior way, or door, into man. 3207. G. is called Lord, in respect to a servant, and father, in respect to a son. (Mal. i. 6; Ps. cv. 17, 20–22.) 4973. From g. all liberation and salvation is derived. 2709. A man does not know what g. is, in reality, before he is in g., and has his perceptions from it. 3325, 3330, 3336. The celestial see truths from g. alone. A.R. 121. If man lives in g., he is a heaven in its least form, or his interiors cor. to the three heavens. 5145. Unless a man is in g., his internal man is not opened, but remains closed. 10.367. No one can do g. which is really g. from himself; but at this day scarce any one knows whether the g. which he does be from himself, or from God, because the church has separated

127

Good of Charity

faith from charity. Dec. 9. He who is in g. is in the faculty of seeing truths which flow from general truths, and this in a continual series. 5527. G. is actually spiritual fire, from which spiritual heat, which makes alive, is derived. 4906. Every g. has its particular delight from use. 3049, 4984, 7038. Although divine g. is united to divine truth alone, it nevertheless flows into interior truths, and joins itself with them; yea, it even flows into scientific and sensual truths, which are scarce any thing but fallacies, and joins itself with them; if it were not so, no man could possibly be saved. 2554. There is *civil* g., *moral* g., and *spiritual* g. Civil g. is that which a man does whilst acting under the influence of civil law; and by this g. and according to it, he is a citizen in the natural world. Moral g. is that which a man does whilst acting under the influence of the law of reason; and by this g., and according to it, he is a man. Spiritual g. is what a man does whilst acting under the influence of a spiritual law; and by this g., and according to it, he is a citizen in the spiritual world. These three kinds of g. follow in this order; spiritual g. is the supreme, moral g. is the middle, and civil g. is the ultimate, or lowest. *Doc. of Life*, 12. Natural g. is not really g., unless also it be made spiritual g. A.E. 619. Spiritual g. flows immediately into natural g., but mediately into natural truth. 3314, 4563. Celestial g. is g. in essence, and spiritual g. is g. in form. A.E. 283. When g. is so formed, that it may be intellectually perceived, it is called truth. 3049. G. has relation to the will, truth to the understanding; from the love of g. in the will, proceeds the love of truth in the understanding; from the love of truth proceeds the perception of truth; from the perception of truth, the thought of truth; hence comes the acknowledgment of truth, which is faith in its genuine sense. Dec. 36, 38. G. is to every one that which is the delight of his affection, and truth is that which is the pleasantness of his thought derived therefrom; from the delights of the affections and the pleasantnesses of the perceptions and thoughts is derived the vital heat. D.P. 195. G. is Lord and truth is minister, and when it is said of a Lord that he gave authority to a minister, or of g., that it gave authority to truth, in the internal sense, it is not s. that it ceded the dominion thereto, but that it applied itself, for in the internal sense a thing is perceived as it is in itself, but in the sense of the letter, it is expounded according to appearance, for g. always has the dominion, but applies itself that truth may be conjoined to it. 4977. G. is called Lord, and truth servant, before they are conjoined, but afterwards they are called brethren. 4267. G. is connate to man, of the middle heaven spiritual, and of the ultimate heaven, spiritual natural. H. and H. 31.

Good of **Charity**, the, like a flame from heaven, illuminates truths, and manifests the deformity of fallacies. 5510.

Good of **Infancy**, the, is not spiritual, but becomes so by the implantation of truth. H. and H. 277. Without the g. of i. and childhood derived from the Lord, man would be worse and more fierce than a wild beast. 3793.

Good of **Love**, the, is celestial good, which is that of love to the Lord; and the good of charity is spiritual good, which is that of love towards our neighbor. A.R. 89. The g. of l. is not good except so far as it is united to the true of wisdom; and the true of wisdom is not true, except so far as it is united to the g. of l. D.P. 2. The g. of l. does not operate any thing from itself, but through the truth of wisdom, nor does the truth of wisdom operate any thing from itself, but from the g. of l. A.R. 649. The g. of l. produces and disposes truths in order with man when he is regenerated, and afterwards holds them in order. 9846. The g. of l. and charity is entirely from the spiritual world. 5951.

Good of the **Natural Principle**, the, is the delight which is perceived from charity, or from friendship which is grounded therein. 2184.

Good of **Remains** are three kinds; viz., good of infancy, good of ignorance, and good of intelligence. 2280.

Good of **Truth**, the, when it is with any one, is the good of life, for truth becomes good by a life according to it; before that, truth is not good with any one, for truth, when it is only in the memory, and thence in the thought, is not good, but is made good when it comes into the will, and from thence into act, for the will itself transforms truth into good, which is manifest from this, that whatsoever man (homo) wills, this he calls good, and whatsoever he thinks, this he calls truth. A.E. 458.

Good Works s. at once charity, and faith in internals, and at the same time their effects in externals. A.R. 949. They who primarily respect goods of charity, which are g. w., are in reality in truths of doctrine, but not on the contrary. A.R. 82.

Goods and **Truths**, all, which are in the natural or external man, are conceived and born from the rational or internal. 3677. G. and t. that are not absolutely genuine, serve as a means of introduction of those which are; and the former are afterwards relinquished. 3665, 3690, 4145. G. and t. internal, are s. by oil and wine; but g. and t. external, by wheat and barley. A.E. 3276.

Gopher Wood (Gen. vi. 14) is a sulphureous wood, and s. concupiscences. 643.

Goshen, land of (Gen. xlvi. 28), s. the inmost of the natural mind. 5910.

Gospel, the, s. the coming of the Lord; and to preach the g. is to announce his coming. A.E. 613. G. is glad tidings, and the everlasting g. is the truths and goods of the Word revealed at the second advent of the Lord, which took place in the year 1757. A.R. 478.

Governments in the heavens are various; of one sort in the societies which constitute the Lord's heavenly kingdom, and of another sort in the societies which constitute the Lord's spiritual kingdom. G. in the Lord's celestial kingdom is called justice, and in his spiritual kingdom is called judgment. There are also g. in the hells. H. and H. 213, 214, 215, 220.

Governors (Gen. xli. 34) s. things common or general, because these are over particulars. 5290. G. of Israel (Judges v. 9) s. the truths of the church. A.E. 355. G. in heaven dwell in the midst of their society, more elevated than others. H. and H. 218.

Governs, the Lord, the human race as one man. D.P. 163. G. hell by opposites. D.P. 299.

Gourd, the, which God prepared to come up over the head of the prophet Jonah (iv. 6) s. the evil and self-love of the Jewish nation. A.E. 401. See *Wild Gourds.*

Grace s. the salvation of mankind. 598, 981. "To find g. in thine eyes," was a customary form of speech on every occasion of respectivity. 2157. To give g. (Gen. xxxix. 21) s. relief, for to give g. in temptations, is to comfort and relieve by hope. 5043. They who are principled in truth, and thence in good, implore only g.; whereas they who are principled in good, and thence in truth, implore mercy of the Lord. 2412. G. is applied to the spiritual, and mercy to the celestial. 598.

Grain s. interior goods and truths. 7112.

Granary, or **Barn**, s. heaven. A.E. 911.

Grand or **Greatest Man.** The three heavens together constitute the g. or g. m. 4330. All who are therein are in heaven, but all who are not, cor. with the various corruptions and diseases of the human body, and are in hell. 4225. The g. m. is heaven. In the head of the g. m. are those who are called celestial; from the breast even to the loins are those who are called spiritual; and in the feet are those who are called natural. A.E. 708. Angels know in what province of the g. m. they are, but spirits do not. 4800. Not

Grape

only these things in the body which are external and visible to the sight according to their functions and uses, cor. to the g. m., but also those things which are internal and not extant to the sight; consequently, both those things which are of the external man, and those which are of the internal man. The societies of spirits and angels to which the things of the external man cor., are in a great part from this earth; but those to which the things of the internal man cor., are for the most part from other earths. 4330.

Grape, the blood of the, s. spiritual celestial good, which is the name given to the divine in heaven proceeding from the Lord; wine is called the blood of g., inasmuch as each s. holy truth proceeding from the Lord, but wine is pred. of the spiritual church, and blood, of the celestial church; and this being the case, wine was enjoined in the holy supper. 5118. G., in a good sense, mean goodness, and in an opp. sense, evil. 2240, 5117. To eat sour g. s. to appropriate to one's self, the false of evil. A.E. 556. Wild g. (Isa. v. 1) s. evils opp. to the goods of charity. A.E. 375. G. and clusters s. works of charity, because they are the fruits of the vine and the vineyard, and by fruits, in the Word, are s. good works. A.R. 649. G. of gall and clusters of bitterness (Deut. xxxii. 21) s. evils from dire falses. A.E. 433. To gather g. s. to collect for use, especially such things as are serviceable to the understanding. (See Jer. vi. 9; Lev. xix. 10; xxvi. 5; Deut. xxvi. 7; xxiv. 21.) A.E. 919. To gather g. (Rev. xiv. 18) s. to bring forth the fruit, and to make an end, the same as to reap. A.R. 649. Gathering of g. s. the devastation of the church. A.E. 919. Gleaning g. when the vintage is done (Isa. xxiv. 13), s. the vastation of the church as to truth. A.E. 313.

Grape-Gatherers (Obad. ver. 5) den. falses which are not from evil; by those falses the goods and truths stored up by the Lord in man's interior natural principle, that is, remains, are not consumed, but by falses derived from evils, which steal truths and goods, and also apply them to confirm evils and falses by sinister applications. 5135. G.-g. s. falses; thieves s. evils which devastate the truths and goods of the church; but robbers s. falses as well as evils. (Obad. ver. 5.) A.E. 919.

Grass s. the scientific principle, for as green g. serves animals for support, so scientific truth serves men for spiritual nourishment. A.E. 507. G. is scientific truth, and flower of the field is spiritual truth. (Isa. xl. 5, 6.) A.E. 507. Green g., in the Word, s. that good and truth of the church, and of faith, which first springs up in the natural man. This is also s. by herb in the field. A.R. 401, 426. Green g. also s. that which is alive with man; and g. burnt up s. that which is dead with him. A.R. 401. G. and the pulse of the herb (Ps. xxxii. 2) s. what is most vile. 996. G. s. science from a spiritual origin, or that by which spiritual truth is confirmed; but reeds and rushes s. science from a sensual origin, or that by which the fallacies of the senses are confirmed. (Isa. xxv. 7.) This science, considered in itself, is only of the lowest natural degree, which may be justly called material and corporeal, in which there is little or no life. A.E. 627.

Grasshoppers s. the same as locusts: the false which vastates the extremes of the natural. 7643.

Grate of **Network** around the altar (Exod. xxvii. 4) s. the sensual external, or that which is the ultimate of life with man. 9726.

Gratis. Truths are given g. from the Lord to those who desire them. A.E. 840.

Gratuitous Gifts. In the heavens all the necessaries of life are given gratuitously. D.L.W. 334.

Grave (Ps. lxxxviii. 5) s. hell. A.E. 659. To come forth out of the g. (John v. 29) s. to come forth out of the material body, which is the case with every one immediately after death. A.E. 659. When the subject treated of is concerning those who are in truth from good, then by g. is s. the removal and rejection of the false from evil; and by burying, is understood exsuscitation and resurrection to life, as also regeneration; for with man, who is in truths from good, the false from evil is removed and rejected to hell, and himself, as to his interiors, which are of his spirit, arises and enters into a spiritual life of truth from good. A.E. 659. G. s. the hell where evils predominate, and from whence they arise; and destruction, the hell whence falses predominate and arise. (Ps. lxxxviii. 12.) A.E. 659. G. (John v. 28, 29) s. places in the inferior earth [of the spiritual world] where were reserved and kept by the Lord those who had previously lived a life of charity, and acknowledged his divine, and at the day of the last judgment were elevated into heaven. A.E. 899. "And the g. were opened, and many bodies of saints which slept arose and came out of the g. after his resurrection, and went into the holy city and appeared to many." (Matt. xxvii. 52, 53.) They appeared in testification, that although they had been detained in spiritual captivity, unto the Lord's coming, they were then liberated by him and introduced into heaven. 8018. See *Monuments, Sepulchres.*

Graven Image (Exod. xx. 4), which we are commanded not to make, s. that which is not from the Lord, but from the proper self-derived intelligence of man; that which is from high intellectual proprium is called g. i., and that which is from his voluntary proprium is called molten image; to adore them, is to love that above all things which proceeds from them. 8869. See *Idol, Image.*

Gravity, in the natural world, cor. to good in the spiritual world, and extension to truth; the reason is, because in heaven, whence cor. are, there is not given either g. or extension, because there is no space; there appear indeed things heavy and extended, but they are appearances arising from the states of good and of truth in the superior heaven. 5658.

Great is pred. of good, and, in an opp. sense, of evil. A.R. 582.

Great Day of God Almighty (Rev. xvi. 14) s. the coming of the Lord, and the establishment of a new church. A.R. 704.

Great Lights (luminaries) s. love and faith, and are called in Gen. i. 14, 15, 16, 17, sun, moon, and stars. 31.

Great Men (Rev. vi. 15) s. those who are in good, and, in an opp. sense, those who are in evil. A.R. 337. G. m. (Rev. vi. 25) s. internal goods, which are goods of the internal or spiritual man. A.E. 408. G. m. of Jerusalem, etc. (Jer. v. 5, 6), s. those who go before the rest in teaching truths and goods. A.E. 780.

Great and Fair. (Isa. v. 9.) The former term is pred. of goods and its affection, and the latter, of truth and its intelligence. A.E. 675.

Great and High. G., in the Word, is spoken of good, and h., of truth. A.R. 337, 898.

Great and Numerous. (Gen. xviii. 18.) G. is pred. of good, and n., of truth grounded in good. 2227.

Great and Wonderful (marvellous), when pred. of the Lord (Rev. xv. 1), have reference to his divine omnipotence, and his divine providence. For man, when he reflects on the greatness of the Lord, naturally looks to his divine omnipotence; and when he thinks of the Lord, as being w., he has respect to his divine providence. A.E. 927. G., in the Word, is said of such things as are of affection and love, and marvellous, of such things as are of thought and of faith. (Rev. xv. 1.) A.R. 656.

Greater and Lesser s. good and truth. 3296.

Greatest. In the g. and in the least things, the Divine is the same. D.L.W. 77–82.

Grecians s. the gentiles who are in falses. A.E. 242.

Greece, in the Word, s. the nations about to receive the truths of doctrine. A.E. 50. It s. the same as isles. A.R. 34. The king of G. rep. the same as the goat. (Dan. viii. 2, 14.) F. 66.

Greeks

Greeks, sons of the (Joel iii. 6), s. the falses of evil. Also the gentiles which are in falses. A.E. 242.

Green s. the scientific and sensual principle. 7691. G., or flourishing, s. what is alive. A.R. 401. A.E. 507. The natural sphere round about the Lord appears g., like the emerald. A.R. 232.

Grey hair s. the last of the church. 5550.

Grief, anxiety of heart or will. 5887, 8.

Grieve at Heart, to, has respect to love, and to repent, to wisdom. (Gen. vi. 6.) 590.

Grind, to collect and learn such things as are serviceable to faith. A.E. 163.

Grind to Powder, to (Exod. xxxii. 20), s. to form what is false from infernal pleasure, thus the infernal false. 10.464. See *Mill.*

Grinders, in the Word, are they who within the church are principled in truth from the affection of good; but in an opp. sense, they who within the church are principled in truth from the affection of evil. 4335.

Grizzled. See *Spotted.*

Grove s. intelligence. U.T. 200. G. have various significations according to the particular kinds of trees growing in them. The g. where olives grew, s. the celestial things of worship; the g. where vines grew, s. the spiritual things thereof; but the g. consisting of fig-trees, of cedars, of firs, of poplars, and of oak, s. various things appertaining to things celestial and spiritual. 2722.

Groves and **Images** in the **Open Air**. (Isa. xvii. 8.) G. s. religion from falses, and i. religion from evils of the false. A.E. 391.

Ground, in a universal sense, s. the church, and the man of the church in particular. 872. In the Word there is an accurate distinction made between g. and earth; by g. is everywhere s. the church, or somewhat relating to the church; hence also is derived the name of man, or Adam, which is g.; by earth (Gen. i.), is meant where the church is not, or where there is nothing relating to the church; earth only is named, because as yet there was no church, or regenerate man. In the second chapter mention is first made of g., because then there was a church. 566. When man is regenerate he is no longer called earth, but g., because celestial seeds are implanted therein; he is also compared to g., and is called g. in every part of the Word. 268. See *Earth.*

Grow, to, s. to be perfected. 2646.

Grub s. the falses and evils of the external man. 9331.

Guard. The literal sense of the Word is a g., to prevent the interior divine truths of its spiritual sense from being injured. A.R. 898. To g. (Gen. xli. 35) den. to store up. 5298. G. (Gen. xxxvii. 36) s. those things that minister. 4790.

Guile s. to deceive and seduce from a deliberate purpose. A.E. 866.

Guilty. He is g. who knows that a thing is evil, and yet does not restrain himself. 9075.

Gulf, great (Luke xvi. 26), is opp. and contrariety of the states of life. 9346.

Gum den. the truth of good. 5620.

Gutters (Gen. xxx. 38) s. good of truth in the natural principle. 4016.

Gyres. There are g. into which recent [newly deceased] spirits are obliged to be inaugurated, to the intent that they may be initiated into the consorts of others, so as both to speak and think together with them. The first introduction into g. is, that they may be accommodated together; the second is, that the thought and the speech may be in concord together; the third is, that they may mutually agree amongst each other as to the thoughts and as to the affections; the fourth is, that they may agree together in truths and goods. 5582.

H

H (the letter) involves infinity, because it is only an aspirate; hence it was added to the names of Abram and Sarai, that each might rep. the divine, or Jehovah. A.E. 38. U.T. 278. The letter H is the only one in the name of Jehovah which implies divinity, and s. I Am, or esse. 2010.

Habit. All that parents contract from actual use or h., is derived into their offspring. 3469.

Habitation (Gen. xxxvii. 39) s. life. 3600. The h. of holiness, s. the celestial kingdom; and the h. of honorableness, the spiritual kingdom. (Isa. lxiii. 15.) 3960. H. and footstool of Jehovah (Ps. cxxxii. 7) s. the spiritual and natural sense of the Word. A.E. 681. See *Tents* and *Tabernacles.*

Hadar rep. things of the spiritual church. 3268.

Hadoram (Gen. xxvii.) s. a ritual of the church called Eber. 1247.

Hadradrimmon (Zech. xii. 11) s. the love of honor, dominion, and power. A.R. 707.

Hagar (Gen. xvi.) s. the affection of sciences of the external man; also the life of the exterior or natural man. 1890.

Hagarenes, the (Ps. lxxxiii. 6), s. those who are principled in the externals of worship and doctrine. 2488.

Hai, or Ai, s. light der. from worldly things. 1453.

Hail s. the false principle destroying good and truth. A.R. 714. H. s. the false from evil in the exterior natural principle. 7677. H. of a talent weight (Rev. xvi. 21) s. direful and atrocious falses. A.R. 714. When divine truth from the heavens flows into the sphere which is about the evil, and appears as a storm, formed from the evil affections and thence the falses of their thoughts, then that influx is turned into various things, and into h. amongst those who from evils and falses think against the good and truth of heaven and the church, and vehemently oppose them. A.E. 704.

Hair is occasionally mentioned in the Word, and it therein s. the natural principle, because h. are excrescences in the ultimate parts of man, as also the natural principle is in his rational principle, and the interiors thereof. 3301. A h. in the Word s. the least of all things. D.P. 159. Grey h. (Gen. xlii. 38) s. the last of the church, for grey h., when the church is treated of, s. its last (or ultimate); this last (or ultimate) is also s. by grey h. in Isa. xlvi. 4. 5550. See *To Comb the Hair.*

Hairs of the **Head,** the **Beard,** and the **Feet.** (Isa. vii. 20.) H. of the h. s. the ultimate of wisdom, of the b., the ultimate of intelligence, and of the f., the ultimate of science. A.E. 569. H. of the h. s. the ultimates of love and wisdom; it was on that account that Samson's strength lay in his h. A.R. 47. H., when pred. of the Lord, as in Rev. i. 14, s. the divine good which is of love and the divine truth which is of wisdom, in the ultimates of the Word. A.R. 47. S.S. 35, 49.

Hairy Garment s. the truth of the natural principle. 3297, 3301.

Hairy Man (Gen. xxvii. 11) s. the quality of natural good respectively. 3527.

Half, the, and the double as to numbers in the world involve a similar signification. 5291.

133

Hallelujah

Hallelujah den. the joy of heart arising from the worship, confession, and celebration of the Lord, as the only God of heaven and earth. A.R. 803.

Hallowed be thy Name (Matt. vii. 9) s. to go to the Lord and to worship him. (See Rev. xv. 4; John xii. 28, etc.) The father is hallowed in the son, and by angels and men, through the son. (See also John xvii. 19–26.) A.R. 839. H. be t. n. is to be understood as relating to the father in his humanity, which is the father's name. U.T. 112.

Halo s. the sphere of divine good. 9407.

Halt. In the original tongue the h. is expressed by one expression, and he that halteth by another; and by h., in a proper sense, is s. they who are in natural good, into which spiritual truths cannot flow by reason of natural appearances and the fallacies of the senses; and in an opp. sense, they who are in no natural good, but in evil, which altogether hinders the influx of spiritual truth; whereas by one that h., in a proper sense, are s. they who are in natural good, into which common [or general] truths are admitted, but not particular and singular truths, by reason of ignorance; but in an opp. sense, they who are in evils, and thereby do not even admit common [or general] truths. 4302. See *Lame*.

Halt upon the Thigh, to (Gen. xxxii. 31), in the supreme sense, wherein the Lord is treated of, s. that truths as yet were not arranged into that order, that all together with good might enter celestial spiritual good. 4302. In the internal historical sense, it also s. that goods and truths were altogether destroyed with the posterity of Jacob. 4314.

Ham, the land of, s. the church destroyed. A.E. 448. The sons of H. are all those who are scientifically skilled in the knowledges of faith, and have no charity; or who are scientifically skilled in the interior knowledges of the Word, and in its very mysteries; or in the science of all things contained in the literal sense of the Word; or in the science of other truths; or in the knowledge of all the rituals of external worship; if they have no charity, they are the sons of H. 1162.

Hamathite s. variety of idolatry. 1204–5.

Hammer (Jer. xxiii. 29) s. the truth of faith in the ultimates. A.E. 411.

Hamor, the father of Schechem, rep. the truth of the church among the ancients. 4442. Also, the good of the church amongst the ancients. He also rep. life, for life is of good, as doctrine is of truth, which is Schechem, H. son; and because H. condescended to the external things of the sons of Jacob. 4471.

Hand s. ability, power, and thence confidence. 878. Under the h. (Gen. xli. 35) den. for disposal in all necessity, for h. s. power, and what is in the power of any one, is at his disposal. 5296. To lay the right hand upon any one, when pred. of the Lord (as in Matt. xvii. 6, 7; Rev. i. 17, etc.), s. to inspire him with his life. The ground and origin of this is, because the presence of the Lord with man is adjunction, and so conjunction by contiguity, and this contiguity is nearer and fuller, in proportion as man loves the Lord, that is, does his commandments. A.R. 55. "Put thine h. in thy bosom" (Exod. iv. 7), s. the appropriation of divine truth. 6965. "To place the h. upon the head" (2 Sam. xiii. 19), s. that there was not any intelligence. A.E. 577. H. upon the head (Jer. ii. 37) rep. shame. A.E. 577. H. s. the omnipotence of truth from good, and arm, the omnipotence of good by truth. (Ps. lxxxix. 21.) A.E. 684. H. s. power; arms, still greater power; and shoulders, all power. 1085. Communication is produced by the touch of the h., inasmuch as the life of the mind, and thence of the body, exerts itself in the arms, and by them in the h.; hence it is, that the Lord touched with his h. those whom he restored to life and healed. A.R. 55. To hold up the h. (Exod. xvii. 11) s. faith looking towards the Lord. 8608. The works of a man's h. s. the things proper to man, which are evils and falses; and the works of the h. of God s. the things proper to him, which are goods and truths. A.R. 457. When h. and feet are mentioned together, the former s. the interiors of man; and the latter his exteriors; or both, whatever is spiritual and natural in man. (Exod. xxx. 19.) 10.241. H. (Gen. xvi. 12) s. falses and truths combating. 1950. H. (Gen. xxvii. 16) s. the faculty of receiving. 3551. H. (Isa. xxxi. 7) s. man's proprium. 1551. See *Right Hand—Ten.*

Handful, an, s. the same as hands. 2177.

Handles s. the faculty of conjunction by good. 9611.

Handmaid s. the affection of things rational and scientific. 2567, 2657. H. (Gen. xxx. 3) s. the affirming medium of conjoining interior truths with natural or external truths. 3913. H. (Gen. xxxiii. 2) s. the affection of sciences and knowledges, and means serviceable to the conjunction of the external and internal man. 3913, 4344. H. (Gen. xxxiii. 7) s. scientifics of external things derived from the world, which are the most common or general of all. 4360.

Hand-Breadth s. conjunction there of truth from the divine. 9534.

Hand-Staff and **Spear** s. self-derived power and confidence. A.E. 357.

Hang, to (Gen. xli. 13), s. to reject. 5242. Hanging rep. the damnation of profanation. 5044.

Hannah, the prophecy of (1 Sam. ii.), treats concerning the deprivation of truth among those of the church who are in no affection of spiritual truth, and concerning the reception and illustration of those who are without the church, because in the affection of spiritual truth. A.E. 357.

Hanoch den. those who are in the truth of faith. 3242.

Happiness must be within joys and flow from them, and this is derived to every angel from the use he promotes. T.C.R. 735.

Happy and **Delightful**. All truth which is celestial, or what is produced from a celestial principle, is h. in the internal man, and d. in the external. 1470.

Haran (Gen. xi. 28) s. interior idolatrous worship. 1367. H. (Gen. xii. 5) s. an obscure state. 1431. H. (Gen. xxviii. 10) s. external good and truth. 3691. H. (Gen. xxix. 4) s. collateral good of a common stock. 3777.

Harbour, or **Haven**, the station where scientifics terminate and commence, or where there is a conclusion of truths from scientifics. 6384.

Hard Things (Gen. xlii. 20) s. non-conjunction, by reason of non-correspondence. 5511.

Harlot, an, s. the affection of falses, thus the church corrupted. 4522.

Harmony, spiritual, is the h. of the goods of love. 8003.

Harpers and **Musicians** (Rev. xviii. 22) have respect to spiritual affections. A.R. 792. Harps s. confessions of the Lord from spiritual goods and truths. A.R. 276. Harps and all stringed instruments have respect to spiritual affections, and wind instruments to celestial affections. A.R. 792. Sound or speech descending from the inferior heavens is sometimes heard like the sound of harps, not that they are playing upon harps, but because the voice of confession of the Lord from joy of heart, is so heard below. A.R. 616.

Harrow, to. To h. the earth s. to deposit in the memory. A.E. 374.

Harshness, the, of the literal sense of the Word when it passes towards heaven, becomes gentle and mild. 4002.

Hart s. the natural affection of truth. 6413.

Harvest s. the church with respect to divine truth; because from h. is procured corn of which bread is made; and by corn and bread is s. good of the church, and that is procured by means of truths. A.R. 645. H. (Joel iii. 13) s. the last state of the church, when the old church is devastated as to all good and truth. A.E. 911. A.R. 646. H. (Mark iv. 29) s. the increase of the church in general and particular. A.E. 911.

Hasten, to, or **Hastiness**, in the internal sense, does not den. what is quick, but what is certain, and also what is full, thus every event, for h. involves

Hatch

time, and in the spiritual world there is not time, but instead of time there is state, thus the haste of time has relation there to such a quality of state as cor., and the quality of state which cor. is, that there are several things which are together efficient, from which results a certain and full event. 5284. To h., pred. of Joseph (Gen. xliii. 30), s. what bursts forth from the inmost, for it follows, because his compassions were moved, whereby is s. mercy from love; when this bursts forth, it bursts forth from the inmost, and this at the first striking of the eye, or at the first moment of thought, therefore, by hastening, nothing else is here s. but from the inmost. 5600.

Hatch, to, **Eggs**. To perform uses. A.E. 236, 721.

Hatchet s. the intellectual proprium. 8942.

Hate, to (Gen. xxvii. 41), s. to be averse to. 3605.

Hatred is contrary to charity, and if it does not murder with the hand, yet it murders in mind, and by all possible methods, being only prevented from committing the outward act by outward restraints; wherefore all h. is blood. See Jer. i. 33, 34; and whereas h. is blood, all iniquity is blood; for h. is the fountain of all iniquities. Hosea iv. 2, 3, etc. 374.

Havilah (Gen. x. 28) s. a ritual of the church called Eber. 1245. The land of H. (Gen. ii. 11) s. the celestial man. 110.

Haven, or **Port**, or **Harbor**. H. den. the station where scientifics terminate and commence, or where there is a conclusion of truth from scientifics. 6384.

Hawk rep. the natural man separate from the spiritual man. A.V.C.R. 30.

Hazarmaveth (Gen. x. 26) s. a ritual of the worship of the church, called Eber. 1247.

Hazel-Tree (Gen. xxx. 37) s. natural truth. 4014.

Hazezon-Tamar, dwelling in, s. falses from which evils are derived. 1679.

Haza s. various religious principles and kinds of worship. 2863.

Hazor, the inhabitants of (Jer. xlix. 30), s. such as possess spiritual riches, which are the things of faith. 382. H. (Jer. xlix. 33) s. the knowledges of truth. A.E. 280.

He Is can only be pred. of Jehovah. 926.

Head, the, in the Word, s. intelligence and wisdom, and in a universal sense, the understanding of truth and the will of good, but in a bad sense, as in Rev. xiii. 3, it s. only science, and sometimes it s. insanity arising from mere falses. A.E. 785. The h. rep. things celestial and spiritual. 2162. The h. s. wisdom originating in love. A.R. 823. The h. cor. to the third heaven. A.E. 65. The h. when mentioned concerning the Lord, means the divine in first principles. A.E. 66. Also, the divine love of the divine wisdom. A.R. 47. Above the h. in heaven, are the celestial men of the most ancient church. 1115. Those who are in the h. in the grand man, which is heaven, are all in good above the rest; for they are in love, peace, innocence, wisdom, knowledge, etc., and consequently, in joy and happiness; these flow into the h., and into those things which are of the h. with man, and cor. to them. H. and H. 96. The h. of a man s. the all of his life; and the all of man's life has relation to love and wisdom. A.R. 47, 534, 565.

Heads, the seven, of the dragon, and of the beast rising out of the sea (Rev. xii. 3, and xiii. 3), s. insanity arising from mere falses. A.R. 568, 576.

Healing, reformation by truth derived by good. A.E. 283.

Healing in his **Wings** (Mal. iii. 20) s. reformation by divine truth from good. A.E. 284.

Heap, a (Gen. xxxi. 46), s. good, because formerly, before they built altars, they made h., and ate together upon them, as a testimony that they were joined together in love. 4192. To h. together (Gen. xli. 49) den. to multiply. 5345.

Hear, to, s. reception and perception, thence also influx, for the things which are received and perceived, flow in. 9926. To h. (Rev. ix. 21) s. the perception which is from the will of good, and thence obedience, because speech enters the ear together with sound; and the truths of the speech enter the understanding and thought, and the sounds, the will, and thence the affection. This originates from the spiritual world. A.E. 588. A.R. 87. To h. a voice, when pred. of the Lord (as in Gen. xxi. 17), s. to bring help. 2691. To h. a voice from heaven (Rev. xiv. 13) s. a prediction from the Lord. A.R. 639. Hearing the words of the prophecy of this book (Rev. xxii. 18) s. to read and to know the truths of doctrine. A.R. 957.

Hearken, to, **to my voice** (Gen. xxvi. 5), being pred. of the Lord, s. to unite the divine essence to the human by temptations. 3381. To h. to father and mother (Gen. xxviii. 7) s. obedience from affection. 3684. To h. (Gen. xxx. 22) s. providence. 3966. See *Obedience.*

Heart, the, cor. to love or charity in the will, which has relation to good, or to evil, according to the pred. of the subject. 2525. U.T. 705. A great h. (Dan. viii. 8) s. the dominion of that false principle of doctrine, called salvation by faith alone. A.E. 418. The h. s. divine celestial love, and the lungs, divine spiritual love. 3858. The h. cor. to the celestial kingdom of the Lord, and the lungs to his spiritual kingdom. H. and H. 95. A.C. 170, 3635.

Heart and **Soul**, when pred. of the Lord, in the Word, as in Jer. xxxii. 41, have relation to the divine good of his love, or mercy, and to the divine truth, which is of faith amongst men. 9050.

Heat (Rev. xvi. 9) s. the concupiscences of evils which are contained in self-love and the delights thereof. A.R. 692. H. does not exist in love itself, but from it in the will, and thence in the body. D.L.W. 95. Spiritual h. in its bosom contains all the infinities of the Lord's love. U.T. 365. Spiritual h. is truly h., which animates the bodies of the angels with warmth, and at the same time their interiors with love. 6032, 9383. Spiritual h. does not flow into man by three degrees, except so far as he shuns evils as sins and looks up to the Lord. D.L.W. 242. Spiritual h. kindles the will, and produces love, therein. A.R. 867. Infernal h., or fire, is changed into intense cold, by any influx of h. from heaven. H. and H. 572.

Heat of the **Sun** (Rev. vii. 16) s. concupiscences to evil. A.R. 382.

Heat and **Light**, in the Word, s. love and wisdom. H. and H. 155, 488. H. and l. from the sun of heaven flow into the will and understanding of man, and produce the good of love and the truth of wisdom. l. 7. The l. of heaven, in its essence, is divine truth, and the h. of heaven, in its essence, is divine good, both proceeding from the Lord, as the sun there. A.R. 611. Natural h. and l. serve as a clothing and support to spiritual h. and l., whereby they may be conveyed to man. U.T. 75. Spiritual l. from the Lord discovers the thoughts which are of the understanding and faith, and spiritual h. discovers the affections which are of the will and love, and spiritual l. together with spiritual h. discovers the intentions or endeavors. A.R. 867.

Heathen, the time of the (Ezek. xxx. 3), s. the h., or wickedness. 488.

Heathenism, of the Christian world, is where the Word is taken away from the people, and replaced by human decissions. A.Cr. 22.

Heave Offering (Exod. xxix. 27) s. the divine celestial which is of the Lord alone, perceived in heaven and the church. 10.093.

Heaven is the love of the Lord, and the love of our neighbor. N.J.D. 237. H. is no other than the divine flowing from the divine. 10.098. H., before the advent of the Lord, was not distinguished into three h., but was one. 8054. H. is distinguished generally into two kingdoms, specifically into three h., and particularly into innumerable societies. H., as to all its cor., could in nowise exist, unless from the inhabitants of many earths. 6698. H. in the whole complex constitutes one man, and is therefore called the grand, or greatest man, and that from the divine humanity of the Lord. H. and H. 78, 86. H. is arranged into innumerable societies, all connected with each

Heaven

other, according to the differences of the affections, which are of love in general and in particular; each society is one species of affection, and there they dwell distinctly, according to the propinquities, and affinities of that species of affection, and they who are in the nearest state of propinquity in the same house; therefore cohabitation, when pred. of a married pair in a spiritual sense, s. conjunction by love. A.R. 883. H. is not confined to any particular place, but is everywhere, with every one, where the divine being is present in charity and faith. 8931. H. is in man, and is only so far an external place of abode, as it is an internal state of mind. 3884, 10.367. The Lord appears in h., both as the sun, and as the moon; as the sun, to those who are in the celestial kingdom; and the moon, to those who are in the spiritual kingdom. 1053, 7078, 7173, 7270, 8812, 10.809. In h., no other divinity is perceived, but the divine human. 6475, 9267, 9303, 10.078. In h. there appear mountains, hills, rocks, valleys, and different kinds of earth, altogether like what we see here. 10.608. In h. there is a state of morning and evening, but not of night. 10.604. In h. there are marriages, as well as upon earth. H. and H. 366, 380. In h. there are administrations, offices, judicial proceedings both in greater and lesser cases, also mechanical arts and employments. C.S.L. 207. There are also writings and books in heaven. H. and H. 258. There is a h., in which are atmospheres of different colors, where the universal aura glitters as if it consisted of gold, silver, pearls, precious stones, of flowers in their least forms, and of innumerable things besides. 4528. There are two things by which h. is shut to the men of the church; the one is a denial of the Lord's divine, and the other is a denial of the sanctity of the Word. G.E.D. p. 36. H. is said to be opened, when the interior sight, which is of the spirit of man is opened. H. and H. 171. They who receive h. in the world, come into h. after death. 10.717. When man is in h., he is without all solitude, restlessness, and anxiety, and thence he is in a state of blessedness. 8890. Few enter into h. immediately after death. 8029. All who come into h., return into their vernal youth, and into the powers appertaining to that age, and thus continue to eternity. C.S.L. 44. They who are not in the life of h., cannot bear the light of h., which is divine truth proceeding from the Lord there as the sun, much less can they bear the heat of h., which is divine love. A.R. 157. H. (Rev. xix. 14) s. the new christian church; the reason why that h. is meant, is because it is the new h. treated of in the Apocalypse. A.R. 826. H. open (Rev. xix. 11) s. a revelation from the Lord, and consequent manifestation. A.R. 820. H. of h. which were of old (Ps. lxviii. 32) s. the wisdom of the most ancient church. 219. The lowest or first h., in the grand man, forms the inferior parts down to the feet, and also the arms to the fingers; for the arms and hands are the extremities of the body, though at the sides; hence also proceeds the distinction of three h. H. and H. 65. In the ultimate or first h., the Lord does not appear as a sun, nor as a moon, but only as light, which light far exceeds the light of the world. 6832. The ultimate h. consists of those who are in the obedience of doing the truths and goods which are commanded in the Word, or in the doctrine of the church in which they were born, or which they have received from a master, or governor, and according to which they have conscientiously acted. A.E. 443. The first h. which perished, was collected out of the whole human race, from the commencement of the christian church till the last judgment. L.J. 29. The middle or second h. forms the breast, down to the loins and knees. H. and H. 65. The supreme or third h. in the grand man, forms the head to the neck. H. and H. 65. The inmost h. is the most perfect; the middle less perfect; and the first, or lowest, the least perfect. H. and H. 211. The new h. was formed of such christians as acknowledged the divinity of the Lord in his human, and at the same time, had repented of their evil works. From this

Heavens

h. will descend the new church, which is the New Jerusalem. Preface to A.R. The new h. was formed of those who lived after the Lord's first coming; this heaven is also distinguished into three h. A.R. 612, 876.

Heaven and **Earth** s. in general, the internal and external church; and in particular, the internal and external, or the spiritual and the natural man. A.E. 751. A.C. 82. H. and e. in scripture, s. the h. and e. which angels and spirits inhabit, and in a spiritual sense, the church amongst men. H. and H. 221-227. A.E. 304. H. and e. (Ps. lxxxix. 13.) s. the superior and inferior h., also the church internal and external; the world and its fulness, h. and the church in general, as to good and truth. A.E. 60. H. and the e. finished, and all the host of them (Gen. ii. 1) s. that man was rendered so far spiritual, as to become the sixth day. 82. H. and the e. s. all the interiors of the church; and sea and dry land, all its exteriors. (Hag. ii. 6.) A.E. 400. In h., upon e., and under the e. (Rev. v. 3), s. the three h. in orderly succession, from the highest to the lowest. A.E. 304.

Heavenly Marriage is between the good of the natural man and the truth of the spiritual man. 3952.

Heavens, the, are things celestial and spiritual, and consequently, inmost things, both of the Lord's kingdom in the h. and in the earths, or in the church, and also with every individual man, who is a kingdom of the Lord, or a church, consequently, the h. den. likewise, all things appertaining to love and charity, and faith grounded therein; as also, all things appertaining to internal worship; and in like manner, all things appertaining to the internal sense of the Word; all these things are h., and are called, "The throne of the Lord." 2162. The three h. are distinguished according to the degrees of wisdom and love. They who are in the ultimate h. are in the love of knowing truths and goods, they who are in the middle h. are in the love of understanding them, and they who are in the supreme h. are in the love of being wise. I. 16. The first h. is the abode of good spirits, the second is the abode of angelic spirits, and the third is the abode of angels. 459. There are three h. in which the Lord appears as the moon, superior, middle, and inferior; or interior, middle, and exterior; but nevertheless, all in those h. are natural, for the natural is distinguished into three degrees, like as the spiritual. A.E. 708. The h. are expanses one above another, and everywhere there is earth under the feet. A.R. 260. Those things which are done in the h., are rep. in the world of spirits, by such like forms, as appear in the world. 4043. In the h., as well as on earth, there is the Word, temples, preachings, and the priesthood. A.R. 533. The superior h. and the inferior act as one by influx. A.R. 286. The ultimate h. are courts, and the interior h. are the house and temple of Jehovah. 9741. In the ultimate h. all those things which are seen and heard are rep. of such things as are thought and spoken by the angels in the superior h. 4043, 10.126.

Heavens, the ancient, were formed before the Lord's first coming, and are above the new h.; all of which acknowledge the Lord alone to be the God of h. and earth. The h. communicate with the new h., by influx. A.R. 612, 617. The christian h. is below the ancient h.; into this h. from the time of the Lord's abode in the world, were admitted those who worshipped one God under three persons, and had not at the same time an idea of three Gods; and this by reason that a trinity of persons was received throughout the whole christian world; but they who entertained no other idea of the Lord's humanity than as of the humanity of another man, could not receive the faith of the New Jerusalem, which is, that the Lord is the only God in whom there is a trinity; these latter, therefore, were separated and removed after the last judgment. A.R. Preface.

Heavens, imaginary. It was permitted those who had lived in externals like christians, but in internals were devils, to form themselves by fantasies, in the world of spirits, as it were h. in great abundance; these fictitious and imaginary h. before the last judgment were like dark clouds between the sun and the earth, consequently, between the Lord and the men of the church, therefore these h. were dispersed, and after the last judgment it was not allowable to form to themselves such h., but then every one was bound to the society to which he belonged. A.R. 791, 804, 865.

Heavens, the former, which passed away (Rev. xxi. 1) s. the societies of those in the spiritual world who were only in external or apparent good. A.E. 675.

Heavens and **Hells**, the, are entirely separated, and as inversely situated with respect to each other as antipodes; therefore evils and falses cannot reach to the h. (see Rev. xviii. 5), but yet when evils and falses are multiplied beyond the degrees of opposition, and thence beyond a certain equal measure, the h. are infested, and unless the Lord then defends the h., which is done by stronger influx from himself, the h. suffer violence, and when this arrives at its height, he then executes the last judgment, and they are delivered. A.R. 761.

Heavy. Falses are h. from the evil within them. 8279.

Hebrew, the. This term is used in the word when any thing of service is s., of whatever nature it be; hence Abraham, in one passage only, is called the H., viz., Gen. xiv. because he rep. the Lord's interior man, to which is adjoined the internal or divine man, and the interior man is such, that it serves the internal or divine man. 1702.

Hebrew Boy, a (Gen. xli. 12), s. the guiltless principle of the church, for b. s. a guiltless principle, and H., one who is of the church. 5236.

Hebrew Church, the, was a church which succeeded that called Noah, and exercised a sort of holy worship which consisted in external rites; this church, in process of time, was varoiusly deformed, and its external worship was changed into idolatrous worship, and then was its consummation. 2243.

Hebron rep. the Lord's spiritual church in the land of Canaan. 2909. H. rep. the church as to good. 2909.

Hedge (Matt. xxi. 33) s. preservation from falses of evil which are from hell. 922. A h. s. the same as a wall, which see.

Heel, the, s. natural things of the lowest order. 259, 2162, 3304. The h. which the serpent should bruise (Gen. iii. 15) s. the lowest natural principle, or the corporeal. 250–255. H. (Gen. iii. 15) s. the literal or ultimate sense of the Word. A.E. 768. To lift up the h. against the Lord (Ps. xli. 10) s. to pervert the literal sense of the Word even unto the negation of the Lord, and to the falsification of every truth. Since the Word is divine truth, therefore, also this before the Lord is in image as a divine man; and its ultimate sense cor. to the h., and as this was perverted by the Jews by application thereof to their false traditions, therefore, this is s. by lifting up the h. against the Lord. A.E. 617. Beneath the h. of the foot at a great depth are situated the hells of the most deceitful, and of the modern Antediluvians. 2754. Beneath the h. backwards is the hell of those who are spiritual murderers and who fascinate to murder. 4951. Under the h. of the right foot is the hell where they inhabit who have taken delight in cruelty, and at the same time in adulteries, and have perceived therein the greatest satisfaction of their lives. 824.

Heifer, the, whereby labor has not been done (Deut. xxi. 3) s. the innocence of the external man, which is in ignorance. 4503. The red h. (Num. xix.) s. unclean truth of the natural principle, which was made clean by burnings, and also by such things as are s. by cedar-wood, hyssop, and double-dyed scarlet; water therefrom rep. the means of purification. 5198. H., ram, and she-goat, each three years old (Gen. xv. 9), s. those things which are representative of the celestial things of the church; a h. of celestial things exterior, a she-goat of celestial things interior, and a ram of celestial things spiritual, the being three years old, was to imply all things appertaining to the church as to times and states. 1821. H., in a bad sense, den. falses. 5202.

Height s. the good and truth of the church in every degree. A.R. 907. A.C. 9489.

Heir, an (Jer. xlix. 1), s. the good of truth. A.E. 435. To become an h., or to inherit, s. life eternal in the Lord's kingdom, or to be conjoined to the Lord. 1799. A.R. 890. H. (Gen. xv. 4) s. those who are principled in love. 1804. H. s. those who are in truths originating in good from the Lord. A.E. 1034.

Hell (Jonah ii. 3) s. the earth below. 247. H. cannot be known, unless the nature of evil is known. 7181, 4997. The diabolical h. cor. by opposition to the celestial kingdom; and the satanic h., by opposition to the spiritual kingdom. D.L.W. 273. As there is the same number of societies in h., as in heaven, so there are as many different h.; for as every society in heaven is heaven in a lesser form, so every society in h. is h. in a lesser form, and as in the general division, there are three heavens, so also three h., the lowest of which is respectively opp. to the inmost or third heaven; the middle h., to the middle or second heaven; and the uppermost, to the first or lowest heaven. H. and H. 542. H. as well as heaven is necessarily under the Lord's government. A.R. 62. H. and H. 536. Every one in h. is tormented by his love and its concupiscences. A.R. 864. All that are in h. speak only the false from evil. 1695, 7357. The h. are eternal workhouses or prisons. A.R. 153. The worst h. are in the west, they operate on the voluntary principle and all the affections appertaining thereto. 8593. The h. in their complex, or the infernals collectively, are called the devil and satan. 694, 968.

Helmet of Salvation (Isa. lix. 17) s. divine truth from divine good by which salvation is effected. A.E. 557. See *Shield*.

Help-meet for him, a, or a **help as before him** (Gen. ii. 18), s. proprium, but whereas the man of the church, who is here treated of, was good in temper or disposition, such a proprium was granted him, that it appeared like his own, wherefore it is called a help, as it were, before him [or with him]. 140.

Hem, Skirt, or **Border** s. the extremes, or the natural principle. 9917.

Hemispheres of the brain. Exp. D.L.W. 384.

Hemlock s. unpleasantness. A.E. 522. See *Bitter*.

Hemorrhoids s. truth defiled by evil of life. A.E. 700, 817.

Herb, every, in the Word, s. some species of scientifics. 7626. H. bearing seed (Gen. i. 29) s. every truth which regards use. 57. Green h. (Gen. i. 30) food for the natural man. 59. H. of the earth s. the truth of the church. 7571. H. of the field (Gen. iii. 18), by eating it is s. that man should live as a beast. (See also Dan. iv. 25.) 272, 274. H. of the field s. spiritual truth. A.E. 507.

Herd (Gen. xxxii. 7) den. exterior or natural good, and also things not good. 2566, 3408. See *Flocks, Animals*.

Hereditary Evil did not come from the first man upon all who live at this day, according to the common idea; but successively, from one generation to another. 313. All evils which man derives from his parents which are called h., remain in his natural and sensual man, but not in his spiritual man, from thence it is, that the natural man (homo) and the extremely sensual are opp. to the spiritual man; for the spiritual man from infancy is closed, and is only opened and formed by divine truths received in the understanding and will, and in proportion to the quality and extent of such opening and formation, the evils of the natural and sensual principle of man are removed, and instead of them, goods are implanted. A.E. 543.

Hereditary Principles

H. e. are those of the love of self and of the world. 694, 5660. Man does not suffer punishment in the other life on account of h. e., inasmuch as he is not in fault, but for his actual sins. 966.

Hereditary Principles. There are two h. p. in man; one derived from the father, the other from the mother, that from the mother is somewhat corporeal, which is dispersed during regeneration, but what man derives from the father remains to eternity. 1414.

Heresies are ever attendant upon the true church, and the ground of h., is, the being intent upon some particular article of faith. 362, 363. Innumerable h. arise from the literal sense of the Word being separated from its internal sense. 10.402.

Heretic. One who confirms himself in falses. D.P. 318.

Heritage of **Esau** (Matt. i. 3) s. falses from evils, and dragons of the wilderness, mere falsifications from which they are derived. A.E. 750.

Heritage of **Jacob**, to feed on the (Isa. lviii. 13, 14), s. the tranquillity and external delight of the celestial man. 85.

Hermon, dew of, s. divine truth. A.E. 375.

Hero. Those who excel in ingenuity and subtlety in adulterating the truths of the Word. A.E. 618.

Heshbon (Jer. xlix. 3) s. the fructification of truth in the natural man. A.E. 435.

Heth (Gen. x. 15) s. the exterior knowledges of things celestial. 1199. Daughters of H. (Gen. xxvii. 46) s. affections of truth from a ground not genuine, here the affections of natural truth, because spoken of Jacob. 3620, 3688. Sons of H. (Gen. xxiii. 7) s. those who were of the new spiritual church. 2928.

Hewers of **Wood** (Josh. ix. 23, 27) in the Jewish church rep. those who place righteousness and merit in good works, and have thus attributed to themselves the effective power of salvation. 1110. Those who extirpate good. (Jer. xlvi. 22.) A.E. 1145. See *Drawers of Water.*

Hiddekel, the river (Gen. ii. 14), s. reason, or the clearness and perspicuity of reason. 118.

Hidden Things. The science of the Egyptians, and especially the science of cor., are called the h. t. of gold and silver, and desirable things. (Dan. xi. 42.) A.E. 654.

Hide, to, from the face of **Jehovah God** (Gen. iii. 8) s. to be afraid of the dictate of, or impression, as is usual with those who are conscious of evil. A.R. 222. To h. themselves in the dens and in the rocks of the mountains (Rev. vi. 15) s. to be in evils and in falses of evil, because they who in the sight of the world have pretended to be in the good of love, and yet were in evil, after death h. themselves in dens; and they who have pretended that they were in truths of faith, and yet were in falses of evil, h. themselves in rocks in the mountains; the entrances appear like holes in the earth, and fissures in mountains, into which they crawl like serpents, and h. themselves there. A.R. 338. It is sometimes said in the Word, that the Lord h. his face from man, on account of his iniquities and sins, when nevertheless he never does so, inasmuch as he is divine love and mercy itself, and wills the salvation of all, wherefore he is present with all, even the most wicked, thereby giving them the liberty of receiving him; the above therefore is only an apparent truth. A.E. 412.

Hieroglyphics. Whereas the ancient churches where rep., therefore the men of those churches made to themselves sculptured things and images of various kinds, which rep. and thence s. things heavenly, and the ancients were delighted with them on account of their s.; wherefore when they looked upon those things they were reminded of the heavenly things which they rep., and inasmuch as they were such as appertained to their religion, they used them in worship; hence came the use of groves and high places, and also of sculptured, molten, and painted figures, which they placed either in groves, or upon mountains, or in temples, or in their houses; hence in Egypt, where the science of rep., which is the same with the science of cor., flourished, they had images, idols, and sculptured things, whence also came their h. A.E. 827. See *Correspondences, Egypt.*

High s. what is inward, also heaven. D.L.W. 103. A.C. 1735, 2148, 8153. See *Altitude.*

Higgaion. See *Music.*

High Places of the **Earth**, to ride on the (Isa. lviii. 13, 14), s. the peace and internal felicity of the celestial man. 85.

High-Priest. H.-p. has respect to divine good. 6148.

High-Way, a, for the **Remains** of the **People** left from **Assyria** (Isa. xi. 16) s. a disposing into order. 842.

Highest den. the inmost, because interior things, with man who is in space, appear as superior things, and exterior things as inferior; but when the idea of space is put off, as is the case in heaven, and also in the interior thought of man, then is put off the idea of what is high and deep, for height and depth come from the idea of space; yea, in the interior heaven neither is there the idea of things interior and things exterior, because to this idea there also adheres somewhat of space, but there is the idea of more perfect or imperfect state, for interior things are in a more perfect state than exterior things, because interior things are nearer to what is divine, and exterior things are more remote thence; this is the reason why what is highest (5146) s. what is inmost. D.L.W. 103.

Hills s. the good of charity. 6435, 10.438.

Hin den. the quantum of conjunction. 10.262.

Hind, a (Gen. xlix. 21), s. the affection of natural truth. 3928.

Hinnom, the valley of, den. hell, and also the profanation of truth and goodness. 1292. See *Tophet.*

Hiram, the Adullamite (Gen. xxxviii. 12), s. the false. 4854.

Hiram (1 Kings x. 22) s. the nations without the church, amongst whom are the knowledge of good and truth. A.E. 514.

Hire (Gen. xxx. 33), pred. of the Lord, s. his proprium; viz., what was acquired from his own proper ability. 3999.

Hirelings. They who speak truth and do good, not from spiritual, but mere natural affection, and think continually concerning a reward, were rep. by h. in the Israelitish church. (See Exod. xii. 43, 45; Deut. xxiv. 14, 15; Mal. xxxv., etc.) They are also mentioned among the poor, the needy, the strangers, the fatherless, and the widows; they are also in the lowest heavens, and are there servants. They also are called h., who do not think of a reward in heaven, but in this world, on account of their good actions, but these are infernal. (See John x. 11, 13; Jer. xlvi. 20, 21, etc.; Isa. xvi. 14; xxi. 16.) A.E. 695.

Historical Faith, whereby the sick were healed. A.E. 815.

Historical Parts of the **Word** are more obscure to man, with respect to the interior arcana contained therein, than the prophetical parts, by reason, that the mind is engaged in viewing and considering the historical subjects. 2176. All things contained in the h. p. of the W. are h. true, except what is written previous to the 12th chapter of Genesis; or rather to the time of Eber, which contains h. circumstances not literally true, but only rep. of truths, being things reduced to an h. form for that purpose. But from the 12th chapter of Genesis, h. truths and rep. are both united in the literal sense. 1401, 1540, 2607. Arcana are so delivered, in the h. of the W., in order that the W. may be read with delight, even by children, and the simple, to the intent that whilst they are in holy delight arising from the h.

sense, their attendant angels may be in the sanctity of the internal sense, which sense is adequate to angelic intelligence, whilst the external sense is adequate to human intelligence; hence the consociation of man with the angels, which man is altogether ignorant of, only he perceives thence a certain principle of delight, wherein is a principle of holiness. 3982. See *Angel.*

History. The custom of the ancients, in speaking and writing, was such, that they marked out times and names, and thence framed a h. resembling a true one. 755.

Hittite, in a good sense, s. the spiritual church, or the truth of the church; for the H. were among the upright Gentiles, who were in the land of Canaan. 2913, 3470. H. s. what is false, and Amorite what is evil. (Ezek. xvi. 45.) 289. H., Perizzite, and Rephaim (Gen. xv. 20), s. persuasions of the false. 1867.

Hivites and **Jebusites.** The former rep. those who were in idolatry, but in which there was something of good, and the latter, those who were in idolatry, but in which there was nothing of good. 6360.

Hoar Frost, in the Word, s. truth in the form of good. 8459.

Hobab, or **Jethro,** den. good of the church. 6827.

Hogs. Swine cor. to the life of avarice and its delight. 1742.

Hollanders. Des. 4630, 5573.

Hold [den, or dungeon] (Rev. xviii. 2) s. hell, because they who are there are in confinement. A.R. 757.

Hole and **Cleft** of a **Rock,** in scripture, s. the obscurity and false of faith. 10.582. The infernal spirits creep into h. and c. when the divine sphere about an angel touches them. H. and H. 488. A.R. 338.

Holiness and **Justice** are the celestial principle of faith, uprightness and judgment are the spiritual principle thence derived. (Ps. xv. 1, 2.) 612.

Hollow of the **Thigh** den. where there is conjunction of conjugial love. "And the h. of Jacob's t. was out of joint in his wrestling with him" (Gen. xxxii. 25), s. that as yet, truth had not ability to conjoin itself altogether to good, for to be out of joint den. that as yet truths were not arranged in that order, that they altogether with good could enter celestial spiritual good. 4277, 4278.

Holon, Jahzah, Mephaath, Dibon, Nebo, Bethgamul, Bethdiblathaim, Kiriathaim, Beth-meon, Kerioth, Bozrah (Jer. xlviii. 21–26), s. the kinds of the false principle, whereby they who are called Moab and Ammon adulterate goodness and extinguish truths, 2468.

Holy is pred. concerning divine truth, hence the church is called a sanctuary, for the Latin word for h. is sanctus, from which sanctuary is derived. A.E. 204. A.R. 666. H. s. the good which reigns in the middle heaven. 9680.

Holy of Holies, the, rep. the very essential divine good and truth in the Lord's divine human, whereunto truth from the human was conjoined; the same thing was s. by the golden altar, the table for the shewbread, the candlestick, the propitiatory, the ark, and most intimately by the testimony. 3210. The glorification of the Lord's humanity even till it became the divine good which is Jehovah, is des. in the internal sense, by the process of expiation, when Aaron entered into the h. of h., within the veil (Exod. xvi.), and in the respective sense, by the same process is des., the regeneration of man, even unto celestial good, which is the good of the inmost heaven. 9670. See *Veil.*

Holy and **Just.** They are called h., who are in the Lord's spiritual kingdom, and they are called j., who are in his celestial kingdom. A.E. 325. H. is pred. of what is true, and righteous or just, or what is good. A.R. 173.

Holy and **True.** (Rev. iii. 7.) The Lord is called h., because all charity is derived from him, and t., because all faith is from him also. A.E. 204.

Holy City New Jerusalem coming down from God out of heaven (Rev. xxi. 2) s. a new church to be established by the Lord at the end of the former church. A.R. 879, 880.

Holy Ghost. See *Holy Spirit.*

Holy Jerusalem, the, s. the Lord's kingdom in the heavens and on the earths. 1298.

Holy One of **Israel,** the Lord as to divine good and truth. A.E. 585.

Holy Spirit, the, is divine truth, and also divine virtue and operation proceeding from one God in whom is a divine trinity, consequently, proceeding from the Lord God the Saviour. U.T. 139. The divine virtue and operation s. by the h. s., consists in general, in reformation and regeneration, and in proportion as these are effected, in renovation, vivification, sanctification, and justification; and, in proportion as these are effected, in purification from evils, remission of sins, and, finally, salvation. U.T. 142. The divine virtue and operation s. by the mission of the h. s., with the clergy in particular, consists in illumination and instruction. U.T. 146. H. s., holy divine, or divine proceeding, is not a person by himself, because the Lord is omnipresent. A.R. 666, 962. The h. s. is the divine presence of the Lord. A.R. 949. The h. s. proceeds from the divinity in the Lord, through his glorified humanity, which is the divine humanity, comparatively, as all activity proceeds from the soul through the body in man. A.R. 962. The sin against the h. s. is the denying the Lord's divinity and the sanctity of the Word, and confirming these to the end of life. D.P. 98, 99. See *Blasphemy.*

Holy Supper, the, is the primary part of external worship. 2811.

Homer, or **Measure,** den. a sufficient quantity. 8468.

Homicides s. the extinction of the understanding of truth, and the perception of good. A.E. 589.

Honesty and **Decorum.** H. is the complex of all moral virtues, and d. is the form thereof. 2915.

Honey s. the delight which is derived from good and truth, or from the affection thereof, and specifically the external delight, thus the delight of the exterior natural principle; inasmuch as this latter delight is of such a nature, that it comes from the world through the things of sense, therefore the use of h. was forbidden in the meat offerings. H. den. delight, because it is sweet, and every thing sweet in the natural world cor. to what is delightful and pleasant in the spiritual; the reason why it is said the delight thereof, viz., the delight of truth derived from good in the exterior natural principle, is, because every truth, and especially every truth of good, has its delight, but a delight arising from the affection of good and truth, and from consequent use. 5620. H. (Deut. xxxii. 13) s. the pleasantness and delight derived from the affections of knowing and learning goods and truths celestial and spiritual. 5620. H. (Isa. vii. 14, 15) s. that which is derived from the celestial principle of the Lord. 2184. H. (Ezek. iii. 3) den. the delight of truth divine as to the external sense; for truth divine as the Word in the external form, or in the literal sense, is delightful, because it suffers itself to be explained by interpretations in every one's favor; but not so the internal sense, which is therefore s. by the bitter taste, for this sense discovers man's interiors. The reason why the external sense is delightful, is, as was said, because the things appertaining to that sense, may be explained in every one's favor, they being only common [or general] truths, and such is the quality of common [or general] truths before they are qualified by particulars, and these by singulars. It is also delightful, because it is natural, and the spiritual principle conceals itself deep within; it must likewise be delightful to the intent, that man may receive, that is, that he may be introduced, and not deterred at the threshold. 5620.

Honey and Oil

Honey and **Oil.** (Ezek. xvi. 3.) H. s. good natural or of the external man; and o., spiritual good, or good of the internal man. A.E. 617. See *Milk and Honey.*

Honey-Comb, the, and the **Broiled Fish,** which the Lord ate with his disciples after his resurrection, s. the external sense of the Word; the fish, as to the truth thereof, and the h.-c., as to its pleasantness. 5620.

Honor s. the good of love. 8897. To h. (Isa. xxiv. 15) s. to worship and adore. A.E. 406. H. thy father and thy mother (Exod. xx. 12), in a spiritual sense, s. to revere and love God and the church; and in a celestial sense, by father is meant our Lord Jesus Christ, and by mother, the new church. U.T. 306. The h. of Carmel and Sharon (Isa. xxxv. 1, 2) s. divine good, which the Gentiles should receive. A.E. 288. H. is pred. of worship from good, and fear of worship from truth. (Mal. i. 6.) A.E. 696. H., virtue, and might (Rev. vii. 12) s. the divine celestial things of the Lord. A.R. 373. To be honored above all (Gen. xxxiv. 19) s. what is primary. 4476.

Honorableness s. the spiritual church. A.E. 504.

Hoof s. truth in the ultimate degree, or sensual truth. 7729. H. of horses s. the lowest intellectual principles. 3727. H. of the horses (Ezek. xxvi. 21) s. scientifics which pervert truths. 2336.

Hook in the **Nose,** a (Isa. xxxvii. 29), s. stupidity and foolishness; for n. s. perception, and h. its extraction, properly immersion in the sensual corporeal principle. A.E. 923. See *Pruning Hooks.*

Hope, the, and victory of those that undergo temptations. 6574.

Horeb, Mount, s. the quality of the divine good of love, that was to appear, and this quality appears from the things which were there seen (Exod. iii.) viz., "from the flame of fire out of the midst of the bush;" thus it is the divine good of love shining forth by truth which is of the divine law. 6830. Mount H. s. divine truth in externals, for H. was a mount round about Mount Sinai, which s. divine truth. 10.543.

Horites (Gen. xiv. 6) rep. those who are principled in the persuasions of what is false, grounded in self-love. 1675.

Horn, when spoken of the Lord, s. omnipotence. A.R. 270. The little h. that rose up (Dan. vii. 3–8) s. the plenary perversion of the Word, by the application of its literal sense to the confirmation of the love of dominion, but it is called little, because such perverted application is not sensibly apparent to the understanding of man, or to the sight of his spirit. A.E. 316. H. s. the power of truth from good, and ten h. much power. 2832. A.R. 539. H. (Rev. xiii. 11) s. power in speaking, teaching, and writing, consequently, in reasoning and arguing. A.R. 595. Because h. s. truths from good, which s. was known to the ancients, it was customary to make h. budding forth and fragrant, whence came the expression cornucopia. A.E. 316.

Horns of **Ivory** and **Ebony** (Ezek. xxvii. 15) s. exterior good things, such as relate to worship or rituals. 1172. H. of the unicorns (Ps. xxii. 21) s. truth as to its fulness and power. A.E. 316.

Hornets (Exod. xxiii. 28) s. falses of a tormenting and destructive kind, striking with formidable terror, or the dread of those who are in falses. 9331.

Horror. Temptations are permitted in order that states of h., at evils and falses may be induced and a conscience formed. 1692.

Horse s. knowledges or understanding of the Word; and in an opp. sense, the understanding of the Word falsified by reasonings, and likewise destroyed, as also self-derived intelligence. A.R. 298. Meditation from the Word appears in the spiritual world as a h., lively, as a man thinks spiritually, but dead, as he thinks materially. A.R. 611. A dead h. s. no understanding of truth from the Word. A.R. 225. A pale h. s. all understanding of the Word destroyed utterly both as to good and truth. A.R. 320. A red h. s. the understanding of the Word destroyed as to good; and a black h., the understanding of the Word destroyed as to truth; but a white h. s. the understanding of the Word as to truth and good. A.R. 839. U.T. 113. White h. s. the understanding of the Word as to the interior things thereof, or what is the same thing, the internal sense of the Word. 2761. H. (Amos vi. 11) s. reasoning. 1488. H. (Hab. i. 8) s. reasoning from the natural man. A.E. 780. The heels of a h. s. the lowest intellectual or scientific principles. 3923. "The strength of a h.," which Jehovah does not delight in (Ps. cxlvii. 10) s. all things which are from man's proper intelligence from which are mere falses. A.E. 355. See *Bells of the Horses, Bridles of the Horses, Fiery Horses*.

Horseman s. intelligence, or one that is intelligent. A.E. 239. H. (Rev. ix. 16) s. reasonings concerning faith alone. A.R. 447. Ratiocinations from falses. A.E. 355.

Hosea, the prophet, from the first chapter to the last, treats of the falsification of the genuine understanding of the Word, and of the consequent destruction of the church among the Jewish nation, and therefore he was commanded, for the sake of rep. that state of the church, "to take unto himself a wife of whoredoms, and children of whoredoms" (chap. i. 1), and again, "to take to himself an adulteress" (chap. iii. 1). U.T. 247.

Hospitable Abode, or **Inn**. The natural principle is an i., or place of rest, or night abode for scientifics. 5495.

Host of **Heaven** (Gen. ii. 1) s. love, faith, and the knowledges thereof. 821. H. of h. (Deut. xvii. 2) s. falses. 606. See *Armies*.

Hot s. to be in spiritual love. A.E. 231.

Hour, in the Word, s. a greater or a less state of duration. A.E. 488. One h. (Rev. xvii. 12) s. a little while, and also in some degree. A.R. 741. One h. (Rev. xviii. 10) s. so suddenly. A.R. 769. Half an h. (Rev. viii. 1) s. greatly, because by an h. is s. a full state. A.R. 389. H., day, month, and year (Rev. ix. 15), s continually and perpetually. A.R. 446. H., days, months, and years, in the Word, s. states of life in particular, and in general. A.E. 571.

Hours s. states. D.L.W. 73.

House, in the Word, is of extensive s., but what it s. in particular may appear from those things whereof it is pred. 1488. H., in the internal sense, is the natural mind, for the natural mind, as also the rational mind, is like a h., the husband therein is good, the wife is truth, the daughters and sons are the affections of good and truth, also the goods and truths which are derived from them as parents; the maid-servants and men-servants are the pleasures and scientifics which minister and confirm. 4982. H. s. celestial good, which is of love and charity alone. 2331. H. s. the church, and in the inmost universal sense, the universal kingdom of the Lord. 3720. H. (Gen. vii. 1) s. the will-principle. 706. H. (Gen. xii. 27) s. scientifics which are collected together, for to collect scientifics is to raise and build up the external man, which is not unlike the building of a h. 1488. H. (Gen. xxvii. 15) s. the rational principle as to good and truth. 3538. The h. built by Solomon for Pharaoh's daughter (1 Kings vii. 8) was rep. alone of scientific wisdom. 1462. H. (Luke xi. 24, 26) s. the natural mind, which is called a h. empty and swept when there are no goods and truths therein. 4982. H. (Amos iii. 15) s. the things of the natural mind separate from the spiritual mind. The winter h. and the summer h. s. those things of the natural man which are called sensual; and the h. of ivory and the great h. s. those things of the natural man which are called rational. The things relating to truth are s. by the h. of ivory, and those relating to good, by the great h., in this passage. A.E. 1146. The great h. and the little h. which the Lord will smite (Amos vi. 11) s. the learned and the unlearned man. A.E. 519. When the subject treated of is concerning the celestial man, by h. is s. celestial good, and by field, spiritual good; but when the subject treated of is concerning the spiritual

Household

man, by h. is s. the celestial principle appertaining to him, which is the good of charity towards the neighbor, and by field the spiritual principle appertaining to him, which is the truth of faith; the former and the latter are s. in Matt. xxiv. 17, 18. 4982. To build a h. (Deut. xx. 5, 8) s. to restore the church; the like is s. by planting a vine, in this passage, but h. relates to good, and vine to truth. A.E. 734. H. of brethren (Gen. xxiv. 27) s. good wherein truth is grounded. 3124. H. of my father (Gen. xx. 31) s. the good of delight arising from the appearances of scientific and rational things. 2559. And in Gen. xxviii. 21, pred. of the Lord, is the essential divine principle, in which the Lord was from conception. 2736. H. of a father (Gen. xxiv. 28) s. internal good. 3128. And in Gen. xli. 51, den. hereditary evils. 5353. H. of my father, and the land of my nativity (Gen. xxiv. 7), s. the Lord's maternal human, which he expelled. 3036. H. of God, in the internal sense, s. the church, and in a more universal sense, heaven; and in the most universal sense, the universal kingdom of the Lord; but, in a supreme sense, it s. the Lord himself as to the divine human. The h. of God also s. the Lord's celestial church; and, in a more universal sense, the heaven of the celestial angels; and, in the most universal sense, the Lord's celestial kingdom; and, in the supreme sense, the Lord as to divine good. 3720. A.E. 204. H. of God (Gen. xxviii. 17) s. the Lord's kingdom in the ultimate principle of order. 3720. The h. of Jehovah means the church where love is the principal; the h. of Judah s. the celestial church; the h. of Israel, the spiritual church. 710. H. of a mother (Gen. xxiv. 28) s. good of the external man. 3128. H. of wood s. things of the quality of good; and a h. of stone the things of truth. 3720. All things in man refer to one h., and good and truth constitute one h., like husband and wife. 3020, 4973. In heaven there is a new h. for every novitiate angel. A.R. 611. It is frequently the case with persons, on their first arrival in the spiritual world, to have a h. provided for them, similar to that which they lived in when in this world. U.T. 797. H. full of every good (Deut. vi. 11) s. all things which are of wisdom. A.E. 638. H. s. goods, and palaces the goods of truth of a nobler degree. (Ps. xlviii. 14.) A.E. 453. H. of Israel, see *Antiquities.* H. of Joseph, see *Israel.* See *Closets.*

Household, foes of his own, den. that the evils and falses by which he is tempted, are those of his own proprium. 4843.

House-Top (Matt. xxiv. 13) s. the superior state of man; consequently, his state as to good. 3652.

Howl, to, s. grief by reason of vastation. A.E. 406.

Hul s. so many several kinds of knowledges derived from the knowledges of good. 1234.

Human Essence of the **Lord**, the, was only an additament to his divine, which was from eternity. 1461.

Human. The Lord assumed the h., that he might put himself in power of subjugating the hells, and reducing all things to order, as well in the heavens as in the earths. This h. he superinduced upon his former h.: the h. which he superinduced in the world, was like the h. of a man in the world; yet both were divine, and therefore infinitely transcending the finite h. of angels and men; because he fully glorified the natural h., even to its ultimates, therefore, he rose again with the whole body, otherwise from any man. D.L.W. 221. The h. of the Lord was made divine, when he received the father's love into the h. 6872. When the h. of the Lord was made divine, it was no more an organ, or recipient of life, but life itself. 2658. The h. of the Lord was divine truth, when he was in the world. N.J.D. 303. The glorified h. of the Lord could not be conceived like h., but like divine love in a h. form. 4735. The h. of the Lord is called the son of God which mediates, intercedes, propitiates, and expiates. U.T. 135. The h. of the Lord from the mother was like the h. of another man, and consequently, material. L. 35.

The h. which the Lord took from the mother by nativity, was such as was capable of being tempted, for it was polluted with evil hereditary from the mother. 5041. The h. which the Lord derived from the mother, he altogether put off, and put on the divine h. when he passed out of the world. 2288. The Lord successively and continually, even to the last period of his life in the world, when he was glorified, separated from himself, and put off that which was merely h.; viz., what he derived from the mother, till at length he was no longer her son, but the son of God, as well with respect to nativity, as to conception, and thus became one with the father, and himself Jehovah. 2649, 2159.

Human Form. The divine being is worshipped under a h. f., by most in the universe of worlds, which is by virtue of influx from heaven. 10.159. The first rudiment of the h. f., or the h. f. itself, with all and every thing appertaining to it, is from principles continued from the brain through the nerves; this form it is, into which man comes after death, and which is then called a spirit and an angel, and which is in all perfection a man, but spiritual: his material form which is added and superinduced in the world, is not a h. f. from itself, but from the above spiritual form; being added and superinduced, in order that man may perform uses in the natural world, and also carry along with him, from the purer substances of the world, some fixed continent for spiritual things, and so continue and perpetuate his life. It is a tenet of angelic wisdom, that the mind of man, not only in general, but in every particular, is in a perpetual effort, tending to the h. f., because God is a man. D.L.W. 388.

Human Industry, the products of, are cor. H. and H. 104.

Human Principle, the, with every man, commences in the inmost of his rational principle. 2194. There are two principles which properly constitute the h. p., viz., the rational and the natural. 3245.

Humble. The Lord continually humbles the proud, and exalts the h. D.P. 183.

Humiliation is the essential of divine worship. 8271. The first principle of h. on man's part, is to acknowledge, that of himself he is nothing but what is evil and false. 4779. When man is in a state of h. from self-acknowledgment, he is in a state of reception of good and truth from the Lord. 4956.

Hundred, a (Gen. xxi. 5), s. a full state of unition. 2636. A h. years (Gen. xi. 10) s. the state of the church in general. 1332. A h. years (Gen. xvii. 17) s. that the rational principle of the Lord's human essence should be united to the divine. 2075.

Hundred and **Fifty**, a (Gen. vii. 24), s. a term last and first; here, the last term of the most ancient church. 812. A h. and f. days (Gen. viii. 3) s. the term of fluctuation, and of a new life. 849.

Hundred and **Forty-Four Thousand sealed** out of the **Twelve Tribes of Israel** s. all who acknowledge the Lord to be the God of heaven and earth, and are in truths of doctrine originating in the good of love from him, through the Word. For by the number 144,000, the same is s. as by 12, because it arises by multiplying 12 into 12, and then by multiplying it by 100, and by 1000: and any number whatsoever multiplied into itself, and then multiplied by 10, 100, or 1000, has the same s. as the original number; therefore, the number 144,000 s. the same as 144, and this last the same as 12, because 12 multiplied by 12 makes 144; in like manner, the 12,000 sealed out of each tribe, being multiplied by 12, make 144,000. A.R. 348. A h. and f.-f. t. s. o. of the t. t. of I. (Rev. xvi. 1) s. the angels of the superior heavens, who are all in the good of celestial love. A.R. 631.

Hunger, or **Famine**, s. evils of life. A.R. 323. To h. s. to desire good from affection, because bread, in the internal sense, is the good of love and of charity, and food, in general, is good. 4958. To h. (Isa. viii. 21) s. to desire knowledge. A.E. 386. To h. s. to desire good, and to thirst s. to desire truth. A.R.

Hungry and Afflicted

889. H. and thirst, when pred. of the Lord, s. the inclination and desire of his divine love, for the salvation of the human race. A.E. 386. Spiritual h. and thirst is the affection and desire towards good and truth. A.E. 617.

Hungry and **Afflicted** (Isa. lviii. 10) have reference to those who desire good and truth. A.E. 750.

Hunt, to, s., in general, to persuade, and in particular, to captivate and ensnare men's minds, by flattering them in the pursuit of the things of sense, such as sensual pleasures and lusts, and by applying doctrinals which they explain at their pleasure, according to their own tempers, or those of others, with a view to their own self-exaltation, or the aggrandizement of wealth; and such persuasion too commonly prevails among those who are principled in faith separate from charity. 1178. H. (Gen. xxv. 27) s. truths appertaining to the natural man, from which are derived goods, or sensual and scientific truths; for h., in an extended sense, den. those things which are taken by h., as rams, kids, goats, etc., which den. spiritual good; and also because the arms used in h., which were quivers, bows, and darts, den. doctrinals of truth; hence it is, that to h. den. to teach from the affection of what is true, in a good sense. 3309. H. s. the good of life derived from natural truths. 3313.

Hur s. the truth of doctrine. 9424.

Hurt, to (Rev. vi. 6), s. to violate and profane. A.R. 316. To h. (Rev. ix. 4) s. to pervert the truths and goods of the church, by crafty ratiocinations from sensual scientifics and fallacies. A.E. 581. To be h. of the second death (Rev. ii. 11) s. to sink under evils and falses from hell. A.R. 106.

Husband (Gen. iii. 16) s. the rational principle. 265. H. (Ezek. xvi. 45) s. the Lord, and all that is celestial. 289. H., in the Word, s. good, and wife, truth. It is otherwise when h. is called man (vir); in this case man s. truth, and wife, good. 2509, 2510, 2517, 2533. H. and wife s. truths in conjunction with goodnesses. 718. The h. does not rep. the Lord, and the wife the church, because both together, the h. and his wife constitute the church. C.S.L. 125. In the heavens, two conjugial partners are there called two, when they are called h. and wife, but one, when they are named angels. C.S.L. 177.

Husbandman (Amos v. 16) s. the man of the church, because field, s. the church as to the implantation of truth. A.E. 652. H. (Joel i. 10, 12) s. worshippers. 368.

Huts (Gen. xxxiii. 17) s. the holy principle of truth, common, general, or exterior. 4392.

Huz den. various religious principles and worship. D.P. 2864.

Hyacinthine, or **Color** of **Jacinth** s. intelligence derived from spiritual love, because that color partakes of the redness of fire, and the whiteness of light; and fire s. love, and light, intelligence; this intelligence is s. by h., or blue, in the coverings and veils of the tabernacle (Exod. xxvi. 31, 36.) A.R. 450.

Hyde, or **Skin,** den. external truth. 6402.

Hypocrisy and **Error.** (Ps. xxxii. 6.) To do h., and to speak e., is to do evil from the false, and to speak the false from evil. A.E. 238.

Hypocrite, a, in the spiritual world, when he comes into the company of the wise, either goes away, or retires to a corner of the room, and makes himself invisible, and sits silent. A.R. 290.

Hyssop (Exod. xii. 22) s. external truth, which is a medium of purification; also external good. (See Num. xix. 6, 18.) 7918. See *Vinegar.*

I

I, in the Angelic Language. E and I properly belong to the spiritual class of affections. S.S. 90. H. and H. 241.

Idea of God, the, is the primary of all, for such as that is, such is a man's communication with heaven, and conjunction with the Lord, and thence is his illustration, affection of the true and the good, perception, intelligence, and wisdom; for these things are not from man, but from the Lord, according to conjunction with him. The i. of G. is the i. of the Lord and his divine; for no other is the G. of heaven, and the G. of earth, as he himself teaches in Matt. xxviii. 16. But the i. of the Lord is more and less full, and more and less clear; it is full in the inmost heaven, less full in the middle heaven, and still less full in the ultimate or lowest heaven. Wherefore they who are in the inmost heaven are in wisdom, they who are in the middle heaven in intelligence, and they who are in the ultimate heaven in science. A.E. 957.

Ideas, the, of man, during his life in the world, are natural, because he then thinks in a natural sphere; but still spiritual i. are concealed therein, with those who are in the affection of truth for its own sake, and man comes into these i. after death. 3310. The i. of thought which flow from acknowledgment, make one with words uttered by the tongue, with those who are in the spiritual world. A.R. 290.

Idealists. Visionaries who are called i. D.P. 46.

Identity. The good and truth received from the Lord, by every angel and man, constitute his i. 10.367.

Idle Person, no, is tolerated, even in hell; every one is obliged to work. A.Cr. 84.

Idleness is called the devil's pillow. A.E. 831. Is a life of self-love, and scatters the thoughts upon every vanity. A.Cr. 112.

Idol, Prophet, and **Unclean Spirit.** (Zech. xiii. 2.) I. s. the false of religion; p., the false of doctrine; and u. s., evils springing up from falses of doctrine; for, whilst man lives according to the false of religion and doctrine, he becomes an u. s. A.E. 483.

Idolaters s. those who establish worship, or are in worship, not from the Word, consequently, not from the Lord, but from self-derived intelligence, as was the case with those, who from a single passage in Paul falsely understood, and not from any word of the Lord, fabricated the whole of their church doctrine, which also is a species of spiritual theft. A.R. 892.

Idolatrous Worship, the origin of. The ancient church accounted the significatives which were with the most ancient people before the flood, as holy, and hence came the rep. w. of that church. They did not w. external things, but by external things remembered internal, and hence were in the holy of w. But when the state of mankind was so changed and perverted that they removed themselves from the good of charity and no longer believed in the existence of a heavenly kingdom or of a life after death, but that they were in a state nearly like that of animals, then holy rep. w. was changed into i., and things external were worshipped. 2722.

Idolatry. There are three universal kinds of it; the first is grounded in self-love, the second in the love of the world, and the third in the love of pleasures; these three kinds of i. are s. by the three sons of Terah, viz., Abram, Nahor, and Haran. 1317.

Idols. Mention is made in the Word, of four kinds of i., viz., of stone, wood, silver, and gold. I. of stone s. worship from falses of doctrine; i. of wood, worship from evils of doctrine; i. of silver, worship from the false, as to doctrine and as to life; and i. of gold, worship from evil, both as to doctrine and life; hence i. of gold s. worship of the worst kind of all. 10.503.

Idols of **Gold, Silver, Brass, Stone,** and **Wood.** I. of g. s. falses concerning things divine; i. of s., falses concerning things spiritual; i. of b., falses concerning charity; i. of s., falses concerning faith; and i. of w., falses concerning good works. And taken collectively, i. s. false principles of worship, from self-derived intelligence. How man fashions them, and afterwards to accommodate them, that they appear as truths, is fully des. in Isa. xliv. 9, 10. A.R. 459. When a false doctrinal is confirmed by the spiritual things of the Word, then that becomes a g. and a s. i.; but when false doctrinal is confirmed by the natural things of the Word, as those in its literal sense, then it becomes an i. of b. and s.; and when from the mere literal sense, it becomes a w. i. A.E. 587. "To eat of things offered to i.," s. the appropriation of evil, and the adulteration of all good. A.E. 161. I. in the Word, s. the false of religion, and images, doctrinals. A.E. 827.

Idumea (Isa. xxxiv. 5) s. those who are in evil, and in falses thence derived. S.E.L.P. p. 10.

Ignominy of **Rachael** taken away, den. the affection of truth no longer barren. 3969.

Ignorance. Man is born in a state of mere i., in consequence of his hereditary evils. 1050. I. excuses, but it does not take away the confirmed false principle; for this false principle coheres with evil, consequently, with hell. D.L.W. 350.

Iim. Interior things of worship appertaining to self-love. 1326.

Iim and **Dragons.** (Isa. xiii. 22.) I. s. truths profaned and adulterated, and d. goods profaned and adulterated. A.E. 714.

Illegitimate conjunctions, of good with truth, are des. as whoredoms. 4989.

Illumination, which is attributed to the holy ghost, is indeed in man from the Lord, but nevertheless it is effected through the medium of spirits and angels. D.L.W. 150. I. is an actual opening and elevation of the soul into the light of heaven. 10.330. Every one is illuminated according to the spiritual affection of what is true and good; and at the same time according to the genuine truths, by which he has opened his rational [mind]. A.R. 414.

Illusions are induced by certain spirits. Exp. 1967. I. originate in the confirmation of apparent truths. D.L.W. 108.

Illustration flows into the natural man, by the affection of truth, when it is initiated in good. 2185. They who have been in vastation or desolation, in another life, after that they are comforted with the hope of help, are elevated by the Lord into heaven, thus they are raised from a state of shade, which is a state of ignorance, into a state of light, which is a state of i., and of refreshment thence arising, consequently, into joy, which affects their inmost principles. 2699.

Image. That an i. of what is infinite, may exist in a perpetual variety of qualities, the creator of the universe has distinguished all and singular the things which he has created into genera, and each genus into species, and has discriminated each species and each discrimination in like manner, and so forth. C.S.L. 479. Graven i. s. the false which belongs to proprium; and molten i., the evil which belongs to proprium. 215. I. has relation to faith, and likeness to love. 481. I. s. spiritual love, that is love to our neighbor, or charity; and a likeness s. celestial love, or love to the Lord. 1013.

Image of **Nebuchadnezzar**. (Dan. ii. 32, 33.) By this statue were rep. the successive states of the church; by the head, which was gold, the first state, which was celestial, as being a state of love to the Lord; by the breast and arms, which were silver, the second state, which was spiritual, as being a state of charity towards the neighbor; by the belly and thighs, which were brass, a third state, which was a state of natural good, which is brass (natural good is of love or charity towards the neighbor, in a degree below spiritual good); by the feet, which were iron and clay, a fourth state, which was a state of natural truth, which is iron, and also of no coherence with good which is clay. 3021. See *Nebuchadnezzar*.

Images of **Men** (Ezek. xvi. 17) s. appearances of truth, which are nevertheless falses. A.E. 725.

Imagination. This faculty is the interior sensual. 3020.

Imitation. Divine worship is not to be imitated for the gratification of the proprium. 10.309.

Imitation of things divine by spirits not allowed. 10.284.

Immanuel, God with us, s. the Lord as to the divine human. A.E. 852.

Immaterial. Ideas called i., or intellectual, are from the light of heaven. 3223.

Immature Fruit. The procedure of good in the regeneration compared with i. f. 3982.

Immensity of heaven so great, that it cannot be filled to eternity. L.J. 11. The angels by the i. of God, perceive his divinity. T.C.R. 31.

Immersion in **Jordan** den. regeneration. I. of the truths of faith in cupidities, causes profanation. 571, 10.239.

Immortal, man's, is his mind in the human form. D.P. 324.

Immortality. Existence of the human spirit after death. 5114. They who in heart deny the Divine, begin to reject their own i. Exp. L.J. 25. Man lives immortal from being conjoined to the Lord by love and faith. A.R. 224. Without liberty and rationality, man would not have i. D.P. 96. Argument for the existence of the human spirit after death. 5114.

Immunity den. the affection of truth and its potency. 2526.

Impatience is a corporeal affection, and so far as man is in it, he is in time. 3827.

Implantation, the, of truth in good, is the means of conjoining the will and the understanding so as to make them one mind. Ill. 5835.

Impieties, all, and glorifyings about them, are permissions. D.P. 249.

Impious, the, in heart, who are in dignities, the Lord governs by the fame of their name, and excites them to doing uses. D.P. 250. S. those who are in falses. A.E. 539.

Implanted. The idea of God, as man is i. in every one. A.Cr. 22.

Imposition of **Hands** rep. communication and reception. By the i. of the h., among the ancients, was s. the communication and translation of the thing treated of, and also the reception thereof from another, whether the thing be power, or obedience, or benediction, or testification. 10.023.

Imposthumes. Description of the spirits who cor. to ulcers, tubercles, i., etc. 5188.

Impurity. Man of himself is nothing but a congeries of the most impure evils. Exp. 10, 239. I. is caused by falses opposed to the truths of wisdom. D.L.W. 420.

Imputation. The faith which is imputative of the merit and righteousness of Christ the redeemer, first took its rise from the decisions of the council of Nice, concerning three divine persons existing from eternity, which faith, from that to the present time, has been received by the whole christian world. U.T. 632. Faith imputative of the merit of Christ, was not known in the apostolic church, which preceded the council of Nice, nor is it declared or s., in any part of the Word. U.T. 636. The i. of the merit and

In

righteousness of Christ, is a thing impossible. U.T. 640. The i. of the new church cannot abide together with the faith and i. of the former church; and that in case they abide together, such a collision and conflict will ensue, as will prove fatal to every thing that relates to the church in man. U.T. 647. The Lord imputes good to every man, and hell imputes evil to every man. U.T. 650.

In is a more interior expression than with. Exp. 5041.

Inapplication, relating to the forming of the rational. Exp. 3128.

Inaugurations into the priesthood were made by things spiritual; by things spiritual, man is introduced to things celestial. 2830. I. of Aaron and his sons into the priesthood (Exod. xxix.), was rep. of the glorification of the Lord's human. 9985. All i. into the holy things of heaven and the church, are by the good of love, which is from the Lord. A.E. 375.

Incantations pred. of the profanation of truth. 1368. A.R. 462.

Incense, or **Odors**, s. worship and confession of the Lord, from spiritual goods and truths. A.R. 277. The smoke of the i. s. what is grateful and accepted. A.R. 394. Propitiations and expiations were made by i. A.R. 393. I. and golden altar (Rev. viii.) s. worship of the Lord from spiritual love. A.R. 393.

Inchanters (Rev. xxi. 8) s. they who inquire after truths which they falsify, that by means of them they may confirm falses and evils as they do, who take up this truth. That no one can do good from himself, and by it confirm faith alone, for this is a species of spiritual theft. A.R. 892.

Inclinations. Infants derive their i. from hereditary evil. 2300, 4317.

Increase, the, of good and truth is den. by growth in various senses. Exp. 2646.

Incredulity. How prejudicial to the reception of truth. Exp. 3399.

Incubus, caused by diabolical spirits. Exp. 1270.

Indefinite, the, is an image of the Infinite. 1590.

Indemnification den. the rendering good. 4172.

Indicate. To tell, or i., is to apperceive. 5601.

Indigence. The conjunction of good with truth takes place when the i., hunger, or want of them is perceived. 5365.

Indignation, spiritual, does not take any tincture of anger from the natural man, and still less celestial i., but it takes its tincture from the interior essence of zeal, which zeal in an external form appears like anger, but in its internal form is not anger, nor even the i. of anger, but is somewhat of sadness attended with a wish, that what caused it might not be so, and in a still interior form, it is only an obscure principle, arising from what is not good and true in another, which intercepts the principle of heavenly delight. 3909. The i. which has place with the angels, is altogether different from that which prevails with man when any thing evil befalls him, which is the i. of anger; with the angels it is not of anger, but of zeal, wherein there is nothing of evil and which is as far removed from hatred or revenge, or the spirit of returning evil for evil, as heaven is removed from hell. 3839.

Inebriation s. truths falsified. A.E. 1035.

Infancy, real essential, by which is s. innocence, does not appertain to i. but to wisdom. 2289. What is once implanted from i. as holy, particularly if it be implanted into children by their fathers, and thereby rooted in them; this the Lord never breaks, but bends, unless it be contrary to order itself. 2180. The good of i. is inseminated from man's i. to the tenth year of his age; the good of innocence, from the tenth to the twentieth; from this year man begins to become rational, and to have the faculty of reflecting on good and truth. It was on this account that the Jews were not permitted to go to war before they were twenty years of age. (See Num. i. 20–45.) 2280, 2289.

154

Infinity of God

Infant. In the Word sucklings, infants, and little children den. three degrees of love and innocence. 430. I. in the street (Jer. ix. 21) s. truth beginning to grow. 655. I. and suckling (Jer. xliv. 7) s. the first degrees of love. 430. I. and suckling (Jer. xliv. 7) s. celestial love, and the innocence thereof. 3183.

Infants are innocences, and their innocence flows into them from the Lord, and affects their parents. C.S.L. 396, 995. They who die i., grow up in heaven, and when they arrive at the stature in which young men of eighteen years and virgins of fifteen years are in the world, they stop therein, and then marriages are provided for them by the Lord. C.S.L. 444. All i. after they are grown up in heaven, are sometimes left to their own hereditary evils for a while, in order to their conviction that of themselves they are only evil, and therefore, delivered from hell by the mere mercy of the Lord. H. and H. 342. I., who die such, and are educated in heaven, and, consequently, without actual evil, as the adult, are still alike in evil, yea, they are nothing but evil; nevertheless, they are, like all the angels, withheld from evil and preserved in good. 2307. Immediately on their nativity, there are angels attendant on i. from the heaven of innocence. 2303. I. do not continue i. in another life; but in proportion as they are instructed in intelligence and wisdom, they become adults. 2304. I. and children, in another life, are easily instructed, because they never committed actual evil. H. and H. 330. The love of i. cor. to the defence of truth and good. C.S.L. 127. I. in heaven, are more especially instructed by rep. adequate to their tempers and geniuses, beautiful and full of wisdom from an interior principle. 2299. In general, i. are of a genius either celestial or spiritual; they who are of a celestial genius are readily distinguished from those of a spiritual genius. 2301.

Inferior, the, is as the throne or seat of the superior. 5313. I. s. exterior. D.L.W. 206.

Infestations are caused by infections of falses against truths, and those falses are repelled by influx from heaven, that is, through heaven from the Lord, with those who are infested; in such a state they are held, who are in a state of vastation as to falses, until they have imbued the truths of faith, and by degrees, interior truths; and in the same proportion that these truths are imbued, those persons are liberated from i. I. are not temptations, for temptations are accompanied with anguish of conscience, for they who are in temptations are held in a state of damnation, from whence anguish and pain come. Vastations also differ from both these. 7474.

Infidelity. The seed of the serpent, the church, being treated of, den. all i. 250–4.

Infinite. Every created thing is finite; and i. is in finite things, as in its recipients, and in men, as in its images. U.T. 33, 34. God is i., by reason that he is, and exists in himself, and that all things in the universe are and exist from him. U.T. 28. God is i., by reason that he was before the world; consequently, before spaces and times had birth. U.T. 29. I. and eternal mean the divine itself, but by finite are meant all things created from the divine. D.P. 52. I. and eternal are two attributes, which are alone pred. of Jehovah; i. relates to his divine esse, and eternal to his divine existere. A.E. 286. A.C. 3701.

Infinity of God, the, in relation to spaces, is called immensity; and in relation to times, is called eternity; and yet, notwithstanding those relations, there is nothing of space in his immensity, and nothing of time in his eternity. U.T. 31. To the end that what is infinite might in some manner be perceived by finite man, it pleased the Lord to des. his i. by these words: "I am Alpha and Omega, the beginning and the end; which is, and which was, and which is to come, the Almighty" (Rev. i. 8), which words include all things that ever angel or man can think, spiritually and naturally, concerning the divine. A.R. 31.

155

Infirm Human

Infirm Human. The human derived from the mother. 1414.

Inflame is pred. of the lusts of man kindling. 7519.

Inflamed s. destruction by evils. A.E. 863.

Influx. There is a continual i. from the spiritual into the natural world. D.L.W. 340. I. from the Lord, is through the internal into the external. 1943. Spiritual i. is founded on the nature of things, which is spirit acting on matter. I. 1, 2, 3. Physical i., or natural, originates from the fallacy of the senses that the body acts on spirit. I. 1, 2, 3. Harmonious i. is founded on a false conclusion; viz., that the soul acts jointly and at the same instant with the body. I. 1, 2, 5. There is a common i., and this i. passes into the life of animals, and also into the subjects of the vegetable kingdom. 1633, 3648, 5850. I. is twofold; immediate from the Lord, and mediate through heaven. 6063, 6307, 6472, 9682, 9683. H. and H. 208. There is an immediate i. into the superior and inferior heavens, and there is a mediate i. of the superior heavens into the inferior. A.R. 286. I. passes from the Lord to man through the forehead; for the forehead cor. to love, and the face to the interior of the mind. H. and H. 251. I. from the spiritual angels to man, is all round, from his forehead and temples to every part under which lies the brain. H. and H. 251. I. of the celestial angels, is on that part of the head which covers the cerebellum, or back part of the head. H. and H. 251. They who are instructed by i. what they are to believe and do, are not instructed by the Lord, nor by any angel of heaven, but by some spirit of an enthusiast, Quaker, or Moravian, and are seduced. D.P. 331. The human soul, as being the superior spiritual substance in man, receives its i. immediately from God; the mind, as an inferior spiritual substance, receives its i. from God mediately through the spiritual world, and the body being of that nature, which is called material, receives its i. from God, mediately through the natural world. I. 8. Naked goods and truths cannot enter by i., for these find no reception, but only truths clothed, such as there are in the literal sense of the Word. A.R. 672. I. of the Lord through heaven is like an i. of the soul through the body, the body does indeed speak and act, and likewise feels something from i., but yet the body does not do any thing from itself as of itself, but is acted upon; this also is the nature of all speech. A.R. 943. The Lord, by various degrees of i. into the heavens, disposes, regulates, tempers, and moderates all things there and in the hells, and through the heavens and the hells, all things in the world. A.R. 346. All things which a man wills and thinks enter by i., or flow in, as all things which a man sees, hears, smells, tastes, and feels; but the former are not perceived by the senses, because they are spiritual, for man is only a recipient of life. A.R. 875. Evil spirits cannot sustain the Lord's i. from heaven, neither his sphere. A.R. 339. When the divine i. from the Lord is remiss in the spiritual world, then the good are separated from the evil; but when it is intense, then the evil are cast into hell. When the last judgment is executed, the Lord's i. is first remiss, and afterwards intense. Such intense i. in the inferior parts of the spiritual world, is like a tempest and a whirlwind; this is called, in the Word, the east wind. A.E. 418. He who is acquainted with the i. of successive order into simultaneous, may comprehend the reason why the angels can see in a man's hand, all the thoughts and intentions of his mind; and also, why wives, from the hands of their husbands on their bosoms, are made sensible of their affections. C.S.L. 314. The divine i. from heaven with the good, opens the spiritual mind, and adapts it for reception; but with the evil, in whom there is not any spiritual mind, it opens the inferiors of their natural mind, wherein evils and falses reside, and from whence there is an aversion to all the good of heaven and a hatred against truth. A.E. 504. To the intent that the natural principle appertaining to man may live, there must be i. from the Lord, not only immediate from Himself, but also mediate through the spiritual world. 6063.

Inform, to, is to apperceive. 5601.

Information. See *Education, Science.*

Ingrafting into a branch of the tree of life. Ill. D.P. 296.

Inhabit s. to live. A.E. 294. Pred. of good. A.E. 417.

Inhabitants (Isa. xxvi. 9) s. the men of the church who are in good of doctrine, and thence in the good of life. A.E. 741. I. (Rev. xii. 12) s. those who are principled in the doctrine of faith alone, and thence in the evils of life. A.R. 558. I. of the rock (Isa. xlii. 11) s. such as are principled in charity. 795.

Inherit, to, in an internal sense, when pred. of the Lord, s. to have the life of the father, consequently, to have life in himself; and when it is pred. of man, is to have the Lord's life, that is, to receive life from the Lord. 2658. To i. land (Gen. xv. 7) s. to possess the heavenly kingdom, which is here pred. of the Lord's human essence, for as to his divine essence, he was possessor of the universe, consequently, of the heavenly kingdom from eternity. 1817. To i. (Gen. xxii. 17) s. to succeed. 2851.

Inheritance s. those who are in goods, and those who are in evils. A.E. 863.

Ingenuity, in the confirmation of dogmas and persuasions, is not intelligence. 6222.

Iniquities. By the Lord's carrying our i., nothing else is meant than to sustain dire temptations; also to suffer the Jews to do unto him what they had done unto the Word, and to treat him in the same manner, because he was the Word. The prophets were also treated after the same manner, because they rep. the Lord with respect to the Word, and consequently, with respect to the church, and the Lord was the real essential prophet. L. 15.

Initiation from the natural to the rational. 3108–10.

Injection, the, of falses and evils from hell. Exp. 7111.

Injucundity. When evil begins to predominate. Exp. 8356.

Injury done to spiritual truth. Exp. 5022.

Inmosts. The Lord acts from i., and from ultimates at the same time. D.P. 124.

Inmost. Such as the i. is, such is the whole. A.E. 313. The life which is man's i. is derived from the Lord's presence with man. A.Cr. 47.

Inmost Principle, may be called the entrance of the Lord to man. H. and H. 39.

Innate. Words, thoughts, gestures, etc., imbued from infancy become as if they were i. 7935.

Inn, an, s. a place of instruction. A.E. 706. I. s. the exterior natural principle in general, which cannot, indeed, be confirmed from parallel passages in the Word, but still may be confirmed from this consideration, that scientifics are, as it were, in their i. when in the exterior natural principle; the natural principle is twofold, exterior and interior; when scientifics are in the exterior natural principle, they communicate immediately with the external senses of the body, and there they repose themselves upon them and are, as it were, at rest; hence it is, that this natural principle is an i., or place of rest, or night abode for scientifics. 5656. I. (Exod. iv. 24) s. the external natural or sensual principle of the church without the internal. 5495, 7041.

Innocence is the primary principle in the Lord's kingdom. 3994. I. is the essential principle of regeneration. 3994. Without i. no one can enter into heaven. H. and H. 281. They who are in i. are content with what they have, whether little or much: and therefore are not solicitous about what shall befall them, calling this the taking thought for the morrow. H. and H. 278, 286, 288, 341. There are three degrees of i.; viz., sucklings, infants, and little children. 430. A lamb den. i. of the inmost degree, its opp. is a wolf; a

Inordinate

kid i. of the second degree, the opp. to which is a leopard; a calf i. of the third or ultimate degree, whose opp. is a young lion. (See Isa. xi. 6–8.) A.E. 314. The i. of infants is only external, and not internal, and inasmuch as it is not internal, it cannot be conjoined with any wisdom; but the i. of the angels, especially of those of the third heaven, is internal, and thus conjoined with wisdom. Man also is so created that when he grows old, and becomes as an infant, the i. of wisdom in such case conjoins itself with the i. of ignorance, which he had in infancy, and thus as a true infant he passes into the other life. 5608.

Inordinate. See *Order.*

Insanity. Such is the i. that prevails amongst the infernal inhabitants, that they are desirous of ruling heaven; and some call themselves God the father, some God the son, and some God the holy ghost; and amongst the Jews, some call themselves the Messiah. U.T. 598. Insanities are wants of bonds, which are affections, which close and terminate influx. 5145. In spiritual things, they are occasioned by the want of charity and its affections. 3938.

Inscribe. To be i. in the book of life, den. that it remains after death such essentially as it had become in the life of the body. 2256.

Insects are in the lowest degree of natural affection; fowls of the air in the next degree; and the beasts of the earth, which were created from the beginning, in the highest degree. A.E. 1201.

Insemination, how the, in truths of good, is to be conceived. 4301, 9269.

Insertion of **Truths** into **Scientifics.** Des. 6052.

Insidious, the, in the other life. Des. 827.

Insinuation. Goods and truths are insinuated into man's affections and thoughts in perfect freedom. 2876–7.

Insition. When good is willed from the heart, flows into the thought, and thus conjoins knowledges to itself, there is an i. of good in truths. 3033.

Inspiration of the **Word** implies that in all and singular parts of it, as well historical as others, are contained celestial things which appertain to love or good, and spiritual things which appertain to faith or truth consequently, divine things. 1887, 9094.

Instinct. The affections of beasts proceed from i., without reason, and lead them to their use. 5198.

Instruction. By i. the interiors are formed, and thereby the internals, and are adapted to the reception of the good things of love, and the truths of faith, and thus to the perception of goodness and truth. 1802. Things divine flow into those things which are in the natural man, according to i. and advancement thereby. 3151.

Instrumental. Things spiritual throughout the Word, are den. by things i., which are the ultimates of nature. A.R. 794.

Instruments, stringed, s. spiritual truth; but wind i., the celestial things of faith. 417–420, 2987. A.R. 276. I. of music according to cor., s. the pleasant and delightful affection of spiritual and celestial things, therefore, also in many of the Psalms of David, it is written and declared how they should be sung; as, upon Neginoth, upon Nehiloth, upon Octava, Schigajon, Gitthith, Muthlabbean, Scheminith, Schuschannin, Machalath. 8337. I. of music have sometimes an opp. or bad sense in the Word, and s. gladness and joy, resulting from the affections of evil and the false. (See Isa. xxiii. 15, 16, and v. 11, 12.) A.E. 323.

Insufflation. The evil have not life, but the i. of the loves of self or appearance of life. 5664 1–2.

Insurgents den. evils and falses from hell. 10.481.

Integument. The external is called an i., because it invests and closes in what is above. 9544.

Integrity is pred. of the good of faith. 2826. Of divine truth in effect, or a life according to divine precepts. 9905.

Intellectual Things, or Things Appertaining to Faith, do not constitute the church, but the things of the will, or such as appertain to love, do constitute the church. 709. I. t. regard the things of the will as different and distinct from themselves, whereas the things of the will regard i. t. united to themselves, or as one. 732.

Intellectuals. There are three degrees of man's i., called intellect, reason, and science. 658.

Intelligence is distinguished from wisdom, by this, that i. is the quality of the understanding of truth in the spiritual, and wisdom is the understanding of truth with the celestial man. A.E. 280. I. has respect to truth; but wisdom has respect to good. 1458. I. is not wisdom, but leads to wisdom; for to understand what is true and good, is not to be true and good; but to be wise is to be true and good. Wisdom is pred. only of life, and has relation to the quality thereof in man. 1555. To have i. (Rev. xiii. 18) s. to be in illumination from the Lord. A.R. 608.

Intention, the, or end, is the very life of man. 6571.

Intentions are thoughts from the will. D.P. 152. Thoughts are conveyed according to i. H. and H. 532.

Intercede, to (Gen. xxiii. 8), s. to be prepared to receive. 2933. Intercession s. the perpetual remembrance of man by the Lord. A.E. 810. Intercession is perpetual mediation, for true love, whence mercy, clemency, and grace proceed, perpetually i., or mediates, for those who do his commandments, and who are thereby the objects of his love. U.T. 135.

Intercourse with Spirits attended with Danger. Exp. A.Cr. 74.

Interior man, the, is the middle between the internal and external man; by means of the i. m., the internal communicates with the external, and without such medium, no communication could possibly exist. The i. m. is called the rational man, and is a mediatory communication between the celestial, spiritual, and corporeal principles. 1702.

Interior Thought, the Lord's, was from the affection of truth intellectual, and this affection was from the essential divine good; such thought never did, nor can, appertain unto man. 1935.

Interiors of the **Interior Natural Principle,** the, are those things in that principle which are called spiritual, and the spiritual things in that principle are what are from the light of heaven, by virtue of which light those things therein are illuminated which are from the light of the world, which things are properly called natural; in the spiritual things in that principle are stored up truths adjoined to good. The spiritual things therein are such as cor. to the angelic societies which are in the second heaven; with this heaven man communicates by remains; this heaven it is which is opened when man is regenerating, and it is this heaven which is closed when man does not suffer himself to be regenerated; for remains, or truths and goods stored up in the interiors, are in nothing else but cor. with the societies of that heaven. 5344.

Interiors of the **Mind,** the, cor. to the interiors of the body, and the interiors of the body cor. to its exteriors. D.L.W. 219.

Interiors and **Exteriors** of **Man** are not continuous, but distinct according to degrees, each degree having its own termination. 3691, 4145, 5114, 6326, 6465, 8603, 10.099. H. and H. 38. N.J.D. 47. Interiors accommodate exteriors to themselves, and reject the things which do not accord with them; for every one's exteriors after death, are reduced to a state analogous to his interiors. A.R. 157.

Intermediate Angels. The third or inmost heaven is conjoined with the second or middle heaven, by i. a., who are called celestial spiritual and spiri-

Intermediate Principle

tual celestial angels; these, together with the angels of the third or inmost heaven, constitute the superior heavens; but the rest in the second or middle heaven, together with those who are in the first or ultimate heaven, constitute the inferior heaven. A.E. 322.

Intermediate Principle. It is impossible to climb up to higher principles, without an i. p. 4585.

Internal Man is called the firmament; the knowledges in the internal man, the waters above the firmament; and the scientifics appertaining to the external man, are called the waters beneath the firmament. (Gen. i. 6.) 24. The i. m. is formed of things celestial and spiritual; the interior man, of things rational; the external man, of things sensual, not such as belong to the body, but such as are derived from bodily things; and this is the case, not only with men, but also with spirits. 978. The i. m. with every man is of the Lord alone, for there the Lord stores up goodnesses and truths with which he endows man from infancy. 1707. If the i. m. looks downwards; viz., to earthly things, and there places his all, it is absolutely impossible for him to look upwards, and there place any thing, inasmuch as earthly things altogether absorb and suffocate; the reason is, because the angels of heaven cannot be attendant on man in earthly things, wherefore they recede, and in such case infernal spirits accede, who cannot be with man in heavenly things. 5449. See *Regeneration of Internal Man.*

Internal and **External Man.** In every person there is an i. m., and an e. m.; the i. m. is called the spiritual man, because it dwells in the light of heaven; the e. m. is what is called the natural man, because it dwells in the light of this world only. *Both* of these must go through their respective processes of regeneration, before the whole man can be regenerate. N.J.D. 38, 179. So far as man is in love to the Lord and love towards his neighbor, so far he is in a *spiritual internal*, from which he thinks and wills, and from which also he speaks and acts; but so far as man is in the love of self, and in the love of the world, so far he is in a *natural internal*, from which he thinks and wills, and from which also he speaks and acts. N.J.D. 42. The i. m. must be regenerated before the external. 3321, 9325. The societies of spirits and angels to which the things of the e. m. cor., are in a great part from this earth; but those to which the things of the i. m. cor., are for the most part from other earths. 4330. When man thinks well, it is from the internal or spiritual man in the external or natural. 9704, 9705, 9707. The e. m. thinks and wills according to his conjunction with the internal. 9702, 9703. The i. m. must be lord or master, and the external his minister, and in a certain respect his servant. 10.471. The i. m. is called heaven, and the e. m. is called earth. (Gen. ii.) 82, 83. The real i. m. thinks no otherwise, than according to the science of cor., or according to the internal sense of the Word; for when the e. m. apprehends the Word according to the letter, the i. m. in such case apprehends it according to the internal sense, although man, during his life in the body, is ignorant of it; this may appear especially from this circumstance, that man when he comes into another life and becomes an angel, knows it without instruction, as it were of himself. 4280.

Internal Sense of the Word. There is an i. s. in the W., in consequence of the Word's having descended from the Lord, through the three heavens, even to man. 2310, 6397. Without an i. s., the prophetical parts of the Word, in many places, are unintelligible, and, therefore, of no use. 2608, 8020, 8398. The i. s. of the W. consists of two principles, viz., a spiritual and a celestial principle. 2275. In the i. s. of the W., the essential truth is exhibited in its purity, and things are exposed such as they really are in themselves. 2026, 8717. The i. s. may be called the soul of the Word. 4857. The i. s. of the W. is the Word of the Lord in the heavens. 1887. The i. s. of the W. altogether coincides with the universal language in which the angels are. 4387. To violate it, is to deny those things which are the principal constituents of that sense, and which are the very essential holy things of the Word, and these are the Lord's divine human, love to him, and love towards our neighbor. These three are also the internal and holy things of all doctrinals which are derived from the Word, and likewise the internal and holy things of all worship; for in them is the Lord's essential kingdom. 3454. The i. s. of the W. is remote from the sense of the letter, but still the sense of the letter rep. truths, and exhibits appearances of truth, in which man may be principled, whilst he is not in the light of truth. 1984. The i. s. of the W. is sometimes of such a nature and quality, that it may be called more universal, as being more remote from the letter, and in this case cannot so well appear from the explication of each particular expression made use of in the letter, unless they are viewed in a kind of general idea. (See Gen. xvii. 4, etc.) 2004. The i. s. of the W. appears scattered and unconnected, when explained and confirmed by similar authorities from the literal sense interspersed, but when collated into one sense, it has a most regular and beautiful coherence. 1756. The i. s. of the W. is the true doctrine of the church. 9025, 9430, 10.401. In the i. s. of the Word the Lord's whole life is des., such as it was about to be in the world, even as to perception, etc. 2523. The reason why it is exhibited in order in the i. s., how the Lord perceived and thought concerning the doctrine of faith, and concerning the rational principle, whether it should be consulted, is because it is angelical to think on these subjects in such a series. 2551. The i. s. of the W. is such, that the expressions and words are almost as nothing, whilst the sense thereof, flowing from the series of things treated of, presents a spiritual idea before the angels, to which idea the external or literal sense serves as the object from which it is derived. 2953. If the i. s. of the W. was left without the external, it would be like a house without a foundation. 9430. In the i. s. of the W., there are singular things, whereof myriads constitute together one particular, which is exhibited in the literal sense; or what is the same thing, in the i. s. there are particular things, where myriads constitute, together, one common or general thing which is, in the literal sense, and it is this common or general thing which appears to man, but not the particular things which are in it, and which constitute it; still, however, the order of the particular things in the common or general thing, appears to man but according to his quality, and this order is the holy principle which affects him. 3438. They who are in the i. s. of the W. can instantly, and indeed from a single expression, discern what is the subject treated of; much more can they discern it from several expressions connected together. When another subject is treated of, immediately other expressions are used, or the same expressions are connected in a different manner. 793. There is a continual change of circumstances in the i. s., with respect to the literal sense of the W. 851. The i. s. of the W. continually shines forth in the external sense thereof, but it is not perceived by any others than those who are internal men of the church. 10.691. The man who is regenerate, is actually in the i. s. of the W., notwithstanding his ignorance thereof, inasmuch as his internal man is open, which is endowed with spiritual perception, and, therefore, man, after death, spontaneously comes into the i. s., and is no longer in the sense of the letter. 3226, 1041. The i. s. of the W. (as now revealed) may testify concerning the divinity and sanctity of the Word, and convince even the natural man, if he is in a disposition to be convinced. S.S. 4.

Internal Worship, which is love and charity, is worship itself. 1175.
Internuncio, or **Messenger,** s. to communicate. 4239.

Interrogation

Interrogation den. thought or knowledge from perception. 2693.

Interpretations, the, given in the Word, are given in a natural sense and not in a spiritual sense, because the natural sense is the basis, continent, and firmament of its spiritual and celestial senses. A.R. 736. 1. (Gen. xl. 22) s. prediction. 5168.

Intestines, the, den. last and lowest things, such as sensual delights. 7859.

Intestines (Exod. xxix. 13) are the ultimate or lowest [principles]. 10.030. Who they are who constitute that province in the grand man, may be manifest in some measure from those who have reference to the stomach; for the i. are continued to the stomach, and the offices of the stomach there increase and are provoked even to the last i., which are the colon and the rectum; wherefore they, who are in these last i., are near to the hells, which are called excrementitious. In the region of the stomach and of the i. are they who in the earth of lower [things or principles], who, inasmuch as they have drawn along with them from the world things unclean, which adhere in their thoughts and affections, are on this account kept there for some time, until such things are wiped away, that is, are cast sideways; when this is the case, they are capable of being elevated to heaven. 5392. See *Bladder*.

Intraction, or **Indrawing**. Des. 5270.

Introductions into a **House** den. introduction into good. 2379.

Intromission into **Heaven** consists in the reception of the spirit into the society of angels. 2130.

Intuition, is from interior sight flowing in, and finally, from the Lord who alone sees. 1954.

Inundation, or **Flood**, in the spiritual sense, is twofold, one being an i. of lusts, and the other of falsities; an i. of lusts is of the voluntary (or will part), and is of the right part of the brain; whereas an i. of falsities is of the intellectual part, in which is the left of the brain. 5725. See *Flood*.

Inventor, or **Contriver**, den. the intellectual principle, which thinks, contrives, and acts. 9598.

Inversion, the state of man before regeneration is completely inverse to his state afterwards. 3539.

Investiture, the, and girding of the body, den. a state prepared to receive and to act. 7863.

Invoked. The Lord alone is to be i. D.P. 257.

Involuntary. The voluntary action of man continually tends to disorder, and the i. to order. 9683.

Involuntary common (or general) **Sense**, at this day, is such with those who are principled in the good and truth of faith; but with those who are principled in evil, and thence in what is false, there is not any longer any i. common sense, which manifests itself, either in the face, or in the speech, or in the gesture; but there is a voluntary principle, which assumes the semblance of what is i., or natural, as it is called, which they have made such by frequent use or habit from infancy. 4327.

Ir Cheres s. doctrines brilliant from spiritual truths in the natural principle. A.E. 294.

Irad (Gen. iv. 18) s. heretical doctrine derived from Enoch, and originally from the first, which was called Cain. 404.

Irrational, he is, who does not perceive good to be good, and truth to be truth. 3108.

Iron (Deut. viii. ix.) s. natural or rational truth. 425. I. s. natural truth, consequently, the natural sense of the Word, and at the same time, the natural light of man; in these two consists the power of truth. A.R. 148. I. (Rev. ix. 9), from its hardness, s. what is strong. A.R. 436. I. s. truth in ultimates, which is called sensual truth; which, when it is separated from rational and spiritual truth, is converted into falsehood. A.R. 847. I. cor. to the truths of faith. A.R. 913.

Is, Was, and **Is to come** s. the Lord who is infinite and eternal. A.R. 13.

Isaac rep. spiritual love. 1025. I. (Gen. xvii. 19) s. the rational divine. 2079, 2083, 2627. I. s. the Lord's divine rational as to divine good. 3679. I. s. the Lord's interior man. 1950. I., in the respective sense, s. the Lord's celestial kingdom; inasmuch as by the rest of Abraham's sons, viz., those which he had by Keturah, is s. the Lord's spiritual kingdom. 3245.

Iscariot, Judas, rep. the Jewish church. A.E. 433.

Ishbak rep. the common lots, or heritable divisions of the Lord's spiritual kingdom. 3239.

Ishmael rep. the first rational principle appertaining to the Lord. 1944. The rational principle separate from good. 1942, 1944, 1950, 2078. The Lord's rational principle merely human. 2661. I. (Gen. xxv. 12) s. the spiritual church. 3262. I. rep. the Lord's spiritual kingdom. 3245.

Ishmaelites, the, rep. those who are in simple good as to life, and thence in natural truth as to doctrine. 3263, 4747.

Island, in an abstract sense, s. the truth of faith. A.R. 336.

Islands s. the natural mind, or the natural man, as to his truths and falses. A.E. 406. They who are in the internal sense of the Word, as the angels, do not know what i. are, for they have no longer any idea of such places, but instead of them they have a perception of more remote worship, such as is of the gentiles out of the church. 1158. When i. are opposed to earth or mountains, they s. the truths of faith, by reason of their being in the sea; thus they s. doctrinals which are rituals. 1158. I. (Ezek. xxvii. 6) s. those in the church who are natural, but nevertheless rational. A.E. 1146. I. s. those who are in truths; and people from afar (Isa. xlix. 1), those who are in goods, and abstractedly truths and goods, both in the natural man. A.E. 406. Isles s. the nations more remote from the worship of God, but yet which will accede to it. A.R. 34.

Israel rep. the Lord, as to the interior natural principle. 1416, 5663. I. den. those who are in divine truths from the Lord. A.R. 96, 350. I. (Gen. xxxv. 21) s. the celestial spiritual principle of the natural. 4598. I. (Gen. xliii. 6) den. spiritual good, and whereas I. den. spiritual good, he den. also the internal spiritual church, for that church is a church by virtue of spiritual good. 5595. I. (Jer. xxiii. 8) s. the church spiritual natural. A.E. 768. I., in the rep. sense, is the good which is procured by truth. 4925.

Israel and **Ephraim.** (Jer. xxxi. 9.) I. den. spiritual good, and E., spiritual truth. 3325.

Israel and **Jacob.** I. s. truth in act, and J. truth in doctrine; and as there is no church from the latter alone, therefore J. was named I. A.R. 17. The children of I. dispersed by falses all the literal sense of the Word. A.R. 47. The children of I. (Isa. xiv. 2) s. the Gentiles. A.E. 811.

Israelitish Church. Circumcision was the principal thing which distinguished the I. c. from the other Asiatic churches. U.T. 674.

Issachar s., in a supreme sense, the divine good of truth, and truth of good; in a spiritual sense, celestial conjugial love, which is the love of goodness and truth; and, in a natural sense, remuneration, or giving rewards. A.R. 358. I., in an opp. sense, s. meritorious good. A.R. 358. I. (Gen. xlix. 14) s. a reward or remuneration, on account of works; and a strong ass, which he is called, s. service of the lowest kind. A.E. 448.

Issue, or **Flux.** (Lev. xv. 4.) To be affected therewith, is pred. of those who are in natural love separate from spiritual. A.E. 163.

Isthmus of the **Brain.** Those who have reference thereto, are amongst wandering societies of good spirits, and are consociated in principles and ends, but speak and act differently in extremes. 4051.

Ithomar

Ithomar s. the good of faith and obedience. 9812.

Itself. God, or the divine esse, is the I., because he is love i., wisdom i., good i., truth i., life i.; which, unless each were i. in God, would not be any thing in heaven and in the world, because there would not be any thing of them having relation to the I. or him. A.R. 961.

Ivory s. natural truth. A.R. 774. See *Bed.*

Ivory, Apes, and **Peacocks** (1 Kings x. 22) s. the goods and truths of the external church. A.E. 514.

J

Jabal. The father of such as dwell in tents and of cattle (Gen. iv. 20) s. doctrine concerning the holy things of love, and the good things thence derived, which are celestial. 412.

Jabboc (Gen. xxxii. 22) s. the first insinuation, because it was a boundary of the land of Canaan; and all the boundaries of that land were significative of the celestial and spiritual things of the Lord's kingdom, according to distance and situation. 4270.

Jacinth s. intelligence from spiritual love, and, in an opp. sense, intelligence from infernal love, which is self-derived intelligence. A.R. 450.

Jacob rep. the Lord's exterior man. 1950, 2083. J., in the supreme sense, in general, rep. the Lord's divine natural; but, whereas, when the Lord glorified his natural, it was other in the beginning, than in the progress, and in the end: therefore, J. rep. various things, viz., in the beginning, the Lord's natural as to truth; in the progress, the Lord's natural as to the good of truth; and in the end, as to good. 4538. J. rep. the Word, as to the literal sense. 3712. J. (Gen. xxxiii.) s. the universal of all principles as to truths. 4352. J. (Gen. xxvii. 19) s. natural truths. 3548. The doctrine of the church. A.R. 137. J. rep. that good which the Lord procured to himself by his own proper power, and this is the good which he conjoined to the divine good; thus he made the human in himself divine. 4641. J., as a father, rep. the Jewish religion derived from the ancient church. 4738. J. (Gen. xxxiv. 5) s. the ancient external church. 4439. By the excellency of J., and by his palaces, which Jehovah hates (Amos vi. 8), is s. the love and faith of the false, among those who are of the church; by pride or excellency, the love of the false, and by palaces, those falses themselves, which are called palaces, because they are of pride. A.E. 675. The names of all the sons of J., s. universal principles of the church. 3861. The sons of J. s., in general, all things which are in the Lord's divine natural. 4610. The ten sons of J., from Leah, s. the truths which are of the external church; and the two sons of J., from Rachel, s. the truths which are of the internal church, as is evident from this: that Leah s. the affection of exterior truth, and Rachel, the affection of interior truth. 5409. Temptations, and combats in temptations were the means whereby the Lord made his human divine, and temptations and victories in temptations are what make man spiritual, therefore, J. was first named Israel when he had wrestled: "Thy name shall not any longer be called J., but Israel, because, as a prince thou hast contended with God and with men, and hast prevailed." See 4286. See *Bed.*

Jacob and **Esau** s. faith and charity; J., faith or truth; and E., charity or good. 367.

Jacob and **Israel.** By J. is s. the external of the church; and by I., the internal thereof. 4286. J. specifically rep. the intermediate principle, which communicates with the external and with the internal; thus by the external with those things which are in the natural world, and by the internal with those things which in the spiritual world; this natural principle is what J. specifically rep., and the internal natural is what I. specifically rep. 4570. J. is taken in each sense by the prophets; in one, when the Jewish church

Jacob's Ladder

is s. in its perverted state; in the other, when the true external church of the Gentiles is s. When the internal is s. it is called I. 422. J. and I. (Jer. xxx. 9, 10) s. those who are in goods and truths within the church. A.E. 677.

Jacob's Ladder. By the truths which were of man's infancy and childhood, the angels of God, as by a l., ascended from earth to heaven; but afterwards by truths appertaining to his adult age, the angels of God, as by a l., descend from heaven to earth. 3701. See *Ladder*.

Jacob's Well s. the Word. S.S. 2.

Jaeser s. those who explain the Word to favor the loves of the world. A.E. 911.

Jah (Ps. cxxii. 4) s. the Lord as to divine truth. A.E. 431. Tribes of J., truths from good. A.E. 431. The song J. s. the celebration and glorification of the Lord. A.E. 326. The reason why J. den the divine truth proceeding from the divine human of the Lord, is because J. is from Jehovah, and is called J. because it is not the esse, but the existere from the esse, for divine truth is the existere, but the divine good is the esse. 8267.

James the **Apostle** rep. those who are in charity, and in the abstract, charity itself. A.R. 5, 356, 790.

James den. faith, charity, and the goods of charity. Preface before 2135. See *Peter, James, and John*.

Japhet. They who are s. by J. constitute the external church, cor. to the internal. 1083.

Jareb, king. (Hosea v. 13.) By the Assyrian and King J. is s. the rational principle, perverted as to good, and as to truth. A.E. 962.

Jared (Gen. v. 15) s. a sixth church from Adam. 510.

Jaser s. false principles. 2468.

Jasher, the book of (Josh. x. 10, 12, 13, and 2 Sam. i. 17, 18), is contained in the ancient Word, which was extant in Asia, before the Israelitish Word, and which is preserved to this day among the people who inhabit Great Tartary. A.R. 11.

Jasper Stone, inasmuch as it is white, s. the things appertaining to the truths of wisdom. A.R. 231. J. s. s. the divine truth of the Word in its literal sense, translucent from the divine truth in its spiritual sense. A.R. 897.

Javan and **Jubal** (Isa. lxvi. 18, 19) den. true internal worship. 1151.

Javanites, sons of the (Joel iv. 6), s. worship in externals, separate from what is internal. 1151.

Jaws, the (Isa. xxx. 28), s. thoughts from the sensual corporeal principle, thus from fallacies. A.E. 923.

Jaw-Bone (Matt. v. 38) s. the perception and understanding of interior truth; the right j.-b. the affection and thence perception thereof; and the left j.-b. the understanding thereof. A.E. 556.

Jazer, Sibmah, Heshbon, and **Elealeh**. (Isa. xvi. 9.) By J., the vine of S., and by H. and E., are s. the men of the external church, who explain the Word to favor worldly love. A.E. 911.

Jealous, or **Zealous** (Gen. xxx. 1), s. somewhat of indignation. 3906. See *Indignation*.

Jebusites, Amorites, Girshashites, Hivites, Arkites, Sinites, Arvadites, Zemarites, and **Hamathites** (Gen. x. 16–18), s. different kinds of idolatry, or of falsities and evil lusts. 1205.

Jebusites s. what is idolatrous. 6860.

Jegar Sahadutha, the heap of testimony (Gen. xxxi. 47), s. the quality of good derived from truth, on the part of those who are principled in goods of works, like the Gentiles. 4195.

Jehoiakim (Jer. xxxvi. 30) after he had burnt the roll written by Jeremiah, it is said, "that his dead body shall be cast out in the day to the heat, and in the night to the frost;" which s. that the truths of the church would perish by concupiscence for the false, and thence by aversion towards truths; for this king rep. the truth of the church about to perish. The roll which he burnt, s. the Word, which is said to be burnt, when it is falsified and adulterated, which is done by the concupiscence of the false from evil. The concupiscence for the false is s. by the heat in the day; and aversion to the truth, by frost in the night. A.E. 481.

Jehoshaphat, the valley of (Joel iii. 12), s. the falsification of the Word. A.E. 911.

Jehovah in the Word of the Old Testament, everywhere means the Lord. 2005. J. s. divine love, or divine good. U.T. 85. J. s. the Lord's internal man. 1793. When it is pred. of J., that he says, nothing else is implied, but that it is so, or not so; or that it is so done, or not so done, for nothing else can be said of Jehovah—but he is. The various things pred. of J. throughout the Word, are spoken in compliance with the conceptions of those who can comprehend nothing, but what has some relation to things human, and this is the reason why the literal sense is such as we find it. The simple in heart may be instructed by appearances, according to human things, for their knowledges are seldom extended beyond the limits of sensual objects; wherefore, in the Word there is an accommodation of expression to their apprehension. 926. When it is said that J. speaks, it means that he wills; and when it is said that he swears, it means that he understands it to be true. 3037. J. repenting that he had made man upon the earth (Gen. vi. 6), s. mercy. 586–590. The right hand of J., the great name of J., the soul of J., the holiness of J., and the height of Jacob, s. the Lord's divine human. (Isa. lxii. 8; Jer. xliv. 26; li. 14; Amos iv. 2; viii. 7.) 2842. J. appeared to Moses in a human form adequate to his reception, which was external, as an aged man with a beard sitting with him, which is the reason why it is said of Moses, that "J. knew him, and spake with him face to face." Hence, also, the Jews had no other idea of J., than as of a very old man, with a long beard white as snow, who could do miracles above other gods. 4299. It is said (Exod. xxxiii.) that Moses saw J. face to face, which s. to see him in the interiors of the Word, of the church, and of worship, which yet is to see him in externals from internals. A.E. 412. At one time this name was lost, or changed into other names by the ancients, and it appears that even Moses did not then know the name of J. (See Exod. iii. 13–15.) 1343. J., prior to his personal incarnate advent, appeared in the form of an angel, for when he passed through heaven, he took upon himself that form, which was a human form; for the universal heaven, from the divinity therein, is like one man; and as J. appeared in human form as an angel, it is evident that it was nevertheless J. himself, and that that very form was also the form of J. himself; because it was the divinity of himself in heaven; this was the Lord from eternity. But since that human form was assumed by transition through heaven, it was necessary, in order to the salvation of the human race, for him to become really and essentially a man, and therefore he was pleased to be born, and actually to assume the human form, in which was J. himself. 10.579. J. descended and assumed the humanity, for the purpose of redeeming and saving mankind. U.T. 82. J. descended as divine truth, which is the Word, nevertheless, he did not separate thence the divine good. U.T. 85.

Jehovah Caused to Rain from **Jehovah out of Heaven**. (Gen. xix. 24.) By these words it appears, in the sense of the letter, as if there were two J., one on earth, and one in heaven; but the internal sense teaches how this is to be understood; viz., that by J. first named is meant the Lord's divine human and holy proceeding, and that by J. named a second time, is meant the essential divine, which is called the father. 2447.

Jehovah

Jehovah going down to see (Gen. xviii. 21) s. judgment and visitation. 2242.

Jehovah God is first mentioned (Gen. ii. 4), because the celestial man is treated of; whereas he is called singly God in the foregoing chapter, wherein the spiritual man was treated of. On the same account mention is here made of ground and field, and heaven is first mentioned before earth. 89. J. G. (Gen. iii. 22) means the Lord, and, at the same time, the angelic heaven; hence he first speaks in the singular, and afterwards in the plural number. 298, 300. J. G. of heaven (Gen. xxiv. 3), as spoken of the Lord, is Jehovah himself, who is called the father, or the divine essence; and J. G. of earth, is, in this case, Jehovah who is called son, or the human essence. Thus J. G. of heaven s. the divine which is in things supreme; and J. G. of earth, the divine which is in things thence derived. But the Lord is called J. G. of heaven, by virtue of his divine, which is in the heavens; and God of earth, by virtue of his divine which is in the earths. The divine in the heavens, is also what is with man in his internals, but the divine in the earths, is what is with man in his externals. 3023.

Jehovah Zebaoth and **Lord**. When it is treated in the Word, concerning the divine power of good, or omnipotence, then it is said J. Z., or J. of hosts, and also Lord, so that J. Z. and Lord are of the same sense and s-ignification. 2921. See *Lord of Hosts*.

Jehovah and **God**. J. is a name most holy, and belongs only to the church; whereas G. is not so, inasmuch as every nation had gods. It was not allowed any one to name the name of J., but those who had the knowledge of the true faith; whereas every one might name the name G. 624. J. is the name adopted in the Word, when the subject is concerning things belonging to the will, or the good things of love; but when the things treated of, are concerning intellectual things, or the truths of faith, the term G. is used. 709. J. means the Lord not yet incarnate, and the word Lord means J. incarnate, which is J. in his humanity. 2921.

Jehovih Lord s. the L. as to divine good. A.E. 850.

Jehudith, the daughter of Beeri the Hittite (Gen. xxvi. 3), s. truth from another source, than what was real and genuine. 3470.

Jerah (Gen. x. 27), a ritual of the church called Eber. 1247.

Jeremiah. Lamentations of J., treat of the vastation of every good and truth among the Jewish nation. A.E. 357.

Jericho s. instruction, also the good of life, because no one can be instructed in the truths of doctrine, but he who is in the good of life. But J., in an opp. sense, s. the profanation of truth and good. A.E. 700. J. s. the good of truths. A.E. 458. J. (Luke x. 30) s. the church, which is in possession of the knowledges of truth and good. A.E. 458. The waters of J. (2 Kings ii. 19–22) s. the truths of the Word in its literal sense; and the waters were healed by salt being cast into them, because salt s. the desire of truth towards good, and from the conjunction of both, health and soundness are produced. 10.300.

Jerusalem s. the church, because in that city, in the land of Canaan, and in no other place, the temple was, and the altar and sacrifices were offered, thus divine worship performed; wherefore, also, three feasts were held yearly there, and every male throughout the whole land was commanded to come to them; hence it is, that J. s. the church as to worship and therefore as to doctrine, for worship is prescribed in doctrine and performed according to it, also because the Lord was in J., and taught in his own temple, and afterwards glorified his humanity there. A.R. 880. J. first s. the ancient church, and afterwards the Israelitish church. A.E. 619. J. (Ezek. xvi. 7) s. the ancient church. 3301. J. (Zech. ii. 4.) The spiritual are understood by those, who are in the midst of J.; and the spiritual natural, by those who are in the suburbs thereof. A.E. 629.

Jerusalem and **Jericho**. (Luke x. 30.) J. s. the truth of doctrine, and J. the good of truth, which is the good of life. A.E. 458.

Jezreel (Hosea ii. 22) s. a new church. 3580.

Jesse, the root of, s. the Lord. 2468.

Jest. To j. from the Word and concerning the Word, is to sprinkle the holy things of heaven with the dust of the earth. A.E. 1064. It is also a profanation. 1064.

Jesuits. The scandals they infuse against the Lord. 8383. Interiorly believe nothing divine, but exteriorly play with divine things like conjurers. D.P. 222. Consulting on the means of keeping the people in blind obedience. L.J. 58.

Jesus. "I J. have sent mine angel to testify unto you these things in the churches," etc. (Rev. xxii. 16.) The reason why the Lord here names himself J., is, that all in the christian world may know that the Lord himself, who was in the world, manifested the things which are des. in the book of Revelations, as also the things which are now opened. A.R. 953.

Jesus Christ. The name J. s. the divine good, and the name C. the divine truth, and by both the divine marriage in heaven. 3004, 3009. The angels sometimes called the Lord, J. C. U.T. 621. J. C. is Jehovah Lord, the Creator from eternity, the Saviour in time, and the Reformer to eternity, who is therefore at once, the father, son, and holy spirit. A.R. 961.

Jesus Christ and the **Lamb**, in the Apocalypse, s. the Lord, as to his divine human, and God there s. the Lord, as to his all-creating divinity. A.R. 6.

Jethro, the father-in-law of Moses (Exod. xviii. 1), rep. divine good, from whence proceeds ordination. 8641. Also the good of the church amongst those who were in the truth of simple good. 8643.

Jetur rep. the spiritual church among the gentiles. 3268.

Jewels, when applied to the ears, s. good in act. 3103.

Jewish Church, the, was not properly a church, but only the rep. of a church. 4281, 4289. The J. c. was instituted, that it might rep. the celestial church. 3727. The J. c. itself, and all things appertaining thereto, were rep. of such things as respect the Lord's kingdom. 1823. The J. c. was not any new church, but it was a resuscitation of the ancient church, which had perished. 4835. The statutes, judgments, and laws of the J. c., as to a part, were like those in the ancient church. 4442. The J. c. by truth, understood the precepts of the decalogue, and also the laws, judgments, testimonies, and statutes, which were delivered by Moses. 4690. The J. c. knew nothing concerning faith, which the christian church did. 4690.

Jewish Nation, the, rep. the celestial kingdom of the Lord, and the Israelitish nation his spiritual kingdom. A.E. 960. The J. or Israelitish nation was such, that they only regarded externals, and not at all internals, and to look to externals alone, is to look to the image of a man without life; but to look to internals also, is to behold a living man. A.E. 412. The Israelitish and J. n. was not elected or chosen above others, but only received, in order that it might rep. a church. 4290.

Jews, in the Word, s. those who belong to the Lord's celestial church. A.R. 96. Their external holy principle was miraculously elevated by the Lord into heaven, and the interior things of worship, of the church, and Word perceived thereby in heaven. 3480, 4309, 4311, 6304, 8588, 10.492, 10.500, 10.602. The J. were forbidden to eat blood with the flesh, because it rep. at that time profanation; for "not to eat flesh with its soul the blood," s. not to mix together things profane with things holy. 998, 1003, 1008, 10.033. The J. being so prone to profanation, had never the mysteries of faith revealed to them, so that it was never even openly declared to them that they should live after death; nor, do they know at this day, that any internal man exists. 302. They think erroneously who believe, that the J. will be

Jezebel

converted in the last time or age of the church. 4847. The J., in another life, appear in front in the lower earth of the spiritual world, beneath the plane of the left foot. 3481.

Jezebel s. faith separate from charity. A.R. 132. J. s. those who are in the doctrine of every false, from the pleasures of self-love, and the love of the world. A.E. 160.

Jidlaph, various religious principles and kind of worship. 2863.

Jishbak rep. the heritable divisions of the Lord's spiritual kingdom. 3239.

Joab den. those in whom there is no longer any spiritual life, by reason of the profanation of good, and the falsification of truth. 9014.

Job, book of. The most ancient books, amongst which is the book of J., were written by mere cor.; for the science of cor. was then the science of sciences, and they were esteemed above all others who could compose books most abounding in the most significant cor.; the book of J. is of this nature; but the spiritual sense therein collected from cor., does not treat concerning the holy things of heaven and the church like the spiritual sense in the prophets, wherefore it is not amongst the books of the Word. A.E. 543. The book of J. is an ancient book, wherein indeed is contained an internal sense, but not in series, or in regular and connected order. W.H. 16. S.S. 20. A.C. 2682. See *Noah.*

Jobal (Gen. x. 28) a ritual of the church called Eber. 1245.

Jobel. To draw J., or what is the same, to hear the sound of a trumpet, den. to be in common perception of the good of the church, and the jubilee thence derived. 8802.

John the **Apostle** s. those who are in the good of life from charity and its faith. A.R. 790. J. (Rev. i. 4) s. the Lord as to doctrine. A.E. 18. Also, doctrine concerning the Lord. A.E. 45. The things which were written by J. in the Apocalypse, were not sent to any church in those places, which are therein mentioned, but were told to their angels, by whom are understood those who receive. A.R. 41.

John as an **Apostle** s. the good of love to the Lord, and consequent good of life, for which reason he was loved more than the other apostles, and at supper lay on the bosom of the Lord. (John xiii. 23, and xxi. 20.) A.R. 879. See *Ezekiel, Peter.*

John the **Baptist** rep. the Lord as to the Word. 9372. It is said of him "that among them that are born of women, there has not risen a greater than J. the B., and notwithstanding, he that is least in the kingdom of heaven, is greater than he;" by which is s. that the Word is more than any doctrine in the world, and more than any truth in the world, but that the Word, in its internal sense, or its quality in heaven, is, in degree, above the Word in its external sense, or such as it is in the world, and such as J. the B. taught. 9372. J. the B. was sent before, to prepare the people for the reception of the Lord, by baptism; because baptism rep. and s. purification from evils and falses, and also regeneration through the Word from the Lord, which rep., unless it had preceded, the Lord could not have manifested himself in Judea and Jerusalem, to teach and to sojourn, because the Lord was the God of heaven and earth, under a human form, who could not be together with a nation, which was in mere falses of doctrine and evils of life; wherefore, unless the rep. of purification from evils and falses, had prepared them for his reception, that nation had perished by his divine presence, with disease of every kind, which is s. by these words, "lest I come and smite the earth with a curse." (Mal. iii. 23, 24.) A.E. 724. A.R. 776. See *Baptism of John.*

Joint, out of, den. the want of that order in which the conjunction of truth with good can take place. 4278.

Joints, torpor of the, occasioned from voluptuous spirits. 5724.

Jokshan. Common lots of the Lord's spiritual kingdom. 3239.

Joktan (Gen. x. 25) s. the external worship of the church called Eber. 1240.

Jonadab, the sons of (Jer. xxxv.) rep. those who are of the celestial church of the Lord, and hence it is said, that they should not drink wine, nor build a house, nor sow seed, nor plant vineyards, which s. to learn and retain those truths of the memory, which constitute the spiritual church; but that they should dwell in tents, which s. to receive and obey in the life. S.E.L.P. p. 26.

Jonah rep. the Jewish nation. A.E. 401. J. description of his being in the belly of the great fish (chap. ii. 5, 6), applies to and rep. the temptations of the Lord in his combats against the hells. 1961. See *Gourd.*

Jonathan s. the truth of doctrine. A.E. 357.

Jordan, land of (Ps. xlii. 6), s. what is lowly, consequently, what is distant from what is celestial, as the external things of man are from things internal. 1585. The plain of J. (Gen. xiii. 11) s. the external man. 1592. The river J. s. that which is first in the church, and this is divine truth, such as it is in the literal sense of the Word. A.R. 367. J. (Ps. cxiv. 5) s. the knowledges of good. 4255. J., as being a boundary, s. initiation into the knowledges of good and truth, for these are the first things; and at length when man is made a church, or the Lord's kingdom, they become the last. 4255. J. being divided, and the sons of Israel passing over on dry [ground], s. the removal of evils and falses, and the admission of those who were principled in goods and truths. The like was s. by the waters of J. being divided by Elias, when he was taken up into heaven, and by Elisha, when he entered upon the prophetic office in the place of Elias. 4255. The passing over the river J. rep. the introduction of the regenerate into the kingdom of the Lord. 901. The swelling of J. s. the things appertaining to the external man, which rise up and want to have dominion over the internal. 1585.

Josedech. See *Joshua the son of Josedech.*

Joseph s. in a supreme sense, the Lord in regard to the divine spiritual; in a spiritual sense, the spiritual kingdom; and in a natural sense, fructification and multiplication. A.R. 360. J. (Rev. vii. 8) s. the doctrine of good and truth, which is among those who are in the Lord's spiritual kingdom; because he is named after the tribe of Zebulon, and before the tribe of Benjamin, consequently, in the middle; and the tribe which is first named in the series or class, s. some love which is of the will; and the tribe which is named after it, s. something of wisdom, which is of the understanding; and the tribe which is named last, s. some use or effect derived from them; thus each series is full or complete. A.R. 360. J. s. the celestial spiritual man. 3969. J. (Gen. xl.) rep. the Lord's internal man; or, the celestial spiritual from the rational. 4962, 4963. J. (Gen. xxix) s. good natural spiritual. 5006. That which J. rep. is called the celestial of the spiritual principle from the natural, nor can it be expressed otherwise, for the celestial principle is good from the divine, the spiritual principle is truth from that good, thus it is the truth of good from the divine human; this the Lord was when he lived in the world, but when he glorified himself, he then transcended above it, and was made the divine good itself or Jehovah even as to the human; this arcanum cannot be specifically explained further, only it may be added, that J. on this account came into Egypt and first served in the house of Potiphar the prince of the guards, and was next detained in custody, and afterwards made ruler over Egypt, that he might rep. how the Lord progressively made the human in himself divine, concerning which the Word was to be written, which Word was to contain things divine in the internal sense, a sense which was to be serviceable more especially to the angels, whose wisdom (incomprehensible and ineffable in respect to human wisdom) is employed on such subjects, and at the same time was to be serviceable to men, who are particularly fond of historical relations, and in this case might have their minds engaged in those circumstances, wherein the angels perceive things divine by influx from the Lord. 5307. By those things which are recorded of J., from beginning to end, was rep. in its order, the glorification of the Lord's human, and consequently, in an inferior sense, the regeneration of man. 5827. J. s. internal good from the rational. 5805. J. s. the good of faith. 5922. J. s. the good of the will in the rational. 6295. J. s. the spiritual church. 6434. The internal of the church. 5469. J. s. natural perception from celestial spiritual. 5325. J. being sold into Egypt, s. the same as the Lord's being sold by Judas Iscariot. 4751. Head of J. s. wisdom appertaining to the internal man, and the top of the Nazarite his brother, intelligence and science appertaining to the external man. (Deut. xxxiii. 16.) A.E. 295.

Joseph and **Benjamin**. J. is the celestial spiritual man, and B. the spiritual celestial. 3969.

Joseph's Brethren (Gen. xxxvii.) rep. the church, which is in faith separate from charity. 4740. J. brethren s. the general truths of the church. 5419.

Joshua, the **Son** of **Josedech** the **High-Priest** (Zech. iii. 1), s. the law, or the Word. A.E. 740. J., the son of Nun, rep. truth combating; also, the truth of the Word illustrating. 8595. 10.454. J., the Son of Nun, rep. the Lord. 901.

Jot, or **Tittle**. The angels have written Word amongst them, composed of letters, inflected with significative little bendings and dots; from whence it may appear what the words of the Lord s., in Matt. v. 18, and Luke xvi. 17. S.S. 90.

Journey, to, s. the institutes and order of life. 1463. Journeyings and peregrinations s. things relating to instruction, and thence to life. 3148.

Joy is spoken of the delight of the love of good of the heart, and of the will; and gladness, is spoken of the delight of the love of truth of the soul, and of the understanding. A.R. 507. See *Dancing.*

Joyful Lips (Ps. lxiii. 5) s. the spiritual principle. 353.

Jubal (Gen. iv. 21) s. the doctrine of things spiritual in the new church which succeeded Lamech; and his being the father of such as handle the harp and organ, s. the truths and good things of faith. 417.

Jubilee. The influx and reception of celestial good. 8802.

Jubilate, to, or make a joyful noise, s. worship from the delight of good. A.E. 361.

Judah and his **Tribe** rep. and thence in the Word s., in a supreme sense, the Lord as to celestial love; in its spiritual sense, the celestial kingdom of the Lord and the Word, and in a natural sense, doctrine of the celestial church from the Word; but J., in the opp. sense, s. diabolical love, which is the love of self. A.R. 350. A.E. 119. The twelve tribes of J. were divided into kingdoms, the Jewish and the Israelitish; and the latter rep. the spiritual church, and the former the celestial church. A.R. 350. City of J. (Isa. xl. 9) s. the doctrine of love towards the Lord, and love towards our neighbor in the whole complex. A.E. 850. J. (Gen. xlix. 11) s. the Lord's divine celestial; "the garment which he should wash in wine," and "the covering which he should wash in the blood of grapes," s. his rational and natural which he should make divine. 2576. J. (Isa. xxxvii. 30) s. the celestial principle of the church; and the king of J. the spiritual principle thereof. A.E. 706.

Judaism. Why it continues. D.P. 260.

Judas Iscariot rep. the Jewish nation, as to the church, or the Jewish church itself. A.E. 433. A.C. 4751.

Judea s. the church. 3654. J. (Mark xiii. 14) s. the church vastated. 795.

Judge of the **Whole Earth**, the (Gen. xviii. 25), s. essential good from whence truth is derived. 2258.

Judges. A j. formerly rode upon a she-ass, and his sons upon he-asses; by reason that j. rep. the good things of the church and their sons truths thence derived; but a king rode on a she-mule, and his sons on he-mules; by reason that kings and their sons rep. the truths of the church. 1672, 1728, 2069, 2781.

Judge, to. It is on no account allowable for one man to j. of another as to the quality of his spiritual life, for the Lord alone knows this; nevertheless, it is allowable for every one to j. of another's quality as to moral and civil life, for this is of concern to society. 2284. A general judgment, as this, for instance, "if you are such in internals as you appear in externals, you will be saved or condemned," is allowed; but a particular judgment, as this, for instance, "you are such in internals, therefore you will be saved or condemned," is not allowed. C.S.L. 523. The Word itself judges every one. A.R. 321. Every one, as well the evil as the good, is judged immediately after death, when he enters the spiritual world, where he pursues his life to eternity, either in heaven or in hell. A.E. 413. Every one is judged according to the nature and quality of his soul, and the soul of man is his life, for it is the love of his will; and the love of every one's will, is entirely according to his reception of divine truth proceeding from the Lord, and this reception is taught by doctrine of the church derived from the Word. A.R. 871.

Judgment appertains to the Lord's divine human and holy proceeding. 2319. J. is twofold, from a principle of good, and a principle of truth; the faithful are judged from a principle of good, but the unfaithful from a principle of truth. 2335. J. is pred. when evil is brought to its height, or, as it is expressed in the Word, when it comes to its consummation. 1311. J. (Rev. xvii. 1) s. the state of the church at its end. A.R. 719. See *Last Judgment*.

Judgments, great, s. the laws of divine order, or divine truths. 7206. J. s. divine truths, according to which man ought to live, whereby it is known what he is, and according to which he will be judged. A.R. 668.

Judgments, Precepts, and **Statutes**. J. s. civil laws, p. the laws of the spiritual life, and s. the laws of worship. A.E. 946.

Jugglers. The arts of juggling den. the falses of the evil of self-love, which destroy the truths of good. 9188. See *Magi*.

Juice of the **Grape**, the, and wine have a similar signification. A.R. 653. See *Wine*.

Juices of **Meats**, the, which are immediately imbibed by the veins, and are conveyed into the circulation, even into the brain, cor. to those who scarcely at all endure the vexation of vastation in the world of spirits. 5174.

Jupiter. The spirits and angels, who are from the earth J., in the grand man, have relation to the imaginative principle of thought, and consequently, to an active state of the internal parts. E.U. 64. The inhabitants of J. made wisdom to consist in thinking well and justly on all occasions of life. They acknowledge the Lord as the supreme, and call him a man, and the only Lord, because in their earth he has been seen as a man; but they do not know that he was born a man on our earth. They are exceedingly cautious on their earth, lest any one should enter into wrong opinions concerning the only Lord. Such of them as have lived in true conjugial love, and have taken such care of their children as becomes parents, do not die of diseases, but in tranquillity, as in sleep. E.U. 62, 84.

Just. He is said to be j., in a spiritual sense, who lives according to divine laws. A.R. 815. They on the right hand being called j., as where it is said, "the j. shall answer him, saying," etc., and "the j. shall go into life eternal," s. that they are in the Lord's justice; all who are in the good of charity, are called the j., not that they are j. from themselves, but from the Lord,

Just and Equitable

whose justice is appropriated to them; wherefore they who in the Word are called j. and holy, are they who know and acknowledge that all good is from the Lord, and all evil from themselves, that is, in the power of themselves from hell. 5069.

Just and **Equitable**. That in the natural principle is called j. and e., which in the spiritual principle, is called good and true. 4167.

Just, and in the **Fear of God**. (2 Sam. xxiii. 2.) J. is pred. of good, and the f. of G. of truth. A.E. 411.

Just and **Upright**. (Gen. vi. 9.) J. has relation to the good of charity, and u. to the truth of charity. 610.

Just and **Wicked**. (Gen. xviii. 23.) J. s. the good, and w. the evil. 2250.

Justice s. both good and truth. A.R. 821.

Justice and **Judgment**. J. is pred. of divine good, and j. of divine truth. A.R. 668. J. and j., in ancient times, with respect to the Lord, s. mercy and grace, and with respect to man, charity and faith. 2235.

Justification by **Faith alone**. Those who are confirmed therein, both in doctrine and life, in the spiritual world, exhale a sphere of the infamous adultery of a mother, or mother-in-law with a son, with which it has a cor. A.E. 237.

Justify, to (Isa. v. 3, 11), s. to save from divine good. A.E. 309.

K

Kadesh den. truths, and contentions about truths. 1678.
Kadmonite. Falses to be expelled from the Lord's kingdom. 1867.
Kalah s. false doctrinals of life generated between falses of reasoning and of lust. 1190.
Kaluch s. varieties of worship. 1180–3.
Kaphtor den. vastation of the church. 9340.
Kaphtorim s. scientific or external rituals of worship. 1193–5.
Kasluhim s. external rituals of worship. 1193–6.
Kedar, or **Arabia** s. spiritual good. 3268. K. den. those of the Gentiles, who are in simple truth; the same is s. by A. 3268. K. s. the knowledges of good. A.E. 734.
Kedemah rep. things of the spiritual church among the Gentiles. 3268.
Kedorlaomer s. apparent goods and truths. 1667.
Keep, to, the Commandments (Rev. xiv. 12) s. to live according to the precepts, of which the decalogue contains a summary. A.R. 638.
Keep, to, the Garments (Rev. xvi. 15) s. to persist in truths, and a life conformable to them to the end of life. A.R. 705. By them who k. the words of this book (Rev. xxii. 9) are s. they who k. and do the precepts of that doctrine, which are now manifested by the Lord. A.R. 946.
Keeper, to be a, (Gen. iv. 9) s. to serve, as is the case with k. of a gate, and the k. of the porch in the Jewish church; faith is called the k. of charity from this circumstance, of its being subservient thereto; but according to the principles of the doctrine called Cain, faith was to have dominion. 372.
Kemuel den. various religious principles and worship. 2864.
Kenan, or **Cainan,** s. a fourth church after Enos. 500.
Kenite, Kenizzite, and the **Kadmonite** (Gen. xv. 19), s. falses, which are to be expelled from the kingdom of the Lord. 1867.
Kesed den. various religious principles and worship. 2864.
Kesia den. inmosts of divine good. 10.258.
Kesib (Gen. xxxviii. 5) s. a state of the idolatrous principle s. by Shelah, in which the Jewish nation was. 4827.
Kesithæ (Gen. xxxiii. 19), which were money, s. interior truths. 4400.
Keturah (Gen. xxv. 1) s. divine truth spiritual, conjoined to divine good spiritual. 3236, 3243.
Key den. power. 9410. The k. which opened the bottomless pit (Rev. ix.) s. communication and conjunction with the hells by falses, into which the truths of the Word were turned by those who falsified them, by applying them to evils of life, and to the principal falses thence received. A.E. 536.
Key of David (Rev. iii. 7) s. the Lord's omnipotence over heaven and hell; and the same that is here s. by the k. of D., is s. by the keys of Peter. (Matt. xviii. 18.) A.R. 174.
Keys of Hell and **of Death.** (Rev. i. 18.) By k. is s. the power of opening and shutting, in this instance the power of opening hell, that man may be brought forth, and of shutting it, lest he should enter it again; for man is born to evils of all kinds, consequently, in hell, for evils are hell; he is brought out of it by the Lord, who has power to open it. A.R. 62.

Kibroth Hattaavah

Kibroth Hattaavah, or the graves of concupiscence (Num. xi. 34), was a name given to the place where the children of Israel were smitten with plagues, on account of their natural and sensual disposition. A.E. 513.

Kick, to. The state of the Jews as to intellectual truth, rep. by a horse kicking. 6212.

Kid s. the truth of the church. A.R. 572. Also, innocence and charity. A k. (Isa. xi. 6) s. the genuine truth of the church. A.R. 572. A k. (Isa. xi. 6) s. the good of interior innocence. 10.132. K. (Isa. xi. 6) s. charity. A.E. 780. "Thou shalt not seethe a k. in his mother's milk" (Exod. xxiii. 19), s. that the good of the innocence of a posterior state, is not to be conjoined with the truth of the innocence of a prior state. This is a celestial arcanum, from which that law proceeded. 9301. K. of the goats s. the innocence of the external or natural man; thus the truth and good thereof. 3519. K. of the goats (Gen. xxvii. 16) s. truths of domestic good. 3540.

Kidneys (Exod. xxix. 13) s. internal truths, or truths exploring, purifying, and correcting. 10.032. They who constitute the province of the k., of the ureters, and of the bladder, in the grand man, are of such a genius and temper, that they desire nothing more ardently than to explore and scrutinize the quality of others, and there are some also who desire to chastise, and punish, provided there be any thing of justice in the case. 5381. See *Reins, Bladder.*

Kill, to. To destroy the souls of men. A.R. 325. To k. (Gen. xxvii. 42) s. to deprive of self-derived life. 3610. To k. her sons with death (Rev. ii. 23) s. to turn truths into falses, for by that means they perish; also to condemn their falses. A.R. 139. To k. (Rev. vi. 4) s. intestine hatreds, infestations from the hells, and internal restlessness. A.R. 307. To k. (Rev. ix. 5) s. to take away from those who are in the faith of charity, the faculty of understanding, and willing what is true and good, for when this faculty is taken away, man is spiritually killed. A.R. 427. By killing and being killed (Rev. xiii. 10) is s. to destroy and be destroyed, or to ruin and perish, which is effected by falses. A.R. 592.

Kiln den. worship derived from falses. 1296.

Kindles, all evil which does not appear itself, is like firewood under ashes. D.P. 278.

Kine, in the genuine sense, s. truths in the interior natural principle, but in the opp. sense, falses there. 5268. K. s. good natural affections; the lowing of the k. in the way (1 Sam. v. 6) s. the difficult conversion of the concupiscences of evil in the natural man into good affections; and the offering the k., with a cart, as a burnt offering, s. that the Lord was thus propitiated. D.P. 326. See *Cow.*

King. It was sacrilege to hurt a k., because he was the anointed of Jehovah. (See 1 Sam. xxiv. 7, 11; xxvi. 9; 2 Sam. i. 16, 19, 22.) A.R. 779. The regulation concerning a k. (Deut. xvii. 14–18) implies, that the Jews should choose genuine truth originating in good, and not spurious, and that they should not defile it by reasonings and scientifics. 2015. K., in an opp. sense, s. one who is in falses from concupiscence of evil, and abstractedly that false itself. A.R. 440. K. den. truth itself, and prince a principal truth. A.R. 548.

King in his **Beauty,** to see the (Isa. xxxiii. 17), s. genuine truth, which is from the Lord alone; and "to behold the land of far distances" s. the extension of intelligence and wisdom. A.E. 304.

King of Assyria (Isa. viii. 7) s. fantasies. 705.

King of Judah s. the spiritual principle of the church. A.E. 706.

King of the **North** and **King** of the **South.** (Dan. xi. 1, to the end.) By the k. of the n. is s. the kingdom or church of those who are in falses; and by k. of the s. is s. the kingdom or church of those who are in truths; for it is a prophecy respecting the churches to come, shewing what the nature of them will be in their beginning, and what afterwards. A.R. 720.

King of **Saints** s. divine truth in heaven and in the church from the Lord. A.R. 664.

King and **Counsellor.** (Micah i. 9.) K. s. the truth of doctrine from the Word, and c., understanding thence. A.E. 721.

King of **Kings** and **Lord** of **Lords.** The Lord, with respect to his divine human is called K. of k. and L. of l.; and he is called K. from divine truth, and L. from divine good; and this also is meant by kingdom and dominion, where it treats concerning him. A.R. 743.

King, Queen, Daughters, and **Virgins.** (Ps. xlv. 10–16.) By the k., in this passage, is meant the Lord; by the q., the church as a wife; and by d. and v., the affections of goodness and truth. A.R. 620.

King and **Ruler,** or **Governor.** (Ps. cv. 20.) The Lord is called k. in the W., from divine truth, and g., from divine good. A.E. 448.

Kingdom, animal. The forms of the a. k. which are called in one word animals, are all in accordance with the flux of spiritual substances and forces; the only difference being in the forms into which the influx is received. A.Cr. 93.

Kingdom, mineral, the, is merely the storehouse in which are contained the substances which compose the forms of the animal and vegetable kingdoms. A.Cr. 96.

Kingdom, vegetable. The vegetative soul is in the effort to produce a vegetable from seed, to new seeds, and so on to infinity; for there is in every vegetable an idea, as it were, of the infinite. A.Cr. 92.

King's Daughter s. the love of truth. 3703. K. d. (Ps. xlv. 13) s. the Lord's spiritual kingdom. 5044.

King's Son (Ps. lxxii. 1) s. the celestial man. 337. K. s. and kings s. those who are in wisdom from the Lord. A.R. 20.

Kings s. those who are in truths originating in good from the Lord, and in the opp. sense, those who are in falses originating in evil, or abstractedly, such truths or falses. A.R. 20, 700, 921. K. are pred. of peoples, but not of nations. 1672. The two k. (Isa. vii. 16) s. the truth of the Word in its internal sense, and the truth of the Word in its external sense. A.E. 304. K. who should come forth of Abraham (Gen. xvii. 6) s. celestial truths, which flow in from the divine good of the Lord; and k. of people who should be of Sarah (ver. 16) s. spiritual truths, which flow in from the divine truth of the Lord. 2069. K. of antiquity (Isa. xix. 11–13) s. the truths of the ancient church. 5044. K. of the earth and rulers (Ps. ii. 2) s. the falses and evils of the church. A.E. 684.

Kingdom of **God,** in its universal sense, means the universal heaven; and in a sense less universal, the true church of the Lord; and in a particular sense, every particular person of a true faith, or who is regenerate by the life of faith. 29. The k. of G. s. both heaven and the church, for the k. of G. on the earth is the church. U.T. 572.

Kingdom of and **Will** of **God.** (Matt. vi.) When all things appertaining to love and faith, which things are of God, or of the Lord, and are from him, are accounted holy, the k. of G. comes, and his will is done in the earths, as in the heavens. 2009.

Kingdoms, the, of this **World,** are become the k. of our Lord, and of his Christ (Rev. vi. 15) s. that heaven and the church, are become the Lord's, etc. A.R. 520.

Kiriathaim. Those who adulterate goodness and extinguish truths. 2468.

Kir den. those who possess the knowledges of good and truth, but pervert them. 9340.

Kirheres s. external worship defiled. 3468.

Kirjath-arba

Kirjath-arba (Gen. xxiii. 2) s. the church as to truth. 2909.

Kiss, to, s. unition, or conjunction from affection. 3574. To k. (Gen. xxix. 13) s. initiation. 3808. To k. s. conjunction and acknowledgment. 4215.

Kites, Magpies, Peacocks, Quails, etc., are seen in the spiritual world, and derive their existence from the affections of spirits. Exp. A.Cr. 89.

Kitthim. Doctrinals respecting ritual observances. 1156.

Kneading Troughs (Exod. vii. 3) s. the pleasantnesses of lusts in the natural principle; the same is s. by ovens in a bad sense. 7356. To k. dough, s. to fabricate doctrine from cupidities, and according to them. A.E. 555.

Knee s. the conjunction of natural good with spiritual good. Bending the k. s. acknowledgment, thanksgiving, and adoration, from spiritual good in the natural man. A.E. 455. K. (Gen. xxx. 5) s. conjugial love. 3915. The k. (Isa. lxvi. 12) s. celestial love. A.E. 365. K. (Ezek. vii. 17) s. the love of good. A.E. 677.

Knife used for sacrifices, den. the truth of faith. 2799.

Knives of **Flints** (Josh. v. 2, 3, 9) s. truths whereby evils may be corrected. 2039. The knife used for sacrifices den. the truth of faith. 2799.

Knock, to. "Behold I stand at the door and knock" (Rev. iii. 20), s. the perpetual presence, and operation of the Lord with man. A.E. 248.

know, to. When pred. of God, s. foresight and providence, for it cannot be said of God, that he knows, inasmuch as from himself he knows all things; and the faculty of knowing appertains to man from him, wherefore to k. is in God to foresee and to provide; to foresee is to k. from eternity to eternity, and to provide is to do it. 5309. By no one knowing the written name but himself (Rev. xix. 12), is s. that no one sees but the Lord himself, and they to whom he reveals it, what the Word is in its spiritual sense. A.R. 824. By Cain's knowing his wife, and her conceiving and bearing Enoch (Gen. iv. 17), is s. that this schism or heresy, produced another from itself. 400.

Known, to make, is to teach. 8695.

Known, to be. From good evil is k., and from truth falsity. From heaven is k. every thing in hell. A.Cr. 110.

Knowledge of the **Lord**, the, is the universal of all things of doctrine, and thence of all things of the church; from it all worship derives its life and soul, for the Lord is all in all in heaven and the church, and hence all in all in worship. A.R. 916.

Knowledges are the things which open the way to behold things celestial and spiritual; by k. the way is opened for the internal man to the external, in which are the recipient vessels, which are as many in number as are the k. of goodness and truth; into these as into their vessels celestial things enter by influx. 1458. Faith and the consequent presence of the Lord is given by means of k. of truths derived from the Word, especially concerning the Lord himself there, but love and consequent conjunction is given by a life according to his commandments. A.R. 937. K. of what is true and good out of the Word, when there is in them the spiritual principle out of heaven from the Lord, are not called k. but truths; but if there is not in them any spirituality, out of heaven from the Lord, they are nothing but scientifics. A.R. 900.

Kor, or **Homer** den. a sufficient quantity, or as much as can be received. 8468.

Korah, Dathan, and **Abiram** s. damnation. 8306.

Koran. The Mahometan, after evils are removed, sees truths from the k. A.Cr. 73.

Korhites, the families of the (Exod. vi. 24), s. the quality of goods and truths. 7230.

Kush s. love and faith. A.C. 117.

L

Laban s. the affection of good in the natural man, or the affection of external good, and properly collateral good of a common stock. 3665. The good rep. by L. is such, that it is merely a useful good, viz., to introduce genuine truths and goods, and when it has answered this purpose of usefulness, it is afterwards left. 3982. L. (Gen. xxxi. 44, etc.) rep. the goods of works, such as have place with those who are aside, that is with the Gentiles. 4189. L. and the flock (Gen. xxxi.) rep. that middle or mediatory good that man is kept in for a while during the process of his regeneration.

Laban and **Aramæan** (Gen. xxxi. 20), s. middle good, in which there is not divine good and truths as before. 4112.

Labyrinths in the grand man. Exp. 5181.

Labor has respect, in a good sense, to the things that are of love; and in an opp. sense, to the things that are of evil. 613. L. (Gen. xli. 51) den. the combats of temptation. 5322. L. s. affliction of soul and crucifixion of the flesh, for the sake of the Lord, and of eternal life. A.R. 640. To eat the l. of the hands s. celestial good, which man receives by a life according to divine truths from the Lord. A.E. 617. In a spiritual sense, l. s. all which man thinks; and patience, or endurance, all which man does. A.E. 430.

Laborers (Matt. ix. 37, 38) s. all who teach from the Lord. A.E. 911.

Lace. Genuine scientific truths appear like l. Exp. 5954.

Laceration, punishments of. Des. 829.

Ladder s. the communication of truth which is in the lowest place with truth which is in the highest. 3699. See *Jacob's Ladder.*

Lake s. where there is truth in abundance; also, where the false principle abounds. A.R. 835. L. of waters s. knowledges of truth. A.E. 405. See *Pool.*

Lake of **Fire** s. hell. A.R. 872. L. of f. and sulphur s. the hell where the love of what is false and the cupidities or the lusts of evil reign. A.R. 864.

Lamb s. the good of the innocence of infancy. 10.132. L. s. the Lord as to his divine humanity. A.R. 256. L. (Rev. xiii. 11) s. the Lord as to the Word. A.E. 816. L. (Rev. xiv. 10) s. divine good. A.E. 888.

Lamb Slain from the **Foundation** of the **World** (Rev. xiii. 8) s. the Lord's divine humanity, not acknowledged from the first establishment of the church. A.R. 589.

Lamb, Kid, and **Calf** (Isa. xi. 6), s. three degrees of innocence and love; wolf, leopard, and young lion, s. their opposites. 430.

Lambs and **Sheep.** L. s. those who are in the good of innocence and love to the Lord; and s., those who are in the good of charity towards their neighbor. A.E. 9.

Lambs, Rams, and **Goats,** cor. to the goods and truths respectively, in which the angels of the third, second, and first heaven are principled. (See Ezek. xxvii. 21, and Deut. xxxii. 14.) A.E. 817. See *Ewe Lambs.*

Lame. That the l. s. those who are in good not genuine, because in ignorance of truth. A.E. 455, 518. That by the l. leaping, is s. joy from perception of truth. A.E. 455.

Lame and **Blind.** The l. and b. s. those who are in their own proprium of self-

Lame in the Feet and Hands

hood. 210. The l. s. those who are in evil, and the b. those who are in falses. 4302.

Lame in the **Feet** and **Hands**, the, rep. such as are in perverted external worship; such were not permitted to offer offerings of fire to Jehovah. (Lev. xxi. 19, 20.) 2162.

Lamech (Gen. iv. 18) s. the vastation of the church, when there was no longer any faith. 405. L. (Gen. v. 25) s. the ninth church from Adam. 523. In this church the perception of truth and goodness was become so common and obscure, that it was next to none, and thus the church was vastated. See *Zillah.*

Lamentation. The children of Israel rep. l. by various things, which, from cor., were significative of some evil of the church among them, for which they were punished; and when they were punished, by such things, they rep. repentance and humiliation. A.R. 492. See *Mourning.*

Lamentation of **David** over **Saul**, treats concerning the doctrine of truth, combating against the falses of evil. 10.540.

Lamentations of **Jeremiah**, treat of the vastation of every good and truth among the Jewish nation, on account of their application of the literal sense of the Word, to favor their own loves. A.E. 357.

Lamp. Light of a l. s. illumination from the Lord. A.R. 796. L. (Rev. xxii.) s. natural light from self-derived intelligence. A.R. 940. L. s. things celestial, from which things spiritual proceed. 886. By the ordination of the l., from the evening until the morning (Exod. xxvii. 20, 21) is s. the perpetual influx of the good and truth from the Lord, always in every state. 9787. L. (Matt. xxv. 4) s. love. 3079. L. and candles s. intelligence in both senses. A.R. 408. L. s. truths of faith. D.P. 328.

Lances s. truths combating. A.E. 557.

Lancet s. truth. 2799.

Land, in the Word, den. the church, for the things significative of the church, are significative also of the things relating to the church, for these constitute the church; the reason why l. den. the church in the Word is, because the l. of Canaan was the l. in which the church had been from the most ancient times; hence, when l. is named in the Word, the l. of Canaan is meant, and when this is meant, the church is meant; for they who are in the spiritual world, when mention is made of l., do not rest in the idea of l., but in the idea of the nation which inhabits it, nor in the idea of the nation which inhabits it, but in the idea of the quality of that nation, consequently, in the idea of the church. 5577. L. or earth (Gen. xx. 15) s. the doctrine of love and charity. 2571. The celestial principle of love. (Gen. xxiv. 4.) 3026. Things rational. (Gen. xxvi. 12.) 3404. The good of the natural principle. (Gen. xxviii. 13.) 3705. The divine of the rational principle. (Gen. xxx. 25.) 3973.

Land of Canaan, or the **Holy Land,** in the Word, is taken for love, and consequently, for the will of the celestial man. 485.

Land of Cush, the (Gen. ii. 13), s. mind or faculty, or the will and understanding. 116.

Land of Drought and of **Thick Shade** (Jer. ii. 2), s. the perception of good, and the understanding of truth obscured. A.E. 730.

Land of Negotiation (Ezek. xvi. 29) (translated, the land of Canaan) s. the origin and source from whence all falses are derived; namely, the sensual principle. A.E. 654.

Land of Seir s. celestial and natural good. 4328.

Land not Inhabited (Lev. xvi. 22) s. hell. A.E. 730.

Land and **Ground.** (Mal. iii. 11, 12.) L. evidently s. that which contains, consequently, it s. man, who is called l., where g. s. the church or doctrine. 566.

Laughter

Lands of different nations are used in the Word to s. the different kinds of love prevalent in the inhabitants. 585.

Lanes. By the servants going into the streets and l., is s. that he should seek everywhere some genuine truth. 2336.

Language. There is a universal l., which angels and spirits use, and this has nothing in common with any l. of men in this world, but every man comes into this l. spontaneously after death, for it is inherent in him from his creation. A.R. 29. The l. of the Word is real angelic l. in its ultimates. 3482. Every spirit and angel, when conversing with a man, speaks that man's own l.; thus French with a Frenchman, English with an Englishman, etc. C.S.L. 326.

Lantern (Ps. cxxxii. 17, 18) s. the light of truth. 2832.

Laodiceans (Rev. iii. 14) s. those who alternately believe sometimes from themselves, and sometimes from the Word, and so profane holy things. A.R. 198. By the church of the L., are meant those who are in faith alone, thus who are in faith separate from charity. A.E. 227.

Lapping Water with the **Tongue**, as a **Dog** (Judges vii.), s. punishment, on account of the falsification of truth. 3242.

Larynx. They who love the Word are in the province of the l. 4791.

Lasciviousness. One of the causes of disease. 5712.

Lasha s. falses and evils wherein knowledges terminate. 1212.

Lassitude, or **Weariness,** den. a state of temptation combat. 3318.

Last. The first and the l. s. that the Lord is the only God. A.R. 92.

Last Judgment, the, was accomplished in the spiritual world in the year 1757; it was executed on those who were in the world of spirits, but not on any one in heaven, nor on any one in hell. A.R. 342. The l. j. is to be considered as general, particular, and singular; general, with respect to the end of a church; particular, as to the last time of every man's life; and singular, with respect to his thoughts, words, and actions. 1850, 4535. L. j. is not executed till devastation takes place. A.R. 676. Unless the l. j. had been accomplished, the heavens would have suffered, and the church perished. A.R. 263. By the l. j., all things are reduced to order in the spiritual world, and thence in the natural world, or in the earths. A.R. 274. The l. j. with every one is when the Lord comes, as well in general, as in particular; thus, it was the l. j. when the Lord came into the world; it will be the l. j. when he shall come to glory; it is the l. j. when he comes to each man in particular; it is also the l. j. with every one when he dies. 900. After the l. j. it was provided and ordained by the Lord, that hereafter no one should have conjunction with heaven, than he who is in spiritual faith, which is acquired by a life according to the truths of the Word, which life is called charity. A.E. 737. The spiritual sense of the Word and the doctrine, that the Lord alone was the God of heaven and earth, was not revealed till after the l. j., for by the l. j. the Babylonians were removed, and likewise such of the reformed, as acknowledged justification by faith only, whose falsities were like black clouds, interposed between the Lord and men upon earth; they were also like cold, and extinguished spiritual heat, which is the love of goodness and truth. A.R. 804.

Latchet, by **Shoe,** is s. evil. 1748.

Latitude s. truth. A.R. 861. See *Degrees of Altitude.*

Latter Days (Jer. xlviii. 47) s. the advent of the Lord. A.E. 811.

Laughter is an affection of the rational principle, and indeed an affection of the true or of the false in the rational principle, hence comes all l.; so long as such affection is in the rational principle, which puts itself forth in l., so long there is somewhat corporeal or worldly, thus merely human; celestial good and spiritual good does not laugh, but expresses its delight and cheerfulness in the countenance, in the speech, and in the gesture, after another

Laurels

manner; for in l. there are many principles contained, as for the most part something of contempt, which although it does not appear, still lies concealed under that outward expression, and is easily distinguished from cheerfulness of mind, which also produces something similar to l. 2216.

Laurels have respect to the affections of truth. H. and H. 520.

Laver of **Brass** (Exod. xxx. 18) s. the good of the natural man, in which purification takes place. L. s. the natural principle, and b., the good thereof. The like was s. by the molten sea, which Solomon made. (1 Kings vii. 23, etc.) 10.235.

Law. By the l., in a strict sense, are meant the ten commandments; in a more extensive sense, all things written in the five books of Moses; and in the most extensive sense, all things that are contained in the Word. L. 8, 9, 10. By the works of the l., mentioned by Paul in Rom. iii. 28, are meant the works of the Mosaic l., proper to the Jews. A.R. 417.

Law Written in their **Hearts** (Jer. xxxi. 33) s. perception of good and truth thence derived, and also conscience. 3654. Those who have the l. w. in their h. are in the third heaven. A.R. 121.

Law and the **Prophets** s. the universal doctrine of faith, and all the Word. 2116. A.E. 250.

Law and **Word** of **Jehovah**. (Isa. ii. 3–5.) L. is the doctrine of the good of love; and W. is truth from that good. A.E. 734.

Lawn, or **Linen**, s. genuine truth. A.R. 814.

Laws, all, even civil and forensic, which are in the Word, have cor. with the l. of good and truth, which are in heaven. 3540.

Laws of the **Jewish Church**, notwithstanding the cessation of their authority in the letter, are yet the sacred Word of God, on account of the interior things which are in it. 9211. All and singular things in the l., judgments, and statutes which were promulgated from Mount Sinai, and which are contained in Exodus xxi. xxii. xxiii., are holy in the internal form; but still that some of them are abrogated as to use at this day, where the church is, which is an internal church; but some of them are of such a quality that they may serve for use, if people are so disposed; and some of them ought altogether to be observed and done. Those which ought altogether to be observed and done, are what are contained in chap. xx. vs. 3, 4, 5, 7, 8, 12, 13–16, 17, 23; xxi. 12, 14, 15, 20; xxii. 18, 19, 20, 28; xxiii. 1, 2, 3, 6, 7, 8, 24, 25, 32. Those which may serve for use if people are so disposed, are such as are contained in chap. xx. 10; xxi. 18, 19, 22, 23, 24, 25, 33, 34, 35, 36; xxii. 1, 2, 3, 4, 5, 6, 7, 8, 9, 10, 11, 12, 13, 16, 20, 21, 22, 24, 25, 26, 30; xxxiii. 4, 5, 9, 12, 13, 14, 15, 16, 23. But those which are abrogated as to use at this day where the church is, chap. xx. 24, 25, 26; xxi. 2, 3, 4, 6, 7, 8, 9, 10, 11, 16, 21, 26, 27, 28, 29, 31, 32; xxii. 15, 29, 30; xxiii. 10, 11, 17, 18, 19. 9349.

Laws of **Permission** are laws of divine providence. D.P. 234–240.

Lawgiver (Num. xxi. 18) s. the Lord. 3424.

Lawyers (Luke xi. 52) s. those who searched the scriptures and taught how they were to be understood. A.E. 536.

Lawn, or **Fine Linen**, s. genuine truth. A.R. 814.

Lay, to, the **Hand** on the **Wall** (Amos v. 19) s. self-derived power and confidence, grounded in sensual things. 195.

Laying on of **Hands** in inauguration, rep. the blessing communicated to the intellectual and voluntary faculties. 6298.

Lazarus s. the Gentiles, who had not the Word. That they were despised and rejected by the Jews is s. by his being laid at the gate of the rich man, full of sores. S.S. 40. A.R. 724. The raising of Lazarus (John ix.) rep. a new church from among the Gentiles. 2916. See *Dives*.

Lazule Stone rep. the appearance of the Lord's divine sphere, in the spiritual heavens. A.R. 232.

Lead, to. The Lord leads and inclines man by his proprium, as well by the fallacies of the senses as by his lusts, to those things which are true and good. 24. The Lord l. those who are in the principles of good and truth, into the life of truth and good, although they know it not. 3773. The divine love l. the evil and unjust in hell, and snatches them out thence. D.P. 337.

Lead us not into Temptation, etc. (Matt. vi.) According to the literal sense, it appears that the Lord leads man into temptation; but the internal sense is, that the Lord leads no one into temptation. 3425.

Leader. What is primary in doctrine. 3448.

Leaf s. truth throughout the Word. 885. L. rep. the external natural church. A.E. 695. See *Medicine*.

Leah and **Rachel**. L. rep. the Jewish church, and R. the new church of the Gentiles. 422. L. s. the exterior affection of truth, and R. the interior affection thereof. 3793.

Lean in **Flesh** (Gen. xli. 19) s. where there was no charity. 5258. To make l. (Zeph. ii. 11) s. to remove evils from falses. A.E. 406.

Leap, to (Lev. xi. 21), when pred. of birds, s. to live. A.E. 543.

Learn, to (Rev. xiv. 3), s. to perceive interiorly in himself, that it is so, which is to understand, and so to receive and acknowledge; he who l. any otherwise, learns and does not l., because he does not retain what he l. A.R. 618.

Learned, from the light of the world. Exp. 206. The l., or wise, who shall shine as the stars, are they who are in good. 3820.

Least. The greatest in heaven are they who are l. in their esteem, and in the greatest affection of serving others. 3417.

Leathern Girdle, the, which John the Baptist wore, s. an external band receiving and containing the interiors. 9372.

Leaven s. evil and the false, which should not be mixed with things good and true; therefore in Lev. ii. 11, it is said, "no meat offering which ye shall bring to Jehovah, shall be made leavened." And therefore it was also enjoined, that on seven days of the passover, they should not eat any but unleavened bread. (Exod. xii. 15, 18–20.) 2342.

Leaves s. truths according to the different kinds of trees. The l. of the olive tree and vine, s. rational truths, from celestial and spiritual light; the l. of the fig-tree rational truths from natural light; and the l. of the fir, poplar, oak, and pine, rational from sensual light. The l. of the latter trees excite terror in the spiritual world, when they are agitated by a strong wind, and these are what are meant in Lev. xxvi. 36; Job xiii. 25. But with the l. of the former it is not so. A.R. 936. L. of the fig-tree (Matt. xxi. 19) s. truths from the literal sense of the Word. A.E. 386. L. and blossoms s. the truths of faith, and fruit the good of love. Dec. 46.

Lebanon s. spiritual good. 10.261. Lebanon s. the church as to the perception of truth from the rational man. A.E. 650. See *Cedars*.

Led. To be l. by the Lord is to be in a state of essential liberty, blessedness, and happiness. 5660.

Led and **Taught**. It is a law of the divine providence, that man is l. and t. by the Lord from heaven, through the Word, by doctrine and preachings from it, and this in all appearance as of himself. D.P. 154. The will of the life of man is l., and the understanding of his life is t. D.P. 156.

Leeks s. the corporeal part of man. A.E. 513. See *Cucumbers*.

Lees s. truths from good. A.E. 1159. See *Feast of Fat Things*.

Left in the **Land** (Isa. vii. 22) s. remains. 680. It is said (Luke xvii. 34) that at the last judgment, "one shall be taken from the mill, and the other left," etc., and by some being left is plainly declared, that the world would not then be destroyed. 931. By those who are left are s. they who neither inquire after, nor receive truths, because they are in falses. A.R. 794.

Left Foot. See *Jews*.

183

Left Hand

Left Hand in a bad sense, the false by which evil is produced. 10.061.

Legions, twelve, of **Angels** (Matt. xxvi. 53) s. the universal heaven, and more than these, divine omnipotence. A.E. 430.

Legislator (Num. xxi. 18) s. the Lord as to the Word, and doctrine from the Word. A.E. 537.

Legitimate. Truth can only be l., multiplied from good. 5345.

Legs s. the exteriors of the natural man. 10.050. The l. of a man (Ps. cxlvii. 10) which Jehovah does not take pleasure in, s. those things which are of man's voluntary proprium, from which are mere evils. A.E. 355. Two l. (Amos iii. 12) s. the will of good, and a small piece of an ear the will of truth. 3869. See *Horse*.

Legs and **Feet** s. natural good conjoined to spiritual good, and f. natural truth separated from good which should not be appropriated by man; it was therefore called an abomination to eat any thing that went upon all four, without l. (Lev. xi. 20, 21.) A.E. 543.

Lehabim. Rituals of external worship, merely scientific. 1149.

Leibnitz. No one can think from himself, ill. in the case of L. D.P. 289.

Lend, to, s. to teach. A.E. 559. Also to communicate the goods and truths of doctrine from the Word. 695.

Length den. good, or the good of the church, which is grounded in the same cause as the s. of breadth; the cause is this; the extent of heaven from east to west is s. by l., and the extent of heaven from south to north is s. by breadth, and the angels who dwell in the east and west of heaven, are in the good of love, and the angels who dwell in the south and north of heaven, are in the truths of wisdom. It is the same with the church on earth, for every man who is in the goods and truths of the church derived from the Word, is consociated with angels of heaven, and as to the interiors of his mind dwells with them; they who are in the good of love in the east and west of heaven, and they who are in the truths of wisdom in the south and north of heaven; this indeed man does not know, but yet every one after death comes into his place. A.R. 906. L. has respect to holiness. 646–650.

Lentiles s. the less noble species of good. 332.

Leopard, a, being an artful and insidious animal, more particularly rep. those who confirm faith separate from good works. A.E. 780. L. s. the affection or lust of falsifying the truths of the Word; and because it is a ferocious beast, and kills innocent animals, it also s. an heresy destructive of the church. That truths of the Word falsified are s. by l., is owing to its black and white spots, and by black spots are s. falses, and by the white intermixed with them is s. truth; therefore, because it is a fierce and murderous beast, by it are s. truths of the Word falsified, and so destroyed. A.R. 572.

Leprosy, the, rep. unclean false principles grounded in what is profane. 3301. A.E. 962. The l. s. the falsification of truth and good in the Word, also the Jewish profanation of the Word; wherefore that nation was afflicted with that disease. A.E. 475, A.R. 678.

Lesser den. truth, greater den. good. 3296.

Let Down, to (Gen. xxiv. 18), s. an act of submission. 3091.

Letushim s. varieties of faith. 3241.

Leummim s. good of faith and its varieties. 3241.

Levi s. truth in act, which is the good of life. A.R. 17. L., in a supreme sense, s. love and mercy; in a spiritual sense, charity in act, which is good of life; and in a natural sense, consociation and conjunction. A.R. 357. L. s. the affection of truth originating in good, and consequently, intelligence. A.R. 357. L. (Mal. ii. 5) rep. the Lord as to divine good. A.E. 701. L., in a bad sense, s. the evil of the false which is opp. to the good of charity. See Gen.

Life of Man

xlix. 5–7, and Luke x. 29–37. A.E. 444. The sons of L. (Deut. xxi. 5) s. the affection of good and truth, which is charity. A.E. 444.
Leviathan (Ps. lxxiv. 14) s. scientifics in general. 7293, 9755, 10.416. L. the straight serpent s. the merely sensual who are without faith, because they do not comprehend, and who reject all things they do not see with their eyes; l. the crooked serpent s. they who therefore do not believe and yet say that they do believe. A.E. 275.
Levites, by, is s. obedience of faith. A.E. 438.
Libanus s. the spiritual church. 5922. The glory of L. or cedars (Isa. lx. 13) s. the celestial spiritual things of the Lord's kingdom and church. 2162.
Libation. See *Drink-Offering.*
Liberation from evils and falses is effected by the holy proceeding from the Lord's divine human. 6864.
Liberty, or **Free-Will,** s. the faculty of thinking, willing, and acting freely. D.L.W. 264. All liberty is from love and affection. 2870, 3158, 9585, 9591. Man first comes into a state of l., when he is regenerated, being before in a state of slavery. 892. The infernal l., or freedom, consists in being led by the loves of self and of the world, and their lusts. 2870, 2873. Spiritual l. is grounded in the love of eternal life. D.P. 73. In temptations man's spiritual l. is stronger than when he is out of them, because it is interior. A.E. 900.
Libration. The salvation and l. of the spiritual, is by means of the divine human. 2833.
Lice (Exod. viii.) s. evils which are in the sensual, or in the external man; and infestations by evils, are s. by their biting. 7419.
Lie Down, or sit at a table, s. conjunction and consociation. A.E. 252.
Lie With, to (Gen. xxvi. 10), s. to pervert and adulterate what is true and good. 3399. To l. w. (Gen. xxxix. 7) s. conjunction, or to the intent, that there might be conjunction. 5007.
Lie and Vastation. (Hosea xii. 2.) L. s. the false, and v. the dissipation of truth. A.E. 419. L. s. falses, and perversity is the evil of the false. (Isa. lix. 3, 7.) A.E. 329.
Life. There is one sole l., which is God, and all men are recipients of l. from him. D.P. 213. A.C. 1954, 2536, 5847. The Lord as to his divine human, is l. in himself. A.R. 58, 961. Good has l. in itself, because it is from the Lord, who is l. itself; in the l. which is from the Lord, there is wisdom and intelligence, for to receive good from the Lord, and thence to will good, is wisdom, and to receive truth from the Lord, and thence to believe truth, is intelligence, and they who have this wisdom and intelligence have l.; and whereas happiness is adjoined to such l., eternal happiness is what is also s. by l. 5070. There can be no such thing as l. in an individual, unconnected with the l. of others. 687, 889. L. appears to man as properly his own, and it is by influx from the Lord. 3742, 4320. L. from the Lord flows in with the evil, and with those who are in hell; but they change good into evil, and the truth into the false, and thus l. into spiritual death; for such as man's nature is, such is his reception of l. 2706, 2743. Spiritual l. is that l. which the angels have in heaven; to this l. man is introduced in the world by the things which are of faith and charity; the very affection of good which is of charity and the affection of truth which is of faith is spiritual life. 5561. A moral l. without a spiritual l., will avail nothing, being like natural l., which is from no other origin than the love of self and the world, and must be vivified by truth and good, which prepares and opens the internal spiritual man. A.E. 188.
Life after Death. Not openly declared to the Jews. See *Jews.*
Life of Man, in its principles, is in the brains, and in its principiates in the body. D.L.W. 365. The l. of m. consists in the freedom of will he possesses in spiritual things, from the Lord. U.T. 489. The l. of m. admits of no change

Lift up the Eyes

after death, for it remains the same that it was in the world, and is in no respect changed, inasmuch as an evil life cannot be changed into a good one, nor vice versa, because they are opposites, and conversion into an opposite is extinction. N.J.D. 239. H. and H. 470. If any man's life had been in the love of evil, every truth which he had acquired in this world, from masters, preachings, and the Word, is taken away from him in the other world. D.P. 17.

Lift up the Eyes, to (Gen. xxiv. 63), s. intention. 3198. To l. u. the e. (Gen. xliii. 29) den. thought and intention, observance and reflection. 5684.

Lift, to, **up the Head** s. to conclude, and in the supreme sense, to provide, for the divine conclusion and execution of a thing concluded is providence. To l. u. the h. was a customary form of judgment amongst the ancients, when the bound, or they who were in prison, were judged either to life or death; when to life, it was expressed by l. u. the h. (2 Kings xx. 27, 28), but when they were judged to death, it was expressed by l. u. the h. from upon him. (Gen. xl. 19.) This form of judgment derived its origin with the ancients, who were in rep. from the rep. of those who were bound in prison, or in a pit, and inasmuch as by these were rep. they who are in vastation under the lower earth; therefore, by l. u. the h. was s. their liberation, for in such case they are elevated or lifted up out of vastation to the heavenly societies; to be lifted up or be elevated is to advance towards interior things, for what is elevated or high is pred. of things interior. 5124.

Lift up, to, the **Voice,** and **Weep** (Gen. xxix. 11), s. the ardor of love. 3801.

Light s. the divine truth of the Word, also the truth of faith. A.R. 897. A.C. 3395, 9684. The Lord is the l. which illuminates the understanding of angels and men, and that l. proceeds from the sun of the spiritual world, in which he dwells. A.R. 796. The delight of love and wisdom elevates the thought, enabling it to see, as in the l., that a thing is so, although the man had never heard of it before; this l. which illuminates the mind, flows from no other source but out of heaven from the Lord; and whereas they who are to be of the New Jerusalem will directly approach the Lord that l. will flow in, in the way of order, which is through the love of the will into the perception of the understanding. A.R. 914. L., which was made the first day '(Gen. i.), s. divine l. which, in itself, and in its essence, is divine truth, consequently, spiritual l., which ill. the understanding, and since in that chapter regeneration is treated of, which is primarily effected by ill. from the Lord, therefore, l. is therein first of all mentioned. A.E. 532. L. (John xi. 9) s. truth grounded in good. 2353. L. (Rev. xxi. 24) s. perception of divine truth by interior illumination from the Lord. A.R. 920. L. of eternity (Isa. ix. 20) is pred. concerning those who are in the good of love to the Lord, and the fulfilling of the days of mourning, concerning those who are in the good of charity towards the neighbor, or in truths from good. A.E. 401. L. of heaven is divine truth, and by that l. falses are discovered, also the thoughts of every one, and this l. is spiritual l. A.R. 754. L. of infatuation arises from the confirmation of what is false. Persons in this situation are called owls and bats. A.R. 566. L. of a lamp (Rev. xviii.) s. illumination from the Lord, and consequent perception of spiritual truth. A.R. 796. "L. of the moon shall be as the l. of the sun, and the l. of the sun shall be sevenfold, like the l. of seven days" (Isa. xxx. 26), s. that then the truth of the Lord's spiritual kingdom shall be such as the truth of his celestial kingdom had formerly been, and truth in the celestial kingdom shall become the good of love. Also, that the Lord should appear in much greater effulgence and splendor in the heavens, at the time of the last judgment, and commencement of the New Jerusalem, than he did before. A.E. 401. The l. of the moon is faith grounded in charity, and the l. of the sun intelligence and wisdom grounded in love, in such case derived from the Lord. A.R. 53. The

l. which the spiritual enjoy, is a sort of nocturnal l., such as that of the moon and stars, in respect to the diurnal l. which the celestial enjoy. 2849.

Light and **Heat**. The l. of the spiritual sun is divine truth, and the h. is the divine good. A.Cr. 3, 17.

Lightnings, Thunderings, and **Voices** s. illustrations, perceptions, and instructions, by influx from heaven. A.R. 396.

Lign Aloes (Num. xxiv. 6, 7) s. those things which are of the natural man. A.E. 518.

Ligure, Agate, and **Amethyst,** the (Exod. xxviii. 19), s. the spiritual truth of good. 9870.

Likeness of God s. the celestial man. 51. L. (Gen. v. 3) has relation to faith, and image to love. 484.

Lily. "To blossom as the l." (Hosea xiv. 5), is pred. of the first state of the new birth, or of regeneration; for a l. s. the blossom which precedes the fruit. A.E. 638.

Limbs and **Joints,** a torpor of the, is occasioned from voluptuous spirits, who spurn at faith. 5724.

Limit to the determination of thought. Exp. 5225.

Line of Emptiness, and **Plumb-Lines of Wasteness** (Isa. xxxiv. 11), s. the desolation and vastation of truth. 5044.

Linen s. the truth of spiritual love. 9873. L. s. divine truth. A.R. 671. L. or lawn s. truth from good. A.R. 671. Fine-twined l. s. truth from a celestial origin; or, the intellectual quality of the spiritual man, or which is in an angel who is in the Lord's spiritual kingdom. 9596. L., clean and shining, s. what is bright, by virtue of good; and pure, by virtue of truths. A.R. 814. L. and fine l., genuine truth. A.R. 814. See *Flax.*

Linger, to (Gen. xix. 16), s. resistance from the nature of evil. 2410. Lingering s. a state of doubt, inasmuch as when the state of the life is in a state of doubt, in such case the external is in a state of lingering; this is also exhibited to view in the man himself, for when his mind rests in any doubt, he instantly stops and pauses; the reason is, because doubt causes the state of the life to be a state of hesitation and fluctuation, consequently, it affects in like manner the external progression, as being the effect. 5613.

Lintel den. the goods of the natural principle; and posts, its truths. 7847, 8989.

Lion, in a good sense, s. divine truth in power. A.R. 241, 471, 574. L. s. the Lord as to his humanity, or the power of his divine truth; hence he is called the l. of the tribe of Judah. A.R. 241. L. s. the good of celestial love. 6367. L., in a bad sense, s. the false principle destroying the truths of the Word. A.R. 573. "The l. shall eat straw, like the ox" (Isa. xi. 6), s. that the infernal false, burning to destroy the truths of the church, shall do no hurt to the good affection of the natural man, as well with man in himself, as with men among themselves, and that neither shall it do any hurt to the Word. A.E. 781. L. and asp s. interior and exterior falses, destroying the truths of the church; and l. and dragon s. interior and exterior falses, devastating the goods of the church. (Ps. xci. 13.) A.E. 714. L. (Ps. civ. 21, 22) s. the angels of heaven. A.E. 278.

Lip s. doctrine. 1284, 1288. L. (Isa. vi. 3, 7) s. the interiors of man, consequently, internal worship, wherein is grounded adoration. 1286. L. (Isa. xxxvii. 29) s. thought of the understanding. A.E. 923. L. (Mal. ii. 6, 7) den. doctrine grounded in charity. 1286.

Liquid, or to **Melt,** den. good from the Lord vanishing before the heat of lust. 8487.

Literal Sense of the **Word.** Such is the nature of it, that it distinguishes what the internal sense unites; and this by reason that man who is to be instructed from the sense of the letter cannot have an idea of one, unless he has first an idea of several, for one with man is formed of several, or, what is the same thing, that which is simultaneous is from things successive. There are several things or principles in the Lord, and all are Jehovah. Hence it is, that the sense of the letter distinguishes, whereas heaven in no sort distinguishes, but acknowledges one God, with a simple idea, nor any other than the Lord. 3035. Unless the Word in that sense, consisted of natural rep. cor. with spiritual and celestial things, it would be like a house without a foundation. 10.559. The l. s. of the W. must pass, as it were, into a shade, before the internal sense can appear, even as the earthly body must die, before man can clearly behold the spiritual things of heaven. 1408. The l. s. of the W. is written according to appearances and cor., but not in the spiritual sense, for in this latter there is no appearance and cor., but truth in its light. A.R. 658. The reason why it is said therein, that Jehovah God not only turns away his face, is angry, punishes, and tempts, but also kills, and even curses, is in order that men might believe, that the Lord governs and disposes all and every thing in the universe, even evil itself, punishment, and temptation; and when they have received this most general idea, might afterwards learn how, or in what manner, he governs and disposes all things, and that he turns the evil of punishment and the evil of temptation into good; the order of teaching and of learning in the Word, is from the most general ideas; for which reason the sense of the letter abounds with such most general ideas. 245. The l. s. of the W. is in the light of the world, because it is the Word for men before they come into the light of heaven from the Lord, from which, in such case, they have illustration; hence it is evident, that the sense of the letter, is serviceable for the simple, to initiate them into the internal sense. 4783. The l. s. of the W. serves the spiritual ideas of angels, as a medium of conveyance comparatively, as the words of speech do with men, to convey the sense of a subject, whereon they discourse. 2143. The l. s. of the W. is called a cloud, because the internal sense, which is called glory, cannot be comprehended by man, unless by one who is regenerated, and thence ill.; the internal sense of the Word, or divine truth in its own glory, if it should appear before the man who is not regenerated, would be as thick darkness, in which he could see nothing at all, and also from which he would blind himself, that is, he would believe nothing. 8106. The l. s. of the Word, is a defence for the divine truths concealed in it. U.T. 260. The l. s. of the W., is the basis, the continent, and the firmament, of its spiritual and celestial sense. U.T. 210–213. See *Jehovah.*

Litigate den. to deny. 3425–7.

Little One, or **Little Child**, a, in the Word, s. innocence, and also charity, for true innocence cannot possibly exist without charity, nor can true charity exist without innocence. 430.

Live Forever, to (Gen. iii. 22), does not s. to live forever in the body, but to live after death in eternal damnation. (See also Ezek. xiii. 18, 19.) 304. "Him that liveth forever" (Rev. x. 26), s. the Lord himself. A.R. 474.

Liver, the (Exod. xxix. 13), s. interior purification, and caul above the l., the inferior good of the external or natural man. 10.031.

Lives, used in the plural, because of the will and understanding, and because these two l. make one. 3623.

Living, the, s. those who have spiritual life. A.R. 525.

Living Soul (Gen. ii. 7) s. the external man made alive, by serving the internal. 94, 95. L. s. (Rev. xvi. 3) s. the truth of faith. A.R. 681. L. s., in the Word, s. every animal in general of every kind. 670.

Living Thing, every (Gen. vi. 19), s. the things which appertain to the understanding, and all flesh, the things which appertain to the will. 670.

Living Water and **Rivers**. (John vii. 38.) L. w. s. divine truth, and r. intelligence. A.E. 518. L. w., or w. of life (Zech. xiv. 8) s. divine truths from the Lord. A.R. 932.

Loathe den. aversion. 6665.

Locust and **Caterpillar**. (Ps. x. 5, 34.) L. s. the false of the sensual man, and c. his evil. A.E. 543.

Locusts s. falses in the extremes, which consume the truths and goods of the church in man. A.R. 424, 430. L. which John the Baptist ate, s. ultimate truths, or truths of a most common or general nature; and wild honey the pleasantnesses or delight of them. 9372.

Lodger (Exod. xii. 45) den. one who from natural disposition does good, and does it for the sake of gain. 8002.

Loftiness. The l. of man s. the pride of man's own intelligence. A.E. 445.

Logic draws down the understanding into the dust. Exp. 3348, 4658.

Loins, in general, s. love, and when spoken of the Lord, divine love. A.R. 830. L. s. the interiors of conjugial love. 9961. L. (Isa. xi. 5) s. those who are in the divine good of love, and reins s. those who are in love towards their neighbor. A.E. 780. The l. (Ezek. xxix. 7) s. the marriage of truth and good. A.E. 627.

London, in the spiritual world. Des. C.L.J. 42, 3.

Long, and thence to prolong, are pred. of good. A.E. 900.

Look, to (Gen. xviii. 22), s. to think, for to see den. to understand. 2245. L. not back behind thee (Gen. xix. 17), means that Lot, who rep. the good of charity, should not have respect to doctrinals. 2414. To l. up, is to l. to things celestial. 248.

Look Back. To regard doctrinal truths, and not the good of life. 2454.

Loops of the **Curtains** of the **Tabernacle** (Exod. xxvi. 4) s. conjunction. 9605.

Lord, the, is essential good and essential truth. 2011. The L. is the Word, and the Word treats of him alone, and he is the God of heaven and earth, and from him alone the new church has its existence. A.R. 820. The ground and reason why so various principles of the L. are rep. is not because there are various principles in the L., but because his divine is variously received by man. 4206. The L. was the God of the most ancient church, and called Jehovah; and also of the ancient church. 1343. H. and H. 327. The L. is called a little one, or a little child (Isa. ix. 5), because he is essential innocence and essential love. 430. The L. is called "who is, who was, and who is to come," because he is eternal, infinite, and Jehovah. A.R. 13, 522. There is in the L., and therefore from the L., the divine celestial, the divine spiritual, and the divine natural; and from thence these three principles are also in heaven, in man, in the Word, and in the church. A.R. 49. The L. as to his divine human is Jehovah, or the father in a visible form. 9310. The L. from eternity, or Jehovah, out of himself produced the son of the spiritual world, and out of it created the universe and all things therein. D.L.W. 290. The L. from eternity could not have created the universe and all things therein, if he had not been a man. D.L.W. 285. Amongst other secret reasons for calling Jehovah L., were the following: viz., that if it had been declared at that time that the L. was the Jehovah so often mentioned in the Old Testament, it would not have been received, because it would not have been believed, and further because the L. was not made Jehovah, as to his human; also, until he had in every respect united the divine essence to the human, and the human to the divine. 2921. The L. came into the world not to save the celestial, but the spiritual church; this is the meaning of his words. (Matt. ix. 12, 13, and also John x. 16.) 2661. The L. came into the world to reduce all things to order in heaven and earth. D.L.W. 14. From the prophet Isaiah unto Malachi, there is not a single thing that does not relate to the L., or that being in the opp. sense does not relate to something contrary to the L. L. 2, 3. The L., as to his humanity,

Lord

was made the divine law, i.e., truth itself. 6716. When the L. made his whole human divine, then his flesh was nothing else but divine good, and his blood divine truth; that in the divine nothing material is to be understood, may be manifest. 3813, 5200. The L. was in two states when in the world, viz., a state of humiliation, and a state of glorification. 2288. The L., by degrees, adjoined the human essence to the divine. 1708. The L. made the very corporeal principle in himself divine. 2083, 5078, 10.121. D.L.W. 221. The L. made his humanity divine, by virtue of the divinity in himself, and thus he became one with the father. L. 29. The L. made himself righteousness by acts of redemption. U.T. 95, 96. By the same acts the L. united himself to the father, and the father united himself to him, and this was effected according to divine order. U.T. 97–100. The L. put off all the humanity taken from the mother by temptations, and at last by death, and put on the humanity from the essential divine; hence it is, that in heaven by his death and burial is understood the purification of his human and glorification. (See John xii. 24, and John xx. 17.) A.E. 899. The L. successively put off the human taken from the mother, and put on the human from the divine in himself, which is the divine humanity and the son of God. L. 35. The L. in the Word made his humanity divine truth from divine good which was in himself, and when he went out of the world he made his humanity divine good, by unition with his essential divinity, which was in him from conception. A.E. 594. A.C. 3210, 10.367. A.R. 193. The L. rising again on the third day implies that truth divine, or the Word, as to the internal sense, as it was understood by the ancient church, shall be raised again in the consummation of the age, which also is the third day. 2813. The L. from his own proper power disposed and reduced all things in himself into divine order. 4251. When the L. subdued the hells, he not only delivered the angels from infestation, but also the men of the church. A.R. 829. The L. spake by cor., rep., and significatives, because from the divine thus before the world and heaven those things which filled the universal heaven. 4807. The L. appeared in the most ancient church as a man, and spake to them by word of mouth. 49. The L. appears above the heavens in a sun, because no one can sustain his presence, such as it is in itself, and he is present with every one by veilings and coverings. A.R. 54, 465. The L. appears to every one according to his state and quality, as a vivifying and creating fire, to those who are in good, as a consuming fire to those who are in evil. 934, 1861, 10.551. The L. flows into man by good, and by this disposes truths into order, but not *vice versa.* 9337. The L. flows into man by a twofold manner, viz., mediately through heaven and immediately from himself. 6472. The L. flows into man in his love or will, and causes the faculty of reception, but in a state of liberty. 10.097. The L. not only knows the quality of the whole man, but also what his quality will be to eternity. 6214. The L. who is the light itself, sees all and singular the things which are in thought and will of man, yea which are in the universal nature, and nothing is in any degree concealed from him. 5477. The L. is not among the angels, as a king in his kingdom, for he is above them, as to his aspect in the sun, and as to the life of love and wisdom in them. D.L.W. 103. The L. only can teach and lead all, because he is God, and because heaven and the church are as one man, whose soul and life the L. is. A.R. 383. Man cannot see the L., such as he is in himself, and live; and therefore he presents himself to be seen in the heavens by angels, whom he fills with his majesty. A.R. 938. The truths of the Word are mirrors or glasses, by which also he causes himself to be seen. A.R. 938. The angels continually behold the L. as a sun before their eyes, and this in every turn of their face and body. A.R. 938. Jehovah, who was in him, appeared to be absent in temptations, and this appearance was proportionable to the degree of his immersion in the humanity, which he received from the mother. 1815. The L. coming forth from the father, and returning to the father, means the humanity proceeding from the divinity and the union and glorification of the humanity. 3194, 3210. By the L. birth from eternity, is meant his birth foreseen from eternity, and provided for in time. A.R. 961.

Lord God Omnipotent and the **Lamb**. (Rev. xxi. 22.) L. G. O. s. the Lord from eternity, who is Jehovah himself; and the Lamb s. his divine humanity. A.R. 918.

Lord God and **Jehovah God** s. the L. as to divine good, and as to divine truth; and J. in the old Testament, is called L. in the new. A.E. 689.

Lord Jehovih is frequently mentioned in the Word, and this especially where the subject treated of is concerning temptations. 1793. L. J. is mentioned when the aid of omnipotence is more especially sought for, and supplicated. 2921. L. J. (Isa. xl. 10, etc.) s. the Lord as to divine good. A.E. 850.

Lord Jesus Christ, the, alone must be worshipped in the New Church, as he is in heaven. A.R. 839.

Lord and **God**. The L., in the Word, is called L., from the divine good of his divine love, and G., from the divine truth of his divine wisdom. A.R. 663.

Lord and **God** of **Jacob**. Where the subject treated of is concerning the good of love, in the Word, the L. is called the L., and when it is concerning goods in act, he is called the G. of J. (See Ps. civ. 2–6.) A.E. 405.

Lord and **Master**. He is called L. as to divine good, and M. as to divine truth. 2921.

Lord's Prayer. In the New Jerusalem Church, the L. alone will be worshipped as in heaven, and thus all will be fulfilled that is contained in the L. P., from beginning to end. U.T. 113. The L. P. is repeated every day in heaven. A.R. 839. U.T. 113. The quality of all spirits and angels, whatever, may be known by the influx of the idea of their thoughts and affections into the contents of the L. P. 4047. That whatever precedes, must reign or prevail in what follows, and consequently, in a series, appears evident from every word which the Lord spake; but more especially from his prayer, which is called the L. P.; all things therein follow in such a series, that they constitute, as it were, a column increasing from the highest to the lowest, in the interiors whereof are those things which precede in the series; that which is the first, there is the inmost; and that which succeeds in order adds itself successively to the inmost, and thus increases; whatever is the inmost, that reigns or prevails universally, in such things as are in the circumference, that is, in all and singular the parts thereof; for hence is what is essential to the existence of the whole. 8864. See *Daily Bread.*

Lot means truth sensual. 1431, 1547, 1584. L., when he was with Abraham, rep. the Lord's sensual principle, consequently, his external man. 2324, 1428, 1434. L. den. the Lord's external man; in a former state he was denominated "a brother's son," being occupied by apparent goodnesses and truths, but he is called "the brother of Abraham," when occupied by genuine goodnesses and genuine truths. 1707. L. (Gen. xix.) rep. the rise of the new church. 2323. L. (Gen. xix.) rep. the external men of the church, who are those that are principled in the good of charity, but in external worship, and he not only rep. the external man of the church, or the external church, such as it is in the beginning, but also such as it is in its progress, and also in its end. 2324.

Lot's Wife s. truth wasted of all good. 2453–5.

Lots, to cast, **upon the People** s. to disperse the truths of the church, by falses. A.E. 863. See *Coat.*

Loud, or **Great Voice**, a (Rev. v. 2), s. divine truth from the Lord, in its power or virtue. A.R. 258.

Louse, Lice, s. evils in the sensual. 7449.

Love

Love, or the **Will**, is the essential life of man. D.L.W. 399. L., or the w., continually makes an effort to the human form, and to all things which are of the human form. D.L.W. 400. L., originating in the Lord as a sun, is the heat of life (or vital heat) in angels and men, consequently, it is their life, and the derivations of l. are called affections, and by these are produced perceptions, and consequently, thoughts; therefore, wisdom in its origin is l. A.R. 875. Every l. follows man after death, because it is the esse of his life; and the ruling l., which is the head of the rest, remains with him to eternity, and together with it the subordinate l. C.S.L. 45–48. Every l. is felt under some species of delight, and, therefore, unless man knew what evil was, he might feel evil as good, and thence by falses confirm it, from which man perishes. A.R. 531, 908. In every one's l., there is the light of his life. 3798. L. is like a fire in the w., and like a flame in the understanding. C.S.L. 360. U.T. 658. The essence of l. is to l. others out of, or without, itself, to desire to be one with them, and to make them happy from itself; and these properties of the divine l. were the cause of the creation of the universe, and are also the cause of its preservation. U.T. 37–57. Three kinds of l. constitute the heavenly things of the Lord's kingdom; viz., conjugial l., l. towards infants, and the l. of society, or mutual l. 2039. Celestial l. from the Lord, continually flows into man, and nothing else hinders and impedes its reception, than the lusts of self-l., and the l. of the world, and the falsities thence derived. 2041. There is celestial l., in which are the angels who are in the Lord's celestial kingdom, and there is spiritual l., in which are the angels who are in the Lord's spiritual kingdom. A.R. 120. Celestial and spiritual l., when they flow in, torment and excruciate those who are in self-l., and in the pride of self-derived intelligence. A.R. 691. Spiritual l. derives its essence from celestial l. A.R. 395. Spiritual l. is l. towards our neighbor, which is called charity. A.R. 128. Infernal l. cannot be transcribed or changed into celestial l. N.J.D. 239.

Love, to, the Lord s. to do his commandments, because he himself is his commandments, for they are from him, therefore, he is in them, and consequently, is in the man in whose life they are engraven; and they are engraven in man by willing and doing them. A.R. 556. L. towards God, and love towards our neighbor, were intended to be joined together, and are so joined with those who live in the exercise of charity or neighborly l., out of l. towards God. U.T. 456–458. There is no other medium given of loving the Lord, than charity. 4776. L. to the Lord is a likeness of him, and charity to our neighbor is an image of him. 3324.

Love of Dominion, the, originating in self-love, and the love of rule originating in the pride of self-derived intelligence, are the heads or sources of all infernal loves, and consequently, the heads or sources of all evils and of all falses, resulting from those evils in the church; when the l. of d. originating from self-love and the pride of self-derived intelligence constitute the head, then the love of uses, which is celestial love, constitute the feet, and the soles of the feet; and so on the contrary. A.R. 502.

Love and Wisdom. L. or the will can be elevated, and receive the things which are of the heat from heaven, if it loves w., its consort in that degree. Otherwise, l., or the will, draws down w., or the understanding, from its elevation, to act as one with it. D.L.W. 414, 416. L. purified by w. in the understanding, becomes spiritual and celestial, but defiled in the understanding, becomes sensual and corporeal. D.L.W. 422–424.

Love, to, and Serve, relate to l., and to walk and seek, relate to faith. (Jer. viii. 2.) 519.

Love your Enemies s. charity; bless them that curse you, instruction; and to pray for them that despitefully use, and persecute you, intercession. A.E. 644.

Lovers (Jer. xxii. 22) s. truths of the church.

Lower, or inferior region of the world of spirits. A.E. 899.

Lower Earth. In the world of spirits, the l. e. is the region under the feet, where well-disposed spirits are, before they are elevated into heaven. 4728.

Lowest. In each kingdom of nature, l. is for the use of the middle, and the middle for the use of the supreme. D.L.W. 65.

Lowing of the **Kine** s. the difficult conversion of the concupiscences of evil in the natural man into good affections. D.P. 326.

Lubim s. rituals merely scientific. 1195.

Lucid s. to be wise. A.E. 1081.

Lucifer s. self-love, profaning holy things. 3387. D.P. 257. L., son of the morning (Isa. xiv.), s. the same as Babel. A.E. 1029. L. and Babylon s. those who profane the goods and truths of the Word. A.R. 24.

Lucre, or **Gain,** s. every thing false derived from evil, which perverts the judgment. 8711.

Lud (Gen. x. 22) s. the knowledge of truth. 1223.

Ludim, Anamim, Lehabim, and **Napthtukim** (Gen. x. 13), s. so many several kinds of rituals of external worship, which are merely scientific. 1194.

Lukewarm. The subject where truths and at the same time falses which are opp. subsist, is called l.; and the subject in which falses and truths are commixed is called l. 5217. To be l. (Rev. iii. 16), is pred. of those who are guilty of profanation, and after death are neither in heaven nor hell, but in a place separate, deprived of human life, where there are nothing but mere fantasies. A.R. 204. D.P. 226, 231. See *To Spew out of the Mouth.*

Lumen, delusive. Spirits who attribute all things to fortune, and to their own prudence, and nothing to the divine, as they have done in the world, have the skill to imitate divine things by various methods; for they present to view palaces almost like those in the heavens, also groves and rural objects nearly resembling those presented by the Lord among good spirits; they adorn themselves with shining garments, yea, the syrens also induce a beauty almost angelical; but all these things are the effect of art by fantasies; nevertheless, however like they appear in the external form, still in the internal they are filthy; which also is instantly made manifest to good spirits by the Lord, for unless it were manifested, they would be seduced; for what is external is taken away, and when this is the case, the diabolical [principle] within comes forth; it is taken away by light let in upon it from heaven, by virtue whereof the delusive l., which is of fantasies, by which they produce such effects, is dispersed. 10.286.

Luminaries. The two l. den. love and faith in the internal man. 30–37.

Luminous. Those in ill. from the Lord have something l. and glowing round the head. D.P. 169.

Lungs, the, cor. to faith in the understanding. 3886. The l. cor. to the spiritual kingdom, which consists of those who are in love to the neighbor. 3635. See *Heart, Respiration.*

Lust and **Concupiscence,** all, is of self-love, and the love of the world. 1668. L. close up and blind the understanding. D.P. 144. The l. of evil impede genuine truths. 3175. The l. of the mind are the origins of diseases. 5712. Infernal spirits dwell in, and excite the l. of others. 5032.

Luther accurses faith alone, and acknowledges that he was warned by an angel of the Lord not to do it. D.P. 258. His lot in the spiritual world. C.L.J. 54, 5.

Luxuries are among the causes of disease. 5712, 5145.

Luz (Gen. xxviii.) s. a state wherein truth is together with good, in the ultimate principle of order. 3730.

Lybia

Lybia s. the same as Phut, which see.

Lydians (Jer. xlvi. 8) s. scientific rituals. 1196.

Lye, in the Word, s. the false of doctrine. A.R. 924.

Lymph. Those who belong to that province, and who are of the viler sort, run about hither and thither, apply themselves to those whom they see, attend to every particular, and tell to others what they hear; prone to suspicion, impatient, restless, in imitation of that l. which is therein and is conveyed to and fro, their reasonings are the fluids there which rep.; but these are of the middle sort; whereas they who have reference to the excrementitious l. therein, are such as draw down spiritual truths to things terrestrial, and there defile them. These appear in front at some distance to the right. 4050.

Lymphatics. The gyres of those who belong to this province are like a lightly flowing stream. Ill. 5181.

M

Machiavelists, or those who make no account of murders, thefts, adulteries, false witnesses, etc. D.P. 310.

Machir s. the like with Manasseh; for M. was the son of Manasseh. A.E. 447.

Machpelah (Gen. xxiii. 17) s. regeneration by truth, which is of faith. 2970.

Mad s. to be spiritually insane. A.E. 960.

Madai (Isa. xxi. 1) s. the external church, or external worship in which is internal. See (Gen. x. 2) where M. is called the son of Japheth. 1228.

Magi and the **Wise.** They who were skilled in and taught the mystic scientifics were called m., and they who were skilled in and taught the non-mystic scientifics, were called the w., consequently, they who were skilled in and taught the interior scientifics were called m., and they who were skilled in and taught the exterior scientifics were called the w.; hence it is that by the m. and the w. such things are s. in the Word; but after that they began to abuse the interior scientifics of the church, and to turn them into magic, then by Egypt also began to be s. the scientific principle which perverts, and in like manner by the m. of Egypt and the w. ones thereof. The m. of that time were acquainted with such things as are of the spiritual world, which they learnt from the cor. and rep. of the church, wherefore also many of them had communication with spirits, and hence learnt illusory arts, whereby they wrought magical miracles; but they who were called the w., did not regard such things, but solved things enigmatical, and taught the causes of natural things; herein consisted the wisdom of that time, and the ability to effect such things was called wisdom. M., in the opp. sense, are they who perverted spiritual things, and thereby exercised magic arts, as they who are mentioned (Exod. viii. 11, 22; viii. 7, 18, 19; ix. 11); for magic was nothing else but perversion, and a perverse application of such things as are of order in the spiritual world, whence magic descends; but that magic at this day is called natural, by reason that nothing above or beyond nature is any longer acknowledged; a spiritual principle, unless by it is meant an interior natural principle, is denied. 5223.

Magi, Soothsayers, or **Jugglers,** were such as studied natural magic, whereby nothing of what was divine could be foretold, but only what was contrary to the divine principle; this is magic. 3698.

Magic is the perversion of order, and abuse of cor. 6692.

Magistrates. Not to have power over the laws, but to administer them. 10.799.

Magnificent s. those who are in love of self and the world. A.E. 410.

Magpies, in the spiritual world, are manifestations of the affections of spirits. A.Cr. 89.

Magog s. those in external natural worship. A.R. 858. See *Gog.*

Mahalaleel (Gen. v. 12) s. a fifth church from Adam. The life of those who constituted this church was such, that they preferred the delight arising from truth, to the joy arising from uses. 506, 511.

Mahalath (Gen. xxviii. 9) s. truth from a divine origin. 3687.

Mahanaim (Gen. xxxii. 2) s. the celestial and spiritual heavens, and, in the supreme sense, the divine celestial and divine spiritual of the Lord. 4237.

Mahomet

Mahomet and **Mahometans** in the spiritual world. Des. C.L.J. 68–72.

Mahometan Religion was raised up by the divine providence of the Lord, and accommodated to the genius of the orientals, to the end that it might destroy the idolatries of very many nations, and was permitted, on account of its acknowledgment of the Lord as the son of God, as the wisest of men, and as the greatest prophet. D.P. 255.

Mahujael and **Methusael** (Gen. iv. 18) s. heretical doctrine. 527.

Maid-Servants s. the affections of the natural principle. 2567. See *Handmaid*.

Maids den. external affections serving the internal. 3835.

Make, to (Hosea viii. 11), is pred. concerning good, and, in an opp. sense, concerning evil. A.E. 391. To m. heaven, and earth, and the sea, and the fountains of waters (Rev. xiv. 7), in a natural sense, s. to create them, but in a spiritual sense, it s. to m. the heaven of angels and the church, and all things appertaining to them. A.R. 630.

Maker and **Holy One** of **Israel** (Isa. xvii. 8) s. the Lord as to divine good and truth. A.E. 585.

Makkedah, cave of (Josh. x. 28), s. the dire false originating in evil. A.E. 665.

Male Son, the, which the **Woman brought Forth**. (Rev. xii. 5.) By m. s. is s. truth conceived in the spiritual man, and born in the natural man; the reason is, because by conceptions and births in the Word, are s. spiritual conceptions and births, all which in general relate to what is good and true, for nothing else is begotten and born of the Lord as a husband, and from the church as a wife. Now since by the woman who brought forth, the new church is s., it is plain that by the m. s. is s. the doctrine of that church. The doctrine here meant, is the doctrine of the New Jerusalem, published in London, 1758; as also the doctrine concerning the Lord, concerning the sacred scripture, and concerning a life according to the commandments of the decalogue, published in Amsterdam; for by doctrine are understood all the truths of doctrine, because doctrine is the complex. A.R. 543.

Male and **Female**, the, were created to be the essential form of the marriage of good and truth. C.S.L. 100. The essential difference between the two principles is this: in the masculine principle love is inmost, and its covering is wisdom; whereas in the f. principle the wisdom of the m. is inmost, and its covering is the love thence derived; so that the m. is the wisdom of love, and the f. is the love of that wisdom. C.S.L. 32, 33.

Malice. Quality and state shown. 4951.

Malignity, how it persuades and leads. 9249. Increases as the spiritual mind is closed. D.L.W. 269.

Mammon of Unrighteousness (Luke xvi. 9), in the spiritual sense, means the knowledges of good and truth, which the evil possess, and which they use only for procuring wealth and dignities for themselves. D.P. 250.

Mamre (Gen. xxxv. 27) s. the determination of the state of a thing, for it was a place where Abraham dwelt (Gen. xiii. 18), and where Isaac dwelt, and whither Jacob came. 2970, 4613. M., Eschol, and Aner (Gen. xiv. 13), rep. and s. the angels who were attendant on the Lord, when he was engaged in combat in his earliest childhood, which angels were of a quality like that of the good and truths then with the Lord; they also have their names from goodnesses and truths, similar to the case of Michael, and others mentioned in the Word. 1705. See *Oak Grove*.

Man, in the Word, s. intelligence and wisdom, derived from the Word, and intelligence and wisdom derived from the Word in m., is the church in him; hence by m. in the concrete, or in common, that is, when a society or assembly is called a m., is meant the church; from this ground it is that the prophets were called sons of m., and that the Lord himself called himself the son of m., and the son of m. is the truth of the church derived from the Word, and when said of the Lord, is the Word itself, from which the church has its existence. A.R. 910. In the Word, especially the prophetic, the expression m. (vir) often occurs, as when it is said, m. and wife, m. and woman, m. and inhabitant, also m. (vir), and m. (homo); and in these passages, by m., in the internal sense, is s. what relates to the understanding, which is truth, and by wife, woman, inhabitant, and m. (homo), what relates to the will, which is good. 3134. M. (vir), in the Word, s. the understanding of truth, and m. (homo) the perception of good; and by both, the church as to truth, and as to good. (Jer. ii. 6.) A.E. 537. M. (vir) s. rational truth, and also, in an opp. sense, the false principle. 265, 2362. M. s. the understanding of truth. 476, 749. M. (Gen. ii. 23) s. the internal m. 156. M. (vir) (Gen. xix. 8) s. the false principle which defiles the affections of good and truth. 2362. M. (Gen. xxxii.) s. good, because the Lord is the alone m., and m. from him is called m. 4287. M. (Ezek. xxxvi. 11, 12) s. the spiritual m., who is also called Israel. 55. M. (Gen. v. 2) s. the most ancient church, consisting of both male and female. 477. M. (homo) s. the spiritual affection of truth, and, in an opp. sense, the lust of the false. (See Ps. cxix. 134.) A.E. 328. M. (homo) (Zeph. i. 3) s. the whole of the church. A.E. 1100. M. (homo) (Rev. iv.) s. a recipient of divine truth. A.E. 280. M. is so created, that the divine things of the Lord may descend through him into the ultimate things of nature, and from the ultimate things of nature may ascend to him, so that m. might be a medium of union between the divine and the world of nature, and thus by m., as by a uniting medium, the very ultimate principle of nature might have life from the divine, which would have been the case, if m. had lived according to divine order. M. is so created that, as to his body, he is a little world, all the arcana of the world of nature being therein reposited, for whatsoever of arcanum there is in the ether, and its modifications, this is reposited in the ears, and whatsoever invisible thing flows and acts in the air, this is in the organ of smell, where it is perceived, and whatsoever invisible thing flows and acts in the waters and other fluids, this is in the organ of taste; also the very changes of state are in the sense of touch, throughout; besides that, things still more hidden would be perceived in his interior organs, if his life was according to order, which is, if m. only acknowledged the Lord as his last and first end with faith of heart, that is, with love; in this state were the most ancient people. 3702. M. is born to the ultimate or lowest degree of the natural world, he is then elevated by sciences to the second degree, and as by means of sciences he perfects his understanding, he is elevated to the third degree, and then becomes rational; the three degrees of ascent in the spiritual world are in him above the three natural degrees, nor do they appear, before he puts off his earthly body; when he puts this off, the first spiritual degree is opened to him, afterwards the second, and lastly the third, but only in those who become angels of the third heaven; these are they who see God. D.L.W. 67. M. is first natural, then he becomes rational, and at length spiritual; when he is natural, he is in Egypt, when he is made rational, he is then in Assyria, and when he becomes spiritual, he is then in the land of Canaan, that is, in the church. A.E. 654, 918. A.R. 503. M. has two minds, one exterior, and the other interior; the former is called natural, but the latter spiritual. The natural mind is opened by the knowledges of worldly things; but the spiritual mind is opened by the knowledges of heavenly things. 126. Inasmuch as there is a cor. more especially of m. with heaven, and by heaven with the Lord, it is from this ground that m. appears in the other life, in the light of heaven, according to the quality in which he cor.; hence the angels appear in ineffable brightness and beauty, but the infernals in inexpressible blackness and deformity. 5377. M. cannot be regenerated till he arrives at adult age. 677. His affections and thoughts cor. with all things of the animal kingdom; his will and understanding with all things

Man upon the Throne

of the vegetable kingdom, and his ultimate life, with all things of the mineral kingdom. D.L.W. 52. The body and the sensual part of m. is the extreme of life. Natural desires and things of the memory are more interior; good affections and rational things are still more so, and the will of good and the understanding of truth are inmost. 6654. In order to man's being m., his will and understanding should act in unity. 3623. M. is not life itself, but only a recipient of life from God. U.T. 470. M., from head to foot, or from the first principles in the head to the ultimates in the body, is such as his love is. D.L.W. 369. The memory is the natural m., the understanding is the rational, and the will is the spiritual. A.E. 654. M. after death is in a perfect human form. H. and H. 453–460. M. after death retains every sense which he had in this world, and leaves nothing behind him but his terrestrial body. H. and H. 461–469. Every m. after death is instructed, and afterwards sent to various societies, and at length he remains with those who are in similar love and faith. A.R. 549. Such as m. is in the world as to his spirit, such does he remain to eternity, only with this difference, that his state becomes more perfect, if he has lived well, because then he is not clogged with a material body, but lives spiritual in a spiritual body. A.R. 937. M. communicates immediately with those who are in the world of spirits, but mediately with those who are in heaven or hell. A.R. 552. M. of himself continually inclines to the lowest hell, but by the Lord he is continually withdrawn. D.P. 69. So long as m. is spiritual, his dominion or rule proceeds from the external m. to the internal, as it is representatively described. (Gen. i. 26.) But when he becomes celestial and does good from love, then his dominion proceeds from the internal m. to the external, as the Lord des. himself, and thus, at the same time, the celestial m. who is his likeness, in Ps. viii. 6, 7, 8. 52. The celestial m. is the seventh day, and the spiritual m. the seventh month. 851. "I have gotten a m. Jehovah" (Gen. iv. 1), s. the doctrine of faith. 340. See *Grand Man.*

Man upon the **Throne** (Ezek. xxvi.–xxviii.) s. the Lord; by the appearance of fire from his loins upward and downward s. his divine love and by the brightness round about, the divine wisdom thence proceeding. A.R. 830.

Man of the **Church**, the, is not only the church itself, but the all of the church; it is a general expression comprehending whatever is of the church, and hence the most ancient church was called man, and other succeeding churches were mentioned by name. 768.

Man of the **New Church**, the, is explored by temptations as to his quality with respect to a life according to the commandments, and with respect to faith in the Lord. A.R. 639.

Man-Angel is one who is in the affection of good, and a man-devil is one who is in the affection of evil. D.P. 69.

Man-Brother (Gen. xiii. 8) s. the union of truth and goodness. 1578. Man (vir) and brother (Isa. xix. 2) s. truth and good, and, in an opp. sense, false and evil; man (vir) and neighbor s. truths among themselves, and, in an opp. sense, falses among themselves. A.E. 734.

Man, Grand, the. Universal angelic heaven in its complex before the Lord as one m. and is called the g. m. A.Cr. 20.

Man-Servant den. the natural as to truth. 8890.

Man and **Son** of **Man**. M. s. m. as to wisdom, and the s. of m., m. as to intelligence. A.E. 507. M. (vir) is truth itself conjoined to its own good, and s. of m. is truth. (Jer. li. 43.) A.E. 63.

Man and **Angel**. (Rev. xxi. 18.) By m. is here s. the church as consisting of men, and by a., is s. heaven as consisting of angels, therefore by the measure of a m. which is of an a., is s. the quality of the church as making one with heaven. A.R. 910.

Man and **Beast** (Jer. xxvii. 5) s. the affections of truth and good in the spiritual and natural m. A.E. 304. M. and b. named together, s. m. with respect to spiritual affection and natural affection. A.R. 567. M. s. the internal m., and b. the external. (Jer. xxxi. 27.) 477. M. is pred. of celestial good; inhabitant, of spiritual good; and b., of natural good. (Jer. xxxiii. 10.) 2712.

Man, Seth, and **Enos.** The three churches so called, constitute the most ancient church, but still with a difference of perfection as to perceptions. 502.

Manesseh s. the voluntary principle of the spiritual church. 3969. M., in the original tongue, s. forgetfulness, thus in the internal sense removal, viz., of evils as well actual as hereditary, for when these are removed the new will-principle arises. 5353. M. (Gen. xlviii.) s. the external of the celestial man. 6295. M. s. those who are in natural good which is the pleasure of doing good and of learning truth. A.E. 440.

Manasseh and **Ephraim.** M. s. the will-principle of the new natural principle, and E., the intellectual principle thereof, or what is the same thing; M. s. the good of the new natural principle, because good is pred. of the will, and E. s. the truth thereof, because truth is pred. of the intellectual principle. 5348. A.E. 440.

Mandrakes (Gen. xxx. 14) s. the things which are of conjugial love, which appears from the signification of the original word dudim, from which the Hebrew dudaim is derived. (See also Solomon's Song vii. 12, 13.) 3942. M. s. the marriage of good and truth, or the conjugial principle which exists between good and truth. A.E. 434.

Man of War s. truth combating against the false and destroying it. A.E. 329; or truth derived from good, and destroying the false, 355; and abstractly, truths themselves combating, 734.

Manger s. spiritual instruction for the understanding; for a horse that feeds therein s. the understanding. A.R. 255.

Manifested s. to be revealed. A.E. 946.

Manifestation. The Lord's m. in man is his presence in good 10.153.

Manna s. the Lord's divine human, or hidden wisdom. 2838. A.R. 120. M. s. the good of celestial love conjoined to wisdom. A.R. 120. A.E. 730. M. s. the good of truth. 8537. M. s. celestial and spiritual good. 10.303. Hidden m. (Rev. ii. 17) s. hidden wisdom, such as they have who are in the third heavens, whose superior wisdom is written in their lives, and not so much in the memories; and hidden m., in a supreme sense, s. the Lord himself. A.R. 120.

Manner den. mutations of state. 4077.

Mansion. (Gen. vi. 14.) The two parts of man which are the will and understanding. 638. M. (lowest, secondary, and third) are scientifics, rationals, and intellectuals. 657. M. of the angels with men are in their affections of good and truth. L.J. 9.

Mantle of **Elijah,** the, s. the divine truth of the Word in common or in general. A.R. 328.

Mantles s. truths in common. A.R. 328. See *Robes.*

Many, pred. of truths. 6172.

Marah den. the quality and quantity of temptation, also what is bitter. 8350.

Marble (Rev. xviii.) s. the sensual principle profaned. In a good sense it s. the sensual principle which is the ultimate of the life of the thought and will of man; for stone s. truth in the ultimates, specifically the appearance of truth. A.E. 1148. Vessels of m. (Rev. xviii.) s. scientifics derived from the appearance of good and truth. A.R. 775.

March Into the **Breadths** of the **Earth,** to (Hab. i. 6), s. the vastation of the church as to truths. 3901.

Mark, a, s. an acknowledgment and a confession. A.R. 605. To receive a mark

Markets and Fairs

on the right hand, and on the forehead (Rev. xiii. 16), s. that no one is acknowledged to be a reformed Christian, unless he receives the doctrine that faith is the only medium of salvation; or that faith, without the works of the law, justifies and saves. A.R. 605, 607. By having the m. of the beast (Rev. xvi.), is s. to acknowledge faith alone, to confirm himself in it, and to believe according to it. A.R. 779. See *Cain.*

Markets and **Fairs** s. acquisitions of good and truth. 3923.

Mariners. Those who are sea-farers, and who look to the Lord, and shun evils as sins, and do their work sincerely, justly, and faithfully, are more devout in their daily and nightly prayers and songs than those who live on land; for they trust more to divine providence than landsmen do. C. 96. See *Ships, Pilots.*

Marriage in a spiritual sense, rep. the celestial m., which is of good and truth. 4865, 6794. C.S.L. 100, 198. M. s. heaven, the church, and the kingdom of God. D.P. 21. Without some kind of m. it cannot be that any thing should exist or be produced; in the organical parts or substances of man, both compound and simple, yea the most simple, there is a passive and active principle; the case is the same throughout universal nature; these perpetual m. derive their beginning and birth from the celestial m., by which an idea of the Lord's kingdom is impressed on every thing in universal nature, as well inanimate as animate. 718. M. in heaven is the conjunction of two in unity of mind. H. and H. 367. The heavenly m. is not between good and truth of one and the same degree; but between good and truth or an inferior degree, and of a superior; that is, not between the good of the external man and the truth of the same, but between the good of the external man and the truth of the internal, or, what is the same thing, not between the good of the natural man and the truth thereof, but between the good of the natural man and the truth of the spiritual man. It is this conjunction which constitutes a m. 3952.

Marriage of **Good** and **Truth**. The celestial are sons from the essential m. of g. and t.; but the spiritual are sons from a covenant not so conjugial. 3246. From the m. of g. and t. which proceeds from the Lord in the way of influx, man receives truth, and the Lord conjoins good thereto, and thus the church is formed of the Lord with man. C.S.L. 62, 83–115, 122.

Marriage of the **Lamb** (Rev. xix. 9) s. the new church, which is in conjunction with the Lord. A.R. 816.

Marriage of the **Lord** and the **Church**. When the Lord's humanity is acknowledged to be divine, there is a full m. of the L. and the c., for it is a known thing in the reformed Christian world, that the church is a church, by virtue of its marriage with the Lord, for the Lord is called "the lord of the vineyard," and the church is "the vineyard;" moreover, the Lord is called "the bridegroom and husband," and the church is called "the bride and wife." A.R. 812. The word is the medium of conjunction, or of the m. of the L. with the c. A.R. 881.

Marriage Ceremony. On earth it is expedient that a priest should be present, and minister at the m. c., but not so in heaven. C.S.L. 21.

Marriage House s. heaven and the church. H. and H. 180.

Marriages on the earths are derived from m. of good and truth. C.S.L. 116–131, 339. The divine providence is peculiarly exercised with respect to m. C.S.L. 316. It is said, that in heaven they are not given in marriage, just in like manner as it is said, that we are to call no one father, doctor, or master; that it is difficult for a rich man to enter the kingdom of heaven, as for a camel to pass through the eye of a needle; that if any man will take away your coat, you are to let him have your cloak; and that the adulteress was liberated by the Lord's writing on the earth. A.E. at end of Index. See *Spiritual Nuptials.*

200

Married Land s. the will and the understanding united. 55.

Married Partners, two, most commonly meet after death, know each other again, associate, and for some time live together; this is the case in the first state; thus, while they are in externals, as in the world. But successively as they put off externals and enter into their internals, they perceive what had been the quality of their love and inclination for each other, and consequently, whether they can live together or not. In case they can live together, they remain conjugal partners; but if they cannot live together, they separate themselves, sometimes the husband from the wife, and sometimes the wife from the husband, and sometimes each from the other. C.S.L. 47–49.

Married Wife and **Mother** of many **Children** (Isa. liv. 1; 1 Sam. ii. 5) s. the Jews who were in possession of the Word. A.R. 535.

Marrow, fat things full of, s. goodnesses. 353.

Mars. The spirits who inhabit that planet are amongst the best of all spirits, who come from the earths of this solar system, being mostly celestial men. They worship the only Lord, and he appears to them at times. E.U. 85, 91. The spirits of M. in the grand man, have relation to thought grounded in affection, and the best of them to the affection of thought. E.U. 88.

Martyr s. confession of the truth, the same as witness. A.R. 6.

Marvellous and **Great** have reference to the Lord's omnipotence. A.E. 927.

Mary. The Lord called himself the son of man as to divine truth, and not as the son of M. 10.053. State of M. in spiritual world. Des. C.L.J. 66. The Lord was really born of her, but he put off all the humanity that he had from her, and became wholly divine. T.C.R. 98.

Mash den. various knowledges concerning good. 1233.

Massa s. things appertaining to the spiritual church. 3268.

Massah and **Meribah** (Exod. xvii. 7) s. the qualities of a state of temptation. 8587, 8588.

Masses, permitted by Providence, though not understood by the common people, and the reason why. D.P. 257.

Master and **Lord**. (John xiii. 13–16.) M. is pred. of the L. as to truth, and L. is pred. of him as to good. 2921.

Material and spiritual ideas compared. 10.216. M. things are in themselves fixed, stated, and measurable. A.Cr. 105. What is m. does not live, but what is spiritual. H. and H. 192.

Matrix s. opening of the spiritual mind. A.E. 865.

Matter. Every thing extended belongs to m. A.Cr. 33. Its origin exp. D.L.W. 302.

Mature. Pred. of the new birth. 5117.

Me. A formula of asseveration, and den. certainty. 6981.

Meadow. That a broad m. s. the Word. A.E. 644. That m. den. those things which are of the spiritual mind, and thence of the rational. A.E. 730. See *Field, Garden.*

Meal, farina, s. the truth of faith, or truth from good. 2177. A.R. 411. A.E. 245. See *Flour.*

Means, by which the three degrees are opened, are a life according to equity or justice; a life according to truths of faith, and goods of charity; and a life of mutual love, and love to the Lord. 9594. The m. of Divine Providence are all those things by which man is made man, and perfected as to his understanding and will. D.P. 335.

Measure, to, s. to know and explore the quality of a thing. A.R. 486, 904.

Measures and **Weights**, in the Word, s. the estimation of goodness and truth. A.R. 313, 315.

Meat (Gen. xl. 17) s. celestial good, because the m. of the angels are nothing else but the goods of love and charity, by which they are not only vivified but also re-created. 5147.

Meat Offerings

Meat Offerings and **Drink Offerings** s. worship from the good of love, and the truths of faith, and, in the opp. sense, worship from evils originating in the love of evil and from falses of faith. A.E. 376.

Mechanics and **Physics**. How inscribed in the organization of man. 6057.

Medan, s. common lots of the Lord's spiritual kingdom. 3239.

Medes, the (Isa. xiii. 17), s. those who are contrary to the truths and goods of the church. A.E. 242.

Media and **Persia**, the kings of, rep. those who are in faith separate from charity. F. 66.

Median s. those who are principled in the false. 3762.

Mediastinum, spirits des. who infest the. 5188.

Mediates. All and each of the things in the vegetable kingdom are m. D.L.W. 65.

Mediately. The Word is taught m. by parents, preachers, and especially by reading it. D.P. 172.

Mediation s. that the human is the medium through which man may come to God the father, and God the father to man, and thus teach and lead him that he may be saved. U.T. 135. See *Intercession*.

Mediatory, or **Middle Good**. During the process of man's regeneration, he is kept by the Lord in a sort of m. or m. g., which good is then separated, when it has served its use. 4063.

Medicine. The intelligence den. by the leaf (Ezek. xlvii. 12), which shall be for the use of the celestial man, is called m. 57. See *Physician*.

Medicines den. the truths of faith considered as preservatives from falses and evils, because they lead to the good of life. 6502.

Meditate, to, in the **Field** (Gen. xxiv. 63) s. to think from the rational principle in a state of good. 3196.

Meditation. The delight of m., thought and reflection, when the end is justice. D.P. 296.

Medium. Every m. with externals alone, without an internal, perishes; for the case with a m. is this: it exists from the internal, hence also it subsists from the internal, for it exists by the intuition [view or looking into] of the internal into the external from an affection and end of associating the external to itself; thus what is a m. is conjoined to the internal, and from the internal with the external, but not with the external without the internal; hence it is evident, that that which is a m., with the external alone without the internal, must perish. 5413.

Medulla Oblongata. See *Bones*. 5560.

Meek s. those who are in the good of charity. A.E. 304.

Meet, to. To cause to m. (Gen. xxiv. 12), s. to provide. 3062. To m. into (Gen. xxiii. 1), s. the influx, whence comes illustration. 4235.

Meeting den. influx and conjunction. 4247.

Megiddon (2 Chron. iii.) s. the same as Armageddon, which see. A.R. 770.

Mehujael s. heresies. 404.

Melancholy, or **Sadness** of **Mind**, proceeds from certain spirits who are not as yet joined to hell, being newly departed from the body, who take delight in things indigested and putrid, such as meats corrupted in the stomach into which they enter. H. and H. 299.

Melancthon, state of, des. in the spiritual world. C.L.J. 4754.

Melchizedek s. the celestial things of the interior man with the Lord. 1724. M., a priest and king in one person, rep. the divine humanity of the Lord, both with respect to good and truth. 1657, 2015.

Melecheth (Jer. vii. 17, 18), or the queen of the heavens, s. falses in the whole complex, also evils in the whole complex. A.E. 324.

Melons s. the lowest natural. A.E. 513. See *Cucumbers*.

Melt den. vanishing before the heat of lust. 8487.

Membrane. Spirits who go in crowds, and are as passive forces, cor. to the m. 5557.

Memorial. For a sign and for a m., den. that a thing should be perpetually remembered. 8066.

Memory, the, is only the entrance into man, and as a courtyard, by which there is entrance to a house, and it is like the ruminatory stomach amongst birds and beasts to which also the m. of man corresponds. A.E. 290. Man has two memories, one interior, the other exterior; the interior m. is proper to his spirit, but the exterior is proper to his body. 2469. Man's interior m. is his book of life, for all and every particular which man has thought, spoken, and done, and all that he has heard and seen, are inscribed in his interior m. 2474, 7398. The exterior m. is the ultimate of order in which spiritual and celestial things are softly terminated, and reside, when goods and truths are there. H. and H. 466. The external m. is not opened after death, except at the Lord's good pleasure. E.U. 160. See *Doctrinal.*

Memphis s. those who desire wisdom in divine things from themselves. 273.

Men (Gen. xiv. 23) s. angels. 1753. The three m. who appeared to Abraham (Gen. xviii. 2), s. the essential divine, the divine human, and the holy proceeding. 2149, 2156. M. (Gen. xix. 11) s. evil rational things and false doctrinals thence derived. 2382. M. (Gen. xxiv. 32) s. all things in the natural principle. 3148. Great m. s. those who are in goods; rich m. those who are in knowledges of truth; mighty or powerful m. are those who are in erudition; and free-m. s. those who are in goods and truths from themselves, but not in a conformable life. (Rev. vi. 15.) A.R. 337.

Men of the **Church** are internal, or external. 7840. The internal consists of the regenerate. 1083.

Men-Servants s. scientifics which are the truths of the natural man. 2567, 4037. M.-s. and maid-servants den. natural and rational truths, with the affections thereof. 2567.

Mene, Tekel, and **Perez.** (Dan. v. 25–28.) By m., or to number, is s. to know his quality as to truth; by t., or to weigh, is s. to know his quality as to good; by p., or to divide, is s. to disperse. A.R. 313. A.C. 3104.

Menstruous Women. (Ezek. xviii. 6.) "He who hast not come near to a m. w.," s. him who has not defiled truths by false lusts. A.E. 555.

Mention, to make, den. communication. 5133.

Mephaatah s. false principle. 2468. See *Holon.*

Mercenary den. the good of lucre, or the good of reward. 9179.

Merchandise s. the knowledges of good. A.E. 1145.

Merchandise of **Babylon,** the, are the holy things of the Word adulterated and profaned. A.R. 772.

Merchants s. those who have the knowledges of good and truth. 2967. M. (Nahum iii. 16) s. those who falsify the Word, and communicate, and sell. A.E. 543.

Merciful s. to do good to the needy from a principle of love. A.E. 295.

Mercury, Minerva, etc., were worshipped by several nations, because they attribute to them the government of the universe, and the attributes of God. A.Cr. 22.

Mercury, the spirits of, in the grand man, have relation to the memory of things abstracted from what is material. E.U. 10. The inhabitants are intellectual, and are desirous of knowing every thing; in consequence of which, they are permitted, in another life, to wander about searching for knowledge; but not so much to reduce knowledge to use, as to know things. E.U. 13, 14, 15.

Mercy of the **Lord,** the, is the influx of good and truth from him and thence spiritual life which is given by regeneration. 6160, 6307, 8714, 8879. Love itself is turned into m. and becomes m. when any one who is in need of help is regarded from love or charity, hence m. is an effect of love towards the needy and miserable. 3063. To do m. (Gen. xxiv. 12) s. an influx of love. 3063. To give m. (Gen. xliii. 14) s. to receive graciously. 5629.

Mercy-Seat (Exod. xxv. 17) s. a cleansing from evils, or the remission of sins, consequently, a hearing and reception of all things which are of worship. 9506.

Meribah s. things appertaining to the spiritual church. 3268. See *Nebaioth.*

Merit belongs only to the Lord. 9715. The m. of the Lord, is, that when he was in the world, he subdued the hells, and reduced all things in the heavens to order, and that he glorified his humanity by his own proper power. A.E. 293.

Mescha (Gen. x. 30) s. truth. 1248.

Meschech and **Thubal** (Ezek. xxxii. 26) s. doctrinals which are ritual observances. 1151.

Mesentery. Spirits who pertain to the province of the lymphatics. 5181. D.P. 164.

Mesopotamia den. knowledges of truth. 3051.

Messenger (Isa. xliii. 19) s. the Lord, as to divine good. A.E. 409. To send messengers (Gen. xxxii. 3), s. to communicate. 4239.

Messiah s. divine truth. 3008.

Messiah and **Prince** (Dan. ix. 25) the Lord is called m. from his divine humanity, and p., from his divine truth. A.E. 684. See *Anointed Christ.*

Metals, all, such as gold, silver, brass, iron, tin, and lead, in the Word s. goods and truths, because they correspond, and because they correspond they are also in heaven; for all things there are correspondences. A.R. 775.

Metaphor. All comparisons in the Word, are also Correspondences. 9828.

Metaphysics. Des. 4658. A.R. 655.

Methusael s. heresies. 404.

Methuselah (Gen. v. 21) s. the eighth church from Adam. 515.

Mibsam. Things appertaining to the spiritual church. 3268. See *Nebaioth.*

Micah and his graven image. 2598.

Mice (1 Sam. vi. 1–21) s. the falses of the sensual man. A.E. 700. See *Emerods.*

Michael (Dan. x., xii.) s. genuine truth from the Word. A.E. 735. By Michaels are meant the men of the new church, and by M., such of them as are wise therein. A.R. 224, 564.

Microcosm. Man was so called by the ancients from his resembling the m., which is the universe in the whole complex. This they derived from the science of cor. D.L.W. 319.

Microscope. Its discoveries cited. 1869, 4224.

Midday in the heavens is from the clear light of truth. 5962. S. knowledges of truth. A.E. 401.

Middim (Judges v. 10, 19) s. the rational principle as to truth. The common version of the Hebrew text has it Meggiddo, which has another s. A.E. 355.

Middle den. what is primary, principal, or inmost. 2940.

Middian s. those who are principled in the truth of faith, and are still in the good of life, but the truths according to which they live, are the sons of M. But, in a bad sense, M. s. those who are principled in what is false in consequence of not being in the good of life. 3242.

Midianites s. those who are in the truth of simple good. 3242.

Midnight. (Exod. xi. 4.) Total devastation from a state of mere falses. 7776.

Midst, the, in an internal sense, s. what is primary, or principal, and also inmost, which arises from rep. in another life; for when any thing good is rep. by spiritual ideas, then the best is presented in the m., and the decreases of good are presented by degrees from the m., and, lastly, at the circumference those which are not good. 2940. In the m. s. in the inmost, and thence in all things around. A.R. 9331. A.E. 313. M. of the land (Isa. vi. 12) s. the internal man. 576.

Midwife (Gen. xxvi.) s. the natural principle. 4588. Midwives (Exod. i. 15–21) s. receptions of truth in the natural principle. 4588.

Might den. the forces or power of truth. 6343.

Mighty, the (Rev. xix. 18), s. those who are in erudition from doctrine derived from the Word; and abstractly, erudition or learning derived from that source. A.R. 832.

Mighty Men (Lam. i. 15) den. those who are in the good of love. A.E. 922.

Mighty Ones (Isa. xxi. 17; Hosea x. 13) s. those who were in faith separate from charity. 1179. The m. o. of Babel (Jer. li. 30) s. those who are intoxicated with self-love. 583.

Migrate s. rejection. A.E. 811.

Migrations den. changes of state. 1463.

Milcah and **Nahor** (Gen. xxii. 20) s. the origin of the affection of truth. 3078.

Milcom rep. those who are in external worship. 3468.

Mildew s. the non-reception of good of love and faith. 9277.

Mildew and **Blasting** s. evil and false in the extremes. A.E. 638.

Mile s. progressions in a series according to thoughts. 942.

Miles s. progressions in a series. A.E. 924.

Military Service. The office of the Levites to war in m. s. is s. the goods and truths of the church, and, in the opp. sense, its evils and falsities. A.R. 500.

Milk, as containing fat in it, s. the celestial spiritual principle, or truth grounded in good, or faith grounded in love or charity; or spiritual good, or the spiritual principle derived from the celestial. 2184, 2643. A.E. 710. M. s. divine truth spiritual natural. A.E. 617. M. of the flock is the celestial spiritual principle of the rational. 2184.

Milk and **Honey**. (Num. xiii. 27.) M. den. the abundance of celestial spiritual things, and h. den. the abundance of happiness and delights thence derived. 5619.

Milk Butter, and **Honey**. (Isa. vii. 22.) M. s. spiritual good; b., celestial good; and h., what is thence derived. 5619. See *Honey.*

Mill. By grinding at the m., in a good sense, is meant examination and confirmation of spiritual truth out of the Word; but, in a bad sense, by m. is s. the search after and confirmation of what is false. A.R. 394, 484.

Millet, etc., s. various species of good. 3332.

Millstone s. truth serving to faith. 9755. "No man shall take the nether or the upper m. to pledge, for he taketh a man's life to pledge" (Deut. xxiv. 6), s. that they should not deprive any one of goods and truths. A.E. 182. M. (Rev. xviii.) s. adulteration and profanation of the truth of the Word. A.R. 791.

Mind. Although the m. appears to be in the head, yet it is also actually in the whole body. C.S.L. 178, 260. It is contrary to the laws of the other world to have a divided m. 250. The three degrees of the natural m., which is a form and image of hell, are opp. to the three degrees of the spiritual m., which is a form and image of heaven. D.L.W. 275. All the things which are of the three degrees of the natural m. are included in works, which are performed by acts of the body. D.L.W. 277. Good and truth are what give orderly arrangement to all and singular things in the natural m., for those principles flow in from within and thereby arrange. 5288.

Minerals are the substances which compose the forms of the animal and vegetable kingdoms. A.Cr. 96.

Mines. Vegetation of minerals in m. wherever an aperture is found. A.Cr. 96.

Mingled. Charity cannot be inseminated when m. with profane things. 408.

Minister, to (Gen. xl. 2), is pred. of scientifics. 4976. M. is pred. of good, and servant of truth. A.R. 128.

Ministers

Ministers. They are called m., in the Word, who operate the things which are of charity. A.R. 128. They are called m. who are in the Lord's celestial kingdom, and they are called servants who are in his spiritual kingdom. A.R. 3.

Minnith and **Pannag**, wheat of (Ezek. xxvii. 17), s. goods and truths in general. A.E. 375.

Miracles, all the, which were done in Egypt s. evils and falses originating in infernal love. A.R. 399. All the m. which were done by the Lord on earth, had a spiritual application, and hence were significative of things done to the blind and lame, the leprous, the deaf, the dead, the poor, in an internal sense, or those who are so called as to doctrine and life; it is from this ground, that the m. wrought by the Lord were divine, as also were those which were wrought in Egypt, in the wilderness, and others recorded in the Word. 2383. Many m. were wrought in consequence of the Lord's presence in his ten words, which are the commandments of the decalogue. Dec. 55, 56. M. and signs reform no man, because they force. D.P. 129, 130.

Miriam (Exod. xv. 20) s. the good of faith. 8337.

Mire of the **Streets** (Zech. x. 5) s. the false doctrine. A.E. 96, 134.

Mirror. Scientifics are as mirrors, which reflect the image of the interiors. 5201.

Mirth. See *Joy, Delight.*

Miry Clay s. evil of life. A.E. 666. See *Pit of Devastation.*

Miry Places and **Marshes** (Ezek. xlvii. 11) s. scientifics inapplicable and impure; or a life defiled with falses and evils. 2702. A.E. 342.

Miserable and **Poor**. (Rev. iii.) M. is pred. of those who are in no knowledges of truth; and p., of those who are in no knowledges of good. A.E. 238. M. and p. (Rev. iii.) s. principally those who are not in the knowledges of what is good and truth, and yet desire them, because by the rich are understood such as are possessed of the knowledges of things good and truth. A.R. 209.

Misery and **Weariness** of the **Hand** (Gen. xxxi. 42) s. temptations. 4182.

Misfortune. No one is reformed in a state of m. if the state is compelled. D.P. 140.

Misgab s. false principles. 2468. See *Nebo.*

Mishmah. Things appertaining to the spiritual church. 3268. See *Nebaioth.*

Mishpat Cadesh s. contention about truths. 1678. See *En-Mishpat.*

Mists, in the spiritual world, cor. to fantasies, and are more or less dense according to the quality of the fantasy. 1512.

Mistress (Gen. xvi. 9) s. the affection of interior truth. 1936.

Mites cor. to evil uses. D.L.W. 338.

Mitre (Exod. xxviii.) s. intelligence and wisdom. 10.008. See *Bonnets.*

Mix s. to falsify truth and to profane it. A.E. 960.

Mixed. Divine truth when first received is m. with evils and falses. Ill. 6724.

Mizpah (Gen. xxxi. 49) s. the quality of the Lord's presence, with those who are principled in goods of works, or with the Gentiles. 4198.

Mizraim s. the same as Egypt. 1165.

Moab, in a good sense, s. those who are in natural good, and suffer themselves to be easily seduced; but, in an opp. sense, those who adulterate what is good. 3242. M. and Ammon s. those with whom good is adulterated and truth falsified. 2467, 3322.

Moat, a, or **Ditch**, s. doctrine. A.E. 652.

Mock, or **Scorn**, is pred. of those in truth, and not in good. 2403.

Mocked, Scourged, and **Crucified**, being pred. of the Lord s. blasphemy, falsification, and perversion of truth, and the adulteration and destruction of the good of the church and of the Word. A.E. 654.

Mode, Manners, etc., den. changes of state. 4077.

Moderation. The Lord moderates. 5497.

Moderators. In the societies of angels, there are m., presiding over the rest, but nevertheless there are not any archangels, who exercise any arbitrary authority, such government not existing in the heavens, for there no one acknowledges in heart any above himself but the Lord alone. (See Matt. xxiii. 8–11.) A.E. 735.

Modes, the, of Divine Providence are all those things by which the means for forming and perfecting man are effected. D.P. 335.

Modifications of the light of heaven take place according to the reception in the angels. 9814.

Molech. (Lev. xviii. 21.) By giving of his seed to M., is s. to destroy the truth of the Word, and then the doctrines of the church, by application to filthy and corporeal loves, as murders, hatreds, revenges, adulteries, and the like, from whence infernal falses are taken for divine truths. M. was the god of the children of Ammon. (1 Kings xi. 7.) A.E. 768. A.C. 2468.

Moles (Isa. ii. 20) rep. those who do not study truths on account of truths, but only on account of fame, name, glory, and gain. A.E. 587. See *Bats.*

Molten Image s. the evil which belongs to proprium. 215.

Molten Thing den. what is from the will-proprium. 8869.

Momentaneous Salvation from immediate mercy, is the fiery flying serpent in the church. (See Isa. xiv. 29.) D.P. 340.

Monads. It is a fallacy of the natural senses to suppose there are simple substances, such as m., etc. 5084.

Monarchical Power, the establishment of, closes up the superior parts of the understanding. Exp. T.C.R. 9.

Money is pred. of truth. 1551.

Monks, s. how they infest with their ideas of religion for the sake of dominion. 10.785.

Monsters. Evil spirits in the light of heaven appear like m. 4533.

Month has respect to the state of truth in man. A.R. 22, 935. M. s. a full or plenary state. A.R. 489. M. (Gen. xxix.) s. the end of a preceding and the beginning of a subsequent state, thus a new state. 3841. See *Forty-two.*

Monuments. By being buried or put into m. s. resurrection and continuation of life. A.R. 506.

Moon, the, s. the Lord in reference to faith, and thence faith in the Lord. 1529, 7083. M. s. spiritual good or truth. 469. The m. s. intelligence in the natural man and faith. A.R. 533. "Until the m. is not" (Ps. lxxii. 5), is that faith should become love. 337. M., in an opp. sense, s. self-derived intelligence and faith grounded in man's self. A.R. 919. The spirits of the m. in the grand man, have relation to the ensiform cartilage, or xiphoides, to which the ribs in front are joined, and from thence descends the fascia alba, which is the fulcrum of the abdominal muscles. E.U. 111. See *Ordinances.*

Moral. What is m. is the receptacle of the spiritual. D.P. 322. M. things are substances and not abstractions. D.L.W. 209.

Moral Good is that which a man does while acting under the influence of the law of reason. D.L. 12.

Moral Life is twofold, spiritual and natural, and in man, who lives from the Lord, life is spiritual moral, but in man who does not live from the Lord, life is natural moral, such as may exist with the wicked, and frequently with spirits in hell. A.R. 386.

Moralists. What becomes of the natural m., who think civil and moral life, with the prudence belonging to it, and the Divine Providence nothing. D.P. 117.

Moravians, in the spiritual world. Des. C.L.J. 86–90. None but M. spirits operate upon M. A.Cr. 74.

Moreh s. the earliest of the Lord's perception. 1442.

Moriah

Moriah, the land of, den. a place and state of temptation. 2775.

Morning, in the Word, s. various things, according to the series in the internal sense; in a supreme sense, it s. the Lord as to his divine humanity, and also his advent: in an internal sense, it s. his kingdom, and the church and its state of peace; it also s. the first state of the new church, and also the state of love; also a state of illustration, from thence a state of intelligence and wisdom; and also a state of the conjunction of good and truth, when the internal man is conjoined to the external. A.E. 179. M. s. the first and most intense degree of love. H. and H. 155. A.C. 7216, 8426, 8427. M. s. the celestial principle of love in general and in particular. 2333. M., in a proper sense, s. the Lord, his coming, and consequently, the approach of his kingdom; also the arising of a new church, for this is the Lord's kingdom in the earths, and this both in general, and in particular, yea, and also in singular; in general when any church is raised up anew on the face of the earth; in particular, when man is regenerated and is made new, for then the Lord's kingdom arises in him and he becomes a church; and in singular, as often as the good of love and of faith is operative in him; for in this is the Lord's coming; hence the resurrection of the Lord on the third day in the m. involves all those things even in particular and in singular, denoting that he arises daily, yea, every moment, in the minds of the regenerate. 2405. M. s. a state of illustration, thus what is revealed and clear; because all the times of the day, as all the times of the year, s. various states according to the variation of the light of heaven; the variations of the light of heaven are not variations as of light in the world every day and every year, but they are variations of intelligence and love; for the light of heaven is nothing else but divine intelligence from the Lord, which is also bright before the eyes, and the heat of that light is the divine love of the Lord, which also is warm to the sense; it is that light which makes the intellectual principle of man, and that heat which makes his warm vital and will-principle of good. 5097. M. (Gen. xxii. 3) s. a state of peace and innocence. 2780. M. (Zeph. iii. 5) den. the time and state of judgment, which is the same thing with the coming of the Lord, and the coming of the Lord is the same thing with the approach of his kingdom. 2405.

Morning, Day, Evening, and **Night** are pred. of the changes of state in the church. By m., is understood the first rise or beginning of the church; by d., the progression of the new church towards light and its intelligence; by e., the declination of the church from good and truth, which is called vastation; and by n., its end and destruction, and which is called consummation. A.V.C.R. 8.

Morning Star (Rev. ii. 28) s. intelligence and wisdom. A.R. 151. The Lord is called the m. s. from the light which from him will rise upon the new church, which is the New Jerusalem. A.R. 954.

Morrow, the, of the paschal supper den. the state in which the Lord is present, and hence liberation from damnation. 8017.

Mortal. That which is m. in man is the material body, which is taken away by death. D.P. 324.

Mortar (bitumen) (Nahum iii. 14) s. falses from evil conjoined. A.E. 540. Untempered m. (Ezek. xiii. 11) s. the confirmation of the false by fallacies, by which the false appears as true; and stones of hail are falses. A.E. 644.

Mortification. The evils that are shut in and do not appear are like m. D.P. 251.

Moses rep. the Lord as to the divine law, which is the Word, and in a respective sense he rep. divine truth amongst the men of the church. (Num. xvii. 17–25.) 6714. M. rep. scientific truth. 6793. M., in an extensive sense, s. all the law written in his five books, and in a more confined sense, the law which is called the decalogue, or ten commandments. A.R. 652.

Moses and **Aaron**. (Exod. vi. 25.) M. rep. the internal of the spiritual church, and A. its external; the internal of the church is called the divine law, and the external doctrine from thence; the divine law which is the internal of the church is also the Word in its internal sense, and doctrine thence is the Word in its external or literal sense. 7089. See *Aaron.*

Moses, Aaron, and **Hur.** (Exod. xvii. 10.) M. rep. divine truth proceeding immediately from the Lord; A., divine truth mediately proceeding from the Lord, and H., divine truth by that again mediately proceeding; thus they are truths in successive order. 8603.

Moses and **Elias** (Luke ix. 30, 31) s. the Word. A.R. 897. The whole historical Word is called M., and the whole prophetical Word is called E. U.T. 222.

Most Ancient Church, the, rep. the celestial kingdom of the Lord, even as to the generic and specific differences of perception, which are innumerable. 483. The m. a. c. above all the churches in the universal globe, was from the Divine, for it was in the good of love to the Lord, their will-principle and intellectual made one, and thus one mind, wherefore they had a perception of truth from good, for the Lord flowed in by an internal way into the good of their will; and through this into the good of their understanding, or truth, hence it is that that c. in preference to the rest was called man. 4454. The m. a. c. was the sabbath of the Lord, above all that succeeded it. 85. In the time of the m. a. c. they performed holy worship in tents. 414. The m. a. c. was fundamental of the Jewish church. 886.

Most High s. the inmost. D.L.W. 103.

Mote s. a lesser false from evil. A.E. 746. See *Beam.*

Moth den. falses and evils in the extreme borders of the natural mind. 9331. Cor. to evil uses. D.L.W. 338.

Mother s. the kingdom of the Lord, the church, and the divine truth. 289, 8897. M. (Gen. xxiv. 55) s. truth in the natural man. 3174. M. (Ezek. xix. 10) s. the ancient church. 289.

Mother of all **Living**. (Gen. iii. 20.) Eve was so called on account of faith towards the Lord. 290.

Mother of the **Whoredoms** and **Abominations** of the **Earth** (Rev. xvii. 5) s. the origin of the adulterations of what is good and true in the Word and also defilements of the same, and the profanations of the holy things of the church, by the Roman Catholic religion. A.R. 729.

Motion s. change of state. 3356. M. of the earth (Isa. ix. 5) s. the perversion of the church by the falsifications of truth. A.E. 329.

Move, to, Live, and **Be.** To m., is pred. of the external of life, to l., of its internal, and to b., of its inmost; hence it was said by the ancients, that "in God we live and move and have our being." 5605.

Mound s. truths not appearing, because falsified. A.E. 543.

Mount of **Holiness** (Isa. lxv. 25) is heaven, specifically the inmost heaven. A.E. 314.

Mount of **Jehovah** and the **House** of **Jacob** (Isa. ii. 3, 2; Micah iv. 3) s. the church where there is love to the Lord and worship from that love. A.E. 734.

Mount of **Olives** s. the celestial church. 9277.

Mount Zion s. truths of celestial good. A.E. 594.

Mountain s. the celestial principle of the Lord, also, the good of love and charity. 1793, 4210. A great and high m. s. the third heaven. A.R. 896. M. of the east (Gen. x. 30) s. charity from the Lord. 1248. M. of holiness (Ezek. xx. 40) s. love to the Lord, and the m. of the height of Israel s. charity towards the neighbor. 795. M. of Jehovah (Isa. xxx. 29) s. the Lord with respect to the good of love, and the rock of Israel, the Lord with respect to the good of charity. 795.

Mountains

Mountains s. celestial and spiritual love. 796, 1691. Seven m. (Rev. xvii.) s. the divine goods of the Word and of the church profaned, and also have relation to Rome. A.R. 737.

Mountains and **Hills**, in a bad sense, s. self-love and the love of the world. A.R. 336. M. and h. (Ps. lxxii. 1–7) s. the most ancient church. 337.

Mountains and **Lands** in the Word have and receive a s. from those who dwell thereon. 1675.

Mountains, Hills, and **Rocks**. The angels who constitute the Lord's heavenly kingdom, dwell for the most part in elevated places, which appear as m. from the ground; the angels who constitute the Lord's spiritual kingdom, dwell in less elevated places, which appear as h.; but the angels who are in the lowest parts of heaven, dwell in places which appear as r. of stone. H. and H. 188.

Mountains, Hills, and **Valleys** s. the higher, the lower, and the lowest things relating to the church. U.T. 200.

Mourn and **Weep,** to. (Gen. xxiii. 2.) To m. relates to grief on account of good, and to w. relates to grief on account of truth. 2909. The days of mourning (Gen. xxvii. 41) s. inversion of state. 3607. Mourning (Rev. xviii. 8) s. internal grief, in consequence of being reduced from a state of opulence to want and misery. A.R. 765.

Mourning and **Bitter Lamentation**. (Jer. vi. 26.) M. is pred. on account of the destruction of truth, and b. l., on account of the destruction of good. A.E. 1129.

Mouse. The sordidly avaricious seem as if infested by mice. 938.

Mouth, in a spiritual sense, s. thought, preaching, discourse, doctrine, and speech; and when pred. of the Lord, s. the Word. A.R. 453, 574. A.E. 235. M. (Gen. xxv. 28) s. natural affection. 3313. To fall into the m. of the eater (Nahum iii. 12) s. to be received only into the memory. A.E. 403. M. of man s. the infernal false, and sepulchre the infernal evil. (Num. xix. 18.) A.E. 659.

Move, to, den. to live. 5605.

Moved. Every thing acted upon or m. seeks to return to an equilibrium. A.Cr. 45.

Mowers. A class of those who expect heaven as a reward of merit, appear to cut grass. 1111.

Much is pred. of truths. 6172.

Mucus. Spirits rep. the m. of the nostrils. Des. 4627.

Mud, Loam, or **Clay** s. ultimates in which are truths. A.E. 355.

Mule s. rational truth, and a she-m., the affection of rational truth. 2781. See *Horse, Ass.*

Mules and **Asses** den. rational and natural truths. 4505, 6. See *Judges.*

Multiplication, the, of any number by 100, does not take away its s., but only exalts it. A.R. 654. To multiply seed (Gen. xvi. 10) s. the fructification of the celestial things of love in the rational principle, which the rational principle submits itself to interior or divine truth. 1940.

Multitude, a, is pred. of truths. 4574. M. is pred. of falses, and a heap, of evils. (Nahum iii. 3.) A.E. 354.

Murders. Three kinds of m. lie concealed inwardly with man from his birth. M., in a natural sense, are enmities, hatreds, and revenges of every kind. By m., in a spiritual sense, are meant all the methods of killing and destroying the souls of men; and by m., in a supreme sense, is meant to hate the Lord. Dec. 67–69.

Murders, Incantations, Whoredoms, and **Thefts**. (Rev. ix. 21.) M. den. the evils which destroy goods; i., the falses thence derived, which destroy truths; w. den. truths falsified; and t. den. goods thereby alienated. 5135.

Murmur den. complaint and pain from the bitterness of temptation. 8351.

Murmuring, the, of the **Children** of **Israel** against Moses and Aaron s. the profanation of the good of celestial love. A.E. 324.

Muscles, composition of. Exp. 9394.

Muses. See *Parnassus*.

Musical Instruments. Stringed appertain to truth; wind, to things celestial. A.E. 323.

Music. The sound of musical instruments cor. to affections of spiritual and celestial love. A.R. 792. See *Instruments*.

Must, or **New Wine**, den. evil produced by false. 2465. M. s. truth derived from the good of charity. A.E. 695.

Mustard Seed, a grain of (Matt. xiii. 31, 32), is man's good before he becomes spiritual, which is the least of all seeds, because he thinks to do good of himself, and what is of himself is nothing but evil; yet whereas he is in a state of regeneration, there is something of good, but it is the least of all things; at length, as faith is conjoined with love, it becomes greater, and an herb; and, lastly, when the conjunction is perfected, it becomes a tree; and then the birds of the heavens, which in this passage s. truths or things intellectual, build their nests in its branches, which are things scientific. 55.

Mutual Love, such as prevails in heaven, is not like conjugial love; the latter consists in desiring to be in the life of another one, but the former consists in wishing better to another than to itself, such as is the love of parents towards their children. 2738. M. l. unites the internal and external man. 1594.

Myriad and **Chiliad**. M., or ten thousand, is pred. of truths, and c., or one thousand, is pred. of goods: for truths are manifold, but goods are simple. A.R. 287. A.E. 336.

Myrrh (Exod. xxx. 23) s. sensual truth. 10.252. Also natural good. S.S. 23. A.C. 9293.

Myrrh, Aloes, and **Cassia**. (Ps. xlv. 9.) M. s. good of the ultimate or first degree; a., good of the second degree; and c., good of the third degree. A.E. 683.

Myrtle Tree (Isa. xli. 19) s. rational truth of an inferior degree. Also spiritual good. A.E. 294, 730.

Mystery of the **Word**, the, is no other than the contents of its internal or spiritual sense which treats of the Lord, of the glorification of his humanity, of his kingdom, and of the church, and not of the natural things of this world. 4923.

Mystery of God (Rev. x. 7) s. the advent of the Lord, in the opening of the spiritual sense of the Word. A.E. 612.

Mystics and **Mystical**. Exp. 4923, 5223.

N

Naamah, the sister of Tubal-Cain (Gen. iv. 22), s. a new church, or the doctrine of natural good and truth out of that church. 421.

Naaman, the Syrian (2 Kings v. 10), rep. those who falsify the knowledges of truth and good from the Word. A.E. 475. N.'s being healed of his leprosy by washing himself seven times in Jordan, according to the command of Elisha (2 Kings v. 1-14), rep. baptism, or initiation into the church, and into those things which appertain to the church; thus it s. regeneration, and the things appertaining to regeneration. 4255.

Naboth's Vineyard (2 Kings ix.) s. the church. A.R. 132.

Nadab s. doctrine from the internal sense of the Word. 3375.

Nahor (Gen. xxii. 20) s. the Lord's church among the Gentiles. 2861. See *Milcah*.

Nail (Zech. x. 4) s. truth supporting. A.E. 355. See *Cords*.

Nails of the Hand (Deut. xxi. 12) s. falses and evils of the sensual man.

Naked, the (Matt. xxv. 35), s. those who acknowledge that there is nothing of good and of truth in themselves. 4956. The celestial angels appear n., but the spiritual, clothed. H. and H. 177, 182. A.E. 240.

Nakedness, when pred. of the head, which is baldness, s. a deprivation of the intelligence of truth, and of the wisdom of good; when it regards the whole body, it s. a deprivation of the truths which are of faith; but when it regards the loins and genital parts, it s. a deprivation of the good of love. 9960. N. s. the evils to which man is born, which, because they are opp. to the good of celestial love, are in themselves profane. N. also s. innocence, and likewise ignorance of good and truth. A.R. 213. N. sometimes s. disgrace, and is pred. of a perverted church. (See Ezek. xvi. 7, 22; Rev. iii. 18.) A.R. 213, 295.

Nakedness of the Land (Gen. xlii. 9) s. the want of truths in the church. 5433.

Name s. the essence of a thing, and by seeing and calling by a n. is s. to know its nature and quality. 145. N. (Gen. xi. 4) s. the reputation of power. 1308. N. (Matt. xviii. 20) s. all things appertaining to love and faith, for these things are of God, or of the Lord, and are from him; and whereas these things are holy, when they are accounted holy, the kingdom of the Lord comes, and his will is done in the earths as in the heavens. 2009. To be called by a new n. (Isa. lxii. 2), s. to be changed. 145. N. which no one knew but himself (Rev. xix. 12), s. the quality of the Word in its spiritual and celestial sense seen by none but the Lord, and they to whom he reveals it. A.R. 824. It was an ancient custom, when an infant was born, to give it a n. significative of a state, and that the state should then also be des., as when Cain was born to Adam and Eve. (Gen. iv. 1.) 2643. In the spiritual world, all are named according to the quality of their life, thus with a difference within the societies and without them; within the societies, the quality of the state of every one's life is constant; but before man comes into that society which accords with his ruling love, he is named agreeably to the idea and perception of the quality of the respective states he passes through. A.E. 676.

Name of the Father, the, is the divine human of the Lord. A.R. 618, 839.

Name of God, in the spiritual sense, s. the Word, and whatever the church thence derives as accessary to the true worship of God. U.T. 298. N. of G. sometimes means the all of worship or the all of love and charity. 2724. N. of G. or of the Lord s. all the doctrine of faith concerning love and charity, which is s. by believing in his name. 2009. The n. of G. s. all the quality by which God is worshipped; for God is in his own quality, and is his own quality. His essence is the divine love; his quality is the divine truth thence proceeding, united to the divine good; thus, with us on earth, it is the Word; wherefore also it is said (John i. 1), "The Word was with God, and God was the Word." And thence also it is the doctrine of genuine truth and good from the Word. A.E. 959. A.R. 584.

Name of Jehovah. By taking the n. of J. in vain (Exod. xx. 7), in a spiritual sense, is meant to take any thing thence, and use it in vain discourse, false assertions, lies, execrations, witchcraft, and incantations; for this is to revile and blaspheme God, and consequently, his name. In a celestial sense, by taking of his name in vain, is meant blasphemy against the holy spirit. U.T. 288, 289.

Name of the Lord, the, in the celestial sense, s. his divine human. U.T. 299. It is highly necessary for man to know the quality of faith and love, which is the n. of the L., and then to love that quality, for the Lord is not loved, except according to his quality. A.E. 815. Every one in the spiritual world is instantly known, as to the quality of his love and faith, only by his pronouncing the name of the Lord Jesus Christ. A.E. 102.

Name of a Prophet, etc. To receive a prophet in the n. of a p., a righteous man, in the name of a righteous man, and to give drink in the name of a disciple (Matt. x. 41, 42), s. to love truth on account of truth, good on account of good, and to exercise charity from the faith of truth. A.E. 102.

Name and **Remnant, Son** and **Nephew** (Isa. xiv. 22), s. all truths from first principles to ultimates. A.E. 724.

Naphish rep. things in the spiritual church. 3268.

Naphtali, in a supreme sense, s. the proper power of the Lord's divine human; in a spiritual sense, temptation and victory; also a perception of use after temptation; and, in a natural sense, resistance on the part of the natural man. A.R. 354.

Naphtuhim s. external rituals of worship. 1193.

Napkin. (Luke xix.) The servant who laid up the pound in a n., den. those who procure to themselves the truths of faith, and do not conjoin them to the good of charity, in which case there is nothing of gain, or fruit. 5291.

Narrate den. to perceive. 3209.

Nathan s. the doctrine of truth. A.E. 555.

Nation (Gen. xxi. 18) s. the spiritual church which should receive the good of faith. 2699. N. from afar (Jer. v. 17) s. the false of evil, which is the false of the sensual man. A.E. 724.

Nations s. those who are in the good of love and charity from the Lord. A.R. 667. Two n. in the womb (Gen. xxv. 23) s. the natural principle as to interior and exterior good. 3293. N. (Jer. xxv. 31) s. falses. 662. N. twice repeated (Ezek. xxix. 15) have reference, in the first place, to the truths of the church, and in the second place, to the goods thereof. A.E. 654. N. (Micah vii. 14–17) s. those who trust in their own selfhood. 249.

Nations and **People.** They who are of the celestial church are called n.; and they who are of the spiritual church are called p. in the Word. A.E. 625.

Nativities (Gen. x. 1) s. the origin and derivation of doctrinals and of worship. 1149, 1330.

Nativity (Gen. x. 32) s. reformation. 1255. "Out of thy n. and out of thy father's house" (Gen. xii. 1), s. corporeal and worldly things of an exterior sort, and things interior of a like kind. 1412.

Natural Good

Natural Good is not really good, unless made spiritual good. A.E. 619.

Natural Domestic Good is that good which a man receives from his parents, or into which he is born, very distinct from the good of the natural which flows in from the Lord. 3518.

Natural Men. There are three kinds of n. m.; one kind consists of those who know nothing of the divine commandments; the second consists of those who know that there are such commandments, but think nothing of a life according to them; and the third consists of those who despise and deny them. D.L.W. 249.

Natural Principle, the, s. the natural mind; for there are two minds, the rational mind is of the internal man, but the natural mind is of the external man, this latter mind or this latter man is what is meant by the n. p. simply so called. 5301, 7693.

Natural and **Rational Principles.** Nothing but a conformity of the n. to the r. and a conjunction of both, can make man blessed and happy, which is only effected by charity, and charity is only from the Lord. 2183.

Naturalism arises from thinking of divine subjects from the properties of nature, which are matter, space, and time. A.Cr. 107.

Naturalists. Those who are mere n. des. 5571. Those who confirm in themselves appearances, make them truth, become n., believing nothing but what they can perceive by the bodily senses. D.P. 310.

Nature. All and every particular in n. exists and subsists continually from what is divine; and that by means of, or through, the spiritual world. 775, 8211, 5013. All n. is a rep. theatre of the spiritual world, that is, of heaven. 2758, 2999, 3000, 4939, 8848, 9280. From the light of n., without the Word, nothing can be known about the Lord, about heaven and hell, or about the life of man after death. 8944, 10.318, 10.319, 10.320. N. contributes nothing at all to the production of vegetables and animals, but that alone which flows in from the spiritual world into the natural. D.L.W. 344. N. is the recipient of love and wisdom, whereby they may produce their effects of uses. C.S.L. 830. N. is the ultimate of creation. D.L.W. 160.

Nauseates. The natural man n. the wisdom of angels. 999.

Nay has respect to the celestial principle. 3246. See *Yea.*

Nazarite rep. the celestial man. 2342. See *Joseph.*

Nazarites, the, rep. the Lord as to his divine human, especially as to his divine natural. 3300. A.E. 364. N., in the Israelitish churches, rep. the Lord as to the Word, in its ultimates, which is its literal sense. A.R. 47. N. rep. the Lord as to his divine human, and thence the man of the celestial church, who is a likeness of the Lord, and the natural of that man by the hair; wherefore when they were sanctified, they were to put off their old or former natural man, into which they were born, and were to put on the new man; which was s. by this, that when the days were fulfilled, in which they should separate themselves to Jehovah, they should let down the hair of their head, and should put it on the fire beneath the sacrifice; for the state of the celestial man is, that he is in good, and from good knows all truths, and never thinks and speaks from truths concerning good, still less from scientifics concerning good. 3301. In order that the conjunction of the external man with the internal, and thus the conjunction of the celestial paradise with the earthly paradise, might be rep., the *Nazariteship* was instituted; which conjunction, although it cannot be effected in man, could nevertheless be rep., and thus an image of the Lord could be exhibited, who alone conjoined both in himself. He is a N. who is holy not only as to his internal faculties, but also as to his body. *Adversaria.* See *Lord.*

Near, in the Word, s. presence and conjunction. A.E. 16. To be n. s. to be in internals. A.E. 1133. N. (Gen. xix. 20) s. truth bordering upon good. 2428. To come n. (Isa. xxxiv. 1) s. to be conjoined by love. A.E. 331.

Nebaioth, Kedar, Addeel, Mibsam, Mischma, Dumah, Massa, Hadar, Tema, Jetur, Naphish, and **Kedmah** (Gen. xxv. 11, 15), s. all things appertaining to the spiritual church, especially among the Gentiles. The ground and reason whereof is because the ancient church, which was spiritual, was amongst them, but their doctrinals and rituals were various, nevertheless, they formed one church, because they made not faith but charity essential. 3268. See *Flock.*

Nebajoth (Gen. xxviii.) den. good which is of the spiritual church. 3688.

Nebo, Kiriathaim, Misgar, Sibmah, Jaser, Chemosh, etc. (Jer. xlviii. 1) s. the false principles wherewith they are tainted who are principled in natural good. 2468.

Nebuchadnezzar rep. the profane principle which vastates. 10.227. N. king of Babylon rep. the Babylonian falsification of the Word and destruction of all truth therein. A.R. 47. See *Dream of Nebuchadnezzar.*

Nebuchadnezzar and the **Chaldeans**. N. s. those who destroy all things of the church by evils; and the C., those who destroy all things of the church by falses; or, abstractedly considered, the evils and falses themselves which destroy. A.E. 811.

Nebuchadnezzar's Image rep. successive states of the church. 3021.

Necessity. Doctrine of philosophical, not true. 6187.

Neck, the, s. influx and the communication of interior and exterior principles and consequent conjunction. The inmost or third heaven has reference to the head, the middle or second heaven has reference to the body. Therefore the n., inasmuch as it is intermediate, s. influx, and the communication of things celestial with things spiritual. 3603, 5328.

Necklace of **Gold upon the Neck** (Gen. xli. 42) den. a significative of the conjunction of things interior with things exterior, effected by good. A n., inasmuch as it encompasses the neck, is a significative of their conjunction; a n. of gold s. conjunction by good, or effected by good, because gold den. good. A sign of the conjunction of interior truth with exterior truth is s. by a n. on the throat, in Ezekiel: "I adorn thee with adorning, and put bracelets on thy hands, and a n. on thy throat: (xvi.), 11. 5320.

Needle, eye of a, s. spiritual truth. H. and H. 365. A.C. 9688, 10.227, 10.236.

Needlework (Exod. xxvi. 36) s. the scientific principle. 9688.

Needlework from **Egypt**, and **Blue**, and **Purple** from the **Isles** of **Elisha**. (Ezek. xxvii. 7.) N. from E. s. the scientific principle, b. and p. from the i. of E., s. rituals cor. to internal worship. 2576. See *Embroidery.*

Needy, in the Word, s. one who is not in goods. A.R. 95.

Negative Principle. In another life they who are in the n. p. when they think of spiritual things, are, as it were, drunken. 1672, 8629.

Negative and **Affirmative Principles**. There are two p. one which leads to all folly and madness, another which leads to all intelligence and wisdom; the former p. is to deny all things, as when a man says in his heart, that he cannot believe such things until he is convinced by what he can comprehend or be sensible of; this p. is what leads to all folly and madness, and may be called the n. p.; the other p. is to affirm the things which are of doctrine from the Word, as when a man thinks and believes with himself that they are true, because the Lord has said to; this p. is what leads to all intelligence and wisdom, and may be called the a. p.; they who think from the n. p., the more they consult things rational, scientific, and philosophical, do but so much the more plunge themselves into darkness, till at length they come to deny all things; the reason is, because no one can from things inferior comprehend things superior, that is, things spiritual and celestial, still less things divine. 2568.

Negro, or **Ethiopian**, changing his skin, s. that companions should not be defrauded of external truths, which are doctrinals according to which they live. 297, 1073.

Neighbor. The n. is not only man singly, but also man collectively, as a less or greater society, our country, the church, the Lord's kingdom, and, above all, the Lord himself; these are the n. to whom good is to be done from love. A society is our n. more than a single man, because it consists of many. Our country is our n. more than a society, because it is like a parent; for a man is born therein, and is thereby nourished and protected from injuries. The church is our n. more than our country, for he who provides for the church, provides for the souls and eternal life of the men who dwell in his country. The Lord's kingdom is our n. in a still superior degree, for the Lord's kingdom consists of all who are in good, as well those on the earths as those in the heavens. N.J.D. 91–95.

Neighings (Jer. xiii. 27) are the profanations of truth. A.E. 142.

Nephilim. See *Giants.*

Neptune, Apollo, Pluto, etc., were worshipped by several nations, because they were regarded as possessing the properties and qualities of God. A.Cr. 22.

Nerve, or **Sinew,** s. truth. 4303.

Nest. To make a n. (Jer. xlviii. 28), when pred. of a bird, s. the same thing as to dwell; viz., to fulfil the duties of active life when pred. of a man. A.E. 411.

Net. To cast the n. on the right side (John xxi. 6) s. to teach the good of life. A.E. 600.

Network, grate of, s. the sensual external. 9726.

Nettles s. vastation of good. 2455. An abandoned place of n. (Zeph. ii. 9) s. the rage or burning of the life of man from self-love. 10.300.

New Birth, or **Creation,** the, is effected from the Lord alone, by charity and faith as two means or mediums, during man's co-operation. U.T. 576–578.

New Birth. The first act of the n. b. is called reformation, and relates to the understanding; the second is called regeneration, and relates to the will. U.T. 571.

New Church. There is at this day a n. c. establishing by the Lord, which is meant by the New Jerusalem in the Apocalypse, in which the Lord alone is worshipped, as he is in heaven. A.R. 839. The n. c. which is the New Jerusalem is formed by those who approach the Lord only, and at the same time perform repentance from evil works. A.R. 69. The n. c. is the crown of all the churches that have hitherto been in the world, because it will worship one visible God, in whom the invisible God, as the soul is in the body. U.T. 787. All who are in truths originating in good are received into the n. c., because they love the light thereof; and the rest cannot bear that light. A.R. 922. The two essentials of the n. c. are an acknowledgment of the Lord, that he is the God of heaven and earth, and that his human is divine; the other is a life conformable to the precepts of the decalogue; and these two are conjoined like the two tables of the decalogue, and like love to God and love towards the neighbor. A.R. 490. The n. c. is first amongst a few, afterwards with greater numbers, and so at last to arrive to its full state. The causes are, first, that its doctrine, which is the doctrine of love to the Lord and charity towards the neighbor, cannot be acknowledged and thence received, except by those who are interiorly affected with truths and who see them, have cultivated their intellectual faculty, and have not destroyed it in themselves by the loves of self and the world. Another cause is that the doctrine of that church cannot be acknowledged, nor, consequently, received except by those who have not confirmed themselves in doctrine and at the same time in life, in faith alone. The third cause is that the n. c. on the earth increases, according to its increase in the world of spirits among those who are in the spiritual affection of truth, and who renounce the doctrine they had been in in the world, and receive the doctrine of the n. c. The numbers there every day increase. A.E. 732.

New Heaven, the, is treated of in the Apocalypse, and is called the Christian heaven, because it is distinct from the ancient heavens, which were composed of men of the church before the Lord's coming. A.R. 876. See *Heaven.*

New Heaven and **New Earth**, a (Rev. xxi. 1), does not mean a natural h. visible to the eye, nor a natural e. inhabited by men, but a spiritual h. is meant, and an e. belonging to that h., where angels are. A.R. 876. N. h. and n. e. s. a new church, h., its internal, and e., its external. A.R. 613.

New Heaven and **New Church**. In proportion as the n. h., which constitutes the internal of the church in man, grows and increases, in the same proportion the new Jerusalem, that is, the n. c., comes down from that heaven. U.T. 784. The n. h. means a n. h. from among Christians. The new Jerusalem is the n. c. upon earth, which will act as one with that n. h. (Rev. xxi. 1, 2.) A.R. Preface.

New Man and **Old Man**. The n. m. is in the affection of spiritual and celestial things, inasmuch as these constitute his delights and blessednesses; whereas the o. m. is in the affection of worldly and terrestrial things, and these constitute his delights and satisfactions, consequently, the n. m. has respect to ends in heaven, but the o. m. to ends in the world. 4063.

New Name of the **Lord** (Rev. iii. 12) s. his divine human, and to write it upon any one, s. to implant the acknowledgment thereof, in his life. A.E. 224.

New Song. To sing a n. s., is to confess out of joy of heart, and out of affection, that the Lord alone is the Saviour, Redeemer, and God of heaven and earth. A.R. 279, 615, 662.

New Testament. As to what concerns the Word of the N. T. written by the Evangelists, inasmuch as the Lord spake from the essential divine, therefore all and single things spoken by him were rep. and s. of divine things, thus of the celestial things of his kingdom and church. 2900.

New Wine is the divine truth of the N. T. A.R. 2466, 316.

Newton. His abhorrence of the idea of a vacuum or of nothing. D.L.W. 82.

Nice, Council of. Imputation originated with the Council of N. U.T. 636.

Nicolaitans (Rev. ii. 60) are they who make works meritorious. A.R. 86. Those who separate good from truth or charity from faith. A.E. 107, 142.

Nigella den. scientifics. 10.669.

Nigh den. truth in affinity with good. 2428.

Night, in the spiritual sense, den. a state of shade induced by the false grounded in evil, thus also an obscure principle of the mind. The obscurity, which is that of n. in the world, is natural obscurity, but the obscurity, which is that of n. in the other life, is spiritual obscurity; the former exists from the absence of the sun of the world, and the consequent privation of light, but the latter, from the absence of the sun of heaven which is the Lord, and the privation of light, that is, of intelligence thence derived; this privation does not exist, in consequence of the sun of heaven setting as the sun of the world, but in consequence of a man or a spirit being in the false grounded in evil, and removing himself, and occasioning to himself obscurity. 5092. N., or winter, s. the end of the church. D.L.W. 73. N. s. a state void of love and faith. 221, 709, 2353, 6000, 6110. N. s. the light of the natural man, for his light, compared to the light of the spiritual man, is like the light from the moon and stars compared to the light of day from the sun. A.E. 401. N. sometimes s. a state of damnation. 7851. N. (Gen. xix.) s. the last time, when the Lord's divine human and holy proceeding are no

Nights

longer acknowledged. 2353. N. (John xi. 9) den. the false principle grounded in evil. 2353.

Nights, forty (Gen. vii. 4). den. anxieties of temptation. 786. N. (Ps. xvi. 7) s. the state of man when falses rise up against him, and excite the combat of temptation. A.E. 168.

Nile, the, or river of Egypt, rep. the sensual things subject to the intellectual part, thus the scientifics which are thence derived, for these are the ultimates of the spiritual things of the Lord's kingdom. 5196.

Nimrod (Gen. x.) s. those who make internal worship external, by depending upon external worship alone. 1173–1179.

Nine s. conjunction. 2075.

Ninety Years, a daughter of (Gen. xvii. 17), s. that truth conjoined with good should effect the union of the rational principle of the Lord's human essence to his divine; or conjunction by remains. 2075. Ninety-nine years (Gen. xvii. 1) s. the time before the Lord fully conjoined the internal man with the rational. 1988. Ninety-nine years (Gen. xvii. 26), the state and time before the union of the Lord's divine essence with his human essence. 2106.

Nineveh s. the falses of doctrinals, also the Gentiles, or the falses originating in the fallacies of the senses, in the obscurity of an unemlightened understanding and in ignorance. 1188.

Nissi, Jehovah. Continual war and protection of the Lord. 8624.

No (Ezek. xxx. 15) den. doubt in a state of temptation. 2334. See *Egypt.*

No One, or **None,** den. the negative of a thing. 5225.

Noah (Gen. v. 29) s. the ancient church, or the parent of the three churches after the flood. 528, 529. N. was not the ancient church, but, as it were, the parent or seed of that church; but N., with Shem, Ham, and Japheth, constituted the ancient church, which immediately succeeded the most ancient church. Every man of the church called N. was of the posterity of the most ancient church, consequently, in a state nearly similar, as to hereditary evil, with the rest of the posterity which perished; and they who were in a similar state could not be regenerated and become spiritual, as those who are not so infected with hereditary evil. 788.

Noah, Daniel, and **Job** (three men), (Ezek. xiv. 16) s. those who are reformed by truths from the Word, and by temptations. A.E. 721.

Nobleman (Luke xix. 12–24) s. the Lord, and his going into a far country; s. his going out of this world, and thence his apparent absence. A.E. 675.

Nobles and **Chaldeans.** (Isa. xliii. 14.) N. s. principal falses, and C. are they who devastate by falses. A.E. 574.

Nobles and **Little Ones.** (Jer. xiv. 3.) N., or great ones, s. those who teach and lead, and the l. o., those who are taught and led. A.E. 644.

Nod, the land of (Gen. iv. 16), s. a state destitute of goodness and truth. 397.

Noise. To shout and n. applies to what is disturbed, and to occasions of festivity. 375.

Noon s. the full state of the church. D.L.W. 73. N. s. wisdom in its most luminous state. H. and H. 155–158. N. den. a state of light, because the times of the day, as morning, n., evening, cor. to ill. in the other life, and ill. in that life are the ill. of intelligence and wisdom, for in the light of heaven is intelligence and wisdom; the vicissitudes of ill. in the other life are of this description, viz., as morning, n., and evening on the earths; states of shade have existence like those in the evening, not from the sun in that world, that is the Lord, who always shines, but from the propriety of the angels; for as they are let into their own propriety, they thus come into a state of shade or evening, and as they are elevated from their own propriety into the celestial propriety, they thus come into a state of light; hence it is evident from what ground it is that n. cor. to a state of light. 5672.

Noph and **Zoan** s. ill. of the natural man from spiritual light. A.E. 654.

North, the, s. those who are in obscurity as to truth. 3708. N. (Isa. xiv. 31) s. hell. A.E. 817. The n. (Jer. iii. 12) s. those who are in ignorance of truth, and are yet in the life of good. 3708. Evil out of the n. (Jer. vi. 1) s. man's sensual principle and the scientific thence derived. 4592.

Northern or what **Cometh** from the **North** (Jer. xv. 12) s. what is sensual and natural; for what is natural in respect to what is spiritual and celestial, is like darkness, or the north, in respect to light, or the south. 426.

Nose, the, s. the life of good, on account of the respiration which has place there, which, in the internal sense, is life, and likewise on account of odor which is the grateful principle of love, whereof good is. 3103. N., or nostrils, s. perception. 3577, 10.292. Those in the province of the n., are in various degrees of the perception of truth, but the more interior, the more perfect. H. and H. 96. See *Hook in the Nose.*

Nostrils. Blast of the breath of the n. s. same as by his anger and wrath. A.E. 741.

Not remains a negative expression in the series of the spiritual sense. 3990.

Nothing. In n. there is no actuality of mind. D.L.W. 82. From n., n. originates. A.Cr. 29.

Nourishment. Spiritual n. is science, intelligence, and wisdom. A.E. 386. N. is from knowledges of good and truth der. from the Word. 5960.

Novitiate Spirits are men newly deceased. C.S.L. 461. A.R. 153. N. s. are carried about and introduced into various societies, as well good as evil, and are examined whether they are affected with truths or falses, and in what manner. A.R. 153.

Noxious Animals der. their origin from man. D.L.W. 339.

Number, to, s. to know the nature and quality of any thing; hence David's numbering the people was a heinous offence, because in the internal sense, the arrangement of those truths and goods which constitute the church in man, can only be effected by the Lord. A.R. 364. A.C. 10.218. To n. (Isa. xxii. 10) s. to falsify. A.E. 454. To n. bones (Ps. xxii. 14–18) s. to desire to dissipate truths by reasonings and false principles. 3812. Number s. the quality of a thing as to truth. A.R. 364. The same n. which s. what is full and sufficient, when it is pred. concerning quantity, s. duration, when pred. concerning time. A.E. 548. See *Mene, Tekel, and Perez.*

Numbers, all, in the Word, s. things or states, and various, according to the respect they have to other n. A.E. 24. The most ancient, who were celestial men, and discoursed with angels, formed ecclesiastical computation by n., whereby they expressed universally those things, which by words, they expressed singularly, but what each n. had involved did not remain with posterity, only what was signified by the simple n., viz., 2, 3, 6, 7, 8, 12, and hence 24, 72, and 77. 5265. N., in the Word, s. things, or rather resemble certain adjectives to substantives, den. some quality in things, because n., in itself, is natural, for natural things are determined by n., but spiritual things, by things and their states. A.R. 10. Spiritual things are not numbered and measured, but still they fall into n. and measures as they descend out of the spiritual world, or heaven where angels are, into the natural world or earth where men are; and in like manner when they descend out of the spiritual sense of the Word into the natural sense. Hence the literal sense of the holy Word, in that respect, is such as we find it. A.E. 429. There are writings in the inmost heaven consisting of mere n. in a regular order. H. and H. 263. When two n. multiplied, the one greater and the other less which s. the same, are both mentioned together, as 10 or 100, or 100 and 1,000, etc., then the less n. is pred. of goods, and the greater, of truths. A.E. 366. There are simple n. which are significative above all others, and from which the greater n. derive their significations,

Numerous

viz., 2, 3, 5, and 7. From the n. 2, arise the n. 4, 8, 16, 400, 800, 1,600, 4,000, 8,000, and 16,000. From the n. 3, arise 6, 12, 24, 72, 144, 1,440, 144,000. From the n. 5, arise 10, 50, 100, 1,000, 10,000, 100,000. And from the n. 7, arise 14, 70, 700, 7,000, 70,000. A.E. 430. The half and the double, as to n. in the Word, involve the like, as twenty the like with ten, and four the like with two, six with three, twenty-four with twelve, and so forth; this is the case also with n. still further multiplied, as with a hundred and also a thousand, which involve the like with ten; so likewise with seventy-two, and a hundred and forty-four, which involve the like with twelve; what therefore the compound n. involve, may be known from the simple n., from which and with which they are multiplied; what also the more simple n. involve, may be known from the integral n., as what five involve may be known from ten, and what two, with a half, from five, and so forth; in general, it is to be noted, that n. multiplied involve the like with the simple n., but what is most full and that n. divided involve the like, but not so full. 5291. A.E. 384.

Numerous and **Great**, is pred. of truth grounded in good. 2227.

Nun, Joshua, the Son of, rep. truth combating. 8595.

Nuptials. To make n. is to be conjoined to the Lord, and to enter into n. is to be received into heaven by the Lord. C.S.L. 41.

Nurse (Gen. xxiv. 59) s. a state of innocence. 3183. N. (Gen. xxxv.) s. hereditary evil. A n., so far as she nourishes and suckles an infant, properly s. the insinuation of innocence, by the celestial spiritual principle, but when it is said that "Deborah the n. of Rebecca died and was buried," etc., it s. that hereditary evil, which the Lord received from the mother, and which was nourished from infancy (like as in the case of other men), but which was afterwards entirely expelled forever. 4562.

Nursing Fathers and **Nursing Mothers**. (Isa. xlix. 22, 23.) N. f., which is pred. of kings, s. intelligence, and n. m., which is pred. of queens, s. wisdom. 3183.

Nut. Turpentine n., or dates, den. goods of life cor. to the truths of natural good. 5622.

Nutriment is greatest when food is eaten joyfully. 5147.

Nymphs. Des. of the n. who have passed from the caterpillar. 8848.

O

O, in the angelic language, is a vowel used among the angels of the third heaven, to express a sound corresponding with affection. S.S. 90. U.T. 278.

Oak s. the sensual good and truth of the church, and consequently, the lowest of the natural principle; therefore either the truths and goods, or the falses and evils that are therein. U.T. 200. O. (Isa. i. 30) s. the natural man, and its leaves the scientifics and knowledges of truth in him. A.E. 504. "To hide under an o." (Gen. xxxv. 4), s. eternal rejection. 4552.

Oak Groves of Mamre (Gen. xiii. 18) s. more interior perception than that which is s. by the o. g. Moreh. 1616. O. g. of M. (Gen. xviii. 1) rep. and s. perceptions, but such as are human grounded in scientifics, and in the first rational principles thence deduced. 2144.

Oak Grove of Moreh (Gen. xii. 6) s. the first or earliest of the Lord's perception. 1442.

Oars and **Benches.** (Ezek. xxvii. 6.) O. s. those things which are of the sensual man by which the understanding speaks; and a bench or board s. that which is rational from which the understanding is led. This also is signified by ebony, mentioned in the same passage. A.E. 1146. See *Rowers.*

Oath, or Swearing, s. confirmation and conjunction. 2720, 3459. Also a covenant. 1996. After the rep. rites of the church were abolished, oaths, as used in covenant, were also abolished by the Lord. A.R. 474.

Obadiah, the prophet, treats in general of those who are in self-derived intelligence and who pervert the letter of the Word, whereby the church perishes, and a new church to be raised up instead thereof, which should be in the understanding of truth, and that they who are therein shall be saved. S.E.L.P.

Obal (Gen. x. 28) s. a ritual of the church called Eber. 1245.

Obduracy s. confirmation against the goods and truths of the Word. A.E. 653.

Obed-Edom, the **Gittite** (2 Sam. vi. 10), rep. those who were in spiritual good. A.E. 700.

Obedience of the **Philistines.** (Isa. xi. 14.) The sons of Ammon, were so called, because they are tainted with false principles derived from them. 2468.

Object. Exp. D.L.W. 70, 293.

Oblation of **Incense** and **Vanity.** (Isa. xvi. 3.) O. of i. is worship from spiritual good, and v. is evil and the false of evil. A.E. 340.

Oblivion. (Gen. xli. 30.) To give to o. den. removal and hence apparent privation. 5278.

Oboli has reference to remains of good and truth. 2959.

Obscure. Man in the body is o., compared with his interior life, that myriads of perceptions merge in one. 2367.

Observe, to, s. things to be kept. 3382. Also, the intention of perverting. A.E. 780.

Observances. Things to be observed have reference to the whole contents of the Word in general; *precepts*, to all its internals; *statutes*, to its externals; and *laws*, to all in particular.

Obsession

Obsession is when natural and corporeal spirits enter into man's body, and occupy all his senses, and speak through his mouth, and act by his members, then not knowing but that all things appertaining to the man are theirs. Such o., however, are not given at this day. H. and H. 257. But there are internal o., occasioned by certain spirits called syrens, who study to destroy conscience and possess the interiors of men, although man is ignorant of it. 1983.

Obstinate and **Obduracy** have relation to those who are principled in the falses of evil. 7272.

Obstipations of the **Brain**. Those cor. thereto who have no end of use, only that they may enjoy the company of their friends and mistresses and the pleasures thence resulting, thus who live in self-indulgence alone. Their sphere induces stupidity, and extinguishes in others the affections of truth and good. 4054.

Obstruction of the interior vessels by evil, as the cause of disease. 5718.

Occiput. Des. of dangerous and clandestine spirits who act under the o. 4227.

Occult, or **Secret**. There is nothing that man does in s., but becomes manifest in the other life, because it forms his sphere. 7454.

Occulation of good and truth. Exp. 5962.

Ocean, or **Sea**. Waters den. knowledges and scientifics; s., their collection, or gathering together in the natural man. 27.

Ochim and **Zim**. Interior things of worship appertaining to self-love. 1326.

Odium, or **Hatred**, is aversion and spiritual antipathy. 5061. H. actually cherished make hell. 1608.

Odor. When the celestial angels attend the dead body of a deceased person, who is to be resuscitated, the smell of the dead body is changed into an aromatic o., on perceiving which, the evil spirits cannot approach. 1518. Fragrant o. which exist in heaven cor. to affections of charity and perceptions of faith. A.R. 278. O. cor. with spheres. 1514. O. of spheres of charity and faith are perceived in another life like those of flowers, lilies, and spices of divers kinds, with an infinite variety. 1519. The infernal spirits are delighted with the most filthy o. 5387. H. and H. 485, 490.

Odor of **Rest** (Gen. viii. 21), when spoken of Jehovah s. the perception of peace. 925.

Offence. The doctrine of the Lord is an o. to many who apparently believe it. Exp. 2034.

Offerings s. worship. 349.

Offerings and the **First Fruits** of **Oblations** with **Holy Things** (Ezek. xx. 40) s. works sanctified by charity from the Lord. 349.

Officer den. doctrines or principles of interpretation. 4790.

Officers s. principles of what is false and evil. A.E. 863.

Offices, or **Uses**, are goods, because the good of charity consists in use. 6073.

Offspring (Isa. lxv. 23) s. those who are principled in the good of love. 613. The spiritual o. which have birth from the Lord's marriage with the church are truths and goods; truths, from which are derived understanding, perception, and all thought, and goods from which are derived love, charity, and all affection. C.S.L. 121.

Og, king of Bashan, s. in evils of every kind. A.E. 163.

Ohalim, Tabernacles, s. the holy principle of good. 4391.

Ohola s. truths falsified. A.E. 355.

Oil s. the holy principle of good, or the good of love. 3728. O. s. celestial good and spiritual good. O. of unction, the good of love to the Lord from the Lord, and the o. of the lamps, the good of charity from the Lord towards our neighbor. A.E. 375. A.C. 10.261. Setting up a statue of stone,

Omega

and pouring o. upon it (Gen. xxxv. 14, 15), rep. the progress of the glorification of the Lord and the regeneration of man from truth to celestial good. 4582. See *To Anoint, Olive, Press.*

Oil and **Wine** s. the good and truth of the internal or spiritual sense of the Word. A.E. 375.

Oil, and **Wine,** and **Wheat,** and **Barley.** See *Goods and Truths.*

Ointment s. celestial good and spiritual good, or the good of love to the Lord and the good of charity to the neighbor. A.E. 375.

Old. To grow o., when pred. of the Lord (Gen. xviii. 10, 12) s. to put off the human. 2204. To be o. (Gen. xxvii. 1) s. the presence of a new state. 3492. See *Days of Old.*

Old Age, in the Word, implies nothing else but the last time. 2198.

Old Estates (Ezek. xxvi. 11) s. the most ancient church after the flood. 55.

Old Man, in the Word, s. a wise man, and in the abstract, wisdom. H. and H. 178.

Old Men and **Women.** O. m. s. confirmed truths, and o. w., confirmed goods. 2348. See *Boys, Decrepit Old Men and Women.*

Old Testament. That the Word of the O. T. contains the mysteries of heaven, and that all and every thing therein regards the Lord, his heaven, the church, faith, and whatever relates to faith is inconceivable from the letter; for the letter or literal sense suggests only such things as respect the externals of the Jewish church, when nevertheless there are internal things contained therein which do not in the least appear in those externals, except in a very few cases, which the Lord revealed and unfolded to the apostles; as that sacrifices are significative of the Lord; that the land of Canaan and Jerusalem are significative of heaven, on which account, we read of the heavenly Canaan and Jerusalem; and in like manner of Paradise. 1. The reason why interior truths are so rarely extant in the literal sense thereof, is because the Jews, who were not willing to know them, would thereby have profaned interior goods and truths, as they had profaned exterior, by their so often becoming open idolaters. 3373.

Old Waste Places and the **Foundations** of **Generation** and **Generation.** (Isa. lxviii. 12.) O. w. p. s. the celestial things of faith and the f. of g. and g., the spiritual things thereof. 613.

Olive (Isa. xvii. 6) s. celestial remains. 886. O. s. love and charity, because the o. tree s. the celestial church, and thence the o., which is its fruit, s. celestial love, which love is love to the Lord; thence it is, that this love is also s. by the oil wherewith all the holy things of the church were anointed; the oil which was called the oil of holiness, was produced from o., and mixed with aromatics. (Exod. xix. 23, 24), and moreover, the lamps of the candlestick in the tabernacle were made to burn every evening with o. oil. (Exod. xxvii. 20; Lev. xxiv. 2.) A.R. 493.

Olive Leaf Plucked Off in the **Dove's Mouth** (Gen. viii. 11) s. some little of the truth of faith; left is faith, and olive, the good of charity; plucked off s. that the truth of faith is from the good of charity as its origin. 879.

Olive Tree. Shaking of an o. t. (Isa. xxiv. 13) s. the vastation of the church as to good. A.E. 313. The oil tree s. the perception of good and truth celestial. A.E. 403.

Olive Trees, two, and **Two Sons** of **Oil.** (Zech. iv. 11, 14.) The two o. t. s. the two churches called celestial and spiritual, and the t. s. of o., their doctrinal truths. A.E. 724.

Olive Yards (Amos iv. 12) s. the celestial things of the church. 1069.

Olives s. good. A.E. 340. See *Plants of Olives.*

Olivet, Mount, s. the celestial church, or celestial good which is of love towards the Lord. Also divine love. 9277. A.R. 493.

Omega and **Alpha** s. the Lord's divinity and infinity. A.R. 29.

223

Omer

Omer, an, s. a sufficient quantity, and has respect to good. 8540. O. and half an o. (Hosea iii. 2) s. so little as to be scarce any thing. A.E. 374.

Omit. They who o. to think of evil, are continually in it. D.P. 101.

Omnipotence of **God**, the, in the universe, and in all its parts, proceeds and operates according to the laws of its own order. U.T. 56, 58.

Omnipotence and **Omniscience**. O. is pred. of quantity in relation to magnitude, and omniscience of quantity in relation to multitude. O. is also pred. of infinite good of divine love, or of the divine will; but omniscience is pred. of infinite truth, or of the divine intelligence. 3934. O., omniscience, and omnipresence are the effect of the divine wisdom derived from the divine love. U.T. 50, 51.

Omnipotent. The Lord is called o. (Rev. xix.) from the power of separating the good from the evil by the last judgment, and also from the power of saving those who receive him. A.E. 1217.

Omnipresent. God is o. in all the gradations of his own order from first to last. U.T. 63, 64. The Lord is o. because he is in love and wisdom, or good and truth, which are himself, and which are not in place, but with those who are in place according to reception. A.R. 961.

Omniscient. God is o., that is, perceives, sees, and knows all and every thing, even what is most minute, that is done according to order, and by that means also whatsoever is done contrary to order. U.T. 59, 62.

On. The priest of O. den. good. 5332.

Onan. (Gen. xxxviii.) By him is des. the evil which is derived from the false of evil in which the Jewish nation was secondarily principled. 4837. O.'s trespass (Gen. xxxviii. 6, 10) s. his aversion and hatred against the good and truth of the church, from whence he was not willing to continue the representation of it, which is understood by his not raising up seed to his brother; it is said, the Lord caused him also to die, by which is s. that there was no representation of a church. But it was the intention or end of evil which influenced the conduct of O., which was contrary to conjugial love and divine order. 4834–4840.

Once in a year that expiation was to be made, den. perpetual purification from evils by the truths of faith. 10.209.

One, the number, is pred. concerning good, and indicates what is perfect. A.E. 374.

One, a, in all cases, is composed, not of same principles, but of various principles in form, which constitute a o. according to the form. 4149. Every o. thing or principle consists of various things or principles, and this by celestial harmony and concord. 4263.

One Hundred s. a full state of unition. 2636.

One Hundred and **Forty-Four Thousand** den. the state of all who are in charity. 7973.

One Hundred and **Twenty** (10×12) s. remains of faith. 575.

Onions s. such things as are of the lowest natural. A.E. 513.

Only Begotten of the **Father** (John i. 14) s. the existing or proceeding from the divine esse in himself. A.E. 1069.

Onycha (Exod. xxx. 34) s. the affection of interior natural truth. 10.293.

Onyx Stones set in **Ouches** of **Gold** (Exod. xxviii. 11) s. that the good of love should enter by influx into the truth of faith. 115. See *Bdellium*.

Open, to (Rev. ix.), s. to communicate and conjoin. A.E. 537.

Open, to, the **Mouth** (Rev. xii. 16) s. to adduce truths out of the Word. A.R. 564.

Open, to, and **Loose** the **Seals** of the **Book**. (Rev. v. 3.) To o. s. to know, and to loose the seals of the book s. to perceive those things which to others were altogether concealed. A.E. 303. To o. or loose the seals (Rev. viii.) s. to explore states of life, or the states of the church, and thence of life. A.R. 388.

Open the Womb, to (Gen. xxx. 22), s. to give the faculty of conceiving and bringing forth, thus, in an internal sense, the faculty of receiving and acknowledging the goods of truth and the truths of good. 3967.

Operate, to, or work a thing into fashion, is to regenerate. 8329.

Operation. The o. of the Lord is upon man's love, and from it upon his understanding. A.Cr. 5. O. by influx into vegetable and animal forms. D.L.W. 346. The o. and progression of the end by its means, is what is called Divine Providence. D.P. 331.

Operations. There are four common o. of heaven by influx into the body. Des. 3884.

Operators, used in the sense of laborers, in the spiritual church. 1069.

Ophir (Gen. x. 28) s. a ritual of the church called Eber. 1245. Gold of O. (Isa. xiii. 13; Ps. xlv.) s. spiritual good. 9881.

Opinion. To have one o. s. unanimity. A.E. 1071. Those who tenaciously adhere to an o. des. 806.

Opposite. Most expressions in the Word have an o. sense, and this by reason that the same things which are doing in heaven, when they flow down into hell, are changed into things o., and actually become o. 1066, 3322, 5268. The things of the literal sense of the Word, in many cases appear o. to what is contained in the internal sense, when, yet, they are by no means o., but entirely cor. 3425.

Opposition. Heaven and hell are in mutual o. D.P. 300. Good is known as to its quality, by relation to what is less good, and by o. to evil. D.P. 24.

Oppression s. destruction of truth by falses. A.E. 328.

Oppressors, Infants, and Women. (Isa. iii. 12.) O. s. those who violate truths; i., those who do not know them, and w. s. lusts which pervert them. A.E. 555.

Opprobrium. Applied to what is against the religion of another. 4463.

Opulence, or **Riches**, are so far good as spiritual good enters into the use of them. 3951. The rich, who have lived for themselves, without conscience or charity, are not tolerated in societies in the other life. 1631. In heaven o. originates in knowledge. A.Cr. 81. O., greater or less, is only something imaginary. D.P. 250.

Opulent is pred. of truths. A.E. 644.

Oracles. See *Representatives.*

Orb, or **World**, s. the church. A.E. 275.

Order. The Lord is o. itself. 1728, 1912. O. consists in celestial things bearing rule over spiritual, and spiritual over natural, and natural over corporeal. 911. Man was created a form of divine o. U.T. 65. Divine truths are the laws of o. 2247, 7995. Divine truth from the Lord constitutes o., and divine good is the essence of it. 1728, 2258. Essential o. requires that the celestial principle, by means of the spiritual, should insert itself into the rational, and thereby into the scientific, and adapt each to itself, and unless this o. be observed, it is impossible to acquire wisdom. 1475. So far as man lives according to o., so far he is a man; but so far as he is not in such a life, so far does he appear as a monster. 4839, 6605, 6626. Both in heaven and in the world, are found two kinds or establishments of o., successive o., and simultaneous o.; in successive o., one thing succeeds and follows another, from what is highest to what is lowest; but in simultaneous o., one thing is next to another, from what is innermost to what is outermost. Successive o. is like a column with degrees from highest to lowest; but simultaneous o. is like a work whose centre and circumference have a regular coherence even to the extremest superfices. The highest parts of successive o. become the innermost of simultaneous o., and the lowest parts of successive o. become the outermost of simultaneous o., comparatively as a column of degrees, when it subsides becomes a coherent body in a plain.

Ordinances

Thus, what is simultaneous is formed from what is successive, and this is the case in all and every thing in the natural world, and in all and every thing in the spiritual world, for there is everywhere a first, a middle, and a last; and the first, by means of the middle, tends and proceeds to its last; but it should be well observed, that there are degrees of purity, according to which both these kinds of o. are established. U.T. 214.

Ordinances, in the prophets, s. changes relative to things spiritual and celestial, both in general and particular, which are also compared to the changes of days and of years. 37.

Ordinances of the **Moon** and of the **Stars** (Jer. xxxi. 35) s. all things which are in the natural man, and which are done according to order. A.E. 401.

Ordinances, Precepts, Statutes, and Laws. O. are all things of the Word in general; p. are the internal things thereof; s., the external things; and l., all things thereof in particular. 3382.

Ordination of the Twelve Tribes rep. the o. of the angelic societies in the heavens from whence it is, that they rep. all things of the church, for heaven and the church make one; the rep. of heaven and the church fall according to the order in which they are named, and the first name, or the first tribe is an index by which those which follow are determined, and from thence the things of heaven and the church with variety. A.E. 431.

Organ s. spiritual good. 419.

Organical Forms are not only those which appear to the eye, and which can be discovered by microscopes, but there are also o. f. still purer, which cannot possibly be discovered by any eye, naked or artificial; these latter forms are of an interior kind, as the forms which are of the internal light, and finally those which are of the intellect, which latter are inscrutable, but still they are forms, that is, substances, for it is not possible for any sight, not even intellectual, to exist, but from something; this is also a known thing in the learned world; viz., that without substance which is a subject, there is not any mode or any modification, or any quality, which manifests itself actually; those purer or interior forms, which are inscrutable, are what form and fix the internal senses, and also produce the interior affections; with those forms the interior heavens cor., because they cor. with the senses thereof, and with the affections of these senses. 4224.

Organical Vessels. The external man cannot particularly and distinctly receive his life from the internal man, unless his o. v. be opened, so as to be receptive of the particular and singular things of the internal man; those o. v., which should be thus receptive, are not opened except by means of the senses, especially those of hearing and seeing, and in proportion as they are opened, the internal man, with its particulars and singulars, may enter in by influx; they are opened through the medium of the senses, by scientifics and knowledges, and also by pleasures and delights, the things of the understanding by the former, and the things of the will by the latter. 1563.

Organization. They who deny God in the world, deny him after death, and the o. induced remains to eternity. D.P. 319, 326.

Organize. Every part of the brain is organized. These variations are infinitely more perfect in the organic things of the mind than of the body. D.P. 279.

Origin, the, of kingdoms and empires, come from the lust of ruling, which entered like a contagion; hence arose degrees of dignities, and honors according to them. O. of the love of possessing wealth beyond the necessaries of life. D.P. 215.

Origin of **Man**. Des. D.L.W. 346.

Original Sin. Not true as commonly understood, yet man is nothing but sin. 5280.

Ornament den. holy truth, also what is divine in externals. 10.536. O. for the nose and bracelets for the hands were give to a bride; the o. on the nose s. good, and the bracelents on the hands truth, because those things constitute the church. 3103. See *Beauty.*

Orphans s. those who are in a state of innocence and charity, and desire to know and to do what is good but are not able. 3703.

Outer Darkness (Matt. viii. 12, etc.) den. the more dreadful falsities in which they are immersed who are in the church, for such persons darken the light, and cause an opposition of falsities against truths which the Gentiles cannot do. 1839.

Outer and **Inner Bark**. How vegetation is produced. D.L.W. 341.

Outermost. Graduated order, from innermost to o. 2973.

Outmost. There is a perpetual connection of the o. with the inmost. Ill. D.P. 180.

Oven (Mal. iii. 19) s. hell, where they are who confirm themselves in false doctrines and in evils of life from earthly and corporeal loves. A.E. 540. O. (Exod. vii. 3) s. exterior goods, which are in the natural principle, and are commonly called pleasant. 7356. See *Kneading Troughs.*

Over, or **Upon**, in the Word, s. within, for, that which is supreme in successive order, becomes inmost in simultaneous order, wherefore the third heaven is called as well the supreme as the inmost heaven. A.R. 900.

Overcome. To o. s. to receive in heart. A.E. 109. To o. s. to conquer in temptations, and to remain in a state of faith der. from charity. 146, 253.

Overflow, to (Dan. xi. 40), s. to immerse in falses and evils. A.E. 355.

Overflowing Stream (Jer. xlvii. 2) s. the false principle. 2240.

Overtake den. communication and influx. 8155.

Overthrow of God, the (Jer. l. 35, 40), s. damnation. 2200.

Overturned s. to punish. A.E. 411.

Ovum, or **Egg**. A man who is born again passes through a succession of ages like an egg. 4378, 1815.

Owl s. the falsification of truth. A.R. 566. By the o., and by the demon of the wood, or satyr, are s. corporeal and merely natural concupiscences. A.E. 586. Daughter of the o., falsities or falsified truths. 586.

Ox, young. The son of a cow s. the celestial natural principle, also natural exterior good. 2184, 4244. See *Lion.*

Oxen, or **Calves**, s. the affections of the natural mind. 2180, 10.407. O. (Exod. ix. 3) s. exterior natural good. 7503. O. and cattle (Isa. vii. 25) s. natural good and spiritual good. A.E. 617. O. and cows s. natural goodnesses. 2179. Five yoke of o. (Luke xiv. 10) s. all those natural affections, or lusts, which lead away from heaven. A.E. 548. Young o. and rams s. things spiritual, but lambs, things celestial (Num. xxix. 12, 14, etc.); for on the feasts [here referred to] they were to be sanctified, and to be introduced by things spiritual. 2830.

P

Padan Aram (Gen. xxviii. 2) s. the exterior knowledges of good and truth. 3664, 4395.

Pagans, or **Gentiles**. The Lord gifts the P. with a conscience according to their religion. 1032.

Pain s. repugnances arising from interior falses, for what is repugnant, that is painful. A.R. 697. Evil spirits, when they approach, occasion p. in the part to which they are opp. So adulterers, in the loins, and this p. greater or less, according to their state. 5659.

Pain after **Circumcision** (Gen. xxxiv. 25) s. lust, for while man is purifying from the love of self and of the world, to which purification circumcision cor., as is the case in regeneration, he is in p. and anxiety, in consequence thereof. 4496.

Pairs, or two and two, den. things cor., as truths and goods and evils and falses. 747. P. entering into the ark (Gen. vi. 19) s. truths and goods. 671.

Pairs of **Hands, Eyes**, etc., have relation to the will and understanding, or to good and truth; the right to the will, or to good, and the left to the understanding, or to truth. C.S.L. 316.

Palace, a (Ps. cxliv. 12), is the rep. of the understanding in which truths are in a beautiful form, and they are in a beautiful form when they are from the affection of truth. A.E. 724. P. (Isa. xxxii. 14) s. the whole church, as to truths from good. A.E. 410. P. (Amos iv. 3) s. the Word, consequently, the truth of doctrine which is from good. 4926. P. and houses s. things of the will. 2348. Walls of p. s. all truths of defence. A.E. 391.

Palace of **Wisdom**. The twelve steps to the p. of w. s. principles of good conjoined to truth, and principles of truth conjoined to good. D.P. 36.

Paleness s. the absence and deprivation of spiritual life. A.E. 381. A.R. 320.

Palestina (Exod. xv. 14) s. the same as Philisthea, which see. 8313.

Pallas. Appearance of a woman to Aristotle. 4658.

Pallium, or **Robe**, rep. the middle degree of the spiritual kingdom. 9825.

Palms. To hold p. in the hands s. confession from divine truths. A.R. 367. P. s. a holy festivity which is from good. 8369. (See John xii. 12, 13; Rev. vii. 9.)

Palms of the **Hands** s. divine truth in ultimates, also the reverse. (See 1 Sam. v. 6.) A.R. 367.

Palm Trees (Exod. xv. 27) s. the spiritual goods of the church, which are the goods of truth, and therefore also the affection of good, and from thence pleasantness. 8369. A.E. 277. P. trees (1 Kings vi. 32) den. wisdom which is of good from the Lord. 8369. P. trees s. the divine wisdom of the Lord, and flowers his divine intelligence. (1 Kings vi. 29, 32.) A.E. 456.

Palmer Worm (Hosea iv. 9) s. the false destroying good. A.E. 403.

Palpitation of the **Heart** den. fear. 5501.

Pan, an iron (Ezek. iv. 3), s. such truth as was falsified and adulterated with the Jewish nation. A.E. 706.

Pan, name of a city, den. doctrine. 4650.

Pancreas. They who belong to the p., act, as it were, by a mode of sawing, also with a noise like that of sawing, which noise is sonorous in the ears of spirits, but does not affect the ears of man, unless he be in the spirit whilst in the body; their region is between the region of the spleen and of the liver, more to the left. They who are in the province of the spleen, are almost directly above the head, but their operation falls thither. 5184.

Pancreatic, Hepatic, and **Cystic Duct.** There are spirits who have reference to the p., h., and c. d., consequently, to the biles contained therein, which the intestines eject. 5185.

Pannicle (Gen. xxxviii. 18) den. truth, because it is amongst the things which has relation to garments. 4875.

Papacy. Origin of the papal authority. Des. 4738.

Papists. Doctrines, etc., des. A.R. 717–842. Elatedness of heart from dominion. A.R. 764.

Paps and **Breast.** (Rev. i. 13.) The paps s. spiritual love, and the breast, the essential good thereof. A.E. 65. P. and b. s. love, and in an eminent sense the divine love. A.R. 46.

Parables. The Lord spake in p., lest the Jews should have understood the Word and thereby have profaned it, the church at that time being vastated among them. 3898. The things which the Lord spake in p., appear in the external form like common similitudes, but in the internal form, they are such as to fill the universal heaven, inasmuch as in singular the things contained in them there is an internal sense, which is such that its spiritual and celestial principle diffuses itself through the heavens in every direction like light and flame; this sense is altogether elevated from the sense of the letter, and flows from singular the expressions, and from singular the words, yea, from every iota. 4637.

Paraclete s. the divine truth proceeding from the Lord. A.E. 16, 27. A.E. 120. P. of God s. heaven. A.E. 110. P. of God s. the truth of wisdom and of faith. A.R. 90. Flying bird of p. rep. the spiritual man, as to his progression in spiritual things. A.V.C.R. 30.

Parallelism. There is a p. and hence communication between interior and exterior good. Exp. 3564. P. between spiritual things. D.L.W. 333.

Paran, or **Elparan,** s. a state of illumination from the Lord's divine human. 2711, 2714. Mount P. s. spiritual love. 2714. See *Teman.*

Parasite, or **Complaisance,** is more or less evil according to the end. 5388. A.R. 717.

Parched with the **East Wind** (Gen. xli. 6) s. full of lusts, or to be consumed by the fire of lusts; for the e. w. and the east, in the genuine sense, den. love to the Lord and love towards the neighbor, hence in the opp. sense, they den. self-love and the love of the world, consequently, concupiscences and lusts, for these are the offspring of those loves; fire is pred. of these, and consequently, parching is pred. of them. 5215.

Parents s. the goods and truths of the church. A.E. 315.

Parnassus, etc., were significatives derived from the ancient church. 2762.

Parrot, or **Goose,** a. The man whose rational principle is merely natural, the ideas whereof being solely derived from this world through the senses, and not by affections and thence perceptions from heaven, if such a person then speaks concerning any spiritual subject of the church, his voice is heard by the angels, not unlike the voice of a p. or a g., for it flows from the respiration only of his body, and not from any respiration of his spirit. A.V.C.R. 7.

Part. Man is said to consist of three parts, corporeal, natural, and rational. Exp. 4038.

Particular. In every form, what is common and what is p., by a wonderful conjunction, act as one. D.P. 180.

Particulars. Every common thing contains thousands of p., and every particular, thousands of singulars. 865. The Divine Providence is in the most

Partition

minute p. of man's life. A.Cr. 68. P. adapt themselves to their common whole. T.C.R. 47.

Partition of the **Israelites**. The twelve tribes den. so many universal divisions of love and faith. 3858.

Partridge (Jer. xvii. 11) s. those who learn many things from the Word and from the doctrine of the church, but not on account of uses of life. To hatch eggs, or to prepare, is to perform uses, that is to live, and so to be reformed. A.E. 236, 721.

Paschal Lamb, the, s. the Lord, also innocence. 3994.

Paschal Supper, the, rep. the consociations of the angels in the heavens, as to good and truth. 7997. P. s. rep. conjunction with the Lord by the good of love. 9965.

Pass, to (Gen. xxxi. 52), s. to flow in. 4205. To p. in peace, implies what relates to the will, and not to go the way with the feet, what relates to the understanding. (Isa. xli. 3, 4.) 683. To p. the night (Gen. xxiv. 54) s. to have peace. 3170. To p. through (Gen. xxx. 32) s. to know and perceive the quality. 3992. To p. through, in the Word, is pred. concerning truths, and to inhabit, concerning goods. A.E. 417.

Passage s. opening and free reception. A.E. 727. P., or opening, has reference, generally, to influx. 6971.

Pass Away. Used in the sense of dying. 5726.

Passed, or **Expired**, den. the conclusion of a state treated of. 6510.

Pass the Night. Said of the angels who visited Lot, den. to judge from truth. 6510.

Passover, the (Exod. 12, 27), s. the presence of the Lord, and his liberation from damnation of those who are of the spiritual church. 7093, 7807, 7938, 9965. Feast of the P. s. celebration of the Lord on account of liberation from damnation, which liberation is effected by regeneration; and, in a supreme sense, it was a memorial of the glorification of the Lord's humanity, because from thence proceeds that liberation. A.E. 401. The p. s. the Lord's glorification, that is, the putting on of the divine as to the human, and, in a rep. sense, it s. the regeneration of man. 3994.

Passion of the Cross, the, was the last temptation of the Lord, by which he fully subjugated the hells and glorified his humanity. A.E. 476.

Passion and **Crucifixion**, Lord's. His being betrayed by Judas s. that he was betrayed by the Jewish nation who had the Word amongst them at that time, for Judas rep. that nation. His being taken and condemned by the chief priests and elders, s. that he was taken and condemned by all the Jewish church. Their scourging him, spitting in his face, smiting him, and striking him on the head with a reed, s. that they did the like unto the Word with respect to its divine truth; all which relates to the Lord. Their putting a crown of thorns upon his head s. that they had falsified and adulterated those truths. Their dividing his garment, and casting lots for his vesture, s. that they had divided all the truths of the Word, but not its spiritual sense, for the vesture of the Lord s. that part of the Word. Their crucifying him s. that they had destroyed and profaned the whole Word. Their giving him vinegar to drink s. that all was falsified and false; and, therefore, he did not drink it, but said, it is finished. Their piercing his side s. that they had entirely extinguished every truth of the Word, and every good thereof. His being buried s. the rejection of the residue of the humanity taken from the mother; and his rising again the third day s. his glorification. L. 16.

Passive and **Active** form, as it were, a marriage through all the organization. 718.

Pastor, or **Shepherd**, s. those who teach truths, and thereby lead to the good of life. A.E. 315.

Pearls

Pastors and **Lovers** (Jer. xxii. 22) s. the goods and truths of the church. A.E. 811.

Pasture, a broad (Isa. xx. 23), s. the Word by which divine influx and spiritual nutrition is der. A.E. 644. To find p. (John x. 9) is to be taught, illustrated, and nourished in divine truths. A.R. 914.

Pastures of the Wilderness (Joel i. 20) s. the goods of doctrine from the literal sense of the Word. That sense is called a wilderness, when only understood naturally, or according to appearances, and not also spiritually, or according to the genuine sense. A.E. 730.

Path den. truths, and, in the opp. sense, falses. 10.422.

Pathros, land of (Ezek. xxix. 13, 16), s. the illustration of scientifics by the knowledges of truth. A.E. 654.

Pathrusim and **Casluhim** (Gen. x. 14) are nations so called, by which are s. doctrinals of rituals merely scientific. 1193.

Patience. (Luke xxi. 19.) "In p. possess ye your souls" s. the conservation of the life of truth among falses. A.E. 813.

Patmos (Rev. i. 9) s. a state and place in which John could be illuminated. A.R. 34. See *Greece.*

Patriotism. The love of one's country becomes, in the other life, the love of the Lord's kingdom, which is then the fatherland. 6821.

Pavilion, or **Tent** (Ps. xviii. 11), s. the Lord's dwelling-place. A.R. 24.

Pawn. To give a p. (Gen. xxxviii. 17), s. a reciprocal principle of conjunction in case of certainty. 4872.

Peace s. the union of the divinity with the humanity in the person of the Lord, and his conjunction with heaven and the church. H. and H. 295. P. is the divine salutation. A.R. 12. P. considered in itself, is not heaven and celestial joy, but these things are in p., and from p.; for p. is like the morning, or the time of spring in the world, which disposes human minds to the reception of heartfelt pleasantness and delightfulness, from those things which appear before the eyes. P. is the blessedness of the heart and soul arising from the conjunction of good and truth among those who are therein; thence there is no more combat of the false and evil against good and truth, or no spiritual discord or war, the consequence of which cessation is p., in which all fructification of good and multiplication of truth is effected, and, therefore, also wisdom and intelligence; and since p. is from the Lord alone, among the angels of heaven and men of the church, therefore, p., in a supreme sense, s. the Lord, and, in a respective sense, heaven and the church, hence also good conjoined with truth among those who are therein. A.E. 365. By p. are s. all things, in their complex or aggregate, which come from the Lord, and, consequently, all things of heaven and the church; and the beatitudes of life in them; these are what belong to p., in a supreme or inmost sense. That p. is charity, spiritual security, and internal tranquillity, follow, of course; for when man is in the Lord, he is in p. with his neighbor, which is charity, in protection against the hells, which is spiritual security; and when he is in p. with his neighbor, and in protection against the hells, he is in internal tranquillity from evils and falses. A.R. 306. Heavenly p. flows in, when the lusts arising from the love of self and of the world are taken away, inasmuch as these lusts are what take away p., for they infest the interiors of man, and cause him at length to place rest in restlessness, and p. in disturbance, because delight in evils; so long as man is in such evils, he cannot, in any wise, know what p. is. 5662.

Peace and **Security**. P. s. the internal pleasantnesses of heaven, and s. its external pleasantnesses. A.E. 365.

Peacock s. the goods and truths of the external church. A.E. 514.

Pearls s. knowledges of truth, and also truths themselves, and the one p. of great price (Matt. xiii. 45, 46) s. the knowledge and acknowledgment of the

Peculiar Treasure

Lord. A.E. 840. A.R. 916. P. s. knowledges of things good and true, as well celestial as spiritual, der. from the Word. A.R. 727. Beautiful p. (Matt. xiii. 45, 46) s. charity, or the good of faith. 2967.

Peculiar Treasure and **Peculiar People** den. those who have the Word, or who form the church, as such are the possession of the Lord. 8768.

Peg den. the conjoining and strengthening principles. 9777.

Pegasus. Significatives derived from the ancient church. 2762.

Peleg (Gen. x. 25) s. the internal worship of the ancient church, called Eber. 1240. P. (Gen. xi. 16) being mentioned as the son of Eber, rep. the external worship of that church. 1345.

Pelican (Zeph. ii. 15) s. the affections of the false. A.E. 650. See *Cormorant* and *Bittern*.

Pellucid. The literal sense of the Word is from the spiritual sense. 9407. The natural mind becomes p. when light from heaven is admitted into it, and when it cor. to the rational. 3493.

Peniel s. a state of temptation. 4298. "Jacob called the name of the place P." (Gen. xxxii.) in the internal historical sense, s. a state that they should put on rep. 4310.

Peniel den. a state of the heaviest temptations. 4298.

Penn, Wm. In the world of spirits. C.L.J. 84.

Penny, a (Rev. vi.), s. what is so little as to be scarce any thing. A.E. 374.

Penuel (Gen. xxxii.) s. a state of truth in good. 4301.

People, in a good sense, have relation to truth, and in a bad sense, to falses. 1259. P. shall prevail over p. (Gen. xxv. 23): the p. mentioned in the first place, s. truth, but the p. mentioned in the second place, s. the good of truth. 3295. P. (Gen. xxiv. 22) s. doctrine. 4485. P. (Gen. xli. 40) s. the knowledges of good and truth in the natural principle. 5342.

People of Jehovah of Zebaoth (Zeph. ii. 10) s. interior truths. 2468.

People and **Inheritance**. (Ps. lxxviii. 62.) P. have reference to those in the church who are in falses; and i., to those who are in evils. A.E. 863.

People and **Israel**. (Micah vi. 2.) By p. are understood they who are in truths and falses, and by I., they who are in goods and evils. A.E. 405.

Peoples, Multitudes, Nations, and **Tongues** (Rev. xvii. 15), s. all who are under the popish dominion of various doctrine and discipline, religion and confession. A.R. 745.

Perceive. If man p. and felt the operation of Divine Providence, he would not act in freedom according to reason. D.P. 176.

Perception is the very essence of every thing celestial, given by the Lord to those who are principled in a faith grounded in love, and exists in the universal heaven with an infinite variety. 536. P. in itself is nothing else but a sort of internal speech which so manifests itself, that it may be perceived what is said; every interior impression or dictate, and even conscience itself is nothing but such an internal speech; p., however, is a superior or interior degree thereof. 1822. P. arises from conjunction of the things appertaining to the external man, with the celestial things appertaining to the internal man. 1615. They who are in the Lord's celestial kingdom are endowed with p.; but they who are in the spiritual kingdom have not p. but conscience in its place. 805, 2144, 8081. P. is a faculty of seeing what is true and good by an influx from the Lord. 202, 895, 7680, 9128. P. is nothing else but the speech or thought of the angels who are attendant on man; when that speech or thought flows in, it occasions a p. that it is so or is not so, but with no others than those who are in the good of love and charity, for by good it flows in; with those, that p. produces thoughts, for what is perceptive is to them the common [or general] principle of thought; but p. from thought is not actually given, but apparently. 5228. The perceptive faculty of the most ancient church not only consisted in a

p. of what was good and true, but also in a p. of happiness and delight arising from well-doing; without such happiness and delight in doing what is good, the perceptive faculty has no life, but by virtue of such happiness and delight, it receives life. 503.

Perdition. To go into p. (Rev. xvii. 8) s. to be rejected. A.R. 734.

Peregrination, or to **Journey,** den. to progress or advance in life. 1456. In the opp. sense to recede. 1290.

Perfect Man. The Lord alone is p. 1414. M. is so called when good is all in all with him. 9568.

Perez (a breach) (Gen. xxxviii. 29) s. the separation of truth from good apparently. 4927. See *Mene, Tekel, and Perez.*

Perezite s. the truth of the church, and in the opp. sense the false. 4517. See *Canaanite.*

Perezite and **Rephaims.** (Josh. xvii. 15.) P. s. the principles of the false, and R., persuasions of the false. 1574.

Perfect. What is perfected to eternity, cannot possibly be p. in an instant. D.P. 338.

Perfection. It appears as if things prior were less perfect than things posterior, or simples than compounds; but nevertheless things prior, from which things posterior are, or simples, from which compounds are, are the more perfect; the reason is, because things prior or more simple are more naked, and less enwrapped with substances and matters void of life; and are, as it were, more divine, wherefore, they are nearer to the spiritual sun, where the Lord is; for p. itself is in the Lord, and thence in the sun, which is the first proceeding of his divine love and divine wisdom; and thence in those things which next succeed, and so in order even to the lowest, which according to their distance are more imperfect. Unless there were such eminent p. in things prior and simple, neither man nor any animal could exist from seed, and afterwards subsist; neither could the seeds of trees and shrubs vegetate and become prolific: for every thing prior, according as it is prior, and every thing simple, according as it is more simple, because it is more perfect, is more exempt from harm. D.L.W. 204.

Perfectness s. the states of those who are in good. A.E. 386.

Perfidy. To act perfidiously den. against divine order, or against truth and good in heaven. 8999. Tact against revealed truths. A.E. 710.

Perforate, or **bore through,** as in the case of the Hebrew servant, den. the addiction of those who do not understand truth, and are not free. 3869.

Perforated den. without terminations or planes, and hence the dissipation of influx. 5145.

Perfumes, Ointment, and **Frankincense** (Rev. xviii. 13) s. spiritual things of worship. A.R. 777.

Pergamos, the church of (Rev. ii.), s. those who place the all of the church in good works, and not any thing in truths of doctrine. A.R. 107.

Period. Any whole p. in the Word is marked either by a day, or by a week, or by a month, or by a year, nay even supposing it to be a hundred or a thousand years, according to the signification of day in the first chapter of Genesis. 893.

Pericardium. Des. of spirits whose influx is into the diseases of p. 5188.

Periods of **Time** are varied according to states of affections and of the thoughts derived from them. A.Cr. 106.

Periostium, an adulterous. Des. 5714.

Periphery, or **Circumference.** The middle s. much, but the c. little. 2936–40.

Perish. A man would totally p. if he had not full liberty to think and to will. D.P. 281.

Perish, or **Die,** to, is pred. of damnation, or the state in hell. 7655.

233

Peritoneum

Peritoneum. Modest spirits, who do not act at all from themselves, but from others, have reference to the p. 5378.

Permanence is pred. of state, when truths become of the life. 9286.

Permission. There are not any laws of p. by themselves, or separate from the divine providence; but they are the same; wherefore it is said that God permits, by which is not understood that he wills it; but that he cannot avert it, for the sake of the end, which is salvation. D.P. 234.

Perpetual, in the literal sense, means to the end of one's life; after death, eternity. 8991.

Perplexed, den. the scientifics, which are mingled in the exterior memory. 2831.

Persecute, to, the **Woman** (Rev. xii. 13) s. to infest the Lord's church. A.R. 560.

Persecutions (Mark x. 29) s. temptations. 4843.

Persevere, to, to the end, is not to be seduced, or succumb in temptations; hence it den. the salvation of those who are in charity. 3488.

Person. According to the angelic manner of speaking, a p. is not named, but that which is in a p., and is constituent of him. A.R. 872. P., in the Word, s. nothing else but things; in a supreme sense, the divine things appertaining to the Lord, and in an internal sense, such things as appertain to man, and are treated of in such case. 3979. The reason why the spiritual sense of the Word is abstracted from p. is because the idea of a p. limits the thought and its extension into heaven every way, for all thought which proceeds from the affection of truth passes through heaven on every side, nor terminates, unless as light into shade, but when a p. is also thought of, then the idea is terminated where the p. is, and with that intelligence also. A.E. 724. Not any p., which is named in the Word, is perceived in heaven, but instead thereof the thing which is rep. by that p., so neither any people nor nation, but the quality thereof; yea further, there is not a single historical relation of the Word concerning p., nation, and people. 5225.

Persuasion. In the spiritual world there exists a power of p. which deprives others of the understanding of truth, and induces stupor and thereby grief upon the mind, but this power of p. is unknown to the natural world. (See Rev. ix. 5.) A.R. 428. A.C. 3895. P. is said to be infatuating, because it carries away the use of reason, until reason, or the rational mind sees nothing but that, which he who is engaged in that p. speaks, for it speedily excites all that which consents, and conceals all that which dissents; whence the mind (mens) is infatuated by that which is in gross darkness and in a state of abstraction from seeing the truth. This p. is also called suffocating, because it deprives the understanding of the faculty of thinking freely, and of extending its sight on every side, as is done by every rational man. A.E. 549. The state of speaking with spirits on this earth is most perilous, unless one is in true faith. They induce so strong a p. that it is the Lord himself who speaks and who commands, that man cannot but believe and obey. *Spirit. Diary* 1622.

Persuasive Principle is s. by a scorpion; because it is of such a nature as to take away from the understanding the light of truth, and to induce infernal darkness. A.E. 549. The p. p. is infatuating and suffocating. It deprives the understanding of thinking freely. A.E. 543–9.

Persuasive Truth is hard, unyielding, and without extension, wherefore it is contrary to order to be persuaded concerning truth in a moment. 7298.

Perturbation of **Mind** caused by spirits. Des. 5716.

Pervert, to, s. to turn truth into false, and good into evil. 9253.

Perversity s. the evil of the false. A.E. 329.

Pestilence den. the vastation of good and truth. 7102.

Peter. In the Word which is in heaven, instead of P., is read truth originating in good which is from the Lord. A.R. 768. The reason why P. was the first of the Lord's apostles was, because truth from good is the primary principle of the church, or that in which man is first instructed in order to his regeneration. A.E. 820. P. three times denying the Lord before the cock crew, s. that there would be no faith nor charity in the last time or state of the church. 6000, 6073. P. (John xxi. 15, 21) s. truth without good, or faith separate from charity. A.E. 443.

Peter, James, and **John.** P. rep. faith, J., charity, and J., the works of charity; in like manner as Reuben, Simeon, and Levi. The rest of the disciples rep. truths and goods which are derived from these, in the same manner as the twelve tribes of Israel, hence those three disciples are mentioned in the Word for all the rest. Preface before 2760. A.E. 411.

Petulantes. Vagabond spirits, so called because of their impertinent curiosity. 5180.

Phantasies and **Lusts.** P. s. falses, and l. s. evils. 4293. See *Heavens (Imaginary).* See *Lumen.*

Phantasy consists in seeing what is true as false, and what is good as evil; and in seeing evil as good, and false as true. 7680.

Pharaoh s. scientifics, or the natural principle in general. 1487, 5192. P. also s. the false principle infesting the truth of the church. 6651, 7031. P. (Gen. xl.) rep. the new natural man, or the new state of the natural man. 5080. "Let P. live" (Gen. xlii. 16), is a formula of asseveration, to den. a thing being certain. 5449. P. and his army s. those who are in falses from evil. A.E. 538. P. and the Egyptians in the Word, s. the sensual and scientific principles. 31.

Phares and **Zarah** (Gen. xxxviii. 28, 30) rep. the dispute about the priority of faith and charity. 3325.

Pharisees. Those who speak things pious and holy, and in their tone and gesture, counterfeit affection of such things. D.P. 231.

Phicol rep. the doctrinals of faith, as grounded in the literal sense of the Word. 3447. See *Abimelech.*

Philadelphia. By the church in P. (Rev. iii. 7), are meant those who are in truths originating in good from the Lord. A.R. 172.

Philantia. One's proprium. 1326.

Philisthea and **Philistines** den. those who hold the doctrine of faith alone, such as prevails in the Protestant churches. D.P. 326. A.C. 1197. P. (Jer. xlvii. 2, 3) rep. those who conceive false principles and reason thence concerning spiritual things which overflow man. 705.

Philosophy and **Philosophers.** Des. 196, 1919.

Phineas (Num. xxv. 12, 13) s. love and the things which are of love, as the priesthood of the Jewish church, rep. by P., s. 1038.

Phlegm of the **Brain,** and spirits who cor. thereto. 5386.

Phut, den. knowledges from the literal sense of the Word. 1163.

Phut, or **Lybia,** s. knowledges collected from the literal sense of the Word and applied to confirm false principles, and also simply such knowledges. 1166. See *Cush.*

Phylacteries (Matt. xxiii. 5) s. goods in external form, for they were worn upon the hands, and hands s. what is done, having relation to action. A.E. 395.

Physician, the **Art** of **Physic,** and **Medicines,** s. preservation from evils and falses, because, in the spiritual world, diseases are evils and falses, spiritual diseases being nothing else, for evils and falses take away health from the internal man and induce sickness in the mind, the thence pains. 6502.

Pia Mater. Those who belong to that province are such as do not trust much to their own thought, and thereby determine themselves to think any thing certain concerning holy things, but depend on the faith of others, not canvassing any point to discover whether it is true, they serve

Pictures of Desire

the angels as mediate spirits, are modest and pacific, and are in heaven. 4047.

Pictures of **Desire**, or **Pleasant Pictures** (Isa. ii. 16) s. false doctrinals favoring the pleasures of earthly loves. A.E. 514.

Pieces, to be broken in, den. good not from the Lord will be dissipated. 9391.

Pierce, to, by piercing Jesus Christ, nothing else is meant but the destruction of his divine truth in the Word. A.R. 26. See *Passion* and *Crucifixion*.

Piety without charity avails nothing, but joined to charity leads to every good. 8252, 8253.

Pigeon, young, s. innocence. A.E. 313.

Pildash s. various religious principles. 2863. See *Uz*.

Piles s. variety of falses from evil. 7524.

Pillar of a **Cloud** by **Day**, and a **Pillar** of **Fire** by **Night** (Exod. xiii. 21) s. state of illustration which is tempered by the obscurity of truth, and a state of obscurity which is tempered by illustration from good. 8106, 8108.

Pillars of **Fire**. (Rev. x. 1.) The reason why the Lord's feet seemed as p. of fire, is because his divine natural which in itself is the divine humanity which he took upon him in the world, sustains, supports, and contains his eternal divinity as the body does the soul, and as the natural sense of the Word, sustains, supports, and contains its spiritual and celestial sense, for feet s. what is natural, p. s. support, and f., divine love. A.R. 468.

Pillars of the **Tabernacle** rep. truths and goods in their ultimates, such as are in the literal sense of the Word. U.T. 220.

Pilling and **Pillings** (Gen. xxx. 37) s. the removal of exterior things, that interior things may be manifested. 4015.

Pillows. (Gen. xxviii. 11.) Those things which are under the back of the head or neck, that is p., or bolsters, s. communication of inmost or divine things, with outermost, thus communication with things external, or communication of a most common or general nature, with the divine. 3695.

Pilots (Ezek. xxvii. 28) s. those who are wise by knowledges from the Word. A.E. 514. A.C. 1201. P. (Rev. xviii.) s. the supreme among the Roman Catholics, who are emperors, kings, dukes, and princes. A.R. 786.

Pine Away. Spiritual life when it perishes. A.E. 617.

Pine Tree (Isa. xli. 19) s. natural truth of an inferior order. A.E. 730. See *Fir Tree*.

Pipers and **Trumpeters** (Rev. xviii. 22) have respect to celestial affections. A.R. 792.

Pipes s. the joys of the affection of the knowledges of good and truth. 8337.

Pison, the river (Gen. xi. 15), s. the intelligence of faith originating in love. 110.

Pit (Gen. xli. 14) s. a state of temptation. 5246. P., or well, in which is no water (Jer. ii. 13) s. doctrines in which are no truths. 2702. P. (Gen. xiv. 10; xxxvii. 20) s. false. 1688, 4728.

Pit of the **Abyss** (Rev. ix. 2.) s. the hell of those, who in their own eyes, and thence in the eyes of many others, seem men of learning and erudition, but quite the reverse in the sight of angels, in consequence of their having confirmed themselves in conjunction by faith alone. A.R. 471.

Pit of **Devastation** and **Miry Clay**. (Ps. xl. 3.) P. of d. s. the false of doctrine, and m. c. s. evil of life. A.E. 666.

Pit of **Salt** s. the vastation of truth. 2455.

Pitch (Gen. xiv. 10) den. lusts. 1688. Burning p. (Isa. xxxiv. 9) s. direful fantasies. 643.

Pitch, to, a camp (Gen. xxxiii. 18) s. application to the goods of truth. To p. (measure) a camp properly den. arrangement according to order: but in the present case, application; for to p. (measure) a camp, here s. to fix a habitation with his (Jacob's) herds and flocks, which were also called a camp. (Gen. xxxiii. 8.) 4396.

Pitch, to, a **Tent** (Gen. xiii. 18) den. conjunction. 1616.

Pitcher, by **Vial**, or, is s. what is contained in them. A.R. 672.

Pithom, Raamses den. quality of doctrine from falsified truths. 6661.

Place, in the spiritual world, cor. to state, for no one can be anywhere else, than where the state of his life is. A.R. 565 1-2. Dry p. (Luke xi. 24) s. states of evil and the false which are of his life who does the work of repentance. A.E. 731.

Plagues s. evils of love, and falses of faith. A.R. 656. The three plagues proposed to David (2 Sam. xxiv. 10, 11) s. those evils which fall upon those who claim to themselves any thing good and true; the first p., which was the seven years of famine, s. the total defect and loss of the goods and truths of faith and love. The second p., which was three months' flight before their enemies, s. continual persecution, or infestation by evils and falses. The third p., which was three days' pestilence, s. the vastation and consumption of all the goods and truths which they had received from infancy. 10.119. P. of Egypt s. the falsities and cupidities whereby the church there perished. A.R. 563. It is said (Rev. xv.) that the p. were poured out upon men by angels from heaven, when nevertheless they are truths and goods sent down by the Lord which are turned into evils and falses by those who are below. A.R. 673, 714.

Plain, a, s. good and truth in the natural man, for they dwell in p., or beneath mountains and hills, who are in the ultimate heaven. A.E. 499. A p. (Gen. xix. 17) s. the all of doctrinals. 2418. P. s. the ultimates of the Word as to doctrine, also the ultimates of the church, or those who are in ultimate truths and goods. A.E. 422.

Plains of the **Earth** (Rev. xx. 7–9) s. the doctrinals of the church, which are laid waste by those who are principled only in external worship. 2418.

Planets. Des. 6695–6701.

Planes. There are three p. for the regeneration and eternal perfection of man; viz., infancy and childhood, adult age, and old age, all formed by progressive sciences and knowledges. 1555. There are with man two p., on which are sounded the celestial and spiritual principles, which are from the Lord; the one p. is interior, the other is exterior; the p. themselves are nothing else than conscience; without p., that is, without conscience, it is impossible for any thing celestial and spiritual from the Lord to be fixed, but it flows through as water through a sieve, wherefore they who are without such a p., or without conscience, do not know what conscience is, yea, neither do they believe that there is any spiritual and celestial principle; the interior p., or interior conscience, is where good and truth, in a genuine sense is, for good and truth flowing in from the Lord is its active principle; but the exterior p. is the exterior conscience, and is where a just and equitable principle in a proper sense is, for what is just and equitable, moral and civil, which also flows in, is its active principle; there is also an outermost p. which also appears as conscience, but is not conscience, viz., acting what is just and equitable for the sake of self and the world, that is, for the sake of self-honor, or reputation, and for the sake of worldly wealth and possessions, also, through fear of the law; these three p. are what rule man, that is, by which the Lord rules man; by the interior p., or by the conscience of spiritual good and truth, the Lord rules those who are regenerated; by the exterior p., or by the conscience of what is just and equitable, that is by the conscience of moral and civil good and truth, the Lord rules those, who are not as yet regenerated, but who are capable of being regenerated, and also are regenerated in the other life, if not in the life of the body; but by the outermost p., which appears like conscience, and yet is not conscience, the Lord rules all the rest of mankind, even the wicked; these latter, without such rule, would rush headlong into

Plane Tree

every species of wickedness and madness, which also they do, when loosed from the bonds of that p.; and they who do not suffer themselves to be ruled by those bonds, are either mad, or are punished according to the laws. These three p. act as one with the regenerate, for one flows into the other, and the interior disposes the exterior; the first p., or the conscience of spiritual good and truth, is in the rational principle of man; but the second p., or the conscience of moral and civil good and truth, that is, of what is just and equitable, is in the natural principle of man. 4167.

Plane Tree (Gen. xxx. 37) s. natural truth. 4014.

Planks, or **Boards** (for the habitation), s. supports from good, because they were of wood, and supported the curtains both of the habitation and of the tent. (Exod. xxvi. 15, 16); and inasmuch as all the rep. in nature have reference to the human form, and have a s. according to that reference, so also have the p. of the habitation; these cor. to the muscular or fleshy part in man, which supports the encompassing coats and skins. 9634.

Plant, to, den. to regenerate. 8326. See *Shrub.*

Plantation and **Germination**. (Ps. xxix. 13, 14.) P. is done in the exterior of man, where there is the good of love and charity; and g. is done in the exteriors of man, where there is the good of life. A.E. 458.

Plants of **Olives**. (Ps. cxxviii. 3.) P. s. truths, and o., good. A.E. 340.

Plate of **pure Gold** (on Aaron's forehead) (Exod. xxviii. 36) s. illustrations from the Lord's divine good, for a p. is illustration, and g. is the good of love. 9930.

Platter. By vials and p. is s. the things contained in them. A.R. 672.

Play, to (Zech. viii. 5), s. that which is of interior festivity arising from the affection of truth and good. A.E. 223. A.C. 10.416.

Pleasures, Appetites, and **Sensual Things**, pursued as an end, are images of hell. 911. P. in a proper sense. 2184.

Pleasant and **Delightful**. P. has respect to the understanding, as d. has respect to the will. A.R. 756.

Pleasantness is pred. of wisdom and thought. D.P. 195.

Pledge. A p. for what has been lent, den. the reception of truth, and a reply to that which is communicated. 9212, 9215.

Plenteous is pred. of truths. A.E. 644. See *Fat.*

Plenum. That is a p. in which there is a good of use. 5214.

Pleura. The common envelope of the heart and lungs, used to ill. the perpetual connection of things outmost with things inmost. D.P. 180.

Pleurisy. Disease of the pleura. Ill. D.P. 180.

Plexuses. Intermediate angels between the celestial and spiritual cor. to p. 9670.

Plough, to (Isa. xxviii. 24), s. to implant truth in good. 10.669.

Ploughing den. preparation from good to receive truths. 5895.

Ploughshares (Isa. ii. 4; Micah iv. 3) s. the goods of the church which by truths are perfected, or set forth. A.E. 734.

Plummet, or **Plumbline** of **Emptiness**, den. the desolation and vastation of truth. 5044.

Plurality of **Worlds**. Des. H. and H. 417.

Poison den. deceit or hypocrisy, in the spiritual sense. 9013. See *Brooks.*

Poll, to, the **Head** and **Beard** s. to reject those things which are of the exterior natural principle, for the hair, which was polled, s. that natural principle; the hair, also, both of the h. and b., cor., in the grand man, to the exterior natural principle. 5247.

Pollution den. the truth of faith defiled. 4504. Conjunction not legitimate. 4433.

Polygamist, a, so long as he remains a p., cannot be made spiritual. C.S.L. 347. With p. there is not given conjugial chastity, purity, and sanctity. C.S.L.

346. P. are saved who acknowledge a God, and from religion live according to the civil laws of justice. C.S.L. 351. P. is not permitted to Christians. C.S.L. 333, 339. P. is not sin with those among whom it is from their religion. C.S.L. 348. P. is not sin with those who are in ignorance concerning the Lord. C.S.L. 349. P. was permitted the Mahometans because they were orientals, who, without this permission, would have burned for foul adulteries. L.J. 72.

Polytheism. A plurality of gods. See *Religion*.

Pomegranates (Exod. xxviii. 34) s. the scientifics of good and truth, which are doctrinals from the Word in the memory, which is in the external or natural man. 9918.

Ponder, to, den. wisdom. A.E. 453.

Pools, in the spiritual sense of the Word, s. intelligence from the knowledges of good and truth. P. of waters, in the opp. sense, den. evils from falses. (See Isa. xiv. 22, 23.) 7324.

Pool of **Siloam** s. the Word in the letter (Isa. viii. 6); so also, in general, the p. that were in Jerusalem. A.E. 239. See *Fish Pool.*

Poor s. one who is not in truths, also those who are ignorant of good and truth, but desirous of instruction. H. and H. 420.

Poor, Maimed, Halt, and **Blind,** the (Luke xiv. 21), s. the uninstructed Gentiles who were in the life of good. 2336.

Pope, seen in the spiritual world, and his imaginary inspiration. 3750. Condition of p. fully des. L.J. 567. Edicts of the p. for the most part from hell. A.E. 1033.

Popery and **Papists,** the judgment of. Fully exp. L.J. 53–64.

Poplar Tree, the, s. the natural good and truth of the church. U.T. 200. See *Oak.*

Poplar Tree den. the good of truth; same falsified. 4013.

Porch s. outward things which cohere with things interior. 7353.

Port, or **Haven,** den. where scientifics terminate and commence, or where there is a conclusion of truth from scientifics. 6348.

Portents, or **Signs,** den. the means of power. 7030.

Portico. The ancients compared p. to the externals of the mind. 7353.

Portion and **Inheritance** (Gen. xxxi. 16) s. conjunction. 4097.

Possess, to, and to **Inhabit.** (Isa. liv. 3.) To p. is pred. of celestial good, and to in., of spiritual good. 2712.

Possessed, to be. The prophets were p. by spirits occupying their bodies. 6212.

Possessions. Spiritual riches, which are knowledges from the Word. A.E. 236.

Postdiluvians. Those who lived after the flood, such as the Canaanites, who were in external worship separate from internal. 1063.

Posteriors den. the exteriors. 3416.

Posterity of **Years** (Ezek. xxxviii. 8) s. the last time of the church. 2006.

Posts of the **Door** (Exod. xii. 7) s. natural truths. 7847.

Pot, that was for holy use, s. doctrine, because containing (8408); since boiling flesh s. to prepare for use of life (1005), and what is boiled with water den. what is from the doctrine of truth. 7857. P. (Ezek. xxiv. 3, 10) s. violence offered to good and truth; the flesh and the bones with which the p. was filled den. good and truth. 3812. To lie amongst the p. (Ps. lxviii. 14) s. to live in statutes or ordinances. A.E. 283. P. den. what is continent of good, and, in the opp. sense, what is continent of evil, because by the flesh which is boiled in it, is s. good, and, in the opp. sense, evil. 8408. See also 8408 for explanation of 2d Kings iv. 38–42. See *Flesh Pots.*

Potent. Truths which constitute the external mind. A.E. 408.

Potiphar, Pharaoh's Chamberlain (Gen. xxix.), s. the interior of scientifics. 4965.

Potiphar's Wife

Potiphar's Wife (Gen. xxix.) s. truth natural not spiritual. 5006.

Pottage and **Pulse**. (Gen. xxv. 34.) P. s. a heap of doctrinals, and p., the good thereof. 3332.

Potter, the (Zech. xi. 12, 13), s. reformation and regeneration. 2276.

Potter's Vessels (Rev. ii. 27) s. the falses which are in the natural man, or the things of self-derived intelligence. A.E. 176. A.R. 149.

Pound s. the knowledges of truth and good from the Word. A.E. 193.

Pour Out, to. By pouring out the vials upon the earth, which contained the plagues (Rev. xvi. 1), is s. influx into the church of the reformed, or into those who study and receive the doctrine of justification by faith alone. A.R. 676. See *Plagues.*

Poured Out and **Multiplied**, to be. (Gen. ix. 7.) To be p. o. is pred. of goods, and to be m., of truths. 1016.

Poverty, s. a defect of the knowledges of truth and good. A.E. 238.

Powder, or **Dust**, has reference to love of self and the world. 3413.

Power. All p. is from divine good by means of divine truths which are from the Lord alone, therefore the Lord in the Word of the Old Testament is called hero, man-of-war, Jehovah of hosts, or of armies. 10.019. A.R. 768. P. (Rev. iv.) s. salvation, because all divine p. regards that as its final end; for man is reformed by divine p., and is thence introduced into heaven, detained from evil, and preserved eternally in good. A.E. 293. To take p. (Rev. xi.) s. divine omnipotence. A.R. 523. To give p. to the beast (Rev. xiii. 4) s. to establish the doctrine of justification by faith alone, and give it authority by means of reception by the laity. A.R. 579. All p. resides in the ultimates of things which are called natural. A.R. 148.

Power and **Glory**. (Matt. xxiv. 30.) P. is pred. of good, and g. of truth. 4060.

Power and **Strength**. (Rev. vii.) P. when concerning the Lord is pred. of divine truth, and s. concerning divine good, and both together omnipotence by divine truth from divine good. A.E. 467.

Praevidence has reference to evil which the Lord foresees. 5155.

Praise God, to, s. to worship him. A.R. 809.

Pray, to, s. all the truth which a man thinks and speaks. A.E. 695.

Prayer, considered in itself, is speaking with God, and at such times a certain internal intuition of those things which are the objects of p., to which cor. something like influx into the perception, or thought of the mind of him who prays; so that there is a kind of opening of man's internals towards God; but this with a difference according to man's state, and according to the essence of the thing which is the object of p.; if the p. be from love and faith, and it be only celestial and spiritual things, concerning which and for which he prays, then in the p. there exists somewhat resembling a revelation, which is manifested in the affection of the person praying, as to hope, consolation, or some internal joy. 2535. P. is nothing else but communication. 3285. The Lord wills that man should first ask and will, and the Lord afterwards answers and gives, for this reason, that it may be appropriated to him. A.R. 376. They who are in the Lord and the Lord in them, whatsoever they will and ask, they obtain, because they will ask from the Lord. A.R. 951. Man is continually praying, when he is in the life of charity, although not with the mouth, nevertheless with the heart, for that which is of the love is always in the thought also, whether man knows it or not. A.E. 325. A.C. 1618. The p. of the Lord was discourse with the divine, and revelation at that time. 2535. See *Lord's Prayer.*

Prayers of **Saints** s. the things which are of faith, and at the same time the things which are of charity. A.R. 278.

Preach to, in the series of the internal sense is to be made known. 3488. Preachings are den. by prophesyings, and by prophetic dreams. 4682. In ancient times from dreams and visions, and from open discourse with angels. 4682.

Preachers, all, in heaven are of the Lord's spiritual kingdom. H. and H. 225.

Precepts are the internal of the Word, statutes its external. 3382.

Precious Stones, in reference to the Word, s. divine truth in the literal sense of the Word translucent from the divine truth in the spiritual sense. A.R. 911. A covering of p. s. (Ezek. xxviii. 13) s. the truths of intelligence. A.R. 90. Ruby, topaz, and carbuncle s. the celestial love of good, on account of their red, flaming color. 9865. Chrysoprasus, sapphire, and diamond den. celestial love of truth. 9868. Lazul, agate, and amethyst den. the spiritual love of good. 9870. Beryl, onyx, and jasper den. spiritual love of truth. Sardine s. divine truth. 9872. Emerald, sphere of divine love and wisdom. A.R. 232.

Precious Things (Gen. xxiv. 53) s. things spiritual. 3160.

Precious Things of **Heaven**, the **Dew** and the **Abyss Lying Beneath** (Deut. xxxiii. 13) s. divine spiritual and spiritual natural things from a celestial origin. A.E. 405.

Precious Wood (Rev. xviii. 12) s. good, and at the same time truth rational; for w. s. good, and p. is pred. of truth. A.R. 775.

Precipitate s. those who easily catch at and believe the things that are said, and consequently, falses also. A.E. 455.

Predestination. All are predestined to heaven, and none to hell. D.P. 329.

Predicate. Whatever exists, derives from that which is called quality. D.P. 4.

Predictions, concerning the future, even when delivered by the evil, are from the divine. 3698.

Prefects, or **Governors**. G. den. common truths in which are particulars. 5290.

Premium, or **Reward**, in its genuine sense, is the delight in well-doing. 6388.

Preparation, and illustration of the natural man, must precede conjunction with the rational. 3138. P. is by instruction in truths and goods. 711.

Prepare. When it is said of goods appropriated, it den. arrangement. 8422. When concerning heaven, it den. to give it out of mercy to those who are in the good of love and faith. 9305.

Prepare, to, the **Way** (Rev. xvi. 12) s. to p. for introduction. A.R. 700. See *Baptism of John.*

Presence and **Conjunction** of the **Lord**. The acknowledgment and worship of the Lord, and reading of the Word, occasion the Lord's p., and these, together with a life conformable to his precepts form a c. with him. A.R. 796.

Present. It was customary in the ancient church, and thence in the Jewish, to give somewhat as a p. to the judges, and afterwards to the kings and priests, when they were approached, and this was also commanded; the reason was, because the p. which were given rep. such things appertaining to man, as ought to be offered to the Lord when he is approached, which things are what proceed from a free principle, consequently, from the man himself, for his free principle is what is from the heart, and what is from the heart is from the will, and what is from the will is from the affection which is not of the love, and what is from the affection which is of the love, is free, thus it is of the man himself; from this principle must be given by man a p. to the Lord when he is approached; it was this p. which was rep., for kings rep. the Lord as to the divine truth, and priests as to the divine good. The offering a p. to Joseph, who is called lord of the land (Gen. xliii. 11) s. to obtain grace. 5619.

Present Time comprehends at once the past and the future. 1382.

Preservation is perpetual creation. 4322.

Press. By an oil p. is s. the good of love, and by a wine p., the truth of faith. A.R. 651.

Prestige

Prestige. See *Providence.*

Prevarications (Lam. i. 14) s. falses. 3542.

Prey den. remains in the internal man. 576.

Priapuses. Those addicted to obscenity. C.L. 44.

Price s. gratis from divine love. A.E. 706.

Price of Redemption. Pred. of truth received by man; of the Lord's union of the human with the divine, and thus the salvation of the human race. 2959.

Pride s. the love of self. 2220. P. extinguishes and suffocates the light of heaven. 4949. P. glues falses together so that, at last, they cohere like concretions formed by the foam of the sea. A.R. 421.

Pride, or **Swelling** of **Jordan,** the, s. the external man continually assaulting the internal, and aspiring to dominion. 1585.

Priesthood, the, rep. the Lord as to the work of salvation, because that proceeded from the divine good of his divine love. 9809. The p. of Aaron, of his sons, and of the Levites, rep. the Lord's work of salvation in successive order. 10.017, 10.119. See *Inaugurations.*

Priests rep. the Lord as to his divine good. A.R. 854. P. are to teach truth, and thereby lead to good, and so to the Lord. 10.794. P. ought to have dignity on account of holy things, but they ought not to attribute the dignity to themselves, but to the Lord, from whom alone they are holy, because the priesthood is not the person, but adjoined to the person. 10.906. P. who do not acknowledge the Lord, have, in the Word, a contrary s. 3670. See *Governors.*

Priests of **Jehovah** and **Ministers** of **God.** (Isa. lxi. 5.) P. of J. s. celestial men, and m. of G., spiritual men. 1097.

Priests and **Elders.** (Lam. i. 19.) P. s. those who teach good, and e., those who teach truth. A.E. 750.

Priests and **Kings.** P. rep. the Lord as to divine good, and k., as to divine truth. 2015, 6148.

Priests and **Prophets.** P. s. those who lead to a life according to divine truth; and p., those who teach divine truth. A.E. 264.

Primary and **Secondary.** What is p. is all in that which is s. A.R. 655.

Primitive, the, of a man is the seed of the father. D.L.W. 432.

Primogeniture of **Faith** and **Charity** was rep. by Ephraim and Manasseh, Jacob and Esau, Phares and Zarah, etc., etc. 3325, 4923.

Prince, in the Word, s. a principal or leading truth. A.R. 548. And, in the opp. sense, princes s. primary falses. A.E. 195, 540.

Prince of the **Bakers** (Gen. xl.) s. the sensual things of the will part. 5167.

Prince of the **Butlers** (Gen. xl.) s., in general, the sensual things subject to the intellectual part. 5165.

Prince of **God** (Gen. xxiii. 6) s. the Lord as to the power of truth. 2921.

Prince of the **Guards** (Gen. xl. 1) s. things primary for interpretation, which are those which primarily conduce to interpret the Word, and thus to understand the doctrinals of love to God and of charity towards the neighbor, which are from the Word. 4966.

Prince of the **House** of the **Prison** (Gen. xxxix. 23) den. truth governing in a state of temptations. 5047.

Prince of the **Kings** of the **Earth** (Rev. i. 5) s. the Lord with respect to divine truth. A.R. 18.

Prince of this **World.** Honors and wealth are given by the devil, and for this he is called the p. of this w. D.P. 216.

Princes, or **Chiefs,** s. the primary things of truth which are precepts. 2089.

Princes of **Zoan** and the **Wise Counsellors** of **Pharaoh** (Isa. xix. 11, 13) s. primary scientifics. 1482.

Princes and **Nobles** of the **People** (Num. xxi. 17) s. those who are intelligent and wise from the Lord, who is there s. by the lawgiver. A.E. 727.

Profanation

Princesses, which shall give suck (Isa. xlix. 23), s. goods, or those who are in goods. 2015.

Principal. That is cailed p. which acts, and that instrumental which it acted upon. A.Cr. 26.

Principality on the **Shoulder** (Isa. ix. 5, 6) s. all divine truth in the heavens from the Lord himself, for the heavens are distinguished into principalities according to truths from good; hence, also, the angels are called principalities. 5044.

Principiates. Exp. D.L.W. 369.

Principles. There are three p. in common appertaining to man, viz., the corporeal, the natural, and the rational p. The corporeal p. is the outermost, the natural, is the middle, the rational, is the interior; so far as one prevails with man above the other, so far he is said to be either corporeal, or natural, or rational; these three parts of man wonderfully communicate, viz., the corporeal with the natural, and the natural with the rational. 4038.

Prior. All things exist and subsist from what is p. to themselves. H. and H. 37. The ultimate is the complex of all things p. A.R. 678.

Priority, by, or **Primogeniture**, is meant superiority in degree and dominion. 3325. P. things exp. D.L.W. 208.

Prison, house of the, den. the vastation of the false, and hence, the false itself. 5085. To be in p. (Rev. ii. 10) s. to be infested by evils from hell, because they are as if they were bound in p., for they cannot think any thing but evil, when, nevertheless, they will what is good, hence proceeds combat and interior anxiety. A.R. 99. See *Bound.*

Prisoners, in the Word, s. the same as captives, or those who are cast into custody. A.R. 99, 678. P. out of the pit wherein is no water (Zech. ix. 11) s. the faithful who were kept in the inferior earth until the advent of the Lord. A.E. 537.

Proceed. Nothing can p. from man but what is temporal, and nothing from the Lord but what is eternal. D.P. 219. P. s. to go forth. 5337.

Proceeding. The Holy Spirit is the holy p. from the Lord by means of spirits and angels. 3704. The infinite from itself is the p. divine, or the Lord in others. D.P. 55.

Procession. Pred. of truth. 9407.

Proclaim s. exploration from influx of the Lord. A.E. 302.

Procurator, or **Steward**, den. the external church. 1795.

Prodigal Son, etc. (Luke xv.) By the p. s. are understood they who misapply spiritual riches, which are the knowledges of truth and good; by his return and confession to his father, is s. penitence of heart and humiliation; by the best robe with which he was clothed are s. general and primary truths; by the ring upon his hand, the conjunction of truth and good in the internal or spiritual man; by shoes upon his feet, the same in the external or natural man; and by both these, regeneration; by the fatted calf, the good of love and charity; and by eating and rejoicing, consociation and celestial joy. A.E. 279.

Prodigy. Signs and prodigies den. confirmations of divine truth, means of divine power. 7273.

Produce den. fruit der. from the good of charity, and truth of faith. 6155.

Produced den. ulterior increase pred. of good. 6647.

Productions are continuations of creation. A.Cr. 97.

Profanation. They are guilty of p. who believe truths and live an evil life; as also they who give no credit to truths, and live in external sanctity. 8082, 8394, 10.287. To prevent p., care is taken by the Lord that no one is admitted further into true acknowledgment and belief of heart than he is capable of being afterwards preserved in. 2357. He who does not acknowledge the Lord's divinity in his humanity, and falsifies the Word, yet not inten-

Profanators

tionally, is indeed guilty of p., but only in a slight degree; whereas they who ascribe to themselves all the power of the Lord's divine humanity, and therefore deny his divine humanity, and who apply every thing in the Word to the purpose of acquiring to themselves dominion over the holy things of the church and of heaven, and for that reason adulterate the Word, these are guilty of grievous p. A.R. 723. Those in the Christian world who defile the holy things of the Word by unclean thoughts and discourses, are guilty thereof. 5390. In order to prevent p., the internal or spiritual sense of the Word was not opened to the Jewish or the Christian churches; hence it was hidden from them that there was any thing as a spiritual internal sense within the natural or literal sense of the Word; and that they might be held in such ignorance, it was provided, that the science of cor., which was the chief science of the ancients, should be lost, so that it was altogether unknown what is meant by cor., according to which the Word is written. The reason why the internal sense of the Word is at this day opened, is because by the last judgment, all things in heaven and hell are reduced to order, and so it is provided by the Lord that p. may not exist. A.E. 375. See also A.C. 10.287.

Profanators after death are not spirits in a human form, as others are, but are mere fantasies, and appear to themselves to fly here and there, without any thought, and at length they are separated from others and cast into the lowest hell of all; they are, therefore, no more called he, or she, but it. A.E. 375.

Profane, to, in the worst manner, is to receive and acknowledge things holy, and afterwards to depart from and deny them. D.P. 228.

Profane, the, are those who profess to believe in God, maintain the sanctity of the Word, and yet with the mouth only. But the impious who deny the Divine Being, and all things divine, have nothing holy in them to profane. D.P. 229.

Progression. In every created thing there is a constant and wonderful p. according to the laws of order. D.P. 332. The Lord was born like a man, and progressed from an obscure to a more lucid state. 1401. He progressed from scientifics to celestial truths. 1402.

Progressions are changes of state. Exp. H. and H. 192.

Prolification is from truth grounded in good in the intellect. C.S.L. 90. P. cor. to the propagation of truth. C.S.L. 127, 137. Spiritual p. and natural p. are from the same origin. C.S.L. 115.

Prolongation of Days s. the felicity of life eternal. 8898.

Prolonged, to be, is pred. of good. 3703.

Prophet. Where any p. is mentioned by name in the Word, it does not mean that p., but the prophetic Word itself; nevertheless, each p. has a distinct signification. 3652. P. is frequently mentioned in the Word, and in the sense of the letter s. those to whom revelation is made, also abstractedly the revelation itself; but in an internal sense, it s. one who teaches, also abstractedly the doctrine which is taught. 2534. P. s. doctrine of the church der. from the Word, and prophecy, the same, because the Word was written by p., and in heaven, a person is considered according to that which belongs to his function or office, agreeably thereto also, every man, spirit, and angel is named in heaven, wherefore when the word p. is used, forasmuch as his function was to write and teach the Word, the Word is understood with respect to doctrine, or doctrine der. from the Word; hence it is, that the Lord, forasmuch as he is the Word itself, was called a p. A.R. 8. P. (Matt. xi. 9) s. the external things of doctrine and of worship. 2576. P. s. the doctrine and thence the science of truth, and, in the opp. sense, the doctrine and thence the science of what is false. A.E. 559.

Prophet and **Dreamer of Dreams**. (Deut. xiii. 2–4.) P. here s. he who gives a sign, and d. of d., one who gives a miracle. A.E. 706.

Prophet, Just Man, and **Disciple**. (Matt. x. 41.) P. s. the truth of doctrine, a j. m., the good of love, and d., the truth and good of the Word and the church. A.E. 695.

Prophets s. all those whom the Lord teaches, that is, all who are in the spiritual affection of truth for its own sake. A.E. 624. P. s. those who teach truths from the Word, and, in an abstract sense, the doctrine of the truth of the church, and, in an extensive sense, the Word itself. A.R. 943. False p. are they who teach falses, and in the abstract sense they s. false doctrines. False p. in sheep's clothing, who are inwardly ravening wolves, are they who teach falses, as if they were truths, and lead a moral life to appearance, but when left to themselves to act from their own spirits, they study to deprive all of truths. A.E. 195. The p. rep. the state of the church as to doctrine, and the Lord rep. it as to the Word. A.R. 8. L. 15–17. When the Word was revealed to the p., it was not by influx into their interiors, but by spirits, whom the Lord filled with his aspect; and the spirit so filled, with the divine from the Lord, knows no otherwise than that he is the Lord, and this even till he is done speaking. H. and H. 254. It is written concerning the p., that they were in the spirit, or in vision, also that the Word came to them from Jehovah. When they were in the spirit, or in vision, they were not in the body, but in their spirit, in which state they saw such things as were in heaven; but when the Word came to them then they were in the body, and heard Jehovah speak: these two states of the p. are carefully to be distinguished; in the state of vision, the eyes of their spirit were opened, and the eyes of their body shut, and then they heard what the angels spake, or what Jehovah spake by the angels, and also saw the things which were rep. to them in heaven; and then they sometimes seemed to themselves to be carried from one place to another, the body still remaining in its place; in such a state was John when he wrote the Apocalypse, and sometimes, also, Ezekiel, Zachariah, and Daniel, and then it is said, that they were in vision, or in the spirit. A.R. 36.

Prophets and **Apostles**. They who taught truths, were called p. in the Old Testament, and a. in the New. A.E. 100.

Prophets and **Priests**. (Lam. iv. 13.) P. s. those who teach, and p., those who live according to what is taught. 382.

Prophets and **Saints**. (Rev. xi. 18.) P. s. those who are in truths of doctrine, and s., those who are in a life conformable to them. A.R. 526.

Propitiation s. the operation of clemency and grace to prevent man from falling into damnation by sin, and at the same time, to be a security against the profanation of holiness, which was s. by the propitiatory, or mercy-seat over the ark in the tabernacle. U.T. 135.

Propitiatory, or **Mercy-Seat**, den. cleansing from evils or remission of sins. 9506.

Proprium. The Lord alone hath p. (something which may be called his own); from this p. he redeemed man, and from this p. he saveth man; the p. of the Lord is life, by virtue of which p. the p. of man is vivified, which in itself is dead. 149. Man's p. is all evil and the false, originating in self-love and the love of the world; and that he believes in himself, and not in the Lord and the Word, and supposes that what he cannot conceive sensually, and scientifically, is nothing, thence come nothing but the evil and false, and thus he sees all things in a perverted view. 210. Man's p. is, as it were, destroyed, when it is vivified or made alive. 731. The p. of man has an innate enmity against the divine providence. D.P. 211. What is divine may be with man as an appurtenance, but not in his p., for the p. of man is nothing but evil. A.R. 758. The Lord is not conjoined with the p. of man,

Prospection

but removes that, and gives to him a new p. from himself in which he abides. A.E. 254. Even the p. of angels is nothing but what is false and evil. 633. The celestial marriage is such, that heaven, and consequently, the church, is united with the Lord by p., so that it consists in p., for without p., no union can exist, into which p. when the Lord out of mercy insinuates innocence, peace, and goodness, in this case in it appears still as p., but celestial and most happy. But the difference between this p. from the Lord, and that from man, is like that which subsists between heaven and hell. 252. The Lord united by his divine power in the world, the divine celestial p. with the human p. in his human essence, so that in him they might be one. 256.

Prospection, or View. Den. to think. 2684. And the extension of influx. 8212.

Prosper s. to be provided; understand, providence so willing it. 3117.

Prostration of **Body** cor. to humiliation. 1999.

Protection. Every one is so far under the p. of the Lord, as he abstains from doing evil. A.E. 643.

Protest s. to be averse. 5584. Also precaution. 8836.

Provender s. the good of scientific truths. 5670. "To give p. to his ass" (Gen. xlii. 27) s. to reflect upon scientifics, for p. is the food with which asses are fed, consisting of straw and chaff, and hence it den. all reflection on scientifics, for reflection principally feeds them. 5495.

Provide. It is provided by the Lord that every one is capable of being saved. D.P. 328.

Providence. The divine p. is the government of the divine love and divine wisdom of the Lord. That the divine p. of the Lord has for end a heaven, from the human race. That the divine p. of the Lord, in all that it does, regards the infinite and the eternal. That it is a law of the divine p. that man should act from freedom according to reason. That it is a law of the divine p., that man should as of himself remove evils as sins in the external man, and that thus and not otherwise the Lord can remove evils in the internal man, and then at the same time in the external. That it is a law of the divine p., that man should not be compelled by external means to thinking and willing, thus to believing and loving, the things which are of religion; but that man should lead, and sometimes compel himself. That it is a law of divine p., that man is led and taught by the Lord from heaven, through the Word, doctrine and preachings from it, and this in all appearance as of himself. That it is a law of the divine p., that man should not perceive and feel any thing concerning the operation of the divine p., but that he should still know and acknowledge it. That one's own prudence is nothing, and only appears to be, and also ought to appear as if it was; but that the divine p. from things most particular is universal. That the divine p. looks to eternal things, and no otherwise to things temporal than as far as they agree with the eternal. That man is not let interiorly into the truths of faith, and into the goods of charity, except so far as he can be kept in them until the end of life. That the laws of permission are also laws of the divine p. That evils are permitted for the sake of the end which is salvation. That the divine p. is equally with the evil as with the good. That the divine p. does not appropriate evil to any one nor good to any one, but that his own prudence appropriates both. That every man may be reformed, and that predestination is not given. That the Lord cannot act contrary to the laws of divine p., because to act contrary to them would be to act contrary to his divine love and contrary to his divine wisdom, thus contrary to himself. D.P. 1, 33, 46, etc.

Provinces of Heaven. Exp. D.L.W. 288.

Provision, abundance of (Gen. xii. 29–31), s. the multiplication of truth, because it is opposed to famine, which s. defect of truth. 6276. P. (Gen. xlii.

2) is here expressed in the original tongue by a term which s. breaking; by a like term also buying and selling are expressed, where it is said, that the sons of Jacob bought it in Egypt, and that Joseph there sold it; the reason is, because in the ancient church bread was broken when it was given to another, and thereby was s. to communicate from one's own, and to appropriate good from one's own, and thus to do mutual love; for when bread is broken, and given to another, then communication is made from one's own; or when bread is broken amongst several, in such case the bread becomes mutual, consequently, there is conjunction by charity; hence it is evident that the breaking of bread was a significative of mutual love; inasmuch as this rite was received and customary in the ancient church, therefore also by the breaking itself was meant the p. which was made common. 5405.

Provoke. See To *Vex.* Anger.

Prudence comes from God. D.P. 191. Self-derived p. proceeds from self-love. D.P. 321.

Prudence and **Cunning.** The former is affirmed of those who are in good; and the latter of those who are in evil. A.E. 581.

Prudence and **Deceit** were regarded as enormities by the most ancient people, and such were cast out as devils from society. 3573.

Prudently. He that thinks and acts p., as from himself, acknowledging that he does so from the Lord, is a man. D.P. 321.

Prune and **Weed,** to (Isa. v. 6), s. to prepare for reception. A.E. 644.

Pruning-Hooks (Isa. ii. 4) s. truths of doctrine, because gardens s. perceptions and knowledges of truth. A.E. 734.

Psalms of David are from the discourse of spirits, which is in a kind of rhythm, or measure. 1648. They were called P. from playing on the psaltery, and also songs from singing. A.E. 326.

Psalteries cor. to spiritual good. A.R. 276. See *Vessels of Cups, etc.*

Psaltery of Ten Strings (Ps. xxxiii. 2, 3) s. spiritual good, cor. with confession of the Lord from spiritual truths. A.E. 323.

Puah and **Shiprhah** s. the quality and state of the natural principle where the scientifics are. 6674.

Publicans and **Sinners** s. the Gentiles who received the Lord, and hence the Lord ate with them. A.E. 617.

Pul s. kinds of external worship. 1158. See *Tarshish.*

Pulmonic Kingdom. That in which wisdom predominates. D.L.W. 381.

Pulsation. Influx into the heart is by regular p. Exp. 3884. See *Respiration.*

Pulsative Instruments have respect to the joy of those who are of the celestial kingdom. A.E. 863.

Pulse of the Herb (Gen. ix. 3) s. what is vile and refuse in delights, because they are only worldly and corporeal, or external; for the pleasures, which are in things corporeal or extreme, der. their origin from interior delights in orderly arrangement; the delights which are perceived in things extreme, or corporeal, are respectively vile and refuse, for every delight is of such a nature, that it becomes viler the more it proceeds to external things, and happier, the more it proceeds to things internal. 996. P. (Gen. xxv. 29) s. doctrinals. 3316. P. (2 Kings iv. 38) s. a heap of scientifics ill-connected together. 3316. See *Beans.*

Pulse and **Respiration.** The variation as to pulses, and as to respirations in the heavens are manifold, being equal in number to the societies therein, for they are according to the states of thought and affection with the angels, which states are according to states of faith and love. 3886.

Punishment is equally the consummation of evil; and because after p., reformation succeeds, therefore, it is said (Deut. xxv. 3), "that no more than forty stripes should be struck, lest thy brother become vile in thine eyes;"

Pure

for by forty is s. the end of evil, and also the beginning of good, wherefore, if more than forty stripes should be given, the beginning of good, or reformation could not be s. A.E. 633. Every evil carries along with it its own p. A.R. 762. No one suffers any p. and torment in another life on account of hereditary evils, but for the actual evils which he himself has committed; when the wicked are punished, there are always angels present to moderate the p., and to abate the pains of the sufferers as much as may be, but they cannot remove them entirely, because, such is the equilibrium of all things in another life, that evil punishes itself, and unless it was removed by p. the evil spirits could not be kept to eternity in any hell, but would infest the societies of the good, and do violence to the order appointed by the Lord, on which the safety of the universe depends. 966, 967.

Pure, pred. of oil, den. genuine celestial good. 9781. Den. inmost truth, which is spiritual truth. 10.296. P. in heart s. those in the good of love. A.E. 340.

Purgatory is a mere Babylonian fiction, invented for the sake of gain. A.R. 784.

Purification from evils is effected in two ways, one by temptations, and the other by fermentations. D.P. 25. Circumcision was to rep. p. from defiled natural loves. 2039. P. is effected by the truths of wisdom. D.L.W. 391. P. cannot take place unless unclean things are seen, acknowledged, and rejected. A.E. 580.

Purple cor. to divine celestial good. A.R. 725, 773. P. s. genuine good. A.E. 118. A.C. 9467.

Purple and **Fine Linen.** (Luke xvi. 19.) P. s. the knowledges of good from a celestial origin, and f. l., the knowledges of truth from a celestial origin. A.E. 1042.

Purple and **Scarlet** s. goods and truths from a celestial origin. A.E. 1042.

Purse and **Scrip** (Luke xxii. 36) s. the like which is s. by pieces of money, namely, the knowledges of truth and good from the Word. A.E. 840.

Purses, large, **Full of Silver** s. knowledges of truth and good in great abundance. A.R. 255.

Pursue, to (Gen. xiv. 16), s. a state of purification; for to p. enemies is here to expel evils and falses, which were with goods and truths, and caused them to appear as goods and truths, and thus to deliver and purify them. 1710.

Push, to, or to **Strike the People**, den. to destroy falses by truths. 9081.

Pustule cor. to blasphemies: filthiness of evil. 7524.

Put, to, has reference to order, arrangement, application, influx. 6725.

Put off, to, is to shake off and annihilate. 4741. The Lord p. o. all that was merely human. 26–49.

Put on, to, is to communicate and imbue. 3539. The Lord p. o. the human from the father. 10.830.

Puth den. knowledges from the literal sense of the Word, understood according to appearances. 1163.

Putridity den. infernal filthiness, pred. of evil. 8482.

Pyropus, or **Sardine Stone**, s. good. A.E. 268.

Pythons. Those who studied natural magic, from which nothing divine could be pred. 3698. Humoring a man's principles, and thus leading, like the blind leading the blind, are p. diviners. A.Cr. 74.

Q

Quails, selav (Exod. xvi. 13), s. natural delight productive of good, because a q. was a bird of the sea, which s. the natural principle, and its flesh, which was desired, delight. Q. (Num. xi. 31, 32) s. the delight of concupiscence. 8452.

Quaker. They who are instructed by influx what they should believe, are not instructed by the Lord, or any angel, but by some Q. spirit, and are seduced. D.P. 321. None but Q. spirits operate upon Q. A.Cr. 74.

Quality s. whatsoever is in a thing as an inward principle. 3935.

Quantity. Pred. of good and truth. 8454.

Quarters. In heaven, as in the world, there are four q., east, west, south, and north, both determined by its own sun: in heaven by the sun of heaven, which is the Lord, in the world, by the sun of the world; but still with much difference between them. H. and H. 141. The four q. in the spiritual world are determined by the sun, which is the Lord, and where the sun is there in the east, the opp. to which is the west, to the right hand is the south, and to the left hand is the north. A.E. 422. H. and H. 116, 125, 141. The q. in the heavens which constitute the celestial kingdom of the Lord, differ from the q. in the heavens which constitute its spiritual kingdom, because the Lord appears to the angels who are in his celestial kingdom as the sun, but to the angels who are in his spiritual kingdom, as the moon; and the east is where the Lord appears: the distance between the sun and the moon there, is thirty degrees, consequently, there is the like distance of the q. H. and H. 146. A.E. 422. In the two q. of the spiritual world called east and west, the Lord flows in with divine good stronger than with divine truth, and in the southern and northern q., he flows in with divine truth stronger than with divine good, from whence these are more in wisdom and intelligence, but the others more in love and charity. A.E. 418. The Lord is the sun of the spiritual world, and in front of him are the east and west, and on the sides are the south and north. The angels who dwell in the east and west of heaven are in the good of love; and the angels who dwell in the south and north of heaven are in the truths of wisdom. It is the same with the church on earth, for every man who is in the goods and truths of the church der. from the Word, is consociated with the angels of heaven, and, as to the interiors of his mind, dwells with them. A.R. 906. H. and H. 148.

Queen (Ps. xlv.) s. the church as a wife. A.R. 620.

Queen of the **Heavens** (Jer. xliv. 17–19) s. falses in the whole complex. A.E. 324. A.C. 4581.

Queen of **Sheba**, the (1 Kings x. 1–3), s. the celestial things of faith. 117. The q. of S. coming to Solomon to Jerusalem with exceeding great riches, with camels carrying spices, gold, and precious stones (1 Kings x. 1, 2), rep. the wisdom and intelligence which was added to the Lord in his natural man. 3048.

Quench, to, the **Smoking Flax**, den. the extinction of cupidities. 25.

Question. It frequently occurs in the Word, that men are questioned of the Lord, concerning their states, but the reason is, because it is agreeable to

Quickly

man's belief, who imagines that no one is acquainted with his thoughts, much less with the state of his affections; a further reason is, that men may hence der. comfort, being enabled to lay open the sensations of the mind, which is commonly attended with a relief from trouble. 1913, 2693.

Quickly s. certain and full, because time s. state and thence q. and speedily, a present state of affection and thought, thus what is certain and full. A.E. 216. A.R. 944.

Quiescence of **Evil** in the **External Man**. The e. which is in the e. m. is incapable of being separated in the case of any man except of the Lord, for whatever a man has once acquired, remains; nevertheless, it seems to be separated, when it is quiescent or at rest, for thus it appears as if it was annihilated; nor, is it thus quiescent, so as to appear annihilated, except from the Lord and when it is thus quiescent, then first good things flow in from the Lord, and affect the e. m. Such is the state of the angels; they know no other than that evil is separated from them, whereas it is only a detention from evil, and thus its q., so that it appears annihilated, consequently, it is an appearance, which the angels also know when they reflect. 1581.

Quills, or Feathers (of yellow gold) (Ps. lxviii. 14), s. spiritual good, from which truth is der. A.E. 283.

Quintate, to, the **Land**, or to **take a fifth Part** (Gen. xli. 34) s. the like with decimating [tithing or taking a tenth], which in the Word s. to make remains, and to make remains is to gather truths and goods, and afterwards to store them up. 5291.

Quiver (Isa. xlix. 2) s. the Word. A.E. 357. Q. s. the doctrinals of good and truth. 3499. See *Arrow*.

R

Raamah, the sons of (Gen. x. 7), s. the knowledges of things celestial. 1172. See *Sheba.*

Raamses. As the journeyings of the sons of Israel, treated of in Exodus, den. states of the life and their changes from first to last, therefore by the journey from R. to Succoth is s. the first state of departure and its quality. 7972.

Rabbah, the sons of, s. the affections of truth in the natural man. A.E. 435. The daughters of R. s. those who are in natural good and falsify the truths of the church. A.E. 637.

Rabbath of the **Ammonites** s. the falsifications of truth. A.E. 163.

Rabbi and **Teacher** s. the doctrine of truth. A.E. 684.

Rabbin. Concerning one in the other life. 940.

Rabshakeh being sent by the **King** of **Ashur** to speak against Jerusalem and King Hezekiah, when the angel of Jehovah, smote in the camp of the King of Ashur one hundred and eighty and five thousand (Isa. chaps. xxxv., xxxvii.) des. the nature and quality of man's rational, when he reasons concerning the truths of faith from the negative principle, and also the overthrow and slaughter of man's rationals when he reasons against divine things, however it may appear to him that he then is wise. 2588.

Raca. To say R. s. to account as nothing, or vile. A.E. 746.

Rachel den. the affection of interior truth. 3758.

Radiation. The Lord's love appears as a radiant belt. 7270. The light of heaven is likened to the sparkling of diamonds, and all manner of precious stones. 1621–5.

Rafter s. that part of the understanding from which is der. what is rational. A.E. 1146.

Rage, to, or go **Mad,** is pred. of the false. 2336.

Rage, to, in the **Streets** (Nahum ii. 4), is pred. of chariots which den. the doctrine of truth, and which are said to r. in the s. when what is false takes place of what is true. 2336.

Raguel, father-in-law of **Moses,** s. good of the church with those who are in simple good. 6827.

Raiment. (Gen. xxvii. 15.) Goodly r. s. genuine truths, and r., inferior truths respectively. 3537. Soft r. (Matt. xi. 9) rep. the internal sense of the Word. 9372. See *Garments.*

Raiment of **Camel's Hair** (Matt. iii. 4) s. the Word in its literal sense as to truth, which sense is a clothing for the internal sense. 5619.

Rain, in a good sense, den. blessing, but, in an opp. sense, damnation. 2443–2445. R. (Gen. ii. 5, 6; Exod. xxxiv. 25–27; Hosea vi. 3) s. the tranquillity of peace when the combat of temptation ceases. 90. An inundating r. s. the vastation of truth (Ezek. iii. 11–14; xxxviii. 23), also temptation. (Matt. vii. 24–27.) A.R. 496. To r. s. influx. A.E. 644. To r. (Gen. vii. 4) s. temptation and vastation. 729.

Rain and **Snow.** (Isa. lv. 10.) R. s. spiritual truth, which is appropriated to man; and s. natural truth, which is as s., while only in the memory, but becomes spiritual by love, as s. becomes r.-water by heat. A.E. 644.

Rainbow

Rainbow s. the quality of divine truth in the spiritual sense of the Word; because the light of heaven, similar to the light of this world, presents variegations of colors, and also r. according to their incidence upon objects. A.E. 595. R. (Gen. ix. 12, 27) s. divine spiritual truth in the natural mind of man who is regenerated; for man, when he is regenerated, from natural becomes spiritual; and inasmuch as then there is a conjunction of the Lord with him, therefore it is said that the bow in the cloud should be the sign of a covenant, which s. conjunction or connection. A.R. 466. R. (Rev. x. 1) s. the Lord's divine spiritual. A.R. 466. In the spiritual world there appear r. of many kinds, some of various colors as upon earth, and some of one color only. A.R. 232.

Ram s. the Lord's divine spiritual appertaining to man. 2830. R. s. the good of innocence and charity in the internal man. 10.042. R. (Lev. xvi. 5–24) s. the natural man as to the good of charity. A.E. 730.

Ramifications of the **Bronchia** cor. to the perceptions and thoughts. D.L.W. 405.

Rams, the **Sons** of **Bashan** (Deut. xxxii. 14), s. celestial spiritual things. 2830.

Rams of **Nebaioth** s. divine spiritual things. 2830. See *Flock of Kedah.*

Ramah den. those things which appertain to spiritual truth der. from celestial. 4592. See *Gibeah.*

Rameses, land of (Gen. xlvii. 11), s. the inmost of the spiritual principle in the natural mind. 6104.

Rampart, a (Lam. ii. 8), s. doctrinals. 402.

Ransom. (Exod. xxx. 12.) "They shall give every man a r. for his soul," s. to be purified or liberated from evil by the truth of faith, which here is to acknowledge that all truths and goods are from the Lord. 10.418.

Raphael s. a ministry in heaven, and not a single angel of that name. 548.

Raphath den. doctrinals of external worship. 1154.

Rapine s. violence offered by the false principle. A.E. 355.

Rat, or **Mice**, rep. the sordidly avaricious. 938. R. cor. to evil uses. D.L.W. 339.

Ratio. There is no r. given between that which is infinite, and that which is finite. A.Cr. 24, 33.

Rational. The superior region of the natural degree is called r. D.L.W. 254.

Rational Man. If a man be r., he speaks from a principle of good thought, and acts from a principle of good will, that is he speaks from faith, and acts from charity; but if a man be not r., in this case, indeed he can act pretendedly as a r. m., and speak in like manner, but still there is nothing of life therein from the r. principle; for the life of evil closes up every way or communication with the r. principle, and causes man to be merely natural and sensual. 5128.

Rational Principle, the, s. the thought of the natural man from knowledges and sciences, for man who is imbued with sciences is able to see things in a series from first and mediate principles to the ultimate, which is called the conclusion, and from thence he can analytically dispose, weigh, separate, conjoin, and at length conclude things even to a further and at length to the ultimate end, which is the use which he loves. Every spiritual man is also r., but the r. man is not always spiritual also. A.E. 569. The r. faculty or principle is the first receptacle of spiritual truths. A.R. 936. The genuine r. p. is, by virtue of good, and exists, by virtue of truth. 3030. The r. p. is conceived of celestial good as a father, but not of spiritual truth, as a mother; which may appear from the conception of the r. p., as being effected by an influx of celestial divine good into the affection of sciences. 2557. The r. p. appertains to the external man which in itself is a kind of medium between the internal and external, for the internal by means of the r. p. operates on the corporeal external. 268. Unless the r. p. submits itself to the influences of the Lord's goodness and truth, it either suffocates, or perverts those influences, especially when they flow into the scientific sensual things of the memory; this is s. by the seed falling in the way, or on stony ground, or amongst thorns. (Matt. xiii. 3–7.) 1940. There appertain to every man who is regenerated, two r. p., one before regeneration, the other after it. The first is procured by exercises of the sciences, the other is formed by the Lord, by the affections of spiritual truth and good. 2657.

Rationality means the faculty of understanding truths and thence falses, and goods and thence evils. D.L.W. 264.

Ratiocination s. thought and argumentation from fallacies and falses. A.E. 569.

Raven (Gen. viii. 7) s. falsities. The spiritual man only knows generals from the Word, and by generals has his conscience formed, and the generals of the Word are accommodated to the fallacies of the senses; therefore innumerable falsities join themselves to, and insinuate themselves into those generals, which cannot be dispersed; these falsities are here s. by the r. which went forth in going and returning. 865. Sons of the r. (Ps. cxlvii. 8, 9) s. natural men who are in a dark lumen arising from fallacies concerning truth divine. A.E. 650. See *Crows.*

Rave, to, or **Rage,** s. to speak falses for truths. A.E. 652.

Raw (Exod. xii. 29) s. without the good of love. 7856.

Reach, to, s. to shut out of heaven. A.E. 1111.

Read. To understand from illustration, thus to perceive. A.E. 12.

Reaction. There is from God in every created thing a r.; life alone has action, and r. is excited by the action of life; this r. appears as if it appertained to the created being, because it exists when the being is acted upon; thus in man it appears as if it was his own, because he does not perceive any otherwise than that life is his own, when nevertheless man is only a recipient of life. From this cause it is that man, from his own hereditary evil, reacts against God, but so far as he believes that all his life is from God, and every good of life from the action of God, and every evil of life from the r. of man, r. thus becomes cor. with action, and man acts with God as from himself. D.L.W. 68.

Real, all is, that is from the Lord. 4623. Objects in the spiritual world are more r. than those in the natural. A.Cr. 105.

Reap, to, s. to execute judgment. A.R. 645. Reaping den. the reception of truth in good. 10.669.

Reason. The Lord wills that a man should r. concerning things divine, to the end that he may see that they are so or not so. D.P. 219.

Reasoners. Sensual men who confirm themselves in favor of nature against God, are more ingenious r. than others, and cunning and craftiness they call wisdom. D.P. 310.

Reasonings and **Ratiocinations concerning Spiritual Things.** Genuine reasonings concerning spiritual things exist from the influx of heaven into the spiritual man, and thence by the rational into the sciences and knowledges which are in the natural man, by which the spiritual man confirms himself. This way of r. is according to order, but ratiocinations concerning spiritual things, which are made from the natural man, and more especially from the sensual man, are altogether contrary to order and spiritual influx. A.E. 569.

Reasons why the Lord was born on this earth—See *Earth.* R. for the Lord's putting on the third degree—See *Human.* R. for calling Jehovah Lord—See *Lord.*

Reaping, or **Harvest Time,** den. the reception of truth in good. 10.669.

Rebecca (Gen. xxiv.) s. divine truth which was to be conjoined to divine good of the Lord's rational, which is Isaac. 3040. See *Damsel.*

Rebel

Rebel, to (Gen. xiv. 4), is pred. of evils appertaining to man, or of evil spirits, when they begin to arise and to infest, after they have been in a state of subjection or servitude. 1660.

Rebuke of Jehovah (Isa. l. 2) s. the destruction and abolition of the church, which takes place, when there is no saving knowledge or perception of truth and good. A.E. 513.

Rebuke and **Chasten,** to. (Rev. iii. 19.) To r. is pred. of temptations with respect to falses, and to c., is pred. of temptations with respect to evils. A.R. 215.

Receive. The very being of men and angels consists in the reception of life from the Lord. 3938. To r. or accept is pred. of affection. 2511. Man may r. wisdom to the third degree; but not love, unless he shuns evils as sins. D.L.W. 242.

Receptacle. The natural man, as to scientifics, is den. by a r., because the good of truth is received in scientifics. 5489. Man was created to be a r. of the divine love and wisdom. D.P. 328. Civil and moral life is a r. of spiritual life. 322. The Lord has formed two r. of Himself; the will and understanding. D.L.W. 358–61.

Reception. The heavens are so formed by the Lord, that one may serve another for r., and that at length man, as to his natural and sensual principle, may serve for ultimate r. 4618.

Rehoboth (Gen. x. 11) s. the false of doctrinals proceeding from ignorance; but attended with the dominion of some evil lust, such as the desire of innovation or pre-eminence. 1188.

Recipient. Man is an organ r. of life from God. A.R. 875.

Reciprocation. There is conjunction of the Lord with man, and a reciprocal conjunction of man with the Lord. Ill. D.P. 92. R. necessary to conjunction. D.L.W. 115.

Reciprocations. A mode of torment by r. exp. 958.

Reciprocality is pred. of the union of the divine and human in the Lord. 2004. Is pred. of action and reaction. 8691. It is by means of r. that conjunction is effected. A.Cr. 48, 51.

Reciprocity. It is by means of r. that conjunction is effected. A.Cr. 48, 51.

Recompense. They who do good with a view to r., desire that others should serve them in another life, and are never satisfied. 6393. The happiness of heaven consists in the love of doing good without any regard to r. 6388.

Reconciled s. the dissipation of anger, enmity, or hatred. A.E. 746.

Recreations. There are diversions of charity, consisting of the various delights and pleasures of the bodily senses, which are of use for the r. of the spirits. Man's nature in his r. or diversions is determined by his affection of charity. The affection of use, the same as it is in the inner man, remains within them all; and during its repose is gradually renovated. Diversions break or terminate the cares of business; for the Lord flows into them from heaven, and implants in them an interior sense of pleasure, of which they who are not in the affection of charity are totally unconscious. But he who is in this affection, inspires his diversions with a fragrance or sweetness which is imperceptible to any but himself. They who are not in diversions from the affection of charity, have none of these things, for their spiritual minds are shut up; and in proportion as they recede from charity, their spiritual minds, in regard to the voluntary part, are compacted, as it were, with glue. C. 117, 121.

Rectitude (Gen. xx. 5) s. innocence and simplicity. 2525.

Rectum, the, in the human body cor. to the first hell. 5175.

Red is pred. of the good of love, because it proceeds from the fire of the spiritual sun. A.R. 167. Because r. s. the quality of a thing as to good, therefore also names and things which are der. from the same word in the original language, s. what proceeds from good. R. in the original language, is called Adam, from thence is the name Adam, and also the name Edom, thence also man (homo) is called Adam, the ground is called Adam, etc. A.E. 364. R., in an opp. sense, s. the infernal love of evil. A.R. 305. R. (Rev. xii. 3) s. the false principle originating in the evils of concupiscences, which is the infernal false principle. A.R. 537. R., or crimson, s. good, and, in an opp. sense, evil of every kind. A.E. 67.

Red Sea, the, s. hell and damnation and also temptation. 842.

Redeem, to, s. to vindicate and to liberate, for there are two words in the original language, by which redemption is expressed. The one s. vindication from evil, and the other liberation from falses. A.E. 328.

Redeemer. Jehovah is called the r., because he assumed the human nature. A.R. 962.

Redeeming Angel den. the divine human. 6276.

Redemption, real, consisted in bringing the hells into subjection, and the heavens into order and regulation, and thereby preparing the way for a new spiritual church. Without such r., no man could have been saved, nor could the angels have remained in a state of integrity. For hereby the Lord not only redeemed men but angels also. U.T. 115, 118, 121. R. was a work purely divine. U.T. 123. R. equally applies to the Lord's second, as to his first, advent. U.T. 772. A.V.C.R. 21.

Redemption, Salvation, and **Regeneration**. R. is deliverance from hell, and s. by conjunction with the Lord, and this is effected by regeneration. A.R. 619.

Reed, a, or **Cane** s. feeble power, such as man has from himself. A.R. 485. A r. s. sensual truth, which is the ultimate, such as is given among natural men, also among the evil. A.E. 627. A bruised r. s. feeble power or faculty. A.R. 285, 904. A bruised r. shall he not break, and the smoking flax shall he not quench (Isa. xlii. 35), s. that the Lord does not break the fallacies nor quench the lusts, but inclines them to truth and good. 25. A r. shaken with the wind (Matt. xi. 8) s. the Word, when explained at pleasure, for a r., in the internal sense, is truth in the ultimate, such as the Word is in the letter. 9372. A golden r. (Rev. xxi. 15) s. a power or faculty originating in the good of love. A.R. 90. R. being given him like unto a rod (Rev. xi. 1), s. power from the Lord; that it means the faculty, and power of knowing and seeing the state of the church in heaven, and in the world. A.R. 485. R. flags and paper r. (Isa. xix. 6, 7) s. natural and sensual truths of the lowest order. A.E. 518. See *Grass*.

Reflect, Intellectual Sight, den. by lifting the eyes. 5684.

Reflection. A derivative from wisdom. D.L.W. 363.

Reflexion. The faculty of r. is from the life of the Lord flowing in by remains. 977.

Reform. Man is r. by the two faculties called liberty and rationality. D.P. 82, 85, 96. No one is r. by miracles and signs. D.P. 130.

Reformation and **Regeneration**. The first act of the new birth is called ref., which relates to the understanding; and the second act is called reg., which relates to the will, and thence to the understanding. U.T. 571, 620. Man who is reformed, first respects truths of doctrine and afterwards goods of life; and when he respects truths of doctrine, he is like unripe fruit, and afterwards as he respects goods of life, he becomes like ripe fruit. A.R. 84.

Reformed. Being r. is removal of evil loves: by means of freedom; and by combat against evils. A.Cr. 55, 53, 80.

Reformed Church. Without the Athanasian doctrine, the r. c. would not have seen the divine in the human principle of the Lord. A.C. 16. Judgment of the R. C. des. L.J.L. 14–31.

Refuge

Refuge. A place of r. den. the state in which man is guiltless of evil. 9011.

Refuge, to, den. aversion. 4990.

Regeneration, by which the new intellectual principle and the new will-principle are formed, is not effected in a moment, but from the earliest infancy even to the close of life, and afterwards in the other life to eternity, and this by divine means, innumerable and ineffable. 5354. When man is regenerated by the Lord, he is first in a state of external innocence, which is his state of infancy, and is afterwards successively led into a state of internal innocence, which is his state of wisdom. 9354, 10.210. All r. proceeds from evening to morning, as it is six times said in the first chapter of Gen., where the r. of man is treated of. 861. The six days, or times, which are so many successive states of the r. of man, are in general as follow: The first state is that which precedes, as well that from infancy as that immediately before r., and is called a void, emptiness, and thick darkness. And the first motion, which is the mercy of the Lord, is the spirit of God moving itself on the faces of the waters. The second state is, when a distinction takes place between the things which are of the Lord, and the things which are proper to man: the things which are of the Lord are called in the Word remains, and here principally the knowledges of faith, which man has learned from infancy, which are stored up, and are not manifested till he comes into this state: which state at this day seldom exists without temptation, misfortune or sorrow, which effect, that the things which are of the body and the world, consequently, which are proper to him, become quiet, and, as it were, die; thus the things which are of the external man are separated from the things which are of the internal: in the internal are the remains, stored up by the Lord till this time, and for this use. The third state is that of repentance; in which from the internal man, he speaks piously and devoutly, and brings forth goods, as the works of charity, but which nevertheless are inanimate, because he considers them from himself: and they are called the tender grass, then the herb of seed, and afterwards the tree of fruit. The fourth state is, when he is affected with love, and illuminated by faith: he before discoursed piously, and brought forth goods, but from the state of temptation and distress, not from faith and charity; wherefore these are now enkindled in his internal man, and are called two luminaries. The fifth state is, that he discourses from faith, and thereby confirms himself in truth and good: the things then produced by him are animated, and are called the fishes of the sea, and the birds of the heavens. The sixth state is, when from faith, and thence from love, he speaks truths, and does goods; the things which he then produces are called the living soul, and beast. And because he then begins also to act from love, as well as from faith, he becomes a spiritual man, which is called an image. His spiritual life is delighted and sustained by such things as are of the knowledges of faith, and of works of charity, which are called his meat; and his natural life is delighted and sustained by such things as belong to the body and the senses, from whence a combat arises, until love reigns, and he becomes a celestial man. They who are regenerating do not all arrive at this state, but some and the greatest part at this day only to the first; some only to the second; some to the third, fourth, and fifth; few to the sixth; and scarcely any one to the seventh. 6–13.

Regeneration of the Internal Man. The i. m. is first regenerated by the Lord, and the external afterwards; for the i. m. is regenerated by embracing the things which belong to faith and charity, and the external, by a life in accordance with them. N.J.D. 181.

Region. The superior r. of the natural mind is called rational, and the lowest, sensual. D.L.W. 5

Rehoboth (Gen. xxvi. 22) s. truths. 3433.

Religious Persuasion

Reign, to (Rev. v.), s. to be in truths and goods, and thence to be in power from the Lord, of resisting evils and falses which are from hell. A.E. 333. To r. on the earth (Rev. v. 10) s. to be in the Lord's kingdom, and there one with him. (See John xvii. 20, 24.) A.R. 284.

Reign, to and to **have Dominion**. (Gen. xxxvii.) To r. implies subjection as to things of the understanding, and to h. d., implies subjection as to things of the will. 4691.

Reins and the **Heart**. The r. s. the truths of intelligence and faith; for as the r. purify the blood from such impurities as are called urinous, and as the h. purifies the blood from such unclean things which are loathsome, so the truth of faith purifies man from falses, and the good of love from evils, hence it is, that the ancients placed love and its affections in the h., and intelligence and its perceptions in the r. A.R. 140. By r. are s. things spiritual, and by h. things celestial, that is, by r. [kidneys] are s. those things which are of truth, and by h. those things which are of good; the reason is, because the kidneys purify the serum, and the h. the blood itself; hence by proving, exploring, and searching the kidneys, is s. to prove, explore and search the quantity and the quality of truth, or the quantity and quality of faith appertaining to man; that this is s., is also manifest in (Jer. xii. 2; David, Ps. li. 6.) That chastisement likewise is attributed to the r. [kidneys], is also clear from David. (Ps. xvi. 7.) 5385.

Rejection of evils and falses briefly exp. 7948.

Rejoice, to, and be **Glad** (Rev. xi. 10) s. to enjoy the delight of the affection of the heart and soul. A.R. 507.

Relapse. Concerning the state of the unregenerate who r. into their cupidities. 2041.

Relate den. that they may know and perceive. 7634.

Relation. Good is not known as to its quality, but by r. to what is less good, and by opposition to evil. D.P. 24. R. to God and to man exp. D.L.W. 254.

Relations, or **Relatives**. The sphere of perception and the extension of its limits, is actually formed from relatives. 2694.

Relationship in the Spiritual World takes its origin from good. 3815. See *Consanguinities.*

Relatives, have respect to the disposition of a variety of things in suitable and agreeable order. T.C.R. 62.

Relaxation. If a r. of the bonds in which man is held were possible, he would madly rush into evil. 987.

Relegation. The return of evil spirits to hell. 6762.

Relent. In all human mercy there is relenting or repentance. 588.

Religion alone renews and regenerates man, for it occupies the supreme seat in his mind, and sees beneath it those civil duties which belong to the world. T.C.R. 601. 1. The Jewish r., though containing truth was not a church, but the representative of a church. 4706. 2. The Roman Catholic r. is external without internal. 10.040. 3. There are two religious corruptions, one by the love of self and the world, and the other by the light of nature. 8941. Duty of each one to search the Word prayerfully for themselves. 5432. 4. Religion must be formed by truths from the Word. 8941. 5. All throughout the world who live according to their r. are saved. 9256. The two essentials, and two universals of r., are acknowledgment of God, and repentance. D.P. 340. The Lord provided that in every r. there shall be precepts similar to those in the Decalogue. D.P. 254. The essence of the christian r. is to shun evils as sins. D.P. 265. A life conformable to doctrine. A.E. 1332.

Religions. The seven hundred wives of Solomon s. the various principles prevailing in the world. D.P. 245.

Religious Persuasion. The church in which there is no longer any good and truth, is not a church but a r. p. A.E. 1037.

Relinquish

Relinquish means to be separated. 5812.

Relish den. the delights of good, and the pleasantness of truth. 3502.

Remains are not only the goods and truths which a man has learnt from his infancy out of the Lord's Word, and which are thus impressed on his memory, but they are likewise all states thence der.; as states of innocence from infancy; states of love towards parents, brothers, teachers, and friends; states of charity towards the neighbor, and also of mercy towards the poor and needy; in a word, all states of good and truth. These states, with their goods and truths, impressed on the memory, are called r.; which r. are preserved in man by the Lord, and are stored up in his internal man, whilst he is altogether ignorant thereof, and are carefully separated from the things which are proper to man, that is, evils and falses; all these states are so preserved in man by the Lord, that there is not the smallest of them lost; as it was given me to know by this, that every state of man, from infancy even to extreme old age, not only r. in another life, but also returns, and that exactly such as they were during man's abode in this world; thus not only the goods and truths in the memory, but likewise all states of innocence and charity; and when states of evil and of the false, or of wickedness and phantasy recur, which also, all and each, even to every smallest circumstance, r. and return, then of the Lord these latter states are tempered by the former; whence it may be evident, that unless man had some r., he could not possibly be otherwise than in eternal condemnation. In case a man had in him no r., he would not be a man, but much viler than a brute; the fewer r. there are, the less he is a man, and the more r. there are, the more he is a man. 530, 561.

Remaliah, the son of, s. the intellectual principle perverted. A.E. 559.

Remember, to (Gen. xli. 9) s. conjunction. The reason why remembering den. conjunction is, because the remembrance of any one in the other life conjoins, for as soon as any spirit r. another, he is presented at hand, and also so present that they discourse together; hence it is, that angels and spirits can meet with all whom they have known, and of whom they have heard, can see them present, and discourse with them, when the Lord grants to r. them. 5229.

Reminiscence. Divine remembrance or r. is salvation; non-remembrance, damnation. 8620.

Remission of **Sins** is a detaining of man from evil, and a keeping him in good by the Lord. 8391, 8393, 9014, 9450. Whensoever sins are removed they are also remitted or forgiven; for repentance precedes r., and without repentance there is no r., wherefore the Lord commanded the disciples, that they should preach repentance for the r. of s. (Luke iii. 3.) D.P. 280.

Remit, to. The Lord r. the sins of all; does not accuse or impute; yet he can only take them away according to the laws of his divine providence. D.P. 280.

Remit, to, **Seven Times**, s. to r. at all times. A.E. 257.

Remiss. The insufficiency of infestation by falses exp. 7118.

Remnant, the, who were affrighted, etc. (Rev. xi. 13), s. those who joined some goods of charity unto faith. A.R. 517. A.E. 676. When a church is vastated a r. always remains, and is continued. 407.

Remnants of **Jacob, Dew** from **Jehovah**, and the **Drop** upon the **Herb.** (Micah v. 7, 8.) The r. of J. s. the truths and goods of the church; and d. from J., spiritual truth; and the d. upon the h., natural truth. A.E. 278.

Removal, or **Remoteness** of place, is an appearance produced by difference of state. 9967.

Renumeration, in its genuine sense, den. mutual love. 6388.

Renal Spirits. The province of r. s. in the grand man is constituted by chaste virgins. 5391.

Representative Humanity

Rend, to, the **Garments** s. mourning for truth lost or destroyed, or the loss of faith. 4763.

Render, to, s. to make tribulation. A.E. 1114.

Rending the **Garments** s. zeal for doctrine and truth, also humility. 2576.

Renew Strength, to (Isa. xl. 31), s. to grow in a will to what is good. 3901.

Renounce, to, the **World** is to remove selfish and worldly love from the heart. N.J.D. 128. A.C. 9382.

Renovation of the natural man is spoken of as regeneration. 3768.

Repay, to, den. emendation or restoration effected by truth. 9087.

Repair, to, s. to raise up that which is fallen, and is pred. in the Word of both evils and falses. 153.

Repentance, actual, consists in a man's examining himself, in knowing and acknowledging his sins, making himself guilty, confessing them before the Lord, imploring help and power to resist them, and thus in desisting them and leading a new life, and all this as from himself. A.R. 531. U.T. 528. It is well to be known, that man, in desiring to repent, ought to look to the Lord alone; if to God the Father alone, he cannot be purified; nor if to the Father for the sake of the Son; neither if to the Son as a man only. D.P. 122. R. and grief of heart are pred. of the Lord, inasmuch as such affections appear to be in all human mercy, wherefore in various parts of the Word, it is spoken according to appearance. But by Jehovah's repenting and grieving at heart is s. mercy. 587, 588.

Repetition. The cause of the r. in the Word, is because the Word treats distinctly of the two faculties in man most distinct from each other, understanding and will. 707.

Rephaim. The R. s. those who, above all others, were in the love of self, and hence most entirely natural, and from the persuasion of their own eminence above others, were in falses of every kind. A.E. 163.

Rephaims, Susims, and **Emims** (Gen. xiv. 5) s. a race similar to the Nephilims. (Gen. vi. 4.) 1673.

Rephidim (Exod. xvii. 1) s. the quality of temptation as to truth. 8561.

Reply. When assent is given by a r., it den. what is reciprocal. 2919.

Repression of Evil, when it is seen to be such, without which man incurs guilt. 9132.

Representation is whatever exists in the things appertaining to the light of the world, that is, whatever exists in the external or natural man, considered in respect to the things appertaining to the light of heaven, that is, appertaining to the internal or spiritual man. 3225. R. are nothing else but images of spiritual things in natural, and when the latter are rightly rep. in the former, they then cor. 4044. In the spiritual world all things appear at a distance according to cor., the forms of such appearances being called r. of spiritual things in objects similar to those that are natural. A.R. 655.

Representative, a, is nothing else but an image of what is rep., and in the image is the himself who is represented. 3393.

Representative Church, a, is when internal worship is in external, but the r. of a c., is when there is no internal worship, yet nevertheless external. 4288. A church merely r., is but a resemblance of a church and not a real church. 3480. All the churches which were before the advent of the Lord, were r., and only saw divine truth in shade, but after his advent, a church was instituted by him, which could see divine truth in the light. S.S. 20. The r. c. had its commencement in Abraham, and was afterwards established amongst the posterity of Jacob. 1409. See *Churches*.

Representative Humanity. Before the incarnation, there was not any divine humanity, except a r. one, by means of some angel whom Jehovah the Lord filled with his spirit, and forasmuch as that was r., therefore, all things of the church at that time were r., and like shadows; but, since the incarna-

Representative Rites

tion, r. have ceased, as the shadows of evening, or night, at the rising of the sun. But the r. h., in which Jehovah was then manifested in the world before his actual advent, was not of such efficacy as that it could spiritually enlighten men; wherefore illumination was then effected only by types and figures. N.Q. No. 6.

Representative Rites in the **Jewish Church.** There were some which originated in r. appearances in the world of spirits, and some which did not. Circumcision was one that did; for when the angels who are in heaven have an idea of purification from natural defilements, there is rep. very swiftly, in the world of spirits, something like circumcision, for angelic ideas pass in the world of spirits into rep. 2039.

Representatives. Every king, whosoever he was, whether in Judah or in Israel, or even in Egypt, and other places, might rep. the Lord; their royalty itself was rep. This was the case with the very worst of kings, as with Pharaoh, Nebuchadnezzar, Saul, etc. In like manner, all priests, whether good or bad, rep. the Lord, the priestly office itself being rep., for the nature and quality of the person is not at all reflected on. 1361, 1409. All things that appear among the angels are r. 971, 3213–3226, 9576, 9577. R. are realities, as being from the light of heaven. 3485. The divine influx assumes the form of r. in the superior heavens, and descends thence to the inferior. 2179, 3213, 9577. R. are more beautiful and perfect in proportion, as they have a more interior birth and existence in the heavens. 3475. R. of the church and its worship ceased when the Lord came into the world, because he opened the internal things of the church, and because all things appertaining to that church regarded him in a supreme sense. 4838. In the most ancient church, their method of expressing themselves was such, that when they made mention of earthly and worldly things, they thought of the spiritual and celestial things rep. thereby; so that they not only expressed themselves by r., but also reduced their thoughts into a kind of historical series, or arrangement, in order to give them life; and in this they found the greatest delight and entertainment. Those r. are called in David, "hidden sayings of old." (Ps. lxxviii. 2, 3, 4.) 66. The Word is rep. before the angels under the most beautiful and agreeable forms. 1767.

Reproach, the, of Rachel taken away den. the office of interior truth no longer barren. 3969.

Require, to, of another den. the state in which one thing is so adjoined to another that it cannot be separated. 5610.

Resemblance, or, **Likeness to God,** s. the divine love. D.L.W. 358.

Reptile s. the sensual principle. A.E. 650. See *Creeping Things.*

Resen between **Nineveh** and **Calah** (Gen. x. 12) s. false doctrinals of life, originating in the falses s. by N. and C. 1184.

Reside, to, and to **Inhabit.** To r. is pred. of truth, and to i., of good. 4600.

Residue of the **Meat Offering.** (Lev. vi. 16.) Aaron and his sons eating the r. of the m. o. s. man's reciprocality and appropriation and consequent conjunction by love and charity, hence it was commanded to be eaten in a holy place. 2177.

Residue of his **People** (Isa. xxviii. 5) s. those among whom the Lord's church will be. A.R. 189.

Resin (Gen. xxxvii.) s. interior truths in the natural principle, but which are from good in that principle. 4748. R. (Ezek. xxvii. 17) s. truth grounded in good. 4748.

Resist. Man cannot of himself r. evils. He can only do so from the Lord. A.Cr. 61.

Respect, to have, **to God** is nothing else than but to think this or that evil a sin against God, and, therefore, not to do it. D.P. 20.

Respective Sense s. the internal sense. 3245.

Respiration. Man has a twofold r., one of his spirit, and the other of his body; the former depends on the fibres from the brains, and the latter on the blood-vessels from the heart, and from the vena cava and aorta. D.L.W. 412. R. cor. to the understanding, consequently, to perception and thought, and likewise to faith, because faith is of the thought according to the perception of the understanding. A.R. 708. In the spiritual world, every one's faith or reception of truth, may be perceived by the r. of his lungs, and the quality of his charity by the pulsation of his heart. F. 19. R. is the life of the body cor. to spiritual things, as the motion of the heart is the life of the body cor. to things celestial: the man of the most ancient church had internal r., consequently, such as was in concord with, and similar to the r. of angels; this r. was varied according to all the states of the internal man; but in process of time, amongst succeeding generations, it was changed, till it was become such with the last posterity, in whom every thing angelic perished, that they could no longer respire with the angelic heaven; this was the genuine cause of their extinction, and hence it is said, "that they expired, and that they died, in whose nostrils was the breath of the spirit of lives." (Gen. vii. 21, 22.) After these times internal r. ceased, and therewith communication with heaven, consequently, heavenly perception, and external r. succeeded; and whereas hereby communication with heaven ceased, the men of the ancient, or new church, could no longer be celestial men, like the most ancient people, but spiritual. 805.

Respond, to, or **Answer**, s. knowledge, for that is implied in answering an interrogation. 5255.

Response, or **Answer**, s. knowledge, perception, thought. 5255, 5468, 6943.

Rest of Jehovah and the **Ark of His Strength**. (Ps. cxxxii. 8.) The r. of J. s. the unition of his humanity with his divinity; and the a. of h. s. is heaven and the church. A.E. 684.

Rest, to, not **Day** and **Night**. (Rev. iv. 8.) The animals not resting day and night s. the Word continually, and without intermission, teaches. A.R. 247. To r. not d. and n. (Rev. iv. 8) s. that the divine providence and protection of the Lord never rests, nor ceases to eternity. A.E. 285. See *Odor of Rest.*

Restitution is pred. of good and truth. 9032.

Restoration, the, of the marriage of good and truth, and the conjunction thereby of the created universe with the Lord, is of the divine providence. D.P. 9.

Resurrection. By r. is s. salvation and life eternal; and by first r., mentioned in Rev. xx. 5, 6, is not meant the first r., but the real and primary essential r., consequently, salvation and life eternal; for there is only one r. unto life, neither is there given a second, neither is there a second anywhere mentioned in the Word. A.R. 851. R. is only the continuation of life in the spiritual world. N.J.D. 221. A.C. 2119, 5070. R. and entrance into the spiritual world generally happens on the third day after death. U.T. 138, 281. A.R. 153.

Resurrection of the Lord den. that he rises every moment in the minds of the regenerate. 2405.

Resuscitation in the other life, des. 178. R. of the church. There is no hope of it, if there is no internal as rep. by Joseph, no medium as rep. by Benjamin, and no charity or faith in the will as rep. by Simeon. 5551.

Retail, to, s. permanence in a state even to the end. A.E. 173.

Retaliation, the law of, consists in this, that evil carries along with it its own punishment, and this law of r. der. its origin from the following divine law: "all things whatsoever ye would that men should do to you, do ye even so to them; this is the law and the prophets." (Matt. vii. 12; Luke vi. 31.) This law, in heaven, is the law of mutual love or charity, whence there exists

Retraction

what is opp. in hell, in that there happens to every one that which he would do to another, not that they who are in heaven do it, but they who are in hell do it to themselves, for the retribution of r. exists from the opposition to that law of life in heaven as an inherent thing in their evils. A.R. 762.

Retraction, the, of the natural man, how he shrinks from coming under spiritual subjection. 5647.

Return, to, refers to state. 2288.

Reu (Gen. xi. 18) s. worship more external than that s. by Peleg. 1347. See *Peleg.*

Reuben. By R. in a supreme sense, is s. omniscience; in a spiritual sense, wisdom, intelligence, and science, as also faith; in a natural sense, sight. In Rev. vii. 5, R. s. wisdom, because it follows after Judah, by whom is s. celestial love, and celestial love produces wisdom, for there does not exist any love without its consort, which is science, intelligence, and wisdom; the consort of natural love is science, the consort of spiritual love is intelligence, and the consort of celestial love is wisdom. The ground and reason why these are s. by R., is, because he was so named from seeing or sight, and spiritual-natural sight is science, spiritual sight is intelligence, and celestial sight is wisdom. Moreover R. was the first-born of Jacob, and was, therefore, called by Israel his might, the beginning of his strength, excelling in eminence, and excelling in worth (Gen. xlix. 3); for such is wisdom originating in celestial love; and whereas R., on account of his primogeniture, rep. and, consequently, s., the wisdom of the men of the church, he, therefore, exhorted his brethren not to kill Joseph, and was grieved when Joseph was not found in the pit (Gen. xxxvii. 21, 22), and, therefore, his tribe encamped on the south, and was called the camp of R. (Num. ii. 10–16); moreover, the south s. wisdom originating in love; for which reason, they who are in that wisdom in heaven, dwell to the south. The tribe of R., in an opp. sense, s. wisdom separated from love, and, consequently, also faith separated from charity; on which account he was cursed by his father Israel (Gen. xlix. 3, 4); and was, therefore, deprived of his birthright (1 Chron. v. 1), for which reason an inheritance was given him on the other side Jordan, and not in the land of Canaan; and also, instead of R. and Simeon, the sons of Joseph, Ephraim, and Manasses were acknowledged (Gen. xlviii. 5); nevertheless, he retained the representation and consequent signification of wisdom. A.R. 351.

Reule den. the good of the church. 6778.

Reumah den. exaltation. 2868.

Revelation in the most ancient church was immediate; in the ancient church by cor.; in the Jewish church, by a living voice; and in the christian church, by the Word. 10.355, 10.632. H. and H. 306. And at this day there exists immediate r., because that is what is meant by the coming of the Lord. H. and H. 1.

Revelation, book of, or Apocalypse, treats in series, of falses in the church. A.R. 700.

Revelations are either from perception, or from discourse with the angels through whom the Lord speaks; they who are in good and thence in truth, especially they who are in the good of love to the Lord, have r. from perception; whereas they who are not in good and thence in truth, may indeed have r., yet not from perception, but by a living voice heard in them, thus by angels from the Lord; this latter r. is external, but the former internal; the angels, especially the celestial, have r. from perception, as also the men of the most ancient church had, and some also of the ancient church, but scarce any one at this day; whereas very many have had r. from discourse without perception, even who have not been principled in good, in like manner by visions or by dreams: such were most of the r. of the prophets in the Jewish church, they heard a voice, they saw a vision, and they dreamed a dream; but inasmuch as they had no perception, they were r. merely verbal or visual without a perception of what they signified; for genuine perception exists through heaven, from the Lord, and affects the intellectual principle spiritually, and leads imperceptibly to think as the thing generally is, with an internal assent, the source of which it is ignorant of; it supposes that it is in it, and that it flows from the connection of things, whereas it is a dictate through heaven from the Lord, flowing into the interiors of the thought, concerning such things as are above the natural and sensual principle, that is, concerning such things as are of the spiritual world, or of heaven. 5121. The Lord acquired to himself intelligence and wisdom by continual r. from the divine. 3382. Revelations are made variously: 1, by dreams; 2, by visions of the night; 3, by visions of the day; 4, by speech which man hears within him; 5, by speech heard without from a visible angel; 6, by speech heard without from an angel not visible. 6000.

Revenge. The origin of r. is self-love. Ill. D.P. 276. Indulgence in r., a cause of disease. 5712. To be avenged seventy and seven fold, den. damnation. 432. The wicked breathes r. against the Lord when he perishes. A.R. 806.

Reverberations. One of the punishments evil spirits bring upon themselves. 829.

Reverence. The fear of God, a holy r. with those in celestial worship. 5459.

Reward s. a means of conjunction; for r. serves as a means, or medium of conjunction with those who are not as yet initiated, for they who are not as yet initiated in good, and the affection thereof, that is who are not as yet fully regenerated, cannot do otherwise than think also of r., because in doing good, they do it not from the affection of good, but from the affection of somewhat blessed and happy in regard to themselves, and at the same time from a principle of fear in respect to hell; but when man is regenerated, this principle is then inverted, and becomes the affection of good, and in this case he no longer has respect to r. 3816. See *Issachar.*

Resin and the **Son of Remaliah.** (Isa. vii. 4.) R., king of Assyria, s. the knowledges of evil, and the son of Remaliah king of Syria, the knowledges of the false. 6952.

Rib (Gen. ii. 2.) s. man's proprium, wherein there is but little of any vital principle, but which indeed is dear to him; for a r. is a bone of the breast, and the breast with the most ancient people s. charity, inasmuch as it is the seat, both of the heart and lungs: and bones s. things of a viler nature, because there is very little of any vital principle in them. 148. By r. of the breast, in the Word, in the spiritual sense, is s., natural truth; this is s. by the r. which the bear carried between his teeth (Dan. vii. 5), for by bears are s. those who read the Word in its natural sense, and see truths therein, without understanding; by the breast of the man (Gen. ii.) is s. wisdom, for truth sustains wisdom, as a r. sustains the breast. C.S.L. 193. R. rep. knowledges imbibed in this life from the Word. A.E. 781. See *Bones.*

Rich Man and **Lazarus.** (Luke xvi. 19, 20.) By the r. m. is meant the Jewish nation, who are called rich because they were in possession of the Word, in which are spiritual riches. By the purple, and fine linen, with which the r. m. was clothed, are s. the good and truth of the Word, by purple its good, and by fine linen its truth, by faring sumptuously every day, is s. the delight which the Jewish people took in possessing the Word, and hearing it often read in their temples and synagogues; by the poor L., are meant the Gentiles, because they were not in possession of the Word; by L. lying at the r. man's gate is meant, that the Gentiles were despised and rejected

Riches

by the Jews; by being full of sores is s. that the Gentiles, by reason of their ignorance of truth, were under the influence of many falses. U.T. 215.

Riches s. the knowledges of good and truth. A.R. 206. R., when pred. concerning the Lord (Rev. v.) s. his divine omniscience. A.E. 338.

Riches and **Merchandise**. (Ezek. xxvi. 12, 13.) R. s. the knowledges of truth; and m. the knowledges of good. A.E. 1145.

Ride, to, s. to be elevated as to the intellectual principle. 3190. To r. upon a cherub (Ps. xviii. 9, 10) den. the Lord's providence, to prevent man's entering of himself into the mysteries of faith contained in the Word. 2761. To r. upon the clouds (Isa. xix. 1) s. to be in the wisdom of the Word. A.R. 24. To r. upon the high places of the earth (Isa. lviii. 13, 14), s. the peace and eternal felicity of the celestial man. 85. To r. upon the Word of truth and of meekness of righteousness (Ps. xlv. 1, 5), is to teach the doctrine of truth and goodness. 1288.

Right, or **Rectitude**, is pred. of truth. 612, 5434.

Right Hand, the, s. the all of man as to intellectual power, consequently, as to faith. A.R. 605. To place the r. h. on the head of any one, s. to regard in the first place. 6292.

Right Hand, man of the (Ps. lxxx. 18), s. the Lord with respect to the Word. He is called "the man of the right hand," because the Lord has power by virtue of divine truth, which also is the Word, and he had the divine power itself, when he fulfilled the whole Word; thus also he said that, "they should see the son of man sitting in power, on the r. h. of the Father." L. 27.

Right Hand and **Left Hand**. (Gen. xxiv. 49.) By not receding and declining to the r. h. or to the l., is s. not to go any other way than that which the Lord himself, and which the good and truth of heaven, and the church lead. A.E. 600. R. h., in a bad sense, s. evil from which the false is der., and the l. h., s. the false by which evil is produced. 10.061. In the spiritual world the south is on the r. h., and the north is on the l. A.R. 933.

Righteous is pred. of what is good. A.R. 173. By the righteousness which exceeds that of the scribes and pharisees, in Matt. v. 20, is meant interior righteousness, in which man is principled who is in the Lord. Dec. 84. To bring in everlasting righteousness (Dan. ix. 24) s. the last judgment, when to every one is given according to his deeds. A.E. 624. The Lord was not born righteousness as to his human essence, but was made righteousness by temptation, combats, and victories, and this by his own proper power; and as often as he fought and conquered, it was imputed to him for righteousness, that is, it was added to the righteousness which he was to be made, as a continual increase, until he became pure righteousness. 1813.

Righteousness and **Praise**. (Ps. xxxv. 28.) R. is pred. of the good of the church; and p. of its truth, as also in other parts of the Word. A.E. 455.

Ring. (Gen. xli. 42; Luke xvi. 22.) To give a r. s. what is confirmative of power. 5317.

Ring upon the Hand s. conjunction of good and truth. A.E. 279.

Rings. (Exod. xxv. 12.) By r. are s. the conjunction of good and truth, and here, that of divine truth with divine good. 9493. See *Earrings*.

Ripe is pred. of the final state of the church. A.R. 650.

Ripen, to (Gen. xl. 10), den. the progress of the rebirth, or regeneration, even to the conjunction of truth with good. 5117.

Riphath (Gen. x. 3) was one of those several nations, which were principled in external worship, and which s. so many several doctrinals, which respected ritual observances, der., from external worship prevailing with Gomer, as appears from the prophetical writings, where the same nations are also mentioned, and by them are s. doctrinals, or rituals, in each sense, sometimes in the genuine sense, sometimes in the opp., as is usual with the prophets. 1154.

Rise, to (Gen. xxvii. 19), s. somewhat of elevation. 3552. To r. (Gen. xxxi. 35) s. to reveal or to discover. 4160. To r. early in the morning s. confirmation in good and truth. 2332. To r. up (Gen. xviii. 16) s. that perception was finished. 2218. To r. day and night s. in every state. A.E. 911.

Rituals were accounted holy, in consequence of their rep. the holy things of heaven, and the church by cor. 4581.

River of Delights (Ps. xxxvi. 8) s. the spiritual which has relation to faith originating in love. 353.

River out of Eden (Gen. ii. 10) s. wisdom proceeding from love, which is E. 107.

River, great, and River Euphrates. (Josh. i. 4.) The great r. s. the influx of spiritual into rational things, and the r. E. the influx of rational into natural, and both together the influx of spiritual things through the rational, into natural things. A.E. 569. See *Euphrates.*

River of Water of Life (Rev. xxii. 1) s. in particular the divine truths in abundance, now revealed by the Lord in the Apocalypse. A.R. 932.

Rivers s. truths in abundance serving the rational man, consequently, the understanding, for the purpose of doctrine and of life. A.R. 683. R. or floods s. temptations. A.R. 409. R. and waters s. difficulties, and also falses. (Isa. xliii. 2.) 790.

Roar as a Lion, to (Isa. xxxi. 4), which is pred. of Jehovah, s. the ardent affection of defending heaven and the church against evils and falses. In an opp. sense, the roaring of a l. s. the desire of destroying and of making desolate. A.E. 278, 304, 605. To r. as a l. (Rev. x. 3) s. grievous lamentation concerning the state of the church; for a l. roars when he sees his enemies and is assaulted by them, and sees his whelps and his prey taken from him; and so does the Lord, comparatively, when he sees his church taken from him by devils, as is evident from many other passages. A.R. 471.

Roast and **Boiled.** (Exod. xii. 9.) In the Word a distinction is made between what is r. and what is b., and by r. is s. good, because by fire; and by b. is meant truth, because by water; and hence the paschal lamb, which rep. the good of innocence, was commanded to be r. with fire, and not sodden at all with water. 7852.

Robbers s. falses as well as evils. A.E. 919.

Robe, Aaron's, s. divine truth in its internal form, which is the medium of the spiritual kingdom; thus the truth itself which is therein. 9825.

Robe of Righteousness (Isa. lxi. 10) s. the good of charity. 2576.

Robes (Rev. vii.) s. truths of defence in general, and before they were washed, falses; for they who are in falses from ignorance, in the spiritual world, appear first in obscure garments of divers colors, and while they are in temptations, in filthy garments; but when they come out of temptations, they appear in white r., clean according to their purification from falses. A.E. 475.

Robes, Mantles, and **Cloaks**, s. truths in common, because they were garments common to the whole body and covered over all. A.R. 328.

Rock s. the Lord as to the divine truth of the Word. A.R. 915. See *Hole and Cleft of a Rock.*

Rock of Israel, the (2 Sam. xxiii. 3, 4), s. the Lord. A.R. 53. R. of I. (Isa. xxx. 29) s. the Lord with respect to the goods of charity. 795.

Rocks s. the good and truth of faith. 8581, 10.580. See *Heaven.*

Rod, or **Staff**, s. power, and is pred. concerning divine spiritual truth. A.E. 726. R. and s. (Ps. xxiii. 3) s. the divine truth and good to which belongs power. 4876. R. and s. have an opp. sense. (Isa. xiv. 5; Ps. cxxv. 3, etc., etc.) A.E. 727. See *Staff.*

Rod coming out of the stem of Jesse (Isa. xi. 5), s. the Lord in his divine humanity. A.R. 46, 954.

Rod of Iron

Rod of **Iron.** By ruling with a r. of i. (Rev. ii. 27) is s. to rule by truths from the literal sense of the Word, and, at the same time, by rational principles der. from natural light. A.R. 148.

Rod of the **Mouth** of **Jehovah** and the **Spirit** of his **Lips.** (Isa. xi. 4.) R. of the m. of J. s. here the divine truth, or the Word, in the natural sense; and the s. of his l. s. divine truth, or the Word, in its spiritual sense. A.E. 727.

Rods, twelve (Num. xvii. 6), s. the same as the twelve tribes, because the same word, in the original language, is used for rod as for tribe. (Num. i. 16; ii. 5, 7.) A.E. 727.

Roe, or **Roebuck,** s. affection of good and truth. 6413.

Roll, to, **away** the **Stone** from the **Door** of the **Lord's Sepulchre** (Matt. xxviii. 2), s. the removal, by the Lord, of all the falsity which intercepted and hindered approach to him, and thus to open divine truth. A.E. 400.

Roll, to, **away** the **Stone** from **over** the **Well's Mouth** (Gen. xxix. 10), s. to uncover the Word as to its interior contents. 5798.

Roll, the, in Ezekiel, and the **Little Book** in the Apocalypse, s. the divine truth. 5620. See *Volume, or Roll.*

Rolls of **Parchment.** In ancient times there were no books, but only r. of p. A.E. 404.

Romans. Italians, Greeks, and R. der. their worship from the ancient church in Canaan. 8944.

Roman Catholic Religion is external without internal; hence the priests only drink the wine, and profanation is thus guarded against. 10.040.

Roof of a **House** s. what is inmost, the like as the head. 3652, 10.184.

Room, or **Place,** den. state. 2625.

Root (Mal. iv. 1) s. charity. 1861. R. dried up (Hosea ix. 16, 17) s. charity which could not bear fruit. 382.

Root of **David** s. the Lord as to divine good united to divine truth in his humanity. A.E. 310. A.R. 266. R. of Isaac (Isa. xi. 10) s. the Lord. A.E. 175. R. of Jesse s. the Lord. 2468. R. of the Serpent (Isa. xiv. 29) s. scientifics. 1197.

Rope, or **Cord,** den. conjunction. 9854.

Roses, bed of, s. the delights of the truth of wisdom. C.S.L. 293.

Rosin, or **Gum** (Gen. xliii. 11), s. the truth of good, or the truth der. from good, because it ranks amongst ointments, and also amongst aromatics; aromatics s. such things as are of truth der. from good, and especially when they are also ointments, and partake somewhat of oiliness, for oil s. good. 5620.

Rotation. Punishment by r. des. 956.

Rough Places made Plain (Isa. xl. 4) s. the falses of ignorance turned into truths. 3527.

Round. What is r. is pred. of good. 8458. A small r. thing (Exod. xvi. 14) is pred. concerning the good of truth in its first formation, for what is small, is pred. of truth. 8458.

Round About den. those things which are most distant from the midst, or from good and truth. 2973.

Rowers, or those that handle the oar. (Ezek. xxviii. 29, 30.) By them that handle the oar are s. the intelligent. A.E. 514.

Royalty of the **Lord** s. heaven and the church. A.R. 664.

Ruby s. the truth of celestial good. 9865. A.E. 364. R. is the appearance of the Lord's divine sphere rep. in the celestial heavens. A.R. 232. The Word is a r. by virtue of its celestial flame. S.S. 42.

Ruddiness is pred. of good, as whiteness of truth. 3300.

Ruin, day of, s. the last judgment. A.E. 538.

Rule, grounded in truths alone, would condemn every one to hell, but r. grounded in goodness raises up out of hell, and elevates into heaven. 2015.

Ruler of the Feast (John ii. 9) s. those who are in the knowledges of truth: by his saying to the bridegroom, "every man at first doth set forth good wine, and when men have well drank, then that which is worse, but thou hast kept the good wine until now," is s. that every church commences in truths from good, but declines into truths without good, but that, nevertheless, now in the end of the church truth from good, or genuine truth is given, namely, from the Lord. A.E. 376.

Ruler, or Governor, s. goods of the church, and, in the opp. sense, falses. A.E. 811, 863.

Ruling Evil, the, in the posterity of the most ancient church, was self-love, and not so much the love of the world, as at this day, for they lived apart from each other, according to their houses and families, and had no desire to accumulate wealth. The r. e. in the most ancient church, which was immediately before the flood, and in the ancient church, which was after the flood, and also in the Jewish church, and afterwards in the new church established amongst the Gentiles, after the coming of the Lord, was this, that they did not believe the Lord or the Word, but themselves and their senses: hence faith became annihilated, and in consequence thereof, neighborly love was annihilated, so that nothing remained but falsehood and evil; and this incredulity is also the r. e. of the present church; however, in the present church, the evil is much greater than in former times, inasmuch as men at this day can confirm the incredulity of the senses by scientifics unknown to the ancients, which have given birth to an indescribable darkness, whereat mankind would be astonished, did they but know how great and terrible it is. 230, 232.

Ruling Love of Man. The end proposed rules in all and every thing that a man thinks and does; the angels attendant on man, being angels of the Lord, rule and govern only the ends proposed by man, knowing that whilst they rule and govern these, they rule and govern also his thoughts and actions, inasmuch as all his thoughts and actions are dependent on the ends proposed; the end proposed by man is his very essential life, and all things which he thinks or does der. life from it, because they are dependent thereon, wherefore, such as is the end proposed, such is the life of man. 1317. See *Love.*

Rumah, Nahor's concubine (Gen. xxii.), s. the Gentiles who are in idolatrous worship and principled in good: her name implies her quality, namely exaltation. 2868.

Rumor and Violence. (Jer. li. 46.) A r. s. such things as belong to understanding; v., such things as belong to will. 622.

Rumors of War den. discussions and strifes con. truths. 3353.

Run, to, to meet any One (Gen. xxix. 13), s. agreement. 3806. To r. to meet (Gen. xxxiii. 4) s. influx. 4350. To r. and tell (Gen. xxix. 12) s. the affection of making known. 3804. To r. and not be weary has respect to the will; and to walk and not faint has respect to the understanding. (Isa. xl. 31.) 8901.

Rupture, or Breach, den. infraction and perversion of truth. 4926. Truths destroyed by falses. A.E. 519.

Rushes. Reeds and r. s. science from a sensual origin. A.E. 627.

Rye (Exod. ix. 32) s. the truth of the interior natural principle cor. to the good which is signified by wheat. 7605.

Rythm. The speech of good and angelic spirits flows into r. 1648.

S

Sabbath-Day. The s. among the children of Israel was the sanctity of sanctities, because it rep. the Lord, six days being s. of his labors and combats with the hells, and the seventh of his victory over them, and of the rest which he thereby attained; and whereas that day was rep. of the close and period of the whole act of redemption, which the Lord accomplished, therefore it was esteemed very and essential holiness. But when the Lord came into the world and in consequence thereof made all rep. of himself to cease, that day was then made a day of instruction in divine things, and thereby also a day of rest from labors and of meditation on subjects that concerned salvation and eternal life, and also a day for the exercise of love towards our neighbor. By the natural sense of the commandment, "to remember the s.-d. to keep it holy," is meant, that six days are for man, and his labors, and that the seventh is for the Lord, and man's rest in dependence on the Lord; for the word s., in the original tongue, s. rest. By this commandment, in a spiritual sense, is s. the reformation and regeneration of man by the Lord, by six days of labor, his warfare against the flesh and its concupiscences, and at the same time against the evils and falses which are with him from hell; and by the seventh day, is s. his conjunction with the Lord and regeneration thereby. The reason why the reformation and regeneration of man are s., in a spiritual sense, by this commandment, is, because they coincide with the labors and combats of the Lord against the hells, and with his victory over them, and the rest into which he then entered. In a celestial sense, by this commandment is meant, conjunction with the Lord and its attendant peace, in consequence of the divine protection from the powers of hell; for by the s. is s. rest, and in this highest sense peace, on which account the Lord is called "the prince of peace," and styles himself peace in the abstract. Hence also the Lord styles himself "lord of the s." U.T. 301, 303. To do no work on the s.-d., s. that nothing should be done from proprium, but from the Lord. 8495. See *Laws of the Jewish Church.*

Sabbaths. (Exod. xxxi. 13.) "Verily my s. ye shall keep," s. holy thought continually concerning the union of the Lord's divine with his human. 10.356.

Sabeans, the merchandise of, den. knowledges of spiritual things ministering to those who acknowledge the Lord. 1164.

Sabtah and **Sabtahikah** s. the various knowledges of spiritual things. 1168.

Sack (Gen. xlii. 25) s. a receptacle, and here a receptacle in the natural principle, because the subject treated of is concerning the truths and scientifics which are in the natural principle; s. in this passage specifically s. the scientific principle, by reason that as a s. is a receptacle of corn, so the scientific principle is a receptacle of good, in the present case of the good which is from truth. 5489.

Sackcloth. By being clothed in s. is s. lamentation on account of the devastation of truth in the church. A.R. 492. S. (Rev. vi. 12) is pred. of destroyed good. 4779.

Sacrament, a, is nothing else but a binding. 3046. A s. (Gen. xxvi. 29) s. consent of doctrinals with the literal sense of the Word. 3452. The s. of bap-

268

tism and the holy supper are the most holy institutions of worship in the christian church. U.T. 699. See *Baptism, Supper.*

Sacrifices and **Burnt Offerings**. All the process of regeneration is des. by singular the rituals of every s. and b. o., and is made manifest, when the rep. are unfolded by the internal sense. They also s. the glorification of the Lord's humanity. 10.042.

Sad. Certain spirits who are in the province of the stomach, induce what is s. and melancholy, likewise anxiety. 6202.

Saddle, to (Gen. xxii. 3), s. to prepare. 2781.

Sages. What their ideas were with regard to the immortality of the soul. D.P. 324.

Sahah den. the offspring of science. 1235.

Sailors trust more to divine providence than landsmen. C. 96. See *Mariners.*

Saints, popish, in the spiritual world des. L.J. 61–5.

Saints s. those who are in divine truths from the Lord. A.R. 586.

Saints and the **Righteous.** S. s. those who are of the Lord's spiritual kingdom, and the r., those of his celestial kingdom. A.R. 393.

Salem s. a state of peace and perfection, or the the tranquillity of peace. 1726, 4993. S. (Ps. lxxvi. 3) s. the Lord's spiritual kingdom where there is genuine truth. A.E. 357.

Salt, s. the desire of conjunction of truth with good, hence nothing but s. will conjoin water, which cor. to truth, and oil, which cor. to good. 10.300. S., in a genuine sense, s. the affection of truth, and, in an opp. sense, the vastation of the affection of truth, that is of good in truth. Inasmuch as s. s. vastation, and cities s. doctrinals of truth, therefore in old time they sowed with s. cities that were destroyed, to prevent their being rebuilt. (See Judges ix. 45.) A.E. 2455. By Lot's wife becoming a statue of s., is s. that all the good of truth in the church rep. by Lot was vastated; for truth averted itself from good, and looked to doctrinals. 2453.

Salvation to the **Lord** our **God** (Rev. xix. 1) s. an acknowledgment and confession that there is s. from the Lord. A.R. 804.

Salvation of **Man**, the, is a continual operation of the Lord in m., from his earliest infancy to the latest period of his life, and this is such a divine work, that it is at once the work of omnipresence, omniscience and omnipotence; and the reformation and regeneration of m., consequently, his s., is all a work of the divine providence of the Lord. The very coming of the Lord into the world was solely for the sake of m. s.; on this account he assumed the human nature, removed the hells, and glorified himself, and invested himself with omnipotence even in ultimates, which is meant by his sitting at the right hand of God. A.R. 798. See *Celestial.*

Salve, eye, s. a medicine whereby the understanding is healed. A.R. 214.

Samaria (Amos iv. 1; vi. 1) s. the spiritual church perverted. 2220.

Samaria, woman of, s. the church to be raised up among the Gentiles. A.E. 537.

Samaria and **Jerusalem.** (Ezek. xxiii.) S. the church which is in the affection of truth, and J. is the church which is in the affection of good. 2466.

Samaritan. By the S. in Luke x. are meant the Gentiles who were in charity towards their neighbor. A.E. 375. The S. s. the Gentiles or nations which would receive doctrine from the Lord and concerning him. A.E. 537. City of the S. (Matt. x. 5) s. the false doctrine of those who reject the Lord. A.E. 223.

Samson rep. the Lord, who, by virtue of the natural man as to truth, fought with the hells and subdued them, and this, before he put on divine good and truth, also as to the natural man. 3301. A.E. 619. S. rep. the only Nazarite, namely, the Lord, and the power of his righteousness, who subjugated all diabolical spirits, that is, conquered death. Adv. See *Nazarites.* See *Hairs of the Head.*

Samuel

Samuel, in a rep. sense, s. the Word. A.E. 750.

Sanctification. It is the divine good which sanctifies, and the divine truth is what is thence holy. A.E. 204.

Sanctify, to, den. being led of the Lord. 8806. Den. not to be capable of being violated. 8887.

Sanctuary s. the truth of heaven and the church. 8330. A.E. 768. S. (Ezek. xxiv. 21) s. the Word. A.E. 724.

Sanctuary and **Habitation** s. heaven and the church, s. as to the good of love, and h., as to truths of that good; for the Lord dwells in truths from good. A.E. 701.

Sand (Matt. vii. 27). s. faith separate from charity. A.E. 212. S. "Treasures hid in the s." (Deut. xxxiii. 19), s. the spiritual things which lie hid in the literal sense of the Word. A.E. 445.

Sand upon the Sea-shore (Gen. xxii.) s. a multitude of scientifics, for sea den. scientifics in general or their gathering together, and s. den. scientifics in particular; scientifics are compared to s. because the little stones of which s. consists, in the internal sense, are scientifics. 2850. S. of the sea (Rev. xiii. 1) s. a state spiritual-natural, such as theirs is, who are in the first or ultimate heaven. A.R. 561 1–2.

Sandal-tree s. things which are of the natural man. A.E. 518.

Sapphire Stone (Exod. xxiv. 10) s. spiritual good. 9407. Work of a s. s. (Exod. xxiv. 10) is the quality of the literal sense of the Word, when the internal sense is perceived therein. 9407.

Sapphire Stone and **Onyx Stone**. S. s., in a general sense, s. the external of the celestial kingdom of the Lord, and the o. s., the external of his spiritual kingdom. 9873.

Sarah den. truth adjoined to good. 1468. Sarai was called S. that she might rep. the divine intellectual principle by the adjunction of the h. in the name of Jehovah. 2603. "Thou shalt not call her name Sarai, but S. shall her name be," s. that the Lord shall put off the humanity, and put on the divinity. 2060, 2063. S. s. divine truth. 2063. S. as a mother rep. truth divine. 3210. S. as a wife (Gen. xviii. 6) s. rational truth appertaining to the Lord. 2173. S. as a wife s. truth intellectual, or spiritual, conjoined to divine good, or what is celestial. 2507. S. as a sister, den. the rational principle. 1495, 2508, 2531.

Sardine Stone, because it is red, indicates the things which appertain to the good of love, or, the goods of the Word in ultimates. A.R. 231.

Sardis. The church in S. (Rev. iii. 1) s. those who are in dead worship. A.R. 154. Also those who live a moral life, but not a spiritual life. A.E. 182.

Sardonyx is supposed to der. its name from participating in the qualities of sardine and onyx. Ap. Rev. 915.

Sarepta. Widow of S. s. obedience and the desire of good to truth. 9188.

Satan and **Devil**. S. has respect to falses and d. to evils. C.S.L. 492. S. s. those who are in the pride of self-derived intelligence. A.R. 97. See *Devil and Satan*.

Satiate. Pred. of as much as one wills, whether it be of good or evil. 8410.

Satiated, to be (Rev. xix. 21), s. to be nourished with concupiscences, as it were, and to draw them in with delight. A.R. 837.

Satiety is pred. of the reception of good, for good is the spiritual nourishment of the soul, as natural food is the nourishment of the body. A.E. 376.

Satisfied with Favor and **full with** the **Blessing of the Lord**. To be filled with the good of love is understood by being s. with f., and to be filled with truths thence, by being full with the b. of the L. A.E. 439.

Satisfy, that which nourishes the soul. A.E. 617.

Saturn. The inhabitants of this planet are upright and modest, and inasmuch as they esteem themselves little, therefore, they also appear little in another life. In acts of divine worship they are exceedingly humble, for on such occasions they account themselves as nothing. They worship our Lord, and acknowledge him as the only God; the Lord also appears to them at times under an angelic form, and thereby, as a man, and at such times the divine beams forth from the face and affects the mind. The inhabitants also when they arrive at a certain age, discourse with spirits, by whom they are instructed concerning the Lord, how he ought to be worshipped, and likewise how they ought to live. The inhabitants and spirits of the planet S. have relation in the grand man, to the middle sense between the spiritual and the natural man, but to that which recedes from the natural, and accedes to the spiritual. E.U. 97, 98, 102, 104.

Satyrs (Isa. xiii. 21) s. goods adulterated. A.E. 1029. S. and priapusses are those who are particularly addicted to obscenity. C.S.L. 44.

Saul, as a king, rep. divine truth. A.R. 166. S. (1 Sam. xvi. 23) rep. the falses which are opp. to spiritual truths, and which were dissipated by the sound of David's harp, for harp cor. to the affection of spiritual truth. A.E. 323.

Saul and **Jonathan**. S. as a king, s. truth from good, and J. the son of a king, s. the truth of doctrine. A.E. 357. See *Bow of Jonathan*.

Save, to. It is of the divine providence that every man is capable of being saved, and those are s. who acknowledge a God and lead a good life. D.P. 325. 332–4.

Saviour. The Lord from the essential divine, through the divine human, is the s. A.R. 961. The Lord became a s., by his spiritual temptations, or combats. L.33.

Saviour and **Prince**. (Isa. xix. 18, 25.) S. is pred. of the Lord as to the good of love; and p., as to the truths of faith from him. A.E. 654.

Savor is pred. of the perception of a thing. A.E. 617.

Savory Meats (Gen. xxvii.) s. the agreeable things which are of truth. 3536.

Say, to, s. to perceive, and to speak s. to think: as for example, when it is said, in the Word, that Jehovah said, it s. that he perceives from the divine celestial principle, and when it is said, that he speaks, it means thought from the divine celestial principle, by the divine spiritual. (See Gen. xxi. 1.) When, however, there is mention made of saying alone, it sometimes s. to perceive, and sometimes to think, because saying involves both. 2619.

Sayings den. to persuade. 4478. When pred. of Jehovah s. to inform or instruct. 8041.

Scab, a (Isa. v. 7), s. evil. 2240.

Scales of a fish (Ezek. xxix. 4) s. scientifics of the lowest order, such as the fallacies of the senses. A.E. 654.

Scandal. A sphere of s. against the Lord, perceived as putrid water. 4629. What is meant by s. 4302.

Scape Goat s. the communication and translation of all the iniquities and sins of the sons of Israel and their remission into hell. 10.023.

Scarlet (Isa. i. 18) s. truth der. from good (A.E. 67); or truth from a celestial origin, such as is the truth of the Word in its literal and natural sense. (Rev. xvii. 3.) A.E. 1038.

Scarlet Double-Dyed (Gen. xxxviii. 28) s. spiritual good. 4922.

Scarlet and **Purple** (Isa. i. 8) s. false and evil. A.E. 1042. See *Purple*.

Scarlet-colored Beast. (Rev. xvii. 3.) By s. is s. truth of the Word proceeding from a celestial origin. By the s. b. is s. the Word with respect to divine celestial truth. And inasmuch as the Roman Catholic religion rests its strength and dignity upon the Word, therefore the woman appeared sitting upon a s. b. as she had appeared before upon many waters (verse 1), by which waters are s. truths of the Word adulterated and profaned. That by b. is s. the Word, appears manifestly from the things said of it in the follow-

271

Scattered Abroad

ing passages of the chapter, as in verses 8, 11, 12, 13, 17: which things can only be said of the Word. A.R. 723.

Scattered Abroad over the face of the **whole Earth** (Gen. xi. 4), s. not to be received and acknowledged. 1309.

Scent s. perception. A.R. 611.

Sceptre and Staff. S. s. divine truth as to government, and staff, divine truth, as to power. A.E. 431.

Schaddai (Gen. xliii. 14) s. temptation, and after temptation consolation. The reason why S. s. temptation and after temptation consolation, is, because the ancients marked the one only God by various names, according to the various things which are from him; and inasmuch as they believed also that temptations are from him, they called God on this occasion S., yet by this name they did not mean another God, but the only God as to temptations; but when the ancient church declined, they began to worship as many gods as there were names of the one only God, and they also of themselves superadded several more; this custom was at length so prevalent, that every family had its own god, and he was distinguished altogether from the rest who were worshipped by other families: the family of Terah, from which Abraham came, worshipped S. for its God, hence not only Abraham, but also Jacob, acknowledged him as their God, and also in the land of Canaan: howbeit this was permitted them, lest they should be forced from their religious principle, for no one is forced from what he regards as holy; but whereas the ancients by S. understood Jehovah himself or the Lord, who was so named when they underwent temptations, therefore Jehovah or the Lord took this name, in appearing to Abraham (Gen. xvii. 1), and also in appearing to Jacob. (Gen. xxv. 11.) The reason why not temptation only, but also consolation, is s. by S., is, because all spiritual temptations are succeeded by consolation, for when any one in another life suffers hardships from evil spirits, by infestations, excitations to evils, and persuasions to falses, no sooner are the evil spirits removed, than he is received by the angels, and is brought into a state of comfort by delight agreeable to his genius and temper. 5628.

Schalem. The tranquillity of peace. 4393.

Schur. Exterior or scientific truth. 2497.

Sciences and languages after death are of no avail, but only the things which man has learnt and imbibed by them. 2480.

Scientific Principle is the natural principle, because the s. p. is truth appearing in the light of the world, but the truth of faith, inasmuch as it is of faith with man, is in the light of heaven. 9568.

Scientific Truth is all scientifics by which spiritual truth is confirmed, and der. its life from spiritual good. A.E. 507.

Scientifics are of three kinds, intellectual, rational, and sensual, all of which are sown in the memory of man or rather in his memories, and in the regenerate are thence called forth of the Lord, by the internal man; these s. which have their birth from things sensual, come to man's sensation or perception during his life in the body, for they are the ground of his thought; the rest, which are more interior, do not so come to his sensation, or perception, before he puts off the body, and enters into another life. 991. S. are what first enter in at the senses, and thereby open the way to the interiors, it being a known thing, that the external sensuals are first opened with man, and next the interior sensuals, and finally the intellectuals, and when the intellectuals are opened, then these latter are rep. in the former, that they may be capable of being apprehended: the reason is, because intellectual things arise out of the things of sense by a method of extraction, for intellectual things are conclusions, and when conclusions are made, they are separated and sublimated; this is effected by the influx of things spiritual, which influx is through heaven from the Lord. 5580. S. must be arranged in order in the natural principle, before the arrangement of the truths of the church can be effected, because the latter are to be apprehended by the former; for nothing can enter the understanding of man, without ideas acquired from such s. as man has procured to himself from infancy. Man is altogether ignorant that every truth of the church which is called a truth of faith, is founded upon his s., and that he apprehends it, and keeps it in the memory, and calls it forth from the memory, by ideas wrought from the s. appertaining to him. 5510. The s. to which those things that are of faith and charity can be in-applied, are very many, as all the s. of the church which are s. by Egypt in the good sense, consequently, all the s. which are true concerning cor., concerning rep., concerning s., concerning influx, concerning order, concerning intelligence and wisdom, concerning affections, yea all truths of interior and exterior nature, as well visible as invisible, because these cor. to spiritual truths. 5213. S. abide after death, but are quiescent. 2476–2479. The interiors of s. are those things which are spiritual in the natural principle, and spiritual things are in the natural principle, when the s. in that principle are illustrated by the light of heaven, and they are then illustrated by the light of heaven, when man has faith in the doctrinals which are from the Word, and he then has faith when he is in the good of charity; for in such case truths, and thereby s., are illustrated by the good of charity, as by flame, and hence have their spiritual light. 5637.

Scientifics and **Knowledges** are the first things on which are raised and grounded the civil, moral, and spiritual life of man, but they are to be learned for the use of life as their end. 1489.

Scientifics and **Knowledges from the Word.** By s. from the Word are understood all things contained in the literal sense, in which the doctrinal appears; but by the k. of truth and good, are understood all things of the literal sense, in which, and from which, there is somewhat doctrinal. A.E. 345.

Scorch, to, Men with Fire (Rev. xvi. 8) s. that love to the Lord torments those who are in concupiscences of evils originating in the delight of self-love. A.R. 691.

Scorpion s. deadly persuasion; for a s., when he stings a man, induces stupor upon the limbs, and, if he be not cured, death. A.R. 425, 427.

Scortations cor. with the violation of spiritual marriage. C.S.L. 515–520.

Scortatory Love, opp. to conjugial love, means the love of adultery, when it is such that it is not reputed as a sin, nor as evil and dishonorable against reason, but as what is allowable with reason. C.S.L. 423–444. The delights of s. l. commence from the flesh, and they are of the flesh, even in the spirit, but the delights of conjugial love, commence in the spirit, and they are of the spirit, even in the flesh. C.S.L. 439.

Scourged s. to pervert. A.E. 655. See *Mocked, etc.*

Scribe (Isa. xxxiii. 18) den. intelligence. A.E. 453. S. (Matt. xxiii. 34) s. the Word from which doctrine is der. 655. Chief priests and s. (Matt. xx. 17) s. the adulterations of good and the falsifications of truth. 658.

Scribes and **Pharisees.** By righteousness which is to exceed that of the s. and p., is s. interior righteousness. Dec. 84.

Scrip and **Purse** s. knowledges of good and truth. A.E. 840.

Scripture, sacred. The sacred s., or word, is divine truth itself. C.T. 189. The whole sacred s. is nothing else but the doctrine of love and charity. N.J.D. 9.

Scroll. (Rev. vi. 14.) The heaven departed as a s. rolled together s. the separation from heaven and conjunction with hell, of those on whom the last judgment was executed. A.R. 335.

Sculptured Thing s. falses from self-der. intelligence. A.E. 304. Images den. things fashioned from man's own intelligence. 8941.

Scum

Scum and **Uncleanness.** s. what is evil and false. 4744.

Sea, the, in which waters terminate and are collected, s. divine truth in its terminations. The s. is an appearance of the divine truth proceeding from the Lord in its terminations, and divine truth in its terminations in the spiritual world, causes the appearance of a s. The s. also in the Hebrew language is called the west, that is, where the light of the sun declines towards evening, or truth into obscurity; s. also s. the natural of man separated from the spiritual, and consequently, hell. A.R. 238. The s. s. the external of heaven and of the church, in which are the simple, who have thought naturally, and but little spiritually of things relating to the church. A.R. 878. The s., considered with respect to the water, s. the scientific principle in general, and considered with respect to waves is s. dispute and ratiocination, which are maintained by scientifics, therefore, the s. s. the natural man. A.E. 511. S. (Rev. xviii. 17) s. the Roman Catholic religion. A.R. 786. "The s. gave up the dead that were in it" (Rev. xix. 13) s. the external and natural men of the church called to judgment. A.R. 869. S. (Zech. xiv. 8) s. the natural man in whom those things descend which are in the spiritual principle; the eastern s. s. the natural man as to good, and the hinder s., the natural man as to truth. A.E. 275. The s. in the spiritual world form the boundaries of the earth eastward and westward. A.E. 406.

Sea of Glass Mingled with Fire. By s. of g. (Rev. iv. 6) is s. the new heaven of christians, who were in truths of a common or general nature from the literal sense of the Word; they who are in common truths, are also in the borders of heaven, wherefore at a distance they seem to be in the sea. But in Rev. xv. 2, by s. of g. is s. the ultimate boundary of the spiritual world, where they were collected who had religion and consequent worship, but not good of life; inasmuch as a collection of these is s., therefore it is said, as it were, a s. of g., and, moreover, it appeared mingled with fire, and by fire there is s. the love of evil, and consequent evil of life, of course, not the good of life, for where there is no good, there is evil. It is this sea also which is meant in Rev. xxi. 1, by the sea which is no more. A.R. 659.

Sea, Red, in which Pharaoh was drowned, s. hell. 7273.

Sea, Red, the **Sea** of the **Philistines,** and the **River Euphrates** (Exod. xxiii. 31.) The R. S. s. scientific truth, the s. of the P., the knowledges of truth and good from the literal sense of the Word, and the r. E., the rational principle; for scientifics serve the knowledges of truth and good from the Word, and these with them serve the rational, and the rational serves for intelligence which is given by spiritual truths conjoined to spiritual good. A.E. 518.

Sea and **Earth.** The s. s. the external of the church, consequently, the church, as consisting of those who are in its externals; and the e. s. the internal of the church, and, consequently, the church as consisting of those who are in its internals; wherefore the s. s. the church among the laity, because they are in its externals, and the e., the church among the clergy, because they are in its internals. A.R. 398, 680. S. den. natural truths, and e., natural goods. (Rev. x. 2.) 2162.

Sea and the **Waves Roaring** (Luke xxi. 25) s. that heresies and controversies, in general within the church, and in particular in every individual, would be thus noisy and outrageous at the last time of the church, or its last judgment. 2120.

Seal, to, in the forehead, s. to distinguish and separate one from the other according to the love. A.R. 347.

Seal up the Vision and **Prophecy,** to (Dan. ix. 24), s. to conclude those things which are said in the Word concerning the Lord and to fulfil them. A.E. 375.

See

Seal up those Things which the Seven Thunders Uttered and **Write them not** (Rev. x. 4) s. that they will not be committed to the heart and receive till after the dragon, the beast, and false prophet are cast out of the world of spirits, because there would be danger if they were received before. A.R. 473.

Seal not the **Words** of the **Prophecy** of this **Book** (Rev. xxii. 10) s. that the Apocalypse must not be shut, for the truths and precepts of doctrine in it are opened by the Lord. A.R. 947. A.E. 1350.

Seal of the Living God. (Rev. vii. 2.) By having the s. of the l. G., as spoken of the Lord, is meant to know all and every one, and be able to distinguish and separate the servants of God from those who are not the servants of God. A.R. 345.

Seals, the seven, mentioned in the Apocalypse, being opened, s. the exploration of the quality and state of those upon whom the last judgment was executed, anno. 1757. A.R. 259.

Search, to (Rev. ii. 23), s. to see. A.R. 140.

Seasons of the **Year,** s. states of the church. D.L.W. 73.

Seba, Havilah, Sabthah, Regmah, and **Sabthecha** (the sons of Cush) (Gen. x. 7), were so many several nations who were not principled in internal worship, but in the knowledges of faith, in the possession whereof they made religion to consist. In an internal sense, by the same nations, are s. the knowledges themselves. 1168.

Seba s. the spiritual things of worship. A.E. 1171.

Second Coming of the Lord, the, is not a coming in person, but in the Word, which is from him, and is himself. The clouds of heaven, in which the Lord is to come, is meant the Word in the sense of the letter. U.T. 776. See *Advent of the Lord, Coming of the Lord.*

Second Death s. spiritual death, which is damnation. A.R. 853.

Second Month (Gen. viii. 14) s. every state before regeneration, which appears from the s. of two in the Word; two s. the same as six, that is, combat and labor which precede regeneration, consequently, in the present case every state which precedes before man is regenerate. 900.

Secret, or **Hidden,** s. inwardly in man. The s. place s. where the Lord is. 638.

Secretions, the, of the human body, and spirits to which they cor. 5380.

Security s. the external delight of heaven. A.E. 365. S. Of life is induced by a belief in instantaneous salvation. Exp. D.P. 340.

Sedge (Gen. xl. 2), or the larger grass, which is near rivers, s. scientifics which are of the natural man; that grass or herb den. scientifics, is clear from the Word. To feed in the s. is to be instructed in scientifics, and by scientifics concerning truths and goods. 5201.

Sediment of the **Waters.** A.E. 741. To persuade falses. A.E. 826.

Seduce, to (Rev. xii. 9), s. to pervert. A.R. 551.

Seduction (Gen. xxvii. 12) s. what is contrary to order. 3528.

See, to, cor. to the affection of understanding, and when pred. of God, means that he knows all and every thing from eternity. 626. To s. (Gen. xix. 1) s. conscience. 2325. To s. afar off (Gen. xxii. 4) s. to foresee. 2790.

See the face of God and **the Lamb,** to. (Rev. xxii.) By seeing the face of G. and of the L., or of the Lord, is not meant to see his face, because no one can see his face, such as he is in his divine love, and in his divine wisdom, and live, he being the sun of heaven and of the whole spiritual world; for to see his face, such as he is in himself would be as if any one should enter into the sun, by the fire whereof he would be consumed in a moment; nevertheless, the Lord sometimes presents himself to be seen out of his sun, but then he veils himself, and so presents himself to their sight, which is done by means of an angel, as he also did in the world to Abraham, Hagar, Lot, Gideon, Joshua, and others, for which reason those angels were called

Seed

angels, and also Jehovah, for the presence of Jehovah at a distance was in them. But by seeing his face here, is not meant to see his face, but to see the truths which are in the Word from him, and through them to know and acknowledge him; for the divine truths of the Word make the light which proceeds from the Lord as a sun, in which the angels are, and whereas they make the light, they are like glasses, in which the Lord's face is seen. A.R. 938.

Seed s. love, and also every one who has love. (See Gen. xii. 7; xiii. 15, 16.) 1025. S. s. faith grounded in charity. 3038. S. s. all who constitute the Lord's spiritual kingdom. 3187. S. s. good and truth from the Lord. 3373. S., in an opp. sense, s. the false of doctrine, and the infernal false. A.E. 768. S. s. the ultimate and primary principles of man. A.R. 936. See *Coriander Seed, Mustard Seed.*

Seed of Evil-Doers, a, and **Children that are Corrupters.** (Isa. i. 4.) A s. of e.-d. s. the false of those who are in evils; and c. that are c., the falses of those who are in falses from that evil. A.E. 768. A.C. 622.

Seed of Holiness (Isa. vi. 13) s. a remnant or remains. 468.

Seed of **Man.** In the s. of m. is his soul in a perfect human form covered with substances from the purest things of nature, out of which a body is formed in the womb of the mother. C.S.L. 183.

Seed of the **Serpent,** the (Gen. iii. 15), s. all infedelity. 250.

Seed of the **Woman,** the (Gen. iii. 15), s. faith towards the Lord. 250. S. of the w. (Rev. xii. 17) s. those who are of the new church, and are principled in the truths of its doctrine. A.R. 565.

Seed as the **Sand,** and the **Offspring** of the **Bowels** as **Gravel.** (Isa. xlviii. 19.) S. as the s. den. good, and the o. of the b. as g. den. truth, or those who are principled in love to the Lord and towards their neighbor. 1803.

Seed and **Offspring.** (Isa. lxv. 23.) S. s. divine truth, and o., a life according to it. A.E. 768.

Seed-Time and **Harvest** (Gen. viii. 2) s. man about to be regenerated, and the church thence der. S. will never cease to be sown into every man by the Lord, whether he be within the church, or out of the church, that is, whether he has been made acquainted with the Word of the Lord, or not; without s. sown in him by the Lord, it is impossible for man to know what is good in any respect; all the good of charity, even amongst the Gentiles, is s. from the Lord, and although they have not the good of faith, as those who are within the church may have, yet they are nevertheless capable of receiving the good of faith: the Gentiles who have lived in charity, as they usually do in the world, embrace and receive the doctrine of truth faith, and the faith of charity, much more easily than christians do, when they are instructed therein by angels in another life. That it will never happen but that a church will exist in some part of the earth, is here s. by s.-t. and h. never ceasing all the days of the earth. 932.

Seek is pred. of the understanding, and to desire of the will. A.R. 429.

Seers. When the prophets were in the spirit, or vision, they saw such things as were in heaven. A.E. 36.

Seethe, to, s. to destroy by falses the truths and goods. A.E. 555.

Seir (Gen. xxxiii. 14) s. the conjunction of spiritual things with celestial in the natural principle, that is, of the truth which is of faith with the good which is of charity; the good to which truth is conjoined in the natural principle, and, in the supreme sense, the Lord's divine natural as to good conjoined to truth therein, is what is properly s. by S. in these passages in the Word, Deut. xxxiii. 2, 3; Num. xxiv. 17, 18; Judges v. 4, 5; and Isa. xxi. 11, 12. 4384. S. (Gen. xiv. 6) s. self-love. 1675. To arise and go forth out of S. (Deut. xxxiii. 2), s. that the Lord would make the natural principle divine, that hence also he might become light, that is, intelligence and wisdom, and thus Jehovah, not only as to the human rational, but also as to the human natural, wherefore it is said, "Jehovah arose from S., and went forth from S." 4240.

Segments den. arrangement of the interiors by regeneration. 10.048.

Seir, the land of, s. in a supreme sense celestial natural good of the Lord; the reason why the land of S. has this signification is, because Mount S. was the boundary of the land of Canaan on one part (see Josh. xi. 16, 17), and all the boundaries, as rivers, mountains, and lands, rep. those things which were ultimate, for they put on rep. from the land of Canaan which was in the midst, which rep. the Lord's celestial kingdom, and, in a supreme sense, his divine human; the ultimates, which are boundaries, are those things which are called natural principles, for in natural principles, spiritual and celestial principles terminate. 4220.

Seir, Mount, den. the human essence of the Lord. 1675.

Seir and Mount Paran. (Deut. xxxiii. 2.) S. has respect to celestial love, and M. P. to spiritual love. 2714.

Selah (Gen. xi. 12) s. what appertains to science. 1339.

Selav den. delight of natural love. 8426.

Self-derived Intelligence is the proprium of the understanding of man. A.R. 452. No false doctrine has any other origin, than in s.-d. i. A.R. 571.

Self-derived Prudence is from the proprium of man, which is his nature, and is called his soul from his parent: this proprium is the love of s., and thence the love of the world; or the love of the world, and thence the love of s.: when the love of s. inspires its love into its mate, the understanding, it then becomes pride, which is the pride of one's own intelligence; hence is one's own p. Thus it is, that one's own p. lies hid in every evil from its origin. D.P. 206.

Self-examination is of no avail, unless man confesses his sins before the Lord, and prays for divine aid, and begins a new life. T.C.R. 530.

Selfhood, or *Proprium*, is nothing but evil. A.C. 210–15.

Self-love consists in wishing well to ourselves alone. N.J.D. 65. S.-l. and the love of the world constitute hell. 2041, 3610, 4225, 10.741, 10.745.

Self-subsisting. The s.-s. principle is omnipresent, omniscient, and omnipotent. D.P. 157. S.-s. who alone is. D.L.W. 45.

Sell, to. (Gen. xli. 56), den. to appropriate to any one. 5371. Jesus said to the young man who was rich, "s. what thou hast, and come, take up thy cross and follow me." (Mark x. 21.) By this, in the spiritual sense, is understood, that he should reject the falses which were the doctrine of the Jewish nation, and receive the doctrine of truth from the Lord, and that he was to undergo conflicts and temptations from falses. A.E. 122. To s. (Rev. xiii. 17) s. to teach doctrine. A.R. 606. Sellers and buyers s. those who make gain to themselves from holy things. To s. and to be sold (Isa. l. 1; lii. 4; Ezek. xxx. 12) s. to alienate truths, and to be alienated from them, and to accept falses for truths, and to be captivated thereby. A.E. 840.

Seminel. Quality des. 5056.

Send, to, s. to reveal. A.E. 8.

Send Away den. to be separated. 3182.

Sennacherib, king of Ashur or Assyria (Isa. xxxvii. 25), s. the rational principle perverted, destroying all the knowledge and perception of truth. A.E. 518, 778. S. the chief captain of the king of Assyria (2 Kings xviii.–xix.), rep. the natural man as to his intellectual principle. A.E. 654.

Sensation. All varieties of s. have reference to the sense of touch, and in the internal sense den. the inmost of and all of perception. 2528. S. which pertain to the body, are der. from love and wisdom. D.L.W. 363.

Sense. The common s. is that in which all particular sensation subsists. 4325–8. See *Involuntary Common (or General) Sense*.

Senses

Senses. The five external s. cor. to the five internal s., and communicate immediately with them. 6404, 4407.

Sensitive is the ultimate of perception. 7691. The sensitive and perceptive exists from good. 3528. All the perceptive and s. are learned and known by relation. D.P. 24.

Sensories. The s. of the body are only recipient and percipient, as if from themselves. Each s. des. A.Cr. 45.

Sensual Life. They who are good, after death, at first live the s. l. in the world or heaven of spirits, afterwards the interior s. l. in the heaven of angelic spirits, and lastly the inmost s. l. in the angelic heaven. 978.

Sensual Man. He is called a s. m. who judges of all things by his bodily senses, and who believes nothing but what he can see with his eyes and touch with his hands; saying that these are something, and rejecting the rest. 5094, 7693. The s. m. thinks in his extremes, and not interiorly from any spiritual light, but he is in a dense natural light. 5089, 5094. S. m. reason acutely and subtilely, because their thought is so near their speech that it is almost in it, and, as it were, in their lips, and because they place all intelligence in speech from memory only; some of them also can dexterously confirm falses, and after confirmation they believe them to be truths. But they reason and confirm things from the fallacies of the senses, by which the vulgar are captivated and persuaded. A.R. 424. Men of learning and erudition, who have confirmed themselves deeply in falses, and still more they who have confirmed themselves against the truths of the Word, are more s. than others. A.C. 6316.

Sensual Principle, the, is the ultimate of the life of man's mind, adhering and cohering to his five bodily senses. 5077, 5767, 9121. The man who is regenerated, especially at this day, is not regenerated as to the s. p., but as to the natural principle, which is next above the s. 7442.

Sensual Things. They who reasoned from s. t. only, and thence against the genuine truths of the church, were called by the ancients "serpents of the tree of knowledge." A.R. 424. A.C. 195–197. S. t. ought to be in the last place, and not in the first, and in a wise and intelligent man, they are in the last place, and subject to the interiors; but in a foolish man, they are in the first place and govern; these are they who are properly called s. A.R. 424. A.C. 5125, 5128, 7645.

Sent, to be. By being s. is everywhere s., in an internal sense, to go forth; as in John xvii. 8. In like manner it is said of the holy of the spirit, that it was s., that is, that it goes forth from the divine of the Lord, as in John xv. 26; xvi. 5, 7. Hence the prophets were called the s., because the words which they spake went forth from the holy of the spirit of the Lord. And whereas all divine truth goes forth from divine good, the expression s. is properly pred. of divine truth. Hence also it is evident what it is to go forth, that is, that he who goes forth, or that which goes forth, is of him from whom it goes forth. 2397. To be s. (Gen. xxxvii. 13) s. to teach. 4710.

Separated from the **Bowels**, to be (Gen. xxv. 23), s. the birth of truth. 3294.

Separation of good from evil exp. 2405. H. and H. 511.

Sephar (Gen. x. 30) s. good. 1248.

Sepulchre, in the internal sense of the Word, s. life, or heaven, and, in the opp. sense, death, or hell; the reason that it s. life, or heaven is, because the angels, who are in the internal sense of the Word, have no idea of a s., because no idea of death, wherefore instead of a s., they perceive nothing else than a continuation of life, thus resurrection; for man rises again as to his spirit, and is buried as to his body, and because burial s. resurrection it also s. regeneration, for regeneration is man's first resurrection, inasmuch as he then dies as to the former man, and rises again as to the new; by regeneration man from dead becomes alive; hence the signification of a

s. in the internal sense. That s., in an opp. sense, s. death or hell is, because the wicked do not rise again to life, and therefore when it is treated concerning the wicked, and mention is made of a s. than there occurs to the angels no other idea than that of hell; this is the reason why hell in the Word is also called a s. 2916.

Serah (Gen. xxxviii. 30) s. the quality of good as actually being first-born, and truth only apparently. S., in the original tongue, s. rise, and is attributed to the sun, and to the first appearance of its light; hence S. was named, because the case is similar with good appertaining to the man, who is regenerating, for it first arises and gives light, by virtue of which light those things are illustrated which are in the natural man, so that they may be seen and acknowledged, and finally believed. 4930.

Seraphim (Isa. vi. 2) s. the Word, properly doctrine from the Word. A.R. 245. See *Cherubim.*

Series. Truths are arranged into s. with man, according to the arrangement of angelic societies. 10.303.

Serpent s. man when he is corporeally sensual, who turns from the Lord to himself, and from heaven to the world; such was the s. who seduced Eve and Adam. A.R. 550. S. (Gen. iii. 15) is evil of every kind; his head is self-love, the seed of the woman is the Lord, the enmity which is put, is between the love of man's proprium and the Lord, thus between man's own prudence and the divine providence of the Lord. D.P. 211. By s., amongst the most ancient people who were celestial men, was s. circum-spection; and, in like manner, the sensual by which they exercised circum-spection, lest they should be injured by the evil; which is evident from the words of the Lord to his disciples, "behold, I send you as sheep into the midst of wolves; be ye therefore prudent as s., and simple as doves." (Matt. x. 16.) 197.

Serpent and Asp. (Gen. xlix. 17.) By s. on the way, and by a. on the path, is s. the sensual principle as to truth, and as to good. A.E. 355.

Sepent's Root, the (Isa. xiv. 29) s. scientifics. 1197.

Serpents. By s. in the Word are s. sensual principles, which are the ultimates of man's life; the reason is, because all animals s. affections of man, where-fore also the affections of angels and spirits in the spiritual world, appear at a distance as animals, and affections merely sensual as s.; and this because s. creep on the ground, and lick the dust, and sensual things are the lowest of the understanding and will, being in close contact with the world, and nourished by its objects and delights, which only affect the material sense of the body. Noxious s., which are of many kinds, s. the sensual things that are dependent on the evil affections, which constitute the interiors of the mind with those who are insane through the falses of evil; and harmless s. s. sensual things that are dependent of the good affec-tions, which constitute the interiors of the mind with those who are wise by virtue of the truths of good. A.R. 455.

Serug (Gen. xi. 20) s. worship in externals. 1349.

Servant. In the Word throughout, there is mention made of s., and thereby in the internal sense is meant what is subservient to another, in general every thing which is below in respect to what is above, for it is grounded in order, that an inferior thing should be subservient to a superior, and so far as it is subservient, it is called a s. 5305. S. den. the humanity apper-taining to the Lord, before it was made divine, which may appear from several passages in the prophets; the reason is, because the humanity appertaining to the Lord, before he put it off, and made it divine, was noth-ing else but a s. 2159. The s. (Gen. xxiv. 17) s. the divine good. 3088. S. (Exod. xxi. 32), in an internal sense, s. labor. 2276. The Lord is as if he did not see and perceive the sins of men; for he leads them gently, thus he

Servants and Elect

bends and does not break in withdrawing them from evil, and in leading them to good; wherefore he does not chastise nor punish, as if he saw and perceived. This is understood by those words, "Who is blind but my s., or deaf as my messenger?" (Isa. xlii. 19.) He is called blind, and thence s., from divine truth, and deaf and thence messenger, from divine good; for blind refers to the understanding and thence perception, and deaf refers to perception, and thence to the will; hence here is understood that the Lord appears not to see, although the divine truth is his from which he knows all things; and that he appears not to will according to what he perceives, although to him belongs divine good from which all things are possible to him. A.E. 409. S., in a spiritual sense, s. those who are in truths, and forasmuch as truths originate in good, by s. are meant those who are in truths, originating in good, therefore also those who are in wisdom originating in love, because wisdom is of truth, and love is of good; also those who are in faith originating in charity, because faith also is of truth, and charity is of good; and forasmuch as the genuine spiritual sense is abstracted from personality, therefore in it by s. are s. truths, and as truths are subservient to good, by teaching it, therefore in general, and properly speaking, by s. in the Word, is meant what is subservient, or he, or that which serves, and in this sense, not only the prophets are called the s. of God, but also the Lord with respect to his humanity. A.R. 3. S. den. those things which are of the exterior natural principle; for when man is regenerated, then inferior things are made subordinate and subject to superior, or exterior things to interior, in which case exterior things become s., and interior things lords. 5161. S., in an opp. sense, s. those who serve the devil, these are in a state of real servitude; but they who serve the Lord are in a state of liberty; as the Lord also teaches in John viii. 32–36. A.R. 3. S. (Gen. xx. 8) s. things rational and scientific. 2541. S. (Gen. xliii. 18) s. light things and things of no account. 5651. The s. which were thrice sent (Luke xx. 10–16) s. the Word given by Moses and the prophets. A.E. 315. See *Men-Servants.*

Servants and **Elect**. S. are they who receive divine truth, and teach; and the e. are they who receive, and lead to divine good. A.E. 409.

Servant of Servants, a (Gen. ix. 25), s. worship in externals without charity, or what is most vile in the church. 1091, 1092.

Serve, to (Gen. xv. 13), s. oppression. 1845.

Serve, to, and **Dwell.** In the Word, to s. is pred. of truth, and to d., of good. A.R. 380.

Service den. all that which is beneath, which is subordinate, and which obeys, consequently, truth as being der. from good, and ministering to good. 3409.

Servitude. Every man wishes to remove slavery from himself. D.P. 148. S. pred. of the unregenerate. 892. S. pred. of the regenerate, or of the external submissive to the internal, is not felt as such, because it is from submission of heart. 5161. To be led by evil is s. D.P. 43.

Servile Fear. In proportion as worship is grounded in s. f. there is less of faith, and still less of love in it. 2826.

Set with Thee, to (Gen. xxxiii. 15), s. to conjoin. 4385.

Set on Edge, to be, s. the appropriation of the false from evil. A.E. 556.

Seth (Gen. iv. 25, etc.) s. a new faith by which comes charity. 434.

Seven. The number s. was esteemed holy, as is well known, by reason of the six days of creation, and of the seventh, which is the celestial man, in whom is peace, rest, and the sabbath; hence the numbers s. so frequently occurs in the rites of the Jewish church, and is everywhere held as holy; and hence times were distinguished into s., both the great and the less intervals, and were called weeks, as the great intervals of times till the coming of the Messiah (Dan. ix. 24, 25); and the time of s. years is called a week by Laban and Jacob. (Gen. xxix. 27, 28.) Wherefore, wheresoever the number s. occurs, it is esteemed holy and sacred, as in Ps. cxix. 164, and in Isa. xxx. 26. As the times of man's regeneration are distinguished into six, previous to the seventh, or the celestial man, so also the times of vastation are distinguished, even till nothing celestial remains; this was rep. by several captivities of the Jews, and by the last Babylonish captivity, which lasted s. decades, or seventy years; it was likewise rep. by Nebuchadnezzar, in Dan. iv. 16, 22, 29. It is also pred. concerning the vastation of the last times, in Rev. xv. 1, 7, 8; and that they should tread the holy city under foot, forty and two months, or six times s. (Rev. xi. 2; and, again, Rev. v. 1.) Hence the severity and increments of punishment were expressed by the number s., as in Lev. xxvi. 18, 21, 24, 28; Ps. lxxix. 12. 395. S. (Rev. xv. 1) s. all in an universal sense. A.R. 657. See *Six.*

Seven-fold and **Seventy-Seven-fold**. As the number seven is holy, so the number seventy has a like s., as comprehending seven ages, for an age in the Word is ten years; whensoever any thing particularly holy or sacred was to be expressed, then the term seventy times seven was applied, as where the Lord said, "that a man should remit to his brother, not only until seven times, but until seventy times seven" (Matt. xviii. 21, 22); by which is meant that they should remit as often as he trespasses, consequently, without end, or forever, which is holy. 433.

Seven Angels (Rev. xv. 1; xvi. 1) s. heaven, and, in a supreme sense, the Lord. A.R. 657, 676.

Seven Churches s. all who were of the church in the christian world, and every one according to reception. A.R. 10, 41.

Seventh Day and **Seventh Month**. (Gen. ii. 2, 3; viii. 4.) S. d. is the celestial man, and the s. m. is the spiritual man. 84, 851.

Seventeen s. both the beginning of temptation, and the end of temptation, by reason that it is composed of the numbers seven and ten; which number, when it s. the beginning of temptation, implies in such case till seven days, or the seventh of seven days, which s. the beginning of temptation. But when s. s. the end of temptation, then seven is a holy number, to which ten is added, which s. remains, for without remains man cannot be regenerated. 755. The seventeenth day (Gen. viii. 4) s. what is new. 853.

Seventy-two den. all things of charity and faith. 5291.

Shaddai s. temptation, and, afterwards, consolation. 5628. See *Schaddai.*

Shade on the **Right Hand**. (Ps. cxxi. 6.) To be a s. on the r. h. s. to be defence against evil and the false. A.E. 298.

Shade of the **Light** of **Heaven**, the, is not similar to the s. of the l. of this world, being an incomprehensibly mild and pure light, equally enlightening the understanding and the sight. 1972.

Shadow s. commonplace. A.E. 324.

Shadow of a **Beam** (Gen. xix. 8) s. a general obscure principle of the good of charity. 2361, 2367.

Shadow of **Death**, the, has respect to the states of those in hell, who are in the falses of evil. A.R. 110.

Shafts s. truths, and spiritual truths. A.R. 299. See *Arrow.*

Shake. To s. bread on the palm of Aaron's hand (Exod. xxix. 24) den. acknowledgment that vivification is of the Lord, and that it is the Lord. 10.082.

Shake Thyself from the Dust, arise, sit down, O Jerusalem (Isa. lii. 2), s. liberation from infernal falses, and elevation to the truths of heaven. A.E. 811.

Shalem den. the procedure of the regenerate to the interior truths of faith. 4393.

Shame s. filthy loves. A.E. 1009.

Sharon

Sharon s. the celestial church, also the internal of the celestial church. 5922, 10.610.

Sharon, Bashan, and **Carmel** (Isa. xxxiii. 9), s. the church as to the knowledges of good and truth from the natural sense of the Word. A.E. 730.

Sharp s. what is accurate, what is exquisite, and altogether, or entirely. A.E. 908.

Shave, to, the **Head** was strictly prohibited the high-priests and his sons, because of the holy rep. of hair, and of the Nazarite. A.R. 47.

Shave, to, the **Head** and **Beard.** See *To Poll the Head and Beard.*

Shaveh s. goods of the external man. 1723.

Shaveh Kiriathaim s. the hells of such as were in persuasions of the false. 1673.

Sheaf s. doctrine, and hence, to bind sheaves s. to teach from doctrine; the ground and reason why s. den. doctrine is, because field is the church, and standing corn in a field den. truth in the church, thus, a s., in which there is corn, den. doctrine in which there is truth. 4686. Joseph's s. (Gen. xxxvii.) s. doctrine from the Lord's divine truth, or the doctrinal concerning the Lord's divine human. 4686, 4689.

Shear, to, the **Flock** (Gen. xxxi. 19) s. to perform use, which is evident from this consideration, that shearing the flock, in the internal sense, is nothing else but use, for thence is wool; that shearing the flock den. use, is manifest also from Deut. xv. 19, where by not shearing the first-born of the block, is meant not to perform thence domestic use. Inasmuch as shearing the flock s. use, therefore, to s. the f., and to be present at shearing, was, in old time, reputed an honorable office and employment, as may appear from what is said of Judah, that "he sheared his flock" (Gen. xxxviii. 12, 13), and from the sons of David in the second book of Samuel xiii. 23, 24. 4110.

Sheba. (Gen. x. 28.) A ritual of the church called Eber. 1245. S. (Jer. vi. 20) s. knowledges and acts of worship. 1171.

Sheba and **Dedan** are those who constitute the first class in the Lord's spiritual kingdom, who are principled in the good of faith, and who have doctrinals of charity; hence it is, that by S. and D. are s. the knowledges of things celestial, or, what is the same thing, those who are in the knowledges of things celestial, that is, who are in the doctrinals of charity, for doctrinals are knowledges, and charity is the celestial principle appertaining to the spiritual man. 3240.

Sheba and **Seba** s. the internal things of worship, namely, S., the celestial things of worship, and S., the spiritual things of worship. 1171.

Shebah (Gen. xxvi. 33) s. the conjunction of confirmed truth. 3465.

Shechem. (Gen. xii. 6.) By Abram's passing through the land unto the place S., is s. a new state of the Lord, when the celestial things of love first appeared to him which is s. by S., which is the first station, as it were, in the land of Canaan, in coming from Syria, or from Haran; Jacob, when he returned from Haran to the land of Canaan, in like manner, came to S., as may appear from Gen. xxxiii. 17–20, where also by S. is s. the first dawn of light. So in David (Ps. lx. 6–8; cviii. 7–9), where by S. also the like is s. That S. was made a city of refuge (Josh. xx. 7), and also a city of priests (Josh. xxi.21), and that there a covenant was made (Josh. xxiv. 1, 25), implies also the like s. 1441. S. (Gen. xxxvii. 12) s. first rudiments of the doctrine concerning faith: first rudiments are also the common [or general] principles of doctrinals, these common [or general] principles are what are first received, special [or particular] principles follow afterwards. 3704. S. the son of Hamor (Gen. xxxiv. 2) s. the truth of the church from ancient time. 4330.

Sheep, in the Word, s. goods. Also, those who are in the good of charity, and thence in faith. 4169, 4809. S., as first mentioned, in John xxi. 15–17, den.

those who are in good from good: and s., mentioned a second time, den. those who are in good from truth. 4169. Other s. which are not of this sheepfold (John x. 16), are meant those who are neither celestial nor spiritual, but natural, and, notwithstanding, are in the good of life according to their religious principles. A.E. 433. See *Lambs.*

Sheep and **Goats** (Matt. xxv. 33–41) do not mean all the good and all the evil; but, in a proper sense, by s. are understood they who are in the good of charity towards their neighbor, and thence in faith; and by g., they who are in faith separate from charity, consequently, all those upon whom the judgment in the last time of the church was about to be executed, for all those who were in the good of love to the Lord were before received into heaven; and all who were in no good of charity, and thence in no faith, were before cast into hell. To the s. it is said, "inherit the kingdom prepared for you," from the foundation of the world, but it is not said that the lot of the g. was prepared from the foundation of the world, for the evil prepare hell for themselves, and the Lord prepares heaven for the good. A.E. 600.

Sheepfolds s. knowledges and scientifics in the natural man. A.E. 434.

Sheet. A punishment des. 964.

Shekel, a, s. the price or estimation of good and truth, and half a s. s. the determination of the quantity thereof. 3104.

Shelah (Gen. xxxviii. 2) s. the quality of evil der. from the false of evil; or the quality of the idolatrous principle with the Jewish nation. 4819, 4826. See *Kesib.*

Sheleph. (Gen. x. 26.) A ritual of the worship of the church called Eber. 1245–1247.

Shem (Gen. x. 21) s. the ancient church in general. 1217.

Shem, Ham, Japheth, and **Canaan.** By S. is understood internal worship, by J. cor. external worship, by H. internal worship corrupted, by C. external worship separate from internal. Such persons never had any existence; but those kinds of worship had such names given them. 1140. See *Noah.*

Shemeber den. evil lusts and false persuasions. 1663.

Shepherd s. the Lord. A.E. 375. S., in the opp. sense, s. those who teach falses, and thereby lead to evil of life. A.E. 388. S., abstracted, s. truths themselves productive of good. 388.

Shepherd of the **Flock**, a, is one who exercises the good of charity, as must be obvious to every one, inasmuch as the expression is commonly used in this signification, in the Word of the Old and New Testament; he who leads and teaches is called s.; they who are led and taught are called the f.; he who does not lead to the good of charity, and who does not teach the good of charity, is not a true s.; and he who is not led to good, and does not learn what is good, is not of the f. 343.

Shepherds of **Abram's Cattle,** and **Shepherds** of **Lot's Cattle.** (Gen. xiii. 7.) S. of cattle s. those who teach, consequently, the things appertaining to worship, as may be obvious to every one. The s. of A's. cattle are things celestial, which appertain to the internal man, and the s. of L's. c. are things sensual which appertain to the external man. 1571, 1572.

Shew, to, s. to instruct to the life. 264.

Shew-bread s. the divine good of the Lord's divine love. 3478.

Shield s. defence to be confided in against evils and falses. In respect to the Lord, it s. defence, and in respect to man, confidence in the Lord's protection, because it was a protection for the breast, and by the breast is s. good and truth, good by reason of the heart being therein, and truth by reason of the lungs. In an opp. sense, s. den. evils and falses, whereby combat is waged, and which is used as a defence, and in which are confided in, as in Jer. xlvi. 3, 4, and other passages. 1788.

Shield, Buckler, and Spear

Shield, Buckler, and **Spear.** (Ps. xxxv. 2.) S., because it guards the head, s. defence against falses which destroy the understanding of truth; and b. because it guards the breast, s. defence against falses which destroy charity, which is the will of good; and s. because it defends all things of the body, s. defence in general. A.E. 734.

Shield and **Helmet** are such things as appertain to spiritual war. 3448.

Shiloh (Gen. xlix. 10) s. the Lord and the tranquillity of peace. 6373. Habitation of S. (Ps. lxxviii. 60, 61) s. the church which is principled in the good of love. A.E. 811. See *Tabernacle and Tent.*

Shinar, land of (Gen. x. 10), s. external worship, whose internal is profane. 1183.

Shinab s. evil lusts, and false persuasions. 1663.

Shine, or **Shining,** s. what is exempt from falsity, and what is pure by reason of truth. A.R. 814.

Ship. A s. s. doctrine from the Word, and its planks, oars, and masts s. the various things of which doctrine consists. They who teach, lead, and rule, are understood by the pilots, the rowers, and mariners, etc. (Ezek. xxvii. 4, 5, 6, etc.) A gallant s. (Isa. xxxiii. 21) s. wisdom from man's proprium, and a s., or galley with oars, intelligence from man's proprium, because it is guided by men with oars. A.E. 514. See *Beam.*

Ships s. knowledges of what is good and truth from the Word, serving for use of life; s. have this s., because they traverse the sea, and bring such necessaries as are of use to the natural man exclusively, and the knowledges of good and truth are the necessaries which are of use to the spiritual man; from these the doctrine of the church is der., and, according to this doctrine, life. S. s. these knowledges, because they are what contain things, and, in the Word, the thing containing is taken for the thing contained. A.R. 406. S. s. the scientifics and doctrinals of the true, and, in the opp. sense, the scientifics and doctrinals of the false. A.E. 355.

Ships of **Tarshish** (Isa. xxiii. 1) s. the doctrinals of truth and good, and, in the opp. sense, false doctrinals. A.E. 514. A.C. 9295.

Shiphrah and **Puah** (Exod. i. 15) s. the quality and state of the natural principle, where the scientifics are. 6674.

Shittah Tree (Isa. xii. 19) has relation to the church in the spiritual or internal man; also to rational truth and its perception; also to genuine truth. A.E. 294, 375, 730.

Shittim Wood s. the good of merit, and in a supreme sense, the mercy of the Lord. 9528. See *Valley of Shittim.*

Shoe. In the Word, the sole of the foot and the heel s. the ultimate natural. The s. is what clothes the sole of the foot and the heel, wherefore the s. s. a natural still more remote, thus the corporeal itself. The s. of s. changes according to the subjects: when it is pred. of what is good, it is taken in a good sense, but when of what is evil, it is taken in a bad sense. By shoe-string (gen. xiv. 23) is s. what is false, and by shoe-latchet what is evil, and indeed by reason of its being a diminutive, such as is the vilest of all. 1748.

Shoe-latchet den. evil; lace or thread what is false. 1748.

Shoot, to, in **Secret** (Ps. lxiv. 4), s. to deceive. A.E. 357.

Shooter of the **Bow** s. a man of the spiritual church, which may appear from the s. of a dart, or an arrow, as den. truth. The man of the spiritual church was formerly called a shooter of the bow because he defends himself by truths, and debates about truths, otherwise than the man of the celestial church. In an opp. sense, by s. of the bow is s. those who are principled in what is false to be shot through (Exod. xix. 13), s. to perish as to spiritual good. 2709, 8800.

Shoots of the **Vine** (Gen. xl. 10) s. derivations from the intellectual principle to the last which is the sensual. 5444.

Shortly. (Rev. i. 1.) "Things which must s. come to pass," s. things that will certainly be, that the church may not perish. For in the divine idea, and thence in the spiritual sense, there is no time, but state instead thereof, and the Apocalypse was given in the first century, since which seventeen centuries have now elapsed; from which it is evident, that by s., is not s. immediately and speedily, but certainly, which spiritually cor. thereto. The like is also involved in the Lord's words. (Matt. xxiv. 22.) A.R. 4.

Shoulder s. all power. 1085. S. (Ezek. xxix. 7) s. the power or faculty of understanding truth. A.E. 627. To dwell between the s. (Deut. xxxiii. 12) s. in security and power. A.E. 449.

Shout, to. To s. from the top of the mountain (Isa. xlii. 11) s. worship from the good of love. A.E. 405. See *To Cry.*

Shouting, Singing, and **Playing** (Ps. xxvii. 6), have respect to what is spiritual. 420.

Shrub, or **Plant** (Gen. xxi. 15), den. perception, but so little as to be scarce any, in like manner as trees, but in a lesser degree. Hence to be cast under one of the s., s. to be desolated as to truth and good, even to desperation. 2682. S. s. the knowledges of truth. A.E. 410.

Shrub of the **Field,** and **Herb** of the **Field** (Gen. ii. 5) s. in general all that the external of the celestial man produces, and in particular, things rational and scientific from a celestial spiritual origin. 90, 91.

Shuah, the daughter of, s. evil, which is der. from the false of evil. 4827.

Shur (Gen. xvi.) s. a scientific principle which is yet as it were in a wilderness, that is, which has not as yet gained life, for S. was a wilderness not far from the Red Sea, consequently, towards Egypt, as appears from Gen. xxv. 18; Exod. xv. 22; 1 Sam. xv. 7; xxvii. 8. 1928. Wilderness of S., s. a state of temptation. 8346.

Shut, to, **after Him.** (Gen. vii. 16.) It is said, that "when they had entered into the ark whom God had commanded, Jehovah s. after h." By Jehovah's shutting after him, is s. that man should no longer have such communication with heaven, as was enjoyed by the man of the celestial church. 784.

Shut up den. what is vastated, or is no more. 9188.

Sibmah s. the men of the external church, who explain the Word to favor worldly love. A.E. 911.

Sichar (John iv. 5) s. interior truth, the same as Shechem. 4430.

Sichem, or **Shechem,** den. a first conscious perception of the Lord's kingdom. 1437.

Sick (Matt. xxv. 35) s. those who acknowledge that in themselves there is nothing but evil, or one who is in evil. 4956, 4958.

Sickness, which precedes death, den. what is progressive to regeneration or resurrection unto life, for man by nature is in a state of spiritual death, but by regeneraiton, he is raised up into a state of spiritual life. 6221.

Sickle (Rev. xiv.) s. the divine truth of the Word, because by a harvest is s. the state of the church as to divine truth, here its last state, and therefore by reaping, which is done with a s., is here s. to put an end to the state of the church, and execute judgment; and whereas this is done by the divine truth of the Word, therefore this is s. by s. A.R. 643.

Siddim, valley of, s. the uncleanness of lusts, and the falsities thence der. 1666.

Side and **Shoulder** (Ezek. xxiv. 21) den. all the soul and all the power. 1085.

Side s. good. A.E. 336. Spiritual love. A.E. 365.

Sides, the, s. the interior or the middle principle between the inmost and the ultimates. 10.185. When by ribs are meant s., they den. truths, but s. properly called s., den. goods. 10.189. S. (Num. xxxiii. 55) s. the things of charity, consequently, goods. A.E. 560. S. of the earth (Jer. vi. 22) s. that which is

Sidon

remote from goods. A.E. 355. S. of the north, (Ezek. xxxviii. 6) s. perverted doctrinals. 1154.

Sidon den. those who possess celestial and spiritual riches which are knowledges. 1156.

Siege, to lay. To straiten by evils and falses. A.E. 633.

Sift, to, the **Nations** with the **Sieve** of **Vanity** (Isa. xxx. 28) s. the adulteration of the Word by means of fictions by those who are in evils. A.E. 923.

Sight. Spiritual s., which is that of the understanding, and thus of the mind, and natural s. which is that of the eye, and thus of the body, mutually cor. with each other. U.T. 346. Spiritual-natural s. is science, spiritual s. is intelligence, and celestial s. is wisdom. A.R. 351. See *Eye.*

Sign is mentioned in the Word in reference to things to come, and then constitutes revelation; it refers also to truth, when it constitutes testification; and it also refers to the quality of any state and thing, when it constitutes manifestation. A.R. 532. S. of the son of man in heaven (Matt. xxiv. 30) s. the manifestation of divine truth. H. and H. 1. The great s. which appeared in heaven (Rev. xii. 1) s. revelation from the Lord concerning his new church in the heavens and on earth, and concerning the difficult reception and resistance which its doctrine meets with. A.R. 532. S. upon the mountains (Isa. xviii. 3) s. the advent of the Lord, and convocation to the church. The like is s. by the sounding of the trumpet. A.E. 741. See *Memorial.*

Sign and **Miracle.** S. s. that which indicates, witnesses, and persuades, concerning a subject of inquiry; but a m. s. that which excites, strikes, and induces astonishment; thus a s. moves the understanding and faith, and a m. the will and its affection; for the will and its affection is what is excited, struck, and amazed, and the understanding and its faith is what is persuaded, indicated to, and for which testification is made. A.E. 706.

Signs and **Prodigies** (Matt. xxiv. 24) s. confirming and persuading principles grounded in external appearances and fallacies, whereby the simple suffer themselves to be seduced. 3900.

Signet and **Seal** den. confirmation and testification. 4874.

Significations. All things in the literal sense are s. of things in the internal sense. 1404.

Sihor, the seed of (Isa. xxiii. 3), s. scientific truth. 9295. To drink the waters of S. (Jer. ii. 18) s. to investigate spiritual things by the scientifics of the natural man. A.E. 569.

Silence has various significations; in general it s. all things which cause it, amongst which is astonishment, whereby it is especially induced. (See Rev. viii. 1.) A.E. 487.

Silk s. mediate celestial good and truth; good, from its softness; and truth, from its shining. A.R. 773. S. the same as fine linen, den. genuine truth, but resplendent from interior good. 5319. Thread of s. s. spiritual truths. A.E. 654.

Siloam s. the Word in the letter; and to be washed therein s. to be purified from falses and evils. A.E. 239, 475.

Silver, in the internal sense of the Word, s. truth, and, in an opp. sense, the false. 1551. The truth which is of faith. 5291. Truth acquired from proprium. 9039. Spiritual good or truth from a celestial origin. H. and H. 115. Scientific truth. 6112. S. (Gen. xx. 16) s. rational truth. 2575. S. purified seven times (Ps. xii. 6) s. divine truth. 1551.

Silver Age, the, was the time of the ancient church, which was a spiritual man. 1551. The people of that age possessed the science of cor., and they had intelligence from spiritual truths and therefrom in natural truths; the like also is s. by s. C.S.L. 76. See *Golden Age.*

Silver, Iron, and **Stone.** The most ancient people compared and likened the inmost spiritual to s.; the inferior spiritual to i.; and the lowest to s. 643.

286

Silver, Iron, Tin, and **Lead** (Ezek. xxvii. 12), s. truths in their order, even to the last, which are sensual. 2967.
Silver. A piece of s. s. a truth, or a knowledge of truth. A.E. 675.
Simeon. (Rev. vii.) By S., in a supreme sense, is s. providence; in a spiritual sense, love towards our neighbor, or charity; and, in a natural sense, obedience and hearing. S. (Judges i. 1–4) s. the Lord as to things spiritual, der. from celestial things. 1574.
Simeon and **Levi,** in respect to the Jewish nation, rep. what is false and evil. 4497.
Similitude, a, **Effigy,** or **Likeness,** den. the celestial man, an image of the spiritual. 51. The Lord spoke by s. and comparisons, which are cor. T.C.R. 215.
Similarities. Extension of distances with the angels are according to s. and dissimilarities of their states: one produces conjunction, the other separation. A.Cr. 106.
Simon. (Luke xxii. 31, 32.) Peter in this passage rep. faith without charity, which faith is the faith of what is false. A.E. 740.
Simon, Son of **Jonah** (John xxi. 15), s. faith from charity: S. s. worship and obedience, and J., a dove, which also s. charity. A.E. 820.
Simran, Jokshan, Medan, Midian, Jishbak, and **Shuah** (Gen. xxv. 2), s. common lots of the Lord's spiritual kingdom, in the heavens and in the earths. 3239.
Simulation and **Deceit** regarded as enormities, and the deceitful cast out as devils. 3573. Such become jugglers and soothsayers. 831.
Simultaneous Order, in, one thing is next to another, from what is innermost to what is outermost. U.T. 214.
Sin, wilderness of (Exod. xvi.), s. the good which is from truth in a prior state of temptation. 8398.
Sin Against the **Holy Spirit** is denying the Lord's divinity, and the sanctity of the Word. D.P. 98, 99.
Sin s. evils arising from a love of self and the world. A.E. 1008.
Sinai, Mount (Exod. xix. 1), s., in a supreme sense, divine truth from divine good: Mount, divine good, and S., divine truth; in the internal sense, the truth of faith from good; and when it is called "the desert of S.," it s. the truth of faith to be implanted in good. 8753. Mount S. s. celestial good. 8819. Mount S. s. heaven. 8931, 9420. Mount S. s. the Word, which is from the Lord, and, consequently, in which the Lord is. 9415.
Sinew, or **Nerve,** s. truth, for truths in good are like s. or n. in flesh; and also truths, in a spiritual sense, are s., and good is flesh. Like things also are s. by s. and flesh. (Ezek. xxxvii. 6, 8.) 4303, 4317.
Sing, to, a **Song,** or **Hymn,** s. glorification of the Lord. 8261.
Singing. Every affection of the heart has a tendency to produce s., and, consequently, to produce whatever has relation to s.; the affection of the heart is celestial, s. thence der. is spiritual. 418. S. s. the testification of gladness from the affection of truth. A.E. 323. The s. of heaven is nothing else but an affection of the mind, which is emitted through the mouth as a tune, for it is sound separate from the discourse of one speaking from an affection of love, which affection gives life to the speech. C.S.L. 155. See *Song.*
Singulars. Every common contains thousands of particulars, and every particular thousands of s. 865.
Sinites s. different kinds of idolatry. 1205. See *Jebusites, etc.*
Sinus. Those des. who have reference to the s. 4048.
Sirens, who are interior jugglers, are they who particularly beset man during night, and, at the same time, endeavor to infuse themselves into his interior thoughts and affections, but they are as often driven away by angels

from the Lord, and are at length deterred from such attempts by most grievous punishments. They are chiefly of the female sex, who, in the life of the body, have studied, by interior artifices, to allure to themselves companions, insinuating themselves by things external, using every method of engaging men's minds, entering into the affections and delights of every one, but with an evil end, especially to gain influence and authority. 1983. S. are such females as have been principled in a persuasion that whoredom and adultery is honorable, and have also been held in esteem by others on account of such persuasion, and of their elegant way of living; the greatest part of them come into another life from christendom. 2744.

Sisera (Judges v. 20) s. the false from evil destroying the church. A.E. 355, 434.

Sister. They are called sisters by the Lord who are in truth from the good of charity from him. (Matt. xii. 50.) A.E. 746. S. den. intellectual truth, when celestial truth is a wife. 1475. S. den. intellectual rational truth. The reason why rational truth is called s. is, because it is conceived by an influx of divine good into the affection of rational truths; the good which is thence in the rational principle is called brother, and the truth which is thence is called s. (See Gen. xx. 12.) 2508.

Sit, to, by the **Flesh Pots** (Exod. xvi. 3) s. a life according to pleasure, and what is lusted after, for this life is the life of man's proprium. 8408.

Sit, to, **Stand,** and **Walk before Jehovah.** To s. before Jehovah is to be with him, consequently, also to will and act from him; to s. before him, is to look to and understand his will, and to w. before him, is to live according to his precepts, thus from himself: forasmuch as to s. involves such a s., therefore, the same word, in the original language which is used to express it, s. to remain and dwell. A.E. 687.

Sitnah (Gen. xxvi. 21), in the original tongue, s. aversion, and here a denial of the internal sense of the Word. 3429.

Situation of spirits in the other life des. 1274.

Six s. combat, as appears from the first chapter of Genesis, where mention is made of s. days in which man is regenerated before he becomes celestial, within which days there is a continual combat, but on the seventh day comes rest; hence it is that there are s. days of labor, and the seventh the sabbath, which s. rest; hence also it is, that an Hebrew servant was to serve s. years, and in the seventh was to be free (Exod. xxi. 2; Deut. xv. 12; Jer. xxxiv. 14) and that they should sow the land s. years, and should gather its produce, but on the seventh they should let it rest (Exod. xxiii. 10–12); and in like manner they should do with a vineyard; and that on the seventh year there should be a sabbath of a sabbath for the land, a sabbath of Jehovah (Lev. xxv. 3, 4); whereas s. s. labor and combat they s. also the dispersion of what is false (Ezek. ix. 2; xxxix. 2), in which passages, s., and to leave a sixth part s. dispersion; and in Job v. 29, it s. the combat of temptations. In some other cases, where the number s. occurs in the Word, it does not s. labor, combat, or the dispersion of what is false, but the holy of faith as having relation to twelve, which number s. faith and all things appertaining to faith in the complex; and as having relation also to three, which number s. what is holy; hence also the genuine derivation of the number s., as in Ezek. xl. 5, where it is said that the man's reed with which he measured the holy city of Israel, was s. cubits; and so in other passages; the reason of this ground of its derivation, is because the combat of temptation is the holy of faith, and also because s. days of labor and combat have respect unto the holy seventh. 737. S. s. all as to truth and good, for s. is composed of three and two multiplied by each other, and by three is s. all with respect to truth, and by two all with respect to good. A.R. 245.

Slain

Six Hundred Years. (Gen. vii. 6.) Noah's being a son of s. h. y. s. the first state of his temptation, which appears from this consideration, that from this chapter, even to Heber, ch. xi. by numbers and by ages of years, and by names, nothing else is s. but things, as also by the ages and names of all that are recorded in chapter v. That s. h. y. s. in this verse the first state of temptation, may appear from the ruling numbers therein, which are ten and six, which are twice multiplied into themselves. 737.

Six Hundred and Sixty-six. (Rev. xiii. 18.) By s. h. and s.-s. is s. all truth of good, and as this is said of the Word, it s. all truth of good in the Word, in the present instance the same falsified, because it is the number of the beast. A.R. 610.

Sixteen and Sixteen Hundred s. the same as four, because s. is the product of four multiplied by itself, and four is pred. of good and of the conjunction of good with truth, consequently, in an opp. sense, of evil, and the conjunction of evil with the false. A.R. 654.

Sixth Part. Because six s. what is full, the word to sextate, or give a s. p., came into use, by which, in a spiritual sense, is s. what is complete and entire; as that the prophet was to drink water by measure, the s. p. of a hin (Ezek. iv. 11); that they were to take for an offering the s. p. of an ephah of a homer of wheat. (Ezek. xlv. 13.) A.R. 610.

Sixty s. a full time and state as to the implantation of truth. A.E. 648.

Skeletons. Profaners appear in the spiritual world like s. D.P. 226.

Skilful. A man s. is pred. of the affection of truth, or of those who are in the affection of truth. 3309.

Skin, the, cor. to truth or to the false in the ultimates. 10.036. The s., from cor. with the greatest man, s. the natural man. A.E. 386. There are spirits who belong to the province of the s., especially that part of it which is rough and scaly, who are disposed to reason on all subjects, having no perception of what is good and true; there are they, who, during the bodily life, have confounded truth and goodness by scientific and philosophical investigations, whereby they seemed to themselves more learned than others, though at the same time they had never taken from the Word any previous principles of truth; hence they have a less share of common sense than the rest of mankind. 1835. S. (Job xix. 26) s. the natural such as man has with him after death. 3540. S. s. things external, because s. are the outermost principles of the animal, in which its interiors are terminated, in like manner as the s., or cuticles in man; this significative is grounded in what is rep. in another life; the s. and also the hides of beasts, s. things external, which is also manifest from the Word. 3540.

Skirt. The s. of a Jew (Zech. viii. 23) s. truth from the good of love to the Lord. To take hold of the s. of a Jew s. the desire of knowing truth from the Lord. A.E. See *Hem.*

Skirts and Heels. (Jer. xiii. 22.) S. s. external truths, and h. outermost goods. 3540.

Skull. They who have lived in deadly hatred, and in the revenges of such hatred, and in falses thence der., have s. perfectly hardened, and some have s. like ebony, through which no rays of light, which are truths, penetrate, but are altogether reflected. 5563.

Slain, when pred. concerning the Lord (Rev. v.), s. the separation of all things from the divine; for by a denial of his divinity, he is spiritually s. among men and denial causes a state of separation from him. A.E. 328. The s. (Lam. ii. 12) s. those who do not know what is meant by the truths of faith. 1071. The s. of Jehovah s. those who turn truths into falses, by which means they perish. A.R. 139. A multitude of s. is pred. of those who perish from falses, and a great number of carcasses, of those who perish from evils. (Nahum iii. 2.) A.E. 354.

289

Slaughter

Slaughter s. perdition and damnation. A.E. 315. S. and a storm of s. s. evils which destroy the goods of the church. The day of great s. s. the last judgment. A.E. 315.

Slave s. those who do not think from themselves but from others. A.E. 836.

Slavery consists in being under the dominion of evil spirits. 892.

Slay, to, or Kill, in the Word, s. to destroy souls, which is to k. spiritually. A.R. 326. To s. a man to his wounding, s. to extinguish faith, and to s. a little child to his hurt, s. to extinguish charity. (Gen. iv. 23.) 427.

Sleep, to, den. an obscure state; s. also, in a spiritual sense, is nothing else, as wakefulness is nothing else but a clear state; for spiritual s. is when truths are in obscurity, and spiritual wakefulness when truths are in clearness: in the degree also of such clearness, or obscurity, spirits are wakeful, or asleep. 5210. By a deep s. (Gen. ii. 21) is meant that state into which man was let, that he seemed to himself to have proprium, which state is like that of s. because in that state he knows no other, but that he lives, thinks, speaks, and acts of himself; but where he begins to know that this is false, he then starts as it were out of s., and becomes awake. 147. "A deep s. fell upon Abram" (Gen. xv. 12), s. that the church was then in darkness; for a deep s. is a dark state in respect to being awake, which state is here pred. of the Lord, who is rep. by Abram; not that a deep s., or a dark state ever has place with him, but with the church; the case herein is as in another life, where the Lord is always the sun, and essential light, but before the wicked he appears as darkness, for the Lord appears to every one according to his state; and so it is in respect to the church when it is in a dark state. Sleeping, when spoken of the Lord, s. his apparent absence. A.E. 514. To s. a perpetual s. (Jer. li. 39) s. never to perceive truths to eternity. A.E. 481. There is a necessity that man should s. in safety, for otherwise the human race must needs perish. 959. Evil spirits have the greatest and most burning desire to infest and assault man during s., but he is then particularly under the Lord's keeping; for love never s. The spirits who infest are miserably punished. 1983. Those spirits who are allotted to involuntary respiration, are present with man during s., for as soon as man falls asleep, his voluntary principle of respiration ceases, and he receives an involuntary principle of respiration. 3893. Certain spirits on their first entrance into the spiritual world, who desire to see the glory of the Lord, before they are in such a state as to be capable of beholding it, are cast into a kind of sweet s. as to their exterior senses and inferior faculties, and then their interior senses and faculties are awakened into an extraordinary wakefulness, and thus they are let into the glory of heaven; but as soon as wakefulness is restored to the interior senses and faculties, they return to their former state. 9182.

Sleights in the **Hand** s. falsifications of truth. 3242.

Sluggishness of spirits who had given themselves up to ease, etc., des. 5723.

Slumber, to, and **Sleep** den. the state of a man who is not in truths. (See Jer. li. 39, 57; Ps. xiii. 3; lxxvi. 5; Luke viii. 23.) A.R. 158. To s., in the internal sense, is, from delay to grow slothful in the things appertaining to the church, and to s. is to cherish doubt. (Matt. xxv. 5.) 4638.

Small and **Great.** The s. s. those who know or are but little in the truths and goods of the church, and the great those who know or are much in them. A.E. 696. S. and g. (Rev. xi. 98) s. who fear the Lord in a lesser or greater degree. A.R. 527. S. and g. (Rev. xix. 5) s. those who, in a lesser and greater degree, worship the Lord from truths of faith, and goods of love. A.R. 810.

Small and **Round** are pred. of truth and good respectively. 8458.

Smell, the sense of, in general cor. to the affection of perceiving. 4404. See *Spheres, Taste.*

Smelling. Instead of taste, spirits have a sense resembling s. 1516.

Smite, to, s. condemn. 7871. To s. (Gen. xiv. 15) s. vindication. 1714. To s. (Gen. xxxii. 8) s. to destroy. 4251. To s. the earth with every plague as often as they will (Rev. xi. 6), is s. to destroy the church by all kinds of evils and falses. A.R. 498. To s. the mother upon the sons was a form of speaking in use amongst the ancients, who were principled in rep. and s., s. the destruction of the church and of all things appertaining to the church, either in general or in particular with the man who is a church; for by mother they understood the church, and by sons the truths appertaining to the church; hence to s. the mother upon the sons den. to perish utterly; man also in such case perishes utterly, when the church, and what appertains to the church with him perishes, that is, when the affection of truth, which is properly s. by mother, and which constitutes the church with man, is destroyed. 4257.

Smith strengthening the **Melter**, the, is pred. of evil, and the smoothing the hammer, of what is false. (Isa. xli. 7.) 3527. S. s. truths in ultimates, the same as iron. A.E. 316.

Smitten s. those who are oppressed by the falses of ignorance. A.E. 357.

Smoke s. divine truth in ultimates, because fire from which s. issues, s. love, moreover, s. s. the same as cloud in many places. A.R. 674. S. (Exod. xx.) s. divine truth, or the Word in its external form. 8916. S. (Rev. ix. 17) s. the pride of self-ascribed intelligence, which is the proprium of man's understanding, issuing from the love of self and of the world, as s. does from fire. A.R. 452. S. of her burning (Rev. lviii.) s. damnation in consequence of adulterating and profaning the Word. A.R. 787. S. of a great furnace (Rev. ix. 2) s. the falses of concupiscences streaming forth from evil loves. A.R. 422. S. of the incense (Rev. viii. 4) s. what is accepted and grateful. A.R. 394.

Smooth is pred. of truth, and, in an opp. sense, of what is false. 3527.

Smooth Man, a (Gen. xxvii. 11), s. the quality of natural truth. 3527.

Smyrna. (Rev. ii.) The church in S. s. those who are in goods as to life, but in falses as to doctrine, which is evident from the things written to it, when understood in the spiritual sense. A.R. 91.

Snake, or **Serpent**. The bite of a s. or s. (Amos v. 19) s. falsification of the Word, from the interior dominion of the false from evil. A.E. 781.

Snare. To be in a s. s. to be taken and seduced by one's own evil and false. 10.641.

Snares of **Death**. (Ps. xviii. 5.) The cords and s. of d. that compassed and prevented, s. temptations which being from hell, are also called the cords of hell, treating of the combats and victories of the Lord. L. 14.

Snorting of **Horses heard from Dan** (Jer. viii. 16), s. reasoning concerning truth from a principle not affirmative. 3923.

Snow s. truth in ultimates, for s. is from water, which s. the truths of faith. A.R. 47. S., or ice, cor. to the state of those who are in truth without good, or faith without charity. N.J.D. 114. S., also, from whiteness, is pred. of truth. 8459.

Soap, Waters of **Snow** and **Pit**. (Job. ix. 30.) Waters of s. den. truths which are or appear genuine; s. den. the good by which purification is effected; and the pit den. the false. A.E. 475.

Society. Every man as to his affections and consequent thoughts, is in s. with those who are in the world of spirits, and mediately through them with those who are either in heaven or in hell: the life of every man depends upon that connection. A.R. 552. If any one in another life be deprived of the s. in which he is, he becomes at first, as it were, almost lifeless, his life at such times being sustained only by an influx of heaven into his interiors. 1506. Heaven is distinguished into innumerable s.; in like manner, hell, der. from an opp. principle; and the mind of every man according to his will and consequent understanding, actually dwells in one

Socinians and Arians

s. and intends and thinks in like manner with those who compose the s. C.S.L. 530. Every one after death is bound to, or in fellowship with a certain s., and this immediately on his entering into the spiritual world; but a spirit in his first state knows nothing thereof, being then in his externals, and not as yet in internals. During his external state, he wanders hither and thither, wheresoever he pleases; but still he is actually where his love is, that is, in s. with those who are in a similar love, while a spirit is in this state, he appears in many other places, and also everywhere as if present in body, but this is only an appearance; wherefore as soon as ever he is brought by the Lord into his governing love, he immediately disappears from the sight of others, and is amongst his like in the s. to which he is bound. L.J. 32. A whole angelic s. appears as one in a human form. But although all who are in one s. when together, appear as one in the likeness of a man, yet one s. is not a like man as another, for they are distinguished one from another, as human faces from one stock. H. and H. 68–70. Every s. of heaven daily increases, and as it increases it becomes more perfect; thus not only that s. is perfected, but also heaven in common, because s. constitute heaven. H. and H. 71.

Socinians and **Arians**, the, although they do not deny the Lord, yet as they deny his divinity, they are without heaven and cannot be received by any angelic society. A.E. 778.

Sockets of **Gold**. To be encompassed with s. of g. (Exod. xxviii. 13) s. to be continued from good, and der. existence and subsistence. 9847.

Sodom den. all evil originating in self-love. 2220.

Sodom and **Egypt** (Rev. xi.) s. two infernal loves, which are the love of dominion grounded in self-love, and the love of rule grounded in the pride of self-der. intelligence. A.R. 502.

Sodom and **Gomorrah**. S. s. the evil of self-love, and G. the false thence der. 2220. See *Cry.*

Sojourn, to, in the Word s. to be instructed, for this reason, because sojourning and migration, or procession from place to place in heaven is nothing else but change of state, wherefore, wheresoever departure, sojourning, and translation from place to place occur in the Word, nothing is thereby suggested to the angels that such a change of state, which has place with those of whom such things are pred.; changes of state have respect to the thoughts and the affections; changes of state in respect to the thoughts are knowledges, which in the world of spirits are exhibited by instructions, which also was a reason why the men of the most ancient church, as having communication with the angelic heaven, by sojourning, had a perception only of instruction. 1463.

Sojourner, or **Stranger** (Matt. xxv. 32), s. one who is willing to be instructed. 4956.

Sojournings, land of (Gen. xvii. 8), in reference to the Lord, s. the life which he procured to himself by knowledges, by temptation combats, and by victories therein, by his own strength. 2025.

Soldiers (John xix. 24) s. those who are of the church and who fight for divine truth. A.E. 64.

Sole-subsisting. He is so called from whom every thing is. D.L.W. 363.

Soles of the **Feet** cor. to the sensual natural principle of man. A.E. 365. A.C. 2162. Beneath the s. of the f., are they, who in the life of the body, have lived to the world and to their own particular taste and temper, delighted with such things as are of the world, and have loved to live in splendor, but only from external cupidity, or that of the body, not from internal, or that of the mind. 4947. See *Love of Dominion.*

Solicitude. They have care for the morrow who are not content with their own lot, who do not trust to the Divine, but themselves, and who look only to worldly and terrestrial things, and not to heavenly. (See Matt. vi. 25, etc.; Luke xii. 11, etc.) 8478.

Solomon was permitted to institute idolatrous worship, for the purpose that he might rep. the Lord's kingdom or church with all the religions in the universal habitable world, for the church instituted with the Israelitish or Jewish nation, was a rep. church, wherefore all the judgments and statutes of that church, rep. the spiritual things of the church, which are its internals; the people itself, the church; the king, the Lord; David, the Lord about to come into the world; and S., the Lord after his coming: and because the Lord after the glorification of his human had power over heaven and earth, as he says (Matt. xxviii. 18), therefore the rep. of him, S., appeared in glory and magnificence, and was in wisdom above all the kings of the earth, and also built the temple; and he moreover, permitted and established the worship of many nations, by which were rep. the various religions in the world; the like things his wives s. who were seven hundred in number, and his concubines who were three hundred in number (1 Kings xi. 3), for a wife in the Word s. a church; and concubine, a religion. From these things it may be evident why it was given S. to build the temple, by which was s. the divine human of the Lord (John ii. 19, 21), and also the church: also that it was permitted him to establish idolatrous worship, and to marry so many wives. D.P. 245. S. rep. the Lord, both as to his celestial and spiritual kingdom. A.E. 654. See *Queen of Sheba*.

Solomon's Song, or the **Canticles**, is not amongst those books which are called Moses and the Prophets, because it has not an internal sense, but it is written in the ancient style, and is full of s. collected from the books of the ancient church, and of several particulars which in the ancient church s. celestial and spiritual love, and especially conjugial love. 3942.

Solomon's Temple rep. heaven and the church. A.E. 220. See *Temple*.

Son (Gen. v. 28) s. the rise of a new church. 526. S. (Gen. xxiv. 3) s. the Lord's rational principle as to good. 3024. S. (Gen. xxx. 7) s. a general truth. 3496. S. (Gen. xxxviii. 4) s. evil. 4823. S. (Gen. xxxviii. 5) s. what is idolatrous. 4825.

Son of God and **Son of Man**. The Lord, at one time, calls himself the S., at another time, the S. of man; and this always according to the subject treated or spoken of. When his divinity, his unity with the Father, his divine power, faith in him, and the life that is from him, are treated of, he then calls himself the S. of G., as in John v. 17-26, and elsewhere. But where what relates to the passion, the judgment, his coming, and in general to redemption, salvation, reformation, and regeneration are treated of, he then calls himself the s. of m.; the reason whereof is, because he is then spoken of as the Word; and he, as the Word, suffers, judges, comes into the world, redeems, saves, reforms, and regenerates. The reason why the Lord calls himself the S. of m. when judgment is treated of, is because all judgment is executed according to the divine truth, which is in the Word; that this judges every one, the Lord himself declares in John xii. 47, 48, and iii. 17, 18. L. 22. When the Lord put off the maternal humanity, he put on the divine humanity, by virtue whereof he called himself the S. of m., as he frequently does in the Word of the New Testament, and also the S. of G.; and by the S. of m. he s. the essential truth, and by the S. of G., the essential good which appertained to his human when made divine. 2159.

Son that is a Stranger (Gen. xvii. 12) s. those who are not born within the church, consequently, who are not principled in the goods and truths of faith, because not in the knowledges thereof; sons that are strangers also s. those who are in external worship. (Isa. lxi. 5.) 2049.

Song, a, s. acknowledgment and confession from joy of heart. A.R. 279.

Sons of the Stranger s. spurious truths, or falses; our s. s. the doctrinals of truth; and our daughters, the doctrinals of good. (Ps. xliv. 11, 12.) 489.

Sons-in-Law. (Gen. xix. 12.) S.-in-l. are truths associated to the affections of good. 2389.

Sons' Wives (Gen. vi. 18) s. truths adjoined to goods. 668.

Sons of **Bereavings** (Isa. xlix. 18) s. truths restored to the vastated church. 5536.

Sons of **Canaan**. (Gen. x.) They who are called the s. of C. were such as maintained external worship separate from internal. 1141.

Sons of **Concubines** s. the spiritual. 3246.

Sons of the **East** s., in general, those who are of the Lord's spiritual kingdom. 3239.

Sons of a **Father** den. truths der. from good, thus from one origin; all truths also are from one good. 5515.

Sons of **God** and **Sons** of **Light**. The spiritual man, who is an image, is called by the Lord a s. of l. (John xii. 36.) But the celestial man, who is a likeness, is called a s. of G. (John i. 12.) 51.

Sons of **God** and **Daughters** of **Man**. (Gen. vi. 2.) By the s. of G. seeing the d. of m. that they were good, and taking to themselves wives of all that they chose, is s. that they conjoined the doctrinals of faith with lusts, and that promiscuously. 569.

Sons of **Ham**. (Gen. x.) They who are named as the s. of H., were such as had a corrupt internal worship. 1141.

Sons of **Israel**, camp of the, rep. the church. C.L. 431.

Sons of **Jacob**, the, in general, s. all things which are in the Lord's divine natural. 4610. See *Jacob*.

Sons of **Japheth**. (Gen. x.) They who are named as the s. of J., were all such as maintained external worship cor. with internal, that is, who lived in simplicity, in friendship, and in mutual charity, and were acquainted with no other doctrinals than external rites. 1141.

Sons of the **Javanites** (Joel iv. 6) s. worship in externals separate from what is internal. 1151.

Sons of **Jerusalem** (Joel iv. 6) s. the spiritual things of faith, consequently, things internal. 1151.

Sons of **Judah** (Joel iv. 6) s. the celestial things of faith. 1151.

Sons of **Levi** (Deut. xxi. 5) s. the affection of good and truth, which is charity. A.E. 444.

Sons of the **Lord**. They who immediately approach the Lord, are his sons, because they are born anew from him, that is, regenerated, wherefore, he called his disciples sons. (John xii. 36; xiii. 33; xxi. 5.) A.R. 890.

Sons of **Nuptials** (Luke v. 35) s. the men of the church. A.E. 1189. A.C. 4434.

Sons of **Oil** s. doctrinal truths. A.E. 724. See *Olive Trees*.

Sons of **Shem**. (Gen. x.) They who were called the s. of S., were internal men, and worshipped the Lord, and loved their neighbor; whose church was nearly such as our true christian church. 1141.

Sons of **Thunder** (Mark iii. 17) s. truths from celestial good. A.E. 821.

Sons of **Zion** (Joel ii. 23) s. those who are in wisdom from divine truth. A.E. 922.

Sons of **Zion** and **Sons** of **Javan** (Zech. ix. 13) s. the truths of the Word, internal and external. A.E. 724.

Sons and **Daughters** s. truths and goods, which may appear from many passages in the prophets: for the conceptions and births of the church in the Word, as of old time, are called s. and d. But according to the nature and quality of the church, such are its s. and d., or such are its truths and goods. 489.

Song (Rev. v. 9) s. glorification, which is confession from joy of heart, because singing exalts, and causes affection from the heart to break out into sound, and show itself intensely in its life. Nor are the Psalms of David any other than s., for they were set to music and sung, for which reason they are also called s. in many places. That s. were used for the sake of exalting the life of love and the joy der. from it, is evident from many passages. A.R. 279. By singing a new s., is s. an acknowledgment and glorification of the Lord, as being the only judge, redeemer, and saviour, consequently, the God of heaven and earth. A.R. 617.

Song of **Moses** and the **Song** of the **Lamb**. (Rev. xv. 3.) The s. of M. s. confession grounded in a life according to the precepts of the law, which is the decalogue; and the s. of the L., confession grounded in faith concerning the divinity of the Lord's humanity. A.R. 662.

Songs in the ancient and Jewish churches were prophetical concerning the Lord, especially that he should come into the world, and subdue the diabolical spirits, and liberate the faithful from their assaults. 8261. Heavenly s. are nothing else but affections made sonorous or affections expressed and modified by sounds, for as thoughts are expressed by discourse, so are affections by s.; and from the measure and flow of the modulation, angels perceive the object of the affection. C.S.L. 55.

Soothsayers. Such as studied natural magic. 3698.

Sorceries. In Rev. ix. 21, s. are mentioned in place of the eighth precept in the decalogue, "Thou shalt not bear false witness," for the three other evils, which are murders, fornications, and thefts, are there named. To bear false witness, s., in the natural sense, to act the part of a false witness, to lie and defame; and in the spiritual sense, to confirm and persuade that what is false is true, and that what is evil is good; from which it is evident, that by sorcery is s. to persuade to what is false, and thus to destroy truth. S. were in use among the ancients, and were performed in three ways; first, by keeping the hearing and thus the mind of another continually intent upon his words and sayings, without retaining aught from them; and, at the same time, by an aspiration and inspiration of thought conjoined with affection, by means of the breath, into the sound of the voice, whereby the hearer is incapable of thinking any thing from himself; in this manner did the lovers of falsehood pour in their falses with violence. Secondly, they infused a persuasion, which was done by detaining the mind from every thing of a contrary nature, and directing the attention exclusively to the idea involved in that which was uttered by themselves, hence the spiritual sphere of his mind dispelled the spiritual sphere of the mind of another, and stifled it; this was the kind of spiritual fascination which the magi of old made use of, and which was spoken of as the tying up and binding the understanding. The latter kind of sorcery pertained only to the spirit or thought, but the former to the lips or speech also. Thirdly, the hearer kept his mind so fixed in his own opinion, that he almost shut his ears against hearing any thing from the speaker, which was done by holding the breath, and sometimes by a tacit muttering, and thus by a continual negation of his adversary's sentiment. This kind of sorcery was practised by those who heard others, but the two former by those who spake to others. These three kinds of s. prevailed among the ancients, and prevail still among infernal spirits; but with men in the world there remains only the third kind, and this with those, who, from the pride of their own intelligence, have confirmed in themselves the falses of religion; for these, when they hear things contrary, admit them no further into their thought than to mere contact, and then from the interior recess of their mind they emit, as it were, fire which consumes them, about which the other knows nothing except by conjecture drawn from the countenance and the sound of the voice in reply, provided the sorcerer does not, by dissimulation, restrain that fire, or what is the same, the anger of his pride. This kind of sorcery operates at the present day, to prevent truths

Sorceries and Inchantments

from being accepted, and, with many, to their not being understood. That in ancient times many magical arts prevailed, and among these, s., is evident from Moses: "When thou art come into the land, thou shalt not learn to do after the abominations of those nations, there shall not be found among you one that maketh his son or his daughter to pass through the fire, or that useth divinations, or an observer of times, or an enchanter, or a witch, or a charmer of incantations, and a consulter with familiar spirits, or a wizard, or a necromancer; for all these things are an abomination unto Jehovah." (Deut. xviii. 9, 10, 11.) On the other hand, incantations s. the rejection of falsity by truths, which was also effected by tacitly thinking and whispering, from a zeal for truth in opposition to falsehood. (See Isa. iii. 1, 2, 5; xxvi. 16; Ps. lviii. 17; Jer. viii. 17.) A.R. 462.

Sorceries and **Inchantments** (Isa. xlvii. 9) are pred. of the profanation of truth. 1368.

Sore (Rev. xvi. 2) s. interior evils and falses destructive of all good and truth in the church; by noisome or noxious is s. destructive, and evil cannot but destroy good, and falsehood truth. The reason why s. has this signification is, because s. of the body proceed from a corrupt state of the blood or some other interior malignity; it is the same with s., when understood in a spiritual sense, these proceed from concupiscences and their delights which are interior causes; evil itself, which is s. by s., and appears pleasant in externals, inwardly in itself conceals concupiscences, from which it proceeds, and of which it is compounded. Ulcers and wounds s. evils in extremes, or external parts, proceeding from interior evils, which are concupiscences, also in the following passages: Isa. i. 6, 7; Ps. xxxviii. 5, 6; Isa. xxx. 26; Deut. xxviii. 15, 27, 35. Neither by the boil breaking out with blains upon man and upon beast in Egypt (Exod. ix. 8–11), was any thing else s.; for the miracles performed in Egypt s. the evils and falses in which they were principled. And inasmuch as the Jewish nation were guilty of profaning the Word, which profanation is s. by leprosy, therefore the leprosy was not only in their flesh, but also in their clothes, houses, and vessels; and the kinds of profanation are s. by the various evils of leprosy, which were tumors, ulcerous tumors, white and red spots, abscesses, scalds, freckled spots, scurfs, etc. (Lev. xiii. 1 to the end.) For the church with that nation was a rep. church, in which internals were rep. by cor. externals. A.R. 678.

Sorrow. The woman condemned to bring forth sons in s. den. the anxieties and combats attending the production of truths. 261–3.

Soul. 1. That the term s., in general, s. man; 2. That the term s., specifically, s. the life of the body; 3. That the term s. s. the life of the spirit of man; 4. That the term s. s. the faculty of understanding; 5. That the term s. s. divine truth; 6. That the term s. s. spiritual life; 7. That the living s. s. life in general. A.E. 750. That the s. of the hungry s. the understanding of good. A.E. 750. S., in the celestial sense, s. the divine proceeding from the Lord. A.E. 750. S. (Gen. ix. 4) is pred. of the life of the regenerate man, which is separate from the will-principle of man. 1000. S. (Isa. xxix. 8) s. the faith of the false der. from no understanding of truth. A.E. 750. S. (Jer. xxxi. 12, 25) s. the affection of truth and good. 2930. S. (Ezek. xxvii. 13; Rev. xviii. 13) s. the science of truth in the natural man. A.E. 750. To require the s. of man is to vindicate profanation. (Gen. ix. 5.) 1004. By not loving their s. (Rev. xii. 11) is s. not to love self and the world more than the Lord; and the things which are of the Lord unto death s. to be willing to die rather; consequently, it is to love the Lord above all things, and one's neighbor as one's self (Matt. xxii. 35–38), and to be willing to die rather than to recede from those two loves. The same is s. by the following passages: Matt. x. 39; Luke xvii. 33; John xii. 25; Matt. xvi. 24, 25; Mark viii. 35, 36, 37; Luke ix. 24, 25. A.R. 556. The s. of every man, from its origin, is heavenly, wherefore, it receives influx immediately from the Lord, for it receives from him the marriage of love and wisdom, or of good and truth, and this influx makes him man, and distinguishes him from beasts. C.S.L. 482. The s. of man is nothing else but the internal man, and the internal man, after death, appears altogether as a man in the world, with a like face, a like body, a like sensitive and thinking faculty. 5511. The s. of man, which lives after death, is his spirit; and this is in perfect form a man, and the s. of this form is the will and understanding, and the s. of these is love and wisdom from the Lord, and these two constitute the life of man. D.L.W. 394, 395. The s. of the Lord was Jehovah. N.J.D. 298. U.T. 167.

Soul and **Heart.** By s. and h. is meant the life of man, is plain, but the life of man is from his will and understanding, or spiritually speaking, from love and wisdom, also from charity and faith; and the life of the will from the good of love, or of charity, is meant by the h., and the life of the understanding from the truths of wisdom, or of faith, is meant by the s.: this is what is meant by s. and h. in Matt. xxii. 3; Mark xii. 30, 33; Luke x. 27; Deut. vi. 5; x. 11; xi. 14; xxvi. 16; Jer. xxxii. 41, and other places; it is the same in those passages where the h. is mentioned by itself, and the s. by itself. The reason of their being named, is grounded in the cor. of the h. with the will and love, and of the animation or respiration of the lungs with the understanding and wisdom. A.R. 681.

Soul and **Body.** The s. of the offspring is from the father, and its clothing from the mother. That the s. is from the father, is doubted by no wise man; it is also manifestly conspicuous from minds, and likewise from faces which are types of minds, in descendants who proceed from fathers of families in just series; for the father returns, as in effigy, if not in his sons, yet, in his grandsons and great-grandsons; and this by reason that the s. constitutes the inmost principle of man, and this inmost principle may be covered and concealed by the offspring nearest in descent, but, nevertheless, it comes forth and manifests itself in the more remote issue. That the s. is from the father, and the clothing from the mother, may be ill. by things analogous in the vegetable kingdom; in this kingdom the earth or ground is the common mother, which in itself, as in a womb, receives and clothes seeds, yea, as it were, conceives, bears, brings forth, and educates them, as a mother her offspring from the father. C.S.L. 206. The human b. exists and subsists by the s., wherefore, in the b., all and singular things are rep. of its s.; the s. regards uses and ends, but the b. is employed in promoting, or bringing into effect, such uses and ends. 1807. See *Lord.*

Soul and **Spirit.** (Isa. xxvi. 9.) S. s. the affection of truth, and s., the affection of good. 2930.

Soul of **Beasts,** the, considered in itself, is spiritual; for affection, of whatever kind it be, whether it be good or evil, is spiritual, for it is a derivation of some love, and der. its origin from the heat and light, which proceed from the Lord as a sun; and whatsoever proceeds thence is spiritual. Beasts and wild beasts, whose souls are similar evil affections, as mice, venemous serpents, crocodiles, basilisks, or cocatrices, vipers, etc., with the various kinds of noxious insects, were not created from the beginning, but have originated with hell, in stagnant lakes, marshes, putrid and fetid waters, etc., with which the malignant loves of the infernal societies communicate. There is also in every spiritual principle a plastic force, where homogeneous exhalations are present in nature; and there is also in every spiritual principle a propagative force, for it not only forms organs of sense and motion, but also organs of prolification, by wombs or by eggs; but from the beginning only useful and clean beasts were created, whose souls are good affections. It is to be observed, however, that the s. of b. are not spiritual in that degree in which the souls of men are, but in an inferior degree,

Soul of Vegetables

for there are seven degrees of spirituality, and the affections of the inferior degree, although viewed in their origin they are spiritual, are yet to be called natural, being similar to the affections of the natural man. There are three degrees of natural affections in beasts, as well as man; in the lowest degree are insects of various kinds; in the superior degree are the fowls of the heaven, and in a still superior degree are the beasts of the earth, which were created from the beginning. A.E. 1201.

Soul of **Vegetables**. By vegetative soul is understood the conatus and effort of producing a vegetable from its seed progressively even to new seeds, and thereby of multiplying itself to infinity, and propagating itself to eternity, for there is, as it were, an idea of what is infinite and eternal in every vegetable; for one seed may be multiplied through a certain number of years so as to fill the whole earth, and also may be propagated from seed to seed without end. This, together with the wonderful propagation of growth from the root into a germ, afterwards into a trunk, likewise into branches, leaves, flowers, fruits, even into new seeds, is not natural, but spiritual. A.E. 1203. The origin of the vegetative soul is also from use, affections having respect to uses: use is the subject of all affection; for man cannot be affected, except it be for the sake of somewhat, and this somewhat is use. Now, since all affection supposes use, and the vegetative soul, from its spiritual origin, is affection, as was said, therefore, it is also use. From this cause it is that in every vegetable there is contained a use, a spiritual use in the spiritual world, and a spiritual and also a natural use in the natural world; the spiritual use is for the various states of the mind, and natural use is for the various states of the body. The external spiritual use from them in the heavens, is recreation of minds: and the internal is the representation of divine things in them, and thereby also the elevation of the mind; for the wiser angels see in them the nature and quality of their affections in a series, the varieties of flowers in their order, and, at the same time, the variegations of colors, and likewise of odors, make those affections manifest, and whatever lies interiorly hid in them; for every ultimate affection which is called natural, although it is spiritual, der. its quality from some interior affection, which is of intelligence and wisdom, and these der. their quality from use and its love. In a word, nothing springs up and flourishes from the ground in the heavens, but use, for use is the vegetative soul. Since use is the vegetative soul, therefore, in those places in the spiritual world, which are called deserts where they dwell who in the world had rejected works of charity, which are essential uses, there appears neither grass nor herb, but mere wastes and sand. A.E. 1214.

Soul going forth and **dying** (Gen. xxxv. 18) s. the ultimate of temptation, which is when the old man dies and the new receives life. 4590.

Soul of thy **Turtle Dove** (Ps. lxxiv. 19) s. the life of faith. 870.

Sound and **Speech**. S. cor. to affection, and s. to thought, wherefore affection utters s., and thought utters s. A.R. 875.

Sound of **Spiritual Language**, the, differs so far from that of natural l. that a spiritual s., though loud, cannot at all be heard by a natural man, nor a natural s. by a s. man. C.S.L. 326.

Sounds in the Spiritual World. Discrete s. excite the affection of truth, in the s. w., and continuous s. excite the affections of good. A.E. 323.

Source, the only, of life is the Lord, and the s. of evil is the love of self and the world. D.P. 292, 139.

South and **Southward** den. truth in light. 9642. Land of the s. (Gen. xxiv. 62) s. divine light, for the s. s. light, and indeed the light of intelligence, which is wisdom, but the land of the s. den. the place and state where that light is. 3195. See *Quarters*.

Special Principles

Sow (Isa. xxviii. 24) s. to learn. A.E. 374. To s. beside all waters (Isa. xxxii. 20) is pred. of those who suffer themselves to be instructed in things spiritual. 2781.

Sow, to, and Reap (Isa. xxxvii. 30) s. the implantation of good and its reception. A.E. 706.

Sower, the parable of the. (Luke viii. 5–8; Matt. xii. 3–8; Mark iv. 3–8.) The s. here is the Lord, and the seed is his Word, thus truth; the seed by the wayside is with those who have no concern about truths; the seed on stony ground is with those who have a concern about truth, but not for its own sake, and thus not inwardly; the seed in the midst of thorns is with those who are in the concupiscences of evil; but the seed in the good ground is with those who love the truths contained in the Word, from the Lord, and practise them in dependence on him, and thus bring forth fruit; that this is the meaning of the parable appears from the Lord's explication of it. (Matt. xiii. 19–23; Mark iv. 14–20; Luke viii. 11–15.) Dec. 90.

Space and **Time**. There are two things, which, during man's life in the world, appear essential, because they are proper to nature, namely, s. and t.; hence to live in t., is to live in the world or nature, but these two things become none in another life; still they appear in the world of spirits as something, by reason that spirits recent from the body have with them an idea of natural things, nevertheless they afterwards perceive, that in the spiritual world there is neither s. nor t., but instead thereof states, and that states in another life cor. to s. and t. in nature: to s., states as to esse, and to t., states as to existere. 2625.

Spaces, in the spiritual world, are appearances arising from the diversity of affection and of thought thence der. A.E. 282.

Sparrow and **Swallow**. (Ps. lxxxiv. 3.) S. here s. spiritual truth, and s. natural truth, from which worship is performed. A.E. 391.

Speak, to, in the internal sense, den. to think, because thought is interior speech, and when man thinks, he then s. with himself; interior things are expressed in the sense of the letter by the exterior things which cor. 5000. To s., in an internal sense, s. both to perceive and to will. 2965. To s. when pred. of Jehovah, s. to perceive. 2287. By God's s. to Noah (Gen. viii. 15), is s. the presence of the Lord with the man of the church, may appear from the internal sense of the Word. The Lord s. with every man, for whatever is good and true, which a man wills and thinks, is from the Lord. There are with every man at least two evil spirits, and two angels, the former excite his evils, the latter inspire him with goods and truths; all good and truth which the angels inspire is from the Lord, thus the Lord continually s. with man, but altogether differently with different men: with such as suffer themselves to be drawn away by evil spirits, the Lord s. as absent, or at a distance, so that it can scarcely be said that he s., but with such as are led by the Lord, the Lord s. more present; which may sufficiently appear from this consideration, that no one can possibly think any thing good and true but from the Lord. 904. To s. (Gen. xxiii. 13) s. influx. 2951. To s. (Rev. xiii. 11) s. affection, thought, doctrine, and preaching. A.E. 817.

Speak, to, **Great Things** and **Blasphemies** (Rev. xiii. 5) s. to teach what is evil and false. A.R. 582.

Speak, to, a **Word against** the **Son** of **Man** s. to interpret the natural sense of the Word according to appearances. A.E. 778.

Speaking with Spirits. See D.P. 135.

Spear. S. and swords s. truths adapted to spiritual warfare. A.R. 299. See *Bow* and *Spear, Shield, Buckler.*

Special Principles of **Doctrine** s. doctrinals of good and truth from the Word. See *Dothan.* But when the church commences from faith and separates from charity, it s. special things of false principles. 4720.

299

Speckled and Variegated

Speckled and **Variegated**. (Gen. xxx. 35.) S. s. good sprinkled and mixed with evils; and v., truth sprinkled and mixed with evils. 4006. See *Spotted.*

Speckled Bird (Jer. xii. 9) s. ratiocinations from falses. A.E. 650.

Speech, angelic, or language, which is spiritual, when it falls into human expressions, cannot fall into any other s. or language than such as is used in the Word, every singular thing therein being rep., and every singular expression being significative; the ancients, because they had commerce with spirits and angels, had no other s. or language than this, which was full of rep., and in every expression of which was a spiritual sense. 3482. In the natural world the s. of man is twofold, because his thought is twofold, exterior and interior; for a man can speak from interior thought and at the same time from exterior thought, and he can speak from exterior thought and not from interior, yea contrary to interior thought, whence comes dissimulation, flattery, and hypocrisy; but in the spiritual world man's s. is not twofold, but single; a man there speaks as he thinks, otherwise the sound is harsh and offends the ear; but yet he may be silent, and so not publish the thoughts of his mind; a hypocrite, therefore, when he comes into the company of the wise, either goes away, or retires to a corner of the room, and withdraws himself from observation and sits silent. A.R. 293. The angels from the sound of the voice know a man's love, from the articulation of the sound, his wisdom, and from the sense of the word, his science. D.L.W. 280. Spiritual s. comprehends thousands of things which natural s. cannot express, and, what is wonderful, which cannot be formed into ideas of natural thought. A.R. 875.

Spelt, or **Fitches,** s. various species of good. 3332. Also knowledges. A.E. 374.

Spermatic Vessels des. 5391.

Spew, to. (Rev. iii. 16.) "I will s. thee out of my mouth," s. to be separated from the Lord, and such separation from the Lord consists in being neither in heaven nor in hell, but in a place apart, deprived of human life, where mere phantasies exist; the reason is, because they have mixed truths with falses, and goods with evils, thus holy things with profane, in such a manner that they cannot be separated. The world of spirits, which is in the midst between heaven and hell, and into which every man first comes after death, and is there prepared, cor. to the stomach, in which all the ingesta are prepared for being converted either into blood and flesh, or excrement and urine, the latter having cor. with hell, but the former with heaven, but the substances that are vomited out of the stomach, are such as have not undergone that separation, but remain commixed. By reason of this cor. the expressions vomited and vomit, are used in the following passages: Hab. xi. 15, 16; Jer. xlviii. 26; Isa. xxviii. 8; besides other passages, as Jer. xxv. 27; Lev. xviii. 24, 25, 28. That warm water excites vomiting, is also from cor. A.R. 204. Shameful spewing (Hab. ii. 16), is pred. of the falsification of divine truth. A.E. 960.

Sphere. There goes out, yea, flows forth from every man a spiritual s., from the affections of his love, which encompasses him, and infuses itself into the natural s. which is from the body, so that the two s. are conjoined; that a natural s. is continually flowing forth, not only from man, but also from beasts, yea from trees, fruits, flowers, and also from metals, is a thing generally known; in like manner in the spiritual world; but the s. flowing forth from subjects in that world are spiritual, and those which emanate from spirits and angels are thoroughly spiritual, because with them there are affections of love, and thence interior perceptions and thoughts; all of sympathy and antipathy has hence its rise, and likewise all conjunction and disjunction, and according thereto presence and absence in the spiritual world, for what is homogeneous or concordant causes conjunction and presence, and what is heterogeneous and discordant, causes disjunction and absence, wherefore those s. cause distance in that world. C.S.L. 171. The divine s. which surrounds the Lord, is from his divine love, and at the same time from his divine wisdom, which, when it is rep. in the heavens, appears in the celestial kingdom red like a ruby, in the spiritual kingdom blue like the lazule stone, in the natural kingdom green like the emerald; everywhere with ineffable splendor and effulgence. A.R. 232. The s. which are perceived in the other life, all arise from loves and consequent affections, in which the spirits had been principled, consequently, from the life, for loves and consequent affections make the very life itself; and inasmuch as they arise from loves and consequent affections, they arise from the intentions and ends, for the sake of which man so wills and so acts, for every one has for an end what he loves, therefore ends determine man's life and constitute its quality, hence especially in his s.; this s. is perceived most exquisitely in heaven, by reason that the universal heaven is in a s. of ends. 4446. See *Odors*.

Sphincter. Spirits des. who cor. with the s. 5389.

Spice (Ezek. xxvii. 22), in an internal sense, is charity. 1171. S. (1 Kings x. 2) s. interior truths. 10.199.

Spices, Resin, and **Myrrh** (Gen. xxxvii. 25), s. interior natural truths conjoined to good in the natural principle. Amongst the ancients, in their sacred worship, things of a sweet smell and fragrant were applied, whence came their incenses and perfumes; like things were also mixed in the oils with which they were anointed; but at this day it is not known in what this originated; the reason is, because at this day it is not known, that the things applied in worship amongst the ancients der. their origin from things spiritual and celestial, which are in the heavens, and that they cor. thereto; man has removed himself so far from those things, and immersed himself in natural, worldly, and corporeal things, that he is in an obscure principle, and many in a negative principle, respecting the existence of any thing spiritual and celestial. The ground and reason why incenses and perfumes were applied by the ancients to sacred purposes was, because odor cor. to perception, a fragrant odor, as of s. of various kinds, to a grateful and agreeable perception, such as is that of truth grounded in good, or of faith grounded in charity. 4748. See *Odors*.

Spiders' Webs (Isa. lix. 5) s. treacherous, falses. L.E. 581.

Spies (Gen. xlii. 9) den. those who learn the truths of the church only to secure gain. 5432.

Spinal Marrow. Des. of spirits who flow into the s. m. 5717.

Spine, or **Thorn,** den. curse and vastation. 273.

Spiral. The contraction of the spiritual degree is like the retortion of a spire. D.L.W. 254.

Spirit. To be in the s. is to be in vision, which is effected by the opening of the sight of a man's s., which, when it is opened, the things which are in the natural world appear to the bodily sight. In this state the disciples were, when they saw the Lord after his resurrection, wherefore it is said that their eyes were opened. (Luke xxiv. 30, 31.) Abraham was in a similar state when he saw the three angels; so were Hagar, Gideon, Joshua, and others, when they saw the angel of Jehovah. A.R. 36. See *Prophets*.

Spirit. By s. is understood the life of man in general; the various affections of life with man, also the life of the regenerate which is called the spiritual life, also spiritual life communicated to those who are in humiliation: but where the s. is spoken of as relative to the Lord, it s. his divine life, consequently, the Lord himself; and in particular the life of his wisdom which is the divine truth. L. 47, 48, 49, 50, 51. S. s. the understanding. D.L.W. 583. The s. which speaketh to the churches, s. the divine truth of the Word.

Spirit of God

A.R. 87. S. (Rev. xviii. 2) s. all that relates to affection and will, and thence to action. A.R. 757.

Spirit of God (Gen. i. 2) s. the divine mercy of the Lord. 19. The s. of G. is his proceeding emanation. D.L.W. 100. The s. of G. den. good from an interior principle, thus from the divine, for the s. of G. is what proceeds from the divine, thus from good itself, for the divine is good itself, and what proceeds from it is truth wherein is good, and this is what is s. in the Word by the s. of G., for the s. itself does not proceed, but the truth itself wherein is good, the s. being the instrument whereby it is produced. 5307.

Spirit of God and the **Holy Spirit**. The s. of G. and the h. s. are two distinct things. The s. of G. did not operate, neither could it operate on man but imperceptibly; whereas the h. s., which proceeds slowly from the Lord, operates on man perceptibly, and enables him to comprehend spiritual truths after a natural manner; for to the divine celestial and the divine spiritual the Lord has united the divine natural also, by which he operates from the divine celestial and divine spiritual. Besides, holy in the Word is alone pred. of divine truth, consequently, of the Lord, who is divine truth, not only in the celestial and spiritual sense, but also in the natural sense; wherefore it is said in the Apocalypse, that the Lord alone is holy. (Chap. xv. 3, 4; see also John vii. 39.) N.Q. 5.

Spirit of Jehovah, the, s. the influx of truth and goodness. 573.

Spirit of Judgment and **Spirit of Expurgation**. (Isa. iv. 4.) The s. of j. s. the understanding of truth, and the s. of e., the affection of spiritual truth, for this purges or cleanses. A.E. 475.

Spirit of Prophecy (Rev. xix. 10) s. the all of the Word, and of doctrine deduced from it. A.R. 819.

Spirit of Storms and an **overflowing Rain** (Ezek. xiii. 11, 13, 14) s. the desolation of what is false. 739.

Spirit of Truth, the (John xv. 26), s. truth itself proceeding from the Lord, wherefore it is said of him, that "he will not speak from himself, but from the Lord." John xiv. 13–16. A.R. 6.

Spirit of Whoredom (Hosea iv. 12) s. the life of the false grounded in evil. 4876.

Spirit and Bird. (Rev. xviii. 2.) S. s. all that relates to affection and will, and thence to action; and b. s. all that relates to thought or understanding, and thence to deliberation; for which reason, by a foul s. and an unclean b. are s. all the evils which pertain to the will and consequent actions, and all the falses which pertain to the thought and consequent deliberations. A.R. 757.

Spirit and Bride. (Rev. xxii. 17.) S. s. heaven, and b. the church. A.R. 955. Also the church as to good and as to truth. A.E. 1189.

Spirit and Life. (John vi. 63.) S. has respect to the spiritual sense of the Word, and life to the celestial sense. S.S. 39. In every particular of the Word there is a s. and l., for the Lord spake the Word, therefore he himself is in it, and he so spake the Word, that every thing in it has communication with heaven, and through heaven, with him, there being a spiritual sense in it, by which this communication is effected; wherefore the Lord said, "the words which I speak unto you, are s. and l." (John vi. 63.) A.R. 602.

Spirits. With every man there are attendant s. and angels, by whom he is ruled of the Lord. 50. S. have sight, hearing, smelling, touch, more exquisite than when in the body, also, lusts, affections, thoughts, and all faculties more excellent: and they discourse one amongst another. 321, 322. S. and angels have every sense except taste. 1880, 1881. S. and angels are attendant on every man, and by them there is communication. 2886. To the intent that man may live, it is altogether necessary that angels from heaven and s. from hell be adjoined to him. 5993. Seven s. (Matt. xii. 45) s.

all falses of evil, consequently, a plenary or total extinction of goodness and truth. A.R. 10. Seven s. (Rev. i. 4) s. all who are in divine truth, and in an abstract sense, the divine true or divine truth itself. A.R. 14. S. of demons (Rev. xvi.) s. cupidities of falsifying truths. A.R. 704. The s. which have intercourse with man put on all things which are man's. 5853. See *Persuasion.* See *Emissary Spirits.*

Spiritual. What is s. is pred., both of the rational and of the natural, for what is s. is the divine truth which is from the Lord, which, when it shines in the rational or in the internal man, is called the s. of the rational, and when it shines in the natural or in the external man, is called the s. of the natural. 4675.

Spiritual Body. Every soul of man is in a s. b., after it has put off its material coverings which it carried about with it in the world. D.L.W. 14. The s. b., or the b. of the spirit of man, is formed solely from those things which man does from his will or love. H. and H. 475. The natural mind of man consists of spiritual substances, and at the same time of natural substances. From its spiritual substances becomes thought, but not from the natural substances, the latter substances recede when a man dies, but not the spiritual substances, wherefore that same mind after death, when a man becomes a spirit or an angel, remains in a similar form to that in which it was in the world; the natural substances of that mind which recede by death, constitute the cutaneous covering of the spiritual body in which spirits and angels are; by means of such covering which is taken from the natural world, their s. b. subsist, for the natural is the containing ultimate; hence it is that there is not any spirit or angel, who was not born a man. D.L.W. 257.

Spiritual Celestial Principle is an intermediate between the natural, or external man, and between the rational or internal. 4594.

Spiritual Church, the, extends over the whole globe, not being limited to those who have the Word, and who thereby know the Lord, and some particular truths of faith; but it is also amongst those who have not the Word, and who therefore are altogether ignorant of the Lord, and consequently, do not know any truths of faith (for all the truths of faith have respect unto the Lord); that is, it is amongst the Gentiles remote from the church, for there are several amongst them who know by rational illumination that there is one God, that he created all things, and that he preserves all things, likewise that from him comes all good, consequently, all truth, and that similitude with him makes man blessed; and who moreover live according to their religious tenets, in love to that God and in charity towards their neighbor; from the affection of good doing works of charity. 3263. The essential of the s. c. is the good of truth. 6426.

Spiritual Fire. Good is actually s. f., from which spiritual heat, which makes it alive, is der. 4906.

Spiritual Good is truth, which has been made good, for truth is made good when the life is according to it, for in such case it passes into the will, and from the will into the act, and is made the life's, and when truth is made the life's it is no longer called truth but good; the will, which transforms truth into good, is the new will in the intellectual part; this good is what is called s. g.; s. g. is distinguished from celestial good in this, that celestial good is implanted in the will part itself of man. 5595. See *Good.*

Spiritual Heaven. With this h. man communicates by remains; this h. it is which is opened when man is regenerating, and it is this h. which is closed when man does not suffer himself to be regenerated; for remains, or truths and goods stored up in the interiors, are nothing else but cor. with the societies of that h. 5344.

Spiritual Light and **Natural Light.** There is s. l. and n. l., both as to external appearance alike, but as to internal unlike, for n. l. is from the sun of the

Spiritual Light

natural world, and thence in itself is void of life, whereas s. l. is from the sun of the spiritual world, and thence in itself is living; this last illuminates the understanding, and not n. l. D.P. 166. When s. l. flows into n. l. with a man who is reading the Word, he is illuminated, and sees truths there, for the objects of s. l. are truths. A.R. 911.

Spiritual Light and **Spiritual Heat.** S. l. flows into man by three degrees, but not s. h., except so far as man avoids evils as sins, and looks up to the Lord. D.L.W. 243. S. l. constitutes the life of the understanding, and s. h. the life of the will; s. l. is from its first origin divine truth from the divine good of the Lord, and hence the truth of faith from the good of charity; and s. h. from its first origin is the divine good of the divine love of the Lord, and hence the good of celestial love, which is love to the Lord, and the good of spiritual love, which is charity towards the neighbor; these two principles constitute all the life of man. 6032.

Spiritual Man, the, is not the interior rational man, but the interior natural; for the interior rational man is what is called celestial. 4402.

Spiritual Natural and **Celestial Natural Angels** are they who are in the first, or ultimate heaven. The s. n. a. belong to the Lord's spiritual kingdom, and communicate with the second heaven; and the c. n. a. belong to his celestial kingdom, and communicate with the third heaven. A.E. 449.

Spiritual Nuptials are understood by the words of the Lord, "that after the resurrection they are not given in marriage." By s. n. is understood conjunction with the Lord, and this is effected on earth, and when it is effected on earth, it is also effected in the heavens, wherefore in the heavens the nuptials are not repeated, neither are they given in marriage. C.S.L. 41. See *Marriages.*

Spiritual Principle, the, consists in comprehending things abstractedly from the letter of the Word, to which things the literal sense serves for an object, as the things which the eye sees, serve as objects of thinking concerning things more sublime. 2275.

Spiritual Sense of the **Word.** There is a s. s. in every particular of the Word, which differs from the literal sense, as that which is spiritual differs from that which is natural. A.R. 768. The true s. s. of the W. is abstracted from persons, spaces, and times, and the like things, which are proper to nature. A.E. 175. The s. s. of the W. is not that which breaks forth as light out of the literal sense, whilst a person is studying and explaining the Word to confirm some particular tenet of the church, for this sense is the literal sense of the Word. But the s. s. does not appear in the sense of the letter, it is within it, as the soul is in the body, or as the thought of the understanding is in the eye, or as the affection of love is in the countenance, which act together as cause and effect. It is this sense, principally which renders the Word spiritual, not only for the use of men, but also for the use of angels; whence also by means of that sense, the Word communicates with the heavens. S.S. 5. The s. s. of the W. is not given to any one except by the Lord alone, and it is guarded by him as the angelic heaven is guarded, for this is in it. U.T. 230. It is owing to the s. s. that the Word is divinely inspired, and holy in every syllable. U.T. 200.

Spiritual Sight. Sight abstracted from such things as are of the world, that is s. s., is nothing else but the perception of truth, that is, of such things as are of faith, wherefore, by seeing in the internal sense nothing else is s.; for the internal sense comes forth, when those things are drawn aside which are of the world, inasmuch as the internal sense relates to such things as are of heaven: the light of heaven, whereby sight is effected there, is divine truth from the Lord, which appears before the eyes of the angels as light, a thousand times brighter than the midday light in the world, and this light, inasmuch as it has life in it, on that account illuminates the sight of the understanding of the angels, at the same time that it illuminates the sight of the eye, and causes an apperception of truth, according to the quantity and quality of the good in which they are principled. 5400.

Spiritual Speech is not twofold, but single; a man there speaks as he thinks. A.R. 293. It comprehends thousands of things which the natural cannot express. A.R. 875. See *Speech.*

Spiritual Sun, in its essence, is pure love proceeding from Jehovah God. I. 5. See *Sun of the Spiritual World.*

Spiritual World. In the s. w., by which is understood both the heavens and the hells, such is the arrangement, that the heavens are as expanses one above another, and under the heavens is the world of spirits, and under this are the hells, one below another; according to this successive arrangement, descends influx from the Lord, thus through the inmost heaven into the middle, and through this into the ultimate, and from these in their order, into the subjacent hells. The world of spirits is in the midst, and receives influx as well from the heavens as the hells, every one there according to the state of his life. But this arrangement of the heavens and the hells underwent changes, from one judgment to another. A.E. 702. In the s. w. there are all the objects that exist in the natural world, but with this difference, that all the things in the s. w. are cor., for they cor. to the interiors of its inhabitants, being splendid and magnificent with those who are in wisdom, der. from divine truths and goods through the Word from the Lord, and the contrary with those who are in a state of madness from falses and evils; such a cor. by virtue of creation, exists when what is spiritual in the mind is let down into what is sensual in the body, for which reason, every one in the s. w. knows the quality of another, as soon as he comes into his apartment. A.R. 772. With the inhabitants of the s. w., the third [degree] which is natural, is wanting. C.S.L. 52. The s. w. is where man is, and not at all removed from him. D.L. and W. n. 92.

Spiritual and Celestial. All those things are called s. which are of the knowledges of faith, and all those things c. which are of love towards the Lord, and towards the neighbor; the former appertain to the understanding of man, the latter to the will. 61.

Spittle. It is said, that the Lord spat upon the ground, and made clay of the s., and anointed the eyes of the blind man with the clay, by which was s. reformation by truths from the letter of the Word. A.E. 239.

Spleen. They who are in the province of the s., are almost directly above the head, but their operation falls thither. 5184.

Splendid Things s. truths and things magnificent hence der. A.E. 1159.

Spoil, to (Gen. xxxiv. 27), s. to destroy. 4503. S. (Deut. xiii. 16) s. the falsification of truth. A.E. 652. Spoiled s. destitute of goods. A.E. 714.

Spoil of Gold, and **Silver**, and **Cattle** (Num. xxv., xxxi.), s. truths falsified. 3242.

Spoil in mine House (Mal. iii. 10) s. remains in the internal man, insinuated, as it were, by theft amongst so many evils and falses. 576.

Spoiled s. destitute of goods. A.E. 714.

Spoiler (Jer. xlviii. 32) s. evil and its derivative false. A.E. 919.

Spoiler of **Moab** (Jer. xlviii. 18) s. the adulteration of the Word, as to its literal sense. A.E. 727.

Sponge (Matt. xxvii. 48) s. the false in the extremes. A.E. 627.

Spontaneity, or **Freedom**, is pred. of whatever is from the affection or love. 4029.

Sport, to, or to **Play**. To s., or to p. (Zech. viii. 5), s. what appertains to interior festivity, which is of the affection of truth and good. 10.416.

Spotted (Gen. xxx. 38) s. truth wherewith falses are mixed. 4020.

Spots

Spots s. falses, properly speaking, falses grounded in evil. A.R. 625. S. s. falses and evils of various kinds. A.E. 867. See *Leopard.*

Spreading Themselves on the **Earth** (Gen. viii. 17) s. the operation of the internal man on the external. 913.

Spread Out, to. (Gen. ix. 27.) By God's spreading out Japheth, is s. his ill.; in a literal sense, to s. o. s. to extend the borders, but in a spiritual sense, it s. to be enlightened; for enlightening is the extension, as it were, of the borders of wisdom and intelligence, as in Isa. liv. 2, s. ill., or enlightening in spiritual things. The man of the external church is s. o. when he is instructed in the truths and goods of faith; and whereas he is in charity, he is thereby more and more confirmed; and the more he is instructed, so much the more the cloud of his intellectual part is dissipated, in which part are charity and conscience. 1101.

Spread Himself Abroad, to (Gen. xxx. 43) s. to be multiplied. 4035.

Spreading Out of **Bones** to the **Sun** (Jer. viii. 1) s. the infernal things attendant upon the lusts of self-love. 2441.

Spring s. the first state of the church, the same as morning. D.L.W. 73.

Spring and **Fountain**. (Hosea xiii. 15.) S. s. doctrine, and f., the Word. A.E. 730.

Sprinkling Blood upon the **Altar** (Exod. xxix. 16), in a supreme sense, s. that the Lord, when he was in the world, made his human divine truth, and united it with divine good, which was in himself, and thus glorified his human. 10.047.

Spue Out s. to separate. To eject truths falsified. A.E. 235.

Square, or **Quadrangular Figure**, s. perfection. 9817, 9861. See *Four-Square.*

Squaring of the **Circle**, comparison of, between angelic and divine wisdom. D.P. 335.

Stables s. instructions. C.S.L. 76. See *Manger.*

Stacte (Exod. xxx. 34) s. the affection of sensual truth. 10.292.

Staff s. power. 4013. The reason why a s. s. power is, because it is a support, for it supports the hand and arm, and thereby the whole body, wherefore a s. puts on the s. of that part which it proximately supports, that is, of the hand and arm, by both which in the Word is s. the, power of truth. From several passages in the books of Moses, it is very evident that the s., as the hand, rep. power, and, in the supreme sense, the divine omnipotence of the Lord; and it is also hence evident, that at that time rep. constituted the externals of the church, and that the internals which are spiritual and celestial things, such as are in heaven, cor. thereto, and that hence was their efficacy. That a s. den. power in the spiritual sense is also manifest from several passages in the prophets. Inasmuch as a s. rep. the power of truth, that is, the power of good by truth, therefore kings had sceptres, and the sceptres were formed like short s.; for by kings the Lord is rep. as to truth. S. (Isa. x. 24, 26) s. power der. from reasoning and science, such as is the power of those who reason from scientifics against the truths of faith, and pervert them or make light of them. 4876. S. (Hosea iv. 12) s. the imaginary power of self-understanding. 2466.

Staff of **Bread** and **Staff** of **Water** (Isa. iii. 1) s. goodness and truth. 4876.

Staff of **Strength** and **Staff** of **Gracefulness**. (Jer. xlviii. 17.) S. of s. s. power from good, and s. of g., power from truth. 4876.

Stag. To leap as a s. (Isa. xxxv. 6) s. to have joy from perception of truth. A.E. 455.

Stakes and **Cords** (Isa. xxxiii. 20) s. strengthening by divine truths, and conjunction by divine good. A.E. 799.

Stall, calves of the, s. those who are filled with knowledges of things true and good from the affection of knowing them. A.R. 242.

Stamen of **Life**. The s. exist in series, or in forms receptive of life. 7408.

Statue

Stammerers (Isa. xxxii. 4) s. those who with difficulty can apprehend the truth of the church. A.E. 455.

Stand, to (Dan. vii. 10), as to go forth, is pred. concerning truth. A.E. 336. To s. above at the fountain of waters (Gen. xxiv. 13), s. a state of conjunction of truth divine with the human. 3065. To s. at the right hand (Zech. iii. 1), s. to fight against divine truth. A.E. 740. To s. before God, s. to hear and do what he commands, as is the case with those who s. before a king. A.R. 366. By standing before God (Rev. xx. 12), that is, before him who sat on the throne, is s. to be present and assembled to judgment. A.R. 866. To s. round about (Rev. vii.) s. conjunction. A.E. 462. S. still, and see the salvation of the Lord (Exod. xiv. 13) s. to have faith. 8172. To s. upon the feet, s. life in fulness, because in the ultimates. A.E. 666. To walk is expressive of the life of the thought from intention, to s. is expressive of the life of the intention from the will, and to sit, of the life of the will. A.E. 687.

Standard den. a congregation gathering together; also the Lord's protection. 8624.

Stand Erect, to, is pred. of those who are in truth, because good softens and produces humiliation. 7068.

Star, in a supreme sense, s. knowledge concerning the Lord. A.E. 422. The Lord is called a s. from the light of his divine wisdom, and from the light with which he comes into the world. A.R. 954. S. (Rev. ix. 1) s. divine spiritual truth or intelligence originating in spiritual love, which is love towards our neighbor. A.R. 420. S. out of Jacob and a sceptre out of Israel (Num. xxiv. 17) s. the Lord's human essence. 3322. See *Morning Star.*

Stars s. the knowledges of truth and good. A.R. 51. S. are frequently mentioned in the Word, and everywhere s. goods and truths, and, in an opp. sense, evils and falses; or what is the same thing, they s. angels, or societies of angels, and also, in an opp. sense, evil spirits and their fellowships; when they s. angels, or societies of angels, then they are fixed s., but when they s. evil spirits and their fellowships, then they are wandering s. 1808. The seven s. (Rev. i.) den. the knowledges of all things pertaining to good and truth, and hence every variety of good and truth. A.E. 88.

Stars of the **Heavens** (Gen. xxii. 17) s. spiritual men. The spiritual are those, who in the Word, throughout are compared to s., and this from the knowledge of good and truth which they possess, but not so the celestial, inasmuch as they have not knowledges but perceptions; and moreover inasmuch as s. enlighten the night, for the light which the spiritual enjoy is a sort of nocturnal light, such as is from the moon and the s., in respect to the diurnal light which the celestial enjoy. 2849.

Stations and **Sittings** are pred. of the rest of man and thence s. the esse of life, from which its existence is der. A.E. 687.

State has relation to love, life, wisdom, the affections, joys, and to good and truth. T.C.R. 30. General s. of regeneration six in number. 6–13. Fulness of s. 7839. Changes of place really changes of s. 1273-7. Varieties of state. 10.200. S. pred. of love, life, wisdom, etc. D.L.W. 7.

States. Man has external and internal s. D.P. 298. Man has three s.; first of damnation, second of reformation, and third of regeneration. D.P. 83.

State and **Form.** By s. in man is meant his love, and by changes of s. the affections of his love; by f. is meant his intelligence, and by variations of f. his thoughts. A.Cr. 45.

Station den. where scientifics terminate and commence, or where there is a conclusion from scientifics. 6384.

Statue s. worship from the truths of faith. S. in the opp. sense, s. worship from falses, and thus idolatrous. A.E. 391. It also s. a holy border, thus the ultimate principle of order, because in the most ancient times, stones were placed at their borders or boundaries, which marked possession or inheri-

Statues

tance one from that of another and were for a sign and a witness that the borders or boundaries were at that place; the most ancient people, in every particular object, and in every particular s., were led to think of somewhat celestial and spiritual; from these stones also which they set up, were led to think concerning the ultimate principles in man, consequently, concerning the ultimate principle of order, which is truth in the natural man; the ancients who were after the flood, received this from the most ancient people who were before the flood, and began to account those stones holy, which were set up in the borders, by reason that they s. holy truth which is in the ultimate principle of order. They also called those stones s. and hence it came to pass, that s. were used in worship, and that they erected such in the places where they had their groves, and afterwards where they had their temples, and also that they anointed them with oil; for the worship of the ancient church consisted of the perceptives and significatives of the most ancient people who were before the flood. The most ancient people, inasmuch as they discoursed with angels, and were together with them whilst they were on earth, were instructed from heaven that stones s. truth, and that wood s. good; hence then it is that s. s. a holy border, or boundary, thus truth, which is the ultimate principle of order with man; for the good which flows in through the internal man from the Lord, terminates in the external man, and in the truth that is therein; man's thought, his speech, and action, which are the ultimates of order, are nothing else but truths grounded in good, being the images or forms of good, for they appertain to the intellectual part of man, whereas the good which is in them, and from which they are der., appertains to his will part or principle. S., in an opp. sense, rep. those things which are contrary to order. 3727, 4580.

Statues of the **House** of the **Sun** (Jer. xliii. 13) s. the worship of self. 2441.

Statute. To appoint for a s. (Gen. xlvii. 26) s. to conclude from consent, for what is appointed for a s. is done from consent on each side, and is referred amongst those things which are ordained from agreement, and thus duly. 6164.

Statutes and **Precepts.** (Deut. xi. 1.) S. s. the external things of the Word, such as rituals, and those things which are rep. and s. of the internal sense; but p. s. the internal things of the Word, such as are the things appertaining to life and doctrine, especially those which are of the internal sense. 3382.

Staves den. the power which is of truth from good. 9496. See *Swords and Staves.*

Steal, to. In a natural sense, by the commandment "Thou shalt not s." (Exod. xx. 15), is meant, according to the letter, not to s., to rob, or to act the pirate in time of peace; and in general, not to deprive any one of his goods secretly, or under any pretext. It also extends to all impostures, illegitimate gains, usuries, and exactions; and also to fraudulent practices in paying duties and taxes, and in discharging debts. Workmen offend against this commandment, who do their work unfaithfully and dishonestly; merchants who deceive in merchandise, either in weight, measure, or accounts; officers who deprive the soldiers of their just wages; judges who judge for friendship, bribes, relationship, affinity, and other causes by perverting the laws or legal cases, and thus deprive others of their goods which they rightfully possess. In a spiritual sense, by stealing is meant, to deprive others of the truths of their faith, by means of false and heretical things; priests, who minister only for the sake of gain, or worldly honor, and teach such things as they see or may see from the Word are not true, are spiritual thieves, since they take away from the people the means of salvation, which are the truths of faith; they are also called thieves in several passages of the Word. In a celestial sense, by thieves are meant, those who take away divine power from the Lord, and also those who claim to themselves his merit and righteousness. These, although they adore God, still do not trust him, but themselves, and also do not believe in God, but in themselves. U.T. 317, 318, 319. S.S. 67.

Stem of Jesse s. the Lord in his divine humanity. A.R. 46.

Stench, a, den. aversion and abomination. 4516.

Steps (Exod. xx. 26) s. ascent to superior or interior principles. 8945.

Steward of the House. (Gen. xv. 2.) An external church is called the s. of the h. when the internal church itself is the h., and the Lord is the father or master of the family. Just so it is with the external church; for all stewardship appertains to the external of the church, as the administration of ceremonies and many things which are of the temple and of the church itself, that is, of the house of Jehovah, or of the Lord. 1795.

Stick of a Reed, the (Ezek. xxix. 6), s. the power of exploring spiritual truths by scientifics. 1085.

Stiff-necked, to be, is pred. of the Israelitish nation, because they would not receive influx from the divine into their interiors. 10.628.

Stings s. falses of a hurtful nature originating in evil. A.R. 439. S. (Rev. ix.) s. craftiness and subtleties to persuade by falses. Also interior falses. A.E. 560.

Stink, to (Gen. xxxiv. 30), s. to abominate. 4516. To s. (Exod. vii. 21) s. aversion. 7319. S. (Isa. xxxiv. 3) s. damnation. A.E. 405.

Stomach. The world of spirits, which is in the midst between heaven and hell, and into which every man first comes after death, and is there prepared, cor. to the s. A.R. 204. They who have been very solicitous concerning the future, and especially they who, on that account have been rendered tenacious and avaricious, appear in the region where the s. is; the sphere of their life may be compared to the nauseous stench which is exhaled from the stomach, and also to the heaviness arising from indigestion; they who have been such, stay long in that region, for solicitude about futurity, confirmed by act, makes dull and retards the influx of spiritual life, for they attribute to themselves what is of the divine providence, and they who do this oppose the influx, and remove from themselves the life of good and truth; inasmuch as solicitude concerning futurity is what causes anxieties in man, and inasmuch as such spirits appear in the region of the s., it is from this ground, that anxieties affect the s. more than the rest of the viscera. 5177, 5178. They, in another life, who induce extreme heaviness in the s., are such as have in the life of the body, not been habituated to any employment, not even domestic, but only to pleasure, and besides have lived in filthy ease and sluggishness, neither had they any concern about others, and also despised faith: in a word, they were animals, not men. The sphere of such with the sick, induces numbness in the members and joints. 5723. See *Intestines.*

Stone, in the supreme sense, s. the Lord, and in the respective sense, his spiritual kingdom or the truth of faith. 6426. S. or rock s. the Lord as to the divine truth of the Word. A.R. 915. S. (Isa. lx. 16) s. sensual truth. 425. Hewn s. (Isa. ix. 10) den. what is fictitious. 1296. Those things which are of self-der. intelligence. (Lam. iii. 9.) A.E. 781. S. s. natural truths, and precious stones, spiritual truths. C.S.L. 76. See *Precious Stones, Millstone, White Stone, Corner-Stone, To roll away the Stone, etc.*

Stone, to, any one s. to extinguish and demolish falses, but, in the opp. sense, when by the evil, it s. to extinguish and destroy the truths of faith. 7456.

Stoning. There were two punishments of death with the Jews, crucifixion and s. The punishment of s. s. condemnation and the curse, on account of the destruction of truth in the church. A.E. 655. See *To Crucify.*

Stones

Stones of the **Altar**. Forasmuch as they s. truths formed from good, or good itself in form, therefore, it was prohibited to fit them with a hammer, an axe, or any instrument of iron, to den. that nothing of self-der. intelligence should enter into the formation thereof. A.E. 391.

Stones of **Hail** are falses. A.E. 644. See *Mortar.*

Stool of the **Feet** (Ps. cx. 1) s. things natural, as well sensual as scientific, and hence the rational things of man, which are called enemies when they pervert worship, and this by the literal sense of the Word, so that there remains only worship in externals, and internal worship either totally perishes or is defiled. 2162. See *Footstool.*

Stoop, to, or **bend himself** as a **Lion** (Gen. xlix. 9), s. to put himself in power. A.R. 241.

Stop up den. the denial and obliteration of truth. 3412.

Storax den. the good of truth. 5621.

Store den. the good of truth as provided for every use of the natural mind. 5299.

Storehouses, or **Treasure Cities**, built by the enslaved Israelites, den. doctrines from falsified truths. 6661.

Storge. Innocence from the inmost heavens. H. and H. 277. Maternal love der. from the womb. A.E. 710.

Storm, a spirit of, den. desolation of the false. 739.

Stoutness (Gen. xlvii. 6), in the original tongue, is expressed by a word which also s. strength and virtue, which, in the internal sense, den. what is prevalent, thus what is more excellent. 6086.

Straight, crooked made, s. the evil of ignorance turned into good. 3527.

Straitness of **Soul** (Gen. xlii. 21) s. a state of the internal, when it is alienated from the external. 5470.

Strange Fire den. infernal love. 10.287.

Strange Fire (Lev. x. 1) s. all love of self and of the world, and every lust of those loves. 934.

Strange Gods den. falses. 4544.

Strange Land den. where the church is not, or where there is no genuine truth. 8650.

Stranger, a (Exod. xii. 49), s. one who is instructed in the truths and goods of the church, and receives them, thus who is not born within the church, but still accedes to it. 7908. S. (Gen. xv. 13) s. what is not born in the land, and thus is not acknowledged as native, consequently, what is regarded as foreign. 1843. See *Sojourner, Eunuch.*

Strangers and **Aliens**. (Lam. v. 2.) Our inheritance is turned away to s., s. the truths of the church converted into falses; our houses unto a. s. the good of the church turned into evils. A.E. 654.

Strangers and the **Violent** of the **Nations**. (Ezek. xxviii. 8.) S. s. falses which destroy truths, and the v. of the n., evils which destroy good. A.E. 537.

Straw (Gen. xxiv. 25) s. scientific truths, because it is pred. of camels, such being their food. 3114. S. (Isa. xi. 6) s. the Word in the letter, which is perverted by the infernal false, but cannot be perverted by them who are in truths from good. A.E. 781.

Straw and **Provender**, to give (Gen. xxiv. 32), s. to instruct in truths and goods. 3146. See *Lion.*

Stray, to, in the **Field**. A wandering or a falling away of the common truths of the church. 4717.

Stream s. those things which are of intelligence. A.E. 6015.

Streams of **Waters** (Isa. xxx. 25) s. the knowledges of good and truth. 6435.

Street of the **great City** (Rev. xi. 8) s. the falsity of the doctrine concerning justification by faith alone. A.R. 501.

Street and **Ditch, the, being Restored** (Dan. ix. 25) s. the restoration of truth and good. 2336.

Streets. By s., in the Word, almost the same is s. as by ways, because s. are ways in a city; but still by s. are s. the truths or falses of doctrine, and by ways are s. truths and falses of the church, because earth s. the church. A.R. 501. On the s. of s., as den. truths, was grounded a rep. rite amongst the Jews to teach in s. (See Matt. vi. 2, 5; Luke xiii. 26, 27.) In the prophets, wheresoever s. are named, in an internal sense, they either s. truths, or what is contrary to truth. 2336.

Streets of the **New Jerusalem** (Rev. xxi.) s. all things of truth which lead to good, or all things of faith which lead to love and charity, and whereas truths, in such case, become of good, and thus transparent from good, the street is said to be pure gold as transparent glass. 2336.

Streets and **Lanes**. (Luke xiv. 21.) By the servant's going into the s. and l. is s. that he should seek everywhere some genuine truth, or truth which shines from good or through which good shines. 2336. See *Mire of the Streets.*

Strength is pred. of what is true, and of what is false. 3727. S. (Luke x. 27) s. the will and understanding brought forth into the ultimates. 9936. S. (Rev. i. 6) s. divine omnipotence, and is pred. of divine love. A.R. 22.

Strength and **Glory**. (Ps. lxxviii. 61.) His s., which he delivered into captivity, s. spiritual truth der. from celestial good, and his g. into the hand of the enemy, s. natural truth from spiritual. A.E. 811.

Strength and **Horn**. (1 Sam. 10.) S. s. the power of good over evil, and h., the power of truth over the false. A.E. 684.

Strength and **Might**. (Gen. xlix. 3.) S. s. the ability which appertains to good, and m. s. the ability of truth; for the expression by which m. is expressed in the original tongue, is, in the Word, pred. of truth, whereas the expression by which s. is expressed, is pred. of good. 6343.

Strength, Throne, and **Power**. (Rev. xiii. 2.) By s. is s. authority, by t., government, and by great p., dominion. A.R. 575.

Strength of a **Horse**. (Ps. cxlvii. 10.) The s. of a h. s. man's proper power of thinking truth. 2826.

Strengthened, to be (Gen. xxi. 18) s. to be supported. 2698.

Stretch Out, to, the **Earth** and the **Heavens** is a common form of speaking with the prophets, when they are treating of the regeneration of man. 25.

Stretched out Arm, a (Exod. vi. 6), s. omnipotence or divine power, because by an a., when it appears s. o. in the heavens, is rep. power from the divine, but when not s. o., but bended, power in the general sense is rep.; hence now it is, that divine power in the Word is very often expressed by a s. o. a., and by a strong hand. 7205.

Strife. Two subjects of s. have infested the church; 1st, whether faith or charity is first born; or 2d, whether faith separate from charity is saving. 9224.

Strike, to, **upon** the **Harp** (Rev. xiv. 2) s. to confess the Lord from spiritual truths. A.R. 616.

Stringed Instruments s. affections of truth. 8337.

Stringed Instruments s. spiritual truth. A.C. 417, 420.

Strip, to (Gen. xxxvii. 23), when it is pred. of divine truth, which in the present case is Joseph, s. to shake off, and also to annihilate. 4741.

Stript and **Naked**. (Micah i. 8.) To be s. s. to be without goods, and to be n. s. to be without truths. A.E. 714.

Stripe (Exod. xxi. 25) s. the extinction, or loss of affection in the intellectual principle; or truth hurt or extinguished. (Jer. xxx. 12.) 9057.

Strong. (Isa. i. 30, 31.) He is sometimes called s. in the Word, who trusts to himself and his own intelligence, for he supposes himself, and the work which he thence produces, to be s. A.E. 504.

Strong Drink

Strong Drink, s. the truth of the natural man. A.E. 376.

Strong Holds, or **Fortresses** of **Munitions** (Dan. xi. 39), s. the things of self-der. intelligence confirmed by the literal sense of the Word. A.E. 717.

Strong Man, Man of **War, Judge**, and **Prophet**. (Isa. iii. 2.) S. m. and m. of w. s. truth combating against evil and the false; and j. and p., the doctrine of good and truth. A.E. 727.

Strong and **Many**. (Isa. xiii. 7.) S. has respect to lust, and m. to falsity. A.E. 518.

Strong and **without Number**. (Joel i. 6.) S. is pred. of the power of evil, and w. n., of the power of false. A.E. 556.

Struggle, to (Gen. xxv. 22), s. combat concerning priority, whether good or truth be prior, or what is the same thing, whether charity, which is of good, or faith which is of truth, be prior. 3289. Strugglings of God, and strugglings den. temptations. 3927.

Struggling, or **Wrestling**, den. temptation, especially as to truth. 4248.

Strumpet, a, s. falsification. S.S. 26. See *Harlot.*

Stubble for Chaff (Exod. v. 12) s. scientific truth; for s. is such truth as is accommodated to the scientific, which is s. by c.; the reason why s. den. such truth is, because it is the stalk in the top of which is seed, and by seeds in the Word are s. truths and goods; thus by the stalk which is beneath them, is s. the common vessel of truth, consequently, scientific truth; for the scientifics of faith and charity are indeed truths, but common or general truths, and thereby the recipient vessels of particular and singular truths: which may also be manifest to every one. 7131.

Stubble, being the grain bearing stalk, den. scientific truth. 7131. To be consumed as s. den. full vastation. 8285.

Stumble, to, den. to be scandalized or offended, and to fall in consequence from truths into falses. 9163.

Stump of the **Roots** of the **Tree** which should be left in **Earth**, (Dan. iv. 15) s. the Word, which is understood as to the letter only and the knowledge remaining in the memory, and passing forth into the speech. A.E. 650.

Stupor, or **Amazement**, is pred. of the understanding, when it has no perception of good, and blindness when there is no apperception of truth. A.E. 355.

Style of the **Word** is a truly divine s., with which no other s., however sublime and excellent it may seem, is at all comparable, for it is as darkness compared with light. The s. of the W. is of such a nature that it is holy in every verse, in every word, and in some cases in every letter; and hence the Word conjoins man with the Lord, and opens heaven. S.S. 3. A.E. 175. There are in general four different s. in the W.; the first is that which was of the most ancient church; their method of expressing was such, that when they made mention of earthly and worldly things they thought of the spiritual and celestial things which they rep. so that they not only expressed things by rep., but also reduced them into a kind of historical series, that they might have more life, which to them was in the highest degree delightful: those rep. are called in David, "dark sayings of old." (Ps. lxxviii. 2, 3, 4.) From the posterity of the most ancient church Moses had these things concerning the creation, concerning the garden of Eden, even till the time of Abram. The second s. is the historical, occurring in the books of Moses, from the time of Abram and in those of Joshua, Judges, Samuel, and the Kings, in which books the historical facts are exactly such as appear in the sense of the letter, but yet they all and each contain things altogether different in the internal sense. The third s. is the prophetical, which took its rise from the s. of the most ancient church, which s. they adored, but it is not continuous as if historical, like the most ancient, but is broken and interrupted, being scarce ever intelligible, but in its internal

312

Substance

sense, wherein are things most hidden, which connectedly follow in harmonious order; and they regard the external and internal man, the several states of the church, heaven itself, and in their inmost the Lord. The fourth s. is that of the Psalms of David, which is between the prophetical s. and that of common speech; there, under the person of David as a king, the Lord is treated of in the internal sense. 66.

Subdue. He who subdues the love of dominion, subdues easily all other evil loves. D.P. 146.

Subjects. In the other life, one society cannot have communication with another, or with an individual, except by the spirits who are sent forth by them, and who are called s., for by them as by s. they discourse. To send forth s. to other societies, and thereby to procure to themselves communication, is amongst things that are familiar in the other life; the spirits and genii attendant on man are nothing else but s., whereby he has communication with hell; and the celestial and spiritual angels are s., whereby he has communication with the heavens. 5983.

Submission. There is a chain of subordination, and thus of application, consequently, of s. from the first of life, or the Lord: the things which are in a lower place, inasmuch as they ought to be subservient to the higher, will be in s., otherwise there is not given conjunction. 3090. The Lord, with a view to render any one blessed and happy, wills a total s., that is, that he should not be partly his own and partly the Lord's, for in such case there are two lords, whom man cannot serve at the same time. (Matt. vi. 24, x. 37; John xii. 25, 26; Matt. viii. 21, 22; Mark xii. 30; Gen. xvi. 9.) 6138.

Subordination. All application and submission must be in succession from the first source of life, that there may be conjunction. 3091. The order of s. is celestial, spiritual, rational, scientific, and sensual. 1486. S. is a law of heaven, but it is of one good to another. In hell it is the reverse. 7773.

Subsist, to. The universe and all things therein s. from heat and light. D.L.W. 32. The internal man, as being prior, can s. without the external, because posterior, but not vice versa; for it is an universal canon, that nothing can s. from itself, but from another, and by another, consequently, that nothing can be kept in a form, but from another and by another; which may also be manifest from the singular things in nature; the case is the same with man, who, as to the external, cannot s. but from the internal, and by the internal; neither can the internal man s. but from heaven and by heaven; and neither can heaven s. of itself, but from the Lord, who alone s. of himself; according to existence and subsistence is influx, for by influx all things s.; but all and singular things s. by influx from the Lord, not only mediately through the spiritual world but also immediately, as well in mediates as in ultimates. 6056.

Subsistence is perpetual existence. The prior flows into the posterior. 3648, 6451.

Substance. S. is pred. of things appertaining to the will, because all things arise or exist, and subsist in man from the will, for the will is the very s. itself of man, or the man himself. 808.

Substance and **Form.** The divine love and the divine wisdom in themselves, are a s. and a f., for they are essence and existence itself, and if they were not such an essence and existence as they are a s. and f., they would only be an imaginary entity, which in itself is not any thing. As the divine love and the divine wisdom are s. and f. in themselves, they are, consequently, the self-subsisting and only subsisting. D.L.W. 43, 44, 198. A s. without a f. is not any thing, neither is a f. any thing without a s. D.L.W. 209.

Substance and **Treasures** (Jer. xvii. 3) s. the spiritual riches of faith, or the things which are of the doctrine of faith. 368.

Substances

Substances. The natural mind consists not only of s. of the spiritual world, but also of s. of the natural world, and the s. of the natural world, from their nature, re-act against the s. of the spiritual world, for the s. of the natural world in themselves are dead, and are acted upon from without by the s. of the spiritual world, and those things which are dead, and are acted upon from without, from their nature resist and consequently, from their nature, re-act. D.L.W. 260.

Substances and **Matters** of which the earths consist, are the ends and terminations of the atmospheres, which proceed as uses from the spiritual sun. D.L.W. 310.

Successive. Influx is according to order, from celestial to spiritual, and from spiritual to natural. 7270.

Successive Order, in, one thing succeeds and follows another, from what is highest to what is lowest. U.T. 214.

Succoth (Gen. xxxiii. 17; Ps. lx. 6, 7; cviii. 7, 8) s. the quality of the holy state of truth from good; for S. s. tents, and tents the holy principle of truth. 4392.

Suck, to. (Isa. lx. 15, 16.) To s. the milk of the Gentiles, s. the insinuation of celestial good; and to s. the paps of kings, s. the insinuation of celestial truth. 6745. To s. (Isa. lxvi. 11) s. influx from the Lord. A.E. 365. To s. the affluence of the sea s. to imbibe truths of doctrine from the Word and intelligence thence. To s. the covered things of the hidden things of the sand, s. the spiritual things which lie concealed in the literal sense of the Word. (Deut. xxxiii. 19.) A.E. 445. See *Elders.*

Suckle, to, den. to insinuate good, for a nurse, or one that s., s. the insinuation of good. 6745. To s. (Gen. xxi. 7) s. to implant the spiritual from a celestial origin, or truth from good; or to implant the Lord's human in the divine, by his own proper power. 2643.

Suckling and **Infants.** (Lam. iv. 3, 4.) S. s. innocence, and i. the affections of good. 3183.

Suckling, Infant, and **Boy.** In the Word, mention is made of a s., and i., and a b., and by them are s. three degrees of innocence, the first degree by the s., the second by the i., and the third by the b.; but whereas with the b. innocence begins to be put off, therefore by b. is s. that innocent principle which is called guiltless; inasmuch as the three degrees of innocence are s. by s., i., and b., the three degrees of love and charity are also s. by the same, by reason that celestial and spiritual love, that is, love to the Lord and charity towards the neighbor, cannot be given except in innocence; it is however to be noted, that the innocence of s., of i., and of b., is only external, and that internal innocence is not given with man, until he be born anew, that is, be made anew as it were a s., an i., and a b.; these states are what are s. by s., i., and b., in the Word, for in the internal sense of the Word nothing is meant but what is spiritual, consequently, spiritual birth, which is called rebirth, and also regeneration. 5236.

Suffocate, to, is to deprive the understanding of the faculty of thinking freely, and of extending its sight on every side, as is done by every rational man. A.E. 549. See *Persuasion.*

Sugar-cane den. acquisitions of truth from which is good. 3923.

Sulphur, or **Brimstone,** s. cupidities or lusts, originating in self-love and the love of the world. A.R. 452, 636.

Sulphur and **Fire.** (Gen. xix. 24.) S. is the hell of the evils of self-love, and f. is the hell of the falses thence. 2446. S. s. the concupiscence of destroying the church by the falses of evil, and f. that concupiscence abounding from self-love. (Luke xvii. 29, 30.) A.E. 578.

Sulphur and **Salt** (Deut. xxix. 23) den. the vastation of goodness and truth, for as what is fiery and s. destroys the earth and its produce, so lust destroys goods, and falsity, truths. 1666. See *Burning, Fire, Pitch.*

314

Sunset

Sum. To take the s. of the sons of Israel (Exod. xxx. 12) s. all things of the church. 10.216.

Summer s. the full state of the church, the same as noon. D.L.W. 73. With the regenerate the changes of things of the will are like winter and s., and the changes of things intellectual like day and night. 935.

Sun, the, s. celestial and spiritual love. A.E. 709. The s. in the Word, when the Lord is spoken of, s. his divine love, and at the same time his divine wisdom; forasmuch as the Lord with respect to his divine love and his divine wisdom, is meant by the s., therefore the ancients in their holy worship turned their faces to the rising s., and also their temples, which custom still continues. A.R. 53. The s. s. the Lord, as to his divine love, and thence the good of love from him, and, in an opp. sense, a denial of the Lord's divinity, and thence adulteration of the good of love. A.R. 332. S. (Jer. viii. 1) s. self-love and its lusts. 2441. Without two s., the one living and the other dead, there can be no creation. D.L.W. 163. There are two s. by which all things were created by the Lord—the s. of the spiritual world and the s. of the natural world; the sun of the natural world was created to act as a medium or substitute. D.L.W. 153.

Sunday, or **Sabbath**, the holy observance of, den. the conjunction of the Lord with the church. 10.326.

Sunrise den. coming of the Lord, or beginning of a celestial state. 2333.

Sunset den. the end of a state. 8615.

Sun Shining in his Strength s. the divine principle itself in its essence. A.R. 53.

Sun-Rising. (Gen. xix. 23.) Forasmuch as times of the day, and also times of the year, in an internal sense, s. successive states of the church, and day-dawn, or morning, s. the coming of the Lord, or the approach of his kingdom, therefore, the rising of the sun, or his going forth upon the earth, s. the Lord's essential presence. In another life, the case is this, the Lord is a sun to the universal heaven, the divine celestial of his love appearing thus to the eyes of the angels, and, in effect, constitutes the essential light of heaven; in proportion, therefore, as the angels are in celestial love, in the same proportion they are elevated into that celestial light which is from the Lord; but in proportion as any are remote from celestial love, in the same proportion they cast themselves from the light into infernal darkness. The ancient church, by the sun, understood nothing else than the Lord, and the divine celestial of his love, and hence came the custom of praying with their faces towards the rising of the sun, not even thinking about the sun at such times; but after their posterity lost this, together with other rep. and s., they then began to worship the sun and the moon, which worship spread itself to many nations, insomuch that they dedicated temples to those objects, and erected statues to their honor; and whereas the sun and moon hereby received an opp. sense, they s. self-love and the love of the world, which are altogether opp. to celestial and spiritual love; hence, in the Word, by the worship of the sun and moon, is meant the worship of self and of the world. 2441. S.-r. (Gen. xxxii. 31) s. conjunction of goods. 4300. S.-r. (Rev. xvi. 12) s. the beginning of a new church from the Lord. A.R. 700. By the rising of the sun is s. the good of love, which is the good of life, and by the setting of the sun is s. the evil of love, which is the evil of life. A.E. 401. From its rising to its going down (Mal. i. 11) s. every place where there is good. A.E. 324. The sun is also said to rise with every one who becomes a church, thus also who becomes rep. of a church. 4312.

Sunset, in the Word, s. the false and evil principle, in which they are, who have no charity and faith, and thus also it s. the last time of the church; and also it s. an obscure principle as to those things which appertain to

315

Sun of the Natural World

good and truth, such as has place with those who are in a degree more remote from divine doctrinals. 3693. The sun was darkened when the Lord was upon the cross, because in the church which was then amongst the Jews, he was entirely rejected, and they were, consequently, in dense darkness, or falsities. A.E. 401. "She that hath borne seven shall breath out her soul, her sun shall set, while it is yet day." (Jer. xv. 9), s. the Jewish church which was to breathe out its soul, or, in other words, would perish; the sun shall set, s. that there will be no longer any love and charity. A.R. 53. "The sun which shall not set" (Isa. lx. 19) is love and wisdom from the Lord. A.R. 53.

Sun of the **Natural World** s. self-love and the pride of self-der. intelligence; and self-love is diametrically opp. to divine love, and the pride of self-der. intelligence is opp. to divine wisdom. To adore the sun of this world, is to acknowledge nature to be creative, and self-der. prudence effective of all things, which implies a negation of God, and a negation of the divine providence. A.R. 53. The s. of the n. w. is pure fire, therefore, dead, and from or by this sun, did exist and does subsist this our world of nature. Hence it follows, that whatever proceeds from this material sun, considered in itself, must be void of life. I. 9, 10. D.L.W. 157.

Sun of the **Spiritual World** is, in its essence, pure love proceeding from Jehovah God, who is in the midst of it. I. 5. That the sphere about the Lord is the s. of the s. w. D.L.W. 291. From the s. of the s. w. proceed heat and light; and as the heat proceeding from it is in its essence love, so the light proceeding from it is in its essence wisdom. I. 6. That sun is not God, but it is an emanation from the divine love and the divine wisdom of God-man: in like manner, the heat and light from that sun. D.L.W. 93. Spiritual heat and spiritual light in proceeding from the Lord as a sun make one, as his divine love and his divine wisdom make one. D.L.W. 99. The s. of the s. w., from which the angels have their light and heat, appears above the earths which the angels inhabit, in an elevation of about forty-five degrees, which is a middle altitude, and it appears distant from the angels, as the sun of this world from men. It appears also constantly in that altitude, and at that distance, neither does it move. D.L.W. 104. The s. of the s. w. is fixed and constant in the east, and has none of those apparent circumvolutions which the sun of this world has, and which produce the various times and seasons of the year. A.E. 610. The distance between the sun and the angels in the spiritual world, is an appearance according to the reception of the divine love and the divine wisdom by them. D.L.W. 108. The Lord from eternity, or Jehovah out of himself, produced the s. of the s. w., and out of it created the universe, and all things therein. D.L.W. 290. The s. of the s. w. is the one only substance from which all things are; and forasmuch as the Divine is not in space, and forasmuch as in the greatest and least things it is the same, so in like manner, is that sun which is the first proceeding of God-man; and that only substance, which is a sun, proceeding by means of the atmospheres according to degrees of continuity, or of latitude, and, at the same time, according to discrete degrees, or degrees of altitude, presents the varieties of all things in the created universe. D.L.W. 300. That the angels of the third heaven see the spiritual sun always, the angels of the second heaven very often, and the angels of the first or ultimate heaven sometimes. D.L.W. 85.

Sun and **Air**. (Rev. ix. 2.) By the s. and the a. is here s. the light of truth, for by the s. is s. love, and by the light proceeding from it divine truth, wherefore when it is said, that the s. was darkened, and at the same time the a., it s. that divine truth had become thick darkness; that this was called by falses of concupiscences, is s. by its being effected by the smoke of the pit. A.R. 423.

Sun and **Moon** and the eleven **Stars**. (Gen. xxxvii. 9.) S. and m. s. natural good and truth, because they are pred. of Jacob and Leah, and Jacob rep. natural good, and Leah, natural truth; s. s. the knowledges of good and truth. 4696. See *Ajalon, Moon.*

Sun and **Rain**. (Matt. v. 45.) By s. is meant here as elsewhere in the Word, in its spiritual sense, the divine good of the divine love, and by r., the divine truth of the divine wisdom, these are given to the evil and the good, and to the just and the unjust, for if they were not given, no one would have perception and thought. D.P. 173.

Sup, to, a **little Water**, etc. (Gen. xxiv. 17), s. exploration whether any thing of truth thence could be conjoined, for to s. s. somewhat similar to drinking, but in a diminutive sense. 3089.

Superior and **Inferior** in the Word s. what is interior and exterior: the same is s. by upwards and downwards, also by high and deep. D.L.W. 206.

Suph. The Sea S. s. damnation, and also hell. A.E. 400.

Supper, the, **Holy** contains both in a general and particular sense, all things relating to the church, and likewise all things relating to heaven. U.T. 711. The Lord and all the effects of his redemption are entirely and completely omnipresent in the holy s. U.T. 716. The Lord is present and opens heaven to those who approach the holy s. worthily, and he is present also with those who approach unworthily, but he does not open heaven to them; consequently, as baptism is an introduction into the church, so the holy s. is an introduction into heaven. U.T. 719. They approach the holy s. worthily who are under the influence of faith towards the Lord, and of charity towards their neighbor, that is, who are regenerate. U.T. 722. The holy s. is to the worthy receivers as a sign and seal that they are the sons of God, and moreover as a key to their house in heaven where they shall dwell to all eternity. U.T. 728–730. N.J.D. 202, 222. A holy principle flows from heaven into the members of the church who partake worthily of the holy s. 676. The holy s. is the primary part of external worship, because it is the Lord's divine human which is there given and communicated. 2811. Bread and wine, in the holy s., in an external sense, s. the Lord's love towards the whole human race and the things appertaining to love, and the reciprocal love of man towards the Lord and his neighbor. 1798. See *Gates.*

Supper, a great, to which all were invited (Luke xiv.), s. heaven and the church, as to spiritual nutrition, or instruction. A.E. 548.

Supper of the **Great God** (Rev. xix. 17) s. the new church, and thereby conjunction with the Lord. A.R. 831. S. of the G. G. s. instruction in truths, and the perception of good from the Lord. A.E. 354. See *Dinner.*

Supplicate, to, den. humiliation. 7391.

Supreme, the head is as, or inmost which continually flows into its derivatives. 10.011.

Surety. To be s. for any one, s. to be adjoined to him. (Gen. xliii. 9.) 5609.

Surname, to, and to **Name** (Isa. xlv. 4), s. to foreknow the quality. 145.

Surface den. what is ultimate. 7687.

Susims den. persuasions of the false. 1673.

Suspend, to, or **Hang**, rep. the damnation of profanation. 5044.

Sustain. To s. exaction (Isa. liii. 7) s. temptations. A.E. 814.

Sustain, or **Hold up**. The sustaining power of good is truth. 3812. In heaven, it is the good of love from the Lord that sustains, includes, and limits all things. 9490.

Sustentation is perpetual creation. A.Cr. 102.

Swaddling Clothes (Luke ii. 16) s. the first truths which are truths of innocence, which also are truths of divine love, for nakedness, when pred. of an infant, s. the deprivation of truth. A.E. 706. See *Nakedness.*

Swallow s. natural truth. A.E. 391. See *Sparrow and Swallow.*

Swallow up

Swallow up, to (Gen. xli. 24), s. to exterminate. 5217.

Swarms of **Flies** (Exod. viii. 21) s. the falses of malevolence. 7442.

Swear, to. Jehovah, that is, the Lord swearing by himself s. that divine truth testifies, for he is divine truth itself, and this testifies from itself and by itself; the reason why it is said that Jehovah s., is, because the church established among the sons of Israel was a rep. church, and therefore the Lord's conjunction with the church was rep. by a covenant, such as takes place between two who s. to their compact; for which reason, as swearing was used for the purpose of ratifying a covenant or compact, it is said that Jehovah s.; by which nevertheless it is not meant that he really did s., but that divine truth testifies or bears testimony to the things asserted. A.R. 474.

Sweat (Ezek. xliv. 18) den. the proprium of man. 9959.

Sweat of the **Face**. (Gen. iii. 19.) "To eat bread in the sweat of the face," s. to have an aversion to what is celestial. 276.

Swedenborg held discourse with angels and spirits for many years. 5, 5978. Let down into hell with a guard. 699, 4940. How and why he opened the interiors of the Word. 4923, 4939. The presence of the Lord in repeating the Lord's Prayer. 6476. Sight opened that he might see things, and describe them. D.L.W. 85. Seeing the sun of heaven, the Lord in the midst. 7173. The Lord was revealed to him, and afterwards continually appeared before his eyes as the sun. D.P. 135.

Swedes, the, in the spiritual world, are arranged towards the west of the centre. L.J. 48.

Sweep the **House**, to (Gen. xxiv. 31), s. to prepare and to be filled with goods, because nothing else is required of man but to s. the h., that is, to reject the lusts of evil, and the persuasions of the false thence; then he is filled with goods, for good from the Lord continually flows in, but into the house, or into man purged from such things as impede influx, that is, which reflect, or pervert, or suffocate the inflowing good; hence was the customary form of speaking with the ancients, to s. or purge the h., also to s. and prepare the way: and by s. the h. was understood to purge themselves from evils, and thus to prepare themselves for the entrance of goods: whereas to s. the way was understood to prepare themselves for the reception of truths, for by h. was s. good, and by way truth. To s. the h. also, in an opp. sense, is applied to man, to s. one who deprives himself of all goods and truths, and thus is filled with evils and falses. (See Luke xi. 24–26; Matt. xii. 43–45.) 3142. To s. the h. s. to run over the whole mind, and to view every thing therein, to discover where the truth has hid itself. A.E. 675.

Sweet s. what is delightful from the good of truth, and the truth of good. A.E. 618. Every thing s. in the natural world cor. to what is delightful and pleasant in the spiritual. 5620.

Sweet and **Harmonious**. Every thing in another life that is s. and h. is from goodness and charity. 1759.

Sweet Calamus s. good. 10.256. See *Calamus*.

Swell, to. (Deut. viii. 4.) "Thy foot hath not swelled these forty years," s. that the natural man was not hurt by the afflictions of temptation. A.E. 730.

Swelling of Jordan, the (Jer. xii. 5), s. the things appertaining to the external man, which rise up and are desirous to have dominion over the internal. 1585.

Swiftness and **Haste** s. excitation from affection and lust. A.E. 281. S. is pred. of affection. 455.

Swift Beasts (Isa. lxvi. 20) s. the external rational principle, which is natural. A.E. 355.

Swine (Matt. vii. 6) s. filthy loves such are in the hells of adulterers. A.E. 1044. By s. (Matt. vii. 6), are s. those who only love worldly riches, and not spiritual riches, which are the knowledges of good and truth, der. from the Word. A.R. 727. To eat the flesh of s. (Isa. lxv. 4) s. to appropriate infernal evils. A.E. 659.

Swooning. There are spirits who infuse unclean colds, such as are those of a cold fever. The same spirits also induce such things as disturb the mind; and likewise they induce s. 5716.

Sword, in the Word, s. 1, the truth of faith combating; 2, the vastation of truth; 3, in an opp. sense, the false combating; and 4, the punishment of the false. 2799. S. on the thigh, s. combat from love; s. in the hand, combat from power; and s. out of the mouth, combat from doctrine. A.R. 826. S. (Ezek. xxi. 9–15) s. the desolation of man, so that he can see nothing that is good and true, but only mere falses and contrarieties, which is meant by multiplying offences. 309. That the dispersion of falses by the Lord, is understood by s. (Rev. i. 16), is evident, because the s. was seen to go out of his mouth, and to go out of the mouth of the Lord, is to go out of the Word, for this the Lord spake with his mouth; and forasmuch as the Word is understood by doctrine thence deduced, this is also s., and it is called "a sharp, two-edged s." because it penetrates the heart and soul. A.R. 52. See *Spears.*

Sword, flame of a, **which turned every Way** (Gen. iii. 24), s. divine truth in ultimates, which, like the Word in its literal sense, is capable of being thus turned. A.R. 329. See *Flame of a Sword.*

Sword and **Famine** are expressions of devastation; the s. as to things spiritual, and f. as to things celestial. 1460.

Sword, Famine, and **Pestilence.** S. s. the vastation of truth; f. the vastation of good; and pestilence, the raging thereof even to consummation. 2799.

Swords and **Staves.** (Matt. xxvi. 47; Mark xiv. 43, 48; Luke xxii. 42.) S. s. falses destroying truths, and woods or s. of wood, evils destroying good. A.E. 1145.

Sycamore and the **Vine** den. truths of the internal and external church respectively. 7553.

Sycamore Tree den. external truth; and fig tree external good. 7553. S. t. (Ps. lxxviii. 47) s. the natural truth of the church. A.E. 503. Also, the natural man as to truths therein, and, in the opp. sense, as to falses. A.E. 815.

Sychar, or **Schechem,** den. tranquillity. 4430.

Syllables and **Letters** of the **Alphabet** in the **Spiritual World,** s. things; and thence originates the speech and writing of those who are there. A.R. 38.

Symbols. Bread and wine were made s. in the holy supper because they rep. celestial and spiritual things. 1727. Were commanded because the greater part of mankind are in externals only. 2165.

Synagogue of **Satan.** (Rev. ii. 9.) It is called s., because Jews are mentioned, and as they taught in s., by s. is s. doctrine; and because by S. is understood the hell of those who are in falses, therefore it is called the s. of S.; therefore by their being the s. of S. is s. that as to doctrine, they are in falses. A.R. 97.

Syria (Ezek. xxvii. 16) s. the church as to knowledges of truth and good. A.E. 195.

Syria of **Rivers** s. the knowledges of truth. 376.

Syrens are interior witches, and prone to infest men by night. 1983.

Systole and **Diastole.** Influx into the s. and d. des. 3884. Changes of state ill. by the expressions and compressions of the s. D.P. 319.

T

Tabernacle. By t. nearly the same is s. as by temple, namely, in a supreme sense, the Lord's divine humanity, and, in a relative sense, heaven and the church. But by t., in this latter sense, is s. the celestial church, which is in the good of love from the Lord to the Lord, and by temple the spiritual church, which is in the truths of wisdom from the Lord. The t. s. the celestial kingdom, because the most ancient church, which was celestial, as being principled in love to the Lord, performed divine worship in temples. T. were of wood, and temples of stone, and wood s. good, and stone truth. Since the most ancient church, which was a celestial church, by reason of its love to the Lord, and consequent conjunction with him, celebrated divine worship in t., therefore the Lord commanded Moses to build a t., in which all things of heaven and the church were rep.; which was so holy, that it was not lawful for any one to go into it, except Moses, Aaron, and his sons; and if any one of the people entered, he would die. (Num. xvii. 12, 13; xviii. 1, 22, 23; xix. 14–19.) In the inmost part of it was the ark, in which were the two tables of the decalogue, over which was the mercy seat and the cherubims; and without the vail, was the table for the shewbread, the altar of incense, and the candlestick with seven lamps; all which were rep. of heaven and the church; it is des. Exod. xxvi. 7–16; xxxvi. 8–37, and we read that the model thereof was shown to Moses on Mount Sinai (Exod. xxv. 9; xxvi. 30); and whatsoever it is given to be seen from heaven, the same is rep. of heaven, and thence of the church. In memory of the most holy worship of the Lord in t. by the most ancient people, and of their conjunction with him by love, the feast of t. was instituted, as mentioned in Lev. xxiii. 39–44; Deut. xvi. 13, 14; Zech. xiv. 16, 18, 19. A.R. 585. T. (Rev. xiii.) s. the church as to doctrine and worship. A.E. 799. See *Feast of Tabernacles.*

Tabernacle of God (Rev. xxi. 3) s. the celestial church, in a universal sense, the celestial kingdom of the Lord, and, in a supreme sense, the divine humanity of the Lord. The reason why t., in a supreme sense, means the Lord's divine humanity, is because this is s. by temple, as may appear from John ii. 18, 21; Mal. iii. 1; Rev. xxi. 22, and elsewhere; the same is s. by t., with this difference, that by temple is meant the Lord's divine humanity with respect to divine truth, or divine wisdom; and by t. is meant the Lord's divine humanity with respect to divine good or divine love. A.R. 882.

Tabernacle and Tent. T. s. the church consisting of those who are in the good of love to the Lord, and tent s. the church consisting of those who are in truths der. from that good. A.E. 799. By God's forsaking the habitation of Shiloh, and the tent which he placed amongst men (Ps. lxviii. 60), s. that the goods of love, and truths of doctrine were destroyed. A.E. 811.

Table. Tables s. all things which should nourish the spiritual life, because by tables are understood the food which is upon them. A.E. 235. Tables full of vomiting and what is cast up s. truths and goods falsified and adulterated. 235. Tables s. instructions. 340. To sit at t. s. to be spiritually nourished. 727. A t. (Exod. xxv. 23) s. heaven, as to the reception of such things which are from the Lord there, and which are the good of love and the good of faith, and beatitude and felicity thence der. 9527.

Tables (Exod. xxxii. 16) s. the external of the Word, because they are here distinguished from the writing, which is its internal. The external of the Word is the literal sense, and that sense is like a table, or a plane, upon which the internal sense is inscribed. 10.453. The second t. (Exod. xxxii.) upon which the decalogue was written, s. the Word in every complex. 10.452.

Tables of the **Decalogue**. There are two tables upon which the precepts of the decalogue are written, one for the Lord, the other for man. What the first table contains is, that a plurality of Gods are not to be worshipped, but only one; and the second, that evils are not to be committed; therefore, when one God is worshipped, and man does not commit evils, a conjunction takes place; for in proportion as man desists from evils, that is, does the work of repentance, in the same proportion he is accepted of God, and does good from him. A.R. 490. God continually operates, that man may receive the things which are in his table, but if man does not do the things which are in his table, he does not receive with acknowledgment of heart the things which are in God's table, and if he does not receive them, he is not conjoined. Wherefore, the two tables are conjoined that they may be one, and are called the tables of the covenant, and a covenant s. conjunction. D.P. 326. See *Decalogue.*

Tabor and **Hermon** (Ps. lxxxix. 13) s. those who are in divine good and in divine truth. A.E. 298.

Tabrets and **Harps** (Isa. xxx. 32) s. the delights of the affection of truth. A.E. 727.

Taches, or **Clasps of Gold,** den. the faculty of being conjoined by good; of brass, den. by external good. 9624.

Tacit Providence. The Lord leads man by his affections, and binds him to good by a t. p., that he may be in freedom. 4364. The invisible action of providence ill. 5508.

Tail. By t. is s. the ultimate of the head, because the brain through the backbone is continued to the t., wherefore, the head and t. make one, as the first and last; when, therefore, by head is s. faith alone, justifying and saving, by t. is s. the sum of all the confirmations of it, which are from the Word, and are, therefore, truths of the Word falsified; every one who, from his own intelligence, assumes a principle of religion, and establishes it as the head, also assumes confirmations or proofs from the Word, and makes them the t., thus does he stupefy others, and so hurts them; wherefore, it is said in Rev. ix., "that they had tails like scorpions," and presently after, that "there were stings in their tails, and that their power was to hurt men;" for by scorpion is s. a power of persuasion, stupefying the understanding. Inasmuch as by t. is s. the ultimate, and as the ultimate is the complex or aggregate of all, therefore, Jehovah said to Moses, "take the serpent by the t., and he took it, and it became a rod." (Exod. iv. 3, 4.) And, therefore, it was commanded, "that they should take off the t. entire, near the back-bone, and sacrifice it, together with the fat that was upon the entrails, kidneys, intestines, and liver." (Lev. iii. 9, 10, 11; viii. 25; ix. 16; Exod. xxix. 22.) A.R. 438. Tails s. scientific sensual principles, because the tails of animals are continuations of the dorsal spine, which is called the medulla spinalis, and this is the continent of the cerebrum, which s. intelligence and wisdom, the ultimates or extremes, whereof are scientific sensual principles. A.E. 559.

Take, to, **a Woman** (Gen. xxxviii. 9) s. to be associated and conjoined. 3688.

Take, to, **Great Power**. (Rev. xi. 17.) Thou hast taken to thee thy g. p. s. divine omnipotence, which is, and was his from eternity. A.R. 523.

Take

Take, to, away Sins. By the taking a. s. is s. the same thing as by redeeming man, and saving him: for the Lord came into the world, that man might be saved, since without his coming, no mortal could have been reformed and regenerated, consequently, no mortal could have been saved; but this became possible after that the Lord had taken away all the power of the devil, that is, of hell, and had glorified his humanity, that is, united it to the divinity of the Father. L. 17.

Taken up into a Mountain, to be (Rev. xxi. 10), s. to be taken up into the third heaven, because it is said "in the spirit," and he who is in the spirit, as to his mind and its vision, is in the spiritual world, and there the angels of the third heaven dwell upon mountains. This elevation is effected in a moment, because it is done by a change in the state of mind. A.R. 896.

Taken and Left. (Matt. xxiv. 40, 41.) By those who are t. are s. they who find and receive truths, and by those who are l. are s. they who neither inquire after nor receive them, because they are in falses. A.R. 794.

Tale of the **Bricks**, etc. (Exod. v. 8.) "And the t. of the b. which they made yesterday, the day before yesterday, ye shall put upon them," s. that things fictitious and false were to be injected in the same abundance as in the former state; for t. den. abundance, in the present case, the same abundance; and b. s. things fictitious and false, and yesterday the day before yesterday s. a former state: and to put upon them s. to inject, because it is pred. of things fictitious and false. 7116.

Talents den. good and truth from the Lord received as remains. 5291.

Talent Weight. (Rev. xvi. 21.) Great hail, the weight of a t., s. direful and atrocious falses, whereby all truth and good in the Word, and, consequently, in the church, is destroyed. The reason why it is said to be of the weight of a t. is, because a t. was the largest weight of silver, and likewise of gold, and by silver is s. truth, and by gold, good, and, in an opp. sense, falsity and evil. A.R. 714. T. (Matt. xxv.) s. the knowledges of truth and good. A.E. 193.

Tapestry den. truths in the ultimate heavens. 9743.

Tar and **Pitch** (Exod. ii. 3) s. good mixed with evils and falses, for t. s. good mixed with evils, and p. s. good mixed with falses; these s. are grounded in this circumstance, that t. and p. are in themselves fiery, and by what is fiery in the Word, is s. good, and, in the opp. sense, evil; but whereas they are sulphurous and also black, they s. evil and the false. 6724.

Tares (Matt. xiii. 30) s. evil and false principles. 3941.

Tares, Wheat, etc. (Matt. xiii. 27–30, 37–42.) The t. are those that are inwardly evil; the w., those that are inwardly good; the gathering them together, and the binding them in bundles to burn, is the last judgment. L.J. 70.

Tarry, to (Gen. xxvii. 44), s. nearly the same as to dwell; but to t. is pred. of the life of truth with good, and to dwell is pred. of the life of good with truth. 3613. To t. (Gen. xxxii. 4) s. to imbibe. 4243. The Lord said to John, that he should t. till he came (John xxi. 22, 23), because John rep. the good of life, and this day is the coming of the Lord, when the good of life is now taught by the Lord, for those who are to be of his new church, which is the New Jerusalem. A.R. 17.

Tarshish (Isa. lxx. 9) s. the natural man, as to the knowledges of good. A.E. 406. T. (Dan. x. 5) s. the good of charity and faith, for T. is a sparkling precious stone. 6135. Gold of T. s. scientific good. 9881.

Tarshish and **Uphaz.** (Jer. x. 9.) Silver from T. s. the truth of the Word in its literal sense, and gold from U., the good of the Word in that sense. A.E. 585.

Tarshish, Pul, Lud, Tubal, and **Javan** (Isa. lxvi. 19), s. kinds of external worship. 1158.

Tartary. Des. of the Word in T. A.R. 11.

Task-masters den. falses by which men are bound to servitude. 6659.

Taste. Inasmuch as food and nourishment cor. to spiritual food and nourishment, it is from this ground, that the t. cor. to the perception and the affection thereof. Inasmuch as the t. cor. to perception and to the affection of knowing, of understanding, and of growing wise, and the life of man is in that affection, therefore it is not permitted to any spirit, or to any angel, to flow into man's t., for this would be to flow into the life which is proper to him. There are, nevertheless, vagabond spirits of the infernal crew peculiarly pernicious, who, in consequence of having been habituated in the life of the body, to enter into man's affections with a view to his hurt, retain also that lust in the other life, and by every method study to enter into the t. with man, into which, when they have entered, they possess his interiors, namely, the life of his thoughts and affections, for they cor., and the things which cor. act in unity; several at this day are possessed by those spirits. 4793. A spirit, or man after death, has all the sensations which he had while he lived in the world . . . but not the t., but instead thereof, something analogous which is adjoined to the smell. The reason why he has not t. is, lest he should enter into the t. of man, and thus possess his interiors; also, lest that sense should turn him away from the desire of knowing and of growing wise, thus from spiritual appetite. 4794. See *Spirits*.

Teach, to, and Seduce. (Rev. ii. 20.) To t. is pred. of truths and falsities; and to s., of goods and evils. A.E. 160.

Teachers s. doctrine, or the doctrine of truth, and, in the supreme sense, divine truth. A.E. 600.

Tear, a, s. grief on account of there being no understanding of truth, and, therefore, on account of the false. A.E. 484.

Tebah, Gaham, Thaash, and Maacah (Gen. xxii. 24), s. the various religious principles and kinds of worship der. from the Gentiles, who are in idolatrous worship, but principled in good, s. by Rumah. 2869.

Teeth s. the ultimates of the life of the natural man, which are called sensuals, of which there are two kinds, one of the will, and the other of the understanding; but the sensuals of the understanding are s. by t. That t. s. the ultimates of man's life, which are called sensuals, which when separated from the interiors of the mind, are in mere falses, and offer violence to truths and destroy them, may appear from many passages. Since sensual men do not see any truth in its own light, but enter into reasoning and altercations about everything, whether it be so or not, and as these altercations in the hells, are heard out of them as the gnashing of t., which, viewed in themselves, are collisions of falsity and truth, it is plain what is s. by the gnashing of t. (Matt. viii. 12, and other places); and also in some measure what by gnashing with the t. (Ps. xxxvii. 12; cxii. 10; Micah iii. 5; Lam. ii. 16). A.R. 435. T. (Gen. xlix. 12), in the genuine sense, s. the natural principle; for the things appertaining to man, which are hard, as t., bones, and cartilages, cor. to the truths and goods which are of the lowest natural principle. 6380.

Teeth whiter than Milk (Gen. xlix. 12) s. the celestial spiritual principle pertaining to the Lord's natural principle. 2184.

Teeth of Beasts, and **Poison of Serpents** of the **Dust**. (Deut. xxxii. 24.) T. of b. s. the sensual principle as to the lusts of evil; and the p. of s. of the d. s. falsities thence der., which by the fallacies of the sensual principle of man, maliciously or craftily pervert truths. A.E. 650. Hypocrites, when it is allowed them to flow in into the parts of the body, to which they cor., from the opp. principle, inject severe and intolerable pain into the teeth, gums, etc. 5720.

Teeth set on Edge s. appropriation of false from evil. A.E. 556.

Tell, to, s. to apperceive, for in the spiritual world, or in heaven, they have no need to t. what they think, there being a communication of all thoughts: wherefore, to t., in the spiritual sense, s. to apperceive. 5601.

Tema

Tema rep. things of the spiritual church among the Gentiles. 3268.

Teman, the inhabitants of (Jer. xlix. 20), s. the evils and falses opposed to the Lord's celestial kingdom. A.E. 400.

Teman and **Paran**. (Hab. iii. 2–4.) T. has respect to celestial love, and Mount P. to spiritual love. 2714.

Tempest and **Whirlwind**. Influx in the inferior parts of the spiritual world is like a t. and w. A.E. 418.

Temple rep. heaven and the church; the sacred place where the ark was, rep. the inmost, or third heaven, and the church among those who are in the inmost principle, which is called the celestial church. The t. without the sacred place rep. the middle, or second heaven, also the church with those who are in similar principles, which is called the internal spiritual church. The inner court rep. the ultimate or first heaven, also the church with those who are in ultimates, which is called the internal natural church, but the outer court rep. entrance into heaven. A.E. 630. T. s. the Lord's divine humanity with respect to divine truth. A.R. 882. T. s. the superior heavens. A.E. 630. T. (Luke xxi. 5–7) s. the church at this day, in which there is no truth left remaining, and which consequently, is at an end. A.R. 191. T. (Rev. xv. 8) s. divine truth, or the Word in the natural sense, in light and potency from the divine truth in the spiritual sense. A.E. 955. By "I saw no t. in it" (Rev. xxi. 22), is not meant, that in the new church, which is New Jerusalem, there will not be t., but that in it, there will not be an external separated from what is internal; the reason is, because by a t. is s. the church as to worship, and, in the supreme sense, the Lord himself as to the divine humanity, who is to be worshipped; and since the all of the church is from the Lord, therefore it is said, "for the Lord God Omnipotent and the Lamb is the t. thereof," by which is s. the Lord in his divine humanity. A.R. 918. See *Court, Vail of the Temple*.

Temple of his **Body** (John ii. 21) s. the divine truth from the divine good. 6135.

Temple of **God**. (Rev. xi. 19.) By the t. of G., is s. the Lord in his divine humanity in the heaven of angels, because it is called the t. of G. in heaven. A.R. 529.

Temple of **Jehovah**. The interior heavens are the t. of J. 9741.

Temple of the **Tabernacle** of the **Testimony**. (Rev. xv. 5.) By "I looked, and behold the t. of the t. of the t. in heaven was opened," is s. that the inmost of heaven was seen, where the Lord is, in his holiness, in the Word, and in the law, or decalogue. A.R. 669.

Temporary. Nothing can proceed from man but what is t., and nothing from the Lord but what is eternal. D.P. 219.

Temptation is a combat between good and evil, therefore each strives for the dominion, that is, whether the spiritual man shall rule over the natural man, and thus, whether good shall have the dominion over evil, or whether, on the contrary, the natural man shall prevail against the spiritual man; consequently, the contest is, whether the Lord shall have the dominion over man, or whether hell shall have the dominion. N.J.D. 199. Whosoever has gained any degree of spiritual life, undergoes t. When a t. is finished the soul is in a state of fluctuation between truth and falsehood, but afterwards truth shines with brightness, and brings with it serenity and gladness. N.J.D. 197. In a state of t. man is near to hell. N.J.D. 197. A.C. 8131. All elevation in a state of t. is effected by divine truth. 8170. T. appertaining to man are spiritual combats between evil and good spirits, which combats are from those things and concerning those things which man had done and thought which are in his memory. 8131. T. are generally carried on to a state of desperation, which is their period and conclusion. N.J.D. 197. A.C. 1787. In t. man is in equilibrium between two opp. powers, one from the Lord in his inner man, and the other from hell in his outer man. N.J.D. 197. A.C. 8168. Infants undergo t. in another world, whereby they are taught to resist evils. N.J.D. 197. A.C. 2294. There are several kinds of t., which in general are celestial, spiritual, and natural, and which ought not in the least to be confounded; celestial t. cannot exist but with those who are in love towards the Lord; spiritual with those who are in charity towards their neighbor; natural t. are altogether distinct from those, and are not t., but only anxieties arising from the assault of their natural loves, being excited by misfortunes, diseases, and a bad temperament of the blood and fluids of the body. In the case of those who are in love towards the Lord; whatever assaults this love produces an inmost torture, which is celestial t.; in the case of those who are in love towards their neighbor, or charity, whatever assaults this love produces torment of conscience, and this is spiritual t.; but in the case of those who are natural, what they mostly call t., and pangs of conscience, are not t., but only anxieties arising from the assault of their loves, as when they foresee and are sensible of the loss of honor, the goods of the world, reputation, pleasure, bodily life, and the like; yet these troubles are wont to be productive of some good. Moreover t. are also experienced by those who are in natural charity; thus they are experienced by all kinds of heretics, gentiles, and idolaters, arising from those things which assault the life of their faith, which they hold dear; but these straitnesses bear some faint resemblance to spiritual t. 847. They who are in good of life, according to their religion, in which there are not genuine truths, in another life, undergo t., by which their falses are shaken off, and genuine truths implanted in their stead. A.E. 452. All persons are tempted who have a conscience of right and wrong, that is, who are under the influence of spiritual love; but they endure most grievous t. who have a perception of right and wrong, that is, who are under the influence of celestial love. 1688, 8693. N.J.D. 197. Dead men, or such as have no faith and love towards the Lord or charity towards their neighbor, are not admitted into t., because they would fall under them. Therefore very few people are at this day admitted into spiritual t. 270. The Lord tempts no man, but on the contrary labors for his deliverance, and the introduction of good. 2768. If man fall in t. his state after it becomes worse than his state before it, inasmuch as evil has thereby acquired power over good and the false over truth. N.J.D. 192. Hour of t. (Rev. iii. 10) s. the time of the last judgment. A.R. 186. There are spiritual t. and there are natural t.; spiritual t. are of the internal man, but natural are of the external man; spiritual t. sometimes exist without natural t., sometimes with them. Natural t. are, when a man suffers as to the body, as to honors, as to wealth, in a word as to natural life, as is the case in diseases, misfortunes, persecutions, punishments, not grounded in justice, and the like; the anxieties which then exist, are what are meant by natural t.; but these t. do not at all affect his spiritual life, neither can they be called t., but griefs; for they exist from the hurt of the natural life, which is of self-love and the love of the world; the wicked are sometimes the subjects of these griefs, who grieve and are tormented the more in proportion as they love themselves and the world more, and thus der. life thence; but spiritual t. are of the internal man, and assault his spiritual life; the anxieties then are not on account of any loss of natural life; but on account of the loss of faith and charity, and consequently, of salvation; these t. are frequently induced by natural t., for when man is in these latter, namely, in disease, grief, the loss of wealth or honor, and the like; if then a thought occurs concerning the Lord's aid, concerning his providence, concerning the state of the evil, that they glory and exult, when the good suffer and undergo various griefs and various losses, in such case spiritual t. is conjoined to natural t. 8164.

Temptations of the Lord

Temptations of the Lord. The L. could in no wise be tempted whilst he was in the essential divine, for the divine is infinitely above all t., but he could be tempted as to the human: this is the reason that, when he underwent the most grievous and inmost t., he adjoined to himself the former human, viz., its rational and natural, and afterwards separated himself from them. But still retained such a principle, that he could thereby be tempted. 2795. His last t. and victory were in the garden of Gethsemane, and upon the cross, whereby he completely subdued all the powers of hell, and made his humanity divine. N.J.D. 201. See *Truth Divine.*

Ten s. all things, because heaven in whole and in part, refers to man, and thence is called the grand man; all the powers of the life of that grand man, or heaven, terminate in two hands and two feet, and the hands as also the feet terminate in t. fingers or toes; wherefore all things of man as to power and support, are ultimately collated into ten fingers, and ultimates in the Word s. all things. A.E. 675. T. s. what is full, also much and many, also every thing and all; hence the things which were written on the tables of the decalogue by Jehovah, are called the t. commandments, which s. all truths, for they include them. And because t. s. all and every thing, therefore the Lord compared the kingdom of heaven to t. virgins. Likewise in the parable, he said of the nobleman, that he gave his servants t. talents to trade with. Many is also s. by the t. horns of the beast which came up out of the sea (Dan. viii. 7), and by the t. horns, and the t. crowns upon the horns of the beast which came up out of the sea (Rev. xxiii. 1), also by the t. horns of the scarlet-colored beast, upon which the woman sat. (Rev. xvii. 3, 7, 12.) From the s. of the number t. as den. what is full, much, and all, it may be seen why it was ordained, that a tenth part of all the fruits of the earth, should be given to Jehovah, and from Jehovah to Aaron and the Levites (Num. xviii. 24, 28; Deut. xiv. 22), also, why Abram gave Melchisedek tithes of all (Gen. xiv. 18, 19), for by this was s., that all they had was from Jehovah, and sanctified. (See Mal. iii. 10.) A.R. 101. That the decalogue consisted of t. precepts or t. words, and that Jehovah wrote them on tables (Deut. x. 4), s. remains, and their being written by the hand of Jehovah s. that remains are of the Lord alone; their being in the internal man was rep. by tables. 576.

Ten and Five. T. s. all, and all things, and f. one part, or one kind. (1 Kings vii. 39.) A.E. 600. See *Tenth.*

Ten Days (Rev. ii.) s. duration for some time, because forty days s. an entire duration of infestation and temptation, and t. den. some part thereof. A.E. 124.

Tenacities of Opinion, to which certain mucous glands cor. 5386.

Tendency, the, to good in the regenerate is from the Lord, even to its least manifestation. 1937. Influx is a continual t. to acts and motions. 3748.

Tender. How the t. ideas of infants are led to wisdom by angels. 2290. Infants confided to angels of the female sex, who had tenderly loved them. 2302. Those who have tenderly loved infants are in the province of the womb, where they live a most sweet life, affected with celestial joys. 5054.

Tender of Age, den. the state of truths newly received not yet genuine. 4377.

Tender and Good den. the celestial natural. 2180.

Tendons, the, of the grand man are composed of those whom the gospel has not reached. D.P. 254, 326.

Tent is used in the Word to s. the celestial and holy things of love, because in old time they performed holy worship in their t., but when they began to profane t. by profane worship, then the tabernacle was built, and afterwards the temple; wherefore what the tabernacle, and afterwards the temple s., that also was s. by t.; a holy man was therefore called a t., and a tabernacle, and also a temple of the Lord. In a supreme sense, the Lord as to his human essence, is a t., a tabernacle, and a temple: hence every celestial man is so called, and hence every thing celestial and holy has acquired those names: and whereas the most ancient church was beloved of the Lord more than the succeeding churches, and men lived among themselves at that time apart, or in their own families, and celebrated holy worship in their t.; therefore t. were accounted more holy than the temple, which was profaned; and for this reason the feast of tabernacles was instituted, when they gathered in the produce of the earth, as a remembrance of those former holy times, and it was ordained, that at this feast they should dwell in tabernacles, like the most ancient people. (Lev. xxiii. 39–44; Deut. xvi. 13; Hosea xii. 9.) 414. The t. (Exod. xxvi. 14) was rep. of the three heavens, thus of the celestial and spiritual things of the Lord's kingdom. 3540. T., in an opp. sense, s. worship which is not holy, or the worship of him who separates himself from the internal. 1566. See *Curtains*.

Tenth Month (Gen. viii. 5) s. truths which are of remains. 856, 868.

Tenth Part, a, s. the same as ten. A.R. 515.

Tenths of All (Gen. xiv. 20) s. remains der. from victory. 1734.

Tenths (Num. xviii. 24, 28) s. benediction in all things. A.E. 675.

Terah (Gen. xi. 24) s. idolatrous worship. 1353. See *Idolatry.*

Teraphim (Gen. xxx.) were idols which were applied to when they consulted or inquired of God, and because the answers which they received were to them truths divine, therefore truths are s. by them. And whereas such things were s. by t., they were also with some, although prohibited, as with Micah in the book of Judges xvii. 5; xviii. 14, 24; also with Michal, David's wife. (See 1 Sam. xix. 14, 16.) That nevertheless they were idols which were prohibited, is evident from 1 Sam. xv. 23; 2 Kings xxiii. 24; Ezek. xxi. 26. 4111.

Terror (Jer. vi. 25) s. spiritual death. A.E. 721.

Terror and **Dread**. Terror is pred. of those who are in evils, and dread, of those who are in falses. 9331.

Terror of **God** den. protection, because it prevents evil spirits from approaching. 4555.

Test, a, is given by which every one may ascertain his real quality; whether evil or good. 1680.

Testament. The blood of the New T., or new covenant, s. the conjunction of the Lord with the church by divine truth. A.E. 960. See *New Testament, Old Testament, Covenant.*

Testicles cor. to conjugial love, and to its opp. Exp. 5060.

Testimony in the **Ark** s. the Lord. 9455.

Testimony den. good from which truth is der., and truth which is from good. 4197. T. is divine truth. A.R. 555. T. (Ps. cxxxii. 12) s. the good of life according to the truths of doctrine. A.E. 392.

Testimonies, Laws, Precepts, Commands, Statutes and **Judgments**, are mentioned together in many parts of the Word, and by t. and c. are s. those things which teach life: by l. and p., those things which teach doctrine, and by s. and j., those things which teach external rites. A.E. 392.

Text. A sentence of Scripture. See *Word.*

Thahash den. religious principles grounded in idolatrous worship, but in good. 2868.

Thamar (Gen. xxxviii.) s. a church rep. of things spiritual and celestial, which was to be established amongst the posterity of Judah. The internal of the church here is T., and the external Judah was the three sons by the Canaanitish woman. 4831.

Thanks being ascribed to the Lord, s. the all of worship. A.R. 249. By giving t. (Rev. xi. 17), is s. an acknowledgment and glorification of the Lord. A.R. 522.

Thanksgiving

Thanksgiving and **Blessing**. (Rev. viii.) T. is pred. of good, and b., of truth. A.E. 466. T. and honor (Rev. vii.) are pred. of the reception of divine good. A.E. 467.

Theatre of the **Universe**. Universal nature is des. as rep. of the celestial and spiritual things of the Lord's kingdom. 1807.

Theft s. the evil of merit, which is, when man attributes good to himself, and imagines that it is from himself, and therefore is willing to merit salvation; this evil it is, which, in the internal sense, is s. by t. See *Murders, Incantations, etc.*

Thema. The inhabitants of the land of T., den. those who are in simple good, such as the well-disposed gentiles are principled in. 3268.

Theology. The science which treats of the attributes of God, and his relations to man. See *Doctrines*.

Thick Darkness s. hatred, instead of charity. 1860.

Thicket den. the scientific natural. To be caught in a t. is to stick in scientifics. 2831.

Thickets (Jer. iv. 7) s. scientifics, because they are respectively such, especially when under the influence of the lusts of self-love and the love of the world, and the principles of the false. 2831.

Thief. (Rev. iii. 3.) It is said that the Lord will come like a t., because man who is in dead worship, is deprived of the external good of worship; for there is something of good in dead worship, because the worshippers think of God, and of eternal life; but still good without its truths, is not good, but meritorious or hypocritical, evils and falses taking it away like a t.; this is done successively in the world, and after death fully, man in the mean time not knowing when and how. A.R. 164.

Thieves of the **Sons Israel** (Deut. xxv. 7) s. those who acquire to themselves the truths of the church, not for the end of living according to them, and thereby of teaching them from the heart, but of making gain thereby themselves: that such a t. is damned, is s. by its being commanded that he shall be slain. 5886. See *Den of Thieves.*

Thigh. (Rev. xix. 16.) By the Lord's t. is s. the Word as to its divine good; the t. and loins s. conjugial love, and inasmuch as this is the fundamental love of all loves, therefore, the t. and loins s. the good of love: therefore when t. is mentioned in speaking of the Lord, it s. himself as to the good of love, in the present instance, it also s. the Word as to the same. A.R.-830.

Thigh Falling, the (Num. v. 21, 27), s. the evil of conjugial love, that is adultery. 3021. To "uncover the thigh passing over the rivers" (Isa. xlvii. 2), s. to adulterate goods by reasoning. A.E. 1182. See *Hollow of the Thigh.*

Thighs and **Loins** (Judg. viii. 30) s. those things which are of conjugial love, also those things which are of love and charity, by reason that conjugial love is fundamental of all love, for they are from the same origin, namely, from the celestial marriage, which is that of good and truth. T. also s. the good of celestial love and the good of spiritual love. By t. and l., therefore, is s. conjugial love principally, and thence all genuine love; but, in an opp. sense, also are s. the contrary loves, namely, self-love and the love of the world. 3021.

Thimnath (Gen. xxxviii. 12) s. a state of consulting for the church. 4855.

Thin (Gen. xli. 6) den. what is of no use, for thin is opp. to full, and that is said to be full, in which there is use, or what is the same thing in which there is good, for all good is of use. Wherefore that is thin which is of no use. 5214. T. in flesh den. not of charity. 5204.

Think, to, freely from his own proper affection, is the very life of man, and is himself. H. and H. 502. To t. spiritually is to t. without time and space, and to t. naturally, is to t. with time and space. C.S.L. 328.

Thirty

Thinking Faculty. In proportion as the t. f. in man is elevated above sensual things, so far he is a man; but no one is capable of such elevation of thought, so as to discover the truths of the church, unless he acknowledge God, and live according to his commandments; for God elevates and illustrates. U.T. 402.

Third. Three den. what is full; a third what is not full. 2788.

Third Day s. the end of a state of preparation for reception, and thus an end of purification. (See Exod. xix. 16.) 8811. T. d. s. the same as the seventh d. (See Hosea vi. 2, 8.) 93. T. d. (Gen. xxii. 4) s. what was complete and a beginning of sanctification. For d. in the Word s. state as does also year, and in general all times, as hour, day, week, month, year, age, and likewise morning, midday, evening, night; and spring, summer, autumn, winter; to which when t. is added, it s. the end of that state, and at the same time the beginning of the following state. In the internal sense of the Word, three days and the t. d. s. the same thing. That the Lord rose again on the t. d. is well known; it was on this account also that the Lord distinguished the times of his life into three, as in Luke xiii. 32. The Lord also endured the last temptation, which was that of the cross, on the t. hours of the d. (Mark xv. 25.) Hence, and especially from the Lord's resurrection on the t. d., the number three was rep. and s. But t. part s. somewhat not as yet full, whereas t. and threefold s. what is complete, and this in respect to evil, as applied to the evil, and in respect to good as applied to the good. 2788. A t. part implies the same as three, and also a t. part of a t. part. 904. T. part (Apoc. xii. 4) s. somewhat not as yet full.

Thirds and **Fourths.** (Exod. xxiv. 7.) T. are pred. of truths and falses; and f. of goods and evils. (See Exod. xx. 5.) 10.624.

Thirst, to. (John xix. 28.) The reason why the Lord said, I t., was because he desired a new church, which should acknowledge him; for to t., in a spiritual sense, s. to desire, and is pred. of the truths of the church. A.E. 83. By t. and thirsting is also s. to perish for want of truths. A.R. 956. See *Hunger and Thirst.*

Thirteen, as between twelve and fourteen, den. the intermediate state. 1668. As the compound of ten and three den. remains. 2108.

Thirteen Years (Gen. xvi. 26) s. a state of holy remains. 2109.

Thirteenth Year (Gen. xiv.) s. the beginning of the Lord's temptations in childhood. 1668.

Thirty, in the Word, s. somewhat of combat, and it also s. what is full of remains; the reason why it has this twofold s. is, because it is compounded of five and six multiplied into each other, and also of three and ten multiplied likewise into each other; from five multiplied into six, it s. somewhat of combat, because five s. somewhat, and six combat; but from three multiplied into ten, it s. what is full of remains, because three s. what is full, and ten remains; and a compound number involves the like with a simple number whereof it is compounded. And whereas man cannot be regenerated, that is, be admitted into spiritual combats whereby regeneration is effected, until he has received remains to the full, therefore it was ordained, that the Levites should not do work in the tent of the assembly until they had completed t. years; their work or function is also called warfare. (See Num. iv. 3, 23, 30.) The like is involved in what is said of David. (2 Sam. v. 4.) From these considerations, it is now evident, why the Lord did not manifest himself until he was of t. years (Luke iii. 23), for he was then in the fulness of remains; and that the priests the Levites, entered upon their functions when they were t. years old, and because David was to rep. the Lord as to the royalty, therefore neither did he begin to reign until he was of that age. 5335.

Thistles

Thistles den. the opp. of fruitfulness and blessing. 273. Thorns and t. den. curse and vastation. 273.

Thorax. The spirits which appear near the t., are they who are in charity. 4403. Dreams are often introduced by spirits who belong to the province of the left t. 1978.

Thorns (Jer. xii. 13) s. the evils and false of self-love and the love of the world. 3941.

Thorns and **Thistles** (Gen. iii. 18) s. a curse and vastation, because cornfields and fruit trees s. things of an opp. nature, such as blessings and increase in multiplication; that the t., the t., the brier, the bramble, and the nettle, have such a s. is plain from many passages in the Word. 273. T. and t. s. mere falsehood and evil. D.P. 313.

Thorns, Briers, Brambles, and **Thistles,** s. falses of evil, from their stings or prickles. A.R. 439. See *Briers and Thorns.*

Thought. The interior t. of man is altogether according to affection, or love. H. and H. 298. T. diffuses itself into the societies of spirits and of angels round about, and the faculty of understanding and perceiving, is according to the extension into those societies, that is, according to the influx thence, and in one idea of the t. there are things innumerable, and more so in one t. composed of ideas. 6599. It is not that which enters into the t., but what enters into the will, that endangers the spiritual life of man, because he then appropriates it. 6308. The t. of man in its first origin is spiritual, and becomes natural in the external man by influx. 10.215. The t. of man, though silent, is audible to spirits and angels at the Lord's good pleasure. 6624. The t. of the angels in the superior heavens, when it descends, appears like flames of light, from which there is a vibration of splendor. 6615. Every man has exterior and interior t.; interior t. is in the light of heaven, and is called perception, and exterior t. is in the light of the world. A.R. 914. The t. of angels and also of man, is caused by variegations of the light of heaven. 4742.

Thoughts. There are t. from perception, t. from conscience, and t. from no conscience; t. from perception, have place only with the celestial, that is, with those who are in love to the Lord; this is the inmost ground of t. with man, and is with the celestial angels in heaven; perception from the Lord is that by which and from which their t. exists; to think contrary to perception is impossible; t. from conscience are inferior, and have place with the spiritual, that is, with those who are in the good of charity and faith, as to life, and as to doctrine; to think contrary to conscience is to them also impossible, for this would be contrary to good and truth, which is dictated to them from the Lord by conscience. But t. from no conscience have place with those who do not suffer themselves to be inwardly ruled by good and truth, but by evil and the false, that is, not by the Lord, but by themselves. 2515. T. grounded in truths, in the spiritual world, when they are presented to the sight, appear as white clouds; and t. grounded in false principles as black clouds. D.L.W. 147. All t., as to the most minute particulars thereof, are made public in another life, before spirits and angels. 2748. The t. of the angels of the supreme, or third heaven, are t. of ends, and the t. of the angels of the middle or second heaven, are t. of causes, and the t. of the angels of the lowest or first heaven, are t. of effects. It is to be observed, that it is one thing to think from ends, and another of ends; also that it is one thing to think from causes, and another of causes; as also that it is one thing to think from effects, and another of effects; the angels of the lower heavens think of causes and of ends, but the angels of the higher heavens from causes, and from ends, and to think from these is of superior wisdom, but to think of those is of inferior wisdom. To think from ends is of wisdom, from causes is of intelligence, and from effects is of science. D.L.W. 202.

Thousand, a, in the Word, s. much and innumerable, and when it is pred. of the Lord, it s. what is infinite. A t. times, as in Deut. i. 11, den. innumerable times, as in common discourse, in which, speaking of many, it is customary to express it by a t., as when you would s. that a thing has been said a t. times, or done in a t. ways. Inasmuch as a t. in calculation is a definite number, it appears in the prophetical parts of the Word, especially when they are connected historically, as if a t. s. a t., when, nevertheless, it s. many or innumerable, without any determinate number; for the historicals of the Word are of such a nature, that they determine the ideas to those s. of expressions which are nearest and most proper to them, as in the case of names also, when yet by numbers, as well as by names, are s. things; hence it is, that some also conjecture, that by t. years in the Revelation (chap. xx. 2–7), are s. a t. years, or a t. times, by reason that things of a prophetic nature are there des. historically, when yet by a t. years, as there applied, nothing is s. but an indeterminate large quantity, and also in other passages, the infinity of time or eternity. 2575. T. (Ps. xc. 4) s. what is eternal, which is the infinite of time. 2575.

Thousand Six Hundred, a (Rev. xiv. 20), s. evils in the whole complex, for by one t. s. h. the same is s. as by sixteen, and by sixteen, the same as by four, because sixteen is the product of four multiplied by itself, and four is pred. of good, and of the conjunction of good with truth, consequently, in an opp. sense, it is pred. of evil, and the conjunction of evil with the false. A.R. 654.

Threats. No one is reformed by t. because they force. D.P. 129.

Three s. what is full from beginning to end. 5708.

Three and Seven are sacred and inviolable, inasmuch as they are each pred. of the last judgment, which is to happen on the third or seventh day. 900.

Three Hundred s. what is full, because the number arises from t. and from a h. by multiplication; and t. s. what is full, and a h. s. what is full; for what the compound numbers s. is manifest from the simple numbers of which they are compounded. 5955. T. h. (Gen. vi. 15) s. remains. 646.

Three Men who appeared to **Abraham** (Gen. xviii. 2) s. the essential divine, the divine human, and the holy proceeding. 2149, 2156.

Three Parts. To be divided into t. p. s. to be totally destroyed. A.R. 712.

Three Years Old (Gen. xv. 9) implies all things appertaining to the church as to times and states, which appears from the s. of t. in the Word, as den. a full or plenary time of the church from its origin to its end, consequently, every state thereof; the last state of the church is therefore s. by the third day, and by the third week, and by third month, and by the third year, and by the third age, which are the same thing; as the state of the church is s. by the number t., so also is the state of every individual who is a church, nay, so also is the state of every thing which is of the church. 1825.

Threefold Principle. In every thing of which any thing can be pred. there is a t. p., which is called end, cause, and effect, and these three are with respect to each other according to the degrees of altitude. D.L.W. 209.

Thresh, to (Micah iv. 13), s. to dissipate evils amongst those who are of the church. A.E. 16.

Threshing-floor. (Gen. l. 10.) T.-f. s. where the good of truth is, for in a t.-f. there is corn, and by corn is s. the good which is der. from truth, and also the truth of good. 6537.

Throat and **Tongue**. (Ps. v. 10.) The t., an open sepulchre, is pred. of evil, the t. speaking smooth things, of the false. 3527.

Throne, when concerning the Lord, s., in general, the whole heaven, specifically, the spiritual heaven, and abstractedly, divine truth proceed-

Throne of the Beast

ing, and, consequently, all things of heaven and the church. A.E. 289. T. (Rev. i. 4) s. the universal heaven. A.R. 14. T. s. heaven, and also judgment. The t. built by Solomon, of which mention is made (1 Kings x. 18, 19, 20), s. both royalty and judgment, because kings, when they executed judgment, sat upon thrones. T. (Rev. iv. 2) s. a representation of judgment, because the things which John saw were visions which rep.; they were seen as he has des. them, but they were forms rep. of things to come, as may appear from what follows, as that there were seen animals, a dragon, a beast, a temple, tabernacle, ark, and many other things; similar were the things seen by the prophets. A.R. 229. T. (Rev. xii. 5) s. the angelic heaven. A.R. 545. T. (Rev. xiii. 2) s. the church as to doctrine. A.E. 783.

Throne of the Beast (Rev. xvi. 10) s. where faith alone reigns; t. s. kingdom, and the b., faith alone. T. also s. the government of falsity and evil in the following passages; namely, Rev. ii. 13, xiii. 2; Dan. vii. 9; Hag. ii. 22; Isa. xiv. 13. A.R. 694.

Throne of David (Isa. ix. 6) s. the Lord's spiritual kingdom. A.E. 946.

Thrust Through, to be, in the Word, is pred. of the extinction of goods and truths; hence in the rep. church, they who touched one who was t. t., were unclean: and on this account inquisition and expiation was made by a heifer. (Deut. xxi. 1–8.) That such laws were enacted, because by one that is t. t. is s. the perversion, destruction, and profanation of the truth of the church, by what is false and evil, is manifest from singular the things contained therein in the internal sense. 4503.

Thumb and the **Great Toe** (Exod. xxix. 20) s. the fulness of the intelligence and power of truth from good in the internal or spiritual, and in the external or natural man. A.E. 298.

Thummim and **Urim**. The word Urim den. lucent fire, and T. brightness thence. In Hebrew language, T. den. integrity. 9905.

Thunder. What the Lord speaks through the heaven, when it descends into the lower spheres is heard as t., and as he speaks through the whole heaven at once and thus fully, they are called seven t. (Rev. x.); for by seven are s. all, all things, and the whole. Wherefore also by t. is s. instruction and perception of truth, and in this instance, the revealing and manifestation thereof. That a voice from heaven is heard as t., when it proceeds from the Lord, is evident from these passages; John xii. 28, 29, 20; Job. xxxvii. 4, 5; 2 Sam. xxii. 14; Rev. xiv. 2; Ps. lxxxi. 8. A.R. 472. Great t. (Rev. xiv. 2) s. the divine g; of divine love. A.R. 615.

Thyatira (Rev. ii.) s. those who are in faith originating in charity, and thence in good works; and also those who are in faith separate from charity, and thence in evil works. That is evident from what is written to the church in T., when understood in the spiritual sense. A.R. 124.

Thyine Wood (Rev. xviii. 12) s. natural good, because wood in the Word, s. good, and stone truth, and t. w. der. its denomination from two, and two also s. good. A.R. 774.

Thymus. There are certain well-disposed spirits, who think not by meditation, and hence they quickly, and, as it were, without premeditation, utter what occurs to the thought; they have interior perception, which is not rendered so visual by meditations and thoughts, as with others, for in the progress of life they have been instructed as from themselves, concerning the goodness of things, and not so concerning their truth. Such belong to the province of the gland called the t.; for the t. is a gland which is principally serviceable to infants, and in that age is soft; with such spirits also there is a soft infantile principle remaining, into which the perception of good flows in, from which perception truth in its common principle shines forth; these may be in great crowds, and yet not to be disturbed, as is also the case with that gland. 5172.

Tidal s. goods. 1685. See *Chedolaomer.*

Tigers rep. the infernal cupidities of self-love. T.C.R. 45. Des. of some internally like. 8622.

Till the Ground from whence he was taken, to (Gen. iii. 23), s. to become corporeal as he was before regeneration. 305. To t. the g. (Gen. iv. 12), s. to cultivate schism or heresy. 380. A tiller of the g. is one who is without charity, however he may be in faith separate from love, which is no faith. 345.

Timbrel (Ps. lxxxi. 2) has respect to what is spiritual. 3969.

Timbrel and **Harp.** (Ps. cxlix. 3.) The t. s. good, and the h. truth. 420. T. cor. to celestial truths. A.R. 276.

Time. (Rev. x. 6.) There shall no longer be t., s. that there cannot be any state of the church, or any church, except one God be acknowledged, and that the Lord is that God. A.R. 476.

Time, and Times, and Half a Time (Rev. xii. 14) s. to the end and beginning, thus during its increase from a few to many, until it grows to its appointed growth. By a t., and t., and h. a t., is s. the same here as by a thousand two hundred and sixty days (verse 6); the same is also s. by three days and a half (chap. xi. 9, 10), also by the three years and six months of famine (Luke iv. 25), and in Dan., by a stated time or stated times and a half, when they will make a consummation of dispersing the hands of the people of holiness. (Dan. xii. 7.) A.R. 562. In the divine idea, and thence in the spiritual sense, there is no time, but instead of time, state. A.R. 4. The reason why time appears to be something, is owing to the mind's reflecting on those things which are not objects of affection, or love, consequently, which are irksome. 3827.

Time, Space, and Person. There are three things in general which perish from the sense of the letter of the Word, whilst the internal sense is coming forth, namely, what is of t., what is of s., and what is of p. 5253.

Times and **Spaces** in heaven do indeed appear like t. and s. in the world, but yet they do not really exist there, for which reason the angels cannot otherwise measure t. and s., which there are appearances, than by states, according to their progressions and changes. A.R. 947.

Timidity, or **Fear.** They who are in evil and false are in f. 390. F. of God s. worship. 2826. F. is of two kinds, holy and not holy. 3718.

Timnath den. state of consultation as to the good of the church. 4855.

Tin (Ezek. xxii. 18) has respect to the things of the literal sense of the Word, or to the goods and truths of the natural man. A.E. 540. See *Silver, Iron, Tin, and Lead.*

Tiras (Gen. x. 2) was one of those nations who were principled in external worship cor. with internal, and by which nations, in an internal sense, are s. so many several doctrinals, which were the same as rituals, which they observed as holy, as appears manifestly from the Word, where mention is made continually of those nations, for by them, wheresoever they occur, is s. external worship, sometimes external worship cor. with internal, sometimes what is opp. thereto. 1151.

Tithes (tenths) s. goods and truths which are stored up from the Lord, in man's interiors, which goods are called remains; when these are pred. of the Lord, they den. the divine goods and divine truths, which the Lord procured to himself by his own proper power. 3740. See *Ten.*

Tittle, the least, in the Word, is rep. of heavenly things. 5147. See *Jot and Tittle.*

To-day. We sometimes read in the Word this expression, even to this day, or t.-d., as in Gen. xix. 37, 38; xxii. 14; xxvi. 33; xxxii. 32; xxxv. 20; xlvii. 26; which expressions, in an historical sense, have respect to the time when Moses lived, but in an internal sense, by this day, and by t.-d., is s. the per-

Toe

petuity and eternity of a state; for day den. state, so likewise t.-d., which is the time present; that which has relation to time in the world, is eternal in heaven, and in order that this might be s., t.-d. is added, or to this day, although it appears to those who are in the historical sense, as if the expressions involved nothing besides; in like manner it is said in other places of the Word, as Josh. iv. 9; vi. 25; vii. 26; Judges i. 21, 26, and in other places; that t.-d. s. what is perpetual and eternal, may appear from David Ps. ii. 7; cxix. 89–91; so also in Jer. i. 5, 10, 18; so in Moses, Deut. xxix. 9, 11, 12, 14; to the same purpose see also Num. xxviii. 3, 23; Dan. viii. 13; xi. 31; xii. 11; Exod. xvi. 4, 19, 20, 23; John vi. 31, 32, 49, 50, 58; Matt. vi. 11; Luke xi. 3. 2838.

Toe. See *Thumb and Great Toe.*

Togarmah (Ezek. xxvii. 14) s. those who are in internal worship. A.E. 355.

Token of a **Covenant** (Gen. ix. 12) s. a mark of the Lord's presence in charity, suggesting thus a remembrance thereof in man. 1038. To give a t. (Gen. ix. 12) s. to cause it to be. 1039.

To-morrow s. to eternity. 3998.

Tones. It is worthy to be remarked, that angels and spirits, according to their differences with respect to good and truth, distinguish t., and this not only of singing and of instruments, but also in the words of speech, and admit only such t. as are in concord, so that there is an agreement of t., consequently, of instruments, with the nature and essence of good and truth. 420.

Tongs and **Snuff-dishes** (Exod. xxv. 38) s. purifiers and evacuators in the natural principle. 9572.

Tongue, the, affords entrance to the lungs, and also to the stomach, thus it rep. a sort of courtyard to things spiritual and to things celestial: to things spiritual, as ministering to the lungs, and thence to the speech, and to things celestial, as ministering to the stomach, which supplies the blood of the heart with aliment; wherefore the t., in general, cor. to the affection of truth, or to those in the grand man who are in the affection of truth, and afterwards are in the affection of good from truth; they, therefore, who love the Word of the Lord, and thence desire the knowledges of truth and good, belong to that province; but with the difference, that there are some who belong to the t. itself, some to the larynx and the windpipe, some to the throat, likewise, some to the gums, and some also to the lips; for there is not the smallest thing appertaining to man, with which there is not cor. But some cor. to the interiors of the t. and of the lips, and some to the exteriors; the operation of those who receive only exterior truths with affection, but not interior, and yet do not reject the latter, flow not into the interiors of the t., but into the exteriors. 4791. T., as an organ, s. doctrine, but as speech, or language, it s. also religion. A.R. 282. T. s. perception of truth, with respect to speech, and the affection of good, with respect to taste. A.E. 455. T. (Luke xvi. 24) s. the thirst and cupidity of perverting the truths of the Word. A.E. 455. To gnaw the t. (Rev. xvi. 10) s. to detain the thought from hearing truths; that by gnawing the t. the above is s. cannot be confirmed from the Word, because the expression nowhere else occurs there; but when any one in the spiritual world utters truths of faith, the spirits, who cannot endure to hear truths, keep their t. between their teeth and likewise bite their lips, and moreover induce others to press their t. and lips with their teeth, and this in such a degree as to give pain; from which it is plain that by gnawing their t. for pain is s. that they could not endure truths. A.R. 696. To speak with new t. s. to confess the Lord and the truths of the church from him. A.E. 455.

Tool. To form an idol with a graver's t. (Exod. xxxii. 4) den. from self-intelligence. 10.406.

Tooth (Exod. xxi. 24) den. the exterior understanding, and hence natural truth. 9052. See *Teeth.*

Tops of the **Mountains Appearing** on the **First** of the **Month** (Gen. viii. 5), s. the truths of faith, which then begin to be seen, as may appear from the s. of mountains, in that they are the goods of love and charity, these tops then begin to be seen, when man is regenerated, and gifted with conscience, and thereby with charity. The t. of the m. are the first dawnings of light which appear. 859.

Topaz (Exod. xxviii. 17) rep. the good of celestial love. 9865.

Tophet and the **Valley** of **Hinnom** (Jer. viii. 32) den. hell. T., hell from behind, which is called the devil; and the v. of H., hell from before, which is called satan. A.E. 659.

Torch of **Fire**, a (Gen. xv. 17), s. the burning of cupidities. And its passing between the pieces s. that it divided those who were of the church from the Lord. 1861, 1862. A.E. 539.

Torment, to (Rev. ix. 5), s. to induce stupor, or to stupefy the understanding. A.R. 427. They who are in hell suffer t. in proportion as they receive the influx from heaven. U.T. 74. All t. in hell results from the love of self and of the world and from cupidities originating in those two loves. A.R. 636.

Tormented, to be. Every one in hell is t. by his love and its concupiscences, for the life of every one there is made up of them, and it is the life which is t., wherefore, there are degrees of torment there according to the degrees of the love of evil and thence of falsity. A.R. 864.

Torments. Infernal t. are not stings of conscience, as some suppose, for they who are in hell have no conscience; such as have conscience are among the blessed. 965.

Torn (Gen. xxxi. 38) s. evil without its fault or (blame). 4171. T. is pred. of good, into which a false principle is insinuated, whence good is no longer alive. 4171.

Torn to **Pieces.** (Gen. xliv. 28.) To be t. to p. s. to perish by evils and falses. The reason why being t. in p. has this s. is, because in the spiritual world no other tearing to pieces has place but that of good by evils and falses; the case herein is like that of death and of the things appertaining to death, which, in the spiritual sense, do not s. natural death, but spiritual death, which is damnation, for there is no other death in the spiritual world; in like manner, tearing to pieces, in the spiritual sense, does not s. tearing to pieces, such as is effected by wild beasts, but the tearing in pieces of good by evils and falses; the wild beasts, also, which tear in p., in the spiritual sense, s. the evils of lusts and the falses thence der., which also in the other life are rep. by wild beasts. 5828.

Torpor. Spirits who have cared to live only in luxurious indolence, induce t. 1509.

Touch, the sense of, in general, cor. to the affection of good. 4404. To t. s. communication, translation, and reception. 10.130. By making to t. (Exod. iv. 25) s. to show, for by the t. it is shown. 7046. The sense proper to conjugial love is the sense of t. The love of knowing objects from the love of circumspection and self-preservation, is the sense of touching. C.S.L. 210. The innocence of parents and the innocence of infants meet each other by means of the t., especially of the hands, and thereby they join themselves together as by kisses. Communications of the mind are effected by this sense, because the hands are the ultimate principles of man, and his firsts are simultaneously in the ultimates, whereby also all things of the body and all things of the mind are kept together in an unsevered connection; hence it is, that Jesus touched infants (Matt. xvii. 6; Mark x. 13, 16); and that he healed the sick by the t.; and that they were healed who touched

Towel

him; hence also it is, that inaugurations into the priesthood are at this day effected by the laying on of hands. C.S.L. 396. See *Hands.*

Towel, a (John xiii. 4), s. divine truths. A.E. 951.

Tower (Gen. xi. 4) s. the worship of self, which consists in a man's exalting himself above another, even so as to be worshipped; wherefore self-love, which is haughtiness and pride, is called height, loftiness, and lifting up, and is described by all those things which are high. The reason why self-love in worship, or the worship of self is called a t. is, because a city s. doctrine, and formerly cities were fortified with towers in which were guards. Towers also were built in the boundaries of a country, wherefore they were called towers of the guards, or watchmen (2 Kings ix. 17; xvii. 9; xviii. 8), and watch-towers. (Isa. xxiii. 13.) When also, the church of the Lord is compared to a vineyard, the things appertaining to worship and to the preservation thereof, are compared to a wine-press, and to a t. in the vineyard, as appears from Isa. v. 1, 2; Matt. xxi. 33; Mark xii. 1. 1306. T. (Matt. xxi. 33) s. interior truths from spiritual good, which is there s. by wine-press. A.E. 929. To build a t. (Luke xiv. 27), s. to procure interior truths. 4599.

Tower of **Eder** (Gen. xxxv.; Josh. xv. 21) s. the progression of what is holy to interior things. 4599.

Towers (Ps. xlviii. 12) s. the interior truths which defend those things which are of love and charity. 4599. T., in the opp. sense, den. the interior things of those who are principled in self-love and the love of the world, thus the falses from which they combat, and by which they confirm their superstitious principles. 4599. T. (Isa. xv. 30) s. doctrines of the false. A.E. 315. Watch-tower (Isal xxiii. 13) s. fantasies. 1306. T. in the Word are pred. of truths, but mountains of goods. 4599.

Trachea. Changes of state ill. by variations of sound in the t. D.P. 279.

Trade, to, s. to procure knowledges to one's self, and also to communicate, because in heaven, where the Word is perceived according to the internal sense, there is not given any trading, for there is neither gold nor silver there, nor any such things as are traded with in the world, wherefore when mention is made of trading in the Word, it is understood in a spiritual sense, and such a thing is perceived as cor., in general the procuring and communication of knowledges, and specifically that which is named, as if gold is named, the good of love and wisdom is understood, if silver, the truth which is of intelligence and faith is understood, and so in other instances. 4453. To merchandise and t. in the Word, s. to procure spiritual riches, which are the knowledges of things true and good, and, in an opp. sense, knowledges of things false and evil, and by the latter to gain the world, and by the former to gain heaven; for which reason the Lord compared the kingdom of heaven to a merchant seeking goodly pearls (Matt. xiii. 45, 46), and the members of the church to servants, to whom there were given talents to t. with and make profit (Matt. xxv. 14–20), and to whom there were given ten pounds, which they were in like manner to t. with and make profit by. (Luke xix. 12–26.) And since as by Tyre is s. the church with respect to the knowledges of things true and good, therefore, her t. and merchandise are treated of throughout the whole of the 27th chap. of Ezekiel. (See also chap. xxviii. 5; Isa. xxiii. 1, 8.) And the perverted church among the Jews in the land of Canaan, is called the land of traffic. (Ezek. xvi. 3, 29; xxi. 35; xxix. 14.) A.R. 759.

Trading den. to procure and communicate knowledge. 4453. T. with reference to the goods and truths of the Lord's kingdom. 4453.

Train. (Isa. vi. 1.) By the t. of the Lord is s. in general the divine proceeding, and specifically the divine truth which is in the extremes of heaven and the church. A.E. 253.

Trample, to, **upon** s. to destroy entirely by sensual and natural principles, which are called the fallacies of the senses. A.E. 632.

Tranquillity is produced from internal peace, when cupidities and falses are removed. 3696. T. is pred. when the spiritual man begins to be made celestial. 91–93.

Transfiguration of the **Lord**. He was not regenerated as a man, but was made divine, and this from the most essential divine love, for he was made divine love itself; what his form then was, was made apparent to Peter, James, and John, when it was given them to see him, not with the eyes of the body, but with the eyes of the spirit; namely, that his countenance shone like the sun (Matt. xvii. 2); and that this was his divine human, appears from the voice which then came out of the cloud, saying, "This is my beloved son." That son is the divine human. 3212. The Word in its glory was rep. by the Lord when he was transfigured. By his face, which shone as the sun, was rep. his divine good; by his raiment which was as light, his divine truth; by Moses and Elias, the historical and prophetical Word, by Moses, the Word which was written by him, and in general the historical Word, and by Elias the prophetical Word; by the bright cloud which overshadowed the disciples, the Word in the sense of the letter; wherefore out of this the voice was heard, which said, "This is my beloved son, hear ye him," for all declarations and responses from heaven are constantly delivered by means of ultimates, such as are in the literal sense of the Word, for they are delivered in fulness from the Lord. S.S. 48.

Transflux. The inflowing of the divine through heaven. 6720.

Transgressions, or **Trespasses**, den. such evils as are done against the truths of faith. 9156.

Transmission of the love of evil from parents to their children. D.S.W. 269.

Travail, to, in **Birth**, s. to conceive and bring forth those things which appertain to spiritual life. A.R. 535.

Travail, to, **with Child**, s. the doctrine of the new church, in its birth, and its difficult reception thereof. A.R. 535.

Travel, to, **or Sojourn**, s. change of state. 1463.

Tread, to, **Down**, or **Bruise** (Gen. iii. 15), s. depression. It has the same s. in Isa. xxvi. 5, 6; xxviii. 2, 3. 258.

Tread, to, the **Holy City under Foot** (Rev. xi. 2), s. to disperse the truths of the doctrine of the new church. A.R. 489.

Tread, to, the **Wine-Press** (Rev. xiv. 20), s. to explore or examine the quality of works, in the present case, works resulting from the doctrine of faith of the church which are evil works, for to t. the w.-p. s. to explore, and the clusters which are trodden s. works. And all exploration or examination of church doctrine is made by the divine truth of the Word, and this not being in that doctrine, but out of it, that also is s. by the w.-p. being trodden without the city. To t. the w.-p. not only s. to explore evil works, but likewise to bear with them in others, also to remove and cast them into hell, in the following places: Isa. lxiii. 1, 2, 3; Lam. i. 15; Rev. xix. 15. A.R. 652.

Treader, the, **Treading out no Wine** in the **Presses** (Isa. xvi. 10), s. that there were no longer any who were in faith. 1071.

Tread-Down, to, den. the depression of evil. 258, 9.

Treasure (Matt. xiii. 44) s. divine truth which is in the Word. A.E. 840.

Treasuries den. knowledges of good and truth, and, in the opp. sense, evil and false. 6660.

Treasure in Heaven (Luke xviii. 22) s. goods and truths from the Lord. 5886. Treasures s. the knowledges of truth and good. 10.406.

Treasures Hid in the **Sand** s. the spiritual things which lie hid in the literal sense of the Word. A.E. 445.

Treasures

Treasures on the **Back** of **Camels** (Isa. xxx. 6, 7) s. knowledges appertaining to the natural principle. 3048.

Treasures of **Darkness**, and **hidden Riches** of **Secret Places** (Isa. xlv. 3), s. interior intelligence and wisdom from heaven. A.E. 208.

Tree s. man; and as man is man by virtue of affection which is of the will, and perception which is of the understanding, therefore these also are s. by t. There is also a cor. between man and a t.; wherefore in heaven there appear paradises of t., which cor. to the affections and consequent perceptions of the angels; and in some places in hell, there are also forests, of t. which bear evil fruits, cor. with the concupiscences and consequent thoughts of those who are there. A.R. 400. The t. is man; the effort to produce means is with man, from his will in his understanding; the stem or stalk, with its branches and leaves, are in man its means, and are called the truths of faith; the fruits, which are the ultimate effects of the effort in a t. to fructify are in man uses; in these his will exists. F. 16. Man who is reborn, in like manner as a t., begins from seed, wherefore by seed in the Word is s. the truth which is from good; also in like manner as a t., he produces leaves, next blossoms, and finally, fruit, for he produces such things as are of intelligence, which also in the Word are s. by leaves, next such things as are of wisdom, which are s. by blossoms, and finally such things as are of life; namely, the goods of love and charity in act, which in the Word are s. by fruits; such is the rep. similitude between the fruit-bearing t., and the man who is regenerated, insomuch that from a t. may be learnt how the case is with regeneration, if so be any thing be previously known concerning spiritual good and truth. 5115.

Tree planted beside the **Waters** that **spreadeth out her Roots** by the **River** (Jer. xvii. 8), has respect to the extension of intelligence from the spiritual man into the natural. A.E. 481.

Tree seen by **Nebuchadnezzar** in a **Dream** (Dan. iv. 7–14), rep. the church which afterwards became Babylon. A.E. 1029.

Tree of **Knowledge** s. the pride of one's own intelligence. D.P. 328. See *Eat.*

Tree of **Life** (Rev. ii. 7) s. the essential, celestial, and, in a supreme sense, the Lord himself, because from him is all the celestial principle, that is, all love and charity. 2187. A.R. 89.

Trees, in general, s. the perceptions when the celestial man is treated of, but when pred. of the spiritual church, they s. knowledges; by reason the man of the spiritual church has no other perceptions that what are der. by knowledges from doctrine, or the Word, for these constitute his faith, consequently, his conscience whence perception comes. 103, 2722. T. (Joel i. 10–12) s. knowledges. 368. See *Groves, Leaves.*

Trees, two, in the **Garden** of **Eden**, one of life, and the other of the knowledge of good and evil, s. that free agency was given to man in spiritual things. U.T. 466–469, 479. The t. of life s. perception from the Lord, and the t. of the knowledge of good and evil, perception from the world. A.E. 739. T. of E. (Ezek. xxxi. 16) s. scientifics, and knowledges collected from the Word profaned by reasonings. 130.

Trees of the **Field** (Ezek. xxxi. 15) s. the knowledges of truth in the church. A.E. 372.

Trees of **Fruit** and **Cedars**. (Ps. cxlviii. 9.) T. of f. s. celestial men, and c. spiritual men. 776.

Trees of **Jehovah**, and **Cedars** of **Lebanon** (Ps. civ. 16), s. the spiritual man. 776.

Tremor. Felt in the nerves and bones when invaded by evil spirits. 3219.

Tremble, to (Jer. x. 10), is pred. of the church, when falses are believed, and called truths. A.E. 400.

Tremble, to, or to be **Amazed** (Ezek. xxvi. 15–18), s. an entire change of state. A.E. 406.

Trembling, dregs of the cup of, s. mere falses from which evils are der. A.E. 724.

Trespass, Onan's, s. his aversion and hatred against the good and truth of the church. 4834.

Triangular s. what is right in the ultimate degree, which is the natural. A.R. 905.

Tribe s. the church with respect to its truths and goods, and, in an opp. sense, with respect to its falses and evils. A.R. 587. T. s. the church with respect to religion. A.R. 282. The t. which is first named in the series or class, s. some love which is of the will, and the t. which is named after it, s. something of wisdom, which is of the understanding, and the t. which is named last, s. some use or effect der. from them; thus each series is full, or complete. A.R. 360.

Tribes. In general the twelve t. s. all things appertaining to the doctrine of truth and good, or of faith and love; these principles, namely, truth and good, or faith and love, constitute the Lord's kingdom, for the things appertaining to truth or faith are the all of thought therein, and the things appertaining to good or love are the all of affection; and whereas the Jewish church was instituted, that it might rep. the Lord's kingdom, therefore the partitions of that people into twelve t. had this s.; this is an arcanum which has not heretofore been discovered. 3859. Love to the Lord is s. by the three first t., namely, Judah, Reuben, and Gad; charity towards our neighbor, by these three t., Asher, Naphtali, and Manasseh; but the obedience of faith is s. by the three following t., namely, Simeon, Levi, and Issachar; the conjunction of them all with the Lord, is s. by the last three t., Zebulon, Joseph, and Benjamin; these things in sum are s. by all these t. named in this order, for their s. are according to the order in which they are named. (Rev. vii.) A.E. 438.

Tribes of **Zebulon, Joseph,** and **Benjamin.** The t. of Z. s. the conjunction of those who are in the third heaven with the Lord; the t. of J., the conjunction of those who are in the second heaven with the Lord; and the t. of B., the conjunction of those who are in the first heaven with the Lord. A.E. 448.

Tribes of the **Earth shall Wail** (Rev. i. 7) s. that there are no longer any goods and truths in the church. A.R. 27.

Tribulation (Matt. xxiv. 29) s. the state of the church when there are no longer any goods and truths. A.R. 27.

Tribute, or **Custom**. (Matt. xvii. 25–27.) By giving t., or c., are meant they who serve, wherefore it is said, "that strangers should give, and sons should be free," for strangers are servants. 6394.

Trine, the, **in One** exists in the Lord only. D.P. 123. In every thing there is a t., called end, cause, and effect. D.L.W. 209.

Trinity. In the Lord God the Saviour there is a divine t., which is, the Divine from which are all things, which is called the Father; the divine human, which is called the Son, and the proceeding divine which is called the Holy Spirit. U.T. 188. That this t. was not before the world was created, but that after the world was created when God became incarnate, it was provided and made; and then in the Lord God, the redeemer and saviour, Jesus Christ. U.T. 170. The t. existing in one person, that is, in the Lord, is the divine essence which is called the Father, the divine human which is called the Son, and the divine proceeding which is called the Holy Spirit; thus there is a t. in unity. 2149, 2156.

Troop, a (Gen. xxx. 11), s., in a supreme sense, omnipotence and omniscience; in an internal sense, the good of faith; and, in an external sense, works. The ground and reason why t., in a supreme sense, den. omnipotence and omniscience, is, because t., in the present case, is a multitude, and when multitude is pred. of the Lord's divine it is an infinite multitude, which is nothing else than omnipotence and omniscience; but omnipotence is pred. of quantity in relation to magnitude, and omniscience, of quantity in relation to multitude; omnipotence also is pred. of infinite good, or, what is the same thing, of the divine love, thus of the divine will, but omniscience of infinite truth, or, what is the same thing, of the divine intelligence. That t., in an internal sense, den. the good of faith, is from cor., for good, which is of charity, cor. to the Lord's divine omnipotence, and truth, which is of faith, to his omniscience. The reason why t., in an external sense, den. works, is, because these cor. to the good of faith, for the good of faith produces works, inasmuch as the good of faith cannot be given without works, just as thinking what is good and willing what is good, cannot exist without doing what is good, the former being an internal principle, and the latter a cor. external. 3934. T. (Gen. xlix. 19) s. works without judgment. 6405. See *Drove.*

Trough (Gen. xxiv. 20) s. the good of truth, for water in the t. s. truth, and the t. itself s. the same as wood, namely, good. The good of truth is what is produced from good by truth, and is an offspring born of truth as of a mother, and of good as of a father; all genuine good which is in the natural man is thence, or from the marriage of good and truth in the rational; this good is what is called the good of truth, and is s. in the Word by t., or place to receive water. 3095. A little t. (Exod. ii. 16) s. the doctrine of charity. The reason whereof is, because it is a wooden t. into which water is drawn from a well to give flocks to drink; for what is wooden, in the internal sense, s. the good of charity; to draw s. to be instructed; the water which is drawn s. the truth of faith; the well from which it is drawn s. the Word; and to give the flocks to drink s. to instruct in good from the Word. From these considerations it may be manifest, that a little t. den. the doctrine of charity. 6777. See *Drinking Troughs, Kneading Troughs.*

True and **Faithful.** (Rev. xxi. 5.) "These words are t. and f.," s. that they may know this of a certainty, because the Lord himself testified and said it. A.R. 886.

Trumpet. Voices as of a t. are heard in heaven, when convocations and ordinations take place; therefore, among the children of Israel, with whom all things were rep. of heaven and the church, it was also commanded, that they should make t. of silver, and that the sons of Aaron should blow with them for the calling of assemblies, and for the journeying of the camps, in days of rejoicing, in festivals, in the beginning of months, over burnt-offerings, for a memorial, and going to war. (Num. x. 1–11.) A.R. 226. To sound a t. as to its effect, s. the revelation and manifestation of divine truth, and, in an opp. sense, the deprivation of truth and desolation. A.E. 502. By sounding with t. is s. to call together upon solemn occasions, and also to explore and discover the quality of the church. A.R. 391, 397. Seven t. which the seven angels sounded (Rev. xvi.) s. the exploring and laying open of the falses and evils in which they are who are principled in faith separate from charity. A.R. 676.

Trumpets and all **Wind Instruments** have respect to celestial affections. A.R. 792.

Trumpets, Timbrels, Psalteries, and **Harps.** T. and t. cor. to celestial goods and truths; and p. and h., to spiritual goods and truths. The cor. is with their sounds. A.R. 276.

Trust, or **Confidence.** All c. draws its esse from the end of life, and hence only exists in good. 4683.

Truth, in its purest and naked principles, is not to be found existing either with men or angels, but only in the Lord. 3207, 7902. Celestial t. is charity, and spiritual t. is faith. 5897. There is a difference between celestial t. and

t. celestial; the former is t. which der. its origin from the celestial; but the latter der. its origin from t. which is implanted in the celestial by means of knowledges. 1545. T. from a celestial origin is the t. of the literal sense of the Word. A.E. 1042. Natural t. is t. in the memory, and not in the life. A.E. 176. There is a difference between scientific t., rational t., and intellectual t., and they succeed each other; scientific t. is of science; rational t. is scientific t. confirmed by reason, and intellectual t. is joined with an internal perception that it is so. 1496. T. is the first or chief of combat, for the combat is supported by t. inasmuch as the knowledge of what is false and what is evil is acquired by t., wherefore such combats never exist before man is imbued with the sciences and knowledges of t. and good. 1685. So far as any one loves t., so far he is desirous of knowing it, and so far he is in heart affected when he finds it, nor can any other attain unto wisdom; and so far as he loves to do the t., so far he is made sensible of the pleasantness of the light in which the t. is. Dec. 89.

Truth Divine in the Lord's human divine, which underwent temptations, is not essential d. t., for this is above all temptation; but it is truth rational, such as belongs to the angels, consisting in appearances of truth, and is what is called the Son of man, but before glorification; whereas d. t. in the Lord's divine human glorified is above appearances, nor can in any wise come to any understanding, not even of the angels, and still less to the apprehension of man, thus in nowise to any thing of temptation; it appears in the heavens as the light which is from the Lord. Concerning this d. t., or the Son of man glorified, it is thus written in John: "Jesus said, now is the Son of man glorified, and God is glorified in him; if God be glorified in him, God shall also glorify him in himself, and shall straightway glorify him." (xiii. 31, 32.) That a distinct idea may be had of this most deep arcanum, it is permitted to call the truth with the Lord, which could be tempted, and which underwent temptations, t. d. in the Lord's human divine, but to call the truth which chould not be tempted, or undergo any temptation, because it was glorified, d. t. in the Lord's divine human. 2814.

Truth of Doctrine. There is no church in man, till t. of d., conceived in the internal man, is born in the external. A.R. 17.

Truth of Good and **Good of Truth**. The t. of g., or t. from g. is masculine; and the g. of t., or g. from that t., is feminine. C.S.L. 88, 90.

Truth and Good. T. is conjoined to g., when a man perceives delight in doing well to his neighbor for the sake of t. and g., but not for the sake of himself and the world; when a man is in that affection, the truths which he then hears, or reads, or thinks, are conjoined to good; which also is wont to be apperceived from the affection of truth for the sake of that end. 5340. T. itself is the spiritual principle of the church, and g. itself is its celestial principle, but with different persons t. and g. are differently understood; such therefore as the understanding of t. is, such is the t. appertaining to every one; the case is similar in regard to the understanding of good. 5354. T. in itself is g. because der. from g. T. is the form of g., that is, when g. is formed that it may be intellectually perceived, then it is called t. 3049.

Truths. The t. which are imbibed by man in his infancy and childhood from the Word, doctrine, and preaching thence, appear indeed as t., but nevertheless they are not t. with him, because they are only like the shell without the kernel, or like the form of the face and body, without the soul and life; but when they are received in the will-principle, then first they become t. and begin to acquire a vital efficacy. A.E. 434. Man is first affected with external t., and afterwards with internal, for external t. are the planes of internal ones, being general principles into which particular ones are insinuated, inasmuch as man, without a general idea of a thing, comprehends nothing particular; hence it is, that in the literal sense of the Word are general t., but, in the internal sense, particular t.; the former are what are called external, but the latter internal; and whereas t. without affection are not t., as not being connected with life, therefore when mention is made of external and internal t., the affections thereof are understood. 3819. T., in a spiritual form, are such as are in the spiritual sense of the Word, but t., in a natural form, are in the natural sense of the Word, which although distinct make one by cor. A.E. 790.

Tubal-Cain, an **Instructor** of every **Artificer** in **Brass** and **Iron** (Gen. iv. 22), s. the doctrine of natural good and truth. T.-C. is called an instructor of every artificer, and not a father, as was the case with Jabal and Jubal; because celestial and spiritual, or internal things, had before no existence, wherefore the term father is applied in the case of Jabal and Jubal, as s. that such internal things then first began to exist; whereas natural or external things existed before, but were now applied to internal things, therefore T.-C. is not called a father, but an instructor of the artificer. 421, 423.

Tubal and **Javan** (Isa. lxvi. 18, 19) den. those who are in external worship, cor. with internal, who were to be instructed concerning things internal. 1151.

Tubercles. Des. of the spirits who cor. to the t. 5188.

Tumult (Isa. xiii. 4) s. eagerness of desire for combating against truths. A.E. 453.

Tun. Des. of an infernal. 820, 947, 948.

Tun. They who are deceitful and think to secure every thing to themselves by deceitful contrivances, and have confirmed themselves in such habits during the life of the body, by being successful herein, they seem to themselves to dwell in a kind of very large t. 947, 948.

Tune. The singing of heaven is nothing else than an affection of the mind, which is emitted through the mouth as a t. C.L. 155.

Turban s. intelligence which is of truth. A.E. 204.

Turn, to, truths into good, is to will and do them. 5820. The interiors of all who love the Lord, are turned to him, while those who love themselves are t. to hell. 10.702.

Turn Aside, to, judgment, den. to pervert and to destroy. 9260. In the case of angels who came to Lot, s. dwelling in the good of charity. 2330.

Turning Aside, like going down, is pred. of elongation from good to evil, and from truth to the false. 4816.

Turpentine-nut den. the goods of life, exterior and interior. 5622.

Turtles, and **Young Pigeons**, s. things spiritual. 1361. 10.132.

Turtle Dove (Ps. lxxiv. 19) s. spiritual good. A.E. 388.

Turtle Dove and **Young Pigeon** (Gen. xv. 9) s. those things which are rep. of spiritual things, exterior and interior. 1827. See *Soul of Thy Turtle Dove.*

Twelve. That t. s. all things of faith, has been heretofore unknown to the world, nevertheless, this is the constant s. of t., wherever that number occurs, either in the historical or prophetical Word; nothing else is s. by the t. sons of Jacob, and hence by the t. tribes which took their names from them; in like manner, by the t. disciples of the Lord, each rep. an essential and primary principle of faith. 2089.

Twelve and **Twenty-Four** s. all things, and are pred. of truths. A.E. 253.

Twelve Angels (Rev. xxi. 12) s. the same as the twelve tribes. 1925.

Twelve Disciples of the **Lord**, the, rep. the church at large, as to all things belonging to faith and charity, in like manner as the twelve tribes of Israel. 2129.

Twelve Gates of the **New Jerusalem** (Rev. xxi.) s. the knowledges in chief of truth and good, by which man is introduced into the church, by twelve pearls is also s. the knowledges in chief of truth and good, hence it is that the gates were pearls; the reason why each of the gates was of one pearl, is, because all the knowledges of truth and good, which are s. by gates and by pearls, have relation to one knowledge, which is their continent, which one knowledge is the knowledge of the Lord; it is called one knowledge, although there are several which make that one knowledge, for the knowledge of the Lord is the universal of all things of doctrine, and thence of all things of the church; from it all worship der. its life and soul, for the Lord is all in all in heaven and the church, and thence all in all in worship. A.R. 916.

Twelve Hours (John xi. 9) s. all the states of truth. 6000.

Twelve Precious Stones in the **Foundation** of the **New Jerusalem** (Rev. xxi.) s. all things of the doctrines of the New Jerusalem in their order from the literal sense of the Word, with those who immediately approach the Lord, and live according to the commandments of the decalogue, by shunning evil as sins. These t. p. s. s. the like as the twelve tribes of Israel respectively, because by the twelve tribes are s., in like manner, all the goods and truths of the church, and of its doctrine in their order; for which reason, it is also said in this chapter, verse 14, that in these twelve foundations were written the names of the twelve apostles of the Lamb, and by the twelve apostles are s. all things of doctrine concerning the Lord, and concerning a life conformable to his commandments. The same is also s. by these twelve stones as by the t. p. s. in the breast-plate of Aaron, which was called Urim and Thummim, as recorded in Exod. xxviii. 15–21, with this difference, that upon the latter were the names of the twelve tribes of Israel, but upon the former, the names of the twelve apostles of the Lamb. A.R. 915.

Twelve Sons of **Jacob** rep. the twelve general or cardinal things, whereby man is initiated into things spiritual and celestial, during the process of regeneration, or of being made a church; for whilst man is regenerating, or is made a church, that is, whilst from a dead man he is made alive, or from corporeal is made celestial, he is led of the Lord through several states; the general states are those which are den. by these t. s., and afterwards by the twelve tribes; wherefore, the twelve tribes s. all things relating to faith and love. 3913.

Twelve Tribes of **Israel** s. all the goods and truths of the church in their order. A.R. 915.

Twenty, when pred. of that number of things, s. all, or what is full, being compounded of twice ten. 10.222. T. (Gen. xviii. 31.) As all numbers which occur in the Word s. things and states, so also it is with t., the s. whereof may appear from its derivation, namely, from twice ten; ten in the Word, as also tenths, s. remains, whereby is s. every good and truth which the Lord insinuates into man from infancy, even to the last period of life; twice ten, or twice tenths, that is, t. s. the same thing, but in a superior degree, namely, good. Good things of a threefold kind are s. by remains, namely, the good things of infancy, the good things of ignorance, and the good things of intelligence. 2280.

Twenty-Four s. all things, and are pred. of truths. A.E. 253.

Twenty-Seventh Day (Gen. viii. 14) s. what is holy, as appears from this circumstance, because it is compounded of the number three twice multiplied into itself: three multiplied into itself is nine, and nine again multiplied by three is twenty-seven, wherefore, in twenty-seven three is the ruling number. 901.

Twilight s. the last time of the church. 10.134.

Twins. T. in the womb (Gen. xxv. 24) s. that both (viz., good and truth, rep. by Esau and Jacob) were conceived together. 3298.

Two s. all, with respect to good. A.R. 245. T. s. conjunction, because all and singular things, which are in the spiritual world, and thence which are in

Two Days

the natural, have reference to t. principles, namely, to good and truth, to good as to what is agent and influent, and to truth as to what is patient and recipient, and because they have reference to those t. principles, and nothing is in any case produced, unless those t. principles are made one by somewhat resembling a marriage, it is from this ground that by t. is s. conjunction; such a somewhat resembling a marriage is in all and singular things of nature, and of her three kingdoms, and without it nothing at all exists. 5194. T., in the Word, s. the same as six, that is, combat and labor which precede regeneration. 900. T. (Gen. vii. 2) s. what is respectively profane, as may appear from the s. of that number. T. s. not only a marriage, but, when the marriage is celestial, it is a holy number, but it s. also the same as six, in that it has the same relation to three that six days of labor have to the seventh of rest, or the holy day; wherefore, the third day, in the Word, is taken for the seventh, and involves nearly the same thing, by reason of the Lord's resurrection on the third day; hence also the Lord's coming into the world and into glory, and also every coming of his, as it is des. by the seventh day, so it is, likewise, by the third day, and hence the t. preceding days are not holy, but respectively profane, as in Hosea vi. 1, 2; and in Zech. xxi. 8, 9. 720.

Two Days (Hosea vi. 2) s. the time and state which precedes judgment. 2405.

Two Olive Trees and **Two Sons** of **Oil** (Zech. iv. 2, 3, 4) are the good of love to the Lord, and the good of charity towards our neighbor. A.E. 75.

Two Times (Gen. xliii. 10) den. exterior and interior life. 5614.

Two and **Two** (Gen. vii. 9) s. things cor. as may appear to every one from this, that they are pairs, which pairs cannot exist unless they cor. with each other, as truths and goods, evils and falses; for there is in all things a kind of marriage, or coupling, as of truths with goods, and of evils with falses, in consequence of the marriage of the understanding with the will; or of things intellectual with things voluntary, and indeed every thing has its marriage, or its coupling, without which, it is impossible for it to subsist at all. 747.

Two-Three and **Four-Five**. (Isa. xvii. 6.) T.-t. s. those who are in good and thence in truths, and f.-f. s. few who are in good. A.E. 532.

Two and **Three**. (Matt. xviii. 19, 20.) T. are pred. of good, and t. of truth. A.E. 411.

Tyrant. The true king and t. contrasted. 10.805.

Tyre (Ezek. xxvii. 13, 14) rep. those who possess the knowledges of things celestial and spiritual. 1154.

Tyre and **Zidon** were the ultimate borders of Philisthea, and were near the sea, and therefore by T. are s. interior knowledges, and by Z. exterior knowledges, and this of things spiritual, which also appears from the Word. 1201.

Tythes, or **Ten**, den. fullness; a tenth part, sufficiency. 8468.

U

U and O. The speech of the heavenly angels sound much from the vowels u and o. From the expressions in the Word in the Hebrew language, it may in some measure be known whether they belong to the heavenly class or to the spiritual class, thus whether they involve good or truths; those which involve good partake much of u and o, and also something of a, but those which involve truth partake of e and i. Because affections manifest themselves chiefly by sounds, therefore also, when great subjects are treated of, as heaven and God, those words are preferred in human discourse, which contain the vowels u and o; musical sounds also have an elevation to the same vowels, when similar things are expressed: it is otherwise when the subjects treated are not of importance; hence it is that the art of music is able to express various kinds of affection. H. and H. 241.

Ulcer den. things defiled, which are from evils. 7524.

Ultimate, the, s. the whole. 10.044. The u. of the will is the pleasurable sensual principle and the u. of the understanding is the scientific sensual principle. 9996.

Ultimate Degree. That the u. d. is the complex, continent, and basis of the prior degrees, is manifestly evident from the progression of ends and causes to effects; that the effect is the complex, continent and basis of the causes and ends, may be comprehended by enlightened reason; but not so clearly, that the end, with all things of it, and the cause with all things of it actually are in the effect, and that the effect is the full complex of them. That the thing is so, may appear from the following considerations; that one is from the other in a triplicate series, and that the effect is no other than the end in its u.; and because the u. is the complex, it follows that the u. is the continent, and also the basis. D.L.W. 212.

Ultimate of Doctrine is the literal sense of the Word, which is called a wall, because it contains and includes the spiritual sense. A.E. 811.

Ultimates. Unless the Lord had come into the world, and so assumed himself, what was u., the heavens which were from the inhabitants of this earth, would have been translated elsewhere, and all the human race in this earth would have perished in eternal death, but now the Lord is in his fullness, and so in his omnipotence in the earths, as he is in the heavens, because he is in u., and thus the Lord can save all who are in divine truths from the Word and a life according to them. A.E. 726. Th u. which are boundaries, are those things which are called natural principles, for in natural principles spiritual and celestial principles terminate. 4240. The end of creation exists in the u., which is, that all things may return to the Creator, and that there may be conjunction. D.L.W. 167.

Ultimates of the Human Body. The cartilages, bones, teeth, and nails, are its u. produced from what is spiritual, in which u., the life, which is derived from the soul, terminates. W.H.

Ultimates of the Lord's Humanity, which he glorified, are called flesh and bones. 10.044.

Ultimates, Mediates, and Primaries. U. are all and every thing of the mineral kingdom, which are materials of various kinds, of stony, saline, oily, mineral and metallic substance, covered over with ground consisting of vegetable and animal matters, reduced to the finest powder; in these lie hid the end and also the beginning of all the uses which are from life; the end of all uses is the endeavor to produce them, and the beginning is the power acting from that endeavor; these are of the mineral kingdom. M. are all and every thing of the vegetable kingdom, which are grasses and herbs of every kind, plants and shrubs of every kind, and trees of every kind; the uses of these are for all and every thing of the animal kingdom, as well imperfect as perfect, they nourish them, delight them, and vivify them; they nourish their bodies with their materials, delight their senses with their taste, smell, and beauty, and they vivify their affections. The endeavor to those things also is in them from life. P. are all and every thing of the animal kingdom; the lowest there are called worms and insects; the middle birds and beasts; and the highest men; for in every kingdom there are lowest, middle, and highest; the lowest for the use of the middle, and the middle for the use of the highest. Thus the uses of all things which are created ascend in order from u. to man, who is the first in order. D.L.W. 65.

Uncircumcised in **Lips** (Exod. vi. 30) s. to be impure as to those things which are of doctrine; for by circumcision was rep. purification from filthy loves, that is, from the loves of self and of the world; hence they who were not circumcised, and were called u., rep. those who were not purified from the above loves, thus impure; and l. den. those things which are of doctrine; thus by u. in l. is s. to be impure as to those things which are of doctrine, for u. is pred. both of doctrine and of life; hence the ear is called u. in Jer. vi. 10, and the heart is called u. in the same Prophet, ix. 26; Ezek. xliv. 7, 9; Lev. xxvi. 41; from which passages it is evident, that u. den. impure; and whereas every thing impure is from impure loves, which are the love of the world and the love of self, therefore by u. is s. that which impedes the influx of good and truth, where those loves are, there inflowing good and truth is extinguished, for they are contraries, like heaven and hell; hence by the u. ear is s. disobedience, and by the u. heart the rejection of good and truth, which is especially the case, when those loves have fortified themselves with the false principle as with a wall. The reason why Moses, inasmuch as he was a stammerer, calls himself u. in l., is for the sake of the internal sense, that thereby might be s., that they who are in falses, who are rep. by Pharaoh, would not harken to the things which would be said to them from the law divine, by reason that they who are in falses give the name of falses to the truths which are of the law divine, and the name of truths to the falses which are contrary to the truths of the law divine, for they are altogether in the opp. principle; hence by them the truths of doctrine are no otherwise apperceived than as impure. 7225. The u. (Ezek. xxxi. 18) s. those who are without the good of charity. A.R. 90.

Unclean Spirit which goes out of a **Man** (Luke xi. 24) s. removal of evils and thence of falses from a man when he performs repentance. A.E. 731.

Unclean Thing. (Rev. xxi. 26.) By u. t. is s. spiritual whoredom, which is adulteration of the good, and falsification of the truth of the Word, for this is uncleanness and impurity itself, because the Word is cleanness and purity itself, and the same is defiled by evils and falses when it is perverted. A.R. 924.

Uncleanness and **Scum** (Ezek. xxiv. 11) s. what is evil and false. 4744.

Unclothed s. to be deprived of the truths of faith. 1073.

Unconnected. There is no u. thing in existence. 5377.

Uncover, to, and **Grind Meal**. (Isa. xlvii. 2.) To u. s. to adulterate the goods of the Word, and to g. m. s. to falsify its truths. A.E. 1153.

Unction is rep., for in ancient times they anointed those who were appointed to the priesthood, and also their garments, inasmuch as by anointing they were consecrated or inaugurated to rep. A.E. 375. See *Oil.*

Under. To be understood as without, thus as external relatively. 4564.

Underneath, or **Below,** in the internal sense, s. without. 4564.

Understand, to, is the companion of volition. D.P. 96.

Understanding, the, of every man is such, that it can be elevated even into the light of heaven, and also is elevated, if from any delight he desires to see the truth. A.R. 914. What is only in the u. and not at the same time in the life, is not in a man, but without, as it were in an outer court; but that which is at the same time in the life, is in a man, it is within him as in a house. A.R. 337. The u. is enlightened in proportion as man receives truth with his will, that is, in proportion as he wills to act according thereto. 3619. The u. receives light from heaven, just as the eye receives light from the world. 1524. The u. takes its quality from those truths der. from good, of which it is formed. 10.064. The u. consists in seeing and perceiving whether a thing be true or not, before it is confirmed, but not in being able to confirm every thing. 4741. Man as to his u. can be in his spiritual mind, and thence in heaven; but he cannot be as to his will in his spiritual mind, and thence in heaven, unless he shuns evils as sins; and unless he be also as to his will in heaven, still he is not in heaven, for the will draws the u. downwards, and causes it to be alike animal and natural as itself. Dec. 86.

Understanding and **Will.** Man without liberty and rationality would have neither u. or w., and therefore would not be a man. D.P. 96.

Unfaithful, the (Rev. xxi. 8), s. those who are in no charity towards their neighbor, for these are insincere and fraudulent, consequently u. A.R. 891.

Unicorn, a young (Ps. xxix. 6), s. the falses of the sensual man. S. S. 18.

Unite. It is the perpetual object of the divine providence to u. in man good to truth and truth to good. D.P. 24.

Union and **Conjunction.** In order that a more distinct idea may be had of the u. of the Lord's divine essence with the human, and of the Lord's c. with mankind by the faith of charity, it may be expedient to call the former u., and the latter c. Between the divine and human essence of the Lord there was a u., whereas between the Lord and mankind, by faith of charity, there is a c. This appears from the consideration that Jehovah, or the Lord, is life, whose human essence was also made life; and there is u. of life with life; but man is not life, but a recipient of life, and when life flows into a recipient of life, there is c.; for it is adapted to it as an active to a passive, or as what in itself is alive to what in itself is dead, which thence obtains life; the principal and the instrumental (as they are termed) appear indeed conjoined, as if they were one, but still they are not so; for the former is by itself, and the latter is by itself. Man of himself is not alive; but the Lord out of mercy adjoins him to himself, and thus causes him to live to eternity; and because they are thus distinct the connection is called c. 2021. See *Conjunction.*

Unity, the, in which is the trinity, is given in the Lord alone. Exp. A.Cr. 13. Reciprocal union makes u. D.L.W. 35.

Universal, the, of all things is love and wisdom. D.L.W. 28.

Universal. No u. can exist but from and with singulars, the totality of these being called an u., even as particulars taken together are called a common subject. 1919.

Universals of **Heaven** and **Hell.** There are three u. of hell, which are diametrically opp. to the u. of heaven; the u. of hell are these three loves, the love of ruling from the love of self, the love of possessing the goods of others, from the love of the world, and scortatory love. The u. of heaven opp. to those are these three loves, the love of ruling from the love of use; the love of possessing the goods of the world, from the love of doing uses by them, and love truly conjugial. C.S.L. 261.

Universe

Universe. In the created u., as well in its greatest as in its least things, there are these three, namely, end, cause, and effect; the reason why these three are in the greatest and least things of the created u., is, because in God the Creator, who is the Lord from eternity, are these three. But because he is infinite, and infinite things in the infinite are distinctly one, therefore, also those three in him, and in his infinite things, are distinctly one. Hence it is that the u., which was created from his being, and viewed as to uses is an image of Him, obtained these three in all and every thing of it. D.L.W. 169. The u. is a work cohering from firsts to lasts, for it is a work continent of ends, causes, and effects, in an indissoluble connection; and because in all love there is an end, and in all wisdom the promotion of an end by mediate causes, and through them to effects, which are uses, it follows also, that the u. is a work continent of divine love, divine wisdom, and uses, and thus a work altogether coherent from firsts to lasts. That the u. consists of perpetual uses produced by wisdom, and originated by love, every wise man may see as in a mirror, while he procures to himself a general idea of the creation of the u., and in that views the particulars; for particular parts adapt themselves to the whole, and the whole disposes them into such a form that they may agree. U.T. 47.

Unjust and **Just**. (Rev. xxxii. 11.) By the u. is s. he who is in evils, and by the j., he who is in good. A.R. 948.

Unleavened Bread s. the holy of love, or the holy of holies, consequently pure love, and the baking of u. b. is purification. 2342. See *Leaven*.

Unspotted. (Rev. xiv. 5.) By the u. are s. those who are not in falsities. (See also Lev. xxi. 17, 23, and xxi. 19–25.) A.R. 625.

Unstring, to, an **Ox** (Gen. xlix. 6) s. to weaken the external good which is of charity. 6357.

Uphaz, gold of, s. celestial good. 9881.

Upon, or **Over**, s. within. A.R. 900.

Upright s. what is true, originating in charity; for truth may be der. from sundry origins, but that which originates in the good of charity from the Lord is called u., and an u. man, as in Ps. xv. 1, 2; xviii. 25; and lxxxiv. 11. 612.

Upwards. To look u., or forwards, s. to look to things celestial, but to look downwards, or backwards, s. to look towards corporeal and terrestrial things. (See Lev. xxvi. 13; Micah ii. 3; Lam. l. 8, 13; Isa. liv. 24, 25.) 248.

Ur of the **Chaldeans** (Gen. xi. 28) s. external worship in which are falses. 1365.

Ureters s. interior truths. 10.032. See *Kidneys*.

Uri and **Hur** (Exod. xxxi. 2) s. the doctrines of celestial truth and good. 10.329.

Uriah rep. the spiritual church. 2913.

Urim (Isa. xxiv. 15) s. the light which is from the divine truth proceeding from the Lord. 5922.

Urim and **Thummim**. The goods and truths of the Word in the sense of its letter, are meant by the U. and T. on the ephod of Aaron. U. and T. s. the brilliancy of divine truth der. from divine good in the lasts or ultimates, for U. is shining fire, and T. is brilliancy, in the angelic language, and in the Hebrew language. U.T. 218. The answers from the Lord, given by U. and T. were resplendencies of light according to the state of the thing in question grounded in order, for all the light of heaven varies according to the states of a thing, and the states of the thing vary according to the order of good and truth. 3862. Responses were given by the variegations of light, accompanied by a tacit perception, or by an audible voice. S.S. 44. What was the order of the precious stones in the U: and T. is mentioned and des. in the Word, but to what tribe each stone cor. is not mentioned, for they rep. all

348

principles of light der. from celestial flame, that is, all principles of truth, grounded in good, or all principles of faith grounded in love, and inasmuch as they had this rep., therefore, celestial light itself was miraculously translucent according to the thing in question, and to which an answer was given, being refulgent and resplendent for the affirmative of good and truth, not to mention variegations as to colors according to differences of the state of good and truth, as in heaven, wherein all celestial and spiritual things are expressed by lights and the discriminations thereof, and this in a manner ineffable and altogether incomprehensible by man; for in heavenly light there is life from the Lord, consequently, wisdom and intelligence: hence, in the discriminations of light, there is every thing which appertains to life, that is, every thing which appertains to wisdom and intelligence, and in the discriminations of flame, of radiance, and of splendor, there is every thing which appertains to the life of good, and to the life of truth grounded in good, or to love towards the Lord and faith thence der. This then was the U. and T., which was on the breastplate of the ephod, and on the heart of Aaron; which is evident also from this consideration, that U. and T. s. lights and perfections, and that the breastplate, on which it was placed, was called the breastplate of judgment, because judgment is intelligence and wisdom; the reason why it was on Aaron's heart was, because by heart is s. the divine love; hence, also, those precious stones were set in bottoms of gold; for gold, in the internal sense, is the good which is of love, and precious stone is the truth which is pellucid by virtue of good. 3862.

Urine. They who have applied divine truths to their own loves, and thus have falsified them, in another life, love urinous things, because such things cor. to the delights of such love. H. and H. 488. The defilements of truth cor. to u. 5390. They who cor. to the u. are most timorous when there is the smallest danger, and most courageous when there is no danger; and they are in the opp. to those to whom the ejection of the u. cor. and study by every means to occasion hurt to it. 5387.

Us. (Gen. i. 26.) Because man is governed by angels and spirits, it is at first said, "Let u. make man into our image." But because the Lord alone governs and disposes, in the following verse it is said, in the singular, "God created him in his own image." (See Isa. xliv. 24.) 50. "Let u. go down" (Gen. xi. 7) s. the execution of judgment, which is effected by means of spirits, and, in fact, by evil spirits. 1320.

Usal (Gen. x. 27) s. a ritual of the church called Eber. 1245.

Uses. All goods which exist in act, are called u., and all evils which exist in act, are also called u., but the latter are called evil u., and the former good u. Now because as all goods are from the Lord, and all evils are from hell, it follows that no other than good u. were created by the Lord, and that evil u. originated from hell. By u. which are particularly treated of in this article, are meant all things which appear upon the earth, as animals of every kind, and vegetables of every kind; the latter and the former, which furnish use to man, are from the Lord; and those which bring harm to man, are from hell. In like manner by u. from the Lord are meant all things which perfect the rational of man, and which cause man to receive a spiritual from the Lord; but by evil u. are meant all things which destroy the rational, and cause that man cannot become spiritual. That the things which bring harm to man are called u., is because they are of use to the evil, for doing evil, and because they conduce to absorb malignities, thus also to cures. Use is said in both senses, like as love is, as a good love, and an evil love, and love calls every thing use, which is done by it. D.L.W. 336. They who are in charity, that is, in love towards their neighbor, from which love is delight in pleasures, which is living delight, do not regard the

Uses for Receiving

enjoyment of pleasures, except for the sake of use: for charity is no charity unless there be works of charity, inasmuch as charity consists in exercise, or use; he who loves his neighbor as himself, never perceives the delight of charity, except in the exercise thereof, or in use, wherefore a life of charity is a life of u.; such is the life of the whole heaven, for the kingdom of the Lord, because it is a kingdom of mutual love is a kingdom of u.; therefore every pleasure which is from charity, receives its delight from use, and the more distinguished the use is, so much the greater is the delight; hence it is, that the angels receive happiness from the Lord according to the essence and quality of use. This is the case with every pleasure, that the more distinguished its use is, so much the greater is its delight, as, merely for examples; the delight of conjugial love, inasmuch as thence is the seminary of human society, and from that seminary the Lord's kingdom in the heavens, which is the most important of all u., therefore so great a delight is in it that it is a heavenly happiness; the case is similar with respect to other pleasures, but with a difference according to the excellence of their u., which u. are so manifold that they can scarcely be arranged into genera and species; nevertheless each of them regards the kingdom of the Lord, or the Lord, some more nearly and directly, others more remotely and obliquely. Hence it may appear, that all pleasures are allowed to man, but for the sake of use, and that thus from the use in which they are with a difference, they partake of and derive life from celestial happiness. 997. U. are provided by the Lord from the conjunction of evil and the false, which is with those who are in hell; for the kingdom of the Lord, which is not only over heaven, but also over hell, is a kingdom of u.; and the providence of the Lord is that there should not be any one, or any thing there by which and through which use is not done. D.P. 26. Influx from hell operates those things which are evil use, in places where there are things which cor. D.L.W. 341. In all forms of u. there is a certain image of man. D.L.W. 317. Also a certain image of infinite and eternal. D.L.W. 318.

Uses for Receiving a Spiritual Principle from the Lord are all things which are of religion, and thence of worship, thus which teach the acknowledgment and knowledge of God, and the knowledge and acknowledgment of good and truth, and thus eternal life; which in like manner as other instructions, are imbibed from parents, masters, preachings and books, and especially by studies of life according to them; in the christian world by doctrines and preachings from the Word, and by the Word from the Lord. These u. in their extent may be described by things similar to those by which the u. of the body were; as by nourishment, clothing, habitation, recreation, and delight, protection, and preservation of state, provided the application be made to the soul, nourishment to the goods of love, clothing to the truths of wisdom, habitation to heaven, recreation and delight to happiness of life and heavenly joy, protection to infesting evils, and preservation of state to eternal life. All these are given by the Lord, according to the acknowledgment that all the things, which are of the body, are also from the Lord, and that man is only as a servant and steward appointed over the goods of his lord. D.L.W. 333.

Usury. An usurer (Exod. xxii. 24) den. one who does good for the sake of gain. 9210.

Uterus, is to the child, what the earth is to the vegetable seed. D.L.W. 316.

Uz, Buz, Kemuel, Kesed, Haza, Pildash, Jidlaph, and **Bethuel** (Gen. xxii. 22, 23), s. various religious principles and kinds of worship, thence der.; those out of the church, who are in brotherhood from good, are s. by Milcah and Nahor. 2863, 2864.

Uz, Hul, Gether and **Mash,** (Gen. x. 23), s. so many several kinds of knowledges der. from the knowledges of good, and the things appertaining to knowledges; knowledges der. from the knowledges of good, are natural truths, and the things appertaining to knowledges are actions according thereto. 1234. **Uzzah** rep. that which ministers, thus truth, for this ministers to good. 4926. **Uzzah** and **Jeroboam**, (2 Sam. vi. 6, 7; 1 Kings xiii. 4, 5, 6.) U.'s putting forth to the ark rep. self-ability, or man's proprium, which being profane, the word hand is not read, but still it is understood, the reason whereof is, lest it should be perceived by the angels, that what was so profane had touched what was holy. Concerning J. in like manner, by putting forth the hand is s. self-ability, or proprium, which is profane, in that it was desirous to violate what was holy by putting forth the hand against the man of God, wherefore the hand was dried up; but inasmuch as he was an idolater, and incapable of profanation, his hand was restored to him. 878.

V

Vacuity den. the state of man before regeneration. 7.

Vacuum, a, is nothing, and from nothing, nothing exists. D.L.W. 373.

Vagabond, is to have no knowledge of what is true and good. 382–8.

Vail (Gen. xxxviii. 19) s. obscurity of the truth. 4883. The essential v. of the tabernacle, which was the first before the ark (Exod. xxvi. 3, and xxxvi. 35, 36), rep. the proximate and inmost appearances of rational good and truth, in which the angels of the third heaven are. The second v., or the tegument of the door of the tent (Exod. xxvi. 36, 37; xxxvi. 37, 38), rep. the appearances of good and of truth, which are inferior or exterior to the former, and which are the middle appearances of the rational, wherein the angels of the second heaven are; and the third v., or the tegument of the court gate of the tabernacle (Exod. xxvii. 16, 17; xxxviii. 18, 19), rep. the appearances of good and truth still inferior or exterior, which are the lowest appearances of the rational, in which the angels of the first heaven are. 2576. See *Veil.*

Vail between the Holy Place and **the Most Holy** (Exod. xxvii. 33) s. the medium which united the divine truth and the divine good in the Lord. 9670.

Vail of the Temple being Rent in Twain (Matt. xxvii. 51) s. that the Lord entered into the essential divine, having dispersed all appearances; and that at the same time he opened a passage to the essential divine, by his human made divine. 2576. V. of the t. being rent asunder (Matt. xxvii. 51; Mark xv. 38; Luke xxiii. 45) s. that when the externals which were of the ancient church, and also of the Jewish, are unfolded, and, as it were, unswathed, the christian church is discovered. 4772.

Vailings, or **Coverings.** By v., or c., man can sustain the presence of the Lord, and thereby the Lord is present in every one who worships him. A.R. 54.

Vain, Vanity. To bring the name of God into what is v. den. to profane divine truths by blasphemies, and to apply divine statutes to idolatrous worship, as the Jews did when they adored a calf. V. den. falsity of doctrine, or of religion. 8882, 9248. See *Wind and Vanity.*

Valley. Mountains, in the Word, s. love or charity, because these are the highest, or, what is the same, the inmost things in worship, and hence a v. s. what is beneath mountains, or what is inferior, or, which is the same thing, the more external in worship. But when worship is not as yet become so profane, it is expressed by the name of a v., as in Isa. xli. 18, which speaks of those who are in ignorance, or who are not instructed in the knowledges of faith and charity, but who, nevertheless, are in charity. V. is used in a like sense in Ezek. xxxvii. 1. 1292. V. (Jer. ii. 23) den. unclean worship. 1292.

Valley of Hinnom den. hell. 1292.

Valley of Jehoshaphat s. the falsification of the Word. A.E. 911.

Valley of Shaveh which is the **King's Valley.** (Gen. xiv. 17.) V. of S. s. the goods of the external man; and the k. v. s. the truths of the same. 1723.

Valley of Shittim (Joel iii. 18) s. illustration of the understanding. A.E. 518.

Valley of Siddim, which is the **Sea of Salt** (Gen. xiv. 3), s. the uncleanness of lusts and the falsities thence der. 1666.

Vastation and Consummation

Valley of **Vision** (Isa. xxii. 1, 5) den. fantasies and reasonings whereby worship is falsified, and at length profaned. 1292.

Valley of **Vision, Sepulchre** on **High**, and **Habitation** in a **Rock**. (Isa. xxii. 5.) V. of v. s. the false of doctrine confirmed by the literal sense of the Word; the love of the false, is s. by the s. on h.; and the faith of the false is s. by the h. in a r. A.E. 411.

Vanity s. evil, and the false of evil. A.E. 340. Vanities of strangers s. falses of religion. 587.

Vapor (Jer. x. 13) s. the ultimate truths of the church. A.E. 304.

Variations, by, of form in man are meant his thoughts. A.Cr. 45. V. of state in the forms of the mind. Exp. D.P. 195.

Variety. There is a v. in all things, so that there does not, and cannot, exist to eternity any one thing the same as another. D.P. 56.

Varieties. There is an infinite variety in the heavens, which is der. from v. of good, and the distinction of things therein is from thence. These v. are manifested by truths, which are manifold, by which every one has his own good. In consequence thereof, all the angelic societies in the heavens, and all the angels therein, are distinct from each other. But they all act in unity by love from the Lord, and thereby regard one end. N.J.D. 26.

Variegated den. truth mixed with evils. 3993.

Variegated Heights s. truths falsified. A.E. 195.

Vastation is nothing else but a deviation, declension, and falling away from rep. worship into idolatrous worship, which two kinds of worship are alike as to the external face, but not as to the internal face. A.V.C.R. 54. V. is of two kinds, first of those who know, and do not wish to know, or who see, and do not wish to see, as was the case with the Jews, and as is the case with christians at this day; the second of those who know or see nothing, by reason of their ignorance, as was the case with the gentiles formerly, and as is the case also with the gentiles at this day; when it is the last time of v. with those who know, and do not wish to know, or who see, and do not wish to see, then a church arises anew, not amongst them, but amongst those whom they call gentiles; this was the case with the most ancient church, which existed before the flood, and also with the ancient church which existed after the flood, and so with the Jewish church. The cause that new light then first beams forth is, because then men can no longer profane the things that are revealed, by reason of their not acknowledging and believing them to be true. That the last time of v. must be present before a new church can arise, is frequently declared by the Lord in the prophets, and is there called v., which respects the celestial things of faith, and desolation, which respects the spiritual things of faith; it is also called consummation and excision, as in Isa. vi. 9, 11, 12; xxiv. 1, to the end; xxiii. 8, to the end; xlii. 15–18; Jer. xxv. 1, to the end; Dan. viii. 1, to the end; ix. 24, to the end; Zeph. i. 1, to the end; Deut. xxxii. 1, to the end; Rev. xv. 16, and the following chapters. 410, 411. V. was rep. by the years of the Babylonish captivity: the beginning of a new church was rep. by the deliverance and rebuilding of the temple. 728. A church vastated is such, that it knows what is true, but is not disposed to understand it. 885.

Vastation and **Breaking** s. evils and falses, because evils vastate the natural man, and falses break him to pieces. A.E. 365.

Vastation and **Consummation** differ from each other just as the shade of evening differs from the thick darkness of night; for v. is a recession from the church, as c. is a full separation from it. V. therefore, is like the case of a person descending from heaven, but not yet arrived at hell, and who tarries in the mid-way standing sideways between both; but c. is like the case of the same person, who, after so standing, turns his face and breast to hell, and his back and hinder part of his head to heaven. V. takes place

Vegetable Kingdom

while man views the holy things of the church from falses and falsified truths; but c. takes place when he lives in evils or in adulterated goods. A.V.C.R. 57.

Vegetable Kingdom. Every thing in the v. k., which is beautiful and ornamental, der. its origin through heaven from the Lord; and when the celestial and spiritual things of the Lord flow into nature, such objects are actually exhibited, and thence proceed the vegetative soul, or life; hence come rep. 1632. See *Influx.*

Vegetables. There are in the heavens, as in the earth, v. of all kinds and species, yea, there are in the heavens such v. as are not in the earth, being compounded of genera and species with an infinite variety. But the genera and species of v. differ there, just as the genera and species of animals do. A.E. 1211. The difference between the v. in the spiritual world, and those in the natural, is, that in the spiritual world they are produced in a moment, according to the affections of the angels and spirits there, and this both with respect to seeds and germinations; but in the natural world the origin of v. is implanted in the seeds, from which they are annually produced. Moreover, there are two things proper to nature, namely, time with its succession, and space with its extension; but these are not given in the spiritual world, as properly belonging thereto, but instead thereof there are appearances of the states of their life; whence also it is, that from the earths there, which are from a spiritual origin, v. spring up in a moment, and also instantly vanish, which yet only happens when the angels depart, for till then they continue. A.E. See *Soul of Vegetables.*

Vegetative Soul. How the spiritual flows into vegetables and produces action. A.E. 1204.

Vegetarians den. the pleasures of the natural man. 996.

Vehement Anger (Gen. xlix. 7) s. grievous aversion from good. 6358.

Veil.- The v. with which brides covered the face, den. the appearances of truth. 3207.

Veins cor. to affections. D.L.W. 412.

Velocity, or **Swiftness,** in the Word, when pred. of intelligence, s. the affection of truth. A.E. 281.

Vengeance, day of, s. a state of damnation. 488.

Venison (Gen. xxvi. 2) s. the truth of the natural from whence is the good of life. 3501.

Venom of **Dragons** and the **Gall** of **Asps** (Deut. xxxii.) s. the enormous false which exists from falsified truths of the Word. A.E. 433.

Ventricles, or **greater Cavities** of the **Brain.** They who have reference to that province are situated above the head, a little in front. They discourse pleasantly, and their influx is tolerably gentle; they are distinguished from others by this, that they have continually an eagerness and desire to come into heaven; the reason is, that the better species of lymph which is in the brain, is of such a quality, namely, that it returns into the brain, and hence it has such a tendency thereto; the brain is heaven, and tendency is eagerness and desire. 4049.

Venus. The planet V., in the idea of spirits and angels, appears to the left a little backwards, at some distance from our earth: it is said, in the idea of spirits "because neither the sun of this world nor any planet appears to any spirit, but spirits have only an idea that they exist; it is in consequence of such idea that the sun of this world, is presented behind as somewhat darkish, and the planets not movable, as in the world, but remaining constantly in their several places. In the planet V. there are two kinds of men, of tempers and dispositions opp. to each other, the first, mild and humane, and second, savage and almost brutal; they who are mild and humane appear on the further side of the earth, they who are

Vessels of Cups

savage and almost brutal, appear on the side looking this way. But it is to be observed, that they appear thus according to the states of their life, for in the spiritual world, the state of life determines every appearance of space and of distance. Some of those who appear on the further side of the planet, and who are mild and humane, during their abode in the world, and more so after they become spirits, acknowledge our Lord as their only God: on their earth they have seen him, and they can rep. also how they have seen him. These spirits in the grand man, have relation to the memory of things material, agreeing with the memory of things immaterial, to which the spirits of Mercury have relation; wherefore, the spirits of Mercury have the fullest agreement with these spirits of V. With respect to those spirits who are on the side that looks this way, and who are savage and almost brutal, the cause of their disposition is this, that they are exceedingly delighted with rapine, and more especially with eating of their booty. These are, for the most part, giants, and the men of our earth reach only to their navels; they are also stupid, making no inquiries concerning heaven or eternal life, but are immersed solely in earthly cares and the care of their cattle. E.U. 105–109.

Verity, or Truth. V. s. t., A.E. 365; also the divine t., 541; also the t. of doctrine, and of faith, 642.

Vermilion. (Jer. xxii. 14.) To paint with v. s. to falsify intellectual and spiritual truths. 3391. To be painted or portrayed with v. (Ezek. xxiii. 14) being pred. of the images of the Chaldeans, which are profane doctrinals der. from the love of self and the world, s. that the exteriors appeared as truths, although within they were profane. A.E. 827.

Vertebræ. Societies of spirits cor. to v. have in them little of spiritual life. 5560.

Vessel. The scientific is a v. wherein is truth, for every scientific is a v. of truth, and every truth is a v. of good; a scientific without truth is an empty v., in like manner, truth without good; whereas a scientific wherein is truth, and truth wherein is good, is a full v.; affection which is of love is what conjoins, so that they may be according to order, for love is spiritual conjunction. 3068.

Vessels, in general, in the internal sense, s. those things which are in the place of a receptacle, as scientifics and knowledges are in respect to truths, and as truths themselves are in respect to good, as may appear from several passages in the Word; the v. of the temple and of the altar had no other s., and by reason of this s., that they were also holy, nor had their holiness any other source; hence it was, when Belshazzar with his grandees and wives drank wine out of the v. of gold and silver, which Nebuchadnezzar, his father, had brought from the temple of Jerusalem, and they praised the gods of gold, of silver, of brass, of iron, of wood, and of stone, that then the writing on the wall of his palace appeared (Dan. v. 2, and following verses); the v. of gold and silver den. the knowledges of good and truth, which were profaned, for they are Chaldeans who are in knowledges, but which are profaned by falses that are therein, so that knowledges serve them for worshipping gods of gold and of silver, for Belshazzar is called king of the Chaldeans (verse 30 of the same chapter); that v. s. the externals of things spiritual, is also evident from the following passages in the Word: Isa. lxvi. 20; Jer. xiv. 2, 3; li. 34; Num. xxiv. 6, 7; Matt. xxv. 4. 3079. V. (Rev. xviii. 12) s. scientifics relating to matters of the church; because scientifics are the continents of goodness and truth, as v. are the continents of oil and wine. A.R. 775.

Vessels of Cups and **Vessels of Psalteries.** (Isa. xxii. 24.) V. of c. s. celestial things, and v. of p., holy spiritual things. 3704.

Vessels of Silver

Vessels of **Silver** and **Vessels** of **Gold**. V. of s. are specifically scientifics, for these are the recipients of truths; and v. of g. are specifically truths, because these are the recipients of good. 3164.

Vestment s. truth, and, in relation to the Lord, divine truth. A.E. 685.

Vesture s. truth investing good, and when said of the Word, s. the Word in its literal sense, for that is like a garment, wherewith its spiritual and celestial sense is clothed. A.R. 825.

Vesture of the **Lord** s. the spiritual sense of the Word. L. 16.

Vetches s. various species of good. 3332.

Vex, or Gall Another, s. resistance by falses. 6420.

Vexations. That aliments or meats in the stomach are by various methods vexed, to the intent that the interior principles thereof may be extracted, and turned to use, namely, may pass off into the chyle, and next into the blood, is a known thing, and also that the same operation afterwards takes place in the intestines; such v. are rep. by the first v. of spirits, all of which are wrought according to their life in the world, that evils may be separated, and goods collected together which may turn to use; whereof it may be said of souls or spirits, some time after their decease or being set loose from the body, that they come, as it were, first into the region of the stomach and are there vexed and purified; in this case, they, with whom evils have obtained the pre-dominion, after that they have been vexed to no purpose, are conveyed through the stomach into the intestines, and even to the last, namely, to the colon and rectum, and are thence voided forth into the draught, that is, into hell; but they with whom goods have had the pre-dominion, after some v. and purifications, become chyle and pass off into the blood, some by a longer way, some by a shorter, and some are vexed severely, some gently, and some scarce at all. 5174. See *Juices of Meats.*

Vials. (Rev. xiv.) By the seven v. the same is s. as by the seven plagues, for they are containing vessels, and by the thing containing in the Word, the same is s. as by the things contained, thus the same is s. by cup as by wine, and the same by platter as by meat. The reason why v. were given them, is because the subject treated of is concerning the influx of truth and good into the church, in order that its evils and falses may be discovered, and naked goods and truths cannot enter by influx, for such are not received, but only truths clothed, such as there are in the literal sense of the Word; and moreover the Lord always operates from inmost principles through ultimates, or in fulness. This is the reason why there were given to the angels v., by which are s. containing truths and goods, such as those of the literal sense of the Word are, by means of which falses and evils are discovered. That by v., platters, cups, and chalices, and by bottles are s. the things which are contained in them, may appear from many passages. V. and also bottle, or pitcher, have the same s. as cup. (Matt. ix. 17; Luke v. 37, 38; Jer. xiii. 12; xlviii. 12; Hab. ii. 15.) By v. and censers containing incense, the same is s. as by incense; and in general by all kinds of vessels, the same as by the things contained in them. A.R. 672.

Vials Full of the **Wrath** of God who **Liveth** for **Ages** of **Ages** (Rev. xv. 7) s. evils and falses which will appear and be discovered by means of pure and genuine truths and goods of the Word. It is said that the "v. were f. of the w. of G.," because they were full of plagues, by which are s. evils and falses of the church; but yet they were not full of them, but full of pure and genuine truths and goods from the Word, by means of which, the evils and falses of the church were to be discovered. Still, however, they were not vials, neither were there in them truths or goods, but by them was s. influx out of heaven into the church. Their being said to be full of the wrath of the living God, is conformable to the style of the Word in its literal sense. A.R. 673.

Viaticum (Gen. xlii. 25 and Ps. lxxviii. 25) s. support from truth and good. 5490. (The common version is provision and meat.)

Vicissitudes of **State**, with the regenerate, are as summer and winter with respect to the will; and day and night, with the understanding. 935.

Victory. Why it seems as if v. declared on the side of prudence, and not on the side of justice. D.P. 252. To fight against evils and falses and be reformed. A.R. 88.

View, to, den. to think. 2684.

Villages s. the external things of faith and thus of the church. The external things of the church are rituals; the internal things are doctrinals when these are not of science but of life. External things were rep. by v., because they were out of cities, but internal things by cities themselves. 3270. V. (Exod. viii. 13) s. the exteriors of the natural mind. 7407. V. (Isa. xlii. 11) s. knowledges and natural scientifics. A.E. 405.

Vindication, punishment or vengeance. Exp. 1711.

Vine s. good and truth spiritual. A.E. 403.

Vine, or **Vineyard**, s. the church where the Word is by which the Lord is known, consequently, the christian church. A.R. 650.

Vine-dressers s. those who are in truths and teach them. A.E. 376.

Vine out of **Egypt** (Ps. lxxx. 8–13), in the supreme sense, den. the Lord; the glorification of his human is des. by it and its shoots; in the internal sense, the v., in this passage, is the spiritual church, and the man of that church, such as he is when made new, or regenerated of the Lord as to the intellectual and will principle. 5113.

Vine of **Sibmah** s. men of the external church who exp. the Word to favor worldly love. A.E. 911.

Vine of **Sodom**, etc. (Deut. xxxii. 32.) Speaking of the Jewish church, their v. being of the v. of S. and of the fields of Gomorrah, den. that the intellectual part was obsessed by falses der. from infernal love; their grapes being grapes of gall, clusters of bitternesses to them, den. that the case was similar with the will-principle therein; for grape, inasmuch as in a good sense it s. charity, is pred. of the will-principle, but of the will-principle in the intellectual part, in like manner, in the opp. sense, for all truth is of the understanding, and all good is of the will. 5117.

Vine and **Choice Vine**. (Gen. xlix. 11.) V. den. the external spiritual church, and a c. v., the internal church. 6375.

Vine and **Noble Vine**. (Gen. xlix. 11.) V. den. the intellectual principle, which is of the spiritual church, and n. v. den. the intellectual principle which is of the celestial church. 5113.

Vine, **Noble**, and the **Degenerate Shoots** of a **Strange Vine**. (Jer. ii. 18, 21.) N. v. s. the man of the spiritual church, who is called a vine from the intellectual principle, and the d. s. of a s. v. den. the man of the perverted church. 5113.

Vine and **Fig Tree**. V. s. the good of the intellectual principle, and f. t., the good of the natural principle, or, what is the same thing, v. the good of the interior man, and f. t., the good of the exterior; therefore, very frequently in the Word, where mention is made of v., the f. t. is also mentioned. 5113.

Vine, the, **shall give her Fruit**, and the **Ground her Increase** (Zech. viii. 12), s. that the spiritual affection of truth produces the good of charity, and the natural affection of good and truth produces the works of charity. A.E. 695.

Vines and **Laurels** cor. to the affection of truth, and its uses. H. and H. 520.

Vinegar s. truth mixed with falses. A.E. 386. Giving the Lord v. mixed with gall (Matt. xxvii. 34) s. the quality of divine truth from the Word such as was with the Jewish nation, namely, that it was commixed with the false of evil, and thereby altogether falsified and adulterated, wherefore he would not drink it. A.E. 519.

Vinegar Mingled with Hyssop

Vinegar Mingled with Hyssop which the Lord received (John xix. 28, 29) s. the quality of the false among the well-disposed Gentiles, which was the false arising from ignorance of the truth, in which there was somewhat good and useful, as this false is accepted by the Lord. A.E. 519.

Vineyard. The ancient church, as being spiritual, is des. by a v., by reason of the fruits, which are grapes, which rep. and s. works of charity, as appear manifest from several passages of the Word; as a v. s. the spiritual church, so also does a vine, for a vine appertains to a v., and in this they are as a church, and a man of the church, therefore, they are the same thing; inasmuch as vine s. the spiritual church, and the primary thing of the spiritual church is charity, in which the Lord is present, and by which he joins himself to man, and by which he alone operates all that is good, therefore, the Lord compares himself to a vine, and des. the man of the church, or the spiritual church, as in John xv. 1, 2, 3, 4, 5, 12. 1069.

Vineyard and **Branch** (Ps. lxxx. 16) s. the spiritual church rep. by the sons of Israel. A.E. 724.

Violation of the **Word** is made by those in the Christian church who adulterate its goods and truths, and those do this who separate truth from good, and good from truth; as they do who assume and confirm appearances of truth and fallacies for genuine truths; as also those who know the truths of doctrine from the Word, and live badly, besides others like them. These v. of the W. and of the church cor. to the prohibited degrees enumerated in Lev. xviii. C.S.L. 519.

Violence s. the outrage which is done to charity, also the destruction of charity and faith. 6353. V. (Jer. xv. 21) s. falses which assault the good of charity. A.E. 328.

Violence of the **Sons** of **Judah** and the **Effusion** of **Innocent Blood.** (Joel iii. 19.) V. of the s. of J. s. the adulteration of the Word as to good, and the e. of i. b., the adulteration of the Word as to truth. A.E. 730.

Violence and **Deceit.** (Isa. liii. 9.) V. relates to the will; and d. in the mouth, to the understanding. 623.

Violent Man and **Evil Man** (Ps. cxl. 2) s. those who pervert the truths of the Word. A.E. 734.

Viper s. mortal hatreds. 2125. V. s. those who are most deceitful. 5608.

Vipers and **Basilisks.** Those who are in the hells where they are who act craftily against innocence, appear as v.; and those who act contrary to the good of love appear as b. A.E. 410. (See Isa. xi. 8.)

Virgin s. the Lord's kingdom and also the church, and hence every one who is a kingdom of the Lord, or who is a church, and this from conjugial love which is in chase v.; in a proper sense, they are v. who are in love to the Lord, that is, who are celestial, thus who are in the affection of good; they are also called v. who are in charity towards their neighbor, that is, who are spiritual, thus who are in the affection of truth. 3081. A betrothed v. has reference to the truth of the church about to be conjoined with good. 3164.

Virgin and **Daughter** of **Zion** s. the church in regard to the affection of good and truth. A.R. 612.

Virgin and **Girl.** In the Word, mention is made of a v., and also of a g., but of this latter, in the original tongue, rarely by the name by which she here is named. (Exod. ii. 8.) A v. s. the good which is of the celestial church, but a g., the truth of good, which is of the spiritual church. 6742.

Virgin and **Woman**, in the Word, s. the affection of good. H. and H. 368.

Virgins (Rev. xiv. 4) s. those who love truths, because they are truths, thus from a spiritual affection. For v. s. the church as a spouse, who desires to be conjoined to the Lord, and to become a wife, and the church which desires this union, loves truths, because they are truths, for by truths, when a life is led according to them, conjunction is effected. Hence it is, that Israel, Zion, and Jerusalem, in the Word, are called v. and daughters, for by Israel, Zion, and Jerusalem is s. the church. That all they who are such in the Lord's church, whether they be v. or young men, wives or husbands, boys or old men, girls or old women, are meant by v., may appear from the Word, where v. are mentioned, as the v. Israel. (Jer. xviii. 13; xxxi. 4, 21; Amos v. 2; Joel i. 8.) The v. daughter of Judah. (Lam. i. 4; ii. 13.) The v. of Jerusalem. (Lam. ii. 10.) The v. daughter of my people. (Jer. xiv. 17; Matt. xxv. 1, and subseq.; Jer. xxxi. 4, 13; Ps. lxviii. 25, 26; xlv. 10–16; Amos viii. 11, 13; Isa. xxiii. 4; Lam. i. 4, 15, 18; Zech. ix. 17; viii. 5; Lam. li. 10, 13, 21, besides other passages, as Jer. li. 20–23; Lam. v. 10, 11, 12; Ezek. ix. 4, 6; Ps. lxxxviii. 62, 63, 64; Deut. xxxii. 25.) Hence it is said (Rev. xiv. 4), "These are they who are not defiled with women, for they are v.," for to be "defiled with women" s. the same as to commit adultery and fornication, namely, to adulterate and falsify the divine good and truth of the Word. A.R. 620. The prudent v. (Matt. xxv. 9, 10) s. those in the Word with whom faith is conjoined to charity; and by the foolish are s. those in the church with whom faith is separated from charity. A.E. 840.

Virtue den. strength and power, and in relation to Jehovah or the Lord, den. all power. 8266.

Viscera and **Members**, or **Organs** of **Motion** and **Sensation**. All and each of the v. and m. or o. of m. and s., cor. to societies, that is, by them, celestial and spiritual things flow in with man, and this into adequate and suitable forms, and present thus the effects which are apparent to man; these effects however do not appear to man otherwise than as natural, thus altogether under another form and under another appearance than what they are in their origin, insomuch that they cannot be known to be from heaven. 3630.

Viscous. The conscientious have reference to the v., exp. 5724.

Vision is the inmost revelation, which is that of perception, for v. are according to the state of man; v. before those whose interiors are closed, is altogether different from what is manifested to those whose interiors are open; as for example, when the Lord appeared to the whole congregation on Mount Sinai, that appearance was a v., which varied according to the states of the beholders, appearing differently to the people from what it appeared to Aaron, and differently to Aaron from what it did to Moses; so again, v. was altogether different as exhibited to MJoses and to the prophets: there are several kinds of v., and they are the more perfect, in proportion as they are more interior; with the Lord it was the most perfect of all; because he then had a perception of all things in the world of spirits, and in the heavens, and had immediate communication with Jehovah; this communication is rep., and s. in the internal sense, by "the v. in which Jehovah appeared to Abram." (Gen. xv. 1.) 1786. V. (Zech. xiii. 4) s. falses. 3301.

Vision of the **Night** s. obscure revelation. 6000.

Visions, are of two kinds, divine and diabolical; divine v. take place by rep. in heaven; and diabolical v. take place by things magical in hell: there are also fantastic v., which are the sportings of an abstract mind. Divine v., which, as was said, take place by rep. in heaven, are such as the prophets had, who, when they were in them, were not in the body, but in the spirit; for v. cannot appear to any man in the wakefulness of his body; wherefore when they appeared to the prophets, it is said also that they were then in the spirit. D.P. 134. See *Prophets, Dreams.*

Visionaries are persons of weak mind, and the things they see are often illusions conjured up from outward objects. 1967.

Visitation. The last time of the church in general, and of each individual in particular, is in the Word called v., and precedes judgment, and thus v. is

Vital Heat

nothing else than an exploration as to the quality, namely, the quality of the church in general, or of man in particular. 2242. V. is spoken of in the Word throughout and thereby is s. either vastation in reference to the church and to individuals, or deliverance, thus exploration as to quality. 2242. V. does not come until evil is consummated, that is, until there is no longer any good of charity, and truth of faith, concerning which consummation much is said in the prophets. 1857.

Vital Heat. The heat of the blood, of man and animals, is the heat of love, to which natural heat cor. T.C.R. 35.

Vivify. To v. or make alive souls which should not live (Ezek. xiii. 19) s. to persuade them that life eternal is from falses. A.E. 186. See *Alive.*

Voice s. what is announced from the Word. V. is often pred. of, and also adjoined to such things as have no relation to a v., as in Exod. iv.; Nahum iii. 2; Ps. lxiii. 3, 4. That v. s. annunciation, and in a good sense annunciation from the Word, which v. is called the v. of Jehovah, is manifest from Ps. xxix. 3, 4, 5, 7, 8, 9, and lxviii. 34; in which passage v. den. divine truth, thus the Word and annunciation from it. 6971. V. s. the quality of the interiors. 10.457. V. (Rev. xix.) s. joy of the worship, confession and celebration of the Lord. A.R. 811. A great v. heard in heaven (Rev. xii. 10), s. the joy of the angels of heaven from the light and wisdom then appertaining to them. A.E. 744. A great v. (Rev. xvi. 1) s. the divine command. A.R. 676. A great v. out of the temple of heaven (Rev. xvi. 17) s. a manifestation from the Lord out of the inmost of heaven. A.R. 709. A great v. (Rev. xxi. 3) s. speech proceeding from love. A.R. 882. One v. (Rev. ix. 13) s. a divine command. A.R. 443.

Voice, a, Crying, and the **Voice** of a **Cry,** are common forms of expression in the Word, and are applied to every case where there is any noise or disturbance, or any thing that infests and is troublesome, yea, and to cases where there is matter of rejoicing, as Exod. xxxii. 17, 18; Zeph. i. 9, 10; Isa. lxv. 19; Jer. xlviii. 3; and in Gen. iv. 10, it is used to express what brings accusation. 375.

Voice, a, Singing in the **Windows** (Zeph. ii. 14) s. reasonings from fantasies. 655.

Voice which came out of the **Throne** (Rev. xix. 5) s. influx from the Lord into heaven; the reason why it was from the Lord, is because he who sat on the throne was the Lord, therefore by a voice proceeding from thence, is meant influx; for the Lord, inasmuch as he is above the heavens and appears to the angels as a sun, does not speak to the angels from thence, but flows in, or influences, and that which flows in the same is received in heaven and promulgated, wherefore that voice, although it came from the throne, was nevertheless heard by John from heaven; consequently from the angels there, and whatsoever the angels speak from heaven, is from the Lord. A.R. 809. To hear the Lord's voice, s. to believe in the Word, for the divine truth of the Word is the voice of Jehovah, and to open the door is to live according to it, because the door is not opened, and the Lord received by barely hearing his voice, but by living in conformity thereto. (See John xiv. 21, 24; Rev. iii. 20.) A.R. 218.

Voice of **Bloods** (Gen. iv. 10) s. violence offered to charity, for there are several passages in the Word, in which the expression voice is taken for whatever accuses, and blood is taken for all sins, particularly for hatred; for whosoever bears hatred towards his brother, kills him in his heart, as the Lord teaches, Matt. v. 21, 22, etc., etc. 375.

Voice of the **Bridegroom** and of the **Bride** (Rev. xviii. 23, and elsewhere) s. spiritual and celestial joy. A.E. 1189.

Voice of a **Great Multitude, Voice** of **Many Waters,** and **Voice** of **Mighty Thunderings.** (Rev. xix.) By the v. of a g. m. is s. the joy of the angels of the lowest heaven; by the v. of m. w. is s. the joy of the angels of the middle heaven; and by the v. of m. t. is s. the joy of the angels of the supreme heaven. A.R. 811.

Voice as of Many Waters, and a **Voice of Great Thunder** (Rev. xiv. 2) s. the Lord speaking through the universal heaven from the divine truths of his divine wisdom, and from the divine good of his divine love. A.R. 615.

Voice of Wings (Rev. ix. 9) s. reasonings, because to fly s. to perceive and instruct. A.R. 437.

Voice and Hand. (Gen. xxvii. 22.) V. is pred. of truth, and h. is pred. of good. 3563.

Voices, great (Rev. xi. 15), s. celebrations of the Lord by the angels. A.R. 520.

Voices of the Seven Thunders (Rev. x.) are three times mentioned, because they contain the very essentials of the new church. A.R. 473.

Voices, Lightnings, and **Thunders** (Rev. xvi. 18), s. ratiocinations, falsifications of truth, and arguings grounded in falsities of evil, in the church among those who are in faith alone, and who turn away from reflecting upon the evils in themselves, because they have no inclination to desist from them even if they come to a knowledge of them. A.R. 710.

Void den. where there is nothing of good. 17.

Volition and **Understanding.** All v. is from love, and all u. is from wisdom. D.P. 89.

Volume of a **Book written within** and **without** (Ezek. ii. 10, and iii. 1–3) s. the then state of the church, consequently, the quality of their life who were of the church. A.E. 222.

Volume, or **Roll** (Zech. v. 2) s. the curse going forth upon the faces of the whole earth. A.E. 675.

Voluntary and **Involuntary,** called will and understanding. The celestial angels cor. to what is i. and spontaneous. 9670.

Vomit, to, is pred. of falsification of divine truth. A.E. 960. A.R. 204.

Vow. (Gen. xxviii. 20.) Vowing a v. den., in the internal sense, to will that the Lord may provide, and, in the supreme sense, in which the Lord is treated of, den. a state of providence. The reason why vowing a v., in the internal sense, den. to will that the Lord may provide, is grounded in this: that in v. there is a desire and affection, that what is willed may come to pass, thus, that the Lord may provide; somewhat also of stipulation is implied, and, at the same time, somewhat of debt on the part of man, which he engages to discharge, in case he comes to possess the object of his wish. 3732.

Vowel, a, inasmuch as it is used for sound, s. somewhat of affection and love. A.R. 29. In all things appertaining to the class of spirituals, the three first v. are commonly prevalent, whereas in things appertaining to the class of celestials, the two last v. prevail. 793.

W

Wafers (Exod. xvi. 31) s. spiritual good. 8522. Also ultimate celestial good in the external man. 10.079. See *Basket.*

Wail and **Howl**, to (Micah i. 8), s. the grief of the angels of heaven, and of the men of the church, in whom the church is, and thus with whom the Lord is. A.E. 695. See *To Weep.*

Wailing. (Rev. xxi. 4.) W. has various s., in all cases having relation to the subject treated of, in the present case to the fear of evils from hell, because the fear of damnation is mentioned just before, and the fear of falses from hell, and of temptations proceeding from them, immediately after. A.R. 884.

Waistcoat den., generally, truth of the natural, by which the spiritual is invested. 3301.

Wakefulness den. a clear state. 5210. See *Sleep.*

Walk, to. To w. with God is to teach, and live according to the doctrine of faith; but to w. with Jehovah, is to live the life of love. To w. is a customary form of speaking, s. to live, as to w. in the law, to w. in the statutes, to w. in the truth. To w. has respect properly to a way, which is of truth, consequently, which is of faith, or of the doctrine of faith. 519.

Walk, to, upon a **Wall** (Gen. xlix. 22) s. to fight against the false. 6419.

Walk, to, upon the **Wings** of the **Wind** (Ps. civ. 2, 4) s. the spiritual sense of the Word contained in the literal sense. A.E. 283.

Walk, to, **Stand**, and **Sit**. (Ps. i. 1.) Here to w., to s., and to s. are mentioned, because the one follows another, for to w. is expressive of the life of the thought from intention; to s. is expressive of the life of the intention from the will; and to s., of the life of the will, thus of the esse of the life; counsel, also, of which walking is pred., has respect to the thought; way, of which standing is pred., regards the intention; and to s. in a seat has respect to the will, which is the esse of man's life. A.E. 687.

Walk, to, **before Jehovah** is to live according to his precepts. A.E. 687.

Walking and **Seeking**. In the prophetical writings the things relating to faith are expressed by w. and s.; and the things relating to love are expressed by loving and serving. 519.

Wall s. truth in ultimates. A.R. 132. W. (Rev. xxi.) s. the divine truth proceeding from the Lord, and hence the truth of faith from the good of charity. 6419. When by the holy city Jerusalem is meant the Lord's new church as to doctrine, by its w. nothing else is meant but the Word in its literal sense, from which doctrine is der., for that sense defends the spiritual sense, which lies concealed within it, just as a w. defends a city and its inhabitants, and the literal sense is the basis, continent, and firmament of its spiritual sense, and that sense is a guard to prevent the interior divine truths of its spiritual sense from being injured; also church doctrine is to be drawn from the literal sense of the Word, and confirmed by it; it is called a w. great and high, because it means the Word as to its divine good and divine truth, great being pred. of good, and high of truth. By w. is s. that which defends, and where the church is treated of, it s. the Word in its literal sense, in the following passages also, Isa. lxii. 6; lx. 14, 18; Zech. ii. 5;

War in Heaven

Ezek. xxvii. 11; Jer. v. 1, 10; Lam. ii. 8, 9; Joel ii. 9; Ps. lv. 11, 12; Isa. xxii. 5; lxi. 5; Jer. i. 15; Ezek. xxvii. 11; Lam. ii. 7. That the Word, in its literal sense, is s. by w., appears clearly from Rev. xxi. where the w., its gates, foundations, and dimensions are much treated of, the reason is, because the doctrine of the new church, which is s. by the city, is der. solely from the literal sense of the Word. A.R. 898. See *Foundations of a Wall.*

Wall daubed Unfitly (Ezek. xiii. 14) s. what is false appearing as true. 739.

Wall, Rampart, Gates, and **Bars** (Lam. ii. 8, 9) s. doctrinals. 402.

Walls and **Palaces**. (Ps. cxxii. 6, 9.) W. s. the exteriors of man, and p. his interiors. A.E. 365.

Wallet, mouth of (Gen. xlii. 27), den. the threshold of the exterior natural principle. The w. was the front part of the sack, therefore by it nothing else is s. than the front part of the receptacle, thus the exterior natural principle, for this is also in front. 5497.

Wander, to, in a **Field** (Gen. xxxvii. 15) s. to fall from the common truth of the church; for field den. the church as to good, and a man of the field den. the good of life der. from doctrinals; it is said a man, because by man [vir] is s. truth, which is of the church. They are said to fall from the common truth of the church, who acknowledge the Lord, but not his human divine; and also they who acknowledge faith as essential, but not charity; each is a common truth of the church, from which when the man of the church recedes, he falls from common truth, and he who falls from this, falls also afterwards from the specific truths, which are treated of in what follows in this chapter; as where any one commences from a false principle, and deduces consequent principles from it, these consequent principles hence become false, because the beginning rules in those which follow, and also by these consequent principles, the first false principle is corroborated. 4717.

Wander, to (Amos iv. 8), s. to inquire. A.E. 532. To w. blind in the streets (Lam. iv. 14) s. not to know what is good and true. 382.

Wanderer den. not to know what is true and good. 382.

Wandering Souls, or **Spirits**. S. and s. to whom there has not yet been allotted a fixed situation in the grand man, are conveyed to divers places, now in one direction, now in another; now they are seen on one side, now on another side; now above, and now another while beneath; these are called w. s., or s., and are compared to fluids in the human body, which, rising from the stomach, sometimes proceed into the head, sometimes to other parts, being translated hither and thither; so it is with these spirits, before they come to the situation designated, and which is conformable to their common or general state; it is their states which are thus changed and are erratic. 1381.

Wandering Stars, encompassing a spirit in the world of spirits, s. falsities, but have a different s. when the stars are not w. 940. See *Stars.*

Want of spiritual nourishment, den. want of the things of science, intelligence, and wisdom. 5576.

War, in the Word, s. spiritual w., which is of the false against truth, and of truth against the false; but it is they who are in falses who combat against truths, but not so they who are in truths against falses, for they who are in falses always assault, but they who are in truths only defend; and as to the Lord, he indeed never opposes, but only defends truths. A.E. 734. See *Fight and War.*

War in Heaven. (Rev. xii. 7.) By w. is s. spiritual w., which is of falsity against truth and truth against falsity, for no other w. can take place in heaven, neither can it take place in heaven when once formed of angels, but it was waged in the former heaven which passed away, as appears (Rev. xxi. 1), for that heaven passed away in consequence of the last judgment being

363

executed on the dragon and his angels, which is also s. by the dragon's being cast down, and his place being no more found in heaven. A.R. 548.

Wars. By w. in the Word, are s. spiritual w., which consist in impugning truth, and are conducted by reasonings from falses. Inasmuch as by w. in the Word are s. spiritual w., therefore the ministry of the Levites was called military service. A.R. 500. All w., how political soever they are, are rep. of states of the church in heaven; and they are cor.; such were all the w. des. in the Word, and such also are all w. at this day. D.P. 251. It is not from the divine providence that w. exist, because they are united with murders, plunders, violence, cruelties, and other enormous evils, which are diametrically against christian charity; but still, they cannot but be permitted. D.P. 251.

Wars of the **Children** of **Israel** with various nations, rep. the Lord's combats with the hells. L. 14. All the w. of the sons of Israel, carried on with the Philistines, rep. the combats of the spiritual man with the natural man, and from thence also, the combats of truth conjoined to good, with truth separated from good. A.E. 817.

Wars of **Jehovah**. By the w. of J., mentioned in the ancient Word, as in ours, the Lord's combats with the hells, are meant and des., and his victories over them, when he should come into the world. The same combats are also meant and des. in many passages in the historical parts of our Word, as in the w. of Joshua with the inhabitants of the land of Canaan, and in the w. with the judges and kings of Israel. S.S. 103.

Wars of **Jehovah** and **Enunciations.** The historical and prophetical parts of the ancient Word, quoted by Moses, were so called. 2897. The w. of J. and the prophetic books which are mentioned by Moses (Num. xxi. 14, 15, 27, 30), are now possessed by the inhabitants of Great Tartary. A.R. 11.

Warmth is from love, and spiritually is love. Such as the love is, such is the w. 2146.

Was, it, involves a new state. 4979.

Wash, to, **us from our Sins** (Rev. i. 5) s. to purify from evils, thus, to reform and regenerate, for regeneration is spiritual washing. A.R. 19.

Wash, to, the **Hands** and the **Feet,** and to **Wash** the **Flesh.** To w. the hands and feet s. to purify the natural man, and to w. the flesh, s. to purify the spiritual man. (See Exod. xxx. 18–21; Lev. xvi. 4, 24.) A.E. 475.

Wash, to, in **Wine** and in the **Blood** of **Grapes,** s. the Lords, rational and natural, which he should make divine. 2576. See *Judah.*

Washing of the **Hands** was an ancient testification of innocence, and s. purification from evils and falses. (See Ps. lxxiii. 13; Matt. xxvii. 24.) A.E. 475.

Washing. (John xiii. 8, 9.) By w. is understood spiritual w., which is purification from evils; by w. the head and hands is understood to purify the internal man, and by w. the feet is understood to purify the external; that when the internal man is purified, the external is to be purified, is understood by this, "He who is washed, needeth only that his feet be washed;" that all purification from evils is from the Lord, is understood by this, "If I wash thee not, thou hast no part with me." W. with the Jews rep. purification from evils, and this is s. by w. in the Word. And by w. the feet is s. the purification of the natural, or external man. D.P. 151. See *Baptism.*

Wash-pot (Ps. lx. 7–9) den. good defiled with falses. 2468.

Waste Places, old, s. the celestial things of faith. 613.

Wasted, to be (Gen. xxi. 15), s. to be desolated. 2680.

Wasters, or **Layers Waste.** (Jer. xii. 12, 13.) W. s. evils and falses, whereby good and truth perish. A.E. 374. W. in the wilderness s. evils in consequence of not having truths. A.E. 730.

Wastes and **Desolations.** (Isa. lxi. 4.) W. in this and other passages, s. evils, and d. 153.

Watch, fourth, s. the first state of the church when it is break of day, for then good begins to act by truth. A.E. 510.

Watching den. a course of life according to the precepts of faith. 4638.

Watchful, to be (Rev. iii. 2) s. to be in truths and in a life conformable to them. By watching in the Word nothing else is s., for he who learns truths, and lives according to them, is like one who is waked out of sleep and becomes w., and he who is not in truths, but only in worship, is like one who sleeps and dreams. Natural life, considered in itself, or without spiritual life, is nothing else but sleep, but natural life, in which there is spiritual life, is watchfulness, and this is no otherwise acquired than by truths, which exist in their own light and in their own day, when man lives according to them. A.R. 158. A.E. 187.

Watchman (Isa. xxi. 11), in an internal sense, s. one who observes the states of the church, and its changes, thus every prophet. 10.144.

Water. (Matt. x. 42.) W. s. truth in affection, and cold w. s. truth in obedience; for obedience alone is a natural affection and not spiritual, wherefore it is respectively cold. A.E. 695. W. s. the spiritual things of faith. 680. To give w. (Gen. xliii. 24) s. the common influx of truth. Such influx is the illumination which gives the faculty of apperceiving and understanding truth; this illumination is from the light of heaven, which is from the Lord, which light is no other than the divine truth. 5668. Foul and filthy w. cor. to that state in which a person is when he acts on account of his own glory and renown. Spirit. Diary. See *Blood and Water, To Boil, To Draw Water, Drawers of Water, Sea.*

Water of **Life** s. divine truths from the Lord through the Word. A.R. 932.

Water and **Spirit**. (John iii. 5.) To be born of w., s. to be born of truths; and of the s., s. by a life according to them. A.R. 50. A.E. 475.

Water-Pot s. scientifics. 3068. See *Cask.*

Water Pots of **Stone placed according** to the **manner** of the **purifying** of the **Jews** (John ii. 1–10) s. all those things in the Word, and thence in the Jewish church, and its worship, which were rep. and s. of things divine in the Lord, and from the Lord, which contained things internal. A.E. 376.

Water-Through s. the doctrine of charity. 6777.

Waters s. truths in the natural man; and in an opp. sense falses. A.R. 50. W. s. particularly the spiritual things of man, or the intellectual things of faith, and also what is opp. thereto. 739. The drying up of the w. from off the earth (Gen. viii. 7) s. the apparent dissipation of falsities. 864. W. (Ps. civ. 3) s. divine truths. A.E. 594. W. going softly (Isa. viii. 6, 7) s. things spiritual, and w. strong and many, s. falses. 790. W. (Ezek. xlvii. 9), where it is concerning the w. from the New Jerusalem, s. things spiritual from a celestial origin. 994. By many w. (Rev. xvii. 1) are s. truths of the Word adulterated. A.R. 719. W. or rivers, s. things spiritual, rational, or scientific, which appertain to truth. 2703. See *Voice of Many Waters.*

Waters above the **Firmament** (Gen. i. 6) s. the knowledges which are in the internal man; and the w. beneath the f. s. the scientifics of the external man. 24.

Waters issuing out of the **Sanctuary** (Ezek. xlvii. 12) s. the life and mercy of the Lord, who is the sanctuary. 57.

Waters of the **lower Fish-pond** (Ps. xxii. 10) s. the traditions whereby they made infractions into the truths which are in the Word. 4926.

Waters, Rivers, and **Depths** (Ps. lxxviii. 15, 16) s. truths from the Lord. 2702.

Wave den. vivification, or life flowing in. 10.082.

Wave-Offering (Exod. xxix. 27) s. vivification by acknowledgment of the Lord. 10.091.

Waves Roaring, Sea and, relates to heresy and controversies in the church. 2120.

Wax and Myrrh

Wax and Myrrh (Gen. xliii. 11) s. truths of good of the interior natural principle, appears from the s. of w., in this case aromatic w., as den. the truth of good, and from the s. of myrrh, as den. also truth from good: the reason why they appertain to the interior natural principle is, because these aromatics are purer than gum or honey, and therefore are named in the second place, for such things are enumerated in the Word according to order. By w. in this passage, is not meant common w., but aromatic w., which is as storax, and which w. is s. by the expression which is used in the original tongue, and by the same expression is also s. an aromatic. 5621.

Wax Warm with their **Gods**, to (Isa. lvii. 5, 6), is pred. of evil; and the smooth things of the valley of the false. 3527.

Way. (Malachi iii. 1.) To sweep the w. den. to make themselves ready and to prepare to receive truth; it is here treated concerning the coming of the Lord, for whom they were to prepare themselves, to receive the truth of faith and by that the good of charity, and thus eternal salvation. 3142. To set a w. (Gen. xxx. 36) s. to be separated. 4010. See *Highway.*

Way, the Truth, and the **Life**. (John xiv. 6.) W. is doctrine, t. is every thing pertaining to doctrine, l. is the essential good which is the life of t. 2531.

Way of the **Tree** of **Life** (Gen. iii. 24) s. admission to the Lord, which men have by the Word. A.R. 239.

Way of **Women** (Gen. xxxi. 35) s. uncleanness. 4161.

Ways of **Jehovah**. To go in the ways of J. (Deut. viii. 6) is to live according to the truths of doctrine. A.E. 696.

Ways. There are eight w. which lead from the places of instruction in the spiritual world to heaven, by which novitiate angels are introduced. There are two w. from each place of instruction, one going up towards the east, the other to the west: they who come into the Lord's heavenly kingdom, are introduced by the eastern w.; but they who come to the spiritual kingdom are introduced by the western w. The four w. which lead to the Lord's heavenly kingdom, appear adorned with olive trees, and fruit trees of various kinds; but those which lead to the Lord's spiritual kingdom, appear adorned with vines and laurels; this is from cor., because vines and laurels cor. to the affection of truth and to its uses, whilst olives and fruits cor. to the affection of good and its uses. H. and H. 520. In the spiritual world there appear w., laid out like the w. in the natural world, some lead to heaven and some to hell; but the w. which lead to hell do not appear to those who go to heaven, nor do the w. which lead to heaven appear to those who go to hell; there are innumerable such w., for there are some which lead to every society of heaven, and to every society of hell; every spirit enters the w. which leads to the society of his own love, nor does he see the w. which tend elsewhere, hence it is, that every spirit as he turns himself to his ruling love, also proceeds. D.L.W. 145.

Ways and **Paths**. (Isa. ii. 3.) W. s. truths, and p. precepts of life. A.E. 735.

Ways, Gates, and **Doors**. In the spiritual world there are actually w. which lead to heaven, and there are here and there g., and they who are led to heaven, by the Lord, take the ways which lead thither, and enter in at the g.; for all things which are seen in the heavens are cor., thus w. also and g., for w. cor. to truths, and thence s. them, and g. cor. to admission, and thence s. it. Inasmuch as the Lord alone leadeth man to heaven, and opens the d., therefore he calls himself "the w.," and also the "d.;" the w. in John, "I am the w., the truth, and the life," xiv. 6; the door in the same Evangelist, "I am the d. of the sheep, by me if any one enter in he shall be saved," x. 7, 9. Since there are both w. and d. in the spiritual world, and angelic spirits actually go those w., and enter into heaven by d., therefore inner d., outer d., and g. are frequently mentioned in the Word, and by which is s. entrance. A.R. 176. See *Gates.*

Weak. Being w. of eyes den. as to the understanding. 3820.
Wealth and **Treasures** s. the knowledges of truth and good from the Word, and in the opp. sense false scientifics from self der. intelligence. A.E. 654. W. s. scientifics, as may be manifest from several passages in the Word; for spiritual w., thus w., understood in a spiritual sense, is nothing else; it consists of scientifics, so far as they are known, which in the Lord's kingdom, consequently in the church, are instead of wealth. 4508.
Wealth of **Sodom** and **Gomorrah** (Gen. xiv. 11). By the w. of S. and G., in an internal sense, nothing else is meant but evil and the false. 1694.
Wealth, Labor, Precious Things, and all the **Treasures** of the **Kings** of **Judah** (Jer. xx. 4, 5), s. the knowledges of faith. 1327.
Wean, to (Gen. xxi. 8), s. to separate, as infants are from the mother's paps. 2647.
Weapons. (Ezek. xxxix. 9.) Shield s. falsity destroying good; buckler falsity destroying truth; bow with arrows, doctrine with its falsities; hand-staff and spear s. self-derived power and confidence, such as belongs to those who place the all of the church and thence of salvation in external worship. A.E. 357.
Weariness den. a state of temptation combat. 3318. A state in which the deficiency of truth is cause of anxiety. 8568. Evil spirits suffer by w. when not permitted to do evil. 7392.
Weary den. a state of temptation combat. 3318.
Weave, to, s. to teach. A.E. 654. See *Flax.*
Weaver (Exod. xxviii. 32) s. the celestial principle, or that which relates to the will, because the will flows into the understanding and fashions it, insomuch that the things which are in the understanding are woven out of the will. 9915. See *Embroiderer.*
Webs (Isa. lix. 6) s. feigned truths which are not for a garment. 2576. See *Spider's Web.*
Webs and **Garments, Iniquity,** and **Violence.** (Isa. lix. 6.) W. and g. s. things belonging to the understanding, or thought; and iniquity and violence, things belonging to the will, or works. 623.
Wedding Garment (Matt. xxii. 11–13) s. divine truth from the Word. A.R. 166. W. g. which the man had not (Matt. xxii. 11, etc.) s. faith towards the Lord as the Son of God, the God of heaven and earth, and one with the Father. U.T. 380. The w. g. (Matt. xxii. 11–13) s. the intelligence of the spiritual man, which is from the knowledges of truth and good; but to be not clothed therewith s. the hypocrite, who by a moral life feigns the spiritual life, when yet he is merely natural; to bind the hands and the feet s. deprivation of knowledges from the Word, by which the spiritual man is assumed; and to cast into outer darkness s. to cast him among those who are in falses from evil. A.E. 195.
Weed, to, and **Prune** s. to prepare for reception. A.E. 644.
Weeds, Bars, Waves, and **Billows.** (Jonah ii. 3, 5.) W. s. falses; b., evils; and w. and b., falses and evils. A.E. 538.
Week s. state, and the seventh w., an holy state. A.R. 480. A w., which is a period of seven days, s. an entire period of every state and time as of reformation, of regeneration, or of temptation, both with regard to man individually, and to the church in general; thus a period whether of a thousand years, or a hundred, or of ten, or of so many days, hours, minutes, etc., is called a w., as may appear from many passages. 2044. The ancients understood by a w., in a proper sense, every period, distinguished into seven, whether it was of days, or of years, or of ages; thus whether it was great or small. 3845.
Weeks, feast of, s. the implantation of truth in good. A.E. 911.
Weep, to, when it is pred. of the Lord, s. to be merciful; that weeping is an

Weep

effect of grief and of love, is a known thing, consequently, it is an effect of mercy, for mercy is love grieving; the divine love is on this account called mercy, because the human race of themselves are in hell, and when man apperceives this in himself, he implores mercy. Inasmuch as weeping is also mercy, in the internal sense, therefore, occasionally in the Word, weeping is pred. of Jehovah, or the Lord. 5480.

Weep, to, and Wail. To w. has respect to mourning of the soul, and to w. has respect to mourning of the heart. A.R. 788.

Weeping is s. both of sorrow and love. 6566. W. s. the last farewell, hence it was usual to weep for the dead when they were buried, although it was known that the carcase was only rejected by burial, and that they, who had been in the carcase, as to their interiors, were living. 4565.

Weeping with a Loud Voice s. the ultimate of grief. 2689.

Weeping and Mourning (Rev. xviii. 15) s. grief of the soul and heart, and has, therefore, reference to the understanding and the will. A.E. 1164.

Weigh, to, the Mountains in a Balance, and **the Hills in Scales** (Isa. xl. 12), s. that from the Lord are the celestial things of love and charity, and that he alone disposes their states. 3104.

Weights and **Measures** are frequently mentioned in the Word, but, in the internal sense, they do not s. w. and m., but w. s. the states of a things as to good, and m., the states of a thing as to truth. 5658.

Well (Num. xxi. 17, 18) s. the Word of the ancient church. 3424. W., or Pit (Luke xiv. 5), s. the false and the evil of the false. A.E. 537. See *Jacob's Well.*

Well of Living Waters s. the Word, in which are truths divine, thus the Word as to the literal sense in which is the internal; that the Word is called a fountain, and, indeed, a fountain of living waters, is well known; the ground and reason why the Word is also called a w. is because the sense of the letter is respectively such, and because the Word, in respect to the spiritual, is not a fountain, but a w. 3424.

Well and Fountain. The Word is sometimes called a w., and sometimes a f.; when it is called a w., the Word is s. as to the literal sense, and when a f., the Word is s. as to the internal sense. 6774.

Wells. (Gen. xxi.) By w. nothing else is s. than doctrinals, about which they disputed, and about which they did not dispute, otherwise the circumstances of digging w., and disputing about them would have been too trifling to be mentioned in the divine Word. 2702. To stop up w. (Gen. xxvi. 15) den. not to be willing to know truths, and to deny, and thereby obliterate them. 3412.

West s. those who are in obscurity as to good; and, in an opp. sense, those who are in evil. 3708. The w. s. the affection of truth. A.E. 439.

Whale (Jer. li. 34) s. those who possess the universals of the knowledges of faith, as scientifics, and apply them to evil purposes. 42. Whales, or great fishes, are sometimes mentioned by the prophets, and are used to s. the universals of scientifics. 42.

Whale and Dragon. The same word, in the original language, is used for both, and both have a similar spiritual s. (See Jer. li. 34.) A.E. 714.

Wheat den. the things which are of love and charity. 3941. The truth of good. A.E. 304. W. (Matt. xiii. 27-30, 37-42) s. those that are inwardly good. L.J. 70. See *Rye.*

Wheat Harvest den. an advancing state of love and charity, because a field s. the church; thus things appertaining to the church, and seeds which are sown in a field, s. the things which are of good and truth; and what springs from those seeds, as wheat, barley, and other produce, den. the things which are of love and charity, and also of faith; states of the church, as to these things, are, therefore, compared to seed time and harvest, and are also called seed time and harvest, as in Gen. viii. 22. 3941.

Wheat of Minnith, and **Pannag Honey, Oil**, and **Balsam** (Ezek. xxvii. 17), den. the good things of love and charity, and the happinesses thereof. 3941.

Wheat and Barley. (Joel i. 11.) W. s. celestial love, and b., spiritual love. 3941.

Wheat, Barley, Beans, Lentiles, Millet, and **Vetches** (Ezek. iv. 9, 12), s. various kinds of good, and its derivative truth. Bread, or a cake, made thereof with human dung, s. the profanation of them all. 3941.

Wheat and Tares. (Matt. xiii. 24–40.) By w., in this passage, are meant the truths and goods of the new church, and by t., the falses and evils of the former church. U.T. 784.

Wheels (Exod. xiv. 25) s. the power of proceeding; also divine intelligence. 8215. W. (Isa. v. 28) s. the doctrine of natural truth. 2686. W. (Dan. vii. 9) are the things which are of wisdom and intelligence, consequently, divine truth. 8216.

Wheels of Chariots s. the faculty of reasoning. A.E. 654. The power of combating which is of the intellectual principle. 8215.

Whelp of a Lion (Gen. xlix. 9) den. innocence with might. 6367. W. of a l. (Deut. xxxii. 22) s. the first principle of truth, which is affirmation and acknowledgment. 3923. See *Bear bereaved of her Whelps.*

Whirlwinds, in the spiritual world, exist from the influx of the divine into the lower parts of that world where they are who are in evils and falses: that influx, as it descends from the heavens towards the earths which are beneath, becomes more dense and appears as clouds, and with the evil dense and opaque according to the quality and quantity of their evils; which appearances entirely arise from their spheres of life. A.E. 419.

Whisperers into the left ear, of an evil character. Des. 4657.

White is pred. of truths, by reason that it der. its origin from the light of the sun. A.R. 167.

White Stone (Rev. ii. 17) s. truths suffragant and united to good. W. s. has this s., because in judiciary proceedings it was the custom to collect votes or suffrages by stones, and by w. s. those which were on the affirmative side; the reason why confirming truths are s., is because white is pred. of truths, hence it is, that by w. s. are s. truths suffragant with good; the reason why they are also united to good, is, because good invites them, and unites them to itself; for all good loves truth, and joins to itself such as accords with it, especially the good of celestial love; this so unites truth to itself, that they make one entirely; hence it is that the celestial see truths from good alone. A.R. 121.

Who is, and **Who was**, den. the Infinite and Eternal. A.E. 972.

Whole, the, exists from the parts, and parts subsist from the w. D.L.W. 367.

Whoredom. By committing w. is s. to adulterate and falsify the Word; the reason why this is s. by committing w., is, because in every particular of the Word there is a marriage of goodness and truth, and this marriage is broken when good is separated and taken away from truth; it is for this reason, that to commit w. s. to adulterate the good and falsify the truths of the Word; and because this is spiritual w., therefore, also they who from their own reason have falsified the Word, after death, when they come into the spiritual world, become addicted to w. A.R. 134. See *Adultery and Whoredom.*

Whore of Babylon. By the great w. is s. profanation of the holy things of the Word and church, and adulteration of good and truth. A.R. 719.

Whorish Gain and the **Whoredom of Tyre** (Isa. xxiii. 17) s. the vaunting and boasting of the false principle. 2466.

Widow. By w. is s. one who is without protection, because without an husband; for, in a spiritual sense, by w. is s. one who is in good, and not in truth, for by man is s. truth, and by his wife good, consequently, by w. is s.

Widow of Zarepta

good without truth, and good without truth is without protection, for truth protects good; this is the s. of w. when it occurs in the Word, as in Isa. ix. 13, 14, 16; x. 1, 2; Jer. xxii. 3; xlix. 10, 11; Lam. v. 2, 3; Ezek. xxii. 6, 7; Mal. iii. 5; Ps. lxviii. 5; cxlvi. 7, 8, 9; Exod. xxii. 20–23; Deut. x. 18; xxvii. 19; Matt. xxiii. 14; Luke iv. 26; xx. 47. A.R. 764. There is frequent mention made of w. in the Word, and he who is unacquainted with the internal sense, cannot believe otherwise than that by a w. is s. a w.; but by a w., in the internal sense, is there s. the truth of the church without good, that is, they who are in truth without good, and yet desire to be in good, consequently, who love to be led by good; husband is the good which should lead; such, in the ancient church, were understood in the good sense by w., whether they were women or men (vir). A w. of a priest rep. the affection of truth der. from good, for a priest, in the rep. sense, den. the good of the church; on this account also it was allowed the w. of a priest, who had no offspring, to eat of the oblations or holy things. (Lev. xxii. 12, 13.) 4844.

Widow of **Zarepta** rep. those without the church who desire truth. 4844.

Wicked, or **Unrighteous**, den. not in truth of faith. 6765. Malice. 7590. Malignity. 9249.

Wicked, the, continually lead themselves into evils, but the Lord continually withdraws them from evils. D.P. 295–6.

Wickedness s. evil, and iniquity s. falses. A.E. 741.

Wife s. the church, and, in an universal sense, the kingdom of the Lord in the heavens and the earths. That the same is understood by mother, follows of consequence. 289. W. s. the celestial church. 3246. W. (Gen. ii. 23) s. proprium. 156. W. (Gen. xx. 7) s. spiritual truth. 2532. By w. (Rev. xix.) is s. the Lord's new church, which is the New Jerusalem, as appears evidently from the following chapter, xxi., which has these words, "I saw the holy city New Jerusalem coming down from God out of heaven, prepared as a bride adorned for her husband," verse 2. And in the same chapter, "And there came an angel unto me saying, come, I will show thee the bride, the Lamb's w., and he showed me the great city the holy Jerusalem, descending out of heaven from God," verse 9, 10. A.R. 813.

Wife, a **Married from Female Captives** (Deut. xxi. 14) s. alien truth not from a genuine stock, which yet may be adjoined in some manner with the good of the church appertaining to man. 5886.

Wife of **Moses**, the (Exod. iv.), in the internal and also in the supreme sense, rep. good conjoined to truth. 7022.

Wife of **Youth** (Mal. ii. 15) s. the ancient and most ancient church, of whose seed or faith the prophet is here speaking. 255.

Wild Ass s. rational truth; in the Word frequent mention is made of horses, of horsemen, of mules, and of asses, and no one has heretofore known that they s. things intellectual, rational, and scientific, but that such is their s. may be abundantly proved; the case is the same with respect to the w. a., for the w. a. is a mule of the wilderness, or an ass of the forest, and s. the rational principle of man, not the rational principle in its complex, but only rational truth. The rational principle consists of good and truth, that is, of those things which are of charity, and of those things which are of faith; rational truth is that which is s. by a w. a. 1949.

Wild Beasts den. affections and lusts. 45–6.

Wild Gourds (2 Kings iv. 39) s. evils der. from the false. 10.105.

Wilderness. By w. in the Word is s., 1st, the church devastated, or in which all the truths of the Word are falsified, such as it was among the Jews at the time of the Lord's advent. 2d, the church in which there are no truths, because they are not possessed of the Word, such as it was among the well-disposed Gentiles in the Lord's time. And 3d, a state of temptation, in which man is as it were without truths, because surrounded by evil spirits who induce temptations, and then as it were deprive him of truths. A.R. 546. W. s. that which as yet has little of life in it, agreeably to what is said in an internal sense in Luke i. 80. 1927. W. s. where there is no good because there is no truth. A.E. 386. W. (Jer. xxiii. 10) s. the Word when it is adulterated. A.E. 730.

Wilderness and **Land** of **Drought**. (Hosea xiii. 5.) W. is a state without good, and l. of d. is a state without truths. A.E. 780.

Wilderness and **Secret Chambers**. (Matt. xxiv. 26.) Truth vastated is what is s. by w., and good vastated by s. or inner c.; the ground and reason why truth vastated is s. by w. is because when the church is vastated, that is, when there is in it no longer any divine truth, because there is no longer any good, or love to the Lord, and neighborly love, then it is called a w., or said to be in a w., for by w. is meant whatsoever is not cultivated or inhabited, and also whatsoever has little life in it, as is the case with truth in the church on such occasions; hence it is evident that w. here den. the church in which is no truth; but s. or inner c., in the internal sense, s. the church as to good, and also simply good; the church which is principled in good is called the house of God, the s. or inner c. whereof are goods and those things which are in the house. 3900.

Wilderness of **Sin** s. the good which is from truth in a prior state of temptation. 8398.

Will. Whatsoever proceeds from the w. is called good, for the essential of the w. is love and thence affection, and all that is done from love and its affection is named good. 4337.

Will and **Understanding**. From the Lord with man there are created and formed two receptacles and habitations of himself, which are called the w. and the u., the w. for his divine love and the u. for his divine wisdom. D.L.W. 358. In these two faculties the Lord is with every man, whether he be good or evil; hence it is that every man, both good and evil, lives to eternity. D.L.W. 240. Every thing in man, both in general and particular has relation to the u. and w., and to the conjunction of both, in order that man may be man. L.J. 39. W. and u., which are the receptacles of love and wisdom, are the brains in the whole and in every part of them, and thence in the body in the whole and in every part of it. D.L.W. 362. There is a cor. of the w. and u. with the heart and the lungs, and thence a cor. of all things of the mind with all things of the body. D.L.W. 374. The w. comprehends in it things intellectual, but the u. does not comprehend in it the things of the w. 712. The w. leads the u., and causes it to be one with itself in action. Dec. 44. Whereas the w. of man is mere lust, to prevent the immersion of the intellectual, or the truth of faith, in his lust, the Lord miraculously provided and distinguished the intellectual from the voluntary of man by a certain medium, which is conscience, into which charity is instilled by the Lord; without this miraculous providence no person could have been saved. 863.

Will, Good Pleasure, Leave, and **Permission** of the **Lord**. The things which proceed from the Lord's w. and g. p., are from the laws of order as to good, also many things which are from leave, and some likewise which are from permission; but when man separates himself from good, he then casts himself into the laws of order which are of truth separate from good, and which are such, that they condemn him, for all truth condemns man, and casts him down into hell, but the Lord, from good, that is, from mercy, saves him, and raises him up to heaven; hence it is evident, that it is man himself who condemns himself. 2447.

Willows of the **Brook** (Lev. xxiii. 40) s. the lowest goods and truths of the natural. A.E. 458.

Wind

Wind. All spirits, both good and bad, are compared and likened to w.; in the original tongue both spirits and w. are expressed by the same word; in temptations they are evil spirits who cause an inundation, entering by influx in great multitudes with their phantasies, and exciting the like phantasies in man; when these spirits or these phantasies are dispersed, it is said in the Word to be done by a w., and indeed by an east w. 842. Inasmuch as a nearer and stronger divine influx, through the heavens, disperses truths amongst the wicked, therefore w. s. the dispersion of truth with them and their consequent conjunction with hell, and destruction. A.R. 343. W. (Jer. xxii. 22) s. the emptiness and vacuity of doctrine. A.E. 811. W., in the spiritual world, arise from the determination of the divine influx, and exist in the inferior parts of the earth there; but in the heavens rarely any w. are apperceived, except such as are soft and gentle. A.E. 419.

Wind and **East Wind.** (Hosea xii. 1.) W. s. fantasies, and e. w. lusts. 5215.

Wind and **Storm** s. reasoning. A.R. 334.

Wind and **Vanity.** (Isa. xli. 29.) W. s. the falses of evil, and v. evils of the false. A.E. 211.

Wind and **Whirlwind.** (Isa. xli. 16.) W. is there pred. of falses, and w. of the evils of the false. A.E. 405. A.C. 842. See *East Wind, Four Winds.*

Window s. truth in the light. A.R. 132. In the Word, the intellectual of man, whether it be reason or ratiocination, that is, his internal sight, is called a w. All the w. of the temple at Jerusalem, rep. the same thing; the highest rep. intellectuals, the middle rationals, and the lowest scientifics and sensuals, for there were three stories (1 Kings vi. 4, 6, 8.) In like manner, the w. of the New Jerusalem, des. in Ezek. xl. 16, 22, 25, 33, 36. Inasmuch as w. s. intellectuals and rationals which appertain to truth, they also s. reasonings, which are grounded in the false, as in Jer. xxii. 13, 14; Zeph. ii. 14. 655.

Wine, in the holy supper, s. the divine truth of the Lord's divine wisdom. U.T. 711. Inasmuch as w. s. faith towards the Lord, therefore faith, even in the Jewish church, was rep. in the sacrifices by a libation of w., concerning which see Num. xv. 2–15; xxviii. 11–15, 18, to the end; xxix. 7, to the end; Lev. xxiii. 12, 13; Exod. xxix. 40; Hosea ix. 2, 3, 4. 1071. W. (Gen. xlix. 11) s. the good of neighborly love and the good of faith, and in the supreme sense, divine truth from the divine good of the Lord; for from this, by influx, man, who receives, has the good of love and faith. Whereas several expressions in the Word have also a contrary sense, so also has w., in which sense it s. the false principle der. from evil. 6377. New w. (Gen. xxvii. 28) s. natural truth. 3580. See *Oil and Wine, Ruler of the Feast.*

Wine of **Fornication** (Rev. xiv. 8, 10; xvi. 19; xvii. 2; xviii. 3; xix. 15) s. the adulterated truths of faith, whereof drunkenness is pred. 1072.

Wine of the **Fury** and **Wrath** of **God.** (Rev. xix.) By the w. of the f. and w. of G., are s. the goods and truths of the church, which are from the Word, profaned and adulterated, and therefore the evils and falses of the church. A.R. 829.

Wine of the **Wrath** of **God mixed with pure Wine** (Rev. xiv. 10) s. the truth of the Word falsified. (See Ps. lxxv. 8.) A.R. 635.

Wine of the **Wrath** of **her Whoredom.** (Rev. xiv. 8.) By w. is s. truth originating in good, and in an opp. sense, the false principle originating in evil; whoredom s. the falsification of truth, and the wrath of whoredom s. adulteration and profanation. A.R. 632.

Wine and the **Blood** of **Grapes.** (Gen. xlix. 11.) W. den. what is spiritual from a celestial origin; the b. of g. den. what is celestial in respect to spiritual churches; thus g. s. essential charity, and w. essential faith. 1071.

Wine and **New Wine.** (Hosea iv. 11.) W. s. what is false, and n. w., evil thence der. 2466.

Wisdom

Wine, New, and Old Wine. (Luke xv. 29.) New w. is the divine truth of the New Testament, consequently, of the new church, and o. w. is the divine truth of the Old Testament, consequently, of the old church. A.R. 316.

Wine and Milk (Isa. lv. 1) s. spiritual and celestial drink. 680.

Wine and Strong Drink. (Isa. xxix. 9.) W. s. specifically the truth of the spiritual and hence of the rational man, and s. d. the truth of the natural man thence der. A.E. 376.

Wine and Vine. (Isa. xxiv. 7.) New w. s. spiritual good, and v. spiritual truth. A.E. 323.

Wine, Oil, Flour, and Wheat (Rev. xviii. 13) s. celestial principles of worship. A.R. 777.

Wine-press (Isa. lxiii. 2) s. combat from divine truths against falses. A.E. 359. W.-p. (Lam. i. 15) s. the production of false from evil, and thence the adulteration of the Word, and aversion of the church. A.E. 922.

Wine-press of the Wrath of God. (Rev. xiv.) W.-p. s. exploration and examination, because in presses wine is expressed from clusters of grapes, and oil from olives, and from the wine and oil which are expressed, is perceived the quality of the grapes and olives; and whereas by vine is s. the christian church, and by its clusters are s. works, therefore the exploring and examining of these in the men of the christian church, is s. by casting them into the press; but inasmuch as they have separated faith from charity and made the former competent to salvation, without the works of the law, and since from faith, separated from charity, none but evil works proceed, therefore it is called the great w.-p. of the w. of G. A.R. 651. See *To Tread the Wine-press.*

Winged Thing s. sensual truth; sensual truths, such as relate to seeing and hearing, are said to be w., because they are extreme truths, and such also is the s. of wing, in reference to other things. 777. See *Fowl.*

Wings. By w. are s. powers, because by them birds lift themselves up, and w. in birds are in the place of arms in men, and by arms are s. powers; that by w. are s. preservation or defences is plain from the following places, namely, Ps. xci. 4; i. 7, 8; xxvi. 8; lvii. 2; lxiii. 8; Ezek. xvi. 8; Malachi iii. 20; Deut. xxxii. 10, 11, 12; Matt. xxiii. 37; Luke 34. A.R. 245. W. spiritual truths. D.P. 20. W. when pred. of the Lord, s. the divine spiritual. A.E. 283. To cover under w. (Ps. xci. 4) s. to guard by the divine truth, which is the divine spiritual. A.E. 283. W., in an opp. sense, have respect to falses and ratiocinations therefrom. A.E. 283. See *Eagle, Healing in his Wings.*

Wings of a Fowl. (Dan. 7.) By the four w., as of a f. on the back of the third beast, are s. confirmations of what is false. A.R. 574.

Wings of the Wind. (Ps. xviii. 11.) It is said, that God rode upon a cherub and did fly, which s. his omnipresence in the spiritual world, and that he was carried upon the w. of the w., which s. his omnipresence in the natural world. A.E. 283. W. of the w. (Ps. civ. 3) s. divine truths which influence. A.R. 343.

Winter, the same as night, s. the end of the church. D.L.W. 73. See *Night.*

Wipe, to, away all Tears from **their Eyes** (Rev. vii. 17) s. that they shall no longer be in combats against their evils and falses, and therefore not in sorrows, but in goods and truths, and thence in celestial joys from the Lord. A.R. 385. "God will w. away all tears from their eyes" (Rev. xxi. 4) s. that the Lord will take away from them all grief, or uneasiness of mind, for tears proceed from uneasiness of mind. A.R. 884. See *Tear.*

Wisdom (Rev. v.) pred. of the Lord, s. his divine providence. A.E. 338. There are three degrees of w., the natural, spiritual, and celestial: in the natural degree of w. is man while he lives in the world: this degree with him can then be perfected to its highest, but still cannot enter the spiritual degree, because this degree is not continued to the natural degree by continuity,

373

Wisdom derived

but is joined to it by cor.: in the spiritual degree of w. man is after death, and this degree is also such, that it can be perfected to its highest, but still cannot enter the celestial degree of w., because neither is this degree continued to the spiritual by continuity, but is joined to it by cor. Hence it may appear, that w. can be elevated in a triplicate ratio, and that in either degree it can be perfected in a simple ratio to its highest. He who comprehends the elevations and perfections of these degrees, can in some measure perceive that, which is said of angelic w., that it is ineffable; it is also ineffable, that a thousand ideas of the thought of the angels from their w. cannot fix above one idea of the thought of men from their w. D.P. 34. W. is der. to man from no other source than from good by means of truths from the Lord: the reason why w. is der. to man through truths is, because the Lord joins or connects himself to man and man to himself, by them, and the Lord is wisdom itself; wherefore w. perishes in man when he ceases to do truths, that is to live according to them, for then he ceases to love w., and consequently ceases to love the Lord. By w. is meant w. in things spiritual, from which, as from its source, is der. w. in other things, which is called intelligence, and through the latter science, which is der. from the affection of knowing truths. A.R. 189. W. with men is two-fold, rational and moral, and that their rational w. is of the understanding alone, and that their moral w. is of the understanding and at the same time of the life, may be concluded and seen from intuition and examination alone. But in order that it may be known what is meant by the rational w. of men, and what by their moral w., we shall enumerate some of the specific distinctions. The things which are of their rational w., are distinguished by various names; in general they are called science, intelligence, and w.; but specifically they are called rationality, judgment, erudition, and sagacity; but because every one has sciences peculiar to his office, therefore they are multifarious, for there are those peculiar to the clergy, peculiar to persons of the magistracy, peculiar to their various offices, peculiar to judges, peculiar to physicians and chemists, peculiar to soldiers and sailors, peculiar to artificers and laborers, peculiar to husbandmen, and so on. To rational w. also pertain all the sciences into which youths are initiated in the schools, and by which they are afterwards initiated into intelligence, which are called likewise by various names, as philosophy, physics, geometry, mechanics, chemistry, astronomy, jurisprudence, politics, ethics, history, and several others, by which, as by doors, entrance is made into things rational, from which there becomes rational w. But of moral w. with the men are all the moral virtues, which have respect to, and enter the life, and also all spiritual virtues which flow forth from love to God and from love towards the neighbor, and flow together into those loves. The virtues, which pertain to the moral w. of the men, are also of various names, and are called temperance, sobriety, probity, benevolence, friendship, modesty, sincerity, courteousness, civility, also carefulness, industry, quickness of wit, alacrity, munificence, liberality, generosity, activity, intrepidity, prudence, and many others. Spiritual virtues with men are the love of religion, charity, truth, conscience, innocence, and many more. The latter virtues and the former in general may be referred to love and zeal for religion, for the public good, for one's country, for his fellow citizens, for his parents, for his conjugial partner, and for his children. In all these, justice and judgment rule, justice is of moral w. and judgment is of rational w. C.S.L. 163, 164.

Wisdom derived from the World. To him who wishes to be wise from the world, things sensual and scientific are the garden; self-love and the love of the world are his Eden; his east is the west, or himself; his river Euphrates is all his scientific which is cursed; the other river where is Assyria is infatuated reasoning and the falsities thence; the third river where is Cush, is the principles thence of evil and the false, which are the knowledges of his faith; the fourth is the w. thence, which in the Word is called magic; wherefore Egypt, which s. science, after it has become magical, s. such a person, and that from the cause, of which see every where in the Word, that he wishes to be wise from himself; concerning such persons see thus in Ezek. xxix. 3, 9. 130.

Wisdom and **Intelligence.** W. is distinguished from i. in this: that the former is from the light of heaven, and the latter is from the light of the world, illustrated from the light of heaven; hence it is, that w. is pred. of spiritual good and truths, and i. of natural good and truths. A.E. 408.

Wisdom, Intelligence, and **Science.** In the Word throughout a distinction is made between w., i., and s., and by w. is meant what is from good, by i. what is from truth, and by s. each in man's natural principle. (See Exod. xxxi. 2, 3; xxxv. 30, 31; and Deut. i. 13.) 5827.

Wise. Those are w. from the Lord who cast out of themselves evil. D.P. 34. Man will be judged, not by the wisdom of his speech, but by his life. D.L.W. 418.

Wise Men, or the **Wise.** W. m. (Matt. xxiii. 34) s. the good of doctrine. A.E. 655. The w. s. they who teach the Word. 1179. They that be w. s. such as are in truths, and they that turn many to righteousness, such as are in goods. (Dan. xii. 3.) A.R. 51.

Witch, Witchcraft (Exod. xxii. 18; 2 Sam. xxviii.) s. the falses of the evil of self-love, conjoined with those things which appertain to the church. 9188.

With. Difference between *in* and w., in the spiritual sense, exp. 5041.

Withdrawal from evil, is effected by the Lord by a thousand secret means. D.P. 296.

Within and on the **Back.** (Rev. v. 1.) By the book written w. and on the b., is meant the Word in every particular and in every general respect; by within in every particular respect, and by on the b. in every general respect; by w. and on the b. is also meant the interior sense of the Word, which is its spiritual sense, and its exterior sense, which is its natural sense. A.R. 256.

Withering. W. and drying up (Ezek. xvii. 10), ascribed to the east wind, s. where there is no good and where there is no truth. A.E. 419.

Witness. By bearing false w., in the natural sense, is meant, to bear false w. before a judge, or before others not in a court of justice, against any one who is rashly accused of any evil, and to asseverate this by the name of God or any thing holy, or by himself, and such things of himself as are of the reputation of any one's name. By this commandment, in a wider natural sense, are meant lies of every kind, and politic hypocrisies, which look to a bad end; and also to traduce and defame the neighbor, so that his honor, name, and fame, on which the character of the whole man depends, are injured. In the widest natural sense, are meant unfaithfulness, stratagems, and evil purposes against any one, originating either in enmity, hatred, revenge, envy, rivalry, etc., for these evils conceal within them the testifying of what is false. In the spiritual sense, by bearing false w. is meant, to persuade that the false of faith is the true of faith, and that the evil of life is the good of life, and the reverse, but to make this false w., it must be supposed to be done intentionally, and not in ignorance, thus to do them after one knows what is truth and good. In the celestial sense, by bearing false w. is meant, to blaspheme the Lord and the Word, and thus to reject the truth itself from the church, for the Lord is truth itself, and also the Word. On the other hand, by bearing w., in this sense, is meant to speak the truth, and by testimony is meant truth itself: on this ground it is that the decalogue is called the testimony. (Exod. xxv. 16, 21, 22; xxx. 7, 8; xxxii. 15, 16; xl. 20; Lev. xvi. 13.) And because the Lord is the truth itself, he says concerning himself, that he testifies. That the Lord is truth itself, may

Witness and Testimony

be seen (John xiv. 6; Rev. iii.), and that he testifies, and bears w. of himself, may be seen (John iii.; viii. 13–19; xv. 26; xviii. 37, 38.) U.T. 321, 322, 323. To w., or bear w., s. to acknowledge in heart and to confess. A.E. 10.

Witness and **Testimony.** W. s. confirmation of good by truth, and of truth from good, and t. s. good from which truth is der., and truth which is from good. 4197.

Witnesses. The command in the rep. church, that every truth shall stand on the mouth of two or three w. (Num. xxxv. 30), is founded in the law divine, that one truth does not confirm good, but several truths, for one truth without connection with others is not confirming, but when there are several in connection, for from one may be seen another; one does not produce any form, thus not any quality, but several connected in a series, for as one tone does not produce any tune, still less any harmony, so neither does one truth; these are the considerations on which the above law is founded, although in its external form it appears founded in the state of civil society, but the one is not contrary to the other, as in the case of the precepts of the decalogue. 4197.

Witnesses, the two (Rev. xi. 3), s. the two essentials of the new church, namely, first, that the Lord is God of heaven and earth, and that his humanity is divine; and the other essential is, that conjunction with the Lord is through a life conformable to the precepts of the decalogue. A.R. 490, 515. The two w. (Rev. xi. 3–11) are good and truth, that is, good in which is truth, and truth which is from good, each confirmed in heart. 4197.

Witnesses of Jesus. (Rev. xvii.) By w. of J. are s., abstractedly, truths and goods from the Lord through the Word in the church, in the present case, those truths and goods profaned, because it says, the blood of the martyrs, or w. of J., and is spoken in relation to Babylon, by which is also s. profanation of the good and truth of the Word and church. A.R. 730.

Wizards den. those who conjoin the falses which spring from the evils of self-love to the truths of faith. 9188.

Woe s. lamentation over evils and falses which devastate the church. A.E. 564.

Wo to Them that are with Child, and **to Them that give Suck in those Days** (Matt. xiv. 19), s. those who have imbibed the good of love to the Lord and the good of innocence; w. is a form of expression s. the danger of eternal damnation; to be with child (to bear in the womb) is to conceive the good of heavenly love; to give suck den. also a state of innocence; those days s. the states in which the church then is. 3755.

Wo, Wo, Wo (Rev. viii. 13), s. extreme lamentation over the damned state of those in the church, who by doctrine and life have confirmed in themselves faith separated from charity. It s. extreme lamentation; for triplication constitutes the superlative, because three s. all and full. A.R. 416.

Wolf s. the infernal false principle. A.E. 783. W. s. the dominion of evil. A.E. 780. W. (Gen. xlix. 27) s. the avidity of snatching away and delivering the good, for a w. den. one who seizes and disperses; and whereas beasts, in the Word, s. lusts, a w. s. the avidity of seizing, as is also evident from the passages in the Word where a w. is named. (See Matt. vii. 15; John x. 12; Luke x. 3; Jer. v. 6; Ezek. xxii. 27; Zeph. iii. 3.) Hence, it is evident that by w. are s. they who seize, but, in the present case, who snatch away from hell those who have been seized. With the s. of w., the case is the same as with the s. of lion, which also is a rapacious animal, concerning which it is likewise said, that he seizes what is seizable, gathereth spoil, and preyeth upon prey, as is here said of a w., and yet a lion, in the good sense, s. truth in ability from good; the case is the same respecting other rapacious beasts, as leopards, eagles, etc. 6441. A w. (Isa. xi. 6; lxv. 25) s. those who are against innocence. 3994.

Wolves of the **Evening** (Hab. i. 8) s. the fallacies of the senses. A.E. 780.

Woman s. the church from the affection of truth, and thence, in an opp. sense, the church from the affection of the false principle. A.R. 620. W. (Gen. ii. 22) s. proprium vivified by the Lord, and by bringing her to the man is s. that proprium was granted to him. The posterity of the most ancient church not desiring, like their parents, to be a celestial man, but to be under their own self-guidance, and thereby inclining to proprium, had a proprium granted them, but still vivified by the Lord, wherefore it is called w., and afterwards wife. 151. By the w. (Gen. iii. 15) is meant the church: by the seed of the serpent, all infidelity; by the seed of the w., faith towards the Lord. 250. The reason why it is said that Rebecca was to Isaac for a w. (Gen. xxiv. 67), and not for a wife, is, because between rational good and truth called forth out of the natural and made divine, it is not marriage which has place, but a covenant resembling a conjugial covenant; the essential divine marriage, which is in the Lord, is the union of the divine essence with the human, and of the human with the divine. This is the reason that Rebecca is called w., not wife. 3211. The w. who seduced the man to eat of the forbidden fruit, s. the affection of the natural man. A.E. 739. The w. fled into the wilderness (Rev. xii. 6) s. the church, which is the New Jerusalem, at first confined to a few. By the w. is s. the new church, and by the wilderness is s. where there are no longer any truths; the reason why that church is s. as being at first confined to a few, is because it follows, "where she had a place prepared of God, that they should feed her there a thousand two hundred and sixty days," whereby is s. its state at that time, that in the meanwhile an increase of its numbers may be provided for, until it comes to its appointed maturity. A.R. 546.

Woman Forsaken, and a **Wife** of **Youth** (Isa. liv. 6), s. in particular the ancient and most ancient church. 253.

Woman encompassed with the **Sun**, and the **Moon** under her **Feet** (Rev. xii. 1), s. the Lord's new church in the heavens, which is the new heaven, and the Lord's new church about to be upon earth, which is the New Jerusalem. That the Lord's new church is s. by this w., appears from all the particulars of this chapter, understood in a spiritual sense. The reason why she appeared encompassed with the sun is, because the church is principled in love to the Lord, for it acknowledges him, and does his commandments, and this is to love him (John xiv. 21–24), the sun s. love; the reason why the moon was seen under the woman's feet is, because the church on earth is understood, which is not yet conjoined with the church in the heavens; by the moon is s. intelligence in the natural man, and faith; and by appearing under the feet is s. that it is about to be upon earth; otherwise, by feet is s. the church itself when it is conjoined. A.R. 533.

Woman sitting on a Scarlet Beast (Rev. xvii.) s. the Roman Catholic or Babylonian religion, for it follows, "Upon her forehead was a name written, Mystery, Babylon the great, mother of the harlots and abominations of the earth." A.R. 723.

Woman, Wife, Bride, Virgin, and **Daughter**. It is by virtue of a celestial and angelic proprium that the church is called a w., and also a wife, a bride, a virgin, and a daughter. 253.

Womb s. where good and truth lies conceived, consequently where that is which is of the church; w., in the genuine sense, s. the inmost principle of conjugial love, in which is innocence, because the w. cor. to that love in the grand man, and inasmuch as conjugial love der. its origin from the love of good and of truth, which is of the heavenly marriage, and this marriage is heaven itself or the Lord's kingdom, and the Lord's kingdom in the earths is the church, therefore by w. is also s. the church; for the church is where the marriage of good and truth is: hence it is, that to open the w.

Womb of the Morning

den. doctrines of the churches thence der., and also the faculty of receiving the truths and goods which are of the church, and that to come forth from the w. den. to be re-born or regenerated, that is, to be made a church, for he who is re-born or regenerated is made a church: inasmuch as by coming forth from the w. is s. re-birth, and hence the church, therefore the Lord in the Word is called "he who formeth from the w," "he who bringeth forth from the w.," and they who are regenerated and made a church, are said "to be carried from the w." 4918. W. (Gen. xlix. 25) s. the conjunction of good and truth. 6433. The term belly is used where truths are treated of, and the term w. where good is treated of. An abortive w. s. falses from evil in the place of truth from good. A.E. 710.

Womb of the **Morning** (Ps. cx. 3) s. the conception of the Lord's divine human from his essential divine, and thence the glorification of his human. A.E. 179.

Womb and **Breasts**. (Hosea ix. 12.) W. s. truths from the good of love, and breasts, truths from the good of charity. A.E. 710.

Women (Gen. xxxi. 50) s. affections of truth not genuine, thus which are not of the church. 4200. W. (Gen. xlv. 19) s. the affections of truth. 5946. W. rep. good and men truth when the spiritual church is the subject treated of. But w. rep. truth, and men good, when the celestial church is treated of. 8337, 4823.

Women, Two, the **Daughters of One Mother** (Ezek. xxiii. 2), s. the Israelitish and Jewish churches. A.E. 141.

Wonder, to. (Rev. xiii. 3.) "All the world wondered after the beast," is s. that faith alone was gladly received and became the doctrine of the whole church. A.R. 578. Wondering attracts, and they whom it attracts follow it. A.E. 787.

Wonderful, Great and. When pred. of the Lord have reference to his omnipotence, and his divine providence. A.E. 927.

Wood, in general, s. such things in the will as are in the lowest degree; precious w., as cedar, and the like, s. such things as are good; the cedar w. used in the temple had this s., so had the cedar w. applied in cleansing the leprosy (Levit. xiv. 4, 6, 7), as also the w. which was cast into the bitter waters at Marah, whereby they were made sweet (Exod. xv. 25); but the w. which were not precious, and which were made into graven images, and also those which were applied to the making of funeral piles, and the like, s. lusts, as do woods of Gopher, mentioned in Gen. vi. 14, by reason of the sulphur they contain. 643. W. s. good, as well the good of love to the Lord as the good of charity towards our neighbor. 3969. Thyine w. (Rev. xviii. 12) s. natural good, because w. is not so precious or valuable as gold, silver, jewels, pearls, fine linen, purple, silk, and scarlet; it is the same with stone; and also with ivory, by which natural truth is s.; by w., in an opp. sense, is s. evil, or what is accursed, as where it is said, that they made graven images out of w. and worshipped them, Deut. iv. 23, 28; Isa. xxxvii. 19; xl. 20; Jer. x. 3, 8; Ezek. xx. 32); also that the being hanged upon w. was a curse (Deut. xxi. 22, 23). A.R. 774. W. s. the good which appertains to works, and which appertains to righteousness, and to cut w. s. to place merit in the good of works, but to cut the w. of a burnt offering s. the merit of righteousness. 2784. The two pieces of w. (Ezek. xxxvii. 16–22), s. the celestial and spiritual kingdom of the Lord. 3969. See *Bears out of the Wood, Hewers of Wood.*

Wood of **Oil** s. good of love. A.E. 277.

Wood which is inquired of (Hosea iv. 12) s. the good of the delight of some lusts. 2466.

Wool s. good in ultimates, for w. is from sheep, by which is s. the good of charity. A.R. 47. White w. (Ezek. xxvii. 18) s. natural good. A.E. 376.

Wool of **She-Goats** s. the ultimate or outermost of innocence, which is in ignorance, such as is with the gentiles, which in the internal sense are the curtains of the tabernacle. It was commanded that the curtain over the habitation of the tabernacle, should be made of the w. of s.-g. (Exod. xxv. 4, etc.) 3519.

Woollen and **Linen** involve that states of good and truth ought not to be confounded. 10.669. See *Garment.*

Word. As to what concerns the term W., in the original tongue it is expressive of thing, hence also divine revelation is called the W., and also the Lord in the supreme sense; and by the W., when it is pred. of the Lord, and likewise of revelation from him, in the proximate sense it s. the divine truth, from which all things, which are things, exist. 5272. W. (Ps. xcix. 6–17) stands for doctrine in general. 1288. The W. (Ps. cxlvii. 18) s. divine good united with divine truth. A.E. 419. W. (Isa. ix. 8) s. the doctrine of internal and external worship. 1288. Few know what is meant by the W. (John i.); that the Lord is meant, is evident from every particular; but the internal sense teaches, that the Lord as to the divine human is meant by the W., for it is said, that "the W. was made flesh, and dwelt in us, and we saw his glory." And because the divine human is meant by the W., thereby is meant also every truth which relates to him, and is from him, in his kingdom in the heavens, and in his church in the earths; hence it is said, that "in him was life, and the life was the light of men, and the light appeareth in darkness;" and because truth, by the W. is meant also all revelation, thus also the W. itself, or holy scripture. 2894. Angels have in the heavens the very same W. that men have in the world, save only, that with men it is natural, whereas in the heavens it is spiritual; and since the W. is divine truth, it is also the divine proceeding, and this is not only from the Lord, but it is also the Lord himself. As this W. is thus the Lord himself, the whole of it in general, and each part in particular, is written in reference to him alone; from the prophet Isaiah unto Malachi, there is not a single thing that does not relate to the Lord, or that being in the opp. sense, does not relate to something contrary to the Lord. That this is the case, has not heretofore been seen by any one; but nevertheless every one has a capacity to see it, provided he is apprized of it, and thinks of it whilst he is reading; and further knows, that there is not only a natural sense in the W., but also a spiritual sense. L. 2. By the W. those also have light who are out of the church, and have not the W. U.T. 267–272. Unless there were a W. no one would know God, heaven and hell, and life after death, and still less the Lord. U.T. 273–276. The sons of Jacob were brought down into the land of Canaan, because all the places in that land, from the most ancient times, were made rep., that thus the W. might be there written, wherein those places should be mentioned for the sake of the internal sense; but nevertheless the W. as to the external sense was changed for the sake of that nation, but not as to the internal sense. W.H. 12. The conjunction of heaven with man is by means of the W., and the W. is called a covenant, because covenant s. conjunction. W.H. 10. In the most ancient time when the church was celestial, the W. was not, for the men of that church had the W. inscribed on their hearts, for the Lord taught them immediately through heaven what was good, and thence what was true, and gave them to perceive each from love and charity, and to know from revelation; the veriest W. to them was the Lord; after this church another succeeded, which was not celestial, but spiritual, and this in the beginning had no other W. than what was collected from the most ancient people, which W. was rep. of the Lord, and significative of his kingdom; thus the internal sense was to them the very W.; they had also a written W., as well historical as prophetical, which is no longer extant, and in this there was in like manner an internal

Word

sense, which had relation to the Lord; hence it was the wisdom of that time both to speak and write by rep. and significatives, within the church, concerning things divine, and out of the church, concerning other things, as is evident from the writings of those ancient people which remain with us; but in process of time this wisdom perished, inasmuch that at length they did not know that there existed any internal sense even in the books of the W.; the Jewish and Israelitish nation was such, and they accounted the prophetic W. holy from this, that it resembled the ancient W. in sound, and they heard the name of Jehovah in the sense of the letter, not believing that any thing divine lay deeper hid within, nor does the christian world think more holily concerning the W. 3432. As to what concerns the W. in particular, it has existed in all times, but not the W. which we have at this day; there was another W. in the most ancient church, which was before the flood, and another in the ancient church, which was after the flood; but the W. written by Moses and the prophets in the Jewish church, and finally the W. written by the evangelists in the new church. The reason why the W. has existed at all times is, because by the W. there is a communication of heaven with earth, and because the W. treats of good and truth, from which man may live happy to eternity; and therefore in the internal sense it treats of the Lord alone, inasmuch as all good and truth is from him. 2895. The art of writing and printing was really provided by the Lord for the sake of the W.; in like manner with all communications by commerce. 9351–4. The W., in its whole complex, is an image of heaven, for the W. is divine truth, and divine truth constitutes heaven, and heaven resembles one man, and therefore in this respect the W. is as it were an image of man. W.H. 11. The sense of the letter and the internal sense are sometimes alike especially when the subject treated of is concerning the essentials of faith, which, because they are necessary to salvation, are expressed in the letter such as they are in the internal sense. (See Gen. xviii. 17; Deut. vi. 4, 5, 6), besides other passages of a similar kind. 2225. The W., which was dictated from the Lord, passed through the heavens of his celestial kingdom, and the heavens of his spiritual kingdom, and thus came to man by whom it was written; wherefore the W., in its first origin, is purely divine; this W., as it passed through the heavens of the Lord's celestial kingdom, was divine celestial, and as it passed through the heavens of the Lord's spiritual kingdom, was divine spiritual, and when it came to man, it became divine natural; hence it is, that the natural sense of the W. contains in itself the spiritual sense, and this the celestial sense, and both a sense purely divine, which is not discernable by any man, nor indeed by any angel. A.R. 959. In the W. of the Old Testament, all the prophetical and historical parts, together with the Psalms of David, refer to the seventeen following points, namely: 1. The coming of the Lord; 2. The successive vastation of the church; 3. The total devastation and rejection thereof; 4. The rejection of the Lord by the church; 5. The Lord's temptations in general; 6. Also, his temptations even to despair; 7. His combats with the hells; 8. His victories over them, or his subjugation of them; 9. The passion of the cross, which was the final temptation; 10. The glorification of the Lord's humanity, or the union of his humanity with his divinity; 11. Concerning a new church in place of the former; 12. A new church, and at the same time a new heaven; 13. The Lord's humiliation before the Father; 14. The states of unition with his own divinity; 15. The last judgment by him; 16. Celebration and worship of the Lord, and 17. Redemption and salvation by the Lord. S.E.L. The whole W. is nothing else but the doctrine of love towards the Lord, and love towards our neighbor. (See Matt. xxii.) A.R. 136. The W., as being divine, contains in it only such things as conduce to salvation and eternal life. 3993. There is not a single contradiction in the W., if viewed in

380

its own spiritual light. S.S. 51. The interiors of the W. are of such a nature, that whatsoever is spoken of the church, is spoken also of each individual of the church, who, unless he were a church, could not be a part of the church, as he who is not a temple of the Lord, cannot be what is s. by the temple, which is the church and heaven. Therefore also the most ancient church is called man, in the singular number. 82. The W. is divine, even in those parts which are repealed, on account of the celestial things which lie concealed in their internal sense. W.H. 13. The books of the W. are all those which have the internal sense; but those books which have not the internal sense, are not the W. The books of the W. in the Old Testament are the five books of Moses; the book of Joshua, the book of Judges, the two books of Samuel, the two books of Kings, the Psalms of David, the Prophets, Isaiah, Jeremiah, Lamentations, Ezekiel, Daniel, Hosea, Joel, Amos, Obadiah, Jonah, Micah, Nahum, Habakkuk, Zephaniah, Haggia, Zechariah, Malachi. In the New Testament the four Evangelists, Matthew, Mark, Luke, and John, and the Revelation. The rest have not the internal sense. W.H. 16. A.C. 10.325. See *Internal Sense of the Word, Literal Sense of the Word, Style of the Word.*

Word of Patience (Rev. iii. 10) s. spiritual combat which is temptation. A.R. 185.

Words, in the original tongue, s. also things, because w. in the internal sense s. the truths of doctrine, on which account all divine truth in general is called the Word, and the Lord himself, from whom comes all divine truth, in the supreme sense is the Word, and whereas nothing, which exists in the universe, is any thing, that is, is a thing, unless it is from divine good by divine truth, therefore w. in the Hebrew tongue den. also things. 5075. W. (Exod. xxxiv. 28) s. all things appertaining to doctrine. 1288.

Words of this Prophecy. (Rev. i. 3.) By the w. of this p. nothing else is understood but the doctrine of the New Jerusalem, for by prophet, in an abstract sense, is s. the doctrine of the church der. from the Word, thus, here the doctrine of the new church, which is the New Jerusalem; the same is s. by p. A.R. 8.

Word of God (Rev. xvii. 17) s. the things fortold in the W. A.R. 750.

Words of this Book (Rev. xxii. 7) s. truths or precepts of doctrine contained in the Apocalypse, now opened by the Lord. A.R. 944.

Work den. use, because it is pred. of the will-principle, or of the sensual principle subject to the will part, and whatsoever is done by that principle, and may be called w., must be use; all works of charity are nothing else, for works of charity are works from the will, which are uses. 5148.

Work of God. The spiritual man, when he becomes celestial, is called the w. of G., because the Lord alone has fought for him, and created, formed, and made him; wherefore it is said, God finished his w. on the seventh day, and is twice said, he rested from all his w.; by the prophets he is everywhere called the w. of the hands and fingers of Jehovah. 88.

Work of the Hands. By the w. of man's h., in the Word, in its natural sense, are meant graven images, molten images, and idols; but in the spiritual sense they s. evils and falses of every kind, which are the things proper to man; for by hands are s. those things in the aggregate which proceed from man; for the powers of the mind, and thence of its body, are determined to the hands, and there terminate, therefore by hands, in the Word, is s. power. All things which are done by the Lord, are also called the w. of his h., which are proper to him, and in themselves are goods and truths. A.R. 457.

Work of Jehovah and the Operation of his Hands. (Isa. v. 12.) W. of J. is pred. of the goods of life, and the o. of his h., of the truths of doctrine, each from the Word. A.E. 376.

Worker of Stone

Worker of Stone den. the good of love, in those who become regenerate. 9846.

Workman (Hos. viii. 6) s. man's proprium. A.E. 279. W. (Zech. i. 20) s. the same as iron, namely, truth in the ultimates. A.E. 316.

Works s. the internal life of every one in externals. There are w. of the mind, and w. of the body, both of them at once internal and external; the w. of the mind are intentions and endeavors, and the w. of the body are words and actions, both the one and the other of these proceed from the internal life of man, which is of his will, or love; whatsoever does not close in w., either internal w. of the mind, or external w. of the body, is not in the life of man, for it flows from the world of spirits, but is not received; wherefore it is like an object which strikes the eye, or like a smell which affects the nose, from which a man turns away his face. A.R. 868. W. (Gen. xlvi. 33) den. goods, because they are from the will, and the things which are from the will are either goods or evils, but the things which are from the understanding, as discourses, are either truths or falses. 6048. In the w. of a man, whose natural mind descends by three degrees into hell, there are all his evils and falses of evil, and in the w. of a man whose natural mind ascends into heaven, there are all his goods and truths; and both the former and the latter are perceived by the angels from the mere speech, and the mere action of a man. Hence it is, that in the Word it is said, that a man is to be judged according to his w., and that he is to render an account of his words. D.L.W. 281. Forasmuch as it is so often said in the Apocalypse, "I know thy w.," it is evident, that by w. are s., in general, all things of the church. A.E. 98. By good w. are s. charity and faith in internals, and at the same time their effects in externals; and as charity and faith exist from the Lord, and according to conjunction with him, it is evident that these are s. A.R. 949. That w. are what constitute man a member of the church, and that he is saved according thereto, the Lord teaches in his parables, several of which imply, that they who do good are accepted, and that they who do evil are rejected. (See Matt. xxiii. 33–44; Luke xiii. 6; Matt. xxv. 14–31; Luke x. 13–25; xxx. 30–37; xvi. 19–31; Matt. xxv. 1–12.) Dec. 2. W. (Rev. xvi. 11) s. falses of faith, and consequent evils of life. A.R. 698.

Works and **Charity**. The internal of the celestial church, is that which is understood by w., and the internal of the spiritual church, that which is understood by c. A.E. 154.

Works, Emeralds, Purple Broidered Work, Fine Linen, Coral, and **Agate** (Ezek. xxvii. 16), s. nothing else but the knowledges of good. 1232.

World. By w., in the most extensive sense, is meant the whole w., and the good as well as the wicked that are therein, and sometimes the wicked only; but in a less extensive sense, by the w. is meant the same as by the globe and the earth, thus the church. The w. also means the people of the church. (John xii. 19; xviii. 20.) A.R. 539. W. (1 Sam. ii. 8) s. the church as to all its goods and truths. A.E. 741. W. (Ps. xiv. 1) s. the church in an universal sense. 6297. W. (Rev. xiii. 3) s. the reformed church. A.R. 578. W., and they that dwell therein (Ps. xcviii. 7), s. the universal heaven as to its truths, and they that dwell therein, the universal heaven as to its goods. A.E. 518.

World of Spirits is like a forum of place of resort, where all are at first assembled, and is as a stomach, in which the food is first collected; the stomach moreover cor. to that w. A.R. 791. All enter into that w. immediately after their decease, and are there prepared, the good for heaven, and the wicked for hell, and some abide there only a month, or a year, and others from ten to thirty years; and they who were permitted to make imaginary heavens to themselves, several centuries, but at this day not longer than twenty years; there is in that w. a vast multitude, and societies there, as in the heavens and in the hells. Upon those who were in that w., the last judgment was executed, and not upon those who were in heaven, nor upon those who were in hell, for they who were in heaven were saved before, and they who were in hell were damned before. A.R. 866. See *Spiritual World.*

World, Prince of the **World, Satan** and the **Devil** (John x. 18) s. hell. L. 13.

Worlds, or **Earths,** are understood all in our solar system. 6695.

Worldly Cares, how, disperse heavenly ideas. 6309.

Worldly Loves. The love of self and the world make hell in man. 7366. Contempt of others is the exterior of self-love. 4750. A man is in the love of self when he regards only his own family and relatives. 7368.

Worm den. the false of evil in the good der. from the proprium. That "dieth not," den. infernal torment pred. of the false. 8481. Den. infernal putrescence, or filth of evil. 8500.

Worms s. the uncleannesses of the false. 8481. See *Canker Worm.*

Wormwood s. infernal falsity, from its intense bitterness, whereby it renders meat and drink abominable. A.R. 410. Waters of w. s. falses of evil. A.E. 521. See *Bitter.*

Worship, to (Rev. xiii. 12), s. to acknowledge a thing to be sacred in the church. A.R. 597. To w. and love the Lord is the all of doctrine, in the Word, as to man. 2859. All w. is from good. 9806. Divine w. consists in the exaltation of the Lord, and in the humiliation of self. 8271. Every one is desirous to observe some kind of w., this being a common disposition, even amongst all Gentile nations. Every man, when he beholds the universe, and particularly when he contemplates the order of the universe, acknowledges a supreme Being and through a desire of promoting his own welfare, worships that being; there is besides, something within which dictates it, which is an effect of the Lord's influx by the angels that are attendant on every man; where this is not the case, man is under the dominion of infernal spirits, and does not acknowledge a God. 1308. No one is compelled to internal w. by the Lord, but this w. is implanted by freedom. 4208. Compelled w. is corporeal, inanimate, obscure, and sad w.; corporeal, because it is of the body and not of the mind; inanimate, because there is not life in it; obscure, bcause there is not understanding in it; and sad, because there is not the delight of heaven in it. But w. not compelled, when it is genuine, is spiritual, living, lucid, and glad w.; spiritual, because there is spirit from the Lord in it; living, because there is life from the Lord in it; lucid, because there is wisdom from the Lord in it; and glad, because there is heaven from the Lord in it. D.P. 137. W. in an internal sense, s. all conjunction by love and charity; man is continually in w. when he is in love and charity, external w. being only an effect; the angels are in such w.; wherefore with them there is a perpetual sabbath, whence also sabbath, in an internal sense, s. the kingdom of the Lord. Man, however, during his abode in the world, ought not to omit the practice of external w., for by external w. things internal are excited, and by external w., things external are kept in a state of sanctity, so that internal things can flow in; moreover, man is hereby imbued with knowledges, and prepared to receive things celestial; he is also gifted with states of sanctity, though he be ignorant thereof; which states are preserved by the Lord for his use in eternal life; for in another life, all man's states of life return. 1618. There are two things which constitute w., namely, doctrine and life, for doctrine without life does not constitute it, neither life without doctrine. A.E. 696. All who come into another life, have at first a w. like what they practised in the world, but they are successively separated from it; the reason is, because all w. remains implanted in man's interior life, from which it cannot be removed and eradicated, but by degrees. E.U. 142. External w. causes the Lord's

Worship in the Jewish Church

presence, but not conjunction with him; but external w., in which the interiors are alive, causes both presence and conjunction. A.R. 160.

Worship in the **Jewish Church**. The principal w. in the J. c. consisted in the offering of sacrifices and incense; wherefore there were two altars, one for sacrifices and the other for incense; the latter altar was within the tabernacle, and was called the golden altar, but the former was without the tabernacle and was called the altar of burnt offerings; the reason was, because there are two kinds of goods, from which all worship exists, celestial good and spiritual good. W. by sacrifices was worship from celestial good, and worship by incense was worship from spiritual good. Whether you call it worship, or confession, it amounts to the same thing, for all w. is confession. A.R. 277.

Worship of **Saints** is such an abomination in heaven, that if they only hear it, they are filled with horror, since as far as worship is ascribed to any man, so far it is withheld from the Lord; for thus he alone is not worshipped, and if the Lord alone is not worshipped a discrimination is made which destroys communion, and the happiness thence resulting. U.T. 824.

Worship of the **Sun** is the lowest of all kinds of worship of God, wherefore that worship in the Word is called abomination. D.L.W. 157.

Worshipper, every, of self and of nature confirms himself against the D. P. and why. D.P. 249.

Worthy, to be. (Rev. iii. 4.) They who are in truths from the Lord, because they are in conjunction with him, are called w., for all worth in the spiritual world is from conjunction in the Lord. A.R. 167. W. (Rev. v.), when pred. of the Lord, s. his merit and righteousness. A.E. 337.

Worthy to **Open** the **Book**, to be (Rev. v. 2), s. to be able or to have power. A.R. 259.

Wound (Exod. xxi. 25) s. an hurt done to the affection which is of love. 9056. To wound s. to injure the mind and spiritual life by falses. A.E. 444. See *Sore.*

Wounds and its **Blackness**. (Gen. iv. 23.) By w. and bruise is s. that there was no longer any thing sound; in particular by w. is s. the desolation of faith, and by bruise the devastation of charity, which is evident from this circumstance, that wound is pred. of a man, and bruise of a little child; by the same expressions are des. the desolation of faith, and the vastation of charity in Isa. i. 6. 431.

Wounded to **Death**, to be (Rev. xiii. 3), s. to disagree with the Word, for all church doctrine which does not accord with the Word, is not sound, but is sick of a deadly disease; for from the Word alone church doctrine is to be der. A.R. 576.

Wrath (Gen. xlix. 7) s. aversion from truth. 6343. Great w. (Rev. xii. 12) s. hatred against the new church. A.R. 558.

Wrath of **God**. By the w. of G. is s. evil among men, which, because it is against G., is called the wrath of G., not that G. is angry with man, but because man, in consequence of his evil, is angry with G., and because it seems to man, when he is punished and tormented for it, as is the case after death in hell, to come from G., therefore in the Word, w. and anger, yea, evil is attributed to G., but this, in the sense of the letter, only because that sense is written according to appearances and cor., but not in the spiritual sense, for in this latter there is no appearance and cor., but truth in its light. A.R. 658.

Wrath of the **Lamb**. The great day of the w. of the L. (Rev. vi. 17) s. the day of the last judgment. A.R. 340.

Wrath and **Anger**. In many parts of the Word w. and a. are mentioned together, and in such cases, w. is pred. of evil, and a. of falsity, because they who are in evil are the subjects of w., and they who are in falsity are subjects of a.;

and both in the Word, are attributed to Jehovah, that is, to the Lord; but it is meant that they take place in man against the Lord. A.R. 635.

Wrestling s. temptation; temptation itself is nothing else but w., or combat, for truth is assaulted by evil spirits, and is defended by the angels who are attendant on man, the apperception of this combat in man is temptation. 4274. The man who wrestled with Jacob (Gen. xxxii.), in the internal historical sense, s. evil spirits, for w. s. temptation, which is so effected. In the internal spiritual sense, by him who wrestled with Jacob is meant the angelic heaven, because the Lord, who is there rep. by Jacob, in a supreme sense, admitted also the angels to tempt him, and the angels on this occasion were left to their own proprium. 4307.

Wretched. (Rev. iii. 17.) By being w. here is s. incoherence, thus by those who are w., such as think incoherently concerning things of the church; the reason is, because they, of whom this is said, at one time deny God, heaven, eternal life, and the sanctity of the Word, and at another time acknowledge them; therefore what they build with one hand, they pull down with the other; thus they are like people that build a house, and presently pull it down; or that clothe themselves in handsome garments, and presently tear them; their houses are therefore rubbish, and their garments are rags. Such is the nature of all their thoughts concerning the church and heaven; but this they are not aware of. This is also meant by wretchedness, or misery, in the following passages: Isa. xlvii. 10, 11; Ezek. viii. 26, 27; Ps. v. 10. Similar is the s. of a ruinous wall (Jer. xlix. 3; Ezek. xiii. 11, 12; Hosea ii. 5). A.R. 208.

Write, to. (John viii. 2–11.) The Lord wrote twice on the ground, when the woman taken in adultery was brought to him, which s. the condemnation of the scribes and pharisees for adulteries in a spiritual sense, they having adulterated the goods and falsified the truths of the Word. A.E. 222. To w. upon any one s. to implant in the life. To w. it upon the heart s. to impress it upon the love. A.E. 222.

Writing. By w., in a natural sense, is s. to commit to paper, and thus to record any thing for the information of posterity; but in the spiritual sense, by w. is s. to commit to the heart for reception. A.R. 473. The most ancient manner of w. was rep. of things, by persons and by words, by which were understood things altogether different from those expressed; profane writers in those times thus framed their historicals, even things appertaining to civil and moral life, so indeed, that nothing was true exactly as it was written as to the letter, but under these things something else was understood. This they carried so far as to set forth certain affections as gods and goddesses, to whom the heathens afterwards instituted divine worship; this may be known to every person of literature, since such ancient books are still extant: this method of w. was der. from the most ancient people who lived before the flood, and who rep. to themselves things celestial and divine by the visible things on the earth, and in the world, and thus filled their minds and souls with joyous and delightful perceptions, when they beheld the objects of the universe, especially such as were beautiful from their form and order; hence all the books of the church of those times, were thus written; such is the book of Job, and in imitation thereof, such is Solomon's song of songs; such were the two books mentioned by Moses (Num. xxi. 14, 27), besides several which are lost. This style of w. in succeeding times became venerated on account of its antiquity, both amongst the Gentiles, and amongst the posterity of Jacob, insomuch that they regarded nothing as divine, but what was thus written; wherefore when they were under the influence of the prophetic spirit, as in the case of Jacob (Gen. xlix. 3–17) and of Moses, (Exod. xv. 1–21; Deut. xxxiii. 2, to the end); of Balaam, who was of the sons of the east

Writing on the Wall

from Syria, where the ancient church then was (Num. xxiii. 7–10, 19–24; xxiv. 5–9, 17–24, and of Deborah and Barak (Judg. v. 2, to the end); and of Hannah (1 Sam. ii. 2–10), and several others; they spake in the manner above mentioned, and this from several secret causes; and although very few understood or knew that the things spoken s. the celestial things of the Lord's kingdom and church, still being touched and struck with a wonderful awe, they felt that the divine were in those things. But that the case is similar with the historicals of the Word, and that they are rep. and s. of the celestial and spiritual things of the Lord's kingdom, as to every individual name and word, is not as yet known to the learned world, only that the Word was as to the smallest iota, inspired, and that all its contents, both generally and particularly, involve heavenly arcana. 1756. The writings of the most ancient people were on tablets of wood and stone, and afterwards on polished tables of wood, and the second age wrote their writings on parchment. C.S.L. 77. The w. in the third heaven consists of letters inflected and variously curved, each of which contains some paticular meaning. S.S. 90.

Writing on the **Wall**, and the **Death** of the **King** (Dan. v.), s. visitation and destruction denounced against those who use divine goods and truths, as means whereby to obtain dominion over the souls of men. L.J. 54.

Written (Rev. xiv. 1) s. acknowledgment in them who were sealed. A.R. 613.

Written Name. (Rev. xix. 12.) By n. is here s. the quality of the Word in its spiritual and celestial sense, and it is called a w. n., because the Word exists as well among men upon earth, as among angels in heaven. A.R. 824.

Written on the **Forehead** (Rev. xvii. 5) s. to be inherent in the love. A.R. 729.

Wrought (intwined or intwisted) is pred. of the natural scientific principle, and in Ps. xlv. 13, of divine natural truth. 3703.

Wrought and **Done.** (Isa. li. 4.) W. has respect to the will, and d. to the understanding. 683.

X

Xavier, a popish saint seen and des. as idiotic as often as he thinks himself a saint. C.L.J. 65.

Xiphoid Cartilage. Spirits of the moon cor. in the Grand Man to. X.C. 9236.

Y

Yards, Olive, s. celestial things of the church. 1069.

Yea, Yea, and **Nay Nay** (in Matt. v. 36), have respect to the celestial principle. 3246.

Year s. an entire period of the church from beginning to end. That y. s. an entire time of a state of the church from beginning to end, or, what is the same, an entire period, and consequently that y. s. times, or periods within the general period, may appear from many passages in the Word. As y. and years s. a full time between each term, the beginning and the end, when they are pred. of the Lord's kingdom on earth, that is the church, so they s. what is eternal, when they are pred. of the Lord's kingdom in heaven. That y. in the internal sense does not s. y., may also appear from this, that the angels, who are in the internal sense of the Word, cannot have an idea of any y., but inasmuch as y. is a full period of time in the natural world, therefore instead of y. they have an idea of what is full in respect to states of the church, and of what is eternal in respect to states of heaven: times with them are states. 2906. Years (Ps. lxi. 6) s. what is eternal. 2906. See *Day and Year.*

Year of the **Good Pleasure** of **Jehovah** (Isa. lxi. 2) s. the time of the new church. 2906.

Year of the **Lord**, acceptable (Isa. lxi. 2), s. the time and state of the men of the church, when they are succored or nourished by love. A.E. 295.

Year of the **Redeemed** (Isa. lxiii. 4) s. a state of blessedness. 488.

Year of my **Redeemed** (Isa. lxiii. 4), and the year of visitation (Jer. xi. 23), s. the time of a new church. 2906.

Year of **Retribution** (Isa. xxxiv. 8) s. the last judgment. A.E. 850. Y. of r. and day of revenge s. the same, only the y. of r. is pred. of falses, whereas the day of revenge has respect to evils. A.E. 413.

Years of Abundance of Provision, and **Years of Famine.** (Gen. xli.) By y. are s. states, by the y. of a. of p. states of the multiplication of truth in the natural principle, and by the y. of f. states of defect and privation of truth in the natural principle; in general, by the seven y. of a. of p., and the seven y. of f. in the land of Egypt, in the internal sense, are des. the states of man's reformation and regeneration, and in the supreme sense the states of the glorification of the Lord's human; to the intent that these things might be rep., such things came to pass in the land of Egypt; the reason why they came to pass in that land was, because by the land of Egypt, and by Pharaoh, in the internal sense, is rep. the natural principle, the glorification of which in the Lord is there treated of. 5275.

Years of Ancient Times (Ps. lxxvii. 5) s. states of the ancient church. 488.

Years of the Babylonish Captivity, etc. Vastation was rep. by the y. of the c.; the beginning of a new church was rep. by the deliverance and rebuilding of the temple. 728.

Years and **Lives** (Gen. xxv. 7, 18) s. rep. states. 3274.

Yellow. The color of good in the other life is presented in blue, y., and red. 8458.

Yesterday, To-Day, and **To-Morrow.** Y. s. from eternity; t.-d., eternity; and t.-m., to eternity. 3998.

Yield Fruit, to (Rev. xxii.), s. to produce goods. A.R. 935.

Yoke upon the neck s. interclusion and interception. 3603. To carry a y. (1 Sam. vi. 7) s. to serve falses which defile good. A.E. 700. To serve the king of Babel and to put the neck under his y. (Jer. xxvii. 8) s. to be altogether deprived of the knowledge and acknowledgment of the good and truth of faith, consequently, of internal worship. 1327. The bonds of the y. s. the delights of evil originating in the love of self and the world. A.E. 365. See *Oxen.*

Young Man and **Virgin** s. the intelligence of truth and the affection of good. A.E. 555.

Young Men s. those who are in truths, and abstractedly truths themselves. A.E. 131. Also, the understanding of truth and intelligence. A.E. 270.

Younger, the (Gen. xlviii. 14), s. to be in the second place. 6270.

Youth, a state of, cor. to the affection of good and truth. 3254. Y. (Ps. cxxvii. 4; cxliv. 12) s. the ancient church which was in genuine truth. Sons of the y. s. the truths of the ancient church, which were natural truths from a spiritual origin. A.E. 724.

Z

Zabuah, the bird, s. reasoning from falses. A.E. 650.

Zachar. The wool of Z. s. natural good. A.E. 376.

Zanzummims, the, who were expelled by the Ammonites (Deut. ii. 19–21), s. falses and evils infesting the regenerate man. 1868.

Zaphnath-Paaneah, the name conferred on Joseph, which means the occult; and the opener of the future den. the quality of the celestial spiritual, as having the divine within it. 5330.

Zarah, Phares and, rep. the dispute about the priority of faith and charity. 3325.

Zarephath. The widow of Z. (1 Kings xvii. 1–13) rep. those without the church who desire truth. 4844.

Zeal of the **Lord**, the, is love and mercy. 8875. In heaven or with the angels there is no such thing as anger, but instead of anger, z.; for anger differs from z. in this, that there is evil in anger, but in z. there is good; or that he who is in anger, intends evil to another with whom he is angry, but he who is in z., intends good to another, towards whom he hath z.; wherefore also he who is in z. can in an instant be good, and in the very act be good towards others, but not so he who is in anger; although z. in the external form appears like anger, still in the internal form it is altogether unlike. 4164. Divine z. is the consequence of divine love, and is a z. for the salvation of men. A.R. 831.

Zebaoth. The Lord is called Jehovah Z., because z. s. an army, or host, which also s. all the truths and goods of the church and heaven. A.E. 727. See *Jehovah Zebaoth*.

Zeboim, Admah and, s. the lusts of evil, etc. 1212.

Zebulon (Gen. xlix. 13) s. the cohabitation of good and truth, or the heavenly marriage. It is called the cohabitation of good and truth, because Z., in the original tongue, s. cohabitation. By Z. are here meant, those who believe the doctrinals der. from the Word, but with whom some affirmative principle universally prevails, and yet faith has not life in truths but in scientifics, for they apply scientifics to doctrinals, and thus confirm their affirmative principle; they therefore, who are Z., do not elevate themselves from scientifics, but when they hear or think concerning any truth of faith, they instantly fall into the scientific principle; several in the world are of this description; the Lord also provides, that things scientific and sensual, should serve them for this use. 6383. By Z., in a supreme sense, is s. the union of the essential divinity, and the divine humanity in the Lord, in a spiritual sense, the marriage of good and truth in those who are in heaven and in the church, and in a natural sense, conjugial love itself; therefore in Rev. vii. by Z. is s. the conjugial love of good and truth; moreover he was so called from cohabitation (Gen. xxx. 19, 22), and cohabitation is pred. of married pairs, whose minds are joined in one, for such conjunction is spiritual cohabitation. The conjugial love of good and truth, which is here s. by Z., is the conjugial love of the Lord, and his church; the Lord is the good of love itself, and gives to the church to be truth from that good; and cohabitation is effected, when the man of the church receives good from the Lord, in truths; in this case, there takes place in man a marriage of good and truth, which constitutes the church itself, and he becomes a heaven; hence it is, that the kingdom of God, that is, heaven and the church, is so often compared in the Word to a marriage. A.R. 359.

Zechariah s. the truth itself of doctrine, and hence those who are in the truth of doctrine. (See Matt. xxiii. 34.) A.E. 329.

Zemarites s. falsities and evil lusts. 1205. See *Jebusites, etc.*

Zerubbabel (Zech. iv.) rep. the Lord. A.R. 43.

Zidon (Isa. xxiii. 2–4) s. exterior knowledges, which having nothing internal in them, are called the seed of Sihor, the harvest of the river, her revenue a mart of nations, and also the sea, and the fortification of the sea; and it is said, that she does not travail, nor bring forth, which expressions in the literal sense seem without meaning, but in the internal sense, they have a clear s., as is the case with other passages in the Prophets; because Z. s. exterior knowledges, it is called, they that are round about Israel, or the spiritual church (Ezek. xxviii. 24, 26); for exterior knowledges are like things that are around. 1201. Z. (Isa. xxiii. 4, 5) s. those who have been in the knowledges of faith, and have destroyed them by scientifics, and thereby become barren. 264. See *Tyre and Zidon.*

Ziim, the people of (Ps. lxxiv. 15), are they who are in falses, or the false itself. 9755.

Ziim, Ochim, Daughters of the **Owl, Satyrs, Iim,** and **Dragons** (Isa. xiii. 21, 22), s. the interior things of worship, appertaining to self-love, or proprium. 1326.

Ziim, and **Ijim, Satyr,** and **Night Monster** (Isa. xxxiv. 14), s. concupiscences corporeal and merely natural, from which all kinds of falses and evils are produced. A.E. 586.

Zillah (Gen. iv.) s. the mother of the natural things of that new church which succeeded Lamech. 405. See *Adah and Zillah.*

Zilpah den. corporeal affection, cor. to the affection of external truth, and serving as a bond. 3835.

Ziplah, Leah's handmaid, s. subsequent affection serviceable to the affection of exterior truth, as a mean or medium. 4609.

Zimram rep. the lots and divisions of the Lord's spiritual kingdom. 3239.

Zinzendorf des. in the spiritual world. C.L.J. 89.

Zion, Mount, s. heaven and the church, where the Lord alone is worshipped. A.R. 612. Mountain of Z., in the supreme sense, rep. the divine good of the Lord's divine love, and in the respective sense, the divine celestial, and the divine spiritual in his kingdom. 6435. Z. (Isa. li. 3) s. the new church amongst the Gentiles, which should acknowledge the Lord. A.E. 739. Z. (Jer. xiv. 19, 21) s. the Lord's celestial kingdom. 5313.

Zion and **Jerusalem,** when named together, s. the celestial church, Z., its internal, and J., its external; but when J. is named without Z., then, in most cases, is s. the spiritual church. 6745. See *Sons of Zion, Daughter of Zion.*

Zipporah (Exod. ii. 21) s. the quality of the good of the church. 6793. Z. (Exod. iv. 25) s. the rep. church. 7044.

Zoan and **Noph** were in the land of Egypt, and s. the illustration of the natural man from spiritual light. The princes of Z. are become foolish, the princes of N. are carried away (Isa. xix. 11, 13), s. that the truths of wisdom and intelligence der. from natural light in the natural man are turned into the falses of insanity. A.E. 654.

Zoan den. truths in the ultimate of order falsified. 5044.

Zoar (Gen. xiii. 10) s. the affection of goodness. Z. was a city not far from Sodom, whither also Lot fled when he was rescued by the angels from the burning of Sodom, concerning which see Gen. xix. 20, 22, 30. Z. is also mentioned Gen. xiv. 2, 8; Deut. xxxiv. 3; Isa. xv. 5; Jer. xlviii. 34; where also it

Zone

s. affection, and because the affection of good, so also, in an opp. sense, as is usual, the affection of evil. 1589. Z. (Gen. xix. 22) s. the affection of good, namely, the good of science, that is, the affection of truth, in the present instance little of truth, for by Z., in the original tongue, is s. little or small, for they who are in the affection of truth, have little of truth, because but little of good, in comparison with those who are in the affection of good. 2439.

Zone, or **Girdle**, in the Word, s. a common band, whereby all things are kept in their order and connection. A.R. 46.

Zuzims (Gen. xiv. 5) s. a race similar to the Nephilims, who are mentioned in Gen. vi. 4, and s. persuasions of the false, or those, who through a persuasion of their own height and preëminence, made light of all things holy and true, and who infused falsities into evil lusts. 1673.